Message in the Music:
Hip Hop, History, and Pedagogy

Edited by
Derrick P. Alridge, *University of Georgia*
James B. Stewart, *Pennsylvania State University*
V.P. Franklin, *University of California, Riverside*

The ASALH Press
Washington, DC

ISBN 978-0-9768111-4-5

CONTENTS

Introduction: Message in the Music: Hip Hop, History,   1
and Pedagogy
   Derrick P. Alridge, James B. Stewart, and V. P. Franklin

Message in the Music: Political Commentary in Black Popular   5
Music from Rhythm and Blues to Early Hip Hop
   James B. Stewart

From Civil Rights to Hip Hop: Toward a Nexus of Ideas   35
   Derrick P. Alridge

Jackanapes: Reflections on the Legacy of the Black Panther Party   62
for the Hip Hop Generation
   V. P. Franklin

In Search of the "Revolutionary Generation": (En)Gendering   70
the Golden Age of Rap Nationalism
   Charise Cheney

Oppositional Consciousness within an Oppositional Realm: 90
The Case of Feminism and Womanism in Rap and Hip Hop,
1976–2004
   Layli Phillips, Kerri Reddick-Morgan, and Dionne Patricia Stephens

"That Supposed to Be Me?": Young Black Women Talk Back to   113
"Hip Hop"
   Aimee Meredith Cox

"I Can Be Your Sun, You Can Be My Earth": Masculinity, Hip Hop,   131
and the Nation of Gods and Earths
   Edward Onaci

Defying Gender Stereotypes and Racial Norms: Naming African   152
American Women's Realities in Hip Hop and Neo-Soul Music
   R. Dianne Bartlow

Scripting and Consuming Black Bodies in Hip Hop Music and   178
Pimp Movies
   Ronald L. Jackson II and Sakile K. Camara

Crossover Collaborations: Towards Realizing Hip Hop's Political   204
  Potential
   Bryan R. Bracey

Commercial Hip Hop: The Sounds and Images of a Racial Project   222
  Bettina L. Love

Hip Hop and Glocal Politics in Caribbean Music: Debates in   239
  Transnationalism and Resistance in Caribbean Hip Hop
   Lesley Feracho

Globalization and the Radical Impact of African American Hip Hop   261
  Culture and Rap in the People's Republic of China
   Bernard W. Bell

"Just Because I Am a Black Male Doesn't Mean I Am a Rapper!":   281
  Sociocultural Dilemmas in Using "Rap" Music as an Educational
  Tool in Classrooms
   Ayanna F. Brown

Transforming the *Carmen* Narrative: The Case of *Carmen the*   301
  Hip Hopera
   Paula Marie Seniors

"Of All Our Studies, History Is Best Qualified to Reward Our   321
  Research": Black History's Relevance to the Hip Hop Generation
   Pero Gaglo Dagbovie

Contributors   345

Index   349

Message in the Music:
Hip Hop, History, and Pedagogy

INTRODUCTION

Derrick P. Alridge, James B. Stewart, and V. P. Franklin collaborated for several years on *The Journal of African American History* (JAAH) Special Issue devoted to "The History of Hip Hop," published in the summer of 2005. The Special Issue sought to "contribute to the scholarship in Hip Hop by examining the movement within the historical context of the African American experience."[1] We argued it was necessary to view Hip Hop from within the African American cultural context and environment in which it emerged, developed, and evolved to fully understand its complexities and assess its potential benefit for current and future generations. After the publication of the Special Issue, a number of scholars asked that we expand it into an anthology that documented the history of Hip Hop, but also included essays from other disciplines and fields of study that brought additional perspectives to interpreting the developments in Hip Hop.

Message in the Music: Hip Hop, History, and Pedagogy examines the messages of Hip Hop music and culture from its beginnings in the early 1970s to the present. With special focus on Rap music, the volume situates Hip Hop in African American, United States, and global history and illuminates the messages and meanings that Rap artists convey through their music. This volume includes perspectives on and thoughtful and empirically-based critiques of Hip Hop as a cultural phenomenon and social movement that offers both emancipatory and self-destructive messages to those in the Hip Hop generation. The essays are written by historians, social scientists, literary critics, and educators for use in high school and college courses on Hip Hop and Youth Culture, American Popular Culture, recent African American and American history, African American Studies, and education. The volume should be valuable to researchers, parents, and fans interested in learning more about the history and global influence of Hip Hop culture and Rap music.

The volume also introduces the important theme of Hip Hop's potential use as a pedagogical tool. Historian Carter G. Woodson believed that education plays a crucial role in liberating the minds of African-descended people in the United States and throughout the world, and we want to challenge the supporters of Hip Hop to take a more intentional role in educating African American youths who have been targeted by the prison-industrial complex and are already struggling to survive in American society. At the same time, the volume seeks to advance the critical intergenerational discourse between the civil rights and post–civil rights generations, while also offering a well-documented discussion of women and gender in Hip Hop; the business and commercial aspects of Hip Hop; and its globalization and relationships to popular culture and alternative modes of representation.

1

The conceptualization of *Message in the Music* has been guided by Alain Locke's notion of "The New Negro" on display in his classic anthology *The New Negro: An Interpretation* (1925), in which the contributors and Locke captured the ethos of the new black consciousness of the post–World War I years. In promoting and celebrating the variety of black artistic expressions, Locke sought to foster a new cultural and artistic renaissance among African American artists and their supporters. In many ways, *The New Negro* projected a cultural and intellectual spirit that was also captured in subsequent black social and cultural movements.

Message in the Music extends the spirit and cultural consciousness of *The New Negro*, as well as the Civil Rights, the Black Arts, and the Black Power movements by offering a critical examination of Hip Hop's potential as an emancipatory pedagogical force. In our quest to engage the most recent manifestations of Hip Hop music and culture, we sought out essays from young scholars, graduate students, and independent scholars, as well as more established authors willing to participate in a scholarly dialogue about Hip Hop as a cultural and social movement.

The tensions between the civil rights and post-civil rights generations have sometimes created suspicions and misunderstanding among members of both cohorts. This tenuous relationship is addressed in James B. Stewart's "Message in the Music: Political Commentary in Black Popular Music from Rhythm and Blues to Early Hip Hop"; Derrick P. Alridge's "From Civil Rights to Hip Hop: Toward a Nexus of Ideas"; V. P. Franklin's "Jackanapes: Reflections on the Legacy of the Black Panther Party for the Hip Hop Generation"; and Charise Cheney's "In Search of the 'Revolutionary Generation': (En)Gendering the Golden Age of Rap Nationalism." These essays recognize and acknowledge the tensions between the generations while also pointing to areas of similarity and the strong potential for further collaborations across the age groups.

Like earlier African American social and cultural movements such as the Blues, Jazz, and the Black Arts Movement, women were often relegated to subordinate roles and status in Hip Hop's emerging years. From that time, however, women artists challenged male dominance in Hip Hop and helped introduce a generation of African American women to a "new feminism." The significance of women in Hip Hop is addressed in Layli Phillips, Kerri Reddick-Morgan, and Dionne Stephens' "Oppositional Consciousness within an Oppositional Realm: The Case of Feminism and Womanism in Rap and Hip Hop, 1976–2004" and Aimee Cox's "'That Supposed To Be Me?': Young Black Women Talk Back to 'Hip Hop.'"

Gender dynamics have been a contested issue in Hip Hop, just as they were in earlier social movements; and several chapters engage the distinctive gender relations that characterize the Hip Hop generation. "'I Can Be Your Sun, You Can Be My Earth': Masculinity, Hip Hop, and the Nation of Gods and Earths" by Edward Onaci; R. Dianne Bartlow's "Defying Gender Stereotypes and Racial Norms: Naming African American Women's Realities in Hip Hop and Neo-Soul Music"; and Ronald Jackson and Sakile Camara's "Scripting and Consuming Black Bodies in Hip Hop Music and Pimp Movies," all offer well-documented and insightful assessments of gender issues in Hip Hop.

Hip Hop artists have had a tempestuous relationship with those in the international music industry who sought to make "big bucks" off Hip Hoppers' commercial aspirations. On the one hand, rappers have tried to "keep it real," emphasizing their continuing connection to the streets and their freedom from commercial influences. On the other hand, mainstream Rap music has been controlled largely by the profit-seeking interests of the music industry, placing many Hip Hop artists in the precarious position of making and promoting CDs with negative and vulgar messages and obscene imagery about the lives of black people. In this volume Bryan Bracey's "Crossover Collaborations: Towards Realizing Hip Hop's Political Potential" and Bettina Love's "Commercial Hip Hop: The Sounds and Images of a Racial Project" explore these tensions and suggest ways Rap artists can promote more progressive political agendas through Hip Hop.

Hip Hop already serves as a vehicle for young people to express themselves and bring attention to social justice issues around the globe. Youths in China express the problems of the younger generation through the embrace of Hip Hop music and culture, and in the Caribbean the young use Hip Hop to rap about the plight of the poor and oppressed. Rap music is becoming a powerful voice for the oppressed, exploited, and the socially engaged. Lesley Feracho's "Hip Hop and Glocal Politics in Caribbean Music: Debates in Transnationalism and Resistance in Caribbean Hip Hop" and Bernard Bell's "Globalization and the Radical Impact of African American Hip Hop Culture and Rap in the People's Republic of China" explore Hip Hop's impact on youth culture around the world.

The chapters in this anthology all have pedagogical implications; but some studies focus specifically on issues related to pedagogy, education, and Hip Hop. Ayanna Brown's "'Just Because I Am a Black Male Doesn't Mean I Am a Rapper!': Sociocultural Dilemmas in Using 'Rap' Music as an Educational Tool in Classrooms"; Paula Marie Seniors' "Transforming the *Carmen* Narrative: The Case of *Carmen the Hip Hopera*"; and Pero Dagbovie's "Of All Our Studies, History Is Best Qualified to Reward Our Research: Black History's Relevance to the Hip Hop Generation," are studies that should prove useful for educators interested in students' making sense of their own experiences and those of others inside and outside the Hip Hop generation.

During his presidential campaign, then Illinois Senator Barack Obama engaged the Hip Hop community in his efforts to appeal to youths of all races and ethnicities to participate in the political reform campaigns. In response to this historic election of Barack Obama as President of the United States, several Hip Hop artists have predicted that this signals a new phase in the Hip Hop movement. This anthology examines a wide array of social, cultural, and educational issues surrounding Hip Hop from a variety of perspectives relevant to issues and concerns raised by President Obama, and makes a substantial contribution to the ongoing dialogue about the role of Hip Hop in shaping the images and cultural realities of U.S. African Americans and people around the world. In offering these interpretations of the messages in the music, we seek to understand the contributions that Hip Hop music and culture has made and will continue to make in educating present and future generations about the significance of African American cultural expressions to world culture in the twentieth and twenty-first centuries.

NOTES

[1]Derrick P. Alridge and James B. Stewart, "Introduction: Hip Hop in History: Past, Present, and Future," *Journal of African American History*, Special Issue "The History of Hip Hop," 90 (Winter 2005): 192–93.

MESSAGE IN THE MUSIC:
POLITICAL COMMENTARY IN BLACK POPULAR MUSIC
FROM RHYTHM AND BLUES
TO EARLY HIP HOP

James B. Stewart

"Music is a powerful tool in the form of communication [that] can be used to assist in organizing communities."

—Gil Scott-Heron (1979)

This essay examines the content of political commentaries in the lyrics of Rhythm and Blues (R&B) songs. It utilizes a broad definition of R&B that includes subgenres such as Funk and "Psychedelic Soul." The investigation is intended, in part, to address persisting misinterpretations of the manner in which R&B influenced listeners' political engagement during the Civil Rights-Black Power Movement. The content of the messages in R&B lyrics is deconstructed to enable a fuller appreciation of how the creativity and imagery associated with the lyrics facilitated listeners' personal and collective political awareness and engagement. The broader objective of the essay is to establish a foundation for understanding the historical precedents and political implications of the music and lyrics of Hip Hop.

For present purposes, political commentary is understood to consist of explicit or implicit descriptions or assessments of the social, economic, and political conditions of people of African descent, as well as the forces creating these conditions. These criteria deliberately exclude most R & B compositions because the vast majority of songs in this genre, similar to the Blues, focus on some aspect of male-female relationships.[1] This is not meant to imply that music examining male-female relationships is devoid of political implications; however, attention is restricted here to lyrics that address directly the relationship of African Americans to the larger American body politic. While a number of commentators have discussed selected aspects of political ideas found in R&B lyrics, the main corpus of this political commentary has not been subjected to systematic analysis.[2]

Historical precedents and theoretical perspectives underlying the present inquiry are discussed in the next section. A typology of commentary types is then presented and used to examine selected political commentary in R&B lyrics from the 1960s through the early 1980s. The concluding section briefly considers the extent to which the typology is useful for understanding political commentary in Hip Hop music.

HISTORICAL PRECEDENTS AND THEORETICAL FOUNDATIONS

There are a variety of classical and more contemporary commentaries about the role of music in African American culture that provide useful insights for the development of a framework for understanding the political role of R&B. Early 20th century perspectives advanced by Zora Neale Hurston, W. E. B. Du Bois, and Alain Locke remain relevant for interpreting contemporary African American musical forms. Hurston insisted that African American folklore was the core component of authentic African American culture.[3] Extending this idea, the most authentic political commentary in music lyrics should originate in the organic everyday experiences of people of African descent. In *The Souls of Black Folk* Du Bois maintained that the "sorrow songs" provided one of the most useful documentations of the long history of oppression and struggle against that oppression.[4] Thus, this form of music became a bearer of historical memory, similar to the role of griots in many West African societies. In addition to the sorrow conveyed in these songs, Du Bois argued that there was also a "faith in the ultimate justice of things" and that "minor cadences of despair change often to triumph and calm confidence."[5] Similar shifts in moods and assessments can be observed in R&B lyrics.

Philosopher Alain Locke went even further than Du Bois by proposing that changes in predominant African American musical genres were closely correlated with major transformations in the sociopolitical and economic milieu for African Americans.[6] Locke's views suggest that in the absence of external efforts to shape the content of African American music, changes in lyrical content should be correlated with changes in the social, political, and economic circumstances for African Americans. Moreover, Locke emphasized that African American music was deeply ingrained in the American cultural fabric to the point that it "furnish[es] the subsoil of our national music."[7] Locke's perspective suggests the need to explore political commentary in black music in terms of not only its impact on African Americans, but also on Americans of European and Asian descent.

Some contemporary commentators echo many of the classical positions about the special role of music in African American life and culture. Samuel Floyd asserts that "all black music making is driven by and permeated with the memory of things from the cultural past and that the viability of such memory should play a role in the perception of and criticism of works and performances of black music."[8] Applying this concept to a subgenre of R&B, historian William Van Deburg argued that, "as an indigenous expression of the collective African American experience, [Soul music] served as a repository of racial consciousness [that transcended] the medium of entertainment [and] provided a ritual in song with which African Americans could identify and through which they could convey important in-group symbols."[9] In a similar vein, disc jockey Reggie Lavong declared, "like Blues, Soul music reflects, defines, and directs the strategies, expectations, and aspirations of black Americans."[10]

These claims about the political efficacy of R&B have been challenged by Brian Ward in *Just My Soul Responding: Rhythm and Blues, Black Consciousness, and Race Relations* who argued that, "on its own Rhythm and Blues had never *made* mass political or social action possible, or even likely, in any direct or simple way." According to Ward, R&B "had always navigated the territory between being a cultural expression of a black insurgency, which was organized by other means and essentially shaped by other intellectual, political, and socio-economic forces; and being a surrogate for such action."[11] While resolution of this controversy is beyond the scope of this investigation, the debate signals the need to ground the current exploration in an interpretation of the general role of music as an influence on individual and collective human behavior.

Some anthropologists argue that music played a functional role in early human development by facilitating transmission and retention of information necessary for individual and group survival. This is accomplished, in part, through the phenomenon of "auditory imagery." Auditory imagery occurs when one has a "song on the brain," that is, one has the experience of hearing the song without auditory stimulation. A study by David Kraemer and others, examining how the brain processes music, found that similar to previous research regarding "visual imagery," auditory imagery is triggered when an individual is familiar with a song. When subjects heard a version of a song with some lyrics missing, the brain involuntarily supplied the missing words. Moreover, the researchers found that this imaging occurred in a specific part of the brain that was not accessed when subjects were not familiar with a song.[12]

In a broader sense, audio and visual imagery induced by music enables listeners to access related memories, an idea used by Samuel Floyd to ground his study *The Power of Black Music*. Floyd argued that "our responses to music are based on our reactions to the artistic embodiment of struggle and fulfillment as depicted in contrived events, relationships, refinements, and idealizations." These constructed scenarios represent analogs to the daily human struggles to achieve balance between what he describes as "various manifestations of tension and repose, including opposition and accommodation, aspiration and hope, and failure and achievement."[13]

The likelihood that listeners supply corroborative content to elaborate on the political messages in music is acknowledged by Ward, who reported that "with relatively few Soul songs and even fewer Soul singers openly embracing the organized struggle during the decades after Montgomery, black audiences sometimes found themselves bestowing political meanings and Movement messages on ostensibly apolitical songs . . . and [that] sometimes involved popular readings of songs which were far removed from the original intentions of those who made the music."[14] One of the thrusts of this investigation is to document the wide variety of political messages available to audiences in using R&B as a vehicle for their personal and collective political affirmations and empowerment.

Ward's dismissal of the political potency of R&B lyrics stems in part from his emphasis on what he perceives as the limited personal involvement of R&B artists in the Civil Rights Movement, the intensifying commodification of the music over time, and the progressive disappearance of radio stations committed to political education and community development that provided outlets for songs with political messages.[15] There is no question that in a world in which black popular music is highly commodified there is no guarantee that lyrical content mirrors the realities existing within the communities from which writers and performers originate. As black music becomes increasingly subject to control by corporate interests seeking to maximize profits, both its organic linkage to community well-being and its sensibilities are weakened, particularly if the controlling financial interests are external to the social orbit of the music's core black constituency. Marc Anthony Neal cautions in *Songs in the Key of Black Life* that one of the principal constraints placed on black radio during the era of "hyperconglomeration" is on "the music that gets played—or, rather, the music that is *never* played on commercial radio stations that specialize in so-called urban formats."[16]

It is also important to recognize that new technologies have significantly reduced the effectiveness of political messages traditionally disseminated through audio recording formats. The music video, for example, has much greater potential than audio recordings to impact the listener's conscious through the combination of auditory and visual imagery. However, the dissemination of political messages through this format is even less likely than with audio recordings due to even stricter control by corporate commercial interests and associated efforts to expand markets for visual media.

As noted by Floyd, the transformation of R&B "into a racially integrated music with African Americans and whites claiming it as their own began in the 1940s" and accelerated with the ascendance of Little Richard and Chuck Berry.[17] The interracial audience of R&B raises the issue of how political messages available to any listener can be shaped in ways that target specific subgroups. Some messages may be simultaneously intended for both black and nonblack audiences. The two groups may interpret messages similarly or dissimilarly depending on the extent of the use of culturally-specific linguistic features and the degree to which conditions are perceived through comparable lenses. When writers and performers engage in intentional audience differentiation to communicate simultaneously with internal and external audiences, this reflects a modern variant of the type of double entendre reflected in many of the Spirituals sung during the era of slavery to promote resistance and provide guidance along the Underground Railroad, such as, "Swing Low Sweet Chariot."[18] In other cases political commentaries may be fashioned to target specific audiences. As an example, some integrationist commentaries are directed primarily to external, non-black audiences, such as with the "crossover" phenomenon in popular music. In contrast, nationalist, anti-establishment, and revolutionary messages are typically shaped to promote internal community political mobilization.

In general, the impact of the lyrical content on the psyche or behavior of single or multiple audiences depends on several factors. These include the forcefulness, sophistication, and creativity of the message content; the efficacy of the style of delivery; and the perceived salience of the message. These elements, in turn, are heavily influenced by changes over time in the technologies of music production, dissemination, and consumption, along with the ever-evolving social-political landscape of race relations and intergenerational differences in musical tastes.[19] In addition, the stylistic conventions that define a particular genre will, of course, set the boundaries prescribing the format of any associated political commentaries. Moreover, the conditions and events specific to a given time period will heavily influence the subjects of political lyrics and will determine the target audiences as well as the content of the commentary.

Audience segmentation is also facilitated through differences in the sites where different subgroups experience music. Guthrie Ramsey introduces the concept of "community theaters," to describe "public and private spaces [that] provide audiences with a place to negotiate with others—in a highly social way—what cultural expressions such as music mean."[20] Before and during the Civil Rights–Black Power Movement, racial segregation demanded distinct spaces in which African Americans listened to and experienced music. These places included family gatherings, informal interactions among friends, parties, organizational meetings, and theaters in the community. These segregated community theaters facilitated the generation of group-specific interpretations of political messages.

The political saliency of R&B songs was further intensified by the efforts of some African American disc jockeys to use their shows as platforms for political education. Brian Ward has provided the most comprehensive account of the role of radio in the southern civil rights struggle. However, in analyzing these initiatives he fails to examine how the disc jockeys carefully selected particular songs to underscore the political messages delivered through other formats.[21] Northern disc jockeys had much greater latitude than their southern counterparts to intermingle narrative political commentary and the judicious play of songs with political messages.

The importance of these diversified community theaters cannot be overstated in gauging the impact of R&B on listeners' political awareness and engagement, but is easily overlooked when only commercial production and distribution channels are examined. This is the context in which Van Deburg maintained that "more overtly political music often made little impact on national record charts, [but] the message of these songs was spread underground via a modern-day 'grapevine telegraph.'"[22] As will be demonstrated in subsequent sections, the wide variety of message content in R&B lyrics provided rich ingredients for robust political discussion.

TOWARD A TYPOLOGY OF POLITICAL COMMENTARIES IN R&B

The traditional lack of attentiveness to the content of political commentaries in R&B is illustrated by Ward's contention that "Rhythm and Blues absorbed changes in mass black consciousness and reflected them primarily by means of certain musical devices and performance techniques, rather than in the form of neat narrative expositions."[23] Even when analysts acknowledge the significance of R&B lyrical content, there has been a tendency to lump very different types of messages together in ways that overlook important distinctions and nuances. As an example, Van Deburg uses the construct of "updated protest songs" to implicitly conjoin a widely diverse list of songs, including the Impressions's, "Keep on Pushing," the Chi-Lites's, "(For God's Sake) Give More Power to the People," the Temptations's, "Message from a Black Man," and Gil Scott-Heron's, "The Revolution Will Not Be Televised."[24]

The traditional use of broad, undifferentiated classifications introduces significant difficulty in fully appreciating the complexity of political thought contained in R&B lyrics. At the same time, some researchers have provided useful hints for developing a more refined typology of commentaries. It is generally agreed that the "documentary" is the most basic type of political commentary found in R&B lyrics. William Van Deburg suggests that the documentary "provide[s] a running commentary on the state of black culture."[25] In general, documentaries highlight negative conditions prevalent in black communities. Brian Ward argued that the "musical and lyrical affinity of R&B to the material circumstances of black lives, dictated that economic factors often loomed large in its songs, just as they did in black life."[26] Descriptions contained in documentaries are often presented using quasi-objective or nonpejorative language. This rhetorical strategy facilitates engagement with both internal and external audiences, with each able to frame distinct interpretations.

Three additional types of documentaries—"Jeremiads," "All God's Children Declarations," and "Defiant Challenges"—typically target an external audience. Borrowing from the analysis of African American speeches and sermons, Jeremiads incorporate three components: an assertion of the significance of core values ascribed to as a covenant with God; a declension detailing America's failure to live up to this promise with respect to its treatment of African Americans; and a prophecy outlining positive outcomes in the case of repentance, or negative consequences stemming from the perpetuation of the status quo.[27]

All God's Children Declarations tout common interests and shared experiences of African Americans and nonblacks to argue for equal treatment, removal of barriers to equality, and a reduction of intergroup conflict. Lyrics sometimes emphasize the role of external agents in changing conditions, but in many cases outsiders and insiders are simultaneously encouraged to work cooperatively to solve critical social problems. Ward claims that most "'engaged' soul songs of the early-to-mid 1960s . . . used quasi-religious imagery and the sounds of soul, rather than direct invocations of race, Jim Crow, or the Movement to make their racial provenance and political relevance obvious."[28] Defiant Challenges demand (rather than entreat) that external forces cease and desist from exploitative behavior. Threats or promises of negative outcomes from failure to terminate oppressive behavior or conditions are standard features. As suggested by the terminology, an aggressive lyrical style is employed with more limited use of nuance than in the other types of commentaries. Van Deburg suggested that such songs emphasize that significant changes in the social order are on the near horizon and are more likely to emanate from revolutionary than evolutionary processes.[29]

The other broad types of internally focused political commentaries can be called "Awareness Raising Self-Criticism," "Collective Self-Help Solutions," "Confrontation Declarations," "Revolutionary Manifestos," and "Spiritual Transcendence Explorations." Awareness Raising Self-Criticism is designed to educate listeners about the seriousness of a particular set of circumstances and to document the need for corrective action. Criticism can be leveled either generally or at specific groups such as politicians, business owners, preachers, or teachers. The primary bases of criticism are the lack of political awareness of the origins and severity of a problem, and the failure to take action to eliminate debilitating predicaments. As Van Deburg asserted, "Black Power era soulsters . . . taught that in order to alter social conditions, African

Americans first had to change the way they looked at themselves."[30] At the same time, external forces are typically targeted as the major culprit producing negative conditions.

Collective Self-Help Solutions also attempt to sharpen political consciousness, but have the further objective of providing guidance for solving community problems. Michael Haralamabos in *Soul Music* observed, for example, that in some R&B, "concern is expressed for conditions in the poorer areas of black society . . . [and they] are condemned as something to be eradicated."[31] These commentaries attempt to mobilize individuals to work collectively in self-help problem solving activities that use local resources rather than relying on external aid. In some cases suggestions for specific strategies to ameliorate problematic conditions are offered.

Confrontational Declarations advocate aggressive self-defense actions to combat direct and indirect manifestations of external control in black communities by any means necessary, including violence. Law enforcement agents are often targeted as the most visible symbols of external political control. However, other external forces, such as purveyors of illicit drugs, are also identified as high priority targets for direct confrontational strategies. Existing neighborhood-based and national organizations are sometimes chastised for exhibiting timidity in protecting the interests of the community. These commentaries address external audiences indirectly through warnings about the consequences of not relinquishing control of key institutions in black communities. Such commentaries flow directly from several variants of black nationalism prevalent during the Black Power era.[32]

Revolutionary Manifestos frame problems in African American communities within the context of broader patterns of global oppression. Calls for the wholesale restructuring of existing political and economic institutions constitute a major distinguishing feature of the lyrics. Global corporate capitalism and its localized manifestations are often the primary focus of revolutionary transformation commentaries. Audiences are called upon to connect with efforts of marginalized groups around the world to struggle for a more humane international order. From this vantage point, local control, as advocated in confrontation declarations may be necessary, but insufficient, to achieve true liberation. Consequently, coordination of efforts to maintain viable local communities and multicultural alliances are sometimes advocated, thus addressing external audiences indirectly. According to Van Deburg, such commentaries are grounded in the view held by some black leftists that, "the black nationalist struggle was one of both race and class and therefore necessarily linked to the struggles of Third World liberation movements."[33]

Spiritual Transcendence Explorations urge listeners to seek solutions to their daily struggles by achieving personal spiritual enlightenment. Presumably a higher spiritual consciousness can be achieved through meditation and diminished focus on the day-to-day confrontations surrounding race and racial inequality. Drug experimentation is often advocated as a means to move to a higher plane of existence. Thus, drug culture is seemingly transformed from a source of oppression into a liberation strategy. Widespread adoption of this lifestyle would presumably reduce racial tensions and contribute to the elevation of the general human condition. Deracialized imagery is sometimes used to increase the attractiveness of performers to external

11

audiences. As suggested by Ward, such commentaries were especially attractive to some members of "the first generation of post-Movement, upwardly mobile, young middle-class African Americans, gamely testing the extent to which traditional barriers to black advancement really had been erased in the new meritocracy."[34] Key elements of each commentary type are summarized in Table 1.

The targeting of multiple audiences introduces complexity in efforts to interpret political themes. In addition, some commentaries do not fit neatly into any single category, exhibiting characteristics of more than one of the typologies. These issues pose no major hurdle because the classification of individual songs in this investigation is undertaken largely in support of exploration of the ways in which artists and writers have worked creatively to convey messages effectively. The classifications' principal value is as a means to ascertain the relative prevalence of particular types of statements. The classifications also facilitate the assessment of the extent to which performers and writers altered the orientation, content, and style of commentaries as social and political conditions changed and new technological capabilities emerged.

Table 1
Political Commentary Typologies in Black Popular Music

Commentary Type	Audience(s)	Key Characteristics
Documentary	Internal/External	Describes negative conditions designed to document the magnitude of problems and possible causes
Jeremiad	External	Challenges outsiders to implement humanitarian beliefs and values
All God's Children Declaration	External/Internal	Calls for equal treatment based on assertions of common interests and shared experiences
Defiant Challenge	External	Demands that external forces cease and desist from exploitative behavior
Awareness Raising, Self-Criticism	Internal	Describes negative conditions designed to broaden concern within the community
Collective Self-Help Solution	Internal/External	Calls for collective problem-solving efforts relying on local resources
Confrontational Declaration	Internal/External	Advocates aggressive self-defense to confront direct and indirect manifestations of external control in black communities
Revolutionary Manifesto	Internal/External	Calls for overturning existing political and economic institutions to advance liberation struggles
Spiritual Transcendence Exploration	Internal/External	Advocates spiritual enlightenment to reduce social tension, with drug use sometimes advocated to heighten consciousness

POLITICAL COMMENTARY IN R&B

Although the typology introduced previously is designed primarily for the classification of political commentary in R&B and Hip Hop, it is important to recognize the potential applicability of this basic approach to other genres. For example, it has been applied directly to the examination of political commentary in the Blues, although it is unrealistic to expect that the Blues would exhibit the full range of political themes encompassed by this classification scheme.[35]

During the Jim Crow era of the early 20th century, Blues artists were subjected to the same forms of social control that were directed at other African Americans. As a consequence, the political commentaries that were advanced were structured to reduce the likelihood of a backlash from offended whites. The type of aggressive, challenging political commentaries that were fueled, for example, by the Black Power Movement were inconceivable to even the most visionary Blues performers. Instead, Blues artists used their finely honed descriptive skills to highlight the effects of oppression in ways designed to raise the awareness of sympathetic external audiences and/or promote solidarity among African Americans by documenting common experiences and enhancing the resolve to survive in the face of daily oppression. Documentaries, Jeremiads, and All God's Children Declarations were the principal Blues commentaries used to communicate with external audiences. Documentaries and All God's Children commentaries were also the principal vehicle for conveying a sense of common destiny among African Americans.[36]

Unlike the Blues, the content and style of political commentaries in R&B have been dominated by northern urban sensibilities, reflecting the influence of the large-scale out-migration from the South during the post–World War II period. The preeminence of Detroit (Motown) and Philadelphia (Philly Sound) as major sites of R&B music production was one outcome of this dramatic demographic shift away from the rural South. Chicago was also a major site of R&B creative production, and Curtis Mayfield emerged as one of the most incisive commentators in the R&B tradition.[37] Highlighting this pattern in no way diminishes the significance of southern-based labels such as Memphis-based Stax; however, the more hard-hitting political commentaries were likely to originate in the North, where African Americans faced less oppressive social controls.[38] Perry Hall has investigated how distinct south to north migration routes reproduced preexisting geographic collectives with distinct cultural elements in specific northern cities. Hall argues that subtle differences in cultural sensibilities and experiences across communities are reflected in the music produced in each locale.[39] In some respects, this is an extension of Locke's arguments, allowing for disaggregation of the broad patterns of correlation between social conditions and music.

Commercialized R&B music was also a form of dance music and developed a highly stylized format with extensive instrumentation and was packaged to maximize record sales. This genre was created by transforming traditional R&B through changes in lyrics and in the rhythmic organization of the music. The modified format was sanitized to ensure that it would not be overtly offensive to white audiences and could be easily duplicated by white artists selected to perform, i.e., cover songs originally performed by black artists.[40] This market orientation also encouraged a high degree of role differentiation among performers, writers, and producers. As a consequence, in many cases it is difficult to identify the precise source of ideas expressed in political commentaries.

A significant body of R&B songs with political commentary did not begin to appear until the mid-1960s after some of the initial victories in the Civil Rights Movement. Some early commentaries continued discussion of issues addressed previously in Blues lyrics. For example, Sam Cooke's "Chain Gang" (1962) is a stark reminder of how the criminal justice system operates as a vehicle of social control.[41] Reflecting the optimism that engulfed many during the early 1960s, R&B writers and performers expressed guarded optimism about the positive long-term outcomes of the freedom struggle. Sam Cooke's "A Change is Gonna Come," released in 1965 after his mysterious death, is a mournful, yet hopeful, call for a new political dispensation: "It's been a long time coming, but I know a change is gonna come, yes it will."[42] The Impressions' "Keep on Pushing" (1965), written by Curtis Mayfield, is another example of an internally directed commentary expressing confidence that the political and economic fortunes of African Americans were improving.[43]

The early successes of the Civil Rights Movement encouraged a flurry of both externally and internally focused commentaries with All God's Children characteristics, but without explicit religious references. Some songs use the metaphor of a train with passengers from different backgrounds traveling toward a common destination to capture the idea of shared interests in pursuing racial justice. The Impressions' "People Get Ready" (1964), written by Curtis Mayfield, is a classic example. Other songs using the train metaphor to invoke interracial unity images with no explicit religious reference include Gladys Knight and the Pips' (1969) "Friendship Train," written by Norman Whitfield and Barrett Strong, and the O'Jays' "Love Train" (1972), written by Kenny Gamble and Leon Huff.[44]

Some internally focused commentaries urged African Americans to institute self-improvement strategies to demonstrate their worthiness of equal treatment. These lyrics combine elements of All God's Children, Awareness Raising Self-Criticism, and Collective Self-Help commentaries. The Staple Singers' "Respect Yourself" (1971), written by Mark Rice and Luther Ingram, is one example of this rhetorical strategy.[45] The Impressions' "Choice of Colors" (1969), written by Curtis Mayfield, uses a more indirect approach to convey a similar message:

> People must say to the people,
> A better day is coming for you and for me;
> And with a little bit more education and love for our nation,
> We'll have a better society.[46]

The Four Tops' "Keeper of the Castle" (1972), written by Dennis Lambert and Brian Potter, emphasizes listeners' responsibility to maintain and improve the physical conditions in urban communities.[47] The cover of the album containing the title song, "Keeper of the Castle," presents two images of the same mansion, one tidy and well kept, the other dilapidated. This imagery suggests two possible futures for black communities, with the actual path depending heavily on choices made by African Americans themselves. The rhetorical strategy thus synthesizes Awareness Raising Self-Criticism and elements of Collective Self-Help commentary.

A more pessimistic body of Jeremiad political commentary began to appear in the early 1970s, induced in part by the failure of the Civil Rights-Black Power Movement to generate any significant changes in the quality of life for urban black residents. This thematic shift parallels the response of some Blues artists to the unrealized expectations associated with New Deal policies in the 1930s and 1940s. Stevie Wonder aptly captures this sentiment in a unique type of All God's Children commentary articulated in "Visions" (1973). Using allusions to the rhetoric and dream of Martin Luther King, Jr., Wonder questions whether significant progress in reducing inequality has occurred:

> People hand in hand,
>> Have I lived to see the milk and honey land?
> Where hate's a dream and love forever stands,
>> Or is this a vision in my mind?
> Or is this a vision in my mind?[48]

The use of Jeremiad-like characteristics in this commentary is subtle—a strategy found in other commentaries as well. Roberta Flack's "Tryin' Times" (1969), written by Donny Hathaway and Leroy Hutson, is another example of a rhetorical strategy using understated Jeremiad features:

> You got the riots and the ghettos,
>> And it's all around;
> And a whole lot of things that are wrong,
>> Are going down.
> I don't understand it,
>> From my point of view,
> Somebody said do unto others,
>> As you would have them do unto you.
> Folks wouldn't have to suffer,
>> If there was more love for each other,
> These are trying times.[49]

Flack goes on to challenge listeners to become active in efforts to change the dynamics producing intergroup conflict, a theme also advanced in the Temptations' "You Make Your Own Heaven & Hell Right Here on Earth" (1970), written by Norman Whitfield and Barrett Strong.[50] Stevie Wonder's "Jesus Children of

America" (1973) is an interesting Jeremiad that takes to task listeners who presumably subscribe to religious values for failing to translate their beliefs into action.[51]

Curtis Mayfield's "(Don't Worry) If There's a Hell Below We're All Gonna Go" (1970) is one of the most innovative examples of this rhetorical strategy. The song begins with a monologue by a woman promoting the view that the simple solution to all of the world's problems is following the prescriptions set forth in the Bible. Mayfield then identifies various groups who are culpable for contributing to social ills, including sisters, brothers, whiteys, blacks, crackers, and the police and their supporters. He then describes various dysfunctional behaviors tolerated by all and enunciates the warning, "if there's a hell below, then we're all gonna go."[52]

In addition to its Jeremiad features, Mayfield's commentary is significant for its focus on the detailed description of oppressive conditions and concrete identification of perpetrators of exploitation. Other writers and performers have used documentary commentaries to convey the same type of message. Stevie Wonder's epic *Living for the City* (1973) is especially noteworthy for ingenious interweaving of several themes. Wonder describes the persistence of southern oppression that led to northern migration, the heroic efforts to inculcate traditional family values in the face of a myriad of dehumanizing forces, differences in the patterns of subordination faced by black males and females, difficulties in applying southern mores and values to conditions in the urban North, and likely outcomes when involvement with illicit drugs leads to engagement with a racist northern criminal justice system.[53]

Marvin Gaye's "Inner City Blues (Make Me Wanna Holler)" (1971), written by Marvin Gaye and James Nyx, and "What's Going On" (1971), written by Al Cleveland, Marvin Gaye, and Renaldo Benson, both paint graphic pictures of deteriorating social conditions and offer stinging critiques of skewed public policy priorities. Portions of "Inner City Blues" exhibit subtle Defiant Challenge commentary characteristics:

> Rockets, moon shots,
>   Spend it on the have nots,
> Money, we make it,
>   'Fore we see it you take it.
> Oh, make you want to holler,
>   The way they do my life,
> Make me wanna holler,
>   The way they do my life,
> This ain't livin', This ain't livin'.

In "What's Going On," Marvin Gaye pleads for allegiance to an alternative value system in an example of an Awareness Raising Self-Criticism:

> Mother, mother
>   There's too many of you crying;

16

Brother, brother, brother,
    There's far too many of you dying.
You know we've got to find a way,
    To bring some lovin' here today—Yeah.
Father, father, father we don't need to escalate,
    You see, war is not the answer,
For only love can conquer hate.
    You know we've got to find a way,
To bring some lovin' here today,
    Picket lines and picket signs
Don't punish me with brutality;
    Talk to me, so you can see,
Oh, what's going on,
    Yeah, what's going on.[54]

The Black Power Movement and the emphasis on black pride arising in the mid-1960s and blossoming in the early 1970s inspired several Defiant Challenge commentaries that incorporated Black Power ideological elements. Representative songs articulating the theme of black pride include James Brown's "Say it Loud" (1969), and Billy Paul's "Am I Black Enough for You?" (1972), written by Kenny Gamble and Leon Huff.[55] James Brown's song is a counterexample to the general claim introduced previously about the relatively limited production of political commentaries by southern record labels, even though the lyrics are not especially creative. Gamble and Huff's lyrics emphasize the need for listeners to continue struggling until the goals have been achieved and to be steadfast in embracing their black identity, as expressed in the turn of phrase, "stay Black enough for you."

The struggle for power and self-determination also found voice in Defiant Challenge commentaries such as the Isley Brothers' "Fight the Power" (1975), written by Ernie Isley, Marvin Isley, O'Kelly Isley, Ronald Isley, Rudolph Isley, and Chris Jasper.[56] Other examples include the O'Jays' "Give the People the Power They Want" (1975), written by Kenny Gamble and Leon Huff, and the Chi-Lites' "(For God's Sake) Give More Power to the People" (1971), written by Eugene Record.[57] The challenge to black oppression was sometimes interwoven with strong anti-Vietnam War sentiment. Edwin Starr's version of "War (What Is It Good For)" (1970), written by Norman Whitfield and Barrett Strong, set the tone for this type of commentary.[58] Freda Payne's "Bring the Boys Home" (1971), written by General Norman Johnson, Greg Perry, and Angelo Bond, links the war to family and relationship disruption.[59]

Marvin Gaye's "What's Happening Brother" (1971), written by James Nyx and Marvin Gaye, is another example of antiwar commentary that has more of a documentary style than Defiant Challenge. In this song, Gaye takes on the role of a black veteran returning home after service in the war who is attempting to find out what changes have occurred in the situation of African Americans:

Hey baby, what'cha know good?
I'm just gettin' back, but you knew I would.
War is hell, when will it end,
When will people start gettin' together again,
Are things really gettin' better, like the newspaper said?

What else is new my friend, besides what I read?
Money is tighter than it's ever been.
Say man, I don't understand,
What's going on across this land.
Ah what's happening brother,
Oh yeah, what's happening, my man?[60]

During the 1950s and 1960s the dissemination of musical political commentaries was facilitated by the heightened consciousness of many black disc jockeys and announcers on AM stations. They were among the first messengers of the Civil Rights Movement—announcing meetings, conducting interviews with civil rights leaders, and keeping listeners informed about developments in the struggle for equality and justice. They were also inclined to give significant airplay to R&B songs with political thrusts. However, as AM radio lost its popularity to FM formats in the 1970s, the new formats de-emphasized both disc jockeys and community affairs programming, and reduced the likelihood of airplay for political commentaries.[61] In addition, the transition from 7" to 12" records (LPs) as the industry standard was underway, although the impact of this transition on R&B was not manifested until the mid-1970s.[62] The shift to the LP as the industry standard facilitated consolidation in the record industry, and as media conglomerates came to exercise more and more control over the content of albums, it became less possible for most artists to have even one song with overt political content included on an album because of concerns about potentially negative effects on sales. As an illustration, Marvin Gaye faced strong resistance from Berry Gordy when he proposed the *What's Going On* album because Gordy saw little commercial potential in the project.[63] Gordy was wrong.

The emergence of the so-called blaxploitation film genre in the early 1970s was perhaps the most difficult challenge that writers and performers faced in seeking to maintain the role of R&B as a major source of political commentary in black communities. In essence, these films were associated with an inauthentic variant of the type of community theater described by Guthrie Ramsey in his book *Race Music*.[64] The brainchild of Hollywood magnates, these films were designed to bolster sagging Hollywood revenues by bringing African Americans into movie theaters. Moviemakers tapped into the growing frustration in black communities about persistent poverty and lack of access to public resources, and they disseminated a perverse political message glorifying conspicuous consumption, gender exploitation, and illegal activities, such as drug dealing, as elements of a viable strategy for "getting over on the man." The powerful combination of visual imagery and audio enhancement had a much more pronounced effect on individual and collective sensibilities than traditional music stimuli. The titles of some of these productions are well known and include *Superfly* (1972) and *Across 110th Street* (1972).[65] In some ways, Berry Gordy's production of *Lady Sings the Blues* (1972), following Motown's relocation to California, was a counterattack on external efforts to define the representation of black life and culture in film. Through an in-depth examination of the tragic life of Billie Holiday (played by Diana Ross), Gordy emphasized the complexity and humanity of African Americans, in contrast to the caricatures offered in the blaxploitation genre. This seemingly progressive move is somewhat ironic given Gordy's resistance to Marvin Gaye's *What's Going On* album, discussed previously.[66]

Some socially conscious black musicians who were contracted to develop the soundtracks for blaxploitation films attempted to neutralize the thematic content and visual imagery by producing audio commentaries challenging the glorification of the underground economy. In effect, these cultural warriors engaged in a type of guerrilla campaign against external cultural manipulation. Two of the more notable examples are Curtis Mayfield's *Superfly* and Bobby Womack's *Across 110th Street* soundtracks.[67]

Curtis Mayfield's, "Freddy's Dead," is a five-and-a-half-minute-tribute to the tragically naïve Freddy, one of the film's main casualties. A good-hearted yet weak-willed man caught up in the life of a pusher, Freddy is killed unceremoniously in the cutthroat world navigated by the Superfly character played by Ron O'Neal. Mayfield asks listeners to think beyond immediate gratification and understand the larger political and economic forces that shape the scenarios producing tragic endings like the death of Freddy:

> We're all filled up with progress,
> > But sometimes I must confess,
> We can deal with rockets and dreams,
> > But reality, what does it mean?
> Ain't nothing said,
> > 'Cause Freddy's dead.

Mayfield goes on to challenge black men to reevaluate their engagement with the underworld via Awareness Raising Self-Criticism:

> If you don't try,
> > You're gonna die.
> Why can't we brothers
> > Protect one another?
> No one's serious,
>
> > And it makes me furious,
> Don't be misled,
> > Just think of Fred.[68]

Bobby Womack's "Across 110th Street," written by Womack and J. J. Johnson also focuses on one character in a larger drama. However, in this case an autobiographical approach is used to describe how black males can easily become entangled in the underworld:

I was the third brother of five,
     Doing whatever I had to do to survive.
I'm not saying what I did was alright,
     But breaking out of the ghetto is a day-to-day fight.
Been down so long it never did cross my mind,
     I knew there was a better way of life I was just trying to find.
You don't know what you'll do 'til you're put under pressure,
     Cause 110th Street is a hell of a tester.

In the closing stanza Womack offers a Collective Self-Help Solution in making a plea for black men to cease and desist from engagement with the drug trade and examine the social function of the ghetto within the larger political economy:

Hey Brother, there's a better way out,
     Snorting that coke, shooting that dope;
Man you're copping out.
     Take my advice, its either live or die,
You gotta be strong if you want to survive.

The families on the other side of town,
     Would catch hell without a ghetto around.
In every city the same thing is going down,
     Harlem is the capital of every ghetto town.[69]

In both examples the individual case studies are used to engage in Awareness Raising Self-Criticism. However, since the commentaries are designed to counteract the negative imagery in the films rather than fully explore alternative survival strategies, the potential to incorporate Collective Self-Help Solutions effectively was limited. To some extent, Curtis Mayfield was able to broaden the dialogue regarding the sources of oppression in the monologue and first chorus of "The Cocaine Song" on the *Superfly* album.

I've met many people over the years,
And in my opinion I have found that people are the same everywhere.
They have the same fears,
Shed similar tears,
Die in so many years.

The oppressed seem to have suffered the most,
In every continent, coast to coast.
Now our lives are in the hands of the pusher man;
We break it all down so you might understand
How to protect yourself.

Don't make no profit for the man.
I'm so glad I got my own;
So glad that I can see,
My life's a natural high,
The man can't put no thing on me.[70]

Mayfield's international references suggest elements of Revolutionary Manifestos while the invocation of "a natural high" is representative of the type of language used in some Spiritual Transcendence Explorations.

Although, as noted previously, southern record labels such as Stax were less likely to produce a significant body of political commentary, artists associated with the Stax label did have a visible impact on the political climate. The film *Wattsax*, originally released in 1973, illustrates how political commentary in R&B and Soul music was introduced into new "community theatre" settings. The live performance community theater approach represented by *Wattsax* constituted another type of musically based counterforce to the blaxploitation films of the early 1970s. *Wattsax* is an interesting combination of documentary and Awareness Raising Self-Criticism embedded in a cinematic format. The film, produced by Mel Stuart, is a retrospective dedicated to the Watts riots of 1965. The primary focus of the film is the Watts Summer Festival's concert held at the Los Angeles Coliseum in 1972. The concert featured various Soul music artists, including Isaac Hayes, Rufus Thomas, the Staple Singers, the Bar Kays, and Luther Ingram. The concert footage is interwoven with interviews dissecting "the State of Black America" in the early 1970s and the effects of the riots on both Los Angeles and the United States.[71]

Philadelphia International Records also exhibited impressive creativity in harnessing its unmistakable "Sound of Philadelphia" to produce some of the best examples of organic Awareness Raising Self-Criticism and Collective Self-Help commentaries of the 1970s. As noted by Nelson George, although the lyrics are carefully crafted to avoid assignment of culpability for problems to outside forces, Harold Melvin and the Blue Notes' "Wake Up Everybody" (1975), written by Gene McFadden and John Whitehead, as well as McFadden and Whitehead's "Ain't No Stoppin' Us Now" (1979), are important examples of this approach.[72]

The album *Let's Clean Up the Ghetto* (1977) captures the essence of the broader Philadelphia International initiative.[73] The record company's ability to mount this type of community empowerment venture, while functioning essentially as a component of CBS's black music department, is an interesting contrast to the more traditional style of corporate control of lyrical content discussed previously. This album features the Philadelphia International All-Stars: Lou Rawls, the O'Jays, Teddy Pendergrass, Harold Melvin and the Blue Notes, Billy Paul, Dee Dee Sharp Gamble, the Intruders, Archie Bell and the Drells, and The Three Degrees. The title song, written by Kenny Gamble, Leon Huff, and Cary Gilbert, is a medley involving most of the All-Stars that implores listeners to participate in a physical clean up effort "because the ghetto is our home."[74] The titles of several of the other songs on the album convey the album's broader thrust including, "Now Is the Time to Do It," "Year of Decision," "New Day, New World Comin'," and "Save the Children."[75] The organization's emergent community development strategy was announced in Kenneth Gamble's prominently placed message on the album cover: "The only way we can clean up the *physical* ghetto is to first clean up the *mental* ghetto. With the help of almighty God, we will be able to turn this community into a positive system. Our first step is cleanliness, 'cause it's the closest thing to godliness." Philadelphia International Records demonstrated its commitment by donating all profits from the album to charity for five years.[76] The religious reference is not easy to interpret using the classification system presented in this investigation. Nelson George observes that by the mid-1970s, Kenneth Gamble viewed Philadelphia International in part as "a platform from which to proselytize, espousing a world view that obliquely revealed his private belief in the tenets of Islam."[77] Gamble's attachment to the Nation of Islam introduces a different perspective on the traditional focus of All God's Children Declarations that reference Christian theology. Nevertheless, the message resonated with adherents to Christianity through its invocation of shared values of community empowerment.

The relocation of Motown from Detroit to Los Angeles circa 1972 raises several interesting issues. It can be argued that the relocation dismantled whatever potential existed for Motown to serve as a significant community theater in which important political commentary originated. Some argue that Gordy provided little notice of his intentions, disrupting the lives of the members of the "Motown family" when the planned move was formally announced, while others claim that plans for the move had been developed well in advance.[78] Whichever version is accurate, there is little doubt that differences in regional culture and political consciousness, along with the departures of several important artists, necessitated a change in Motown's orientation and operations so that by the mid-1970s, it was no longer a significant source of incisive political commentaries. The Commodores' "Visions" (1978), written by Thomas McClary and Lionel Ritchie, is illustrative of the few attempts by Motown to produce political commentary during this period. Released on the album titled, *Natural High*, the lyrics essentially sample earlier commentaries by slightly modifying phrases like "one day a change is gonna come" (recall Sam Cooke) and "I see visions in my mind" (Stevie Wonder).[79] The song fits easily into the Spiritual Transcendence commentary classification, with the focus on a "natural high."

The use of the "natural high" and "visions" metaphors is one indicator of the influence of a new style of political commentary that emerged during this period in Funk music. James Brown is often credited with originating the upbeat musical style characterized as "Funk," that relies heavily on syncopated rhythms, a thick bass line, extensive use of rhythm guitars and a rhythm-oriented horn section, and chanted or hollered vocals.[80] The West Coast was an important community theater production site for Funk music that incorporated political commentaries. In some respects the West Coast locus of this genre represented a counterreaction to the high levels of confrontation emerging out of the Watts Riot of 1965 and the activities of the Black Panthers and United States.[81] Thus, although the titles of "Don't Call Me Nigger, Whitey" (1969) and "Stand" (1969), performed by Sly and the Family Stone, seemingly imply an assertive political line, the lyrics and the musical format project a very different perspective.[82] "Don't Call Me Nigger, Whitey" is most notable for the use of synthesized voices, the extensive use of the electric guitar to produce discordant sounds, and minimalist lyrics, all of which become important elements of Funk music. "Stand" actually promotes an individualistic notion of empowerment, deliberately avoiding any mention of specific groups. A similar rhetorical strategy is employed in "Everyday People" (1969), in which references to blue and yellow people, long hair and short hair, and rich ones and poor ones appear to be used to avoid potential damage to the "crossover" potential that might result from language explicitly addressing black-white relations.[83]

The Motown group, led by writers/producers Norman Whitfield and Barrett Strong, responded to the challenge posed by the new format with its own variant of this genre, "psychedelic soul." The primary examples were the well-known Temptations' hits "Cloud Nine" (1969) and "Runaway Child Running Wild" (1969). These songs focus respectively on drugs and teenage rebellion, and are largely documentaries that offer little guidance for overcoming the problems dramatized in the lyrics.[84] The "new" Temptations were greeted as representatives of the counterculture, a status solidified when they recorded Norman Whitfield's outspoken protest against the Vietnam War, "Stop the War Now."[85]

Spiritual Transcendence commentaries began to proliferate in the early and mid-1970s. To some extent such commentaries reflect disillusionment with the failure of political advocacy and the Civil Rights–Black Power Movement to overcome structural inequalities. Between 1972 and 1975 the median income of black families was stagnant and the unemployment rate for black men jumped from 7.0 to 12.5 percent.[86] In addition, widespread resistance to busing to obtain public school desegregation also arose during this period. These social conditions provide a context for the type of Spiritual Transcendence commentaries exemplified by Earth, Wind, and Fire's "Keep Your Head to the Sky" (1973), written by Maurice White, and "That's the Way of the World" (1975), written by Maurice White, Charles Stepney, and Verdine White. Listeners are told in "That's the Way of the World":

> You will find, you will find peace of mind,
> If you look way down in your heart and soul,
> Don't hesitate, 'cause the world seems cold,
> Stay young at heart, 'cause you'll never, never part.[87]

At the same time, however, there are a few cases where Funk artists produced Defiant Challenge commentaries. Housing segregation persisted in most major urban areas between 1960 and 1970, including Atlanta, Boston, Chicago, Cleveland, Los Angeles, New York, Philadelphia, San Francisco, and Washington, DC, enabling the election of black mayors in many of these cities in the late 1960s and early 1970s.[88] Parliament's examination of majority black urban centers in "Chocolate City" (1975), written by George Clinton, William Collins, and Bernard Worrell, uses an interesting combination of spoken word and abrupt chord changes to present a euphemistic tribute to black control of urban centers. The "Chocolate City" and "CC" metaphors are used to characterize cities where black majorities were likely to emerge and to stake a political claim on those spaces:

Hey CC, they say you jive and game, and can't be changed.
But on the positive side, you're my piece of the rock,
And I love you, can you dig it?[89]

Black majorities in many central cities are suggested to be one outcome of the failure of external forces to address long-standing injustices: "Hey, we didn't get our forty acres and a mule, but we did get you, CC." The chorus "gaining on you" is used extensively as a subtle warning to external audiences about unspecified consequences from demographic shifts producing urban black majorities. The implicit message is that outsiders would be well advised to support policies that reduce structural inequalities.

In many respects, Parliament is an outlier in the Funk genre. Nelson George argues that this group's orientation was shaped by its Detroit origins and influenced by the radical politics found in this metropolitan area. More generally, Funk and Disco, popular in the 1970s, do not fit readily into any of the categories in Table 1, with their orientation toward party and dance music. Nelson George argues that Disco was a disruptive outside force that helped to pull R&B "away from its roots." More pointedly, he maintains that between 1976 and 1980 Disco music evolved into "a sound of mindless repetition and lyrical idiocy that, with exceptions, overwhelmed R&B."[90] A more charitable assessment might conclude that both Funk and Disco were not wholly devoid of political connotations. Both are prime examples of the phenomenon described by Thomas Poole as the creation of party music in circumstances where there is no reason to party as a form of defiant celebration in the face of "dehumanizing" hostility and oppression.[91]

Revolutionary commentaries, as exemplified by the music of Gil Scott-Heron and the Last Poets, served as a counterforce to the tendency toward muted political commentary in black popular music in the mid and late 1970s. A self-described "Bluesician," Scott-Heron positioned himself to resurrect the tradition of political commentary in the Blues. Tracing his lineage directly to Langston Hughes, Scott-Heron stated his intent to "adapt certain theories [used by] . . . Robeson, Hughes, and others [and] . . . [work] these theories in our own context around South Africa, life concerns, and daily living."[92] Hughes's poem "Letter to the Academy" (1933) exhibits a cadence and content similar to many of Scott-Heron's compositions:

But please, all you gentlemen with beards who are so wise and old
And who write better than we do,
And whose souls have triumphed,
(In spite of hungers and wars and the evils about you),
And whose books have soared in calmness and beauty
Aloof from the struggle to the library shelves,
And the desks of students and who are now classics-come forward
And speak upon the subject of the Revolution.
We want to know what in the hell you'd say?[93]

Scott-Heron's debt to the Blues is demonstrated most concretely in the internal-ly oriented commentary, "The Get Out of the Ghetto Blues," in which he attacks the lack of political consciousness among African Americans, irrespective of their social circumstances:

I know you think you're cool,
    Lord, if they bus your kids to school,
I know you think you're cool,
    Just 'cause they bus your kids to school.
But you ain't got a thing to lose,
    You just got the "Get Out of the Ghetto Blues."
I know you think you're cool,
    If you gettin' two welfare checks.
You done told me you think you're cool,
    Because you gettin' two welfare checks.
Yeah, but you got ten years to lose (if you get caught),
    Just trying to fight the "Get Out of the Ghetto Blues."[94]

Scott-Heron's best known composition, "The Revolution Will Not Be Televised," is directed at both internal and external audiences. In this spoken word treatise Heron lambasts popular culture, the police, traditional civil rights leaders, and advertising by multinational corporations, using rhetorical strategies similar to those employed in the earlier commentary, "When the Revolution Comes," (1970) written by Oyewole, and performed by The Original Last Poets:

There will be no pictures of pigs shooting down brothers on the instant replay,
There will be no pictures of pigs shooting down brothers on the instant replay,
There will be no pictures of Whitney Young being run out of Harlem on a rail
    with a brand new process.
There will be no slow motion or still lifes of Roy Wilkins strolling through Watts
    in a red, black, and green jumpsuit he has been saving just for a special occasion.
Green Acres, Beverly Hillbillies, and Hooterville Junction will no longer be so
    damn relevant.

25

And no one will care if Dick finally got down with Jane on "Search for
Tomorrow,"
Because Black people will be in the streets looking for a brighter day
The Revolution will not be televised.[95]

PASSING THE TORCH—FROM THE BLUES AND R&B TO HIP HOP

Of course, the revolution envisioned by Gil Scott-Heron and the Last Poets did not
materialize, and a complex of economic, political, sociological, and technological forces
would converge in the 1980s and delimit the prevalence and range of political commentaries in R&B. Conditions in inner-city black communities worsened considerably following Ronald Reagan's election as President. Reagan moved swiftly to discredit and/or
dismantle federally funded antipoverty, job training, and affirmative action programs.
He appointed archconservatives to head the Equal Employment Opportunity
Commission (EEOC) and the United States Civil Rights Commission (USCRC) who,
in turn, reduced sharply or invalidated thousands of discrimination suits filed against
employers. White racists and hate groups were emboldened by Reagan's anti–civil rights
posture. Racial attacks and harassment of African Americans and other minorities
increased dramatically during his second term in office, including racial incidents on several major college campuses. The Reagan administration also introduced sharp cuts in
financial aid that limited college access for poor black and other nonwhite students.[96]
At the same time, the number of black elected officials continued to expand, creating the illusion of broad inclusion and creating difficulty in identifying the agents
responsible for the worsening conditions. This ambiguity, in turn, inhibited political
awareness and the articulation of easily digested political commentaries. Many members of the black middle class were able to escape the dismal conditions in inner cities
and relocate to the suburbs—segregation actually declined between 1980 and 1990 in
most of the major urban centers.[97] This exodus accelerated disinvestment processes
in inner cities and heightened social isolation. Overall, the real median incomes of
African American men, women, and families were stagnant between 1975 and 1985.
The black male unemployment rate, which was 12.5 percent in 1975, rose even higher to 13.2 percent in 1985, and remained in double digits at 10.4 percent in 1990.[98]
Correspondingly, the number of African Americans newly incarcerated in federal and
state prisons escalated from approximately 58,000 in 1980 to 87,000 by 1985—a figure that would almost double by 1990 to 169,500.[99]
Thus, since the 1980s, R&B, and Hip Hop political commentators have been
forced to address worsening social problems, including high unemployment, police
brutality, incarceration, inadequate public schools, political apathy, and dysfunctional
behaviors that perpetuate oppression. In the R&B tradition, Fatback's R&B-influenced
documentary, "Is This the Future?" (1983), written by Gerry Thomas, uses the spoken
word format, a staple of Hip Hop, and an R&B musical background, to draw connections between deplorable conditions in black communities and public policies.[100]

26

During the same time period, the Hip Hop classic, "The Message," was released, exploring many of the same issues. Grandmaster Flash and the Furious Five's "The Message" (1982), written by Ed Fletcher, Melvin Glover, Sylvia Robinson, and Clifton Chase, is more of a Defiant Challenge commentary. While the lyrics are articulated in a classic Hip Hop spoken word cadence, the background music infuses both traditional R&B and Funk elements. The song contains the type of graphic description of oppressive conditions found in the best Blues and R&B commentaries, and issues the type of subtle warnings to external audiences found in some of the more assertive R&B commentaries:

> It's like a jungle sometimes, it makes me wonder
> > How I keep from going under.
> It's like a jungle sometimes, it makes me wonder
> > How I keep from going under.
> Broken glass everywhere,
> > People pissing on the stairs, you know they just don't care.
> I can't take the smell, can't take the noise,
> > I got no money to move out, I guess I got no choice,
> Rats in the front room, roaches in the back
> > Junkies in the alley with a baseball bat.
> I tried to get away, but I couldn't get far,
> > A man with a tow truck repossessed my car.
> Don't push me cause I'm close to the edge,
> > I'm trying not to lose my head.[101]

Hip Hop, as a new community theater project, initially emerged as a form of mass expression, largely unfettered by corporate attachments, fueled by the harsh realities of inner-city life. Its origins in street performance reflected, in part, the pervasive stultifying effects of commercial control of media outlets. The general black media climate is characterized by a pattern of growing consolidation in ownership and control. This process has had especially negative effects on black radio news, a key complement to R&B political commentaries in the 1960s and early 1970s. The decline of black radio news has conditioned listeners to expect mundane news broadcasts, thereby dulling listeners' receptivity to incisive political commentaries by progressive Hip Hop artists. *Black Commentator* argues that "the near death of black radio news has been a major factor in the erosion of black political organization nationwide" and that "chains like Radio One gradually eliminated news from the mix, offering syndicated or local talk instead, and pretending that morning radio jockeys could double as news people."[102]

Even given these major constraints, Hip Hop's organic linkages to R&B suggest that its approaches to conveying political commentary will exhibit many of the same developmental patterns observed for R&B. As a consequence, the classification scheme introduced in this investigation can be used both to recognize patterns and track general tendencies in the evolution of commentaries.

27

Nas, for example, uses the documentary format effectively to describe historical and contemporary patterns of oppression in black communities in the song "Black Zombie," and the Jeremiad commentary has been creatively adapted by the British alternative Hip Hop group, Jamiroquai, in the song "Emergency on Planet Earth."[103] Michael Franti offers an innovative All God's Children commentary in "Stay Human (All the Freaky People)." Franti calls on people of all cultures, races, and ethnicities to address common problems and to stop perceiving each other as "freaky people" and recognize that they are "all God's children."[104] Mos Def's "Umi Says" is a solid example of a Spiritual Transcendence Exploration in which he calls on Umi (his mother) and Abi (another spiritual being) to help black people overcome their problems in the face of moral uncertainty.[105]

Tupac Shakur provides a paradigmatic example of a Defiant Challenge commentary in the song "Troublesome 96," in which he declares "in your wildest dreams, you couldn't picture a nigga like me."[106] In what is probably the classic Confrontational Declaration commentary, "Fuck tha Police" by NWA, the promise is made that "Ice Cube will swarm on any muthafucka in a blue uniform."[107] The link between earlier and contemporary political commentaries is illustrated by Common's collaboration with the Last Poets on the composition "The Corner." In this Awareness Raising Self-Criticism, Kanye West laments that "on the corners niggaz rob or kill and dyin' just to make a livin'," while the Last Poets remind listeners that "the corner was our Rock of Gibraltar, our Stonehenge, our Taj Mahal, our monument, our testimonial to freedom, to peace, and to love."[108] To address these issues, Jurassic 5 proposes that the people take it back to the concrete streets (the community) in the Collective Self-Help commentary "Concrete Schoolyard."[109] Finally, The Coup issue a powerful Revolutionary Manifesto in "Ride the Fence," challenging imperialism and corporate greed and calling for proactive and direct challenges to global oppression.[110]

Unfortunately, some of the evolutionary parallels between Hip Hop and R&B are problematic for the continuing production of incisive Hip Hop political commentaries. Despite unprecedented success in establishing and maintaining independent record labels, paralleling the early years of Motown, many Hip Hop moguls seem singly oriented toward the pursuit of profit, with little concern for the social and political content of their products. In the representational arena, Hip Hop artists face many challenges, not the least of which is the rebirth of dysfunctional and denigrating imagery propagated through blaxploitation in both films and music videos. Interestingly, Nelson George argues that the old blaxploitation films have been appropriated by some Hip Hop artists for their own purposes.[111] To the extent that these purposes mirror the precedents set by Curtis Mayfield and Bobby Womack (discussed previously), there will be cause for optimism, but no such figure has yet emerged on the Hip Hop scene. Instead, the traditional images of the "pimp" and "hustler" are alive and well and have been introduced into product lines such as Nelly's "Pimp Juice," a recent addition to the energy drink market.

There are, however, a few encouraging signs. The Hip Hop community-sponsored "Stop the Violence" and "Get Out the Vote" initiatives clearly follow in the footsteps of some of the more progressive efforts by R&B artists. As an example, the "Stop the Violence" movement bears some similarities to Philadelphia International's community development initiatives.[112] Efforts by Hip Hop artists to encourage greater voter participation can, to some extent, offset the depoliticizing influences of the changes in black owned radio discussed previously.[113] Several major figures in the world of Hip Hop have also established foundations to promote community development in the spirit of previous Philadelphia International efforts.[114] While the jury is still out on the success and sustainability of these initiatives, one can hope that these are early indications of a political re-awakening that can realize the liberatory potential of Hip Hop.

NOTES

I am deeply indebted to Thomas Poole for lending his knowledge of the Blues to assist in this research. I also owe a special thanks to Caryl Sheffield for invaluable assistance in researching political commentary in Rhythm and Blues and for helpful comments on earlier drafts. My deepest gratitude to Derrick Alridge for identifying Hip Hop compositions that fit into each of the thematic categories. Detailed comments by Perry Hall and V. P. Franklin have been invaluable in the refinement of the analytical framework.

[1]For a treatment of black male-female relationships in black music using a similar methodology, see James B. Stewart, "Relationships Between Black Males and Females in Rhythm and Blues Music of the 1960s and 1970s," *The Western Journal of Black Studies* 3 , no. 3 (1979): 186–96.

[2]A partial list of monographs that include some discussion of political commentary in R&B or related genres would include Samuel A Floyd, Jr., *The Power of Black Music* (New York, 1995); Nelson George, *The Death of Rhythm and Blues* (New York, 1988); Michael Haralambos, *Soul Music, The Birth of a Sound in Black America* (New York, 1974); Marc Anthony Neal, *Songs in the Key of Black Life, A Rhythm and Blues Nation* (New York, 2003); William L. Van Deburg, *New Day in Babylon, The Black Power Movement and American Culture, 1965–1975* (Chicago, 1992); and Brian Ward, *Just My Soul Responding, Rhythm and Blues, Black Consciousness, and Race Relations* (Berkeley, CA, 1998).

[3]See Zora Neale Hurston, "Characteristics of Negro Expression," in *Negro: An Anthology*, ed., Nancy Cunard (New York, 1970), 39–46.

[4]Du Bois describes the "Sorrow Songs" in Chapter 14 of *The Souls of Black Folk*, entitled "Of the Sorrow Songs." W. E. B. Du Bois, *The Souls of Black Folk* (Chicago, 1903).

[5]Ibid., 264.

[6]Alain Locke, *The Negro and His Music* (New York, 1969).

[7]Ibid., 13.

[8]Floyd, *The Power of Black Music*, 10.

[9]Van Deburg, *New Day in Babylon*, 205.

[10]Quoted in Haralambos, *Soul Music*, 118.

[11]Ward, *Just My Soul Responding*, 429.

[12]David Kraemer, C. Neil Macrae, Adam E. Green, and William M. Kelley, "Musical Imagery: Sound of Silence Activates Auditory Cortex," *Nature* 434 (10 March 2005), 158.

[13]Floyd, *The Power of Black Music*, 226–27.

[14]Ward, *Just My Soul Responding*, 203.

[15]Ibid.

[16]Neal, *Songs in the Key of Black Life*, 142.

[17]Floyd, *The Power of Black Music*, 179.

[18]For an impressive audio collection of songs that facilitated movement on the Underground Railroad, see Reggie and Kim Harris, *Steal Away, Songs of the Underground Railroad*, Appleseed Recordings (1997). Samuel Floyd discusses how the chariot trope has been "repeated and revised many times in many titles" in *The Power of Black Music*, 213.

[19]Many of these issues are discussed extensively in George, *The Death of Rhythm and Blues*.

[20]Guthrie Ramsey, *Race Music* (Berkeley, CA, 2003): 77.

[21]Brian Ward, *Radio and the Struggle for Civil Rights in the South* (Gainesville, FL, 2004).

[22]Van Deburg, *New Day in Babylon*, 215.

[23]Ward, *Just My Soul Responding*, 14.

[24]Van Deburg, *New Day in Babylon*, 213.

[25]Ibid., 215.

[26]Ward, *Just My Soul Responding*, 204.

[27]See, for example, David Howard-Pitney, *The Afro-American Jeremiad: Appeals for Justice in America* (Philadelphia, PA, 1990).

[28]Ward, *Just My Soul Responding*, 300.

[29]Van Deburg, *New Day in Babylon*, 212–13.

[30]Ibid.

[31]Haralambos, *Soul Music*, 121.

[32]Assertions of the need for African Americans to control key community institutions were endorsed by most nationalists; however, claims advancing the right to engage in retaliatory violence had significantly fewer adherents. See the discussion of these issues in Van Deburg, *New Day in Babylon*, 152–55.

[33]Ibid., 154.

[34]Ward, *Just My Soul Responding*, 428. Ward refers specifically here only to the attractiveness of Disco.

[35]James B. Stewart, "Message in the Music: Political Commentary in Pre–Hip Hop Black Popular Music Lyrics," unpublished manuscript.

[36]This interpretation of the essence of the Blues has been presented by various researchers, for example, see Daphne Harrison, *Black Pearls: Blues Queens of the 1920s* (New Brunswick, 1988).

[37]The important role of northern urban centers in the development of R&B has been discussed by several authors, including Nelson George in *The Death of Rhythm and Blues* and Brian Ward in *Just My Soul Responding*.

[38]For an in-depth discussion of Stax and southern R&B or Soul, see Peter Guralnick, *Sweet Soul Music: Rhythm and Blues and the Southern Dream of Freedom* (New York, 1986).

[39]Perry Hall, *In the Vineyard: Working in African American Studies* (Knoxville, TN, 1999).

[40]This interpretation is found in Jonathan Kamin, "Parallels in the Social Reaction to Jazz and Rock," *The Black Perspective in Music* 3 (1978): 278–98.

[41]Sam Cooke, "Chain Gang," *The Best of Sam Cooke*, vocals by Sam Cooke, RCA Victor (1962).

[42]Sam Cooke, "A Change is Gonna Come," *The Best of Sam Cooke, Volume 2*, vocals by Sam Cooke, RCA Victor (1965).

[43]Curtis Mayfield, "Keep on Pushing," *Keep on Pushing*, vocals by the Impressions, ABC-Paramount (1965).

[44]Norman Whitfield and Barrett Strong, "Friendship Train," *Gladys Knight & the Pips Greatest Hits*, vocals by Gladys Knight & the Pips, Soul (1969); Kenny Gamble and Leon Huff, "Love Train," *Back Stabbers*, vocals by the O'Jays, Philadelphia International Records (1972).

[45]Mark Rice and Luther Ingram, "Respect Yourself," *Bealtitude: Respect Yourself*, performed by the Staple Singers, Stax Records (1972).

[46]Curtis Mayfield, "Choice of Colors," *The Young Mods' Forgotten Story*, vocals by the Impressions, Buddah Records (1969).

[47]Dennis Lambert and Brian Potter, "Keeper of the Castle," *Keeper of the Castle*, vocals by the Four Tops, ABC Records (1972).

[48]Stevie Wonder, "Visions," *Innervisions*, vocals by Stevie Wonder, Tamla Records (1972). For an in-depth discussion of political themes in the music of Stevie Wonder, see Deborah Atwater, "Political and Social Messages in the Music of Stevie Wonder" in *African-American Rhetoric: A Reader*, ed., Lyndrey Niles (Dubuque, IA, 1995): 139–49.

[49]Donny Hathaway and Leroy Hutson, "Tryin' Times," *First Take*, vocals by Roberta Flack, Atlantic Recording Corporation (1969).

[50]Norman Whitfield and Barrett Strong, "You Make Your Own Heaven and Hell Right Here on Earth," *Psychedelic Shack*, vocals by the Temptations, Gordy Records (1970). My thanks to Caryl Sheffield for recommending this song.

[51]Stevie Wonder, "Jesus Children of America," *Innervisions*, vocals by Stevie Wonder, Tamla Records (1972).

[52]Curtis Mayfield, "(Don't Worry) If There Is a Hell Below We're All Gonna Go," *Curtis*, vocals by Curtis Mayfield, Curtom Records (1970).

[53]Stevie Wonder, "Living for the City," *Innervisions*, vocals by Stevie Wonder, Tamla Records (1972).

[54]Marvin Gaye and James Nyx, "Inner City Blues (Make Me Wanna Holler)," *What's Going On*, vocals by Marvin Gaye, Tamla Records (1971); Al Cleveland, Marvin Gaye, and Renaldo Benson, "What's Going On," *What's Going On*, vocals by Marvin Gaye, Tamla Records (1971).

[55]James Brown and James Ellis, "Say It Loud—I'm Black and I'm Proud," *Say It Loud—I'm Black and I'm Proud*, vocals by James Brown, King Records (1969). James Brown is, of course, a contradictory figure in terms of political stances. His songs "America Is My Home" and "Living in America" extol a much more integrationist message. This contradiction has been highlighted by Nelson George in *The Death of Rhythm and Blues*, 103. Kenny Gamble and Leon Huff, "Am I Black Enough for You," *360 Degrees of Billy Paul*, vocals by Billy Paul, Philadelphia International Records (1972).

[56]Ernie Isley, Marvin Isley, O'Kelly Isley, Ronald Isley, Rudolph Isley, and Chris Jasper, "Fight the Power," *The Heat is On*. T-Neck (1975).

[57]Kenny Gamble and Leon Huff, "Give the People What They Want," *Survival*, vocals by the O'Jays, Philadelphia International Records (1975); Eugene Record, "(For God's Sake) Give More Power to the People," *(For God's Sake) Give More Power to the People*, vocals by the Chi-Lites, Brunswick Records (1971). My thanks to Caryl Sheffield for suggesting this song.

[58]Norman Whitfield and Barrett Strong, "War (What Is It Good For)," *War & Peace*, vocals by Edwin Starr, Gordy Records (1970). Originally recorded by the Temptations.

[59]General Norman Johnson, Greg Perry, and Angelo Bond, "Bring the Boys Home, *Contact*, vocals by Freda Payne, Invictus (1971). My thanks to Perry Hall for suggesting this song.

[60]James Nyx and Marvin Gaye, "What's Happening Brother," *What's Going On*, vocals by Marvin Gaye, Tamla Records (1971).

[61]For more information about the history and activities of disc jockeys and announcers on black AM stations, see the Smithsonian programs exploring various dimensions of black radio at http://www.si.edu/sp/onair/radpgms.htm. Nelson George insists in *The Death of Rhythm and Blues* that AM stations that are black owned and oriented are culpable, along with FM, for diluting their black image in order to attract more ad revenues.

[62]For a useful discussion of the impact of technological changes on R&B, see April Reilly, "The Impact of Technology on Rhythm and Blues," *The Black Perspective in Music* 1 (No. 2, 1973): 136–46; Dave Marsh argued that singles still dominated R&B through the mid-1970s—see *The Heart of Rock & Soul: The 1001 Greatest Singles Ever Made* (1989; reprinted New York, 1999).

[63]For an account of the tensions between Gordy and Gaye surrounding the album, *What's Going On*, see Bill Dahl, *Motown: The Golden Years* (Iola, WI, 2001), 79.

[64]Ramsey, *Race Music*.

[65]In *Across 110th Street* actors Paul Benjamin and Ed Bernard play two Harlem residents driven by desperate circumstances to steal $300,000 from the local mob. In *Superfly*, actor Ron O'Neal plays Youngblood Priest, a Harlem coke dealer who wants to get out of the business but must outwit the cops who have a vested interest in the Harlem dope trade.

[66]See note 64.

[67]Curtis Mayfield, *Superfly*, Curtom Records (1972); Bobby Womack, *Across 110th Street*, United Artist Records (1972).

[68]Curtis Mayfield, "Freddy's Dead," *Superfly*, vocals by Curtis Mayfield, Curtom Records (1972).

[69]Bobby Womack and J. J. Johnson, "Across 110th Street," *Across 110th Street*, vocals by Bobby Womack and Peace, United Artist Records (1972).

[70]Curtis Mayfield, "No Thing on Me," *Superfly*, vocals by Curtis Mayfield, Curtom Records (1972). Thanks to Perry Hall for this recommendation.

[71]A review of the film *Wattsax* by George Singleton can be found at http://www.reelmoviecritic.com/movies20034q/id1947.htm. My thanks to Tom Poole for suggesting this source.

[72]Gene McFadden and John Whitehead, "Wake Up Everybody," *Wake Up Everybody*, vocals by Harold Melvin and the Blue Notes, Philadelphia International Records (1975); Gene McFadden and John Whitehead, "Ain't No Stoppin' Us Now," *McFadden & Whitehead*, vocals by Gene McFadden and John Whitehead, Philadelphia International Records (1979).

[73]Kenny Gamble, Leon Huff, and Cary Gilbert, "Let's Clean Up the Ghetto," *Let's Clean Up the Ghetto*, vocals by the Philadelphia International All-Stars, Philadelphia International (1977).

[74]Ibid.

[75]John Whitehead, Gene McFadden, and Victor Carstarphen, "Now Is the Time to Do It," *Let's Clean Up the Ghetto*, vocals by Teddy Pendergrass, Philadelphia International (1977); Kenny Gamble and Leon Huff, "Year of Decision," *Let's Clean Up the Ghetto*, vocals by The Three Degrees, Philadelphia International (1977); Kenny Gamble and Leon Huff, "New Day, New World Comin'," *Let's Clean Up the Ghetto*, vocals by Billy Paul, Philadelphia International (1977); G. Heron, "Save the Children," *Let's Clean Up the Ghetto*, vocals by the Intruders, Philadelphia International (1977).

[76]This commitment is printed on the album jacket.

[77]George, *The Death of Rhythm and Blues*, 145.

[78]For a brief account of the difficulties experienced by many associated with Motown in connection with the move from Detroit to Los Angeles, see Dahl, *Motown: The Golden Years*, 41–43. The case that Gordy's intentions were well known in advance is made in Nelson George's *Where Did Our Love Go?: The Rise and Fall of the Motown Sound* (New York, 1985).

[79]Thomas McClary and Lionel Ritchie, "Visions," *Natural High*, vocals by the Commodores, Motown Records (1978).

[80]For a more attenuated description of Funk, see Ward, *Just My Soul Responding*, 350–57.

[81]While a large number of books have been written about the Black Panthers, the only effort to provide an analytical examination of the U.S. organization is Scot Brown's *Fighting for US, Maulana Karenga, the US Organization, and Black Cultural Nationalism* (New York, 2003).

[82]Sylvester Stewart, "Don't Call Me Nigger, Whitey," *Stand!*, vocals by Sly & the Family Stone, Epic Records (1969); "Stand!," *Stand!*, vocals by Sly & the Family Stone, Epic Records (1969). My thanks to Caryl Sheffield for suggesting these songs.

[83]Sylvester Stewart, "Everyday People," *Stand!*, vocals by Sly & the Family Stone, Epic Records (1969).

[84]Norman Whitfield and Barrett Strong, "Cloud Nine," *Cloud Nine*, Gordy (1969); Norman Whitfield and Barrett Strong, "Run Away Child, Running Wild," *Cloud Nine*, Gordy (1969).

[85]Norman Whitfield, "Stop the War Now," *Solid Rock* (1972), vocals by the Temptations. This interpretation is presented in "Classic Motown, 1959–1988," http://classic.motown.com/artist.aspx?ob=ros&src=lb&aid=52.

[86]For historical family income data see U.S. Census Bureau, "Historical Income Tables," table F-7B. http://www.census.gov/hhes/income/histinc/f07b.html; For unemployment data, see U.S. Census Bureau, *Current Population Survey*, http://data.bls.gov/servlet/SurveyOutputServlet.

[87]Maurice White, "Keep Your Head To the Sky," *Head to the Sky*, vocals by Earth, Wind & Fire, Columbia (1973); Maurice White, Charles Stepney, and Verdine White, "That's the Way of the World," *That's the Way of the World*, Columbia (1975).

[88]For detailed segregation data, see Cutler/Glaeser/Vigdor Segregation Data, http://trinity.aas.duke.edu/~jvigdor/segregation/.

[89]George Clinton, William Collins, and Bernard Worrell, "Chocolate City," *Chocolate City*, vocals by Parliament, Casablanca (1975).

[90]George, *The Death of Rhythm and Blues*, 155.

[91]Thomas Poole, "Theological, Moral, and Existential Themes in the Blues," paper presented at the Society of Christian Ethics, Washington, DC, 6 January 1995.

[92]"BBB Interviews Gil Scott-Heron," *Black Books Bulletin* 6, no. 3 (1979): 36.

[93]Langston Hughes, "Letter to the Academy (1933)," in *The Collected Works of Langston Hughes, Volume 1, The Poems: 1921–1940*, ed., Arnold Rampersad (Columbia, MO, 2001), 231–32.

[94]Gil Scott-Heron and Brian Jackson, "The Get Out of the Ghetto Blues," *The Revolution Will Not Be Televised*, vocals by Gil Scott-Heron, RCA Records (1974).

[95]Ibid.; Abiodun Oyewole, "When the Revolution Comes," *The Last Poets*, Douglas (1970).

[96]For a useful discussion of how former President Reagan's social policies disadvantaged African Americans and other similarly situated groups, see John L. Palmer, ed., *Perspectives on the Reagan Years* (Washington, DC, 1986).

[97]See Cutler/Glaeser/Vigdor Segregation Data, http://trinity.aas.duke.edu/~jvigdor/segregation/.

[98]Family income and unemployment data is extracted from U.S. Census Bureau, "Historical Income Tables," Table F-7B and *Current Population Survey*.

[99]Data for admissions to federal and state prisons are taken from various issues of *Prison and Jail Inmates at Midyear*, Bureau of Justice Statistics Bulletin, U.S. Department of Justice, Office of Justice Programs.

[100]Gerry Thomas, "Is This the Future?," *Is This the Future?*, vocals by Fatback, Spring Records (1983).

[101]Ed Fletcher, Melvin Glover, Sylvia Robinson, and Clifton Chase, "The Message," *The Message*, Sugar Hill Records (1982).

[102]"Many Ways to Pressure Black Radio," *The Black Commentator*: E-Mailbox, Issue 46, http://www.black-commentator.com/46/46_email.html.

[103]Nas, "Black Zombie," *The Lost Tapes*, Sony (2002); Jamiroquai, "Emergency on Planet Earth," *Emergency on Planet Earth*, Sony (1993).

[104]Michael Franti, "Stay Human (All the Freaky People)," *Stay Human*, Six Degrees (2001).

[105]Mos Def, "Umi Says," *Black on Both Sides*, Rawkus (2002).

[106]Tupac Shakur, "Troublesome 96," *Greatest Hits*, Interscope Records (1998).

[107]N.W.A., "Fuck tha Police," *Straight Outta Compton*, Priority Records (2002).

[108]Common (featuring the Last Poets), "The Corner," *Be*, Geffen Records (2005).

[109]Jurassic 5, "Concrete Schoolyard," *EP*, Interscope Records (1997).

[110]The Coup, "Ride the Fence," *Party Music*, Tommy Boy (2001).

[111]Nelson George, *Hip Hop America* (New York, 1999).

[112]KRS-One, former leader of Boogie Down Productions, founded the "Stop the Violence Movement" in 1989 and organized the all-star charity single "Self-Destruction," which raised half a million dollars for the National Urban League in 1989. Russell Simmons is another Hip Hop mogul who is involved in various Stop the Violence initiatives.

[113]Russell Simmons and several Hip Hop artists including LL Cool J, Rev. Run, and Jadakiss, are spearheading the "One Mind. One Vote" campaign that has a goal of registering two million voters between the ages of 18 and 34 by the November presidential election and a total of twenty million voters over the next five years. The nonpartisan initiative is reaching out to Hip Hop fans through the syndicated radio show hosted by Doug Banks and through voter registration booths set up on the 2004 Doug Banks Jam Session concert tour.

[114]Puffy Coombs (Bad Boy Records), Damon Dash (Rockefeller Records), Master P (No Limit Records), Jermaine Dupri (So So Def Records), and Dee and Wakym (Ruff Ryders) all donate heavily to charities and have created their own foundations.

FROM CIVIL RIGHTS TO HIP HOP:
TOWARD A NEXUS OF IDEAS

Derrick P. Alridge

The most radical ideas often grow out of a concrete intellectual engagement with the problems of aggrieved populations confronting systems of oppression.[1]

The preceding quotation from historian Robin D. G. Kelley captures the manner through which socially and politically conscious (SPC) Hip Hop emerged from the social, economic, and political experiences of black youth from the mid- to late 1970s.[2] Hip Hop pioneers such as Kool Herc, Afrika Bambaataa, and Grandmaster Flash and the Furious Five, among others articulated the post–civil rights generation's ideas and response to poverty, drugs, police brutality, and other racial and class inequities of postindustrial U.S. society.[3] In many ways, early hip hoppers were not only the progenitors of a new form of black social critique, they also represented the voice of a new generation that would carry on and expand upon the ideas and ideology of the civil rights generation.[4]

Since the early years of Hip Hop, SPC hip hoppers have continued to espouse many of the ideas and ideology of the Civil Rights Movement (CRM) and Black Freedom Struggle (BFS), but in a language that resonates with many black youth of the postindustrial and post–civil rights integrationist era.[5] For instance, on Michael Franti and Spearhead's 2001 compact disc (CD) *Stay Human*, Franti uses rap and reggae-style lyrics to critique U.S. capitalism, imperialism, racism, and globalization and to offer analyses of discrimination, prejudice, and oppression similar to those of activists and theorists of the CRM and BFS. In "Oh My God," Franti lays out what he believes are the hypocrisies of U.S. democracy by pointing out its discriminatory practices against the poor and people of color, its use of the death penalty, its indiscriminate bombing of other countries, and its counterintelligence activities that subvert the rights of U.S. citizens. He states:

> Oh my, Oh my God,
> out here mama they got us livin' suicide,
> singin' oh my, oh my God
> out here mama they got us livin' suicide. . . .
>
> Listen to my stethoscope on a rope,
> internal lullabies, human cries,
> thumps and silence, the language of violence,
> algorithmic, cataclysmic, seismic, biorhythmic,

you can make a life longer, but you can't save it,
you can make a clone and then you try to enslave it?
Stealin' DNA from the unborn
and then you comin' after us
'cause we sampled a James Brown horn?
Scientists whose God is progress,
a four headed sheep is their latest project,
the CIA runnin' like that Jones from Indiana,
but they still won't talk about that Jones in Guyana,
this ain't no cartoon, no one slips on bananas,
do you really think that that car killed Diana,
hell I shot Ronald Reagan, I shot JFK,
I slept with Marilyn, she sung me "Happy Birthday."[6]

The lyrics in "Oh My God" and other songs on *Stay Human* are potent, analytical, and reminiscent of the critiques and ideas of such black leaders as W. E. B. Du Bois, Marcus Garvey, Ida B. Wells-Barnett, Malcolm X, Martin Luther King, Jr., Kwame Toure, Angela Davis, and the Black Panthers. Franti's ideas as expressed in "Oh My God" and *Stay Human* regarding U.S. imperialism, racism, discrimination, and the usurpation of individual rights are similar to those expressed in Du Bois's essay, "The Freedom to Learn"; King's book, *Where Do We Go From Here: Chaos or Community?*; Gil Scott-Heron's song, "The Revolution Will Not Be Televised"; and Angela Davis's numerous writings on the prison-industrial complex. Other socio-political rappers and hip hoppers, such as Public Enemy, Sister Souljah, KRS-One, Me'Shell Ndegeocello, Goodie Mob, The Coup, Blackalicious, Jurassic 5, Kanye West, dead prez, Mr. Lif, Mos Def, Immortal Technique, Hieroglyphics, and Ms. Dynamite are among the many artists of the SPC genre of Hip Hop who offer cogent analyses and commentary on race, poverty, and discrimination that build on the ideas and ideology of CRM and BFS.

Despite the shared ideas and ideology of Hip Hop and the CRM and BFS, the two generations have, for the most part, been skeptical, if not outright suspicious of one another, and scholars have tended to portray them in opposition and conflict. For instance, some activists and scholars of the civil rights era criticize the Hip Hop generation for failing to carry on the struggles of the CRM.[7] Moreover, some scholars of the civil rights generation, such as Martin Kilson, believe that Hip Hop is devoid of a sound intellectual activist tradition. Kilson declared that,

The "hip-hop worldview" is nothing other than an updated face on the old-hat, crude, anti-humanistic values of hedonism and materialism. . . . It is ironic, in fact, that black youth in poverty-level and weak working class families, who struggle to design a regime of self-respect and discipline in matters of education and interpersonal friendship, get no assistance whatever in these respects from hedonistic, materialistic, nihilistic, sadistic, and misogynistic ideas and values propagated by most hip-hop entertainers.[8]

Activists and scholars of the Hip Hop generation, in turn, often criticize the civil rights generation for being out of touch with contemporary "real world" problems of black youth, for failing to reach out to black youth, or failing to understand the complexities of the postindustrial society in which black youth live.[9] According to cinema scholar Todd Boyd, the disconnect between the civil rights and Hip Hop generations has made civil rights seem largely irrelevant and has made Hip Hop the primary voice of contemporary black youth. He argued that, "Hip Hop has rejected and now replaced the pious, sanctimonious nature of civil rights as the defining moment of Blackness."[10]

As a child of the civil rights era who came of age during the formative years of Hip Hop, I understand the conflicts between the two generations, but I can also see the largely overlooked commonalties between them. While Hip Hop has not dramatically changed oppressive institutional structures or organized itself at anywhere near the level of civil rights organizations, such as the Student Nonviolent Coordinating Committee (SNCC), the Congress of Racial Equality (CORE), or the NAACP, it shares with the CRM a critique of the problems that plague U.S. African Americans and other oppressed people throughout the world. These shared ideas and common ideology present possibilities for an improved discourse between the two generations.

This inquiry, therefore, illuminates this common ground by examining four ideas that Hip Hop carries on from the CRM and the larger BFS. I argue that SPC Hip Hop reinvigorates and expands these four ideas and ideologies of the CRM and BFS and in doing so presents a cogent and intellectually engaged analysis in a language that resonates with contemporary black youth. In making a case for the shared ideas and ideology of these generations, I will also show how SPC Hip Hop has roots in the CRM and BFS. My aim is to help the Hip Hop and civil rights generations recognize their common ideology and goals and help facilitate a discourse grounded in a history of ideas found among both generations.[11]

IMAGING, SAMPLING, AND SCRATCHING: TRANSCENDING LINEAR NOTIONS OF TIME IN HIP HOP

The fact that the Hip Hop generation of today is thirty-five or more years removed from the CRM has made it difficult for either generation to recognize the commonalties in their ideas. In addition, linear approaches to examining history have reinforced a temporal disconnect between Hip Hop and the CRM. Such approaches obscure the ideological connections between the civil rights era and Hip Hop, disguise the fluidity of ideas between the two generations, and conceal the influence of past ideas on Hip Hop.[12] As a result, it is more difficult to see, for example, how the ideas of Martin Delany, Ida B. Wells-Barnett, Marcus Garvey, Frantz Fanon, Malcolm X, and Martin Luther King, Jr., to name a few, are reflected in and similar to the ideas proposed by rappers such as Public Enemy, Sister Souljah, Michael Franti, and dead prez.

SPC Hip Hop, however, attempts to address these temporal limitations through techniques that morph time and provide a wider lens for seeing the organic, metaphorical, symbolic, and concrete connections between Hip Hop and the CRM and BFS. Many hip hoppers, for instance, employ techniques such as imaging, sampling, and scratching to transcend space and time and to place their ideas into closer temporal proximity to the CRM and BFS. *Imaging* is a general term I use to describe the process by which hip hoppers reproduce or evoke images, events, people, and symbols for the purpose of placing past ideas into closer proximity to the present. Hip hoppers employ imaging by appropriating, for example, the voices and images of civil rights figures and events in their music or videos.

Sampling is a type of imaging in which hip hoppers digitally replicate sounds or voices into a song, performance, or video. Sampling is typically practiced by DJs through the use of sampling machines (via keyboards and computers) that lift sounds from one source and place them into another. James Brown's songs and Malcolm X's voice, for instance, have been appropriated by many SPC hip hoppers as means of promoting and capturing the ideas and aura of Malcolm and Brown's day. Sampling, therefore, has provided a way for the Hip Hop generation to rethink the temporal barriers that separate them from the CRM, and it provides an opportunity for scholars to reconsider how we conceptualize the relationship between these two generations. Hip Hop scholar William Eric Perkins provides further insight into sampling as a means of transcending time, noting that, "sampling was and is hip hop's ongoing link with history and tradition, including all of the African and African American musical genres; so one can say that hip hop generates its own history by recycling music and reintroducing the previous musical genres to new audiences and markets."[13]

Scratching is another type of imaging that complements sampling. Using two or more turntables, DJs employ this technique by sliding the needles on their turntables back and forth across the surfaces of records as a means of lifting snippets of songs and sounds and transporting them to another source (i.e., record, tape, compilation, or live performance). Over time, the scratching sound itself became a musical form and part of the songs. The art of scratching is taking on new forms as digitized music becomes widely used. Many purists, however, continue to develop the art of scratching by using albums. Like sampling, scratching allows the DJ to image the past onto the present, creating a greater awareness of the relationship between the past and present-day problems of the African American community.[14]

Public Enemy has been one of the most visible rap groups using imaging, sampling, and scratching to connect the Hip Hop generation to the CRM and BFS. In their music, Public Enemy has consistently explored contemporary problems of urban strife, poverty, and discrimination in the context of the black experience, and articulated their ideas in relationship to the long history of black struggle. In their video for "Fight the Power" in *Fear of a Black Planet*, for instance, marchers carry cardboard placards with pictures of Harriet Tubman, Frederick Douglass, Paul Robeson, Marcus Garvey, Adam Clayton Powell, Jr., A. Philip Randolph, Martin Luther King, Jr., Malcolm X, and Jesse Jackson.[15] Public Enemy's purpose is to visually connect Hip Hop to the larger BFS and

38

to show Public Enemy as the progeny of previous black leaders. Front man Chuck D asserts that Public Enemy's link to icons of the CRM and BFS is not happenstance, but rather the product of his upbringing in an activist family during the 1960s:

> My parents were young in the 1960s, and had radical ideas. My mother wore an Afro, and I remember wearing an Afro myself, as well as singing the "Free Huey Newton" song. My crucial developmental years took place right smack-dab in the middle years of the Black Power movement.[16]

In 1999 the Atlanta-based, Hip Hop and rap group OutKast forged further connections between Hip Hop and the CRM and BFS with their controversial song "Rosa Parks" on the CD *Aquemini*. Simply using Rosa Parks's name as the song's title connects Hip Hop to the CRM. As an icon of the movement, Parks has become known as the "mother" of the CRM and her name has come to symbolize the birth of the movement. Moreover, although OutKast does not explicitly discuss Rosa Parks, they allude to her participation in the CRM by stating, "Ah-ha, hush that fuss, Everybody move to the back of the bus. Do you wanna bump and slump with us? We the type of people make the club get crunk."[17] The use of Parks's name and the simple refrain in the song provides OutKast with a way of imaging the CRM into Hip Hop. Moreover, the song, though subtle, illuminates Parks's participation in the CRM and preserves her legacy for a new generation. Nevertheless, the tension between the two generations emerged even in this effort, as Rosa Parks and her attorney viewed OutKast's use of her name not as reverence, but as the wrongful manipulation of her name and story for their own profit. Eventually, the lawsuit was settled and OutKast agreed to perform on a CD tribute for Parks and help produce a nationally televised broadcast of Parks's role and participation in the Montgomery Bus Boycott.[18]

Hip Hop activist and rapper Common, formerly known as Common Sense, consistently and consciously uses imaging to illuminate the ideological connections between Hip Hop and the CRM and BFS. In "A Song for Assata" on *Like Water for Chocolate* (2000), Common and Cee Lo, of the socially and politically conscious rap group Goodie Mob, recount the life of civil rights era activist and Black Panther Assata Shakur. The precision and detail in Common's lyrical narrative and composition evoke a vivid image of Assata's participation in the BFS. Common's opening words in "A Song for Assata," however, provide imagery that fuses Hip Hop to its ancestral and spiritual roots in the BFS:

> In the Spirit of God,
> In the Spirit of the Ancestors,
> In the Spirit of the Black Panthers,
> In the Spirit of Assata Shakur,
> We make this movement towards freedom,
> For all those who have been oppressed,
> and all those in the struggle.[19]

Common expresses gratitude for Assata's activism and commitment to her cause and metaphorically places himself in her era when he repeats the refrain, "I wonder what would happen if that woulda been me? All this shit so we could be free."[20] Common completes the imaging of Assata and the CRM and BFS by sampling Assata's voice in the refrain and at the end of the song. Her message to the Hip Hop generation is that freedom is the "right to be yourself, to be who you are, to be who you wanna be, to do what you wanna do."[21] Assata's advice to Common and his generation reflects that of a sage of an earlier era who provides wisdom to the Hip Hop generation.

Another song from the same CD that poignantly connects Hip Hop to the CRM and BFS is "Pops' Rap . . . All My Children." This song is extremely effective because Common's father, Lonnie Lynn Sr., whom Common calls Pops and who sings on the song, uses the imagery of the Underground Railroad to connect Hip Hop metaphorically to the CRM and BFS. Pops informs hip hoppers that Hip Hop is the "language of the Underground Railroad." Pops utilizes the imagery of the Underground Railroad through which numerous people helped enslaved African Americans escape from the South to freedom in the North and Canada.

Pops visualizes African Americans' struggle for equality as an Underground Railroad in which various generations of African Americans take responsibility for guiding their people to freedom. He commends the Hip Hop generation for taking responsibility for carrying on the struggle, for "feeding the children" of their generation knowledge in a language they understand, and for preventing "99" in the year 1999 from turning upside down to become the year 1966. Pops also credits Hip Hop with carrying on the tradition of self-determination and knowledge dissemination.[22] Pops's use of the Underground Railroad metaphor and his inversion of "99" to "66" is highly effective in showing the connections between the Hip Hop and civil rights generations. He goes even further by pointing to Erykah Badu, Cee Lo, Jazzy Jeff, A Tribe Called Quest, and De La Soul as conductors on the modern-day Underground Railroad.[23]

Rhythm and Blues (R&B) artist Me'Shell Ndegeocello, a member of the Hip Hop generation who infuses rap into her socially and politically conscious music, has been another potent force in simultaneously merging and critiquing Hip Hop and the CRM. Since entering the music scene during the early 1990s, she has consistently evoked images and symbolism of the CRM to connect it to the circumstances of her generation. In her song "Hot Night" on *Cookie: The Anthropological Mixtape*, Ndegeocello samples Angela Davis's CD, *Angela Davis: The Prison-Industrial Complex*.[24] In Davis's own words we hear her critique of capitalism as a force that exploits single black mothers by keeping them dependent on government welfare. The juxtaposition of Davis's voice with a driving Hip Hop beat is highly effective in educating hip hoppers about a 1960s black revolutionary such as Angela Davis. It also illuminates the problems of the 1960s that persist for the Hip Hop generation. Ndegeocello completes the connection in the song's chorus by proclaiming herself the heir to Davis, as a "revolutionary soul singer" for her own generation.

The Philadelphia-based rap group The Roots also provides civil rights era imagery to connect Hip Hop to the CRM in their CD, *The Tipping Point* (2004). A picture of the young Malcolm X graces the cover, conveying the nature of the CD's content. In addition, in the song, "Why? (What's Going On?)," the Roots borrow from the theme of Marvin Gaye's civil rights and anti-Vietnam War anthem "What's Going On" to deliver a critique of the war in Iraq. For instance, front man Black Thought declared, "Young teen joins the Marines, said he'd die for the corps. Inducted in the government's war, is it for land or money or oil?"[25] Just as Malcolm X and Martin Luther King raised questions about African Americans' participation in the U.S. armed forces in Vietnam, Black Thought raises questions about their participation in the U.S. war in Iraq, which he asserts is being fought for the acquisition of land and money. In raising such an issue, Black Thought and the Roots renew the concerns of activists of the CRM and BFS and carry on a tradition of exposing the oppressors of African Americans within the United States, even as U.S. politicians claim to be liberating the oppressed abroad.[26]

While Hip Hop lyrics are replete with connections to the CRM and BFS, a number of rappers also attest to an even more direct and personal influence of the CRM and BFS on their ideas and music. In an interview with "underground" Atlanta rapper, John Miles Lewis, son of civil rights leader and icon John Lewis, John Miles provides a firsthand account of the organic ideological connections between Hip Hop and the CRM.[27] In discussing the influence of his father and the CRM on his ideas and work, John Miles, recalled that:

> With me, I grew up around it [civil rights]. Like all I knew really was what was out here. Both of these worlds [civil rights and Hip Hop] was [sic] together within me. You know it's hard as hell growing up in the house and, you know, you got pictures of your pops getting hit with billy clubs and getting dogs sicked on him, that shit goes into your head.[28]

John Miles asserts that the stories he heard about the movement from his father are etched into his mind and have profoundly influenced his lyrics as a SPC rapper. John Miles admits that while his father does not listen to his music, he carefully and consciously listens to the music of his father's generation and merges both the music and ideas of the CRM into his ideas and music for the Hip Hop generation.[29]

The Witchdoctor, a rapper and member of the Atlanta-based Dungeon Family (DF), which includes OutKast and Goodie Mob (which stands for the "Good Die Mostly over Bullshit"), and others, points out the strength of the ideological connections between Hip Hop and the CRM. He believes that, "we [the civil rights and Hip Hop generations] are basically pretty much the same, it's just the timing is different. Martin saying some of the same things we saying now, Malcolm saying some of the same things we saying now."[30] The Witchdoctor, however, offers a critique of the civil rights leadership model and suggests that the Hip Hop generation must address leadership differently. He suggests that, "the time we living in now, it's not a time where we gonna have just one Martin Luther King, one Malcolm X, and everybody following behind one leader. That way our enemy can't say 'there go the enemy, let's get the enemy.'"[31]

According to the Witchdoctor, the Hip Hop generation must serve in a "mass" leadership role that is not as easily identifiable or vulnerable to forces such as the police, politicians, and government agencies that brought down black leadership during the CRM.[32]

Khujo, a member of the Dungeon Family and Goodie Mob, echoes the sentiments of the Witchdoctor. Khujo pays much reverence to activists of the CRM and sees Hip Hop as part of the same continuum as the CRM and BFS. Sounding strikingly like historian and former civil rights activist Vincent Harding, who describes the BFS as a winding and tumultuous river on which each generation must take its turn to navigate, Khujo describes Hip Hop's relationship to the CRM and BFS:

> We [the civil rights and Hip Hop generations] are on the same page. Those guys [civil rights activists] just got a little more gray hair than what we got. . . . The only difference is that we just doing it to music. It was a lot of struggle going on in Marvin Gaye's times, Smokey's . . . times, it's the same struggle though. We all living in the same struggle. It's just different times and it's almost time for our deliverance right now.[33]

These are only a few examples that illustrate the ideological connections between the civil rights and Hip Hop generations. Through imaging, sampling, and scratching, SPC Hip Hop attempts to make a seamless connection between the past and present struggles and experiences of African people. Through an analysis of Hip Hop's language and techniques we can observe four shared themes between Hip Hop and the Civil Rights Movement—self-determination, economic solidarity, liberatory education, and Pan-Africanism.

CONNECTIONS: HIP HOP, THE CRM, AND THE BFS

Since its emergence in the late 1970s, SPC Hip Hop has explored such themes as police brutality toward African Americans, black incarceration, the need for black leadership, black nationalism, black love, and African American solidarity. A comprehensive examination of socially and politically conscious themes and ideas in Hip Hop is beyond the scope of this essay. However, the following sections examine several of the ideas espoused by SPC hip hoppers to illustrate how their messages in many ways echo those of earlier generations, while also resonating with the socio-political issues of their own generation.

SELF-DETERMINATION

Historically, African Americans' desire to control their own destinies can easily be traced to the first Africans who resisted enslavement during the Middle Passage and later in North and South America. During the 18th and 19th centuries, Toussaint L'Ouverture, Nat Turner, Gabriel Prosser, and Denmark Vesey were only a few of the many Africans and African Americans who sought to gain freedom and to control their social, economic, and political destinies. The quest for freedom has been perhaps the defining struggle for people of African descent worldwide during the past three centuries. In *Black Self-Determination: A Cultural History of African American Resistance*, historian V. P. Franklin points out that whether through politics, education, religion, or violent and nonviolent resistance, self-determination has been a central goal of African Americans throughout their history. Moreover, African Americans' quest for self-determination, Franklin argues, is not merely the story of great men, but a narrative encompassing the struggles of the masses.[34]

Historians Lawrence Levine and Sterling Stuckey have provided cogent analyses of black culture and language that testify to the history of African Americans' pursuit of self-determination.[35] In his work on African American folk thought, Levine departs from the "traditional historical practice" that presents black southerners or the "folk" as inarticulate and illiterate observers of their own oppression who are acted upon by others. Instead, Levine presents African Americans as a group that actively developed religion, music, art, and other cultural forms that serve to chronicle their oppression and resistance, and express their hope for a better future. Through Spirituals and secular songs, African Americans have always articulated a quest for greater certainty about and control over their lives. Developed within the confines of slavery and Jim Crow laws, black songs provided a means for African Americans to convey their hardships and express their desires in a dialect and language that was often foreign to whites.[36]

Like African American Spirituals, the Blues also emerged from the racial caste system and discrimination of the U.S. South and developed into an epistemology for understanding and articulating black oppression. According to Blues scholar Clyde Woods, the Blues evolved out of the black working-class experience of the plantation and sharecropping system of the late 1800s and early 1900s. In addition to providing an analytical cultural framework, the Blues represented an ontology as well as a response to the horrendous conditions of plantation life and Jim Crow segregation. Woods points out that the Blues "provided a sense of collective self and a tectonic footing from which to oppose and dismantle the American intellectual, cultural, and socioeconomic traditions constructed from the raw material of African American exploitation and denigration."[37] For rural black southerners, the Blues was both a way of interpreting their experience (explaining reality and change) and a means of coping successfully with the oppressive conditions of their lives. Other examples of black self-determination expressed through culture and language are the Gullah and Geeche peoples of South Carolina and Georgia, respectively. Their languages, perceived by many whites as "bad English," provided a means by which these African American cultures could express themselves within an oppressive situation. Merging English and African words and dialects, Gullah and Geeche provided a cryptic but socially empowering way for African Americans to communicate with one another.[38]

Ultimately, self-determination focuses on African Americans' quest to control their own lives and communities and has historically been articulated through their culture, religion, language, and music. Spirituals, Gullah and Geeche dialects, and the

Blues, during early periods of their development, were viewed by the dominant culture as inept, corrupt, and illegitimate, but over time each has become a recognized means for African Americans to articulate their pain, struggles, and hopes for the future.

Hip Hop, like the Spirituals, the Gullah and Geeche languages, and the Blues emerged from the oppression of African Americans and people of color. During the early 1970s, many black residents in the North were crowded in urban areas with deteriorating economic infrastructures, with a cultural void left by the large number of black men fighting in Vietnam. Hip Hop photographer and griot Ernie Paniccioli, who witnessed and photographed the early years of Hip Hop, described the social environment of the early 1970s:

> Pain, oppression, and art, and in this case Hip Hop, came not only from the Vietnam War, but from the oppression of the streets, the oppression of not being able to get a job, the oppression of not being able to have a stake in your own future. It came from the oppression of not getting a proper education. What happened was that these young kids created their own language of the streets.[39]

Artists such as Afrika Bambaataa and Kool Herc used the burgeoning advancements in recording technologies along with the potent "language of the streets" to create a bombastic and gritty response to their conditions. Their response appealed to many youth because it reflected the mood, feel, and ideas of urban youth culture. Such an environment fostered the emergence and development of a language and cultural form that offered a response and resistance to the conditions of black life during the period.

By the mid to late 1980s, black nationalist and other groups inspired by the teachings of the Nation of Islam, the Five Percent Nation of Islam, and the resurgence in the popularity of black nationalist icons such as Malcolm X were weighing in on the black condition and espousing a philosophy of self-determination. Front man Grand Puba of Brand Nubian, for instance, explicated the conditions in which many African Americans lived during this period and provided them with a mantra for self-determination. In "Wake Up" (Reprise), Puba exclaimed, "Drugs in our community (that ain't right), Can't even get a job (that ain't right), Lying who is God (that ain't right)." Puba, however, provides a solution: "Knowledge of self to better ourself 'cause I know myself, that we can live much better than this." The conclusion of the song leaves an echoing message of self-determination: "Move on black man, move on, you gotta move on black man move on. . . ."[40]

Even Gangsta rap of the late 1980s and early 1990s, as nihilistic and misogynistic as it often was, sometimes advocated self-determination by illuminating problems of police brutality, deterioration of black urban schools, and unjust political and judicial systems, and then provided strategies for addressing these problems. Gangsta rappers such as NWA and Ice-T critiqued the structure of capitalism, the judicial system, and the consignment of African Americans to overcrowded ghettos as attacks on black self-determination. They called for African Americans to resist "the man," oppressive institutional entities, particularly the police; to take control of their own communities; and to use the capitalist system to improve their economic and social conditions.[41]

"Knowledge of self" as a means of bringing about self-determination for African Americans was a consistent theme throughout the 1990s, as artists such as Mos Def and Talib Kweli demonstrate on their classic Hip Hop CD and treatise *Black Star*. As two of Hip Hop's most politically aware rappers, Mos Def and Kweli called themselves "Black Star" after Marcus Garvey's 1919 Black Star Line, the first black-owned steamship line. Just as the title of the album and the duo's name signify an advocacy of self-determination, so do the CD's contents. On "Black Star-K.O.S. (Determination)" (1998), Kweli extols the importance of black emcees in African Americans' quest for self-determination and outlines the role they can play in fanning the flames of self-determination among those in their generation:

So many emcees focusin' on black people extermination
We keep it balanced with that knowledge of self-determination
It's hot, we be blowin' the spots with conversations,
C'mon let's smooth it out like Soul Sensation
We in the house like Japanese in Japan, or Koreans in Korea
Head to Philly and free Mumia with the Kujichagulia true
Singin' is swingin' and writin' is fightin', but what
they writin' got us clashin' like titans it's not excitin'
No question, bein' a black man is demandin'
The fire's in my eyes and the flames need fanning (3x)
With that what (Knowledge of Self) Determination.[42]

Kweli then points out the contemporary impediments to black self-determination and encourages African Americans to take control of their destiny:

Inner-city concentration camps where no one pays attention
or mentions the ascension of death, 'til nothing's left.
The young and dead are black, and sprung addicted to crack
All my people where y'all at cause, y'all ain't here
And your hero's using your mind as canvas to paint fear
With broad brush strokes and tales of incarceration,
You get out of jail with that Knowledge of Self-Determination
Stand in ovation, cause you put the Hue in Human
Cause and effect, affect everything you do,
And that's why I got love in the face of hate.
Hands steady so the lines in the mental illustration is straight,
The thought you had don't even contemplate,
Infinite like figure eight there's no escape,
From that what (Knowledge of Self) Determination.[43]

Throughout the song Kweli acknowledges the material needs of African Americans, but preaches that it is knowledge of their history that ultimately prepares them to determine their own future.

Similarly, throughout their work OutKast has asserted that "knowledge of self" is critical to black self-determination because it helps free black people from "mental slavery." In "Liberation" on *Aquemini*, Andre and Big Boi join Erykah Badu and Dungeon Family members Cee Lo and Big Rube to provide an historical odyssey of black oppression and express hope for a brighter future. Ultimately, "Liberation" is a call for African Americans to become aware of their conditions and to use whatever means are necessary to improve their situation. Hip Hop philosopher Big Rube delivers a message that is cryptic, yet profound:

> I must admit, they [the oppressors] planted a lot of things
> in the brains and veins of my strain,
> Makes it hard to refrain, from the host of cocaine,
> From them whores from the flame,
> From a post in the game,
> Makes it hard to maintain focus.
> There from the glock rounds, and lockdowns, and berries,
> The seeds that sow, get devoured by the same locusts.[44]

Big Rube argues that black liberation and self-determination have historically been thwarted by the oppressors planting misinformation in the minds of generations of African Americans. This misinformation is further entrenched through a subculture of deadly vices such as cocaine addiction and illicit sex. Such vices, Rube posits, make it difficult for African Americans to "maintain focus" on their own self-preservation. Rube's advocacy of black self-determination is buttressed by the words of Big Boi, who informs African Americans that they have a choice in determining their future:

Now [you] have a choice to be who you wants to be. It's left uppa' to me, and my momma n'em told me (yes she did). I said I have a choice to be who you wants to be. It's left uppa' to me, and my momma n'em told me.[45]

"Liberation" catalogues the litany of problems faced by African people in the Diaspora and ultimately calls on them to take control of their own destinies. For instance, Big Rube advocates a philosophy of self-determination by evoking the imagery of Latin American liberation movements through simply stating *Libertad*, meaning "freedom" or "liberty" in Spanish.

dead prez is one of the most recent and popular underground groups to call for black self-determination. Discovered by Lord Jamar of Brand Nubian, in 2000 this duo released *let's get free*, its groundbreaking treatise on black self-determination. In the tradition of other SPC rappers such as Public Enemy and KRS-One, dead prez see themselves primarily as activists who use music as a platform to deliver their message of black self-determination. On *let's get free*, they devote considerable time to assessing the problems in the black community (illegal drugs, racism, police brutality, self-hate, sexism) and call for African American and other oppressed people to lead a revolution for freedom, liberation, and self-determination. In their song and video "hip hop," dead prez advocate for African peoples to prepare themselves mentally, physically, and emotionally to resist and liberate themselves from oppression. The video is replete with messages and symbolism of blacks' historical quest for self-determination. Groups of black men and women hold placards bearing words and phrases such as "food," "clothes," "shelter," "freedom," "I'm an African," and images of the Black Power fist and the African continent. In the video, dead prez intermittently display maxims and pictures pertaining to poverty, revolution, and solidarity.[46]

Public Enemy, Mos Def, Talib Kweli, and dead prez are only a few of the many SPC rappers who promote an ideology of self-determination. While these hip hoppers continue to promote self-determination, currently their music and videos receive little to no airplay on mainstream radio or television.

LIBERATORY EDUCATION AND PEDAGOGY

The acquisition of a liberatory education as a theme in Hip Hop is rooted in the long history of African Americans' quest for self-determination.[47] Scholars have thoroughly documented that within the U.S. slave system of the 18th and 19th centuries, African Americans educated themselves despite laws forbidding them to obtain literacy or "book knowledge," and the harsh punishments that often resulted from any attempt to do so. Under oppressive conditions and threats of punishments such as flogging, whipping, and sometimes death, enslaved Africans and their African American-born children strove to develop educational institutions and pedagogies of resistance that countered the brutality and ignorance perpetuated by the slaveocracy.[48] Philosopher Stephen Haymes argued that enslaved African Americans developed an elaborate existential philosophy of education and a pedagogy of resistance that helped them resist the "dehumanizing project of American slavery."[49] Under harsh conditions, Haymes asserted, enslaved African Americans not only continued to educate themselves, but taught themselves that they were "a Chosen People" and that their existence had meaning and purpose.

After the end of U.S. slavery, African Americans continued to strive to take control of their education away from whites, who propagated educational institutions and practices that reinforced existing social and economic hierarchies. Through the Freedmen's Bureau and white philanthropic organizations such as the Slater Fund, black southerners were often subjected to a curriculum designed to reinforce a social order that relegated them to the lowest position. A survey of U.S. history reveals that despite the hardships African Americans faced, they attempted to control their own education, from the secret schools in slave communities, to the Sabbath schools of the postbellum period, to the freedom schools of the 1960s, and to the independent black schools of today.[50]

In the midst of external control of black schooling, W. E. B. Du Bois, Carter G. Woodson, and Anna Julia Cooper were only a few of the many African American educators who developed pedagogies that called for African Americans to become self-sufficient and take control of their own futures. In his *Mis-education of the Negro*, for example, Woodson pointed out that African Americans remain enslaved mentally when they attempt to imitate the education of whites instead of developing curricula that reflect their own culture, history, and economic reality. Echoing the sentiments of Du Bois, Washington, Cooper, and others, Woodson argued that education for African Americans should be pragmatic, rigorous, critical, and grounded in the culture and historical experiences of African peoples.[51]

Hip Hop artists from the late 1970s have also criticized the U.S. educational system and argued that the public schools often perpetuate "mis-education." Perhaps the most influential and well-known rapper to criticize the educational system and its practices, and to advocate for a liberatory pedagogy, is Hip Hop artist KRS-One, also known as "The Teacha." Since emerging on the Hip Hop scene in the mid-1980s, KRS-One has offered a scathing critique of the American educational system and its curricula, while calling for more historically accurate portrayals of African Americans in textbooks and other classroom materials. In particular, "The Teacha" has been concerned about what he sees as a "Eurocentric" version of history in U.S. public school curricula, which ignores the contributions of African-descended people. He raps, "It seems to me in a school that's ebony, African history should be pumped up steadily, but it's not and this has got to stop."[52] KRS-One further educates his generation about their "real" history: "No one told you about Benjamin Banneker, a brilliant Black man [who created an] almanac. . . . Granville Woods made the walkie talkie, Louis Latimer improved on Edison, Charles Drew did a lot for medicine, Garrett Morgan made the traffic light, Harriet Tubman freed the slaves at night, Madame CJ Walker made a straightening comb."[53]

KRS-One's advocacy of a liberatory education and pedagogy continues to impact and educate a new generation of hip hoppers. Washington, DC-born, but Georgia-based rapper Ishues, who has toured with KRS-One, also sees himself carrying on the tradition of black educators of previous generations. His moniker hints at his concept of educating the masses about issues in contemporary society. Ishues's CD *Reality Flow* (2004) is part autobiography and part political and historical lesson. Ishues holds a view of formal education similar to that of Carter G. Woodson; he believes that education and schooling as practiced in the United States denies students access to the truth and provides them with illusions rather than an understanding of reality.[54]

As a "rapper of the streets," Ishues sees himself as a teacher whose job is to bring reality and truth to the masses, no matter how painful that reality and truth might be. In "Game Time" on *Reality Flow*, Ishues expresses his problem with what he believes is mis-education perpetrated by schools:

The only lesson teachers taught me in school
Was propaganda and pictures of Jesus on the cross. . . .

So, I despise what you teach me,
I despise you completely.[55]

Ishues argues that curricula in U.S. schools offer sanitized and inaccurate information about black history that denies "truth" to children. Such mis-education, Ishues believes, emanates not only from formal educational institutions such as schools, but also from informal education sources such as the media.[56]

Education for liberation is also a dominant theme in the music of dead prez. In "they schools," dead prez offers a scathing critique of one of the most important battlegrounds in the Black Freedom Struggle: the education and schooling of African American children. They announce, "They schools can't teach us shit. My people need freedom, we trying to get all we can get. . . . Tellin' me white man lies straight bullshit. They schools ain't teachin' us what we need to survive, they schools don't educate, all they teach the people is lies."[57] Throughout the "they schools" video, dead prez shows images of nooses in the background to equate U.S. education with slow death for students who are subject to it. dead prez, however, does not merely offer a critique of U.S. education, but also encourages African Americans to take control of their own education and urges students to think long term about their future.[58]

Rapper Nas has consistently served as an educator and teacher from his first CD, *Illmatic*, to his most recent, *Street's Disciples*. Nas's most popular treatise on self-determination in education is his song, "I Can." Like Woodson with the *Negro History Bulletin* and Du Bois with the *Brownies' Book*, Nas educates black children about their rich history to show them that they can succeed in life:

> Before we came to this country,
> We were kings and queens, never porch monkeys,
> There [were] empires in Africa called Kush, Timbuktu, where every race came to get books,
> To learn from black teachers who taught Greeks and Romans.

Nas further explains the role that education can play in helping black children achieve the greatness of their ancestors:

> Read more learn more, change the globe
> Ghetto children, do your thing,
> Hold your head up, little man, you're a king.
> Young Princess when you get your wedding ring
> Your man is saying "She's my queen."[59]

While Hip Hop is far from perfect in addressing the problem of education in black communities, it has carried on the tradition of calling for African Americans to take control of their education and to obtain the educational tools that will enable them to improve their lives. KRS-One, Ishues, Nas, and dead prez are only a few of the rappers who have been in the forefront of calling for a more liberatory education. Hip hoppers and rappers such as A Tribe Called Quest, Lauryn Hill, Poor Righteous Teachers, and Sister Souljah have also put forward an educational philosophy for liberation in their work.

ECONOMIC SOLIDARITY AND ENTREPRENEURSHIP

The quest of African Americans to control their economic future is a prevalent theme in Hip Hop, the CRM, and the BFS. Since the Reconstruction era of the 1860s and 1870s, African Americans have promoted economic solidarity and entrepreneurship as a means of gaining civil rights. Grounded in a philosophy of self-determination and self-help, many African Americans believed that building strong economic bases within their communities would inevitably bring about political equality within the capitalist and democratic society of the United States.[60]

One of the earliest promoters of black economic cooperation was the Episcopal priest and leading black intellectual Alexander Crummell. Crummell stated that African Americans should collaborate "not for idle political logomacy, but for industrial effort, for securing trades for youth, for joint-stock companies, for manufacturing, for the production of the great staples of the land . . . for mental and moral improvement."[61] Similar economic agendas were promoted from the late 1870s through the 1890s by educators such as Robert Terrell, Charles Purvis, Anna Julia Cooper, and Kelly Miller.[62]

The themes of economic solidarity and entrepreneurship are particularly central to the ideas of Booker T. Washington and W. E. B. Du Bois. Despite the antithetical manner in which the ideas of Washington and Du Bois are often portrayed, both men believed that economic security would provide leverage for African Americans to achieve greater social and political advancement. For Washington, social progress would come about more quickly if African Americans focused their efforts on developing industrial and agricultural skills that would help them build a solid business class. This business class would eventually move into higher areas of industry and should strive to own land and enterprises that would employ black workers. By building a strong laboring class and obtaining land and businesses, Washington believed, African Americans would eventually gain greater civil rights.[63]

While Washington adopted an entrepreneurial philosophy of black economic empowerment that often emphasized the individual's acquisition of wealth, Du Bois called for a communal approach to building strong economic communities. In 1898, for instance, Du Bois pointed to Farmville, Virginia as a model city of communal economic cooperation in which black southerners successfully pooled their resources to build a strong local economy. In Farmville, a black man owned and controlled the entire brick-making business, while other African Americans owned several grocery stores, all the barbershops, and the only steam laundry business in the county. Du Bois's study of African Americans in Farmville was one of the first instances in which he emphasized the potential of separate black business institutions. Du Bois would

50

later point to other instances of successful business enterprises in places such as Durham, North Carolina.[64] Throughout much of the 20th century, African Americans promoted ideas of economic solidarity and entrepreneurship as means of building economic strength. Individuals and groups such as the Nation of Islam, Malcolm X, the Black Panthers, and Martin Luther King, Jr., at various points all stressed that economic power could play an important role in improving African Americans' lives and status.

The economic conditions out of which Hip Hop emerged made the artists receptive to the ideas of economic cooperation and entrepreneurship advocated during the BFS. The mid-1970s was a period of high inflation and economic stagnation, and the deterioration of black urban centers was well underway. While the black middle-class expanded as a result of social advances during the civil rights era, the economic status of the black poor continued to lag disproportionately behind that of the vast majority of white Americans. Deindustrialization encouraged companies to move factories out of urban areas and into the suburbs and eventually into parts of South America, Southeast Asia, and other less developed areas. African Americans were negatively affected by deindustrialization, and the black poor and working classes' chances of earning a living wage decreased. At the same time that the federal government was abandoning urban centers, the proportion of African Americans residing in metropolitan urban centers increased from 33 percent in 1970 to 50 percent in 1990.[65]

Juxtaposed against the backdrop of the economic problems of the 1970s were poverty and crime, which were often concentrated in urban areas and black housing projects. For many African Americans, a sense of hopelessness set in as they felt they had lost control of their destinies. African American sentiment about these conditions was expressed in the exploding rap music of the period as early rappers responded to the dismal economic conditions. In "The Message," for example, Melle Mel of Grandmaster Flash and the Furious Five stated:

> Broken glass everywhere, people pissing on the
> stairs like they just don't care,
> I can't take the smell, can't take the noise,
> Got no money to move, I guess I got no choice.
> Rats in the front room, roaches in the back,
> Junkies in the alley with a baseball bat.
> I tried to get away, but I couldn't get far,
> 'Cause the man with the tow truck repossessed my car.[66]

Hip Hop responded to the economic conditions of the times by advocating economic solidarity and entrepreneurial strategies that would empower black communities both economically and politically. Rappers such as dead prez, KRS-One, the Coup, Hieroglyphics, Public Enemy, and Mos Def called for African Americans to "give back" to their communities and build strong economic institutions. M-1 of dead prez articulates a strategy of economic cooperation:

Mostly I envision justice. A just system which will share the resources of the world which come from the earth and belong to no one. I envision those resources being shared equally amongst the masses of the people—including white people—who will only have it after working for it, the same way we all do. I see a system that's classless. Erasing the ruling class and the middle class that leave the lower classes—which is about 90 percent of the people—with little or none, and the ruling class—2 percent of the people—with everything. I envision a place which recognizes this land was stolen from the indigenous people and they have a right to it. Whatever should happen to this land should be the determination of the people who this land was stolen from—and I mean stolen in the most vicious way. Ultimately, [I support] social justice, economic development, and a standard of freedom in life.[67]

dead prez's economic perspective on black liberation is similar in many ways to those of Du Bois, sociologist Oliver Cox, and other social theorists who have written about the social and economic conditions for African peoples. Clearly influenced by a Marxist analysis of their economic condition, dead prez points to unbridled capitalism as the culprit in black poverty and advocates a cooperative, communal, and classless economic system as a viable solution. Their economic philosophy reflects views similar to those of Du Bois in the 1930s and 1940s and the Black Panther Party of the late 1960s and early 1970s.

The late rapper Tupac Shakur offered a dialectical critique of black economics that reflected the ideas of several thinkers of the CRM and BFS. As the son of a Black Panther, Tupac was influenced by the Marxist analyses that exposed the evils of capitalism and the negative impact it has had historically on the black masses. At the same time, Tupac did not dismiss capitalism as a means of improving his life. In an interview, Tupac's friend and former publicist, Talibah Mbonisi, provides some insight into Tupac's ideas about capitalism. She noted that, "he [Tupac] was sporting bling bling and everything else and participating in a system that he certainly had been taught was destructive to us. So there's that contradiction."[68] Mbonisi explains Tupac's struggle as someone who had grown up poor, with the contradiction of embracing a capitalistic ethos while understanding how unbridled capitalism and greed often harmed black communities.

Mutulu Shakur, Tupac's mentor, helped him reconcile this "two-ness" through the social and economic philosophy of "Thug Life," which stands for "The hate u give little infants fucks everybody." Mbonisi explains Mutulu's efforts:

What Mutulu did was to work with them [Tupac and his friends] to build a set of principles around it. Kinda the underlying principle was that there is this underground economic structure that will always be functional as long as we are an oppressed people. You will have pimps, drug dealers, and everything else because people gotta feed their families and they can't do it because they are not allowed to participate in the capitalist structure in the United States.[69]

52

Mutulu taught Tupac that the contradictions of embracing capitalism and wanting to help his people were an understandable reflection of the contradictions inherent in a capitalist-driven economy. Mutulu, however, believed that those contradictions had to be mediated by principles, which included not selling drugs to pregnant women or schoolchildren and not involving civilians (those not involved in the drug trade) in these affairs. As an economic perspective, Thug Life incorporates both economic solidarity and entrepreneurship into its philosophy. Tupac referred to the Thug Life as a "contemporary version of Black Power."[70]

Originally advocated during the BFS and then during the CRM, black entrepreneurship has been an appealing strategy for Hip Hop artists to adopt as a means of overcoming black poverty. Perhaps the best example of the Hip Hop entrepreneur and mogul is Russell Simmons. During the 1970s and 1980s, Simmons embraced the burgeoning art form of Hip Hop and saw its potential as both a tool to organize African Americans and a means of making money. Embracing the entrepreneurial strategy of Booker T. Washington, he has used this strategy in the political manner in which Du Bois believed African Americans should use economic power. By the mid-1980s, he had founded his own management company, Rush Productions, and co-founded Def Jam Records, which over the years has represented LL Cool J, Public Enemy, the Beastie Boys, DMX, Method Man, Jay-Z, and other highly successful recording artists. Today, Simmons uses much of his political and economic clout to fund socially and politically conscious causes such as Def Poetry Jam and his Hip Hop Summit.[71]

In the December 1999 issue of *Black Enterprise*, Hip Hop moguls Master P and Sean (P-Diddy) Combs are presented as entrepreneurs of Hip Hop. Through their savvy economic moves and shrewd negotiations, the article states, these hip hoppers use the medium of Hip Hop culture to help build a stronger black business class while also working to ameliorate the social, economic, and political conditions of black communities. For instance, in the 2004 elections, Simmons and P-Diddy used their economic and social clout to help register thousands of Hip Hop generation youth to vote for the first time in their lives.

Since the late 19th century, the theme of economic freedom and independence has often manifested itself in pro-capitalist and communal ideologies defining the nature of black economic life. SPC hip hoppers are still developing their thinking in this area and continue to draw from ideas of the past to make sense of their present economic status and to formulate strategies for future economic development.

PAN-AFRICAN CONNECTION

Since African people arrived in North America over four centuries ago, many African Americans have called for a spiritual and intellectual recognition of and connection to African people throughout the Diaspora. While the origins of Pan-Africanism can be traced to the 17th and 18th centuries, it gained much recognition at the Pan-African Conference in London in 1900, which was attended by such notable leaders as W. E. B. Du Bois, Anna Julia Cooper, and others. This conference added Pan-African perspectives to the liberation agenda for African peoples in the 20th century. The ideas of Pan-African solidarity and placing the BFS within the context of a global struggle were major themes throughout the CRM and BFS. Marcus Garvey, Malcolm X, Ella Baker, and Martin Luther King, Jr., each saw the CRM and BFS as parts of a larger African and global struggle to alleviate the oppression of people of color. Michael Franti also sees the connection between Hip Hop and Africa. Illuminating the artistic connections, Franti states that Hip Hop is "the African tradition of talking over rhythm. And you know hip hop music has all of the traditional elements of African storytelling: . . . braggadocio, dissing, . . . humor."[72]

Hip Hop from its beginnings called for a spiritual and cultural connection among African-descended people throughout the Diaspora. In fact, Hip Hop itself represents an art form that is spiritually connected to Africa and its people. Afrika Bambaataa was one of the first hip hoppers to make the spiritual connection between Hip Hop and Africa. He recalls that growing up in the South Bronx, many young blacks lacked a sense of pride and gravitated to gangs and violence as a means of dealing with oppressive conditions. As a young child, he saw a television show about the Zulu tribe and was impressed with the Zulu's resistance to the British. He began to think about the Zulu's concept of community and cohesion as a way for African Americans to deal with contemporary problems in the United States:

> Just to see these Black people [Zulus] fighting for what was theirs against the British, that always stuck in my mind. I said when I get of age, I will start this organization and put all these ideologies together in this group called the Zulu Nation. So what I did, with myself and a couple other of my comrades, is get out in the street, start talking to a lot of the brothers and sisters, trying to tell them how they're killing each other, that they should be warriors for their community.[73]

The 1980s witnessed the zenith of Pan-African idealism in Hip Hop. During this period, artists such as Public Enemy, X-Clan, Poor Righteous Teachers, KRS-One, and Queen Latifah exploded onto the rap scene promoting culturally positive images of African and African American culture. Many sported African Adinkra necklaces, leather necklaces of the African continent, and kente cloth. Queen Latifah, aka Dana Owens, called for African Americans to embrace their African culture and led the way by wearing African inspired headdresses and clothes. Her moniker, Queen Latifah, she said came from other "Muslim sounding" names she heard in her native Newark, New Jersey. Latifah explains that she uses her name to pay homage to her African ancestors: "The African queens have a unique place in world history. They are revered not only for their extraordinary beauty and power, but also for their strength and for their ability to nurture and rule the continent that gave rise to the greatest civilizations of all time."[74]

Similarly, the Fugees exploded on the scene during the mid-1990s, calling for a spiritual connectedness among African peoples in the United States, Africa, and the Caribbean. The group represents a Pan-African connection, with an African American, Lauryn Hill, as its lead singer and group members Wyclef Jean and Pras Michael claiming Haiti as their homeland. The group's name, the Fugees, is a derivation of "refugees," which refers to the Haitian refugees. Pras Michael explains his existence as a Pan-African refugee: "As people of African descent, we are all refugees. . . . Everyone came to this country on a boat at one time or another." They also reflect their Pan-African ethos and the rhythmic feel of African music by blending elements of R&B, Jazz, rap, and reggae.[75]

Other hip hoppers also promote a Pan-African philosophy of self-determination. French female hip hoppers Helene and Celia Faussart known as Les Nubians, released in 1999 their Pan-African musical treatise *Princesses Nubiennes*. Like the Fugees, Les Nubians integrate an eclectic blend of musical genres from throughout the Diaspora, including Jazz, R&B, Soul, reggae, and rap music. Of their Pan-African philosophy, Helene Faussart declared:

> One of the things we're trying to do with our music is to show that black people are united. We are one! Even though blacks have developed different styles of music in the different places they've ended up, we are one and the same people. That's why we chose to call ourselves "The Nubians"—it's a way of talking about blacks without using labels like Afro-American, Afro-Caribbean, Ghanaian and what have you. We're talking about one people coming together and using the process of getting in touch with their roots to move forward into the future.[76]

dead prez also espouses a Pan-African philosophy in their music that is comparable to Les Nubians':

> No, I wasn't born in Ghana,
> but Africa is my momma
> And I did not end up here from bad karma
> Or from B-Ball,
> selling mad crack or rappin'.
> Peter Tosh try to tell us what happened.
> He was sayin' if you black then you African. . . .
> A-F-R-I-C-A, Puerto Rico, Haiti, and J.A.
> New York and Cali, F-L-A
> No it ain't 'bout where you stay, it's 'bout the motherland.[77]

Perhaps the most comprehensive and compelling example of Pan-Africanism is the Hip Hop generation's CD tribute to legendary Nigerian musician and political activist Fela Anikulapo Kuti, who died of AIDS in 1997. Titled *Red Hot + Riot: The Music and Spirit of Fela Kuti*, the purpose of the CD was to pay homage to Kuti and his ideas of activism and Pan-African unification. Hip hoppers needed to call attention to the AIDS epidemic that has killed so many African people in Africa and throughout the Diaspora. Fela Kuti is popularly known for developing what was called "Afrobeat" in the early 1970s. Inspired by the music of James Brown, Kuti's "Afrobeat" was a form of "politico-funk" that merged elements of African American funk with traditional African beats and drums. His music addressed the social and political issues of Nigeria and of African people throughout the Diaspora.[78]

The combination of artists on *Red Hot + Riot* demonstrates the Pan-African connections in Hip Hop. Fela's son, Femi Kuti, who is himself recognized as a socially and politically conscious musician of the Hip Hop generation, is featured on the CD with a host of SPC hip hoppers, including dead prez, Blackalicious, Talib Kweli, Me'Shell Ndegeoshello, Common, Macy Gray, and Les Nubians. This ensemble is joined by Cameroonian saxophonist Manu Dibango, Senegalese singer Baaba Maal, and Nigerian-born Sade. The titles and content of the songs call for Africans around the globe to unite. The first song, "Fela Mentality (Intro)," appropriately introduces the Afrobeat genre of music, while songs such as "Shuffering and Shimiling," "Years of Tears and Sorrow," "Gentleman," and "Colonial Mentality" speak to the contemporary problems and challenges faced by African peoples.[79]

The idea of African-descended people across the globe recognizing their common ancestry, cultural threads, and historical struggle has not been lost on the Hip Hop generation. While the concept has not reached a mainstream U.S. audience in any substantive way, SPC hip hoppers are making significant strides in collaborating with other black artists throughout the Diaspora. Artists and groups such as Roots Manuva, Ms. Dynamite, Tego Calderon, K-Os, Dizzee Rascal, Estelle, Wale, Speech Debelle, and Booba, to name only a few, hail from throughout the Diaspora and their music has helped build Pan-African and global connections. Hip Hop is ripe for Pan-African and global movements given the utility of present-day technologies that transcend space, time, and geographical boundaries. Advances such as computers, satellites, e-mail, the Internet, and social networking sites provide the Hip Hop generation with opportunities for significant Pan-African and global unification that were not possible for previous generations of African peoples.

CONCLUSION

In an interview with Cleveland Sellers, a civil rights scholar and former SNCC program director, he acknowledged the tensions between the civil rights and Hip Hop generations and offers a cautionary critique of many hip hoppers for failing to develop a vision for their generation. However, he also notes the failure of his generation in reaching out to the Hip Hop generation. Sellers observed, "We did not assure the Hip Hop generation of their ability to learn from the struggle of our generation. We left the teaching of that process and that methodology to others."[80] Despite the mistakes on behalf of both generations, Sellers sees the potential for greater dialogue and collaboration between them. To help facilitate such discourse, he has worked with the Boston-based Project Hip Hop, which introduces Hip Hop generation youth to the geographical sites and stories of the CRM. Programs such as Project Hip Hop, he argued, brings the two generations together, opens lines of communication between them, and helps them begin to see the commonalties between the struggles of both generations.[81]

Initiatives such as Project Hip Hop and recent Hip Hop summits that bring together people across generations represent steps in the right direction. However, such efforts must only be the beginning if we hope to build a bridge between the civil rights and Hip Hop generations. Hip Hop historians can play a role in facilitating a discourse of common ground by illuminating the historical linkages and shared ideas of the two generations. In doing so, we help build a solid base from which the two generations can more easily see their commonalties, engage in a historically contextualized discourse, and move toward greater collaborative efforts to ameliorate contemporary social problems.

Like Carter G. Woodson and other historians of the BFS, and as Hip Hop historians, we must provide understanding and analyses of the social, economic, and political issues that confront the Hip Hop and civil rights generations. The civil rights generation must seek out and connect to the Hip Hop generation and recognize their similar and divergent views. The Hip Hop generation, in turn, must continue to seek knowledge and information about their social circumstances within the context of the larger BFS. Members must also critique their actions by promoting positive messages to youth and helping ameliorate the problems of their generation. Only when both generations heed these concerns will we have the collective strength to "fight the power" of discrimination, racism, and poverty that continues to impede the progress of African American communities.

NOTES

[1] Robin D. G. Kelley, *Freedom Dreams: The Black Radical Imagination* (Boston, 2002), 9.

[2] I use the term *Hip Hop* in this essay to denote the alternative black art form that emerged in northern urban areas during the 1970s. The elements that compose Hip Hop include graffiti writing, breakdancing, rapping (MCs), and dj-ing. For the purposes of this essay, I focus primarily on the element of rap. For a thorough analysis of rap as a form of Hip Hop, see Tricia Rose, *Black Noise: Rap Music and Black Culture in Contemporary America* (Middleton, CT, 1994).

[3] In this study, I define Hip Hop and rap as socially and politically conscious, or "socio-political," when they focus on the social, economic, and political situation of oppressed people—in this case African Americans. This genre of Hip Hop or rap examines historical problems within black communities, such as racism, police brutality, crooked politicians, greed, poverty, and substandard education. Socially and politically conscious Hip Hop and rap often espouse racial solidarity, community empowerment, and liberatory education as ways to ameliorate problems in black communities. A few of the groups and individuals who promote this genre of Hip Hop and rap include Public Enemy, Poor Righteous Teachers, and Blackalicious. It should be noted that other rappers who may not identify with the socially or politically conscious genre of Hip Hop sometimes have socially and politically conscious lyrics or messages in their music. Such artists include Jay Z, T. I., and Trina, among others. For an informative definition of "message rap" and a discussion of other categories, see Ernest Allen, Jr., "Making the Strong Survive: The Contours and Contradictions of Message Rap," in *Droppin' Science: Critical Essays on Rap Music and Hip Hop Culture*," ed., William Eric Perkins (Philadelphia, PA, 1996), 159–91.

[4] According to Hip Hop scholar Bakari Kitwana, the Hip Hop generation is comprised of those born

between 1965 and 1984 who identify with the language, culture, and music associated with Hip Hop. For a discussion of the Hip Hop generation, see Bakari Kitwana, *The Hip Hop Generation: Young Blacks and the Crisis in African American Culture* (New York, 2002), xiii, and Mark Anthony Neal, *Soul Babies: Black Popular Culture and the Post-Soul Aesthetic* (New York, 2002), 99–130. Also, see Derrick P. Alridge, "Hip Hop As a Social Movement and Radical Pedagogy of Resistance." (Paper presented at the Annual Meeting of the Association for the Study of African American Life and History, Orlando, FL, October 2002).

[5]Historians typically periodize the CRM as occurring between 1954 and 1968. Historian Vincent Harding and others suggest that this periodization is too restrictive and excludes many significant people and events that lie outside these dates. Instead, he argues that the BFS dates back to when the first blacks landed in North America and continues to this day. This broad and inclusive periodization includes people and events beyond the 1954–1968 time frame. See Vincent Harding, *There Is a River: The Black Freedom Struggle in America* (San Diego, CA, 1981), xi–xxvi.

[6]See Michael Franti and Spearhead, "Oh My God," *Stay Human*, Six Degrees Records (2001). For a discussion of Franti's activism that is reminiscent of the CRM, see Michael Franti, interview by Amy Goodman, 31 August 2004, http://www.democracynow.org/article.pl?sid=04/08/31/1455236&mode=thread&tid=25.

[7]See Julian Bond in Michael Hurd, "Civil Rights vs. Hip Hop: Chasm of Disrespect Separates Two Generations," *The Southern Digest*, online edition and Stanley Crouch, "Hip Hop's Thugs Hit New Low," *Daily News*, http://www.nydailynews.com/08-11-2003/news/story/108046p.97644c.html. Also see discussion on rap by Michael C. Dawson, *Black Visions: The Roots of Contemporary African-American Political Ideologies* (Chicago, 2001), 76–82.

[8]See Martin Kilson, "The Pretense of Hip Hop Black Leadership," *The Black Commentator*, http://www.blackcommentator.com/50/50-kilson.html. To a certain extent, the views of Kilson and others of his generation are understandable because they have been exposed primarily to "party rap" and "gangsta rap," which have received more airplay than SPC rap in mainstream media outlets. In his essay, Kilson does not include SPC Hip Hop in his analysis.

[9]See Todd Boyd, *The New H.N.I.C.: The Death of Civil Rights and the Reign of Hip Hop* (New York, 2002). For a response to Boyd, see Derrick P. Alridge, "'Hip Hop Versus Civil Rights?': Essay Review of Boyd's *The New H.N.I.C.*" in *The Journal of African American History* 88 (Summer 2003): 313–16.

[10]Boyd, *The New H.N.I.C.*, xxi.

[11]See Kitwana, *The Hip Hop Generation*. Kitwana has written an excellent book examining some of the core beliefs of the Hip Hop generation. His book acknowledges the tensions between the generations. My essay hopes to connect the ideas of both movements.

[12]See Derrick P. Alridge, "Teaching Martin Luther King, Jr., and the Civil Rights Movement in High School History Courses: Rethinking Content and Pedagogy" in *Teaching the American Civil Rights Movement: Freedom's Bittersweet Song*, eds., Julie Buckner Armstrong, et al. (New York, 2002), 3–18.

[13]William Eric Perkins, "The Rap Attack: An Introduction," in *Droppin' Science: Critical Essays on Rap Music and Hip Hop Culture*, ed., William Eric Perkins (Philadelphia, PA, 1996), 9.

[14]Many identify Grandmaster Theodore as the originator of "scratching." Other early DJs also credited with the development of scratching are Grandmaster Flash and Kool Herc who popularized a technique that was the predecessor to scratching, called "cutting."

[15]Public Enemy, "Fight the Power," *Fear of a Black Planet*, Def Jam (1994).

[16]Chuck D with Yusuf Jah, *Fight the Power: Rap, Race, and Reality* (New York, 1997), 26.

[17]OutKast, "Rosa Parks," *Aquemini*, La Face (1998).

[18]See "Outkast Settles Suit by Parks; Duo to Help on TV, CD Tributes," *Atlanta Journal-Constitution*, 15 April 2005, 1G.

[19]Common, "Song for Assata," *Like Water for Chocolate*, MCA (2000).

[20]Ibid.

[21]Ibid.

[22]Common, "Pops' Rap . . . All My Children," *Like Water for Chocolate*.

[23]In his most recent work, "The Corner," Common continues to connect Hip Hop with the CRM and BFS by collaborating with 1960s era poets, The Last Poets. At the print time of this essay, the video may be viewed at http://www.common-music.com/.

[24]Angela Davis, "The Prison Industrial Complex," *Prison Industrial Complex* (Alternative Tentacle, 1999).

[25]The Roots, "Why (What's Goin On?)," *The Tipping Point*, Geffen Records (2004).

[26]The Roots have consistently connected Hip Hop to the CRM and BFS. On their 1996 CD, *Things Fall Apart*, the Roots use the title of Chinua Achebe's seminal 1958 book about the colonization of Nigeria. On the cover, the Roots use black and white pictures that evoke images of colonial oppression and blacks living in a police state; see, The Roots, *Things Fall Apart*, MCA (1999).

[27]Underground Rap is an unconventional form of Hip Hop typically not heard on mainstream media venues such as MTV, BET, or VH1. This genre does not typically embrace the glitz of mainstream Hip Hop, but retains its connections to the streets, masses, or alternative communities—what Marx called the proletariat and lumpenproletariat. Some, but not all, underground artists lose their underground appeal when they receive heavy airplay on mainstream venues. SPC underground artists, at the writing of this article, include Ishues, Immortal Technique, Mr. Lif, and Aceyalone, to name a few. For discussions and references on underground Hip Hop, see *Hip Hop: The Definitive Guide to Rap & Hip Hop*, eds., Vladimir Bogdanov et al. (San Francisco, CA, 2003), x.

[28]John Miles Lewis, interview by author, tape recording, Atlanta, GA, 10 May 2004.

[29]Ibid.

[30]The Witchdoctor, interview by author, tape recording, Athens, GA, 21 February 2004.

[31]Ibid.

[32]The Witchdoctor did not assert that his leadership model for the Hip Hop generation was influenced by the work of others who advocated a group model of leadership. However, the concerns he expressed about the reliance on a single leader were similar to those expressed by W. E. B. Du Bois in the 1940s and Ella Baker and the Student Nonviolent Coordinating Committee (SNCC) in the 1960s.

[33]Khujo, telephone interview by author, 21 January 2005.

[34]See V. P. Franklin, *Black Self-Determination: A Cultural History of African American Resistance* (Brooklyn, NY, 1992). Also, see Cornel West, *Prophesy Deliverance!: An Afro-American Revolutionary Christianity* (1982; reprinted Louisville, KY, 2002).

[35]Lawrence W. Levine, *Black Culture and Black Consciousness: Afro-American Folk Thought from Slavery to Freedom* (New York, 1978) and Sterling Stuckey, *Slave Culture: Nationalist Theory and the Foundations of Black America* (New York, 1988).

[36]Levine, *Black Culture and Black Consciousness*, 8–15.

[37]Clyde Woods, *Development Arrested: Race, Power, and the Blues in the Mississippi Delta* (London, 1998), 29.

[38]Levine, *Black Culture and Black Consciousness*, 146–49.

[39]Ernie Paniccioli, telephone interview by author, 13 March, 2005.

[40]Brand Nubian, "Wake Up" (Reprise), *One for All*, Elektra/Asylum (1990).

[41]NWA, "Niggaz 4 Life," *Niggaz4life*, Priority Records (1991). For an excellent discussion of "gangsta rap," see Robin D. G. Kelley, *Race Rebels: Culture, Politics, and the Black Working Class* (New York, 1994), 183–227.

[42]Mos Def and Talib Kweli, "Black Star-K.O.S. (Determination)," *Black Star*, Rawkus (1998).

[43]Ibid.

[44]OutKast, "Liberation," *Aquemini*, La Face Records (1998).

[45]Ibid.

[46]dead prez, "Hip Hop," *let's get free*, Loud Records (2000). At the writing of this essay, the video may be viewed at www.mtv.com/bands/az/dead_prez/artist.jhtml.

[47]Kevin K. Gaines, *Uplifting the Race: Black Leadership, Politics, and Culture in the Twentieth Century* (Chapel

Hill, NC, 1996), 32–34.

[48]Thomas L. Webber, *Deep Like the Rivers: Education in the Slave Quarter Community, 1831–1865* (New York, 1978).

[49]Stephen N. Haymes, "Pedagogy and the Philosophical Anthropology of African American Slave Culture," *Philosophia Africana* 2 (August 2001): 63–92.

[50]See James D. Anderson, *The Education of Blacks in the South, 1860–1935* (Chapel Hill, NC, 1988).

[51]Carter G. Woodson, *The Mis-education of the Negro* (Trenton, NJ, 1990).

[52]See Boogie Down Productions, "You Must Learn," *Ghetto Music: The Blueprint of Hip Hop*, Jive/Novus (1989).

[53]Ibid.

[54]Ishues, interview by author, tape recording, Athens, GA, 15 January 2005.

[55]Ishues, "Game Time," *Reality Flow*, Attica Sound (2003).

[56]Ishues interview.

[57]dead prez, "they schools," *let's get free*, Loud Records (2000).

[58]See dead prez, "they schools."

[59]Nas, "I Can," *God's Son*, Sony (2002).

[60]John Silbey Butler, *Entrepreneurship and Self-Help among Black Americans: A Reconsideration of Race and Economics* (Albany, NY, 1991).

[61]Quote from August Meier, *Negro Thought in America, 1880–1915* (1963; reprinted Ann Arbor, MI, 1988), 45; see also V. P. Franklin, "Alexander Crummell: Defining Matters of Principle," in *Living Our Stories, Telling Our Truths: Autobiography and the Making of the African American Intellectual Tradition* (New York, 1995), 21–58; Gregory U. Rigby, *Alexander Crummell: Pioneer in Nineteenth Century Pan-African Thought* (Westport, CT, 1988); Alfred Moss, Jr., "Alexander Crummell: Black Nationalist and Apostle of Western Civilization," in *Black Leaders of the Nineteenth Century*, ed., Leon Litwack and August Meier (Urbana, IL, 1988), 237–51; and Wilson J. Moses, *Alexander Crummell: A Study of Civilization and Discontent* (New York, 1989).

[62]V. P. Franklin, "'They Rose or Fell Together': African American Educators and Community Leadership, 1795–1954," *Journal of Education* 172, no. 3 (1990): 39–63.

[63]See Booker T. Washington, *Working with the Hands: Being a Sequel to "Up from Slavery" Covering the Author's Experiences in Industrial Training at Tuskegee* (New York, 1969).

[64]See W. E. B. Du Bois, "The Negroes of Farmville, Virginia: A Social Study," *Bulletin of the Department of Labor, Washington, DC* (January 1898): 1–38; and "The Upbuilding of Black Durham: The Success of Negroes and Their Value to a Tolerant and Helpful Southern City," *World's Work* 23 (January 1912): 334–38.

[65]Joe William Trotter, Jr., *The African American Experience* (Boston, MA, 2001), 605–06.

[66]Grandmaster Flash and the Furious Five, "The Message," *Message from the Streets: Best of Grandmaster Flash*, Rhino Records (1994).

[67]M-1, interview by Chris Witt, *The Knitting Factory*, http://www.knittingfactory.com/articles/get feature cfm?feature num=50&head=M-1%20.

[68]Talibah Mbonisi, telephone interview by author, 7 January, 2004.

[69]Ibid.

[70]See *Tupac Resurrection: In His Own Words*, co. prod., Dinal Lapolt and Michael Cole, Paramount Video, 2003, videocassette.

[71]Kevin Chappell, "The Half-Billion Dollar Empire of Russell Simmons," *Ebony* (July 2003), 168–78; Christopher Vaughn, "Simmons' Rush for Profits," *Black Enterprise*, December 1992, 67–70.

[72]Interview with Michael Franti in Ishmael Reed, Michael Franti, and Bill Adler, "Hiphoprisy," *Transition*

56 (1992): 155.

[73] Afrika Bambaataa quoted in "Afrika Bambaataa and the Mighty Zulu Nation," in *Yes, Yes, Y'all: The Experience Music Project Oral History of Hip Hop's First Decade*, eds. Jim Frick and Charlie Ahearn (Cambridge, MA, 2002), 44.

[74] Queen Latifah quoted in James G. Spady, "Queen Latifah Expands the Boundaries of the Rap Artist through Mega-Media," in *Street Conscious Rap*, eds. James G. Spady, et al. (Philadelphia, PA, 1999), 74.

[75] Edwidge Danicat, "Hanging with the Fugees," *Essence*, August 1996, 86; and Bogdanov, *Hip Hop: The Definitive Guide to Rap and Hip Hop*, 182.

[76] Helene and Celia Faussart, interview by Loic Bussieres, http://www.rfimusique.com/siteEn/cd_semaine/cd_semaine_7072.asp.

[77] dead prez, "i'm a african," *let's get free* (Loud Records, 2000).

[78] See *Red Hot + Riot: The Music and Spirit of Fela Kuti* (MCA, 2002). For a discussion of Fela Kuti and "Afrobeat," see Michael E. Veal, *Fela: The Life and Times of an African Music Icon* (Philadelphia, PA, 2000), 10–15.

[79] Ibid.

[80] Cleveland Sellers, interview by author, tape recording, Columbia, SC, 16 December, 2004.

[81] Also, in March 2004, a group of rappers and hip hoppers met with 1960s civil rights activists at the National Hip Hop Summit in New Jersey to discuss what could be done to bridge the gap between their generations. The group recognized the tensions between them and called for more discourse aimed at building bridges of communication. Within the past year, such conversations have been occurring throughout the United States.

JACKANAPES: REFLECTIONS ON THE LEGACY OF THE BLACK PANTHER PARTY FOR THE HIP HOP GENERATION

V. P. Franklin

In Bobby Seale's *Seize the Time: The Story of the Black Panther Party and Huey P. Newton*, first published in 1970, in the chapter on "Pigs, Problems, Politics, and Panthers," there is a section devoted to describing the activities of the "Jackanapes, Renegades, and Agent Provocateurs." The renegades were those individuals who joined the Black Panther Party (BPP), but continued to "goof off" and failed to obey the rules until they were "busted" by Seale or Huey Newton or other Panther leaders. One time when the party needed money to bail Bobby Seale out of jail after he was arrested for carrying a shotgun, Newton asked a group of Panthers to go out and sell copies of the *Black Panther Paper* to raise money. However, rather than selling the papers, "they got to jiving around with some chicks in North Richmond. When they got back three or four hours later, they had sold only about twenty-five papers and used a lot of gas." When Newton questioned them, one finally shouted, "To hell with selling these papers right now, man! I'm gonna jive with these chicks." After Newton told them to take the girls back and try and sell some papers, they fooled around again. Newton reminded them that when they were in jail in Sacramento, Bobby Seale had worked hard to raise their bail money; "now you guys are jiving around and the brother's in jail and you won't do the same thing for him." So they were "busted" by Newton, but this time they were thrown out of the party.

But the renegades had learned their lesson. After Seale's bail money was raised and he returned to the Oakland office, he found that these busted renegades were still hanging around. They took Seale aside and tried to explain what had happened: "We goofed off, man. We should have been working to help get bail money to help you get out. Bobby, we're sorry man." Newton explained to Seale, "They're going to have to learn how to get themselves together." However, Seale told Newton, "They asked me to forgive them for it and I did." Newton relented and let them back in the party.[1]

Much more dangerous, however, were the "agent provocateurs" and "jackanapes." The agent provocateurs were police and FBI agents who had infiltrated the party and attempted to provoke party members into illegal activities that theoretically they would not have engaged in without this outside provocation. Seale declared, "Agent provocateurs have come into the Party and have deliberately stirred problems and done things in violation of the Party's principles and rules."[2] Information on the activities of the FBI to try and destroy the Panther organization from within was published in the 1976 three-volume report by the U.S. Senate, the "Church Commission Report."[3] However, Seale discussed these agents' destructive operations in *Seize the*

Time in 1970 and explained how agent provocateurs used the renegades to undermine the party.

> The agent provocateurs used the cats who refused to be politically educated and to follow the revolutionary principles and rules. Half of the cats who didn't follow the program were being led astray by agent provocateur activity. We didn't know it at first, but we felt and knew that something was definitely going wrong.[4]

Even more dangerous than the renegades were the "jackanapes" who not only refused to become "politically educated" and follow the party rules, but also failed to give up their criminal behavior once they became Panthers.

> A jackanape is a fool. He's foolish, but he's not scared of the police. He's foolish in that he'll get himself killed. If you don't straighten him out, and try to politically educate him, *he will definitely bring the Party down*. If there is an agent provocateur around, the agent will hinder your attempts to politically educate these cats, and will lead them to do crazy things based on emotions rather than work based on understanding social change. For example, a jackanape will come walking down the street with a gun in his hand, talking about, "F*** the Pigs, To hell with the pigs, I ain't going to jail." Then he'll be surrounded by 25 cops with shotguns pointed at his head, and he'll go to jail.[5]

Seale contrasted the jackanapes with the "real revolutionaries" who "are like the brothers in the L.A. shootout, where the pigs attacked the office and pulled a predawn raid on them." Seale pointed out that, "those brothers defended that office because they were really defending the community programs that we were trying to set up.

> They defended themselves because they realized that *the power structure wanted to rip them off and systematically exterminate them*, that [the power structure] wanted to prevent the organizing and uniting of the people around revolutionary programs. . . . As a citizen in the community and a member of the Black Panther Party . . . [the real revolutionary will] follow the rules and be very dedicated. He is constantly trying to politically educate himself about revolutionary principles and how they function, to get a broad perspective. He'll also defend himself and his people when we're unjustly attacked by the racist pigs.[6]

And what about the jackanape? Seale noted that "the jackanape generally works from the opportunistic position. He centers things only around himself; he's still selfish. He thinks his pot and his wine are above the Party. He thinks his gun is something that he can use at will, to rip off stuff at will."[7]

David Hilliard, who served as the chairman of the Black Panther Party in the early 1970s while Seale and Newton were imprisoned, published his autobiography

This Side of Glory in 1993. Hilliard provided details on an incident of jackanape activity that had also been mentioned by Bobby Seale in 1970 in *Seize the Time*. It is the incident where two members were sent out to pick up eight others using the Panthers' "big white van," which had *"Black Panther Newspaper"* painted in large black letters on the side. After picking up the others, they stopped the van at a diner, and while one Panther went to use the restroom, the other—the jackanape—decided to rob the place. When the other Panther returned, he was shocked by what the other had done, but both jumped into the van and decided to make a run for it. "Within five minutes," the van was spotted by the police and in the ensuing shootout the jackanape wounded a police officer.[8] In *Seize the Time*, Bobby Seale goes on to relate similar incidents, and at one point quotes David Hilliard at that time declaring in frustration, "These jackanapes and fools are going to try and destroy the Party, if we don't watch them."[9]

According to David Hilliard, however, Eldridge Cleaver recommended that the party tolerate the jackanapes and their behavior. Cleaver had settled in San Francisco after being released on parole from Soledad Prison in December 1966. He had been serving time for rape; however, through the efforts of his attorney Beverly Axelrod and several writers who were impressed by his prison writings, he was granted parole. After writing several articles for *Ramparts* magazine, Cleaver was recruited by the Black Panther Party to work on their newspaper, and soon assumed the title "Minister of Information." Following the publication in 1968 of his book of essays *Soul on Ice*, Cleaver gained national and international celebrity.[10] David Hilliard recalled that in 1968 when the party was confronted by the dangerous antics of the jackanapes, "Eldridge insists we protect them, saying they have good value: they'll be the fighters on the first day of the revolution."[11] In 1972 in a well-known article published in *The Black Scholar*, entitled "On Lumpen Ideology," Cleaver provided his explanation for his support of the former criminals who were causing so many problems for the party. For Cleaver, these jackanapes were members of the "lumpen proletariat," or the "permanently unemployed," "who have no secure relationship or vested interest in the means of production and the institutions of a capitalist society." They "have never worked and never will and can't find a job; [they] are unskilled and unfit." They are also "the so-called Criminal Element, those who live by their wits, existing off that which they rip off, who stick guns in the faces of businessmen and say, 'Stick 'em up' or 'give it up.' These 'forgotten people' have been locked out of the economy and robbed of their rightful social heritage."[12]

In the early sections of *Seize the Time*, Bobby Seale noted that initially Huey Newton endorsed this position, pointing out that Newton wanted to recruit "brothers off the block, brothers who had been pimping, brothers who had been peddling dope, brothers who ain't gonna take no shit." The objective was to give them some "political education" (and it was not much political education since it consisted primarily of the Panthers' "Ten-Point Platform and Program"), and then to organize them, and "you get black men, you get revolutionaries who are too much."[13] However, by the end of *Seize the Time*, Newton is quoted also denouncing some of these "brothers off the block" as jackanapes who will help destroy the party.

In his introduction to the excellent anthology *The Black Panther Party Reconsidered*, the editor Charles E. Jones discussed what he considered the mythologies surrounding the Panthers, including the idea that "the BPP was a 'lumpen-based' organization." Jones examines the educational background of Panther leaders and concluded that most were college students and high school graduates and that "the diversity of the Party membership is often overlooked." He argued that "the socioeconomic profile of the rank-and-file Panthers contradicts the lumpen perception of the organization," and he suggested that "the typical Panther" was a "high school or college student." Indeed, Jones believes that Eldridge Cleaver, "who spent much of his adult life in prison on an assortment of criminal charges," was the Panther leader who closely reflected the profile of the "black lumpen."[14]

The issue of the black lumpen component of the Black Panther Party is revisited in the section of Jones's volume devoted to "The Decline of the Party." There are three essays in that section. Winston Grady-Willis focused on external factors, especially state repression and the commitment of various law enforcement agencies at the local, state, and federal levels to destroy the Black Panther Party. The second article is by Ollie A. Johnson. Utilizing what he refers to as "elite theory," Johnson argues that in the 1970s the Panther leadership centralized the organizational structure, which facilitated an "abuse of power." The leaders became more authoritarian, and "oligarchization" occurred in which "a numerical minority" had gained and misused power and control of the organization. Pointing specifically to Huey Newton, Johnson argues that he used power "irresponsibly and destructively" and his return to power in 1977 after Elaine Brown had been leading the group along a reformist line, "signaled the eventual demise of the Party."[15]

The third article is by Chris Booker and is entitled "Lumpenization: A Critical Error of the Black Panther Party." Booker acknowledges at the outset that "political repression, tactical disagreements, and authoritarianism" all contributed to the demise of the party. However, he argues that "the emphasis on the lumpen was a decisive factor in the Black Panther Party's eventual decline as a national political force."[16] Booker concludes that the recruitment of "that segment closely aligned with the criminal element created a crisis, one that would contribute to the demise of the organization." Booker also pointed out: "One important lesson gleaned from the experience of the Black Panther Party is that organizations that seek to focus on the recruitment of the lumpen should have effective mechanisms to reform new members. The Nation of Islam, for example, recruits heavily from prisons, but stresses personal transformation with much apparent success. By promoting the personalities and lifestyles of the lumpen, the Black Panther Party contributed to its own demise."[17] It should be noted that in Charles Jones's lengthy introduction and Booker's twenty-five page essay, "Lumpenization and the Black Panther Party," they never addressed the numerous problems with the "jackanapes" mentioned over and over in the Panthers' published writings.

At the same time, Booker's point about the success of the Nation of Islam in turning "black lumpen" into the "Fruit of Islam" is an important topic I discussed in my book *Autobiography and the Making of the African American Intellectual Tradition*.[18] In the discussion of the *Autobiography of Malcolm X*, I focused on the fact that the personal transformation that took place for Malcolm and other "black lumpen" who joined the Nation of Islam was considered "miraculous" because it involved a "resurrection from the dead." By most accounts, when someone is raised from the dead, it is generally considered a miracle. And that is how Malcolm characterized his "personal transformation" from Detroit Red to Malcolm X. In relating his exploits as a hustler, for example, Malcolm commented over and over and that his survival during that time was a miracle. "Sometimes recalling all of this, I don't know, to tell the truth, how I am alive today. They say God takes care of fools and babies. I've so often thought that Allah was watching over me. Through all this time of my life, I really *was* dead—mentally dead. I just didn't know that I was." Moreover, every issue of the Nation of Islam's newspaper *Muhammad Speaks* (and continued in the *Final Call*) there is a statement explaining "What the Muslims Believe." Number five among the twelve points states: "We believe in the resurrection of the dead—not in physical resurrection—but in mental resurrection. We believe that the so-called Negroes are the most in need of mental resurrection; therefore, they will be resurrected first."[19]

The personal transformation that occurred for members of the "criminal element," the black lumpen, once they joined the Nation of Islam was often considered "miraculous" by those who witnessed it. Unfortunately, the political education that was offered to the black lumpen who joined the Black Panther Party many times did not produce "real revolutionaries." Charles Jones's conclusion that the Panther membership base included a large number of high school and college students may be accurate, but it was also the case that the party was weakened internally by the antics of the jackanapes.

Calling attention to the jackanapes among the members of the Black Panther Party serves as a perfect segue into a discussion of the Hip Hop generation. *The Journal of African American History* examined many aspects of Hip Hop culture in the Summer 2005 issue devoted to "The History of Hip Hop." This was an attempt to move beyond "pop culture," and offered a scholarly analysis of various aspects of Hip Hop cultural development and evolution.[20] One important theme that is emphasized in the Special Issue is the continuity from the Black Power era to the early years of Hip Hop, especially with the creation of "socially conscious Hip Hop" by artists such as Public Enemy, Professor X, Africa Bambaataa, Brand Nubian, KRS-One, and others. Historian Derrick Alridge pointed out that "by the mid to late 1980s, black nationalist and other [Hip Hop] groups, inspired by the Nation of Islam, the Five Percent Nation of Islam, and the resurgence in the popularity of black nationalist icons such as Malcolm X, were weighing in on the black condition and espousing a philosophy of self-determination."[21] Alridge and the other contributors to the Special Issue pointed to the direct connections that exist between members of the Black Panther Party and Hip Hop artists such as Tupac Shakur.

At the same time, however, the authors also analyze the "cultural baggage" carried over from the Black Power era with regard to misogynistic and homophobic attitudes and positions. Charise Cheney, in her article "In Search of the 'Revolutionary Generation': (En)gendering the Golden Age of Rap Nationalism," documents the male chauvinist and misogynist beliefs and practices of black male leaders in the Civil Rights and Black Power Movements that were re-voiced in the lyrics of male Hip Hop artists during the "Golden Age of Rap" in the late 1980s and early 1990s. Male chauvinist, misogynistic, and homophobic ideas and practices are problematic continuities from the Black Power era to the Hip Hop generation.[22]

In discussions of the black freedom struggle during the middle of the 20th century, historian Peniel Joseph pointed out that the "good" and "heroic" Civil Rights Movement is often contrasted with the "bad 1960s, characterized by the omnipresent Black Panthers, urban rioting, and black separatism."[23] However, the Black Power era brought a significant shift in the social, political, and cultural consciousness of people of African descent, not just in the United States, but throughout the Diaspora, comparable to the New Negro Movement of the post–World War I era and 1920s. The New Negro Movement brought about significant changes in music, arts, literature, politics, education, and economics for people of African descent.[24] While we have had over eight decades to assess the impact of New Negro consciousness on African American life and culture, we are just beginning to assess the enormous legacy of the Black Power Movement.[25]

While the Black Power era was extremely important and brought about many positive changes in African American life and culture, we also must be vigilant in identifying the negative aspects as well. And specifically with regard to the Black Panther Party, which in many ways was an iconic Black Power organization, we must recognize that those who brought aspects of the "thug life" into the organization helped to destroy it. In the documents created by the Panthers in the 1960s and 1970s, and in the various memoirs, autobiographies, and other eyewitness accounts, the jackanapes were clearly involved in activities that contributed to the undermining of the Black Panther Party. Unfortunately, it appears that the jackanapes are alive and well and doing a number on the Hip Hop generation. The numerous shootouts that occur between rap artists and their "posses," as well as the widely publicized murders of Tupac Shakur, the Notorious BIG, and other gangsta rappers suggest that there is a need for the members of the Hip Hop generation to learn the hard lessons from their more politically aware predecessors in the Black Panther Party. This is extremely important because in the case of the jackanapes, their criminal behavior helped bring about the destruction of an organization dedicated to black self-determination and the redistribution of wealth from the "haves" to the "have nots" in capitalist America. In the case of the gangsta rappers, gang bangers, thugs, murderers, and other criminals who are lionized and made into Hip Hop celebrities, they are aiding and abetting the destruction of an entire generation (or more) of African American youth. It seems that the more Hip Hop artists and rappers participate in and advocate gun violence for settling conflicts and disputes, the more acceptable it becomes for black youths to use guns to shoot and kill other black youths, particularly young black men who are being murdered in alarming numbers. Instead of contributing to the high rates of black-on-black crime, the Hip Hop artists and celebrities need to do much more with the resources they have to promote alternatives to gun violence for resolving conflicts among black youths.

In presenting an analysis of the positive and negative aspects of the Black Panther Party and the Black Power era in general, it is our hope that members of the Hip Hop generation will come to understand the complicated legacy of the Black Panther Party and will seek to avoid those ideas, beliefs, and practices that contributed to the untimely demise of one of the most heroic and tragic organizations in the history of the black liberation movement.

NOTES

An earlier version of this paper was delivered as the opening address at the conference on "Race, Roots, and Resistance: Revisiting the Legacy of Black Power," held at the University of Illinois, Urbana-Champaign, 29–31 March 2006.

[1] Bobby Seale, *Seize the Time: The Story of the Black Panther Party and Huey P. Newton* (1970; reprinted Baltimore, MD, 1991), 374–75.

[2] Ibid., 376.

[3] Frank Church, *Final Report of the Senate Select Committee to Study Governmental Operations with Respect to Intelligence Activities and the Rights of Americans*, 3 Volumes (Washington, DC, 1976); see also Kenneth O'Reilly, *"Racial Matters": The FBI's Secret File on Black America, 1960–1972* (New York, 1989), 293–324.

[4] Seale, *Seize the Time*, 379.

[5] Ibid., 379–80.

[6] Ibid., 380.

[7] Ibid., 380–81.

[8] David Hilliard and Lewis Cole, *This Side of Glory: The Autobiography of David Hilliard and the Story of the Black Panther Party* (Boston, MA, 1993), 155.

[9] Seale, *Seize the Time*, 382.

[10] For background information on Eldridge Cleaver, see Kathleen Cleaver, "Introduction," *Target Zero: A Life in Writing—Eldridge Cleaver* (New York, 2006), xi–xxvi.

[11] Hilliard, *This Side of Glory*, 147. In response to Cleaver's statement, Hilliard also mentioned that another Panther suggested that the jackanapes could serve as the "vanguard for the stupid revolution."

[12] Eldridge Cleaver, "On Lumpen Ideology," *Black Scholar* 3 (1972): 2–10.

[13] Seale, *Seize the Time*, 64.

[14] Charles E. Jones, ed., "Introduction: Reconsidering the Panther History: The Untold Story," *The Black Panther Party Reconsidered* (Baltimore, MD, 1998), 45–46.

[15] Winston Grady-Willis, "The Black Panther Party: State Repression and Political Prisoners," and Ollie A. Johnson III, "Explaining the Demise of the Black Panther Party: The Role of Internal Factors," in ibid., 337–414; quote on 392.

[16] Chris Booker, "Lumpenization: A Critical Error for the Black Panther Party," in ibid., 337.

[17] Ibid., 357.

[18] V. P. Franklin, "Malcolm X and the Resurrection of the Dead," in *Living Our Stories, Telling Our Truths:*

Autobiography and the Making of the African American Intellectual Tradition (New York, 1995), 319–45.

[19]Malcolm X and Alex Haley, *The Autobiography of Malcolm X* (New York, 1965), 125.

[20]Derrick P. Alridge and James B. Stewart, "Introduction: Hip Hop in History: Past, Present, and Future," *The Journal of African American History* 90 (Summer 2005): 190–95.

[21]Derrick Alridge, "From Civil Rights to Hip Hop: Toward a Nexus of Ideas," ibid., 235.

[22]Cherise Cheney, "In Search of the 'Revolutionary Generation': (En)gendering the Golden Age of Black Nationalism," ibid., 278–98.

[23]Peniel E. Joseph, "Introduction: Toward a Historiography of the Black Power Movement," *The Black Power Movement: Rethinking the Civil Rights Black Power Era* (New York, 2006), 3–4; see also, Joseph's "Black Liberation without Apology: Reconceptualizing the Black Power Movement," *Black Scholar* 31 (Fall–Winter 2001): 3–19.

[24]One of the best volumes that presents an overview and historical documents from the 1920s New Negro Movement is Michael W. Peplow and Arthur P. Davis, eds., *The New Negro Renaissance: An Anthology* (New York, 1975).

[25]For a comprehensive analysis of the differences between the Civil Rights Movement and the Black Power era, see Sundiata Cha-Jua and Clarence Lang, "The 'Long Movement' as Vampire: Temporal and Spatial Fallacies in Recent Black Freedom Studies," *The Journal of African American History* 92 (Spring 2007): 265–88.

IN SEARCH OF THE "REVOLUTIONARY GENERATION": (EN)GENDERING THE GOLDEN AGE OF RAP NATIONALISM

Charise Cheney

In the 1988 Public Enemy release "Party for Your Right to Fight" rap nationalist and lead lyricist Chuck D ushered in a new moment in Hip Hop history when he defiantly stated: "Power, equality and we're out to get it, I know some of you ain't with it. This party started right in '66, with a pro-black radical mix. . . ."[1] As a trailblazer of the consciousness movement within rap music, Chuck D claimed his legacy as the political progeny of the Black Panther Party. The Black Panthers, remembered by the Hip Hop generation as righteous revolutionaries, are deified and belong to an elite class of politicized "prophets of rage." They are black nationalists whose standard for black manhood is preserved and emulated. In fact, Chuck D told a *Toronto Sun* reporter in May 1998 that when he and his friends from Adelphi University entered the "rap game," they did so in a deliberate manner. "We wanted to be known as the Black Panthers of Rap, we wanted our music to be dissonant."[2] With songs like "Party for Your Right to Fight," "Fight the Power," and "Power to the People," these pioneers of rap nationalism purposefully invoked the rhetorical and political styling of the Black Panther Party and the Black Power Movement of the late 1960s, complete with its envisioning of black nationalism as a politics of masculine protest. Like their idols, Chuck D and his crew believed that they were the representatives of a "revolutionary generation," a group of endangered young black males considered by the state to be "Public Enemy #1." And as Public Enemy, Chuck D argued that it was black men's responsibility to "get mad, revolt, revise, realize" for black liberation;[3] for, as he stated on their 1990 album *Fear of a Black Planet*, "it takes a man to take a stand."[4]

So began the "Golden Age of Rap Nationalism," a period in rap music history bracketed by the release of two Hip Hop classics: Public Enemy's *It Takes a Nation of Millions to Hold Us Back* in 1988, which staged the debut of the "Prophets of Rage" and Ice Cube's *Lethal Injection* in 1993, which signified an end to the profits of rage. Although the use of rap music as a form of cultural expression was not a revolutionary idea (young blacks and Latinos had begun to rediscover poetry in musical motion over ten years prior to the introduction of rap nationalism), the use of rap music as a site for political expression was radical—both because of and despite its lyrical content. This was especially true prior to the mass commodification of rap music (instigated by the popularity of "gangsta rap" music), when artists like Public Enemy, KRS-One and Boogie Down Productions, X-Clan, Poor Righteous Teachers, Ice

Cube, and Paris appropriated black nationalist rhetoric to critique the historical development of racial hierarchies and their legacy in contemporary social, political, and economic institutions.[5] The political positions assumed by black neo-nationalist rap group X-Clan is a case in point. On their 1992 release *Xodus*, lead lyricist Brother J not only rejected bourgeois humanism, but also exposed the hypocrisy of American democracy and refuted white claims to moral superiority:

> Revolution, evolution the solution; No amendments so burn the Constitution. You check the authors a bunch of old Whiggers, who strategized extinction of the pro-black niggas. Know why? 'Cause I'm that nigga that they can't stand. Teach the African how to say 'Black Man.' And I'm that nigga they can plainly see, with the nationalist colors of the red, black, green.

According to Brother J's lyrical thesis, black nationalism is the culmination of a collectivist ethic that is both the legacy of a cultural tradition defined by Africans and a byproduct of the oppressive conditions that defined African America. It is the latter determinant that fuels his black nationalist "politicking." Racial terrorism is at the center of X-Clan's historical memory and at the core of their contemporary social commentary. Brother J highlights the political struggles against legalized violence and cultural expropriation of people of African descent in the United States. He does so with a sense of irony. "Point blank livin'-ism is a check; 'cause there's just some things that I'll never forget. . . . I remember all the times that you called me an animal, but in Milwaukee there's a cannibal."[6] As Brother J passes the mike to his partner in rhyme Professor X (son of Brooklyn nationalist-activist Sonny Carson), the group unveils their antidote to centuries of anti-black discrimination and exploitation. Their revelation: "pro-black dedication"; their strategy: armed rebellion. "The solution, revolution/evolution, the conclusion/the trigger." X-Clan's 1992 song "Fire and Earth (100% Natural)" is a tribute to revolutionary nationalism during which the "ever-nappy crew set[s] the mood" by claiming an inalienable right to self-determination and warning those who attempt to transgress that right: "Our nation is protected by some pro-black niggas."[7] While it is tempting to take this lyrical composition for granted, to assume it is a manifestation of postmodern, postindustrial, post–civil rights black nationalism, it is nonetheless important to interrogate the parameters of its political content.

For more than a generation, researchers and practitioners of U.S. black nationalism have debated its definition; in fact, historian William L. Van Deburg wittily remarked that trying to encapsulate the political phenomenon "is a bit like trying to eat Jell-O with chopsticks."[8] That struggle is due to the fact that observers of U.S. black nationalism must first deal with an obvious theoretical dilemma: African Americans who consider themselves "nationalists" are a nation within a nation, or more accurately, a nation without a nation. Therefore, the discourse surrounding the definition of nationalism is centered on a dispute over whether or not the configuration of the nation-state should figure prominently within—or is fundamental to—

black nationalism in the United States. There are those, such as historian Wilson Jeremiah Moses, who put geopolitical concerns at the center of their definition of black nationalism. Their perspective concurs with that of Malcolm X in 1963 who stated most directly in his "Message to the Grass Roots": "When you want a nation, that's called nationalism."[9] Indeed, there is much evidence in the oral and literary texts of black nationalists to support this point of view. The idea of nation formation—both within and without the United States—is featured prominently in the work of many black nationalist theorists, particularly those who advocated emigration or "internal statism," including charismatic leaders like Martin R. Delany, Bishop Henry McNeal Turner, Marcus Garvey, and organizations and groups such as the Exodusters movement, the African Blood Brotherhood, and the Republic of New Africa.[10] However, limiting the scope of nationalists to those who advocate these tenets excludes or minimizes the importance of theorists and activists who were anti- or nonemigrationist yet clearly nationalist.

This project falls in line with scholarship produced by Sterling Stuckey, V. P. Franklin, Wahneema Lubiano, and others who recommend that definitions of black nationalism go beyond the nation-state configuration to be comprehensive enough to include its cultural manifestations.[11] For example, it is hard to deny the political standpoint of those nationalists in the Black Power and Hip Hop movements who defended the connection between cultural production and psychological liberation from white domination.[12] They may not have advocated the construction of a separate nation-state, but rap artists such as Ice Cube consciously used a "politics of transvaluation" to instill race pride in young African Americans, a common strategy in the black nationalist tradition.[13] "You say Ice Cube is a problem—well you're right, he's two people in the same body, one African, one American," he wrote, invoking W. E. B. Du Bois in the liner notes of his 1992 release *The Predator*. By virtue of his political awakening, Ice Cube was no longer afflicted by the "unreconciled strivings" that once plagued "the souls of black folk" ("I see myself through the eyes of Africa and I will continue to speak as an African," he proclaimed), and this newly discovered consciousness allowed him to confront the contradictions between racial rhetoric and racial realities in post–civil rights America: "I will become African American when America gives up oppression of my people."[14]

As Ice Cube's statement maintains, at its most fundamental level black nationalism is a political philosophy that promotes group self-consciousness and advocates black self-determination. Black nationalist theory is founded upon the conviction that black people in the Diaspora—by virtue of African ancestry, a common historical experience of slavery, as well as a legacy of racial oppression in the forms of political disfranchisement, economic exploitation, social discrimination, and cultural degradation—share a cultural identity and therefore constitute a nationality, or nation, separate and distinct from other (read: white) Americans. "Nationalism is the belief that Black people in this country make up a cultural Nation," articulated Maulana (Ron) Karenga, founder of the cultural nationalist US Organization, in 1967. "The cultural nation is a people with a common past, a common present and, hopefully, a common future."[15]

Yet while black nationalism is a politics that creates a sense of collective identity, it is deceptively hierarchical. Since its inception during the early-to-mid-nineteenth century, black nationalist theory has been shaped, in part, by a hegemonic masculinity that undermines its communal ideal. "[W]e do not believe in 'equality' of men and women," Amiri Baraka wrote of his organization the Congress of African People, founded in 1970. "We could never be equals . . . nature has not provided thus."[16] This paradigmatic statement reveals a style of politicking—an "embodied-social politics"—that demarcates, not only race, but also gender and sexuality.[17] Yet this approach to black nationalist theory and practice is not unique to the Black Power movement. With virtually exclusive access to the public sphere, African American men have historically enabled themselves with the power and authority to determine the black political agenda. Many black nationalists have consistently abused that power and defined the boundaries of the imagined black nation in terms of a sexual politics that institutionalized male domination and the subordination of the "feminine." For instance, black women's sexuality was the subject of scrutiny by classical black nationalists such as Alexander Crummell who suggested that one of black women's primary (political) duties was to protect their virtue and maintain sexual purity, while modern black nationalist Stokely Carmichael conversely asserted that the only position for women in his movement was prone. Black nationalists not only frame their political agenda in masculinist ways, but the masculinist discourse of black nationalism mandates a sexual politics that is based in heteronormativity. This phallocentrism thus necessitates the subordination of not only women, but "effeminate" men as well. To prove their manhood, heterosexual black male nationalists strictly patrolled the borders of their masculine domain, a fact manifest in the heteronormativity. This was displayed by 19th century theorists like Henry Highland Garnet, who demanded both freedom and franchise in terms of patriarchal privilege, and was confirmed by the explicit homophobia exhibited in the mid-20th century by Black Power advocates who deemed homosexuality "counterrevolutionary."[18]

Like their predecessors in the classical and modern periods, rap nationalists created lyrical compositions that rationalized and supported structures of domination in African America. Since the early 19th century, black nationalism has proven to be a politics obsessed with (and therefore limited by) the reclamation of black manhood.[19] Rap nationalists, perhaps unwittingly, reclaimed that legacy during the late 1980s and early 1990s, because, much like their 19th and early 20th century forerunners, they were impelled by a sense of gender deprivation. Allowing for historical nuances, it is clear that the self-perceived "crisis" of masculinity, apparent in the oral and literary works of black nationalists from David Walker's 1829 seminal *Appeal* to Ice Cube's 1991 classic *Death Certificate*, was inspired by the material realities of racism. Specifically, a history of political disfranchisement, economic exploitation, and social discrimination denied black men the patriarchal "right" to provide for and to protect their families and communities. "Raptivists" in the "Hip Hop Nation" were not supported by community organizing or social activism, thus their cultural production more closely resembled a "politics of symbolism" than a political movement.[20] Nevertheless, the political standpoint disseminated in their lyrics represents continuities with the pre-modern and modern periods, particularly in the ways they envisioned their neo-nationalism, in a manner akin to what psychologist Alfred Adler deemed "masculine protest."[21] However, before engaging in a critical analysis of the engendering of rap nationalism as a culture and/or politics, it is important to take a quick survey of the historical and canonical development of "raptivism," its influences, and its philosophical imperatives.[22]

BRING(IN) THE NOISE: THE POLITICIZATION OF RAP MUSIC

Although the social activism of old-school DJ Afrika Bambaataa during the mid-1970s stands as evidence of his early recognition of the possibilities of merging Hip Hop culture and political consciousness, the politicization of rap music evolved slowly and unevenly during the 1980s. It first appeared via social criticisms of "ghetto life" in rap classics such as Kurtis Blow's "The Breaks" (1980) and Grandmaster Flash and the Furious Five's "The Message" (1982). In 1983 the politics of rap music became more explicit, manifest in the "nation-conscious" release "How We Gonna Make the Black Nation Rise" by Brother D and in Keith LeBlanc's "No Sell Out," which, although produced by a white man, utilized excerpts from the speeches of Malcolm X. Four years later, Hip Hop pioneers Run DMC wrote the spirited cultural nationalist song "Proud to be Black," emphatically stating for their audiences: "Ya know I'm proud to be black, ya'll; and that's a fact, ya'll."[23] But it was not until 1988 that two groups—Public Enemy and Boogie Down Productions—fully realized rap music's potential as a vehicle to express black rage and represent a legacy of militant, masculinist black politics. As Jon Pareles observed in the *New York Times*, the power of these two groups resided in their ability to read the social, political, and economic concerns of young African America. "Public Enemy and Boogie Down Productions registered the sense of urgency as urban ghettos grew increasingly desperate and audiences wanted to know why and what to do."[24] Highly regarded by music critics, the lyrical innovation of these two groups is also acknowledged by their fellow rap artists, some of whom they inspired. In an interview published in *Nation Conscious Rap* (1991), rap nationalist Paris paid respect to these Hip Hop pioneers. "It was only a matter of time before our people started to come around," he maintained, "and I think as far as Hip Hop was concerned I think it was sparked by brothers such as KRS-One [of Boogie Down Productions], and brothers such as Public Enemy." Paris contextualized the groundbreaking contributions of these artists, describing the tremendous influence they had on the consciousness of black youth communities during a time when, for most male rap artists, success was measured by conspicuous consumption and sexual conquests. "It made it okay to be conscious where before everybody was talking about women and the gold chains they had, and the Benz they rolled around in," he attested.[25]

74

Paris's enthusiasm unveiled the promise of a new political moment in Hip Hop history. Although Public Enemy's *It Takes a Nation of Millions to Hold Us Back* and Boogie Down Productions' *By All Means Necessary* exchanged one form of gendered politicking for another, they nevertheless established Hip Hop music as an uncompromising voice for black (primarily male) youth. From East Coast groups such as Public Enemy, Boogie Down Productions, and X-Clan to West Coast artists Ice Cube, Paris, and Kam, rap nationalists intentionally conjured a tradition of model, and militant, black manhood. With these politicized rap artists the performative race/gender politics of the black nationalist tradition (re)emerged with a vengeance. Raptivists offered young black males the opportunity to reassert a masculine presence in the public domain. This effort was, in part, a response to both the popular music of mid-1980s and the political culture of the Reagan-Bush administrations. During an era when black male artists like Michael Jackson and Prince dominated the charts, Public Enemy's "Sister of Instruction" Sister Souljah effused: "Rappers are bringing back the notion of strong, masculine voices." Souljah promised that with Hip Hop music, "you will not find a black male rapper who sounds like DeBarge or some other soprano singer."[26] Souljah's viewpoint was affirmed by her band-mate Chuck D. In the 1991 documentary *Tour of a Black Planet*, he maintained that the "black man is already emasculated and this standard is projected to black males" through R&B music. Hip Hop provided an alternative to the effeminate representation of African American men in popular culture, he proclaimed, because black men needed counterimages, an "intellectual, pro-black point of view" represented by men like Malcolm X, Louis Farrakhan, even Martin Luther King, Jr.[27]

While rap artists rebelled against the black male image in popular culture, there was a noticeable void in the black political arena. Black men and women held more elected positions on the local, state, and federal level; however, political representation did not translate into a marked difference in the material conditions of life for many African Americans, in part, because the move from protest politics to electoral politics after the Second Reconstruction rendered black political leaders and organizations—rigidified in civil rights strategy—ineffective and ill prepared to address the multiple needs of African America, particularly the poor.[28] "Most people I grew up with in Newark grew up under black rule," attested Hip Hop activist and spoken word artist Ras Baraka. "They didn't grow up under [white mayor, Hugh] Addonizio. They grew up under [black mayors, Kenneth] Gibson and Sharpe James, with predominantly black city councils, black police directors, black county prosecutors, and went to Malcolm X Shabazz or George Washington Carver elementary school." Meanwhile, the Deputy Mayor of Newark explained, "[black] folks are still disenfranchised. People thought if blacks gained power in the city, then somehow that translated into power for all black people. And it did not."[29] In fact, the gap between the white haves and the black have-nots widened during this period. The crisis in black leadership, which intensified during the Reagan and Bush administrations, did not go unnoticed by those in the Hip Hop generation. "Back in the '60s, there was a big push for black senators and politicians, and now we have more than we ever had before, but our communities are so much worse," reported raptivist Talib Kweli. "A lot of people died for us to vote; I'm aware of that history, but these politicians are not in touch with people at all. Politics is not the truth to me, it's an illusion."[30] As the limitations of electoral politics became glaringly and painfully apparent to the post–civil rights generation, rap artists idolized the words and works of political personalities such as Marcus Garvey, Malcolm X, and Louis Farrakhan, men whose uncompromising public personae and urban, poor/working-class roots stood as an example to those young black men whose status was undermined in the postindustrial capitalist economy. "God knows, when I heard Farrakhan, I had never heard a black man talk like that. It blew my mind, absolutely blew my mind," Hip Hop journalist/activist Kevin Powell recalled of his introduction to Farrakhan during the mid-1980s. "It was intoxicating, as intoxicating as crack was for a lot of people in our community in the '80s." For Powell that event at New York City's Madison Square Garden was affirming; it bolstered his sense of manhood and gave him an opportunity to—at least symbolically—defy white male domination. "I really believe that a lot of black nationalism that is embraced by black men has to do with fear," he confessed, betraying a thinly veiled preoccupation with status common among many young black men during the mid-1980s. "You feel powerless your entire life. And all of a sudden you have this space. You can be Marcus Garvey, and talk stuff to white folks. You can be Malcolm X and talk stuff to white folks."[31]

Powell's experience reveals how, for some males (and females) in postindustrial, post–civil rights African America, the masculinist discourse of black nationalism led to a feeling of empowerment. When understood in the context of the perceived crisis of masculinity that arose, in part, as a response to the popular and political culture of the mid-1980s, it becomes less remarkable that, by the end of the decade in Hip Hop communities across the nation, rap music became a vehicle for the dissemination of black neo-nationalist politics. "With the forced exile, incarceration, and execution of black leaders, rappers have become the spokesmen for the black community," declared Disposable Heroes of Hiphoprisy frontman, Michael Franti.[32] Much like their 19th and 20th century black nationalist predecessors, these artists and activists in the Hip Hop Nation used an embodied-social politics to impart meaning and significance to the increasingly depressed state of urban black America. They interpreted the effects of postmodern, postindustrial, post–civil rights social, economic, and political transformations with a language of masculine dispossession and, thus, endorsed a masculinist agenda for empowerment.

Therefore, during the Golden Age of Rap Nationalism, rap music was used as a tool to both inspire and translate what French philosopher Michel Foucault called an "insurrection of subjugated knowledge"—the sometimes radical, always subversive thinking and/or activism that characterizes the politics of dominated and exploited peoples. And yet, it is important not to overstate the case for the existence of seditious thinking within Hip Hop culture. Contrary to the suppositions of some highly noted scholars who have studied rap music as a form of social commentary (including Todd Boyd, Michael Eric Dyson, and Russell A. Potter), not all rap music can be categorized as political expression. The impulse to legitimate an art form that is consistently under attack is understandable, particularly when those attacks convey a thinly veiled racism. Nevertheless, not all rap music is counter-discourse. There is much within Hip Hop culture in general, and rap music specifically, that supports mainstream American social, political, economic, and cultural values. For example, with few exceptions the Hip Hop generation's construction of a counter-discourse to white supremacy did not disclude the incorporation of a sexual politics that parallels bourgeois notions of male domination. As cultural critic Russell A. Potter testifies, at times the politicking of rap artists "matches Rush Limbaugh in its emphasis on the centrality of black male authority for moral redemption."[33] Indeed, those rap artists who appeared to be most radical on issues of race, were in reality, extremely conservative when it came to issues of gender and sexuality. And yet, retrogressive gender politics were not unique to raptivism: they were pervasive throughout the oral and literary works of 19th and 20th century U.S. black nationalists. In fact, the embodied-social politics of rap music in the late 1980s and early 1990s was similar to the sexual politicking of such Black Power notables as Eldridge Cleaver, Stokely Carmichael, and H. Rap Brown—it was profound, as well as profane—and it stands as the postmodern revisioning of black nationalism as a politics of masculine protest.

FROM EUNUCHS TO AN ENDANGERED SPECIES: BLACK NATIONALISM AS A POLITICS OF MASCULINE PROTEST REVISITED

"I heard payback's a muthafuckin' nigga. . . ."
—Ice Cube, "The Nigga You Love to Hate" (1990).[34]

Rapper Ice Cube opens the second track on his post-gangsta rap release *AmeriKKKa's Most Wanted* with a simple, yet clever, twist on a vernacular expression. By changing its gendered modifier and adding an expletive, he turned a benign declaration ("payback is a bitch") into a declarative threat: "I heard payback's a muthafuckin' nigga." It is a warning of the possibilities of collective defiance, steeped in the kind of indirection that is reminiscent of David Walker's *Appeal* or the use of eschatology in slave religion. From the preaching of Nat Turner to the teachings of Elijah Muhammad, many black nationalist texts are framed by the type of vengeful thinking reflected in Ice Cube's imagining of an (ex)slave revolt: "Just think if niggas decide to retaliate."[35] The recurring theme of violent resistance is a staple of U.S. black nationalism and is certainly a persistent subject of Ice Cube's work as a "gangstAfronationalist."[36] While provocative, the theme of violent resistance is also rooted in an identity politics that, by its very nature, involves a rigid and hierarchical gender order that dictates—and, therefore, limits—the configuration of power and empowerment.

After his break with gangsta rap pioneers Niggaz With Attitude (NWA), Ice Cube moved his act from Los Angeles to New York City where he joined ranks with Public Enemy's production team, the Bomb Squad and, under the influence of Chuck D, began crafting his neo-nationalist politics. The result was *AmeriKKKa's Most Wanted*, a CD that combines the macho posturing of West Coast gangsta rap with the masculinist discourse of East Coast raptivism. Whether his transition is considered a political awakening or a brilliant strategy for marketing "unmitigated black rage prepackaged for . . . cathartic or voyeuristic convenience," Ice Cube's first solo effort demonstrates how black nationalism as an embodied-social politics is dependent not only on performative blackness (e.g. "ghettocentricity"), but on performative mas(k)ulinity.[37] Like "Ice Cube," O'Shea Jackson's race/gender/class identification was that of "nigga," an identity that affiliated him with an imagined community of black men who were hard-core, fearless, and aggressive and who often expressed themselves in violent ways; in fact, at times the more violent, the more "authentic." For the self-proclaimed "nigga," vulnerability is not an option, and is an emotional state reserved for their "feminine" counterparts—the gender-inclusive "bitches." Women and gay men were held in contempt by Ice Cube in *AmeriKKKa's Most Wanted*. For instance, he claimed to "love black women with a passion"; however, fictional violence against women is more prevalent on *AmeriKKKa's Most Wanted* than any expression of affection.[38] From his declaration that he is a "bitch-killah" in "The Nigga Ya Love to Hate" to the misogynistic "You Can't Fade Me," a venomous mother's-baby-father's-maybe tale that concludes with a murderous fantasy. Ice Cube's lyrics thus demonstrate the flip side of a liberatory politics based on race and gender rationales. "[T]he problem with unmitigated black rage," declared author and journalist Joan Morgan, is that "[i]t grabs white people by the jugular with one hand, and strangles black folks with the other."[39]

Indeed, the transformation of gangsta rap also proved that this race/gender performance was a dangerous form of identity politics. Once hijacked by major corporations, gangsta rap, which began as a critique of the criminalization of black male youth, became increasingly devoid of its subversive edge and, unfortunately, started to contribute to the dehumanizing representations of black men that its originators had intended to deconstruct. In fact, as a result of its meta-minstrelsy, gangsta rap became the most popular genre of rap music and contributed to the decline of rap nationalism as a marketable force in the rap music business. Although gangsta rap gained both critical acclaim and widespread criticism for its masculinist and misogynist sexual politics, this type of gender politicking was also rampant among rap nationalists. There has been a great hype about rap music's sexism, misogyny, and homophobia; but few critics have placed this issue within its proper context: the socio-political struggle for the re-masculation of black men. To truly understand and appreciate the subtle distinction between pro-male celebration and anti-female sentiments (without assuming the position of an apologist), it is necessary to assess the sexual politics of Hip Hop culture in the context of the masculinist traditions of black cultural politics and political culture. For example, in a brilliant essay that places male rap artists' machismo/masochism within the context of black vernacular culture, historian Robin Kelley argued that issues of sex and violence tend to converge in communities among men whose limited access to resources jeopardizes their claim to a gendered position of

78

power: "[I]n a world where male public powerlessness is often turned inward on women and children, misogyny and stories of sexual conflict are very old examples of the 'price' of being baaad."[40]

During the post–Civil Rights-Black Power era in communities where the majority of male children were raised in female-headed households—masses were imprisoned, more were under- or unemployed, and too many died a premature and violent death—the reclamation of black manhood reemerged as the primary issue on the political agenda. Despite the fact that a multitude of African American families were in the care of "abandoned and abused young black women" who tended to be "over-arrested, over-indicted, under-defended and over-sentenced" and for whom AIDS was increasingly becoming the leading cause of death, a perceived crisis of masculinity once again seized the spotlight in the black public arena.[41] This situation speaks directly to the perilous ways in which nationalisms are invented and institutionalized, and it is consistent with the tradition of black nationalist thought.

As previously stated, since the 19th century, black nationalism has evolved as a politics of masculine protest. Therefore, for young black men in search of what it meant to be a "man" in a postindustrial economy, the political philosophy of black nationalism was particularly attractive. It is in this context that rap nationalist Ice Cube was able to audaciously, albeit naïvely, suggest to freedom fighter and feminist Angela Davis the retrograde argument that black men's struggle takes precedence over that of black women.[42] And Afrocentric rap artists like the Jungle Brothers confidently recycled the retrograde idea that "with every great man there's a woman behind him."[43] In the midst of declining opportunities for gainful employment and with the ability to provide central to heteronormative definitions of masculinity, rap nationalism became an outlet for black male frustrations over their compromised gender identity. In black nationalist thought, masculinity is defined as not-femininity; and as an embodied-social politics, black nationalism, more often than not, sanctions the subordination of the feminine, which is symbolized by women and gay men. And yet, among raptivists, it was not only men who bought into concepts of male power and powerlessness. Female rap artists also engaged in the anti-woman/anti-gay discourse that characterized rap music's sexual politics. Public Enemy's Sister Souljah, for example, defined black liberation in masculinist terms when she exclaimed: "Every brother and sister has got to be a soldier in the war against the white man."[44] Therefore, it is imperative, as Hip Hop historian Tricia Rose writes, that scholars both observe and examine these "apparent inconsistencies and contradictions in rap's sexual politics within the complexity and contradictions of everyday life and protest."[45]

In the Hip Hop Nation, raptivists propagated the Madonna/whore dichotomization of women: cultural nationalist/Nation of Islam-inspired tributes to the black woman as the "mother of civilization" co-existed with profane narratives reminiscent of a Cleaver/Carmichael depiction of black women as hyper-sexual creatures in control of a dangerous, yet delicious, "pussy power." The sexually explicit lyrics of rap nationalists were a direct descendant of the raunchy poetry of artists/activists of the

Black Power movement. Note H. Rap Brown's x-rated verse in *Die Nigger Die* (which is even more scandalous because it is akin to a "yo mamma" joke): "I fucked your mama, till she went blind. Her breath smells bad, but she sure can grind. I fucked your mama, for a solid hour. Baby came out screaming, Black Power."[46] Like their Black Power predecessors, rap nationalists were no strangers to salacious prose. Raptivists like Public Enemy, Boogie Down Productions, Brand Nubian, and Jeru the Damaja all celebrated the virtues of black womanhood, and, at one point or another, bragged about their sexual exploits with women, or their ability to "mack." For example, in a manner reminiscent of Stokely Carmichael's now infamous declaration, Ice Cube once argued that the only position for women in "a man's world" is that of sexual service: "Women, they good for nothin', naw maybe one thing—to serve needs to my ding-a-ling."[47] On the surface, this kind of sexual politics appears to be incongruous with nationalist values, but as Oakland-based rapper Too Short (who is not a raptivist) attempted to explain, this "pimp attitude" is less about the exploitation of women than it is about the re-masculation of black men: "To me, it's positive, it's not really about degrading women, it's about the black man," the rapper rationalized. "It's almost like the Muslims. Being a Muslim is like keeping your mind straight. The mack thing is about keepin' your mind correct. It's a self-esteem thing, if you ask me."[48]

While Hip Hop chronicler William Eric Perkins argued that this comparison is "sheer folly," it is not as ridiculous as it may seem. The assertion of male power in the sex industry and in the public sphere both depend on the control of black women's sexuality and involve a politic predicated upon women's complicity in their own subjugation. Furthermore, the extraordinary popularity of the "pimp narrative" during black nationalist moments in both the 1970s and the 1990s suggests that both the pimp and the protester represent a potent response to a perceived sense of male powerlessness as it is translated into a politics of masculine protest. For example, during the late 1960s and 1970s, the sensational gender ideals of pimp narratives—both in literature, such as Iceberg Slim's *Pimp: The Story of My Life* (1969), and in films such as *The Mack* (1973)— converged with that of their black nationalist peers. Iceberg Slim's seminal best-selling novel *Pimp* describes pimping as (infra)politics, a tool with which black men are able to challenge white hegemony. Slim's cinematic counterparts in blaxploitation films like *The Mack* and *Dolemite* (1975) also "stick it to The Man" and engage in what philosopher Tommy L. Lott deems a politics of self-defense against the urban reality of police brutality and Hollywood's (sur)reality of black male emasculation.[49] Or as the closing line of Melvin Van Peebles' pioneering 1971 film *Sweet Sweetback's Badasssss Song* warned, "Watch out. A baad assss nigger is coming back to collect some dues." It is no coincidence that Iceberg Slim expressed great respect for Black Panthers Eldridge Cleaver and Huey Newton, whom he deemed "miraculous" and "beautiful," respectively.[50] Or that Newton, in turn, praised the politics of *Sweetback* as the "first truly revolutionary Black film."[51] Furthermore, when understood in context of these testimonials, it is no surprise that almost thirty years later former rap nationalist Ice Cube announced that he would produce and star in a film documenting the life of Iceberg Slim.

IT'S A MAN'S WORLD:
DEFINING WOMEN'S ROLE IN THE HIP HOP NATION

Perhaps the appeal of the pimp to black nationalists in the 1970s and 1990s is conceivable because it is consistent with the gender and sexual politics of the Black Power and Hip Hop movements. The promise to respect and protect the black woman by male black nationalists is conditional, contingent upon black women maintaining a level of sexual purity that rivals that of the Virgin Mary. This degree of chastity is valued because in nationalist circles, a woman's power lies in her ability to (re)produce the nation. In fact, procreation is perceived to be the primary responsibility of women in the struggle for black liberation: "Love" is "the woman's weapon," the Jungle Brothers explained in their 1989 song "Black Woman." "Her womb is the chamber that produces life. Her breast provides the nutrition for growth."[52] Like her Native Tongues brothers, Monie Love also celebrated women's childbearing capabilities and embraced a sexual division of labor in the ironically titled "Ladies First": "We are the ones that give birth, to the new generation of prophets," she pronounced, "because it's ladies first."[53] Not to be outdone by her Afrocentric peers, X-Clan's resident goddess of fertility Isis described her revolutionary power in conventional terms. "I am a self coming forth, a creature bearing life, a renaissance, a rebirth."[54] Even Queen Latifah, who is hailed by many rap observers as a feminist-nationalist, propagated a masculinist position on women and political struggle. Despite her strong voice and imposing cultural nationalist stature, Latifah revamped the campaign for separate spheres endorsed by her 19th and 20th century black nationalist sisters as she identified her role in the Hip Hop movement as "secondary but necessary to reproduce."[55]

While it is tempting to criticize female raptivists for participating in a gender politics that reinforces women's subjugation, their reluctance to publicly castigate their male peers reflects a double bind that has haunted black women freedom fighters since the 19th century: when faced with the prospect of counter-posing race with gender, black women have historically put "race first." And in the post–Civil Rights-Black Power era when rap music reigned as one of the premier forums for black politicking, the reluctance of some female artists, journalists, and even scholars to address issues of sexism and misogyny in Hip Hop culture was largely due to their unwillingness to be used in the anti-rap propaganda machine. In 1994, journalist dream hampton aptly articulated the experience of many Hip Hop aficionados in her "Confessions of a Hip Hop Critic." "I find myself in the uncomfortable and precarious position of defending great poets like Tupac, Snoop Doggy Dogg, and Kool G Rap when outsiders want to reduce them to monster misogynists and murderers," she writes. "Because I love rap music. . . . I've recognized and struggled to reconcile the genius and passion of my brothers—even when it meant betraying my most fundamental politics. I'm in the same position I imagine I would have assumed had my peers been the eloquently sexist Ishmael Reed or genius/woman-beater Miles Davis."[56] The burden of silence afflicting women in Hip Hop was not remarkable, for it is reminiscent of a long tradition of black women's participation in the public sphere. What *is* surprising, however, is that this dynamic continued to handicap some black women in the post-second-wave feminist era.

Even after women of color revolutionized feminist theory and politics during the 1970s and 1980s, a history of racism in the women's movement taints black women's associations with "feminism."[57] Furthermore, as black lesbian-feminist Barbara Smith argued: because feminism threatens the very foundation of intra-racial, inter-gender interaction, black men have been instrumental in cultivating myths that reinforce black women's fears about the women's movement.[58] Consequently, during the early 1990s the anti-rap campaign, combined with female rap artists' rejection of "feminism," conspired to reinforce a discourse of male dominance in the Hip Hop movement. This retrogressive development evokes the period directly following the publication of the 1965 *Moynihan Report* when, in response to the matriarchy thesis and the concomitant image of the black woman as castrator of black men, women in the Black Power movement felt compelled to publicly support female subordination. A generation later, when confronted with the prospect of critiquing sexism in African America, or racism in white America, raptivists such as Queen Latifah of the Native Tongues coalition, Isis of X-Clan, and Sister Souljah of Public Enemy had but one option before them. It was an option that echoed forth from times past: race first.

The embracing of a traditional sexual division of labor by male and female rap nationalists—even in the midst of third-wave feminism—is not as shocking as it may seem given Hip Hop's primary audience. As Hip Hop commentator Nelson George argued, the rap music scene is more than merely male-centered; it reflects a solipsism that is suggestive of an underlying desire for male affection and attention. "There was, and remains, a homoerotic quality to Hip Hop culture," he writes, "one nurtured in gangs and jails, that makes women seem, aside from sex, often nonessential."[59] The return to "tradition" that characterized the gendered discourse in rap nationalism appears to have been motivated by a number of factors. Taking for granted the most obvious reasoning (that male domination is a cultural value both in mainstream and in African America), its reappearance in rap music was, as previously stated, a result of young black men's anxiety over their aggrieved sense of masculinity, and betrays an underlying fear of women inspired by an inability to live up to traditional standards of manhood in a postindustrial economy. Simply put, the sexism prevalent in the Hip Hop Nation signifies male bonding over disappearing economic opportunities.

At the 1994 congressional hearings convened to target violence and sexism in rap music, Robin Kelley urged critics to keep the real issues of sexism in perspective. Unlike the wage gap and sexual harassment in the workplace, profane rap lyrics do not represent the most dangerous manifestations of sexism in American culture, he testified.[60] Yet while Kelley advocated equal rights for women in mainstream America, many raptivists argued that in the context of African America, women had more than their fair share of gender rights and privileges. In fact, the viewpoint of nationalists in the Black Power and Hip Hop movements was that "The Black Woman Is Already Liberated," as artists and activists in both periods pronounced black women guilty of being a dominant and domineering force in black communities.[61] "Historically, Afro-

American women have had to be the economic mainstays of the family," Black Arts Movement theorist Larry Neal observed in a 1968 essay. "The oppressor allowed them to have jobs while, at the same time, limiting the economic mobility of the black man. Very often, therefore, the woman's aspirations and values are closely tied to those of the white power structure and not to those of her man."[62] Over thirty years later, in a manner strikingly similar to Neal's, some members of the Hip Hop Nation employed this line of argument as an explanation for what they perceived to be the contentious state of gender relations in African America; and, like their Black Power predecessors, they subscribed to the notion that black women were a pawn in a conspiratorial plot to maintain white supremacy over black people, particularly black men, in the United States.

According to Bill Stephney, co-founder of Public Enemy and president of StepSun Music, social programs sponsored by the government after the Civil Rights Movement created favorable socioeconomic conditions for black women at the expense of black men. Stephney took particular exception to government aid to women and children, which he believed not only ignored the fact that black men also experience poverty, but also strengthened what he perceived to be a matriarchal family and community structure in African America. While Stephney considered gender equality an important political issue, he declared that a politics of black female empowerment—be it via social programming or feminism—is redundant. "How much more power do [women] need in the black community?" he queried. "If we look at issues of mortality, life expectancy, employment, family structure, executive income, black women are above black men on every level in every standard and statistic."[63] After establishing the argument that local and federal governments purposely created economic disparity (and, therefore, a power differential) between black women and men, Stephney concluded that rap music evolved as a response to the systemic devaluation of black men's experiences within their families and communities, or as he articulated: "Hip Hop wanted to be a soundtrack for this marginalization."[64]

Writer and activist Kevin Powell also believed Hip Hop culture was a response to the increasing estrangement of black men from their families and communities. Like Stephney, he subscribed to the notion that black women received certain privileges denied black men. "Hip Hop was created by black and Latino men, who were left out of the advancements of the Civil Rights movement," he contended. "Black women were allowed to advance in a certain way that a lot of black men were not. Not to say [women] had it better than us," Powell asserted, "but black men represent a certain type of threat that black women don't represent to this white power structure. That's why hip-hop was very male-centered. For a lot of us working-class cats, it was the one space where we're visible, where we could say whatever we want and be free."[65]

This assessment of the social and economic dispossession of black male youth during the 1970s and 1980s provides a context for understanding a song like Public Enemy's "Sophisticated Bitch," which along with "She Watch Channel Zero?!" led some cultural critics to label the group "misogynist." While its hostile condemnation of black women somewhat tarnished Public Enemy's reputation as rap nationalism's pioneers, according to Hip Hop historian Nelson George, "Sophisticated Bitch" spoke to an "uncomfortable truth" about black professional women. It "was a bench-mark," he writes, "in that the critique wasn't about money alone but the class differences between an upwardly mobile woman and a working-class man."[66] However "uncomfortable" (or inaccurate) this revelation may be, it reflects a sense of male powerlessness not only in the economic realm, but within the sexual domain as well, suggesting a more literal interpretation of the Black Panther's concept of "pussy power." Like that old Hip Hop proverb "never trust a big butt and a smile," this reading of Public Enemy's sexual politics indicates, as Tricia Rose observed, "many men are hostile toward women because the fulfillment of male heterosexual desire is significantly checked by women's capacity for sexual rejection and/or manipulation of men."[67] As Stephney, Powell, and George's statements intimate, that threat to black masculinity was made even more perilous by black women's historic participation in the workforce. Therefore, in a curious way, Hip Hop provided a safe space, a nurturing place, for those young men who felt under attack from "The (white) Man" and black women. "These brothers are mad at a whole bunch of folks," not just women, Stephney stated assuredly. "It's safer to get into the discussion of black male anger against white cops, the white corrections system, and the government in general," he claimed, while discussions of their anger toward women, black and white, are "like the third rail." Since Stephney understood the sexual politics of rap artists to be indicative of their declining status in local and national arenas, he regretted that their artistic expression "winds up being reduced to [accusations that] black men are misogynist." He believed this is a one-dimensional reading of a multifaceted experience. "There are some black men, I assume, who are misogynist, just as there are some black women who are anti-male. But there is a specific condition that needs to be ameliorated that these young brothers have been talking about."[68] That condition is believed to be the systematic emasculation of black men, instigated by the government and carried out by black women.

Thus, like their predecessors in the 1960s and 1970s, a significant number of rap nationalists portrayed black women as an accessory to the "crime" of their systemic oppression. For example, Tricia Rose argues that when Ice Cube identifies himself as "the bitch-killah/cop-killah" in "The Nigga Ya Love to Hate," he alludes to an affiliation between black women and "state authority figures" in the "disempowerment and oppression" of black men.[69] When coupled with "You Can't Fade Me" and "I'm Only Out for One Thing," Ice Cube's narratives in *AmeriKKKa's Most Wanted* "are obviously symptomatic of underlying anxieties about the consequences of sexual desire."[70] Similarly, in a manner that contradicts his humanist standpoint, KRS-One of Boogie Down Productions delivered two chilling, anti-woman songs dealing with sexual exploit(ation)s on his 1992 album *Sex and Violence*. In "13 and Good," KRS-One boasts about a sexual escapade with a minor. She may have been 13 years old, he says, "but she was good." And then there's "Say Gal," a song written in response to a number of highly publicized celebrity rape cases in late 1991 and early 1992, including that involving former heavyweight boxing champion Mike Tyson. "All you see in the newspapers nowadays is 'nuff gal talk 'bout them been raped and them been molested and them been feel up and them been all sexed up," he prefaces in the song's opening line. "Say Gal" then proceeds to absolve public figures of any responsibility for acts of sexual violence and, instead, holds women accountable for their style of dress and behavior. This line of self-defense, a classic rationale in U.S. rape culture, is evidence of male sexual frustration and reveals an underlying sense of subordination—male panic even—in the realm of sex and (hetero)sexuality. In his lyrical interrogation, KRS-One argued defensively that if women don't want "sex," they should not dress provocatively. "Don't tell me you can wear what you want," he anticipates, "'cause nowadays a most dem gals a dressin' like a slut."[71]

It is important to note that not all rap nationalists supported a reactionary sexual politics. Mutulu Olugbala (M-1) of dead prez repudiated sexism in rap music. "I think it's fucked up," he exclaimed. "And I think it's not just on sisters to represent that for sisters, I think the brothers should represent that. And we don't. We be frontin' on it, saying 'Put it on the backburner.' And it's not right."[72] Even those artists—such as Public Enemy, KRS-One, and Ice Cube—who at times exhibited outright and outrageous misogyny, at other times displayed more progressive gender politics. For example, when questioned in 2002 about the prevalent image of underdressed, hypersexual women in rap music videos, Chuck D responded: "Being a heterosexual man, artistically, I never have a problem. Exploitation-wise, I have a problem."[73] As this statement demonstrates, the relationship between raptivism and sexism was a conflicted one, and the desire to challenge sexism in rap music was often just as conflicted. "The last thing any of us want is for another man to question how we treat women," admits Kevin Powell. "Aren't we, black men, the endangered species, anyhow?"[74] Reluctance aside, the presence of retrogressive gender politics in rap nationalism did not represent an entirely hopeless scenario for women in the Hip Hop movement; for unlike the Black Power activists who argued that women should be "off the front lines and in the home," many raptivists could imagine a role for women in the masculinist struggle for black liberation, as long as their "gender identity as *women* is effaced."[75] Sister Souljah explained that delicate balance in a 1991 interview with Hip Hop documentarians James G. Spady and Joseph D. Eure: "[A] lot of times, when you're a sister in a leadership position, you always have to deal with someone saying, 'you're manly or masculine.' Or somebody thinking because you're a leader you're a lesbian. My thing is the last thing on earth I would ever be is a lesbian, because I love black people, and I love black men of course."[76] Building on her blatant homophobia and unrestrained heteronormativity, Souljah imagined a way for women to maintain their gender identity and assume leadership positions in the political arena, unwittingly using the moral suasion argument originated by many 19th century female suffragists. "I think that feeling has to be put back into the movement, whether it's Hip Hop or politics," she claimed in 1991. "That emotional side comes from women, so we have to be included in the leadership in order to impact and shape the ways things are going to move forward."[77]

CONCLUSION:
IN SEARCH OF THE "REVOLUTIONARY GENERATION"

Although extremely sensational, the sexual politics of rap nationalists was an extension of a centuries-old tradition of black male politicking that has never been apologetic for or restrained in its desire for male power. While many critics, both black and white, have made male rap artists the poster boys for sexism and misogyny, it is quite clear that the masculinist discourse of rap music is not an anomaly, and that it has its roots in institutions and attitudes that are prominently located within American communities. The "most nefarious expression of sexism and misogyny" in American society, particularly in African American communities, is in the "nuclear family, religious communities, and educational institutions,"[78] Michael Eric Dyson argues, sites in which anti-woman attitudes and behaviors are "nurtured and rationalized."[79]

Perhaps radical documentary filmmaker Marlon Riggs was onto something when he boldly pronounced that "black men loving black men is the revolutionary act of our times." Once black men—particularly heterosexual black men—begin to address their own gendered oppression, redefine the masculine ideal, and learn to love themselves and their communities without fear or anxiety, they can discover and appreciate the value of freedom. For, as black feminist pioneer Toni Cade Bambara wrote in 1970, "it perhaps takes less heart to pick up the gun than to face the task of creating a new identity, a self, perhaps an androgynous self, via commitment to the struggle."[80] Of course, that is easier said than done in a country that values male supremacy while simultaneously undermining black male agency through various forms of institutional racism. Nevertheless, when black men and women realize that our power lies not in the subordination of others, but in collective and democratic struggle, then we as a people can truly get down to the business of liberation. Until that day arrives, we are still in search of a revolutionary generation. As spoken word artist Sarah Jones declared in her controversial 1999 Hip Hop song, "your revolution will not happen between these thighs." "Because the real revolution, that's right; I said the *real* revolution; I'm talkin' about the revolution, when it comes, its gon' be real."[81]

NOTES

[1] Public Enemy, "Party for Your Right to Fight," *It Takes a Nation of Millions to Hold Us Back*, Def Jam (1988).

[2] Errol Nazareth, "A Powerful Noise, Public Enemy's Chuck D Has a Lot to Say About Race, Society and the Media," *Toronto Sun* 3 May 1998; available from http://interact.canoe.ca/JamMusicArtistsP/public_enemy.html.

[3] Public Enemy, "Brothers Gonna Work It Out," *Fear of a Black Planet*, Def Jam (1990).

[4] Public Enemy, "Revolutionary Generation"; ibid.

[5] Gangsta rap, also referred to as "reality rap," exploded in popularity during the late 1980s and early 1990s, as signified by the success of the groundbreaking West Coast group Niggaz With Attitude (NWA).

[6] This last line is a reference to serial killer Jeffrey Dahmer.

[7]X-Clan, "Fire and Earth (100% Natural)," *Xodus*, Polygram Records, Inc. (1992). For an examination of the cultural basis for the demand for self-determination, see V. P. Franklin, *Black Self-Determination: A Cultural History of African American Resistance* (Brooklyn, NY, 1992).

[8]William L. Van Deburg, *Modern Black Nationalism: From Marcus Garvey to Louis Farrakhan* (New York, 1997), 1.

[9]George Breitman, ed., *Malcolm X Speaks: Selected Speeches and Statements* (New York: Grove Press, Inc., 1965), 10.

[10]Writer Theodore Draper notes that U.S. black nationalism has taken two predominant forms: e/migrationism and "internal statism." The first genre is exemplified by organizations that promoted black emigration to Africa or the Caribbean (especially Haiti), the second by those organizations, like the Republic of New Africa, that wanted to establish an independent black nation within the borders of the United States. See Theodore Draper, *The Rediscovery of Black Nationalism* (New York, 1970).

[11]Sterling Stuckey, *The Ideological Origins of Black Nationalism* (Boston, MA, 1972); Franklin, *Black Self-Determination*, 62–81; Wahneema Lubiano, ed., *The House That Race Built: Black Americans and the U.S. Terrain* (New York, 1997).

[12]The term "Hip Hop movement" is used here in reference to the golden age of rap nationalism. Similarly, the term "Hip Hop Nation" will be used to refer to a cohort of black nationalist rap artists, although the term is most often applied to Hip Hop artists and fans regardless of their political standpoint.

[13]Eddie S. Glaude, Jr. writes that a "politics of transvaluation is best understood as a reassessment of 'blackness.'" Eddie S. Glaude, Jr., "Introduction: Black Power Revisited," in *Is It Nation Time? Contemporary Essays on Black Power and Black Nationalism*, ed., Eddie S. Glaude, Jr. (Chicago, IL, 2002), 4.

[14]Ice Cube, liner notes, *The Predator*, Priority Records, Inc. (1992).

[15]Clyde Halisi and James Mtume, eds., *The Quotable Karenga* (Los Angeles, CA, 1967), 6; Scot Brown, *Fighting for US: Maulana Karenga, the US Organization, and Black Cultural Nationalism* (New York, 2003).

[16]Imamu Amiri Baraka, *Raise, Race, Rays, Raze: Essays since 1965* (New York, 1971), 148.

[17]R. W. Connell, *Masculinities* (Berkeley, CA, 1995), 66. Sociologist R. W. Connell suggests that gender politics are, in fact, an embodied-social politics.

[18]For more on the sexual politics of classical black nationalists, see Alexander Crummell, "The Black Woman of the South," in *Destiny and Race: Selected Writings, 1840–1898*, ed., Wilson Jeremiah Moses (Amherst, MA, 1992); Henry Highland Garnet, "Address to the Slaves of the United States of America," in *The Ideological Origins of Black Nationalism*, ed., Sterling Stuckey (Boston, 1975); Carmichael's comment was reportedly made in 1964 at a SNCC meeting in Mississippi.

[19]For more on the framing of black nationalism as a politics of masculine protest, see Charise Cheney, "'We Men Ain't We?': Mas(k)ulinity and the Gendered Politics of Black Nationalism," in *Time Longer than Rope: African American Activism, 1860–1960*, eds., Charles M. Payne and Adam Green (New York, 2003), 536–64.

[20]Andrew Ross, "The Gangsta and the Diva" in *Black Male: Representations of Masculinity in Contemporary American Art*, ed., Thelma Golden (New York, 1994), 163.

[21]Alfred Adler, *The Individual Psychology of Alfred Adler: A Systematic Presentation in Selections from His Writings* (New York, 1956); quoted in R. W. Connell, *Masculinities* (Berkeley, CA, 1995), 16.

[22]"Raptivist" is being used as a descriptive term for the politicized rap artist. It is not intended to suggest that any or all rap nationalists were activists or involved in community or political organizing.

[23]Run DMC, "Proud to Be Black," *Raising Hell*, Def Jam (1987).

[24]Jon Pareles, "Radical Rap: of Pride and Prejudice," *New York Times*, 16 December 1990, sec. 2, p. 1.

[25]Joseph Eure and James G. Spady, eds., *Nation Conscious Rap* (Brooklyn, NY, 1991), 82.

[26]David Mills, "Reality in a New Rapping; Arrested Development, Drawing Raves with a Message of Maturity," *Washington Post*, Sunday, 19 July 1992, Sunday show section.

[27] *Tour of a Black Planet*, Sony Music Entertainment (1991).

[28] For a discussion of this topic, see Robert C. Smith, *We Have No Leaders: African Americans in the Post–Civil Rights Era* (Albany, NY, 1996).

[29] Ras Baraka, telephone interview by author, 10 January 2002.

[30] Jeff Chang, "'Stakes Is High': Conscious Rap, Neosoul and the Hip Hop Generation," *The Nation* 276 (13–20 January 2003): 20.

[31] Kevin Powell, interview by author, tape recording, Brooklyn, NY, 12 November 2001.

[32] Farai Chideya, "Homophobia: Hip Hop's Black Eye," *Step into a World: A Global Anthology of the New Black Literature*, ed., Kevin Powell (New York, 2000), 96.

[33] Michael Foucault, *Discipline and Punish: The Birth of the Prison* (New York, 1977); Michael Eric Dyson, *Between God and Gangsta Rap: Bearing Witness to Black Culture* (New York, 1996); Todd Boyd, *Am I Black Enough for You?: Popular Culture from the 'Hood and Beyond* (Bloomington, IN, 1997); Russell A. Potter, *Spectacular Vernaculars: Hip Hop and the Politics of Postmodernism* (Albany, NY, 1995), 135.

[34] Ice Cube, "The Nigga You Love to Hate," *AmeriKKKa's Most Wanted*, Priority Records, Inc. (1990).

[35] Ibid.

[36] Dyson, *Between God and Gangsta Rap*, 172.

[37] Joan Morgan, "The Nigga Ya Love to Hate" in *Rap on Rap: Straight Up Talk on Hip Hop Culture*, ed., Adam Sexton (New York, 1995), 119. For a discussion of "ghettocentricity," see Nelson George, *Buppies, B-Boys, Baps, and Bohos: Notes on a Post-Soul Black Culture* (New York, 1994), 95.

[38] Ice Cube, "The Bomb," *AmeriKKKa's Most Wanted*.

[39] Morgan, "The Nigga Ya Love to Hate," 123.

[40] Robin D. G. Kelley, *Race Rebels: Culture, Politics, and the Black Working Class* (New York, 1994), 187.

[41] Cornel West, "On Afro-American Popular Music: from Bebop to Rap," *Sacred Music of the Secular City*, Special Issue of *Black Sacred Music: A Journal of Theomusicology* 6 (Spring 1992): 294; Nancy Kurshan, "Women and Imprisonment in the United States: History and Current Reality," *The Prison Issues Desk*, available from http://www.prisonactivist.org/women/woman-and-imprisonment.html.

[42] Ice Cube and Angela Y. Davis, "Nappy Happy," *Transition* 1 (No. 6, 1992): 182.

[43] Jungle Brothers, "Black Woman," *Done by the Forces of Nature*, Warner Brothers (1979).

[44] Jeffrey Louis Decker, "The State of Rap: Time and Place in Hip Hop Nationalism," *Social Text* 11 (Spring 1993): 109.

[45] Tricia Rose, *Black Noise: Rap Music and Black Culture in Contemporary America* (Hanover, NH, 1994), 149.

[46] H. Rap Brown, *Die Nigger Die* (New York, 1969), 26.

[47] Ice Cube, "It's A Man's World," *AmeriKKKa's Most Wanted*.

[48] William Eric Perkins, "The Rap Attack: An Introduction," in *Droppin' Science: Critical Essays on Rap Music and Hip Hop Culture*, ed., William Eric Perkins (Philadelphia, PA, 1996), 28.

[49] See Tommy L. Lott, "A No-Theory Theory of Contemporary Black Cinema," *Black American Literature Forum* 25 (Summer 1991): 221–36.

[50] Helen Koblin, "Portrait of an Ex-Pimp Philosopher, Iceberg Slim," *Los Angeles Free Press* (25 February 1972): 4.

[51] Huey Newton, "He Won't Bleed Me: A Revolutionary Analysis of Sweet Sweetback's Baadasssss Song" in *To Die for the People: The Writings of Huey P. Newton* (New York, 1972), 113.

[52] Jungle Brothers, "Black Woman," *Done by the Forces of Nature*.

[53] Queen Latifah, "Ladies First," *All Hail the Queen*, Tommy Boy Music, Inc. (1989).

[54] Isis, "The Power of Myself Is Moving," *Rebel Soul*, 4th & B'Way Records (1990).

[55] Queen Latifah, "A King and Queen Creation," *All Hail the Queen*. Not all female raptivists supported the separate spheres rhetoric that characterized most rap nationalism. Sister Souljah, who declared the re-mas-

culation of black men the primary struggle of the Hip Hop Nation, paradoxically challenged those men who believed in female subordination: "I'll never keep quiet, so don't even try it. Sit in the back row, I won't buy it. Necessary but secondary, that's your insecurity." Sister Souljah, "360 Degrees of Power," *360 Degrees of Power*, Sony (1992).

[56] dream hampton, "Confessions of a Hip Hop Critic," *Step into a World*, 107.

[57] For further discussion on female rappers' discomfort with the term "feminist," see Tricia Rose, "Never Trust a Big Butt and a Smile," *Camera Obscura* 23 (1991): 109–31; and "Bad Sistas: Black Women Rappers and Sexual Politics in Rap Music," in *Black Noise*, 146–82.

[58] See Barbara Smith, "Some Home Truths on the Contemporary Black Feminist Movement," in *Words of Fire: An Anthology of African-American Feminist Thought*, ed., Beverly Guy-Sheftall (New York, 1995), 254–67.

[59] Nelson George, *hip hop america* (New York, 1998), 186.

[60] House Subcommittee on Commerce, Consumer Protection, and Competitiveness of the Committee on Energy and Commerce, *Music Lyrics and Commerce*, 103rd Cong., 2nd sess., 11 February 1994, 145.

[61] Barbara Smith, "Some Home Truths," 255. Smith identified "The Black Woman Is Already Liberated" as "Myth No. 1" in this essay that highlights five major fallacies that curb the advancement of feminist thought and politics in black communities.

[62] Larry Neal, "The Black Arts Movement" in *Visions of a Liberated Future: Black Arts Movement Writings*, eds., Larry Neal and Michael Schwartz (New York, 1989), 76.

[63] Bill Stephney, interview by author, tape recording, New York, NY, 18 January 2002.

[64] Ibid.

[65] Powell, interview.

[66] George, *hip hop america*, 187.

[67] Rose, "Never Trust a Big Butt and a Smile," 115.

[68] Stephney, interview.

[69] Rose, *Black Noise*, 151.

[70] Benj DeMott, "The Future is Unwritten: Working-Class Youth Cultures in England and America" *Critical Texts* (1 May 1988): 45.

[71] KRS-One, "Say Gal," *Sex and Violence*, Zomba Recording Corporation (1992).

[72] Mutulu Olugbala, interview by author, tape recording, Brooklyn, NY, 16 January 2002.

[73] Chuck D, interview.

[74] Powell, "Confessions," 77.

[75] Decker, "The State of Rap," 71.

[76] Eure and Spady, *Nation Conscious Rap*, 252.

[77] Ibid, 243.

[78] Michael Eric Dyson, *Making Malcolm: The Myth and Meaning of Malcolm X* (New York, 1995), 94.

[79] Dyson, *Between God and Gansta Rap*, 186.

[80] Toni Cade Bambara, "On the Issue of Roles," in *The Black Woman: An Anthology*, ed. Toni Cade Bambara (New York, 1970), 103.

[81] Sarah Jones's "Your Revolution" appears on DJ Vadim's *U.S.S.R.: Life from the Other Side* (Montreal, Canada, 1999).

OPPOSITIONAL CONSCIOUSNESS WITHIN AN OPPO-
SITIONAL REALM:
THE CASE OF FEMINISM AND WOMANISM IN
RAP AND HIP HOP, 1976–2004

Layli Phillips, Kerri Reddick-Morgan, and
Dionne Patricia Stephens

Hip Hop is an oppositional cultural realm rooted in the socio-political and historical experiences and consciousness of economically disadvantaged urban black
youth of the late 20th century.[1] By numerous accounts, Hip Hop originated in the
South Bronx section of New York City during the mid-1970s from a confluence of
factors, including ethnic dislocations spurred by the construction of the South Bronx
highway, and a rapid decline in municipal services induced by severe cuts in federal
funding at the end of the Great Society era. The local job loss and worker obsoles-
cence precipitated by the national shift from an industrial to a service, information,
and finance economy generated an artistically productive "crossroads of lack and
desire" that ultimately gave birth to the culture known as Hip Hop.[2] Tricia Rose has
characterized this time and place as an intersection of "social alienation, prophetic
imagination, and yearning" where postindustrial conditions, technological innovations, and Afrodiasporic cultural frames and priorities came together to produce the
"techno-black cultural syncretism" known as rap music.[3]

Braiding strands of protest and pleasure together into a seamless flow, rap initially expressed both gleeful and aggressive views of survival, social critique, and revelry
to neighborhood audiences comprised primarily of African American and Latino
youth.[4] Over time, however, and due in part to signal shifts in both commercial culture and the mass media, rap's audience grew beyond the bounds of neighborhood to
encompass first the larger city of New York, later the nation (emerging first in a variety of regional flavors, then becoming regionally syncretized), and ultimately the
globe. Today, Hip Hop culture, which encompasses not only rap music and videos but
also particular forms of dress, dance, language, and attitude has been described as the
new global cultural dominant. One thing that has not changed about Hip Hop, however, is that it continues to represent the voices and visions of the culturally, politically, and economically marginal and disenfranchised. Even as Hip Hop becomes global, its perspective is still centered in the experiences of the underdogs and it still
expresses the cultural flair of African American and Latino people.

Women have been integral to the evolution of Hip Hop culture, especially rap
music, since the beginning.[5] Yet, historical accounts and critical analyses of the Hip
Hop phenomenon have tended to downplay the contributions of women. Women

have played pivotal roles as artists, writers, performers, producers, and industry executives. Women have influenced rap style and technique, ultimately shaping aesthetic standards and technological practices utilized by both women and men. Nevertheless, certain facts remain undeniable. First, men have outnumbered women in both the artistic arena and the corporate end of Hip Hop. Male rappers have outnumbered female rappers and male industry leaders have outnumbered female industry operatives. The production pipeline, from writers and performers to producers and executives, has effectively functioned like a modified "old boys' club," hampering women's entry and ascent to power within the industry in ways both subtle and overt. Now that Hip Hop has expanded beyond music into video production, clothing design, and other lifestyle enhancement domains, the processes impeding women's participation and power-sharing have only become more widespread.

Second, a masculinist discursive strand is clearly identifiable in both rap music and its parent culture, Hip Hop.[6] The numerical preponderance of men, combined with preexisting masculinist scripts and sexist practices in virtually all occupational and commercial realms as well as the society at large, has ensured the greater visibility of men's prerogatives and perspectives relative to women's in both rap music and Hip Hop. Due largely to masculinist biases already in place in the domains of advertising and news reporting, the public face of both Hip Hop and rap is masculine and the mainstream discourse of rap as Hip Hop's mouthpiece is masculine.

Third, both women and men have participated in Hip Hop culture and rap music in ways that have been both oppressive and liberatory for women. To assume that men's voice or influence in Hip Hop or rap music has been uniformly sexist and that women's has uniformly opposed this sexism is to accept a false dichotomy that misrepresents the complexity of Hip Hop and rap with respect to gender. Furthermore, to assume that women have been the only feminist voices or influences within Hip Hop and rap is to negate the contributions of progressive, anti-sexist men within the movement. To claim that rap music and Hip Hop culture are purely and simply misogynistic is to view rap and the Hip Hop realm uncritically from the perspective of an outsider. In sum, Hip Hop, including rap music, is a complex and contradictory arena in which regressive and oppressive elements sometimes complicate and at times even undermine what fundamentally remains an oppositional and potentially liberatory project.

The purpose of this essay is to demonstrate, through the examination of women's rap music from 1976 to the present, that women in rap have maintained a dually oppositional stance within Hip Hop culture. On the one hand, this stance has allowed African American and Latino women to critique the sexism of men of their same race or ethnicity, using Hip Hop as a platform. On the other hand, this stance has enabled African American and Latino women to express solidarity with men of their same race or ethnicity in their critique of and struggle against mainstream society's racism, classism, and race-d sexism (which affects both women and men of color). One feature of the second aspect of women's oppositional stance in Hip Hop is that it has allowed "everyday" women of color to critique and contest certain aspects of mainstream (including academic) feminism.[7] After presenting a brief historical overview, we will buttress our central thesis by advancing three major propositions: Hip Hop presents feminism and womanism at street level;[8] women in rap and Hip Hop, through their engagement with street-level communities, redefine and expand the discursive territory covered by feminism and womanism; and by redefining and expanding the discursive territory covered by feminism and womanism, women in rap and Hip Hop co-construct the meaning for feminism and womanism for both women and men in the Hip Hop universe as well as for the entire culture, including academic feminists and womanists. We will support our development of these themes using illustrations of lyrical content by women rappers and their musical kin.

WOMEN IN RAP: A BRIEF HISTORICAL OVERVIEW

Women have been rapping at least since 1976, when Sharon Jackson, a/k/a Sha-Rock, appeared at DJ Kool Herc's parties and got on the microphone.[9] The legendary DJ Kool Herc, a Jamaican immigrant who brought the "yard music" tradition to the South Bronx and is credited with inventing the technique known as "scratching," is regarded by most rap historians as the father of Hip Hop, circa 1974. Sha-Rock later joined the early rap group known as the Funky 4 + 1 More, who released several records between 1979 and 1984, and who in 1981 was the first rap act to appear as a featured musical guest on the national television program *Saturday Night Live*.

Between 1978 and 1986, when rap went largely commercial and became firmly established in the mainstream, more than sixty records featuring over thirty female MCs or DJs were released. In 1977 the first all-women crew, the Mercedes Ladies, composed of two DJs and as many as four MCs, was formed in the South Bronx. Despite many years of holding their own on the party circuit, not until 1984 did they appear on record and, ironically, only to back up male rapper Donald D.

The first women to rap on vinyl were school-aged Paulette Tee and Sweet Tee, who released the single "Vicious Rap" in 1978, recorded by their father, Harlem-based doo-wop producer Paul Winley. In 1979 they were joined by Lady B of Philadelphia, who recorded and released the single "To the Beat Y'All." Lady B had encountered the New York City rap scene while traveling with her friend World B. Free, a New Yorker who played for the Philadelphia 76ers basketball team. Lady B was perhaps the first to export rap from New York City and she was among the first to establish a rap program on a radio station, namely, WHAT-FM in Philadelphia. Today, she is a noted radio personality in Philadelphia.

Around this same time, former R&B singer Sylvia Robinson founded the Sugar Hill Records rap label. Her company produced rap's undisputed first hit record, "Rapper's Delight," by the Sugarhill Gang in 1979. Robinson's stewardship of Sugar Hill Records presaged other women's involvement on the production side of Hip Hop, such as that of Sylvia Rhone at Elektra Records. Robinson's label went on to introduce many of rap's early performers. Among these was the female trio Sequence, featuring Cheryl the Pearl, Blondie (not to be confused with Deborah Harry), and

MC Angie B (who later re-emerged in the mid-1990s as Neo-Soul artist Angie Stone), who released the hit single "Funk You Up" in 1980. An interesting fact about Sequence is that some of its members were from South Carolina, an indication that rap's reach was beginning to extend far beyond New York City.

Around 1980, Queen Lisa Lee began to rap as part of Afrika Bambaataa's Zulu Nation crew, recording and releasing "Zulu Nation Throwdown." Like DJ Kool Herc, Afrika Bambaataa is one of the recognized progenitors of rap. He is credited with popularizing the term "Hip Hop," having borrowed it from a couple of disco DJs, Lovebug Starski and DJ Hollywood, who used it as a party chant. Later, in 1984, Lisa Lee, Sha-Rock, and another rapper, Debbie Dee, formed the first all-women rap "supergroup" known as Us Girls for Harry Belafonte's rap-based film, *Beat Street*. Lisa Lee had rapped previously in the 1982 rap-based underground film *Wild Style*.

By 1982 rap was making its mark outside the United States when white, French-speaking Bee Side recorded "Change the Beat," the first non-English rap record. Other early white rappers included Teena Marie, a/k/a Lady Tee, a protégé of black funk artist Rick James, who rapped on the record "Square Biz"; and Debbie Harry of the new wave group Blondie, who paid homage to the New York City rap scene in her 1981 single "Rapture." On the industry side, Chicago-native Monica Lynch played an important role in the establishment and promotion of rap as the first employee and later president of Tommy Boy Records, perhaps the earliest major rap label.

From the beginning, Latinos, particularly Puerto Ricans, were integral to the evolution of Hip Hop. Women of Latino descent shared the stage with African American women. In 1984, Puerto Rican-Jewish MC Brenda K. Starr performed her song "Vicious Beat" in the movie *Beat Street*. Also in 1984, a Puerto Rican MC by the name of the Real Roxanne became the first Latina on wax with her response record "The Real Roxanne."

The Roxanne phenomenon deserves special focus in any history of women in rap. In 1984, a 14-year-old rapper by the name of Roxanne Shanté (discussed in more depth below) issued the first female response record to a male rap, in this case U.T.F.O.'s 1984 hit "Roxanne, Roxanne." Roxanne Shanté's record was followed up by numerous response records by other female artists, including two women each calling themselves "The Real Roxanne" and a third woman who went by Sparky D, whose 1985 response record was called "Sparky's Turn (Roxanne You're Through)." Incidentally, Sparky D became the first rapper to receive a commercial endorsement, rapping in a radio ad for Mountain Dew in 1985. The numerous response records generated by the original U.T.F.O./Roxanne Shanté dispute ultimately spawned not only a compilation record, but also concert tours featuring the battling female MCs as the main attraction. Scholars agree that Roxanne Shanté's original response to U.T.F.O. launched the "dis" tradition in rap—a tradition wherein artists responded in kind to one another's recorded boasts and taunts, taking each other to task and attempting to establish their own credibility as "the best." The dis tradition has been compared to the act of signifyin' in African American and African oral traditions.[10]

In 1985 a girl-group known as Supernature recorded and released a song called "The Show Stoppa (Is Stupid Fresh)" in response to Doug E. Fresh and Slick Rick's hit single, "The Show." Not long after, Supernature became Salt-n-Pepa, the first female rap superstars. Salt-n-Pepa went on to record gold and platinum albums. In 1987, their album *A Salt with a Deadly Pepa* became the first gold record (a half million copies sold) by a female rap group. Also in 1987, California's J. J. Fad's "Supersonic" became the first single by a female rap group to sell a million copies; however, since it was on a minor label (Eazy-E's Ruthless label), it was not officially certified platinum. It was not until 1991, with MC Lyte's "Ruffneck," that a single by a solo female rapper achieved certified gold status. It was not until 1994, with Da Brat's *Funkdafied*, that the first compact disc (CD) by a female rapper was certified platinum.

From the mid- to late 1980s, rap was transformed from a largely underground phenomenon to a largely mainstream, commercial one. Around 1990, a proliferation of female artists began to hit the scene, most introduced by established male crews. For instance, East Coast political rap phenom Public Enemy, fronted by Chuck D, launched Sister Souljah as its female mouthpiece. KRS-One launched Ms. Melodie. Gangsta rap originators N.W.A., including members Eazy-E, Dr. Dre, Ice Cube, DJ Yella, and MC Ren, largely responsible for establishing the West Coast "gangsta rap" scene, launched Yo-Yo. Then newcomer Puff Daddy (Sean Combs, now known as both P. Diddy in the rap world and Sean Jean in the fashion world) introduced Mary J. Blige, ushering in a whole new sound—Hip Hop Soul. Atlanta-based La Face Records, headed by L. A. Reid and Kenneth "Babyface" Edmonds introduced TLC. Jermaine Dupri's Atlanta-based So So Def Productions launched Da Brat. New Orleans-based Master P of No Limit Records introduced Mia X. West Coast-based Death Row Records introduced the Lady of Rage, a product of Farmville, Virginia. In New York City, Biggie Smalls's Junior M.A.F.I.A. launched Lil' Kim, and Jay-Z's Rockafella crew launched Foxy Brown. Miami's Trick Daddy launched Trina, and the Ruff Ryders crew launched Philadelphia-based Eve. While this is certainly not an exhaustive list of female rappers whose careers were born after rap became commercial, it illustrates a trend in the industry and contextualizes the emergence of many of the women whose lyrics and personae are the necessary fodder of feminist and womanist analyses.

During this same period, several notable female artists were launching themselves, without the "help" of established male crews. These included MC Lyte, Queen Latifah, Lauryn Hill, Erykah Badu, and Missy Elliott. MC Lyte's career, like that of Salt-n-Pepa, bridged the pre- and post-commercialization phases of rap. Queen Latifah, who will be discussed in more depth below, became the first female solo superstar of rap when she emerged with her 1989 CD *All Hail the Queen*. Lauryn Hill got her start as a member of the critically acclaimed trio the Fugees, comprised of two men—Wyclef Jean and Pras, of Haitian descent—and herself during the mid-1990s; while on a motherhood-induced sabbatical from the group in 1998, she presented her now legendary solo CD, *The Miseducation of Lauryn Hill* (1998). Dallas-based Erykah

Badu came out of what seemed like nowhere with her critically acclaimed hit CD *Baduizm* in 1997, which presented politically charged Neo-Soul music with rap-flavored undertones. Missy Elliott, a Portsmouth, Virginia native, entered the Hip Hop scene together with childhood friend and fellow producer Timbaland (although notably, he did not "introduce" her; rather, he introduced Ms. Jade); her innovative debut album *Supa Dupa Fly* also came out in 1997. All of these artists have established themselves as major influences in rap music and Hip Hop culture and, like those mentioned in the previous paragraph, are obvious subjects of feminist and womanist analyses of rap and Hip Hop.

In the sections that follow, we will examine how rap and Hip Hop function as a platform for feminist and womanist themes at ground level, how women involved in rap and Hip Hop culture mold feminist and womanist meanings in ways that are relevant to their everyday experiences and aspirations, and how these meanings subsequently inform the larger meanings of feminism and womanism for the entire culture. Before proceeding, however, in order to contextualize the experience of women in rap and Hip Hop, we will briefly consider how this history relates, thematically and materially, to the broader history of African American women in the United States.

AFRICAN AMERICAN WOMEN IN U.S. HISTORY: CONNECTING THEMES

Scholars of African American women's history have consistently identified a number of themes that have defined U.S. African American women's experiences and perspectives over time.[11] These themes include the intersection of race, gender, and class; African American women as the symbolic linchpins of conflicts between black men and white women; African American women's solidarity with African American men, particularly as expressed through African American women's support for black nationalism and militancy; African American women's history of confronting black men about sexism; relational tensions between African American women and men; black women's ambivalence about feminism and white feminists; fighting stereotypes of African American women, especially negative sexual stereotypes; reclaiming sexual autonomy and self-determination; black women's economic independence and general self-reliance; black women's solidarity, networks, and sisterhood; the uplift tradition; African American women as representatives of an alternative tradition of womanhood (in contrast to white traditions, particularly the "cult of true womanhood"); the importance of motherhood to African American women; divisions among African American women based on vectors of difference other than race and gender (such as color, class, sexuality, nationality, religion, education, or ideology); and African American women as the key to the future of the race or humanity. Women's discourses in rap and Hip Hop unambiguously reflect these themes, as we will demonstrate below (although a full exploration of this topic is beyond the scope of this paper). As historian Darlene Clark Hine observed in another context, African American women demonstrate "a special brand of female militancy"; arguably, this militancy is detectable in women's rap and Hip Hop.[12] Women in rap and Hip Hop personify the concluding assertion of the famous 1991 "Black Women in Defense of Ourselves" statement, which proclaimed that, "No one will speak for us but ourselves."[13]

"THE STREET": FEMINISM AND WOMANISM AT GROUND LEVEL

Popular music, as the folk music of the modern and postmodern eras, articulates the stories, philosophies, and yearnings of the masses.[14] Hip Hop, encompassing one form of popular music (rap) and the culture that surrounds it, presents feminism and womanism at ground level or "the street."[15] In the case of Hip Hop, "the street" is a site where the sensibilities of black lower class people prevail. Rap and Hip Hop artists come from and speak to a population that is not defined in terms of its academic credentials. While many rap and Hip Hop artists, like many members of their audience, are well educated and have college degrees, the erasure of distinctions related to educational attainment is generally valued over the emphasis on such distinctions. "Street knowledge" and "street smarts" are valued over formal education because of the history of African Americans' exclusion from formal education as a result of centuries of enslavement, colonization, legal segregation, and other forms of oppression and discrimination across the African diaspora. Street knowledge and street smarts are also valued because they facilitate the negotiation of postmodern living conditions.[16]

While the pursuit of material wealth is generally condoned in Hip Hop culture, hierarchies based on economic attainment are eschewed, given that a focus on economic distinctions tends to undermine black solidarity unless a pipeline of wealth is created that benefits a group or network of people. While material possessions are lauded as a source of pleasure and status, and competition for material resources is taken as a fact of life, the bottom line is usually about advancement not only for oneself, but also for others, whether members of one's family, crew, or sometimes the entire race, or all oppressed people. Rap lyrics may or may not contain an overt critique of capitalism, but they are generally supported by a communal value system where linkages between people are held together by loyalty and blood. Often, this communal value system bears striking similarities to various African ethical and ontological systems.[17]

In terms of feminism and womanism specifically, Hip Hop culture in general and rap music in particular provide a platform for African American women at street level to process and produce feminist and womanist ideas. Whether or not they endorse the labels "feminist" or "womanist" for themselves, women in Hip Hop are exposed to feminist and womanist ideas circulating within the general culture.[18] Like other women, female hip hoppers discuss, adapt, translate, and sometimes even reject these ideas. One purpose of women's rap is to educate women and to motivate or inspire women to succeed in the face of problems they are likely to encounter in their lives. In rap, women speak to each other about various kinds of everyday occurrences as well as about recurring issues in the larger sociopolitical domain. In this realm, women

96

support each other, critique each other, conscientize each other, challenge each other, and bear witness to each other. Another purpose of women's rap is to air women's concerns to men and provide a forum for discussion. Because gender is an accepted divide within the African American community, the discursive space created by women for women in rap is in many respects inviolate, even when women are using that space to communicate to or with men. Thus, while men may disagree with or reject what women rappers say, they generally engage them and respect women's right to utilize that platform.

One caveat: It must be remembered that, despite 30 years of history, Hip Hop is essentially a youth-driven subculture. Although its participants vary in age, its themes, values, and viewpoints often reflect the interests of teenagers and young adults more than they reflect those of people from other age groups.[19] While the dimensions of this fact may change as the Hip Hop generation itself ages and Hip Hop, like previous youth subcultures, is ultimately supplanted by something else, at this time, the youthful quality of Hip Hop must be borne in mind. Like Rock 'n' Roll before it, themes of sex and relationships, drugs, partying, and opposition to "the Establishment" prevail at a higher rate in Hip Hop than they might in the musings of older or younger people. What markedly distinguishes Hip Hop from Rock 'n' Roll, however, are its black racial underpinnings, combined with its rootedness in the life-space of the economically disadvantaged, which infuse it with an oppositional sensibility that transcends age in some respects. In addition, Hip Hop differs from Rock 'n' Roll politically in that it responds to a markedly different "Establishment" than the one critiqued by "Rock 'n' Rollers." Stated succinctly, Rock 'n' Roll represented the youth of the post–World War II baby boom responding to a modernist establishment, while Hip Hop represents the post-60s, post-desegregation, Generation X and Y youth's response to a postmodern establishment.[20]

The specific ways rap music serves as a platform for women of color to process feminist and womanist themes and issues is made more apparent by an examination of actual lyrical content written and performed by women in Hip Hop. Some of these women rap; others write and perform in hybrid genres that have evolved from rap, such as "Hip Hop Soul," "Neo-Soul," and "Hip Pop" (Hip Hop-influenced popular music). In the section that follows, we present and discuss some of this lyrical content. Since it is difficult to detach the lyrical content from the musical (and often visual) fabric in which it is embedded, but because we cannot adequately convey the sonic (or videographic) features of songs in written form, readers are urged, where possible, to listen to the songs in question (see Discography) and, where relevant, to view the videos to obtain additional meaning.

WOMEN'S DISCURSIVE STRANDS IN RAP AND HIP HOP

Women's rap and related music maintain a number of major discursive strands or themes. Although it is beyond the scope of this paper to review all of them, we will present several to illustrate some of the ways that feminist and womanist themes are engaged by women in rap and Hip Hop.[21] Although space considerations prevent us from adequately representing the full array of female artists who address even the few themes we include, we have attempted to sample both well-known and lesser-known artists, as well as artists from a broad span of Hip Hop's historical spectrum. In this essay, we will discuss three discursive strands that serve to highlight women's dual oppositionality within in Hip Hop culture, namely:

- talking back to men in defense of women and demanding respect for women;
- women's empowerment, self-help, and solidarity;
- defense of black men against the larger society.

Let us now take a closer look at these themes as they are discussed in specific works by specific artists.

TALKING BACK TO MEN IN DEFENSE OF WOMEN

Women's defense of themselves against sexist assault takes many forms in Hip Hop and rap, from the presentation of playful boasts and taunts designed to reclaim women's respect and restore injured pride to bloody fantasies of revenge and vigilante action intended to mete justice out upon men who have exploited women or committed acts of violence against them. In these songs, women rappers engage the classic feminist theme of fighting patriarchy. Because the men being addressed in these songs are typically men of color, these songs serve as a within-group critique of African American (or Latino) men's sexism. While many of the artists who perform these songs do not claim the label "feminist" for themselves, their lyrical messages nevertheless counteract and contradict masculine power assertion and serve to raise women's consciousness about sexism. This discursive strand characterized by women's talking back to men, defending themselves, reclaiming their respect, and resisting sexist violence has a long history within rap.

As mentioned previously, Roxanne Shanté launched the whole "dis" tradition in rap in 1984 when she responded to U.T.F.O.'s "Roxanne, Roxanne" with her own basement recording, "Roxanne's Revenge." "Dis" songs usually serve one of three purposes: to reclaim the respect of someone who has been put down; to put a person exhibiting hubris in his or her place; or to bait another person and rustle up "drama." In the case of "Roxanne's Revenge," all three purposes of the "dis" were invoked. While no single line in "Roxanne's Revenge" stands on its own, the song achieved a number of ends, including conveying to the three men who had designs on Roxanne in "Roxanne, Roxanne" that Roxanne was not just easy prey (thus establishing women's respectability), thereby knocking all men with excessive confidence down a few notches, all while conveying to the world at large that women had lyrical skills and could rap, and thus compete in what had been established as a man's world. The following lines give a flavor of her rap: "Yeah, I am fly but I don't take this, and everybody knows I don't go for it. So if you're tryin' to be cute and you're tryin' to be fine, you need to cut it out 'cause it's all in your mind. Tryin' to be like me, yeah, is very hard—you think you are God, but you do eat lard."[22]

Another early "dis" record was Salt-n-Pepa's "Tramp" in 1985.[23] The song begins with the retort "What'd ya call me?" with the implication that the female speaker has been called a "tramp." In an era when women's sexual prerogatives were being re-negotiated in the larger social sphere, this song was a timely expression of women's demands for both sexual agency and respect. Salt-n-Pepa rap: "Homegirls, attention you must pay, so listen close to what I say. Don't take this as a simple rhyme, cuz this type of thing happens all the time. Now what would you do if a stranger says Hi? Would you dis him or would you reply? If you answer, there is a chance that you'd become a victim of circumstance. Am I right, fellas? Tell the truth—or else I'm-a have to show and prove you are what you are, I am what I am. It just so happens that most men are . . . tramps." Later in the song, the rappers address a prospective "trampy" male thus: "You's a sucker! Get your dirty mind out the gutter. You ain't gettin' paid, you ain't knockin' boots, you ain't treating me like no prostitute!" Returning their attention to their female audience, they say, "Then I walked away, he called me a teas-er. You're on a mission, kid—yo, he's a . . . [implied: "skeezer"] tramp!" This song functions not only as a wake-up call to women considering subjugating themselves to get a man, but also to men who assumed their preying game was not transparent to women.

A more serious "dis" record, focused like Salt-n-Pepa's song on both reclaiming women's respect and also challenging sexist language use, as well as making the streets safe for women, was Queen Latifah's 1993 anthem, "U.N.I.T.Y." This song begins with the angry shout, "Who you callin' a bitch?!" which is followed up by the state-ments "You gotta let him know . . . You ain't a bitch or a ho." Latifah continues: "Instinct leads me to another flow . . . Everytime I hear a brother call a girl a bitch or a ho, trying to make a sister feel low, you know all of that gots to go. . . ." Later in the song, Latifah talks about walking down the street in her cutoff shorts due to the hot weather and talking back to a man who reaches out to grab her buttocks: "Huh, I punched him dead in his eye and said 'Who you callin' a bitch?'"

In some songs, women's rage at men escalates, and the songs reflect violent, ret-ributive fantasies. For example, in Ms. Jade's 2002 "Why You Tell Me That?" the issue is a male partner's failure to put as much into the relationship as his female mate. Ms. Jade prefaces her rap with a sisterhood-inducing round-up call: "Yo, this one's for all my ladies that been through a similar situation. . . ." She then launches into her main tale: "If I had that thing on me woulda shot you right then, if I had that thing on me woulda popped you right then. Nigga, yeah, you played me and said you was down for me. . . . Listen up, wasted skin, I'm much better without you." Lil' Mo, another female rapper, who performs on the song with Ms. Jade, chimes in with some clarification: "Niggas, you toyed with my teenage years and my womanhood. I hate you, hope I make it understood—good-bye. Why you tell me that you love me, why you tell me that you care for me, when you didn't do it? Why you thought you was there for me when you wasn't at all?" Throughout the song, Ms. Jade recounts sacrifices she had made for her man—"Pushed keys overseas, went to jail for you. . . . You had beef, I was there bustin' shells for you. If I ain't miscarry, woulda had a kid for you"—in hopes of obtaining the ultimate affirmation of the relationship; "Led me on, told me I was gonna be your wife." Although throughout the song Ms. Jade has the fantasy of killing the man who hurt her this way, in the end she turns philosophical: "Yo, I just wanna thank the guys, the guys who made us feel like this, made us understand how strong we are as women."

Another example of a revengeful fantasy involving a gun is Trina's 2000 song "Watch Yo Back." Again, the issue is men who chronically disrespect the women who make sacrifices for them: "And it's so sad how I do for you, be the woman come through for you when you do wrong, police, come through for you, I'll even bend the truth for you." The song also includes allusions to domestic violence; "Motherfuckers is so crazy, deranged; let 'em into your brain brings misery and pain, cause they call us lame, bitches, and heffers, and sluts. You think your nut [sex] is gonna heal my bruises and cuts." Trina's conclusion, "Bitches, y'all better get tough and at the same time y'all better lock the game and re-rock the game, get a Glock ready, sit back and cock and aim and try to stop the pain, 'cause you got a lot to gain." Her last line, directed at the men, is "Better watch yo back." The impact of the song's message to men is reinforced by the fact that the chorus is rapped by a man: "Better watch yo back there, boy, and get on your square or my gun'll beat you changed. Got the nigga figured out, shawty [woman], you walk, tell him shit ain't the same, go ahead and kick him out, cut him up, catch him sleepin', fuck him up—only he must not know your name. Pimpin' is a deadly game. . . ."

In Eve's 1999 rap "Love Is Blind," the abuse of women takes center stage.[24] In this case Eve is concerned not about violence being meted out to her, but to another woman. In the song she rises to the other woman's defense and confronts the male perpetrator: "Hey, yo, I don't even know you and I hate you. See, all I know is that my girlfriend used to date you. How would you feel if she held you down and raped you? Tried and tried, but she never could escape you. She was in love and I'd ask her how, I mean, why? What kind of love from a nigga would black your eye? What kind of love from a nigga every night make you cry? What kind of love from a nigga make you wish he would die?" In the next verse, she asserts, "I don't even know you and I'd kill you myself. You played with her like a doll and put her back on the shelf. Wouldn't let her go to school and better herself. She had a baby by your ass and you ain't giving no help. . . . How could you beat the mother of your kids? . . . Had to deal with fist fights and phone calls from your bitches. . . ." Even though the friend in the song returns to the man several times, Eve is not content to stay out of her friend's business: "Floss like you possess her, tellin' me to mind my business, said that it was her life and stay the fuck out of it. I tried and said, just for him, I'll keep a ready clip." The song reaches a climax in the third verse: "I don't even know you and I want you dead. Don't know the facts, but I saw the blood pour from her head. . . . [You] had the nerve to show up at her mother's house the next day to come and pay your respects and help the family pray, even knelt down on one knee and let a tear drop, and before you had a chance to get up, you heard my gun cock. Prayin' to me now, I ain't God, but I'll pretend—I ain't start your life, but, nigga, I'm-a bring it to an end. . . ." In the concluding lines of the song, Eve asserts that the love between sisters (i.e., women's solidarity) is stronger than the love between women and men.

As these excerpted lyrics demonstrate, in rap "talking back" to men in defense of women can take a variety of forms, from light verbal sparring to homicidal fantasies. In all cases these lyrics demonstrate women's commitment to addressing forms of disrespect, deprecation, negation, and violence that they experience in their everyday lives, typically at the hands of men in their own communities. Women attempt to change men's behavior (and, by extension, to dislodge patriarchy) in a number of ways, from "dissing" men, to confronting them, to threatening them. Although mainstream discourses about rap often suggest that women in rap accept, condone, and even valorize male sexism in Hip Hop culture, these songs demonstrate a far more complex picture in which women take their men to task. Although these songs address men, they also highlight women's solidarity, whether in the form of women trying to educate one another in order to help one another avoid life's pitfalls, or overt assertions of sisterhood.

WOMEN'S EMPOWERMENT, SELF-HELP, AND SOLIDARITY

Women's autonomy and solidarity are more directly demonstrated in songs of female empowerment and self-help that are addressed directly to women. In these songs artists attempt to bring women to consciousness about their oppression as well as to provide direct messages of support to each other that counter the many disempowering messages women receive in the dominant discourse. These messages from the dominant discourse are funneled not only through black men, but also through various members of the larger, predominantly white society and the mass media it controls. Thus, within this discursive strand, women of color at street level operate from the base of both forms of oppositionality simultaneously. Although women often talk about their experiences with men in this strand of discourse, men are not the primary intended audience; rather, women are. Thus, black women's unique viewpoint is directly invoked.[25]

In "Girl, Don't Be No Fool" (1992), for example, Yo-Yo says: "Here's a message to the ladies—married, single, and even the ones with babies: Listen to Yo-Yo once again as I conversate about the ways of men. In your life, girl, keep an open mind and you'll find a lie in each and every line. They [men] say, 'Hah, sure, we're from the new school.' What I'm tryin' to say is, girl, don't be no fool." Later, she returns to the theme of her own consciousness-raising influence when she says, "I'm here to open your eyes so you can smell the coffee. Guys ain't nothin' but dirt, and they'll flirt with anything dressed in a mini-skirt." This verse of the song refers to men who cheat on their female partners. In the next verse, Yo-Yo turns to the subject of domestic violence: "Homegirl, what's up with the black eye? (Ehm, I fell . . .) Hah, now that's a damn lie. The man you got is just bad for your health. You can lie to me, but not to yourself. So when you gonna leave him?" Later in the song, Yo-Yo refers to her own women's self-help organization, the Intelligent Black Women's Coalition, referred to as the I.B.W.C.—an organization she actually founded and ran for a time in the early 1990s. On a subsequent CD, Yo-Yo presented a similarly direct message to women in the song "Black Pearl": "Comin' at'cha, can you feel what I'm feelin'? Some soul sisters need some natural healing—gifted, but shifted, so come follow me. 'Cause I'm-a take you on a sister-to-sister journey. Run to get mine, better get 'fore they grab it—like cold Pepsi-Cola, gotta say 'I gots-ta have it.' Stayin' back too long, when you really got it goin' on. . . . Ain't nothin' wrong with being strong. . . ."

In their 1995 song "Ain't Nuthin' but a She-Thing," Salt-n-Pepa offer a similarly inspirational and solidarity-building message about women's empowerment: "I could be anything that I want to be. Don't consider me a minority. Open up your eyes and maybe you'll see: It's a she thing and it's all in me. . . . Ladies help me out if you agree." Later, they rap, "The thing that makes me mad and crazy upset, got to break my neck just to get my respect. Go to work and get paid less than a man when I'm doin' the same damn thing he can. When I'm aggressive, then I'm a bitch; when I got attitude, you call me a witch. Treat me like a sex-object (that ain't smooth), underestimate the mind, oh yeah, you're a fool. Weaker sex, yeah, right—that's the joke (ha!). Have you ever been in labor? I don't think so, nope." The song achieves true anthem like proportions by the end when the rappers offer the following lines: "Don't be fooled by my S-E-X; it ain't that simple, I'm more complex. We've come a long way, and, baby, that's a fact. Let's keep moving forward, girls—never look back. Fight for your rights, stand up and be heard. You're just as good as any man, believe that. Word!"

An example of an even more focused message of empowerment came from Salt-n-Pepa in their earlier hit song, "Let's Talk about Sex" (1991). This song, which was released at a time when AIDS awareness among heterosexuals was just beginning, and "safe sex" was still a controversial topic, offered the following lines: "Let's talk about sex for now to the people at home or in the crowd—it keeps coming up anyhow. Don't decoy, avoid, or make void the topic, 'cause that ain't gonna stop it. Now, we talk about sex on the radio and video shows—many will know, anything goes. Let's tell it how it is, and how it could be. Those who think it's dirty have a choice—pick up the needle, press pause, or turn the radio off. Will that stop us, Pep? I doubt it. All right, then—come on, Spin!" In this song, Salt-n-Pepa work at breaking down barriers to communication about sex by striving for realism and connection with their audience's lived experiences.[26] By the end of the song, this spoken exchange between Salt and Pepa make this plain: "Yo, Pep—I don't think they're gonna play this on the radio. (And why not? Everybody has sex.) I mean, everybody should be makin' love. (Come on, how many guys you know make love??)" Salt-n-Pepa's effort to raise awareness of AIDS and promote safe sex was further strengthened when they made an AIDS public service announcement and also remade their song "Let's Talk about Sex" as "Let's Talk about AIDS."

Like Salt-n-Pepa, the all-female Hip Hop group TLC wrote and performed many songs that raised awareness about AIDS, safe sex, and women's sexual empowerment. But they also addressed other issues of vulnerability for women, such as women's body image and appearance concerns. An early song "Hat 2 Da Back" (1993), encouraged young women to wear comfortable clothes, even if such clothes were considered masculine. "Being that I am the kinda girl that I am. . . . Nobody can make me do what I don't want to. I can be myself a lot and I'm proud of what I got, so I'll never change for you. Being that I am the kinda girl that I am, tight jeans don't hit the scene with one like me. I got to be feeling free and you better believe I'll do what pleases me." Later in the song, the women chide a young man who dares to challenge their choice of clothing: "Shoot, he made another bad move sayin' that girls shouldn't wear baseball caps. He can go take a hike, 'cause it's the style I like. . . ."

On a much later CD, TLC present the song "Unpretty" (1998), which critiques those social forces that make women feel ugly. Chilli sings, "My outsides look cool; my insides are blue. Every time I think I'm through, it's because of you. I try different ways, but it's all the same. At the end of the day, I just have myself to blame." T-Boz sings, "Never insecure until I met you, now I'm bein' stupid. I used to be so cute to me, just a little bit skinny. Why do I look to all these things to keep you happy? Maybe get rid of you, and then I'll get back to me, yeah. . . ." In the chorus, the group sings: "You can buy your hair if it won't grow, you can fix your nose if he says so. You can buy all the make-up that M.A.C. can make, but if you can't look inside, you find out who I am to be in the position that makes me feel so damn unpretty, I'll make you feel unpretty, too." This song's impact was enhanced by the video, which showed the members of the group applying make-up and tearfully smearing it off in disgust over recognition of their own subjugation to external beauty standards.

Queen Latifah offered a different kind of women's empowerment song, "Ladies 1st," on her 1989 debut CD, *All Hail the Queen*. This CD, hailed in the Hip Hop community as a turning point in women's rap discourse, encapsulated an omnibus message of women's power. On this song, Latifah shared the microphone with black British rapper Monie Love, whose lines in the song contribute equally to the song's meaning and impact. Latifah rapped, "A woman can bear you, break you, take you; now it's time to rhyme—can you relate to a sister dope enough to make you holler and scream?" Later, Monie Love embellishes this theme of women's power: "Strong, stepping, strutting, moving on, rhyming, cutting, and not forgetting—We are the ones that give birth to the new generation of prophets, because it's 'Ladies First.'" Latifah then rejoins (with Monie Love's back-up): "I break into a lyrical freestyle, grab the mic, look at the crowd and see smiles, 'cause they see a woman standing up on her own two—sloppy slouching is something I won't do. Some think that we can't flow (can't flow)—stereotypes, they go to go, got to go. I'm-a mess around and flip the scene into reverse (with what?)—with a little touch of 'Ladies First.'" To paint a picture of women's superiority, Latifah raps, "I'm divine and my mind expands throughout the universe—a female rapper with the message to send: Queen Latifah is the perfect specimen!" Later, she states, "Queens of civilization are on the mic." This song, which clearly invokes the mythology of African queens, played well into, yet challenged, the environment of burgeoning Afrocentricity during the early 1990s.

Another artist known for presenting socially conscious music is Lauryn Hill. In her 1998 song "Doo Wop (That Thing)" from her debut solo CD, *The Miseducation of Lauryn Hill*, she uses the old method of "reading" someone, combined with sister-ly empathy, to make a point and encourage women to increase their self-respect. Because her lyrical style does not lend itself to short excerpts, a longer passage will be reproduced here. The chorus exhorts: "Girls, you know you'd better watch out. Some guys, some guys are only about that thing, that thing, that thing. . . ." The verses dedicated to women continue:

It's been three weeks since you've been looking for your friend—the one you let hit it and never called you again. 'Member when he told you he was 'bout the Benjamins? You act like you ain't hear him, then give him a little trim. To begin, how you think you're really going to pretend like you wasn't down then you called him again? Plus, when you give it up so easy, you ain't even foolin' him—if you did it then, then you'd probably fuck again. Talking out your neck, saying you're a Christian, a Muslim, sleeping with the gin [Gentiles]—now, that was the sin that did Jezebel in. Who're you going to tell when the repercussions spin? Showing off you're ass 'cause you're thinking it's a trend—girlfriend, let me break it down for you again! You know I only say it 'cause I'm truly genuine—don't be a hardrock when you really are a gem. Baby girl, respect is just the minimum. Niggas fucked up and you still defending them. Now, Lauryn is only human—don't think I haven't been through the same predicament. Let it sit inside your head like a mil-lion women in Philly, Penn. It's silly when girls sell they souls because it's in. Look at where you be in—hair weaves like Europeans, fake nails done by Koreans . . . Come again! Yo, when, when—come again! My friend, come again!

Later in the song, Hill poses the stinging rhetorical question, "How you gon' win, when you ain't right within?" Although this line is technically embedded in a verse "dedicated to the men," this message pervades the song for members of both genders.

Many more examples of songs containing messages of women's empowerment, self-help, and solidarity could be provided; the examples presented here demonstrate that women rappers present not only sisterly messages of inspiration and encouragement, but also harsh critiques of one another designed to elicit a higher consciousness about women's oppression as well as women's inherent worth and dignity. These songs indi-cate women rappers' awareness of societal messages, from within communities of color as well as the white mainstream, that degrade, discourage, depress, and confuse women, and they show how many women rappers have taken the role of "my sister's keeper."

DEFENSE OF BLACK MEN AGAINST THE LARGER SOCIETY

Black women in rap, as in real life, also take the role of "my brother's keeper." Recognizing that gendered racism affects not only women of color, but also men of color, women rappers articulate a politics of solidarity with their men that is closely aligned with womanism.[27] While the politics of women's solidarity with men have always been controversial in feminism, a stance better described as a loving critical engagement with men is advocated within womanism. In rap and Hip Hop, this latter stance takes the form of celebrations of black men, which counteract standard stereotypical messages of black men's inferiority and brutality that circulate in the wider society, and "ride or die" songs, in which black women express "us against the world" sentiments with regard to black men who are "fighting the system," often in ways that are illegal, dangerous, or alien to mainstream culture. By demonstrating such alliance and solidarity with men of color, women rappers demonstrate a complex "unbought and unbossed" political consciousness and exercise their oppositionality to mainstream racism, classism, and race-d sexism that affects both men and women in the community.[28]

A classic song in praise of black men is Salt-n-Pepa's 1994 "Whatta Man." The chorus is purely celebratory: "Whatta man, whatta man, whatta man, what a mighty good man. . . ." The song's esteeming tone is set in the first few lines: "I wanna take a minute or two and give much respect due to the man that's made a difference in my world. . . . I know that ain't nobody perfect; I give props to those who deserve it, and, believe me, y'all—he's worth it." In the remainder of the song, Salt and Pepa list the man's many attributes and discuss how they will reward the man for his goodness. The "good" man is compared with negative male archetypes, including male "ho's," "macks," pimps, wannabes, suckers, those who are "corny," and "wham-bam-thank-you-ma'am" men. This good man is faithful, sexy, generous, dapper, loving, sexually skillful and attentive, smart, a good conversationalist, never disrespectful, "a lover and a fighter," and humorous. In addition, he spends time with his kids. In sum, "He's a God-sent original, the man of my dreams." By defining a good man, Salt-n-Pepa create and project an archetype for men to follow as well as set a standard for fellow women who may be settling for less.

Respect for the black man is shown in another way in Erykah Badu's 1997 song, "Other Side of the Game." In this song, Badu expresses support for a man who is making a living by illegal means—"Work ain't honest, but it pays the bills." Although the man's line of work causes stress on the family, namely, Badu and her unborn baby, Badu understands the forces that are aligned against him and loyally supports him as best she can. "Now, me and baby got this situation. See, brotha got this complex occupation. And it ain't that he don't have education, 'cause I was right there at his graduation. Now I ain't sayin' that this life don't work, but it's me and baby that he hurts. 'Cause I tell him right, he thinks I'm wrong—but I love him strong. He gave me the life that I came to live, gave me the song that I came to sing. . . ." Later, she continues: "Don't I know there's confusion. God's gonna see us through. Peace out to revolution. . . ." Interestingly, Badu continues the storyline of this song on a much later CD in a song called "Danger" (2003). In this song, the man has gone to jail, and Badu, with the baby, is awaiting his return on the heels of a jailbreak. As she paces the floor with the baby awaiting him in her full make-up (because he's been gone for so long), she keeps the car running and the clip in her "mama's gun." She has saved up money "in a box under the bed" and is prepared to run with the man once he returns. Yet, again, she reflects on the stress of their lifestyle for both herself and her man, at times effectively chiding him: "Well, there ain't no mistakin', that the money you're makin' leaves you nervous and shaken, 'cause at night you're awake and thinkin' about lives that you've taken, all the love you've forsaken, in your zone. Niggas gone, get they fuckin' head blown." "Danger—you're in danger," she warns. "No hard feelings, right or wrong, weak or strong. I don't make the laws." Yet, she has supported her black man in this complex situation.

Women in rap tend to show appreciation for men, rich or poor, from the black "ghetto," recognizing it as a complex of forces constraining life's options and cultivating a particular mix of hardness and vulnerability. An example of such a song is Lauryn Hill's tender and wistful ballad "The Sweetest Thing" (1998), in which she extols her "sweet prince of the ghetto" for "the way you walk, your style of dress" and his "precious, precious, precious, precious dark skin tone." While as much is conveyed in the music of this song as the words, its overall message is one of appreciation for black men. Similarly, in her 2000 song "Brotha," Hip Hop spoken-word artist Jill Scott writes, "If'n nobody told ya, brotha', I'm here to let you know that you're so wonderful, you're so marvelous, you're so beautiful, you're splendid, you're fabulous, brilliantly blessed in every way. Y'all can't touch we. Brotha', don't let nobody hold you back. . . ."

As mentioned, another type of song in which black women support black men could be characterized as "ride or die" songs or "Bonnie and Clyde" anthems. In these songs, lyrics tend to convey women's willingness to help men in dangerous situations and a sense of shared risk in some sort of dangerous endeavor. Often the endeavor involves the drug trade or the redemption of the man's honor in a gang-related conflict. Two examples of this type of song are Yo-Yo's "The Bonnie and Clyde Theme" (1993) and Eve's "Dog Match" (1999). As is common in this genre, both songs are duets; Yo-Yo raps with Ice Cube and Eve raps with DMX. In "The Bonnie and Clyde Theme," Ice Cube starts off: "It's a man's world, but check the girl with the Mac 11, 187. . . ." He compares himself and Yo-Yo to a diverse array of famous male-female teams: "Ike and Tina, Marie and Donnie, Ashford and Simpson, Clyde and Bonnie." Yo-Yo picks it up: "I'm the type of girl that's down for my nigga, I'll lie for my nigga, peel a cap for my nigga. . . . You ain't seen nothing 'til you seen us both jacking, pulling the side of fools, straight ratpacking. . . ." In the chorus they alternate, "Got me a down girl on my team, the Bonnie and Clyde theme, yeah. Got me a down-ass nigga on my team, the Bonnie and Clyde theme, yeah." Later, Ice Cube asserts, "Bonnie and Clyde, equal homicide, yeah." Yo-Yo rejoins, "You can lock us up if you want, don't matter—But give 'em a bail and we'll be right back at cha. . . ." The point of this song is not so much to advocate actual violence as to posture together and express double toughness and fierce loyalty in a "street" context.

In "Dog Match," DMX opens up with, "Now for every real dog, there's that bitch that's behind him, that bitch that when that nigga get to missin', she gon' find him. Old girl gonna stand with the dog, hand in hand with the dog, and whatever the fuck went down, she ran with the dog." Eve matches him with, "Always been the bitch that could roll with a thug and wipe up the blood, roll in the mud with your other ducks, nigga. What you need when the chips is down. I'll abide on the stand when evidence is found. I give pound to ya niggaz—they respect this bitch." Later in the song, the duo speculates about how tough their "pups" would be as a result of their own equally matched and superior toughness.

Foxy Brown presents a similar theme in "Letter to the Firm (Holy Matrimony)" (1996). In this case, however, the "marriage" is to an entire crew rather than to an individual. She raps, "Me and you forever, hand in hand, I'm married to the Firm, boo, ya got to understand. I'll die for 'em, give me a chair and then I'll fry for 'em. And if I got to take the stand for 'em, I'm-a lie for 'em." In "Bonnie and Clyde, Part II" (1999), a duet with male rapper Jay-Z, Foxy Brown invokes the famous fugitive duo directly. The chorus of the song is a sort of call-and-response in which Foxy [F] and Jay-Z [J] trade lines. In the first section, Jay-Z leads: [J] "Now, would you die for your nigga?" [F] "Yeah, I'd die for my nigga." [J] "Would you ride for your nigga?" [F] "I gets lie for my nigga." [J] "Would you live for your nigga?" [F] "Do up big for my nigga." [J] "Would you bid for your nigga?" [F] "Shit, you my nigga." In the second one, Foxy leads: [F] "Would you ride for me?" [J] "Rapper robbery." [F] "Would you die for me?" [J] "I hang high from a tree." [F] "They ain't ready for us, nigga." [J] "Obviously." [F] "Sound like Bonnie and Clyde to me." While this sort of exchange might sound macabre to someone outside this linguistic universe, within it, this exchange represents an expression of mutual loyalty and, to an extent, relational reciprocity. It is a way of saying, on a gendered level, "I would go to the lengths of the earth for you," while also recognizing, from a racial and class positionality, that "it's us against the world."

These songs recognize African American men's gendered vulnerability in a highly racialized society, sending a message to black men, as well as to the world-at-large in which they are frequently put down, that black women are black men's allies. These songs also reflect the complexity of black male-female relations within the Hip Hop generation.[29] These lyrics suggest that the women who pen them know that the criticism of black women's support of black men that occurs within some corners of mainstream society, even in "progressive" circles, is subject to vestigial and often unchallenged racist, classist, and sexist attitudes and sentiments. Thus, while this stance on the part of women of color is, on the one hand, overtly "with" men of color, it is also a veiled assault on mainstream society and, in particular, those hypocrisies which continue to pollute the discourses of its more progressive representatives. Through their expressions of solidarity and alliance with their men, women of color demonstrate clear oppositionality to violent and oppressive aspects of mainstream society and the dominant discourse.

WOMEN IN RAP: EXPANDING THE DISCURSIVE TERRITORY OF FEMINISM AND WOMANISM

As these foregoing examples illustrate, in Hip Hop and rap, women of color, particularly African American women, translate feminist and womanist ideas already circulating in the larger culture into street-level languages and contexts at the same time as they generate autonomous articulations of personal and political struggle and aspiration that then inform others in the larger conversation and, in particular, challenge mainstream feminists. For instance, while women rappers exhibit a traditional feminist orientation when they "talk back" to men to reclaim women's respectability and fight back against violence against women, they push the envelope on feminist discourse when they express alliance with men who are viewed as antisocial by the larger society, or when they advocate violence in their own right. Yet, by containing the contradiction of these positions—as they do, for instance, when they exhort one another towards self-empowerment, agency, and solidarity—women rappers and their musical kin manifest a dual oppositionality that allows them to contest sexism within the Hip Hop universe as well as confront sexism, racism, classism, and other oppressions vis-à-vis mainstream society (which includes some feminists). Ultimately, the process of feminist/womanist knowledge construction, then, becomes not only dialogic, but also inscribed in multiple texts and contexts.[30]

Thus, it can be said that women in Hip Hop and rap participate in and co-construct the larger feminist and womanist conversation as well as the overall meanings of feminism and womanism in society. Like all women, they are both subjects and agents in the process of defining, articulating, and using (or contesting) feminism and womanism. Thus, women rappers and hip hoppers redefine and expand the discursive territory covered by feminism and womanism, not just for the consumers of Hip Hop and rap, but for everyone. Central to their ability to redefine and expand these discourses is their dual oppositionality.

Hip Hop is a complex arena in which not all women address sexism or promote women's empowerment. Certainly, even those women who do promote women's interests and well-being do not always call themselves feminists or womanists, choosing instead to let their lyrics and actions speak for themselves. Yet, at a time in the feminist history of consciousness when the relationships between the academy and the street, between theory and activism, are at issue, rap and Hip Hop are particularly productive and informative sites of inquiry and activity.

Women in rap and Hip Hop exhibit differential consciousness and utilize a form of differential social activism to enact social change in a multiplicity of contexts, at micro and macro levels. Differential consciousness and social movement challenge vectors of oppression in postmodern society by using ideologically eclectic philosophies and methods to intercept and intervene upon rapidly changing and heterogeneous exploitative and violent forces and discourses.[31] By rejecting rigid ideological templates that necessarily draw lines of "insider" and "outsider," "with us" and "against us," differential activists—including, we would argue, women in rap and Hip Hop—retain their ability to generate and maintain relationships of identification and transformation with a wide variety of people. Thus, they retain a certain politically productive connection to "the masses" that is often lost by activists who strive to distill neatly refined, internally consistent, often more academic, and, ultimately, utopian discourses. Hip Hop feminism and womanism, as much as they often fly beneath the radar of the feminist mainstream, survive and thrive because they "keep it real."

The type of nonideological feminist/womanist theory and movement we are describing here is a significant development not only in the larger arena of feminism, but also in the wider fields of critical theory and progressive social activism. Although rap and Hip Hop in general and women's rap and Hip Hop in particular, could be criticized for underutilizing their feminist/womanist potential, both can be lauded for maintaining a lively and perpetually self-reinventing space of liberatory possibility for a broad segment of the youth worldwide. It remains to be seen to what extent this liberatory potential will be realized, but, no doubt, women of color will be in the forefront.

NOTES

[1] The term "Hip Hop" is reputed to have been coined by either Lovebug Starski or DJ Hollywood, two DJs who worked collaboratively in New York during the early and mid-1970s. According to William E. Perkins, DJ Afrika Bambaataa imported this term into the South Bronx party scene in the mid-1970s. Early Hip Hop culture was constituted by three distinct forms of oppositional cultural expression: rap music (comprised of music made by DJs and rap lyrics provided by MCs), graffiti writing (known simply as "writing"), and breakdancing (a/k/a "breaking"). Although all three forms of expression survive today, rap music has entered into a relationship with the cultural mainstream, while writing and breaking retain currency as largely underground activities. For detailed discussions of the origins of Hip Hop, see Tricia Rose, *Black Noise: Rap Music and Black Culture in Contemporary America* (Middletown, CT, 1994); William E. Perkins, *Droppin' Science: Critical Essays on Rap Music and Hip Hop Culture* (Philadelphia, PA, 1996); and Nelson George, *Hip Hop America* (New York, 1998).

[2] Houston A. Baker cited in Rose, *Black Noise*, 21.

[3] Rose, *Black Noise*, 21.

[4] T. Mitchell, *Global Noise: Rap and Hip Hop Outside the U.S.A.* (Middletown, CT, 2001); C. Watson, "With Volume! Hip-hoppers and Their Responses to Social and Political Issues before Rap's Golden Age," *African American Research Perspectives 8* (Spring 2002): 117–23; Jamal Shabazz, *Back in the Days* (New York, 2003).

[5] Nancy Guevara, "Women Writin' Rappin' and Breakin'," reprinted in Perkins, *Droppin' Science*, 49–62; Christine Verán, "First Ladies: Fly Females Who Rocked the Mike in the '70s and '80s," in *Hip Hop Divas*, ed., Vibe (New York, 2001), 5–20; Nelson George has tended to downplay the importance of women in rap; however, see his "Rap's Tenth Birthday," *Village Voice* (24 October 1989), 40, as well as *Hip Hop america*.

[6] T. L. Dixon and T. Brooks, "Rap Music and Rap Audiences: Themes, Psychological Effects, and Political Resistance," *African American Research Perspectives 8* (Spring 2002): 106–16; Johnetta Betsch Cole and Beverly Guy-Sheftall, *Gender Talk: The Struggle for Women's Equality in African American Communities* (New York, 2003).

[7] Joan Morgan, for instance, is credited with bringing the intersection of feminism and Hip Hop together in her book *When Chickenheads Come Home to Roost: A Hip Hop Feminist Breaks It Down* (New York, 1999). By academic feminist standards, this book did little to advance or reconfigure feminist discourse, but what this book did do successfully was instigate a broad discussion of feminism within the Hip Hop community at "street" level and express a Hip Hop-situated, vernacular perspective on feminism. In the time since Morgan's book was published, Hip Hop feminism has also consolidated as a formal academic discourse in its own right, thanks in part to a younger generation of feminist scholars who grew up in the Hip Hop era. See, for instance, Gwendolyn Pough, *Check It While I Wreck It: Black Womanhood, Hip Hop Culture, and the Public Sphere* (Boston, 2004).

[8] An extensive discussion of feminism, black feminism, womanism, and their differences is beyond the scope of this article. For purposes of this discussion, feminism is both a social movement opposed to sexism and a critical theory that emphasizes the role of patriarchy in diminishing women's lives, and the term "feminism" denotes the most generic level of this perspective. Black feminism is an anti-sexist perspective rooted in African American women's distinct history of activism that focuses on the multiple and interlocking oppres-

sions and identities that constitute people's experiences as oppressors or members of the oppressed class. Womanism is a relatively vernacular anti-oppressionist perspective devised and espoused by African American and other women of color that partially overlaps with black feminism but contains elements distinctive from either black or white feminism, and is more broadly conceived. Some black feminists consider themselves womanists, while others do not, and vice versa. Use of the term "street level" in conjunction with feminism, black feminism, and womanism in this article refers not to a class distinction per se, but rather to a common historical and experiential thread that all African American women and other women of color share as "everyday women," outside or beyond those social roles and statuses that differentiate them to serve the purposes of bureaucratic society.

[9]Paulette Tee and Sweet Tee, "Vicious Rap," Winely Records (1978); Paulette Tee & Sweet Tee, "To the Beat Y'all," produced by Sylvia Clemments, 1979; Sequence (Cheryl the Pearl, Blondie, and MC Angie B), "Funk You Up," Sugar Hill Records (1980); Queen Lisa Lee, "Zulu Nation Throwdown," Zulu Nation Cosmic Force, 1980; Lisa Lee, Sha Rock, Debbie Dee, "Us Girls," from the film *Wild Style*, 1982; B-side, "Change the Beat," Celluloid Records (1982); Tina Marie, a/k/a Lady Tee, "Square Biz," Motown Records (1981); Debbie Harry and Blondie, "Rapture," Chrysalis Music (1981); Brenda K. Starr, "Vicious Beat," from the film *Beat Street*, 1984; Roxanne Shanté, "The Real Roxanne," produced by Marley Marl, 1984; Eve, "Love is Blind," Interscope Records (1999); Yo-Yo, "Girl, Don't Be No Fool," East West Records (1992); Yo-Yo, "Black Pearl," East West Records (1991); Salt-n-Pepa, "Ain't Nuthin' but a She Thang," Polygram Records (1995); Salt-n-Pepa, "Let's Talk about Sex," Next Plateau Records (1991); TLC, "Hat 2 Da Back," La Face Records (1993); TLC, "Unpretty," La Face Records (1999); Lauryn Hill, "That Thing," Sony Records (1998); Salt-n-Pepa, "Whatta Man," Polygram Records (1993); Erykah Badu, "The Other Side of the Game," Universal Records (1997); Erykah Badu, "Danger," Motown Records (2003); Lauryn Hill, "Sweetest Thing," Sony Records (1998); Jill Scott, "Brotha," Hidden Beach Records (2000); Yo-Yo, "Bonnie and Clyde Theme," Atlantic Records (1993); Eve, "Dog Match," Interscope Records (1999); Foxy Brown, "Letter to the Firm (Holy Matrimony)," Def Jam Records (1996); Foxy Brown, "Bonnie and Clyde Part II," Def Jam Records (1999). For information about the certification of gold and platinum albums mentioned in the text, see Vibe, *Hip Hop Divas* (New York, 2001).

[10]Elliot Liebow, *Tally's Corner: A Study of Negro Street Corner Men* (Boston, 1967).

[11]Bonnie Thornton Dill, "The Dialectics of Black Womanhood," *Signs* 4: 543–55; Paula Giddings, *When and Where I Enter: The Impact of Black Women on Race and Sex in America* (New York, 1984); Beverly Guy-Sheftall, *Daughters of Sorrow* (Brooklyn, NY, 1990); Darlene Clark Hine, "Lifting the Veil, Shattering the Silence: Black Women's History in Slavery and Freedom," in *Black Women in United States History, Vol. 9,* ed., Darlene Clark Hine (Brooklyn, NY, 1990), 235–61; Deborah Gray White, *Too Heavy a Load: Black Women in Defense of Themselves, 1894–1994* (New York, 1996); Angela Y. Davis, *Blues Legacies and Black Feminism* (New York, 1998).

[12]Hine, "Lifting the Veil," 246.

[13]White, *Too Heavy a Load*, 16. See also Combahee River Collective, "A Black Feminist Statement," in *Home Girls: A Black Feminist Anthology*, ed., Barbara Smith (New York, 1982), 272–82, for a similar statement.

[14]Angela Y. Davis, "Black Women and Music: A Historical Legacy of Struggle," in *Wild Women in the Whirlwind: Afro-American Culture and the Contemporary Literary Renaissance*, ed. J. M. Braxton and Andrée Nicola McLaughlin (Brunswick, NJ, 1990), 3–21; George Lipsitz, *Time Passages: Collective Memory and American Popular Culture* (Minneapolis, MN, 1990); Tricia Rose, "Never Trust a Big Butt and a Smile," in *Black Feminist Cultural Criticism*, ed., Jacqueline Bobo (Malden, MA, 2001), 233–54.

[15]For treatments of feminism and womanism at "street" level, see K. Chappell, "Eve and Missy Elliott: Taking Rap to a New Level," *Ebony* 36 (2001): 68–74; K. Dobie, "Love's Labor's Lost," *Vibe* (September 2001): 194–202; dream hampton, "Confessions of a Hip Hop Critic," *Essence* (August 1994); dream hampton, "Flick: Girls Interrupted," *Vibe* (June/July 2000): 169–70; T. Roberts and E. N. Ulen, "Sisters Spin Talk on Hip Hop: Can the Music Be Saved?," *Ms.* (February 2000): 69–74; Linda Villarosa, "Our Girls in Crisis: The War on Girls," *Essence* (September 2002): 92–121.

[16]These have been described as physical, psychological, and economic dislocation, mobility, and insecurity, the fractionation and hybridization of identity, the cannibalization of cultures, the dissolution of social and moral norms, rapid oscillation between euphoria and despair, and the constant barrage of possibilities (par-

ticularly for consumption), among other things. In this environment, consciousness is the chief terrain for both oppression and resistance, and the symbolic/representational realm becomes a crucial site for activism. Fredric Jameson, "Postmodernism, or the Cultural Logic of Late Capitalism," *New Left Review* 1/146 (July/August 1984): 53–92; Chela Sandoval, *Methodology of the Oppressed* (Minneapolis, MN, 2000), 15–37.

[17]Asa G. Hilliard, III, *SBA: The Reawakening of the African Mind* (Gainesville, FL, 1998); John S. Mbiti, *African Religions and Philosophy* (New York, 1970).

[18]T. L. King, "Who You Calling a Feminist? Creating New Feminisms in Popular Music, 1986–1994," doctoral dissertation, Bowling Green State University, 1999; Tracy E. Hopkins, "Eve on Being a Lady," *Essence* (June 2000); Queen Latifah, *Ladies First: Revelations of a Strong Woman* (New York, 2000); Ann O'Connell, "Women in Hip Hop: A Feminist Approach to Female Rap Music," retrieved from http://www.rap.about.com/cs/womeninrap, 15 February 2003.

[19]Dionne Stephens and Layli Phillips, "Freaks, Gold Diggers, Divas, and Dykes: The Sociohistorical Development of African American Adolescent Females' Sexual Scripts," *Sexuality and Culture* 7 (Winter 2003): 3–49.

[20]As an anonymous reviewer pointed out, this comparison begs additional questions, such as "How does Hip Hop compare with R&B as the younger generation's response to the oppressive social, political, and economic establishment?" and "How does Hip Hop compare with Hard Rock in its response to postmodernism?" Although a complete response to these interesting questions is beyond the scope of this paper, at the most basic level, it could be stated that R&B corresponded in tone to the tactical timbre of the Civil Rights Movement, while Hip Hop, like Rock 'n' Roll, is more strident and provocative. As for Hard Rock and its spinoffs, including heavy metal, speed metal, death metal, and perhaps even punk (which isn't a technically a spin-off, but a distinct genre), these responses to postmodernity were distinctly white and reflected white culture's distraught and somewhat pessimistic response to conditions of its own creating. While Hip Hop can be comparably violent and "real," overall (and there are a few exceptions), it tends to be more optimistic about both human nature and humanity's future.

[21]We are currently preparing a more complete discussion of women's discursive strands in rap and Hip Hop in another article. These discursive strands, when viewed in their entirety, give a clearer perspective on the liberatory potential of women's Hip Hop and rap as well as a more detailed picture of the progressive racial, sexual, and class politics implicit within their lyrics and videos.

[22]Rap lyrics, particularly those that are captured in their recorded rather than their published form, are transcribed differently by different people. In this paper, we will present lines from rap songs not in the typical "poetic" form, which uses slashes (/) between rhyming lines, but, rather, in "sentence" form, which uses regular punctuation to mark the beginning and end of ideas which may or may not correspond with rhyming lines. The reason for this choice is the authors' desire to highlight female rap performers' complete thoughts about the topics in question, with less regard for their artistic presentation or packaging.

[23]Rose provides an insightful dissection of this song and its video in "Never Trust a Big Butt and a Smile."

[24]Insightful analyses of the video for this song are provided by R. A. Emerson, "'Where My Girls At?': Negotiating Black Womanhood in Music Videos," *Gender and Society* 16 (Spring 2002): 115–35, and Donna Troka, "'You Heard My Gun Cock': Female Agency and Aggression in Contemporary Rap," *African American Research Perspectives* 8 (Spring 2002): 82–89.

[25]Patricia Hill Collins, *Black Feminist Thought: Knowledge, Empowerment, and the Politics of Consciousness, 2nd Ed.* (New York, 2000); M. Foreman, "'Movin' Closer to an Independent Funk': Black Feminist Theory, Standpoint and Women in Rap," *Women's Studies* 23 (Spring 1991): 35–55; Patricia Hill Collins, *Black Sexual Politics: African Americans, Gender, and the New Racism* (New York, 2004).

[26]C. E. Stokes and L. M. Gant, "Turning the Tables on the HIV/AIDS Epidemic: Hip Hop as a Tool for Teaching African-American Adolescent Girls," *African American Research Perspectives* 8 (Spring 2002): 70–81.

[27]Alice Walker, *In Search of Our Mothers' Gardens: Womanist Prose* (New York, 1983). Walker wrote that the womanist is "a black feminist or feminist of color" who is "committed to survival and wholeness of entire people, male *and* female" (xi, italics original).

[28]This phrase is borrowed from Shirley Chisholm, *Unbought and Unbossed* (New York, 1970).

[29]Angela Ards, "Where Is the (Black) Love?," *Ms. Magazine* (August/September 2001); Bakari Kitwana, *The Hip Hop Generation: Young Blacks and the Crisis in African-American Culture* (New York, 2002).

[30]Rafael Peréz-Torres, "Mouthing Off: Polyglossia and Radical Mestizaje," in *Movements in Chicano Poetry: Against Myths, Against Margins*, ed., Rafael Peréz-Torres (New York, 1995), 208–42.

[31]Chela Sandoval, *Methodology of the Oppressed* (Minneapolis, MN, 2000).

DISCOGRAPHY

Erykah Badu, "Other Side of the Game," *Baduizm*, Kedar International (1997).
Erykah Badu, "Danger," *World Wide Underground*, Motown (2003).
Bee Side, "Change the Beat," no title, Celluloid Records, France (1982).
Blondie, "Rapture," Chrysalis (1981).
Da Brat, *Funkdafied*, So So Def Recordings/Chaos (1994).
Doug E. Fresh (feat. MC Ricky D), "The Show," Reality (1985).
Missy Elliott, *Supa Dupa Fly*, Gold Mine/East West (1997).
Eve, "Love Is Blind," *Ruff Ryders' First Lady*, Interscope Records (1999).
Eve (feat. DMX), "Dog Match," *Ruff Ryders' First Lady*, Interscope Records (1999).
J. J. Fad, "Supersonic," *Supersonic*, Dream Team Records (1987).
Foxy Brown, "Letter to the Firm (Holy Matrimony)," *Ill Na Na*, Violator/Def Jam Music Group (1996).
Foxy Brown (feat. Jay-Z), "Bonnie and Clyde Part II," *Chyna Doll*, Violator/Def Jam Music Group (1999).
Lauryn Hill, "Doo Wop (That Thing)," *The Miseducation of Lauryn Hill*, Ruff House/Columbia (1998).
Lauryn Hill, "Sweetest Thing," *Love Jones: The Music*, Ruff House/Columbia (1998).
Lady B, "To the Beat Y'All," Tech Records (1979).
Lisa Lee, "Zulu Nation Throwdown," Paul Winley (1980).
MC Lyte, "Ruffneck," Atlantic (1991).
Ms. Jade (feat. Lil' Mo), "Why You Tell Me That?," *Girl Interrupted*, Beat Club Records/Interscope Records (2002).
Queen Latifah (feat. Monie Love), "Ladies 1st," *All Hail the Queen*, Tommy Boy (1989).
Queen Latifah, "U.N.I.T.Y.," *Black Reign*, Motown (1993).
The Real Roxanne, "The Real Roxanne," Select (1984).
Roxanne Shanté, "Roxanne's Revenge," Pop Art Music (1984).
Salt-n-Pepa, *A Salt with a Deadly Pepa*, Next Plateau Records (1987).
Salt-n-Pepa, "Ain't Nuthin' but a She-Thing," London Records (1995).
Salt-n-Pepa, "Let's Talk about AIDS," London Records (1991).
Salt-n-Pepa, "Let's Talk about Sex," *Blacks' Magic*, Next Plateau Records (1991).
Salt-n-Pepa, "Tramp," *Hot, Cool & Vicious*, Next Plateau Records (1985).
Salt-n-Pepa, "Whatta Man," *Very Necessary*, Next Plateau Records (1994).
Jill Scott, "Brotha," *Who Is Jill Scott? Words and Sounds, Vol. 1*, Hidden Beach Recordings/Epic (2000).
Sequence, "Funk You Up," Sugar Hill (1980).
Sparky D, "Sparky's Turn (Roxanne You're Through)," Nia (1985).
Brenda K. Starr, "Vicious Beat," Mirage (1984).
Sugarhill Gang, "Rapper's Delight," Sugar Hill (1979).
Supernature, "The Show Stoppa (Is Stupid Fresh)," London Records (1985).
Paulette Tee & Sweet Tee, "Vicious Rap," Winley Records (1978).
Teena Marie (a/k/a Lady Tee), "Square Biz," Gordy (1980).
TLC, "Hat 2 Da Back," *Ooooooohhh . . . On the TLC Tip*, La Face Records (1993).
TLC, "Unpretty," *CrazySexyCool*, La Face Records (1998).
Trina, "Watch Yo Back," *Da Baddest Bitch*, Slip-N-Slide/Atlantic (2000).
U.T.F.O., "Roxanne, Roxanne," *U.T.F.O.*, Select Records (1984).
Yo-Yo, "Girl, Don't Be No Fool," *Make Way for the Motherlode*, Atlantic/East West Records of America (1992).
Yo-Yo, "Black Pearl," *Black Pearl*, Atlantic/East West Records of America (1992).

"THAT SUPPOSED TO BE ME?" YOUNG BLACK WOMEN TALK BACK TO "HIP HOP"

Aimee Meredith Cox

Unlike the pre-civil rights era, the mechanisms of racism and the mark left by the color line are not so easily distinguishable, their sources not so readily identified. Part of this, it has been argued, is due to an increased visibility of the black middle class in positions that appear to be ones of power, influence, and significance.[1] I believe that it is additionally due to the construction and representation of an urban black lower-class. The increased visibility of black urban culture occurs through its presentation as a product to be consumed or appropriated. Black youth, in particular, populate the radio airwaves, sell products with their bodies, music, and style and generally represent the oddly profitable mix of danger, excitement, modernity, and otherness that mainstream American culture (comprised of all races) is so eager to consume. And yet, rather than celebrating the profound creativity, resourcefulness, and intelligence of this youth culture, identified as Hip Hop culture, it is often denigrated as a culture based primarily in criminal or deviant behavior. This essay explores how young African American women who have been categorized as at-risk, high-risk and, homeless, articulate their understanding of Hip Hop culture, along with the relevancy of Hip Hop to their own self-defined identities as young black women striving to improve their life chances.

The contradictory approach to the promotion of black youth culture presents it as both a symbol of progress and vehicle of aesthetic pleasure while also implying through its representation that it is a threat to the sanctity of middle-class norms, conservative idealizations of the nuclear family, and white youth.[2] The black youth engaged in cultural productions understand their creations to involve the contestation over public space, expressive meaning, interpretation, and cultural capital.[3] The corporate, institutional, and legislative bodies involved in this struggle for representation are just as keenly aware of the power of marginalized youth giving voice (and more importantly being heard). Thus, the marketing and consumption of Hip Hop culture becomes a way to regulate and control the image of black youth. At the same time, the hyper-visibility of black youth as thugs, criminals, and deviants gives permission for us all to ignore the structures of inequality and neglect that have relegated low-income young blacks to the margins of society.[4]

An important element that facilitates the appropriation and consumption of black youth culture is the idea of authentic identities. What it means to be authentically black is context dependent. However, the most prominent image of real or true blackness portrayed in the mass media relies on stereotypes that present blacks as inferior and unable to meet ideals associated with whiteness and middle class culture. More recently, authentic blackness has been tied to Hip Hop culture. Both those who claim

113

to be representatives of Hip Hop culture as well as those who assess and represent it from the outside, manipulate the meanings in these cultural productions to reflect an idea of true blackness. Depending on who you talk to and under what circumstances, this true or real blackness can be associated with surviving poverty and danger in the inner city, simply living in the inner city, being politically conscious and active in the black community, wearing clothes designed by rap moguls and listening to rap music, being a murderous drug dealer or fearlessly championing the freedom of all oppressed people on a global level. The range of descriptors and definitions for members of Hip Hop culture demonstrates the highly contested nature of Hip Hop as a locus of potential power by those who chose to identify with it as well as those who attempt to identify what it is. Marginalized young black women's tensions in defining Hip Hop reveal the complicated and continually shifting nature of their own racial, cultural and gender identifications.

The ethnographic data presented here is drawn from nearly three years of fieldwork and a total of five years of engagement with a homeless shelter and transitional living program for young women located in Detroit called Fresh Start. The Fresh Start shelter is much more than just a warming center or temporary reprieve from the streets. The goal of the shelter program is to provide social support, training, and structured guidance to young women between the ages of 15 and 21 who do not have a safe or viable place to live, so that they may transition out of homelessness and into safe independent living situations or reunification with their families. A third of the Fresh Start residents at any given time are young women with children in their care. Historically, the racial makeup of the program mirrors that of inner city Detroit: the vast majority (98.5%) of the young women being African American.

Fresh Start has a reputation as a trail-blazing agency known for its strength-based approach to ensuring positive youth development. This, in lay terms, means that the organizational practices of the shelter are guided by the belief that young people can chart positive courses for their lives, and that the best way to support them in doing this is by focusing on their capabilities, strengths, and talents. This philosophy extends to all branches of the agency's programs in the form of leadership development, peer training and education, and cooperative planning between the staff and the young women. In addition, Fresh Start claims to honor the diversity of the girls and young women by promoting a highly individualized program of service delivery. The quality and type of services advocated by Fresh Start combined with the demographics of the young women in the program provided an ideal site from which to consider issues of self-concept and identity negotiation among black girls. *Ghetto, adolescent, poor, early pregnancy, teen mother, urban, high school drop-out, gang-affiliated, drug abusers, drug sellers*—these are some of the labels attached to Fresh Start's target population. These labels, by and large considered social stigmas, create an image of these young women that makes them identifiable in society primarily by their level of risk and potential threat.

"At risk" and "high risk" are terms that have become interchangeable with inner-city youth of color, yet Fresh Start attempts to override the negative assumptions attached to their target population through an environment meant to celebrate and promote positive identity formation. Based on this information, the question for me became: How can an environment that works to nurture and validate the experiences of young black women impact the way its participants view themselves and their potential to produce positive, sustainable change in their lives? And, additionally, how do the young black women at Fresh Start respond to the agency's self-defined strategies for empowering and "improving" them in light of the strategies they have learned to employ on their own.

It is probably not surprising that media culture and its specific focus on the ever-evolving cultural productions known as Hip Hop had a significant impact on how the young women of Fresh Start framed the discussion of the larger social landscape and their particular location within it. Similar to the multiple ways that they imagined themselves, their conceptions of Hip Hop were often conflicting, context dependent, and complicated by overly simplistic mainstream assumptions of what they and it can and should be. The young women whose voices are presented in this essay represent a range of experiences and perspectives even though these experiences and perspectives are never accurately captured under the umbrella of their collective identity as a target population. Among the group of informants who share their critical insight on the meaning and impact of Hip Hop in their lives, Crystal at 16 is the youngest and Shavon at 21 is the oldest. The circumstances that led to homelessness for these adolescent girls range from Jaycees's eviction for inability to pay rent after her boyfriend moved out to Crystal's refusal to share space with her mother's emotionally abusive boyfriend. All but one of the young women, Ty, were participants in a peer education outreach project called the Move Experiment.

THE MOVE EXPERIMENT: RECLAIMING "HIP HOP"

The Move Experiment was a project that emerged in the shelter as a response from a group of residents to their overidentification as a target population, frustration with the challenges of asserting their individual identities and what they believed to be the staff's overemphasis on the superficial, exterior aspects of how they looked, dressed, and carried themselves. Within the Move Experiment dance, choreography, poetry, and storytelling became the tools that the shelter residents used to rearticulate their identities and speak back to the assumptions and expectations of the Fresh Start staff, the larger society outside of the shelter as well as an all-pervasive media culture that simultaneously exploited and silenced them.

Although I fulfilled many roles during the five years that I was both researching and working at Fresh Start (including case planner, program coordinator, and even interim Shelter Director), most of the young women in the shelter knew me as the "dance lady" due to my initial and, apparently in their eyes, most relevant position in the organization as the volunteer coordinator of a once-a-week dance workshop. I was no longer officially employed but still officially conducting my field research at Fresh Start when Shavon and Jaycee, two of the longest term Fresh Start residents, asked if

I would help them coordinate what would eventually become the Move Experiment. This request came at the height of the infamous "headscarf riot." The fact that the incident known as the "headscarf riot" was called a riot even though no actions remotely close to riot behavior were ever demonstrated speaks to the always present, underlying assumption that the shelter residents are, by nature, violent, threatening, and ready to act out of the social order. What actually happened sounds much less thrilling than the word riot would imply. Nearly two-thirds of the resident population refused to attend the mandatory educational workshops or participate in job searching activities as a form of protest against a new program policy that forbade them from wearing headscarves in public shelter spaces like the computer, activity, and dining rooms.

The staff's position was that the bandanas and brightly colored fabric scarves tied around the heads of the young women "looked ghetto" and mocked the environment of professionalism and productivity the shelter was trying to create and promote. The young women's perspective on the headscarves was purely utilitarian. To them, the headscarves were a practical way to extend the life of the fairly expensive hairstyles they needed to maintain in order to make the appropriate impression as they searched for jobs and applied for entrance into other training and vocational programs. The residents referenced their financial literacy classes and talked about the headscarves as a critical cost saving strategy. Wrapping their heads was a conscious, rational choice to extend the life of hairstyles that added to the professional appearance they needed to exhibit in the various professional settings they were required to mediate outside of the shelter.

"It don't make no sense," Trina, a long-term resident told me, "for them to try to tell us that we need to do this and that and look a certain way to get a job and when we try do that we get called ghetto. We are homeless, how are we supposed to have money to get our hair done every week?" Trina's comment encapsulates the contradiction that many of the young women identify in the implementation of the program: the focus is more on appearances than actual skill development and resource building; that as program participants they are simply prepped to appear as if they could attain jobs that in reality don't exist in inner-city Detroit.

In my conversations with staff members, "ghetto" and "Hip Hop" were terms that were used interchangeably to define aspects of the young women's dress, style, attitude, language, and behavior that they found unacceptable. Used in this way, Hip Hop was the antithesis of progress, success and productivity and, perhaps, the biggest threat to social mobility for the shelter residents. It is interesting, then, that out of frustration with the hypocrisy exhibited by the program staff in the appropriation of the term Hip Hop, the young women combated this misidentification with their own Hip Hop weapon: the fearless expression of their self-defined identities. Although, as will be shown in the conversations and interactions with the Fresh Start residents, there was no singular idea of what Hip Hop was, most of the young women agreed that what it could and should be was the empowered performance of self in everyday life. The Move Experiment provided this performance space.

Together five young women from the shelter and I wrote a grant proposal so that the Move Experiment (like the other peer education outreach programs focused on alcohol and drug abuse education, safer sex, and academic success) could receive enough funding to actually hire young women in the shelter to facilitate the program they envisioned. Choreographed and spontaneous dance movements, passion-driven words scrawled in composition books, and the rhythmic tones of scratchy voices reciting these words were the young women's reconstituted performances meant to replace the acts of self-erasure they were asked to perform in their daily navigation of shelter duties, case planning meetings, welfare appointments, low-wage work shifts, and ongoing family drama. The peer educators, then, took what they learned from their performative processes and shared this with other young women through movement and storywriting workshops held in the shelter, at after-school programs, in juvenile justice facilities, community centers, and high schools. Giving other marginalized young women the permission to express a critical, individual voice was something the peer educators identified as distinctly Hip Hop.

The Move Experiment peer educators as well as the larger population of Fresh Start residents were constantly, if not always consciously, reacting to the Hip Hop aesthetic that has become almost synonymous with popular culture. In the process, they demonstrated their frustrations in locating space and a voice for themselves in a culture that is marketed and popularly conceived as their own, but is often foreign and alienating. And yet these young women managed to devise new definitions of what it means to be "authentically female," "really black," and "truly young" upsetting the unchecked arrogance of these terms in the process.

Much of the recent proliferation of work done in the academy on Hip Hop culture has focused almost exclusively on rap music (glossing over or ignoring other cultural forms such as visual art, dance, and narrative writing). Within the literature on rap music, two extremes of the form are most commonly examined: gangsta rap and politically conscious rap. The focus on these two genres makes it appear as if Hip Hop culture is either violent and nihilistic or only concerned with producing art with the purpose of fighting the system. Lyrics are dissected for both their superficial and assumed deeper meanings and connections made between the reality framed by the rappers' words and the reality of life on the actual streets and communities they reference. The cultural productions of male artists dominate this literature. Female voices enter the conversation through third wave black feminists interested in defining the misogynist contours of the music and assessing what the image of black women within it says about the heterosexual relationships in the black community. How young women most affected by these images process and respond to them is rarely considered. Their voices are instead replaced with the prioritized knowledge of the scholars who speak in their place. The first consideration I had in thinking about how the young women at Fresh Start critically engage with Hip Hop was the nature of Hip Hop itself.

In trying to articulate what it is, I realized that my conception of Hip Hop is directly tied to the way it has been sold to me through the media. Hip Hop is, in this common-sense media driven view, related to the aesthetics of black youth culture now co-opted and commodified as a global youth culture. But how is this so-called black culture different from the music, clothing styles, dances, language, and other cultural productions of black kids when I was growing up, before it was officially stamped with the label: Hip Hop? Was it just black music, black dance, and slang before the emergence of Hip Hop? Is the only difference the change in its financial capital; directly linked to the cultural capital where the stigma of "acting black" can be erased in middle-class homes now that Hip Hop is universal? Hip Hop scholars[5] take a more proactive approach by tracing the emergence of Hip Hop to the Bronx in the late 70s where the innovative use of turntables over spoken work rhythmic verses, street battles (that used words instead of weapons and break dancing bodies instead of fists) became the symbols of a new urban youth aesthetic. I still wondered, however, how break dancing differed so much from the made up dance battles we had in the driveways on our all black block or the combative style of crumpin' dance that came out of the West Coast. What is so different about the space in between those bootleg teen dance battles and the crumpin' featured in the film *Rize*[6] that allows it to be deemed Hip Hop? Or maybe they all fit under the rubric, depending on your definition. Through my conversations and interaction with the young women at Fresh Start, I sought to understand how they reconcile their personal histories, memories, aesthetics, and beliefs with Hip Hop culture as they know it.

In my work with the Move Experiment peer educators as well as more generally with the larger community of young women at Fresh Start, several significant themes emerged in their discourse on Hip Hop culture: the difficulty in defining its parameters; Hip Hop as a reflection of an enlightened community consciousness; Hip Hop as marketable commodity; Hip Hop's historical ties to jazz and the blues as something definitively African American and absolutely carried and felt in the blood; and the representations of black female bodies.

DIFFICULT DEFINITIONS

Okay. Hip-hop is a way of life to me. It is a culture. It is not just like . . . most people want to put Hip Hop like it is just music. No, Hip Hop got so many more elements to it. It is a way of life. It is how you carry yourself.

—Crystal 16

Crystal makes this statement after going verbally back and forth with Sophie, Ty, and Shavon for the past twenty minutes in an attempt to define Hip Hop. The conversation started after Sophie, an eighteen-year-old white girl who has come to the shelter to teach yoga,[7] mentions that the majority of the kids in her suburban predominantly white school listen to Hip Hop music almost exclusively. When Crystal tells Sophie that she and her friends may enjoy Hip Hop but can never be included as part of what she calls "the Hip Hop life," Sophie and the other girls press Crystal to define what constitutes a Hip Hop life. Crystal pauses for a long time, thoughtfully considering how to answer the question posed to her.

"To me, I think, living the Hip Hop life is like everybody . . . like things . . . like most things in Hip Hop is kind of negative but it is that positive aspect to it like you wanna help people, you wanna make changes through music," Crystal spoke these words slowly taking in the reactions of the other young women scattered around the shelter's large activity room. Crystal continued fueled by the attention of all eyes on her, "Or they may be active in the community. And they be taking from the old Hip Hop kind of style like people who had the messages out there and like...we need to empower each other. That's the kind of Hip Hop that I see like the positive aspect of it. And like the older Hip Hop people not coming out talking about they jewelry and they bling-bling or whatever and they was talking about where they grew up and how they want to change us and like the difference they want to see happen in the community."

Crystal reinforces the idea that there are two different kinds of Hip Hop after telling us that it is a way of life as well as the way people carry themselves. To explain the positive aspects of what she calls living the Hip Hop life she talks about helping people, making change through music and referencing one's roots and community as a way to make a difference. Crystal has a clear idea of Hip Hop as based in the urban community and beneficial primarily for its ability to make change there. This link between Hip Hop and the community and the idea that music, art and performance should and must lead to affecting social change is the mission that Crystal and the other peer educators work from in the Move Experiment. It became apparent to me after the first few weeks of working with the peer educators in the Move Experiment that the young women were developing a sense of themselves as artists and community educators in a way that empowered them to think differently about the potential significance of Hip Hop as a vehicle for developing social and personal change among the members of their identified community. It is important to note that the way community was referenced by all of the young women described poor black urban communities similar to the pockets of neighborhoods in which they grew up in surrounding metropolitan Detroit. Even Sophie used community in this way and understood that the bodies and spaces implicated within the word did not necessarily reference her experience as a young economically privileged white woman in America.

In other conversations about Hip Hop that I both overheard and participated in at Fresh Start, some of the other young women demonstrated more ambivalence than Crystal regarding what they believed to be the definition of Hip Hop. In these conversations, Hip Hop and blackness or black culture were talked about synonymously. Hip Hop was used as another way to call someone or something black. However, when this racialized definition of Hip Hop became challenged by its consumption by the nonblack and nonpoor, the young women made the distinction between their ownership of Hip Hop and the televised, media driven version that they saw primarily as a commodity.

For example, when Sophie talks about the prevalence of Hip Hop music in her all white school, Shavon lets her know that "You can be a part of Hip Hop culture but you can't be a part of black culture. Black culture is what I am from, Boo; Hip Hop is what they want you to buy."

Through this discursive move, Shavon lets Sophie know that Hip Hop is the commodified version of black culture that Sophie may be able to partially identify with but will be able to fully claim as her own. The marketing, packaging, and selling of Hip Hop music and aesthetics is something that the young women at Fresh Start see as the continuation of an historical legacy of appropriation of black cultural productions.

When Jaycee explains this to me she says, "You can like it and take it and then try to make money off of it. Just like with blues and, like, with Elvis Presley and all that junk, but that don't make it yours."

Who is allowed attribution for the creation and ownership of Hip Hop is a question that informs, for these young women, the legitimacy in using the term Hip Hop in the first place. And yet, the majority of the younger women at Fresh Start (those under the age of 17) have difficulty relating to the term at all. This slightly younger generation saw no utility in using the term and appeared to blatantly avoid voicing the word.

As one 15 year old resident told me, "I don't use the word Hip Hop because it don't mean nothing to me." This did not mean, however, that these younger women were unfamiliar with the cultural productions, lifestyle, aesthetics, and personalities that the older young women talked about in their discussions of Hip Hop. Upon further probing of these young women it became clear that several things were at play. First of all, in their minds, Hip Hop was a term manufactured by the media and pushed on them by a mainstream society that could pick and choose the aspects of black culture it found appealing and, therefore, profitable. They were defiantly responding to the power in naming and identifying by choosing to not use language that did not belong to nor respect them. These younger women were highly suspicious of language that could be used in one instance to compliment and promote and in the next to criminalize and condemn. So, they chose to entirely renounce Hip Hop as a meaningful label and moniker.

Crystal, Sophie, Shavon, Jaycee, and the other Fresh Start residents represent conflicting views on the term Hip Hop, and even within their own definitions struggle for coherence. It seems as if Hip Hop is connected to, emblematic of and yet separable from their ideas of black culture. Hip-hop is brushed off as meaningless in one breath and then hotly contested in the next when it appears threatened by another young woman's definition. Additionally, all of the young women made a clear distinction between the word Hip Hop and what the word was meant to signify. In some cases, the young women assert that usage of the term denies and disrespects black culture. In other cases, as in Crystal's interaction with Sophie, Hip Hop is used to represent the whitening of black artistic productions. In this way, Hip Hop becomes the official name assigned to the mimicry of an authentic blackness.

"THIS JUNK IS IN YOUR BLOOD": TRUTH TELLING AND THE BLUES TRADITION

"What is wrong with you? This junk is in your blood. You can do this! You was born to do this." Crystal was beyond frustrated with Ashley at this point. She was coaching Ashley along as she ran through the African dance solo she choreographed for herself for the performance less than three weeks away.

Crystal's comment to Ashley above was made is an attempt to pull out of Ashley a certain feeling or emotive quality that she felt was lacking. Crystal, like the other peer educators would often use phrases like "I can't feel you," "you aren't feeling it," and "make me feel something" to express what they believed to be the most significant property of good dance: the ability to move an audience and to express, as the dancer, your own emotional vulnerability in the process. Along with the comments related to wanting to feel something the dancers also talked about dancing being something that comes naturally to them, that is organic and therefore somehow in the blood. Consequently, all of the peer educators assumed that by virtue of having this dance ability in their blood they possessed the innate capacity to become good dancers.

In much the same way that the peer educators at Fresh Start discussed dance as something deeply rooted in bodily memory and bloodlines, their discourse on Hip Hop often emphasized their belief that real Hip Hop or good Hip Hop was carried in the blood and revealed often painful truths. In terms of the music and performance of Hip Hop artists, the ability to convey a personal story with sincerity and passion seemed to be the hallmarks of artistry for most of the young women I worked with both within and outside of the Move Experiment. Mary J. Blige, a soulful R&B singer alternately known as the Queen of Hip Hop, ranked #1 at the top of 12 out of 13 shelter resident's favorite performers list in an informal survey I conducted during one of the in-house workshops.

"She is just real and sings from the heart," "You feel everything she sings like it is coming straight out of her skin through her pores," "Man, I don't even like her voice but I always feel something when she tells her story," are just some of the ways the respondents characterized why they enjoyed listening to Mary J. Blige and felt that she rightfully earned her title as Hip Hop royalty. It was not that Mary J. was deemed the best singer with the best voice or musical arrangements; it was her emotional vulnerability and clear embodiment of her lyrics that won praise from the young women. In her lyrics and in media interviews, Mary J. Blige is very open about her past drug abuse, unhealthy relationships and battles with self-hatred and depression. This willingness to express a depth of feeling and self-consciously tell her personal story both within and outside of her artistic medium makes Mary a role model for the young women as they seek templates for positive choices in their own journeys through life.

The effort to transcend current life circumstances and move toward more socially and economically empowered positions is an enormous focus and expenditure of energy for the young women at Fresh Start. They call this effort "the struggle" and created the term *struggly* to define anyone and anything that outwardly bears the mark of this effort. On any given Friday or Saturday night over the sound of music videos playing in the background in harmony with the rise and fall of laughter in the activity room, I often heard the word *struggly* emerge in casual conversation as a compliment to describe why the vocals of a particular rap artist were considered emotionally moving or intellectually challenging. Jay-Z and 50 Cent both fell into this category even though they often rap about the excess of money and substantial positions of power they have attained in their lives. "It," as Jaycee tells me, "is still a part of their voice. They may have some money and gotten out of their old environment, but they still struggly just by being black and still communicating with all of us in the 'hood."

In *The Black Dancing Body* Brenda Dixon-Gottschild outlines some of the key distinctions made between Africanist and European dance.[8] In this important, innovative work, Dixon-Gottschild talks about how in African-centered or emergent dance, energy determines form and that there is a "go for broke" "give it your all" African American aesthetic that places emotion rather than motion as the primary means of expression. In the Move Experiment emotional intensity and focused engagement in the dance was an important component of making the dance believable in the minds of the peer educators. And, all of the peer educators, including Sonya and Rosetta who were not African American, were seen as having this emotional intensity by virtue of their experience in the struggle. Sonya's homeless status and experience growing up in a black neighborhood meant that she was automatically included among the "struggly" even though she was Italian American. Rosetta's Mexican-Americanness, residence in southwest Detroit, economic status, and identification as a "brown girl" meant that she was also a part of the struggle and carried the ability to convey this in her blood. For the peer educators, all dance was about telling a story and using the body as the vehicle through which energy motivated by emotion could be channeled. This process of testifying and witnessing was an important part of how they defined true Hip Hop expression.

On our half-hour breaks in between our series of summer workshops with groups of middle-school girls, Shavon, Jaycee, Rosetta, Crystal, and I would sit, rest, and talk on the carpeted floor of the multipurpose room in the agency. It was during one of these breaks that Crystal told us about her uncles, jazz musicians from the south who moved to Detroit in the early 1960s to seek fame as performers and wealth as workers in the then booming automotive industry.

Crystal: They [her uncles] played the blues and they was a trip but they used to let all the boys in the family learn how to play instruments but they was said no to the girls. But they played all this blues stuff for us. Ma Rainey, like she was sweet to me. I don't care. Like that is the first time I had heard that kind of music like of somebody talking like that like old blues women. And I like them because they just came out straight with it. If they had it on they minds, they was saying it. I like that. I like people like that who are going to speak their minds and be real with it. And it's like a whole lot of poets too. Like there's like a whole lot of poets now that just come out and tell you, like this is what I'm feeling and I'm going to let you know.

The other young women were ready to respond to Crystal:

Jaycee: I like when celebrities speak they mind. Like, Kanye West. Most of his stuff is about uplifting or whatever but of course he made his little comment about Bush. And now everybody can't stop talking about it, one little comment. He just said it like, "Oh Bush don't care about black people," like he was just talking to anybody and then just went on.

Rosetta: I thought that was cool. It was out of the blue.

Shavon: But people like, "Oh Kanye West this, Kanye West that" but he ain't the first black person to say that. Blacks been saying that since he got in office. Why is they on him like that? Like, if anybody positive is in Hip Hop they going to have the most stuff said about them. They going to find the most dirt.

And, then, Crystal brings the conversation back to the connection between contemporary performers and what she identifies as an enduring jazz legacy.

Crystal: I like just don't like people who don't respect they self or like conform to like what they think they need to do. So, cause it is like a whole lot of people in the music industry who come out strong and them all of a sudden they just so commercial and I'm like, "Why am I listening to this? I can hear this song any old kind of day." There is nothing that is standing out about it. Alicia Keyes when she first came out people want her to change the way she sing, the way she feel, like her soulful everything. So, she was like, "No. Imma wait cause either way it go I'm going to make it with our without you." And she waited and she made it just the way she wanted to. I like that. I think the determination and focus of that. And like she like the blues women. Like they was sayin some real stuff in those songs. It was like everything we go through today, they was talking about it then.

Celebrities have the potential to be role models but are also harshly judged for behavior that demonstrates self-disrespect. Lil' Kim for example was strongly criticized by the young women for both her physical appearance and behavior that they labeled as symptomatic of a poor self-image. Lil' Kim morphs herself into a new indistinguishable being through plastic surgery and capitalizes on the media attention around her impending jail sentence by playing up her obnoxious antics rather than passing on a lesson. People like Mary J. Blige, Queen Latifah, Alicia Keyes, and Kanye West were respected because they take risks musically that challenge expectations, remain true to their convictions, and represent strength and individuality.

123

It is also interesting that Alicia Keyes is compared with the tradition of blues women—specifically Ma Rainey. Crystal can boast familiarity with Ma Rainey, Bessie Smith, and Billie Holiday from the exposure her great uncles provided. The other young women, even if they had not heard their music actually played, were familiar with their names and understood that strength, assertiveness, resiliency, and humor were characteristic of their music. Crystal understands, and later shares in more depth with the other girls, how these qualities were also central to these women's lives. Kanye West's speaking out against President Bush's dismissal of poor black communities is a part of this blues tradition where people were honest and just "came out straight with it." The blues is a conscious memory shared with Crystal from her uncles and a blood memory for the other girls as they discuss how current artists perform the truth in their music and appear to lead their lives in ways that these young women both easily recognize and respect.

IMPLICATIONS OF VIDEO CULTURE: BLACK DANCING BODIES (BOOTIES) AND ARTISTIC FREEDOM

A point of contestation among the young women at Fresh Start was the image of women portrayed in rap music and videos. When the conversation turned to "the disgrace that is the rap video" as Linda put it, everyone had something to say. The shelter residents started off by stating that they only get to watch music videos when they visit their friends or relatives since the shelter does not have cable. When I tell them that I made the decision to take cable out of the shelter when I was the shelter director (a decision that apparently stuck), the discussion expands to include questions of censorship and the assumed inability of young people to critically engage with media. It also revealed my own biases and assumptions regarding the impact of the representations of rap music on young women. Here, my professional role as the Shelter Director ungracefully collides with my personal values as a youth advocate and researcher.

Linda: Oh, you was the one!

[Linda points at me in mock anger making everyone laugh.]
Linda: Why you do that?

AC: To be honest, initially it was a financial decision. We needed to cut down on expenses in the shelter and cable seemed like an extra. I didn't want to take away from the food or supply budget. But, I won't act like I wasn't happy to see the changes after it was cut off. No more fighting over the TV was definitely a plus.

Linda: But there is a bunch of educational stuff that you can only get from cable. Like the nature channel and those shows where they show people traveling to different continents.

124

AC: Right. But I guarantee you that nobody was interested in watching the nature channel. It was booty videos all day long.

Crystal: I know, right! I bet even them staff was up there watching BET all day long too from what I hear.

Ty: I mean but damn for real, though . . . ya'll like . . . man! We only get to watch like .00001 hours of TV a day anyhow. You been out working all day and can't sit down for a minute with a little Jay-Z?

Sophie: That does seem a tad harsh.

AC: Okay, so now you are all going to come for me? In an ideal world where residents were active during the day and used TV as a break that is one thing. But, music videos all day long? How is that an effective program?

Ty: What you got against videos?

AC: In general nothing but as the only activity is somebody's day. . . .

Macy: I can see that. I mean if I was running a program for girls how I look letting them watch booty shakin' all day long? I get tired of that mess myself. I be like, turn that crap off, when I'm at my boyfriend's house.

Linda: I know . . . I be like If I see one more shaking black ass. . . .

Ty: But ya'll just sitting up here acting like all music videos are about showing ass. There are a lot that are off the hook and real artistic. Like using special effects and cartoons and stuff. Like images that really bring out the beat in the music. Like Outkast has some creative ideas.

Sophie: Plus a lot of artists use videos to make social messages like what Crystal was talking about before.

Crystal: Yeah. and most still about shakin' ass.

The exchange above allowed me to see how even though my research is motivated by the belief in the critical consciousness of marginalized black women and their ability to strategically read and respond to hegemony, my innate response to them does not always reflect this belief. My actions as a Fresh Start employee were often influenced, for better or for worse, by my personal experiences and orientations as a middle-class adult black woman. I did turn off the cable to save money but was more than happy to also cut off the seemingly never-ending stream of half-naked brown and black bodies gyrating across the screen. It was not that I found these bodies offensive or was unable to see their beauty. I was simply tired of them being the overwhelming representation of brown and black female bodies presented to the residents; there was no balance in the distribution of images of black women on the screen. This was, in my opinion, potentially unhealthy to the way these young women formed opinions of themselves. I had not considered the action I took as censorship even by default (we couldn't afford digital cable). It felt like common sense. So much so, that I had not fully reflected on it until this group interview.

The actual impact on young women of the image of the female body in videos cannot be simplistically identified for each young woman reads these images based on the way she feels about herself at the time, what she believes to be the intention of the image, comparisons to other representations, the influence of peers, and a myriad of other factors. Artists such as Andre 3000 and Big Boi from OutKast create innovative music that contests the boundaries of rap and what is typically considered black or Hip Hop musical style. Their creativity translates to the imagery in their videos where half-clothed women are nowhere to be found. They, instead, turn the focus of the camera to the fantastical costuming and eclectic dance steps that cover and move their male bodies. The booty shakin video, however, is the genre that seems to be compelling as the topic of conversation for these five young women.

Ty: Anyway, I like the way they make the girls look in videos. They look sexy—ya'll just jealous. You should be striving to have bodies like that not hatin'!

Linda: I should strive to have plastic titties and look like a ho? Okay. What gets me so irritated is that that is all that they can think to do in a video? I mean, can you gets a bit more creative? How many times do I have to watch the same idea over and over again? Okay we get it . . . you a big star and you can get the pussy . . . let's move on to something more interesting.

Sophie: At least in most black videos the women look like normal people. I am so tired of seeing anorexics in magazines and on TV.

Crystal: Black men love the booootay! So you got to have badunkadunk in the trunk.

Macy: My personal opinion is that there is too much emphasis on sex and women just being like objects to have sex with but Imma be honest it don't mean that much to me cause I don't relate to none of 'em hoes in the video. That is fantasy not reality. Just like, who has twenty cars in they driveway and sit round drinking Hennessy in the club all damn day long? Let's get real. It is called show business for a reason. You look at the girls up in the video anyway nowadays and ain't hardly none of 'em really black anyway. They all trying get Puerto Rican looking girls in there. When the last time you seen somebody chocolate like me in a video?

126

Sophie: Yeah all the girls in the rap videos are starting to look like JLo. That's true. But you can take it as fantasy but it does have a real effect on people.

Macy: I don't see how if you smart enough to know fact from fiction.

Linda: But that is how they get us. You watching a bunch of stuff you calling fiction and some folks living it like it is real. You take that reality out in the club and it makes a dude step to you disrespectfully cause he think he a baller like that and you that ho in the video. But, probly wouldn't step to nobody here anyway cept Sophie. We all too dark.

The young women alternately relate to and disengage from the bodies in videos. These bodies that are seen as fake (both plastic and from a fantasy world) and overly sexualized (look like a ho) are understood to somehow represent them collectively while being so far afield from how these young women see themselves both physically and behaviorally. There is a noticeable difference in the physical type of woman that is now presented in rap and R&B videos by the large majority of black male artists. In the early to late 1990s there was a much broader representation of black women with diversity in skin color, hair texture, and body shape and size. It should also be mentioned that these much lower tech video productions incorporated real friends and family of the artists as extras and romantic interests in the videos. Therefore, the girl in the video was more likely to look like you or your friend down the street than a stripper or model. More recently, there appears to be a focus on flaunting bodies that are racially ambiguous in many rap videos. These darker than white but definitely not black female bodies seem to represent the global nature and proliferation of rap music; a music, lifestyle, and aesthetic that, in its postmodern fluidity can no longer be tied to any one geographic location or racial category.

Although Ty is the only young woman who expresses admiration for the female images in videos, I had plenty of occasions to observe the young women in the shelter discussing their desire to look like the video vixen and styling their clothes and hair to mimic their look. There was a very different commentary occurring during these times around the television when a Nelly or 50 Cent video of the over-the-top variety that Macy mentions (which combines vulgar materialism with female objectification) came on the screen. "Oooh, her hair is fierce. Do you think my hair could do like that? Is that a weave?" "That girl look better than Beyonce, he know he better get with that." "You see her butt? She be doing them press up exercises. Ya'll need to try that." Alright, I see you with the off the hook body." These are some of the comments I found written down in my field notes from a midnight shift I worked in the shelter before the cable was disconnected. I am aware that some of these comments were tongue-in-cheek, and I do not mean to imply that admiration of another woman's body is a negative statement symbolizing low self-confidence, envy or poor body image. What I want to demonstrate here is that there was none of the critical engagement around the implications of the prevalence of these back-to-back portrayals of young

127

brown women clearly waiting and ready for sex with the hyper-masculine rap stars that is shown in the focus group discussion above. It could be that in the more informal setting of the shelter activity room on a late Friday night it is simply bad form to discuss the racial and sexual politics of the rap video. Here it can simply be entertainment and judged primarily on its aesthetic value.

The ability to engage with media on various levels is something we all do. I have paid to see poorly written and even more poorly acted black romantic comedies at the movie theater just for the aesthetic pleasure of seeing black bodies on a large screen in loving, if hokey, situations. I can forgive the amateur script and underdeveloped plot because I am coming for the visual therapy. The rap video could, in a related way, be an escape into a world where black and brown women are desirable to the point of being fetishized. However, there is a danger in the isolation of bodies from the individuals who own them. Abuse, oppression, marginalization, objectification and erasure become all the more easy when you are dealing with *just bodies*. Crystal continues the conversation highlighting the representation of black women in videos as an issue of respect, and more than a matter of taste.

> Crystal: At 3 o'clock in the morning all the videos is basically girls with they butts in the camera the whole time it is like butt shakin like straight out of a stripper club type video.

> Ty: You talking about BET uncut?

> Crystal: Yeah and I don't think that is . . . I just think they is disrespecting themselves. Even if you have a female singer or rapper on Uncut, I am thinking that her video would be better . . . but no her video still have girls shaking they butts. And, I'm like, "Oh my goodness that is crazy." But nowadays, Nick Cannon just made his video and he calls it dime piece and he say that he is looking for a dime piece. He was like, "You ain't gonna see no booty shots. If you is trying to see that you might as well turn the channel now. . . ."

> Sophie: He did a making of the video?

> Crystal: Yeah on BET and he was like, "The most sexy part I'm looking for is ankles and knees." I was cracking up. He was like, "So ladies get that lotion." So he start off the video with all those girls you see in all the other little videos. He was like, "I don't want her in my video." Nick Cannon is so silly but his definition of a dime piece is not just looks. He like explained that you gotta be smart and have all those aspects together. And I thought that was cute because nobody does that anymore and I just don't like that when everybody's music be about shaking butts and I hate it when they disrespect you in the music, of course they going to disrespect you in the video.

Crystal discusses Nick Cannon as a black male Hip Hop artist who consciously chooses to challenge the booty shaking video trend. His "dime piece" or ideal woman is someone who is more than just a body. She must be smart and have "all her aspects together." I am guessing that in the BET making of the video interview Nick also mentioned personality and class two buzzwords often used to describe an "ideal woman." And yet, Nick Cannon is not entirely unproblematic. He is holding a contest[9] to see which young woman will meet his standards and we are supposed to assume that beyond his celebrity status there are other reasons to compete for his favor and attention. However, he does not need to reveal these because he is, after all, Nick Cannon and desirable because he is a celebrity. Nonetheless, it is significant that he actively condemns representations that focus solely on the body parts of young black women. Disrespectful images are not just promoted by male artists. Crystal assumes that a female artist would veer away from the demeaning focus on oversexualized female bodies in her video but is surprised to find that a woman reinforces this form of representation in her work.

Rap videos and representations of black women in Hip Hop are characterized as the most significant media form impacting the self-image of black girls. The young women at Fresh Start are aware of the impact these images can have but do not digest them as fact or translate them wholesale as physical, behavioral, or aspirational standards in their lives. Can these young women enjoy booty shaking videos without having their sense of self demeaned in the process? Formulating an answer to this question was difficult for me in my role as shelter director and is still complicated after reviewing the interview tapes, field notes, and my own written reflections on my time in the Fresh Start shelter.

Any image that is meant in some way to reflect you or your experience has the potential to be internalized when disseminated and viewed repeatedly. The danger in the oversexualized objectification of black women in rap videos is that these images dominate the media outlets most frequently watched by young black women. These same outlets, such as BET and MTV fail to offer a balance of alternative images and ways of being. Even the most astute, young woman schooled in media literacy, cannot help but be affected on some level by the fact that she sees women most like herself represented primarily as bodies, objects, flesh without intellect or emotion. In this context, there is only room to discuss sex and sexuality for young women as something that is done to them or attributed to them from some external source. The version of sex and sexuality in these incarnations of Hip Hop obscures questions of sexual agency, female pleasure, and love.

However, the young women at Fresh Start demonstrated time and time again that their relationship to Hip Hop (as defined by them) was one characterized by producing rather than consuming. The Move Experiment represented just one very obvious and concrete way that the young women acted as cultural agents. And yet, beyond the structured performance and educational space created within the Move Experiment, on a moment-by-moment basis, the young women constructed new meanings out of popular cultural representations of Hip Hop that aligned with their own personal values and identifications. Their critical reflections revealed that they recognized how Hip Hop simultaneously referenced and excluded them, while also recognizing that they had control over how they chose to engage or disengage with these cultural productions, lifestyles, and expressed values. What is most compelling beyond how any individual reacts to an existing cultural form is how new cultural forms are created out of the needs and desires of individuals and the communities they inhabit. Crystal, Sophie, Jaycee, Shavon, and Ty demonstrate that we should be less concerned with how they define and react to Hip Hop and more attuned to how they use their intellect and artistry to mobilize and inspire within their community of *struggly* young women, while also working to actualize change in their own lives. This is a cultural production that has yet to be named and commodified.

NOTES

[1] The visibility of individuals like Condoleeza Rice, Oprah Winfrey, Halle Berry, and Jamie Foxx along with various younger Hip Hop and R&B artists (although relatively small in number) appears as a threat to white racial and cultural supremacy evidenced through visibility in the media. In fact, it was Oprah whom a disgruntled elderly white man invoked in a mall in the suburbs of Cincinnati, Ohio, when he told my cousin that she needed to get to the back of the line because "you crazy, bold Negro women think you can take over the world." The ramifications of what looks like increasing images of token blacks gets even more interesting when public figures like Bill Cosby (forever the idealized face of the black upper-middle class) openly critique the black urban lower-class by focusing on their choices and behaviors with no mention of the larger systematic factors that contribute to the realities of life in the "ghetto."

[2] A reoccurring theme in the literature on youth and youth cultures.

[3] Tricia Rose provides a compelling example of this in her article, "'Fear of a Black Planet': Rap Music and Black Cultural Politics in the 1990s," *The Journal of Negro Education* 60, no. 3 (1991): 276–90.

[4] Howard Winant argues that we are now in a period of racial dualism where everyone's racial identity is problematized. Understanding racial dualism should prevent claims of authenticity (whether hegemonic or subaltern) from going unchallenged. John L. Jackson interrogates the idea of authentic blackness in his latest work, *Real Black: Adventures in Racial Sincerity*. For Jackson, racial sincerity is a more complicated and useful way to understand how agency, strategy, and intent become implicated in the process of identity construction for blacks. Jackson wants to move us away from ideas of authenticity that objectify and render impotent individuals to manipulate and actively construct the social worlds they inhabit.

[5] See Nelson George, *Buppies, B-Boys, Baps and Bohos: Notes on Post-Soul Black Culture* (Cambridge, MA: Da Cappo Press, 2001) as well as Mark Neal, *Soul Babies, Black Popular Culture and the Post Soul Aesthetic* (New York: Routledge), 2002.

[6] *Rize* was released in theatres in 2005. Directed by Dave LaChappelle, this documentary chronicles how young people in Watts and Compton use dance as a form of competition, emotional release, solidarity building, and identity formation.

[7] Sophie was a niece of one of the board member's friends. As punishment for a school senior prank she played during the last week of school, her principal was requiring that she complete 40 hours of community service. When Sophie approached the Move Experiment peer educators and I and asked if she could participate in the program, we were prepared to dismiss her. After all, we viewed the Move Experiment as freedom not punishment and did not want to feel forced into working with her because of her board connections. Sophie, however, was not what we expected. She was genuine, funny, humble, and immediately engaged in the Move Experiment. After her 40 hours were up, Sophie continued working with us through the end of the summer until she went away to college.

[8] Brenda Dixon Gottschild, *The Black Dancing Body: A Geography from Coon to Cool* (New York: Palgrave MacMillan, 2003).

[9] I watched Nick Cannon discussing the details of his contest on BET with a group of shelter residents.

"I CAN BE YOUR SUN, YOU CAN BE MY EARTH": MASCULINITY, HIP HOP, AND THE NATION OF GODS AND EARTHS

Edward Onaci

"*Peace!* Ladies and gentlemen, *Gods and Earths* . . . I'd like to welcome you all. . . ." (emphasis mine)

—J-Live[1]

The above invocation proclaimed by the rap artist J-Live might seem like a standard greeting to anyone who consistently listens to rap music. However, the origins of this greeting extend far beyond Hip Hop to a "way of life" that is unknown to most Americans, even those who proclaim allegiance to the Hip Hop nation. The greeting of "Peace," was first proclaimed by black Muslims from the Moorish Science Temple. A man named Father Allah later used the greeting and made it popular with the Gods and Earths who followed him and believed in his teachings.[2]

Father Allah (a.k.a. Clarence Smith or Clarence 13X) created the Five Percent Nation of Islam—they also go by the Nation of Gods and Earths (NGE)—in the 1960s after he left the Nation of Islam (NOI).[3] Allah combined some of NOI's basic principles with his own knowledge to create what he claimed were the "Divine Sciences," the "Supreme Mathematics" and the "Supreme Alphabet." Further, he and his followers who also defected from the NOI made this knowledge available to New York City youth. The foundation of Allah's message was that the black man was the original man, and that Allah lived within him, making him God. To get his message out to the masses, Allah encouraged each God in his nascent organization to teach another person the knowledge they received. He reasoned this would create a chain reaction that would eventually spread Five Percenters across the nation. His predictions were accurate.

The Five Percenters' most effective tool to spread their message is oral tradition. One can find a group of Gods in a "cipher" (a group of people in a circle "building," or engaging in stimulating conversation) testing each other's knowledge while simultaneously spreading it to any person within earshot who might take the time to listen.[4] For Africans in America, the oral tradition is most noticeable through music. Hip Hop music, to be specific, serves as the most efficient vehicle for Five Percenters to spread their knowledge to mass audiences.

From the early to mid-1990s, groups such as Brand Nubian and Poor Righteous Teachers, as well as Busta Rhymes and Eric B. and Rakim dominated the radio waves and delivered Five Percenters' message of "black righteousness" to receptive audiences.

131

Since their 1993 debut album *Enter the Wu (36 Chambers)*, the Wu-Tang Clan exponentially increased rap music fans' consciousness of, and knowledge about, the Five Percenters, and made their beliefs acceptable and palatable even to white listeners. Still, even with their vast popularity and influence, the NGE has received little scholarly attention. In her study of Islamic groups and practices in the United States, Jane I. Smith briefly discusses the Five Percenters. Casting them as a "sectarian movement," Smith claims that their ideology, "a complex combination of vaguely Islamic symbolism, black supremacy theory, and popular culture," reaches people through the "staccato lyrics of rap music." Yusuf Nuruddin uses interviews and the NGE's publication *The Word* to explore NGE's history, organizational structure, and ideology. Even though they provide readers with a basic understanding of the Five Percenters, neither Nuruddin nor Smith devote much attention to the NGE's relationship with and influence in Hip Hop. And they both tragically mischaracterize the Five Percenters as a gang.[5]

Hip Hop scholars also give little attention to the Five Percenters. Notable exceptions include Ernest Allen, Jr., Charise L. Cheney, and Juan Floyd-Thomas who reference the Five Percenters in their respective studies of "message rap," the "Golden Age" of rap nationalism, and "A Jihad of Words." Allen uses God rappers to demonstrate how emcees "often obscure and contaminate the legitimate demand by African Americans for justice in a white-dominated capitalist world." Because their messages becomes fragmented within an "intersubjective" jumble of "resignation and resistance, raunch and redemption" often present in their rhymes, "socially conscious" rappers typically fall short of achieving any true impact on a political plane. Cheney interweaves examples of Five Percenters and their rap lyrics as she explicates how masculinity and politics converged within Hip Hop culture during the late 1980s and 1990s. Floyd-Thomas attempts to be more comprehensive in his essay, dedicating his short explanation of the NGE to everything from their history to gender relations. Most importantly, he mentions how Five Percenter ideology finds its way into rap lyrics. Out of these texts, none of the authors fully explains the Five Percenters' importance in Hip Hop culture.[6]

Two book-length studies have recently joined the rather slender body of Five Percenter scholarship and begin to disseminate information about this largely overlooked, though essential, part of Hip Hop history. The first is Felicia Miyakawa's, *Five Percenter Rap: God Hop's Music, Message, and the Black Muslim Mission*. Seeking to undermine the image of NGE as a gang with terrorist connections, Miyakawa's fascinating study evaluates the Five Percenters' ideology, their influence in Hip Hop culture, and their use of language, sampling, and even album packaging in Five Percenters' efforts to spread knowledge of the NGE. Miyakawa concludes that although God emcees seek to spread their message to the "blind, deaf, and dumb," "rap fans may easily miss the God Hop message when it is buried beneath heavily coded doctrinal language."[7] On the other hand, Michael Muhammad Knight suggests that a God emcee "can use the medium to teach the world, but while millions listen, he can also engage his Five Percenter family in private conversation." Knight's publication, *The Five Percenters: Islam, Hip Hop and the Gods of New York*, provides readers with a comprehensive narrative presentation of the Nation of Gods and Earths. Although he focuses mainly on Father Allah's New York progeny, his text delivers a thorough explanation of the NGE's history, their current victories and challenges, and their influence in the creation and development of Hip Hop. Knight successfully challenges the assumption that the NGE is merely a racist offshoot of the NOI while giving the Gods and Earths a voice that they have yet to possess outside of their fading influence in rap music.[8] Even with these two important texts, there is more room for scholarly research about the NGE, especially within the realm of masculinity. With this said, the purpose of this paper is to examine the message of the Five Percenters as articulated through Hip Hop music in order to gain an understanding of the current state of masculinity in "socially conscious" rap (see Table 1).

This analysis highlights the problems associated with the co-optation and marketing of black nationalism through Hip Hop. Several scholars have positioned rappers as purveyors of 1960s and 1970s black nationalism. Ernest Allen, Jr., Jeffrey Louis Dekker, Kalamu ya Salaam, and Charise Cheney all analyze rappers' nationalistic tendencies. While they all clearly demonstrate how rappers exhibit black pride and other positive results of black nationalist consciousness, only Cheney fully examines how "socially conscious" rappers wed their gender politics with their nationalist ideology.[10] She builds her argument on a foundation of feminist, womanist, and queer scholars and activists of color who have been challenging the more pernicious forms of black nationalist masculinity since the mid-1960s. Responding directly to the Civil Rights movement and white feminists, Frances Beale, Toni Cade (Bambara), and organizations such as the National Black Feminist Organization presented scathing critiques of the multiple systems of oppression—what Patricia Hill Collins calls the "matrix of oppression"—through which they were trying to affirm their humanity. Out of this response also came groups like the Combahee River Collective and individuals, including Audre Lorde, who ensured that black queer women also had space to voice their dissent from the status quo. The arts were an arena where they could pose many of these critiques. Within the Black Arts Movement, Cheryl Clarke, June Jordan, and others challenged gender and sexual norms. By the late 1970s and into the 1980s, Ntozake Shange and Alice Walker used "choreopoetry" and the novel to help create the "Black Feminist Thought" which, by the 1990s, became an undeniable force that challenged some black nationalist trends for discursive space.[11]

Typically, critiques about gender and Hip Hop fall disproportionately on "commercial" rappers.[12] This paper examines the Five Percenters in order to illuminate gender themes in the rap lyrics of so-called "socially conscious" rappers. It mainly argues that we can gain a more complete understanding of how "socially conscious" Hip Hop presents masculinity to listeners by exploring the themes in the lyrics of "socially conscious" and Five Percenter rappers. This approach allows us to decode and understand the complex rhetoric and metaphors endemic in Five Percenter ideology, so that listeners do not miss the nuances of the artists' lyrics. By decoding these messages, we can simultaneously expose the masculinist tendencies inherent in their lifestyle and ethos, as well as in Hip Hop culture more broadly.[13]

Table 1
Rapper Proximity to Five Percenters Based on Lyrical Content

Degree of Five Percenter Ideology in Rap Lyrics	Characteristics	Artist Examples
God/Earth	Lyrical content mostly or totally informed by Five Percenter ideology and rhetoric. Such artists are, or probably have been, a part of the Nation of Gods and Earths.	Wu-Tang Clan, Busta Rhymes, Erykah Badu, Doodle Bug (from Digable Planets), J-Live, Nas, Poor Righteous Teachers, Brand Nubian, Gang Starr, POETREE Chicago
Informed but not Prevalent	The Five Percenter influence is apparent, but does not compose the prevailing themes and rhetoric in these artists' lyrics. Some, such as Mos Def, participate in other Islamic sects or Islamic inspired subcultures.	Common, Mos Def, Jeru the Damaja, KRS-One, Digable Planets, Medina Green, dead prez, Pete Rock and C.L. Smooth
Barley/Noninformed	Five Percenters may influence these artists, but such ideology is not very visible in their lyrics. Other spiritual forces and/or social and political phenomena inform these artists' lyrics.	Strange Fruit Project, Immortal Tecnique, The Roots, Jean Grae, Soul Students, Queen Latifah, The Coup, Talib Kweli, Asheru, OutKast, Cee-Lo

The above table demonstrates how one may categorize rap artists based on how closely their lyrics resemble Five Percenter ideology and rhetoric. Not all of the artists reviewed and quoted in this essay are members of the Nation of Gods and Earths. However, they fit within the rubric of black nationalist or "conscious" rappers and display particular characteristics typically ascribed to the Islamic rappers, Five Percenters specifically. The primary examples of this are Common and Jeru the Damaja whom I have placed within the middle category. Both of the artists' lyrics definitely exhibit tendencies attributed to the Five Percenters because they utilize key concepts and terms such as "God." However, these categories are by no means definite or static. Some rappers' lyrics may at times seem be heavily laced with Five Percenter ideology and rhetoric, while at others times contain none at all. Further, some artists may be Five Percenters but do not use NGE rhetoric in their lyrics. For example, Felicia Miyakawa asserts that Black Thought is a Five Percenter and that Queen Latifah used to be one; however, their lyrics do not tend to resemble those in the "God/Earth" or even "Informed but not Prevalent" categories.[9]

In accordance with the argument that many of today's rappers are carrying on the traditions of black nationalism (specifically those commonly associated with the cultural nationalists and the Black Arts Movement), we must also grapple with gender and masculinity in black nationalism.[14] Black nationalism is a multifaceted ideology that promotes self-determination, group unity, cultural pride, and self-reliance either within or outside of mainstream U.S. society. Several scholars have categorized it to highlight individuals' and organizations' emphasis of specific trends. One category, cultural nationalism, stresses that African Americans must achieve mental liberation through understanding their connections with Africa. Only then can they successfully struggle for political liberation. It often values the exhibition of that connection and black liberation through artistic media.[15] Regardless of which category of black nationalism one promotes, it often mirrors the patriarchal system present in broader American society in that manhood for black nationalists and rappers largely depends on control over women.

Analyzing patriarchy in Hip Hop also provides one lens with which to clarify and evaluate how corporate America has co-opted and commodified Hip Hop nationalism to its benefit. Ultimately, the "Hip Hop Nation's" relationship with large corporations resembles the exploitation of colonized nations. Exploring Hip Hop from this angle helps us determine how it can best aid social movements that seek to effect liberatory changes for the oppressed.[16] Therefore, before we delve into the full analysis of the Five Percenters use of Hip Hop, it is important to briefly explore the NGE's history and ideology as well its connections with Hip Hop and black nationalism.

"THE GREATEST STORY": ORIGINS OF THE FIVE PERCENTERS[17]

Clarence 13X (born Clarence Smith) joined the Nation of Islam in April 1961, after a short career in the United States Army.[18] He joined Temple No. 7 in Harlem and rose quickly through their ranks to become a lieutenant with the responsibility of training the Fruit of Islam in karate. Clarence 13X's progress even earned the attention of the Honorable Elijah Muhammad who granted him the original name "Abdullah." However, being the independent thinker people knew him to be, the young man began to question the ideology taught to him. Specifically, he questioned the validity of W.D. Fard's divinity because it contradicted Fard's and Muhammad's teaching that Allah was a black man, the original man. Seeing the inconsistency, Clarence 13X began teaching the younger ministers the "truth" as he understood it. His message conflicted with the NOI, and in 1963, Clarence 13X left the organization, taking his followers with him.[19]

With his newfound knowledge and access to the secret Nation of Islam lessons, Clarence 13X changed his name to Allah (he would later be referred to as Father) and developed his program of proselytizing Harlem youth. His goal was to teach young black men their divinity with hopes that black people would eventually rise above their impoverished conditions in the United States. After doing so, they would bring about true liberation from the evil American political and social system to live in peace and harmony. Allah strategically utilized the NOI's Lost-Found Muslim lessons to "teach the babies" their mission. The lessons stipulated that 85% of the population was deaf, dumb, and blind—those African Americans needed redemption from their own ignorance. The 10% kept them ignorant. These people were devils or religious "bloodsuckers" who knew the truth, but intentionally taught the 85% about the "mystery god" so that they could profit off their ignorance. Allah taught that the remaining 5% were the poor righteous teachers, whose main concern was to master equality (or gain knowledge, wisdom, and understanding) and spread their message of redemption to the 85%, especially focusing on the youth. To supplement his message, Allah developed the "Divine Sciences" of "Supreme Mathematics" and the "Supreme Alphabet."[20]

Allah also maintained many of the teachings about diet and health popular in the Nation of Islam. He taught his disciples to clean themselves physically, mentally, and spiritually. "They should abstain from smoking cigarettes, drink[ing] alcohol, and eating pork." He suggested that clean living was necessary for people to regain their "lost stature and prominence in this world."[21] In addition, he retained the patriarchal gender framework and black nationalist thought which the NOI built upon. He instilled in the Gods and Earths who followed him, a sense of responsibility toward building a nation. In order to achieve this goal, Allah expected them to produce as many children as possible.[22]

Father Allah's teachings took root in Harlem and spread to other parts of New York City and led the city government to perceive him as a gang organizer and threat. Because he worked mostly with youth from the streets, people perceived him as encouraging criminal activities.[23] Yet, he was also known to assist then New York City Mayor John V. Lindsay in trying to keep black youth out of trouble. In return, the Five Percenters received a building in Brooklyn where they built a school, which remains at that location today. However, Allah's work did not last long because an unidentified assailant murdered him on June 12, 1969. Barry Gottehrer states, "no natural leader emerged or replaced Allah."[24] One may argue that this speaks to the deficient leadership ability in the logical successors and to the Nation's loose-knit organizational structure even when Father Allah was alive. On the other hand, it speaks to Allah's teaching that each man was God and leader of himself and his family; therefore, the NGE did not need formal leadership.[25] With respect to the latter idea, being sole controller of one's self provides Gods with the freedom to accept or reject anything on the basis that they may decide what is right for them. However, several Gods and Earths have criticized those who claim to be Five Percenters, but do not at least adhere to the basic interpretations of Allah's teaching; or they cannot show and prove how they come to interpret certain ideas.[26] Regardless of which position one takes, the fact remains that the lack of organization and leadership make it difficult for the Nation of Gods and Earths to exhibit a unified ideology that holds members to one interpretation of Allah's teachings.

Regardless, Father Allah's teachings resulted in the proliferation of his group. The NGE continued to grow after 1969 until its reach spanned from New York to Chicago and California, as well as to the south.[27] In this sense, it would seem that Allah has, and still is, achieving his goal of building a nation of Gods and Earths. Of the youth who embraced his teachings, many of them aided the birth of Hip Hop culture and continue today to manifest his message through their lives as emcees, DJs, b-boys/girls, and graffiti artists. Rap music is most important out of these elements to the Five Percenters. To recognize Five Percent rappers' discourse on gender, we now turn to their rhetoric and rap lyrics.

"SPEECH IS MY HAMMER": BUILDING THE HIP HOP NATION THROUGH LANGUAGE[28]

Frantz Fanon suggests that for an oppressed group, one avenue toward achieving liberation lies in mastering their oppressors' languages.[29] Because words are power, mastering them affords the speaker the ability to possess the world expressed and implied by that language. African Americans traditionally use the English language to express their contempt toward oppression, often in coded language. Further, Geneva Smitherman argues that "[H]ip Hop/rap culture is a resistance culture." It utilizes "a resisting discourse, a set of communicative practices that constitute a text of resistance against White America's racism and its Eurocentric cultural dominance."[30] In accordance with Fanon's thinking and in the tradition of black American culture, Five Percenters make a strong practice of using words with hidden meanings. The emphasis on coded language helps us recognize how the Gods fit into Hip Hop culture. Rappers (especially God rappers) load their words with multiple meanings that may confuse someone who resides outside of their particular culture. They purposely keep the outsiders ignorant of the messages in their songs so that they can maintain distinct black speech uncorrupted by mainstream American society.

In order to decode many rap lyrics, one must at least understand the basic principles behind the Allah's "Divine Sciences." In the "Supreme Alphabet," letters A thru Z all have designated meanings and may be combined to delineate "true" meanings of words used in American Standard English. The quintessential example is their rendering of "Islam." Typically, "Islam" connotes one's submission to a higher being. For the Gods its meaning lies within an acronym that stands for "I, Self, Lord, And Master." Since the Gods are the highest beings, they only submit to themselves.[31]

Gang Starr's song "Above the Clouds," featuring Inspectah Deck from the Wu-Tang Clan, further illuminates these themes. Guru, of Gang Starr, begins by stating, "I, Self, Lord, And Master shall bring disaster to evil factors/ Demonic chapters shall be captured by kings. . . . With a force that can't be compared/ To any firepower, for it's mind power shared/ The brain weight, causes vessels to circulate/ Like constellations reflect at night off the lake."[32] These militant lines, which may mean nothing to the untrained listener (or they may leave one to wonder why he refers to himself with such reverence), suggest that Guru is not only God of himself, but that he cannot be overcome by "the devil," or the white man. The key reason for his confidence in victory lies in the line about firepower versus mind power. Guru is referring to the belief that black men's brains weigh approximately seven and one half ounces, while white men's brains weigh only six.[33] Therefore, even though the oppressor may apply guns and other technology against him, they cannot compare to the higher capacity for intelligence that, if effectively utilized, Guru possesses to defeat them.

Next, Inspectah Deck displays the same verbal mastery to suggest that, "Poison bars from the dodge bust holes in your mirage. . . . I span the universe and return to Earth to claim my throne/ The maker, owner, plus sole controller/ Ayatollah rest in the sky, the cloud's my sofa.[34] Deck's line is slightly more entertaining in that he employs the typical braggadocio associated with Hip Hop and rap by letting any potential competitors know that they cannot defeat him in a battle. His "poison bars from the dodge" that "bust holes in your mirage" signify Deck's use of his lyrics to conduct a drive-by styled murder of his competitions' dreams of ever defeating him. They do not stand a chance because he is "the maker, the owner, plus sole controller," which implies that his competition have neither mastered self nor equality and, therefore, are not a match for him.

As the illustration from Gang Starr reveals, coded language pervades Five Percenters' rap lyrics. Understanding how to decode them not only enhances listeners' enjoyment, but also affords one the ability to identify a rapper's political and social ideology. The latter is important because the inability "to analyze Hip Hop lyrics and ideology critically and intellectually may lead one to dismiss an art form capable of transmitting ideas to a community in dire need of positive solution."[35] Many of the ideas in "socially conscious" Hip Hop reflect themes of self-determination and empowerment, black pride, and Third World solidarity. Talib Kweli exhibits such themes when he states concisely, "We in the house/ Like Japanese in Japan, or Koreans in Korea/ Head to Philly free Mumia with the *kujichagulia* (true)."[36] In these lines, Talib not only recognizes the international solidarity organized around the "Free Mumia" campaign, but he illustrates his personal connection with black nationalist tradition by affirming black self-determination through the popular Kiswahili term. With these lines, he also acknowledges that African culture in the United States must engage with a variety of cultures from all over the world. Black nationalists of the 1960s and 1970s popularized these sentiments amongst African Americans.

"THE SOVEREIGN STATE OF THE HAVE-NOTS": BLACK NATIONALISM IN THE HIP HOP NATION/CORPORATE COLONY[37]

Black nationalism has always been a male dominated manifestation of black political ideology. Many scholars trace its roots back to when the first enslaved Africans arrived, not by their own volition, in the "New World."[38] Black nationalism, as we presently know it, took form during the 1950s and 1960s when Malcolm X was a prominent voice for the Nation of Islam. He, along with the NOI and other black leaders, gendered their peoples' liberation in very masculine terms. They expected men to fight for their freedom, protect their women and children, and regain their lost masculinity through their struggle for civil and human rights. To be sure, the attempt to regain their masculinity was not the only reason to struggle for freedom; nor does it mean that black women in the NOI or the broader black community exercised no agency. As several scholars including Jeffrey Ogbar and Trayce Matthews illustrate, women played a major role in shaping black nationalism, and the Black Liberation Movement.[39]

However, a considerable cohort of black men either did not recognize or disavowed the contributions and agency of women. This is most evident when we take into account the cultural nationalism and the Black Arts Movement made famous by intellectual leaders such as Maulana Karenga and such poets as Amiri Baraka and Haki Madhubuti (then Don L. Lee). They delivered their thoughts on black liberation and constructed their ideas about suitable manifestation of black manhood in masculinist—often homophobic—terms that excluded women (or at least relegated them to the "proper" female position they mistook to replicate African tradition).[40] Interestingly, the major tenets of black masculinity and black cultural nationalism exhibit the same tendencies as broader American (or white) masculinity. The display of masculine bravado and bellicose behavior, the perspective that true masculinity is tied to heterosexuality, and especially the need for authority and control. These are all characteristics of white manhood.[41]

The forms of black nationalism displayed by Malcolm X and actors in the Black Arts Movement still have currency today and may be observed through the Five Percenters in Hip Hop. Juan Floyd-Thomas, who argues that "there has been a synergy of African American Islam and Hip Hop over the past few decades which has forged a profound and complicated relationship between these two phenomenological forces that must be studied more closely" begins putting this connection in perspective.[42] Melvin Gladney places Hip Hop in an ideological continuum rooted in the Black Arts Movement based on the use of art to express rage and aggression, the attempt to establish independent institutions and recording companies, and "the development of a 'Black Aesthetic' as a yardstick to measure the value of Black art."[43] Finally, Bakari Kitwana and Ernest Allen, Jr. show how Hip Hop follows the tradition of black nationalism in several ways, two of which are important for this research. First, many of the Hip Hop's central figures were influenced by the religious and economic nationalism of Malcolm X and the Nation of Islam. The prevalence of Five Percenters and NOI (inspired) rappers speaks to these influences. Next, the images and rap lyrics present in Hip Hop, project images of black empowerment and contain themes of cultural nationalism and Afrocentricity.[44]

In the early 1990s Public Enemy, Digable Planets, and Queen Latifah displayed these themes and symbols in their rhymes, videos, and apparel. More recently, rappers Nelly and the St. Lunatics celebrated black pride with shirts commemorating the

Black Panther Party and the 1968 Olympics, as well as red, black, and green "Africa" jerseys. Typical Hip Hop fashion now includes red, black, and green wristbands, and shirts featuring Miles Davis and John Coltrane, Malcolm X and Martin Luther King shaking hands. Some gear features Angela Davis or call for U.S. and New Jersey state government "Hands Off Assata!" Even through the seemingly empty lyrics of "commercial" rap songs, one may observe how Hip Hop culture as a whole embraces and embodies black nationalism while continuing to flaunt its themes.

Using the National Black Politics Study (NBPS), Darren Davis and Ronald Brown claim, "most African Americans endorse at least half of the components of black nationalism."[45] They tend to acknowledge their African heritage and advocate incorporating it into their children's education, support African American business, and support systematic challenges to racial oppression. Yet, African Americans are less likely to support tenets of black nationalism that seem unrealistic, including establishing an autonomous black nation.[46] In a similar study that also draws on the NBPS, Robert Brown and Todd Shaw display comparable results, which they divide into two main streams of black nationalism, "community nationalism" and "separatist nationalism." Community nationalism combines the ideas of "black civil autonomy strategies with control over public institutions," and "reconciles a belief in black autonomy with American ideals of ethnic and racial pluralism." Those who support separatist nationalism seek autonomous African American territory or "at least a symbolic representation of" black independence. Using the demographic data from the NBPS, the authors determine that the older, more economically prosperous respondents, black women, and those who generally view their fate as being linked to other ethnic groups tend to support the former while younger black males with less economic stability are more likely to support the latter.[47] In both studies, the authors claim that people who most seek to assimilate into the dominant social structure tend to express a visible level of pride in their heritage, but not enough to alienate them from other ethnic and racial groups. Many "commercial" *and* "socially conscious" rappers reveal this tendency in their Hip Hop nationalism.

Hip Hop nationalism, as practiced by many rappers, reveals corporate capitalists' calculated efforts to co-opt those black nationalist ideals that align with the social structure's economic and political goals. The current manifestations of the rapper-corporate capitalist relationship mirrors what Robert Allen discusses in *Black Awakening in Capitalist America: An Analytic History*. His 1969 study argues that during the Black Power era an elite class of African Americans assisted the Ford Foundation and other such agencies as they sought their own personal empowerment. As a buffer class, they endorsed a "passive nonresistance to oppression" that ultimately helped quell the masses' political discontent.[48] Many rappers work with the large media corporations to promote images of African Americans that do not threaten the daily operations of the power structure. They embrace the American dream of "making it," which inevitably manifests as black capitalism, but includes male domination and other oppressive forms of black masculinity as an accoutrement. As Angela Davis suggests, theses versions of Hip Hop nationalism ignore the most progressive aspects of the past, which includes Huey Newton's 1970 appeal to reject homophobia and sexism; it "militates against the very revolutionary practice it appears to promote."[49] Many artists from the Hip Hop nation do not take the time to fully consider the culture they perpetuate. Instead, they accept what corporate America markets as "black" and sells to consumers because many of them ultimately desire assimilation into the corporate colonizers' social system.[50] Whether rappers' intentions are to celebrate black culture or not does not matter, because their lack of knowledge precludes their ability to communicate it constructively for others to use in their pursuit of political power. Thus, they do nothing to help achieve the more progressive goals of their black nationalist predecessors, but instead remain products of co-optation and commodification.[51]

"PREPARING YOU TO MAKE FRUIT BEARABLE": HOW BLACK MEN RELATE TO WOMEN IN "SOCIALLY CONSCIOUS" RAP LYRICS[52]

Just as many black males who subscribed to black nationalist ideals in the mid-twentieth century sought to redeem black manhood through collective political struggle against white supremacy and racial oppression, many "socially conscious" rappers manifest such tendencies through their song lyrics and sexist behaviors. The Five Percenters' organization of their family and social institutions replicate this model of manhood based primarily on the members' retentions of beliefs and practices from the NOI. They believe that man, woman, and child all play a particular role in the ideal family or "cipher." The man, symbolized by the number one or "sun," is the original man. He corresponds to knowledge and is the center of his cipher. He is God. The woman, symbolized by the number two or "moon," is the black man's queen or the Earth that revolves around her sun. She represents wisdom. And the child, or "Star," symbolized by the number three, signifies understanding. This order is the dominant idea behind their symbol, a sun with eight points, enclosing a crescent moon, a star, and the numeral seven. Five Percenters and non-Five Percenters alike utilize the sun, moon, and star metaphor in their song lyrics.[53]

Erykah Badu's song, "Orange Moon," provides a wonderful display of how Gods and Earths are supposed to interact with one another when she opens with, "I'm an orange moon/ I'm an orange moon/ Reflecting the light of the sun."[54] The Five Percenters' sun-moon metaphor signifies the relationship that a God and his queen are supposed to have. The God is the leader, or the center of his universe (cipher or family). He expects his moon to "show equality," or reflect everything that her God is, both good and bad. Earths resemble many orthodox Muslim and NOI women (Five Percenter women are often also referred to as Muslims—Muslim means to submit or to bear witness that her man is God) in that they often cover their heads and their bodies with loose-fitting clothing called "culture" or "refinement." Their designated name "Earth," also indicates that they are supposed to be at least three-fourths covered as our planet is with water. An Earth should submit to her man because he is closer to the truth than she is and, therefore, he will lead her along the righteous path to wisdom and knowledge. Submission simultaneously provides a means of protection and punishment. Protection because other men will be attracted to the woman and try and take advantage of her or lead her to an unrighteous path; punishment because of the role that they allegedly played in assisting the devil capture and enslave the black man.[55]

While some people may wonder why women would willfully identify with an organization that relegates them to a lower position than men, Juan Floyd-Thomas suggests a few possible answers. First, he flirts with the idea that to these women, many of whom did not grow up with a father present, the idea of constructing the American nuclear family is appealing. And with the alarming number of black men absent from the home or ever-present in the street, the prospect of meeting strong black men is equally attractive. In addition, the Five Percenters' rhetoric speaks highly of women, calling them queens and such, causing Earths to expect to be treated with respect when they are a part of the Nation of Gods and Earths.[56] Considering Anne Campbell's interview with the "Muslim" woman named Sun-Africa, Floyd-Thomas's assertions are correct. Sun-Africa claims that Gods do not run away from their responsibility to their children. The "Divine Sciences" stipulate Gods and Earths should procreate, so that they can play their part in continuing the NGE's way of life. Also, the Gods and Earths concern themselves with perpetual building, or passing their knowledge on to others. It serves a duel purpose of lifting and elevating each other's consciousness while simultaneously sharing a portion of each other's souls so that even after death the knowledge giver remains in spirit. Gods and Earths especially want to pass all of their knowledge down to their seeds (children) to ensure their own immortality. It should come as no surprise that Earths refrain from using birth control. As their Earth lessons (or knowledge specifically designed for women) explain, Earths should not, "accept birth-control or control birth unless they are trying to destroy us. . . abortion is the modern way to mislead the black woman. Birth control is not good because God will not and cannot fall victim to the devil's civilization."[57]

The possibility of a strong man who will protect his *women* and children, as well as educate and respect them also appeals to some women who later become Earths. Sun-Africa finds the relationships between Gods and Earths appealing, because she expects her God(s) to prevent her from poisoning herself with the wrong foods (pork, candy, soft drinks, etc.) and cigarettes. She is confident that he will not lead her to do or think anything less than righteous. "He ain't going to tell you nothing stupid anyway. . . . If we think it's wrong, we gonna speak on it . . . if it's wrong and we can show and prove that it's wrong, then it wrong and we don't have to deal with it." Sun-Africa displays the level of agency that Earths exercise within their Nation. She does not have to submit herself to someone that she views as harmful or wrong. In addition, for her the ability to produce babies and "show equality," provides everything that she desires or needs.[58]

Some Earths and Gods have attempted to reinterpret many of the ideas that guide their relationships. For example, some Earths have challenged patriarchy, arguing that it prevents them from making their fullest contributions to their Nation. Some Gods have openly supported them at group meetings, called Parliaments, as well as in print and online literature. Michael Muhammad Knight claims that these progressive Gods and Earths found such arguments on the idea that women are comprised of arm, leg, leg, arm, head, which makes them the body of Allah too. They also use Father Allah's assertion that a particular black woman was a goddess as evidence of their truth. Of course, such arguments have not gone uncontested. Some Gods claim that these progressive ideas go against Father Allah's original ideas and do not align with their Nation's mores.[59] Currently, it appears that the voice of tradition still dominates within the NGE.

To examine relationships in the NGE from the Gods' perspective, we once again turn to rap lyrics. An initial listen to Five Percenter rappers may seem to support the notion that Gods treat Earths with a higher regard for equality and respect than many other nationalist orientated black men. In his song "The 4th 3rd," J-Live positions a woman from a past relationship as an equal. He even gives her credit for teaching him about himself and guiding him to higher level of thought and self-consciousness. He states, "The way I live for you was as if I die with you/ Cause not a moment I spent with you was artificial. . . . You puttin' me open to Stephanie and Giovanni" indicating that his muse taught him about prominent black women from the Black Arts Movement.[60] However, he still regards himself as "sole controller" of the situation when he states, "Regrettin' how I ever let you let me let you/ escape fools' paradise," and "With legs entwined, tradin' profound lines/ Lendin' fingers to spines aligned diggin' in your mind like it's mine." In a tricky display of verbal mastery, J-Live indicates at these two points that even though their relationship contained a higher level of reciprocity than traditional NGE ideology seems to advocate, he ultimately controlled the relationship from sexual to mental engagement. His regrets, however, come from his foolish acceptance of this woman as an equal with whom he shared some of his control over their fate. He more explicitly privileges Gods' control over Earths in the precursor to "The 4th 3rd," titled "Get the 3rd." Interestingly, "Get the 3rd" is about women who did not respect J-Live mentally and attempted to use him for sex in a society where one would expect such behavior from *him*. Still, he strategically aligns himself with (and even references) two other songs of the same caliber, by Kool G. Rap and Ghostface Killah when he claims, "I set/ the speed at which you twist upon your axis/ From changin' your thoughts to turnin' over on the mattress," to indicate that *he* still maintained control over the women, mentally and sexually.[61]

The same theme is also present in Masta Killa's song, "Queen," when he states:

> Excuse me, miss, how you feel? Can we build?
> Could it be the mind you see, guidin' you to me?
> Extendin' my hand to welcome you in paradise
> Supreme observation, di-tect hesitation
> Your mind flashed back to other shit you've been through
> Others left you questionable, what's acceptable?
> The first sight of this divine light might shy you

143

> Warm words melt the ice between us
> My thoughts penetrate and begin to break through

Masta Killa's words sound inviting. He first acknowledges the past ill treatment the woman experienced and speaks as if he is sensitive to her emotional needs by presenting himself to her as a man who will treat her with respect and love. In the final lines quoted, he implies that he is the one who will give this mental virgin the experience she needs to become a true queen. Killa realigns himself with the typical patriarchal practice in the next verse when he states, "Watch the God/ As I'm shapin' and moldin' this planet I'm holdin'/ In suspended animation love is the highest ele/vation of understanding I will show."[62] Like J-Live, Masta Killa has control over this woman. He views his own willingness to reach out and become her God as her only hope for protection from pain and disrespect that other men offer. Their relationship will culminate in the creation of seeds (children), which he will always take care of. In these lines, Masta Killa perpetuates the masculinist tendencies of the black nationalist tradition and replicates the patriarchy found in the broader American society.

Method Man provides more lyrics that illustrate the Gods' perspective on relationships with Earths when he states, "Even if I'm locked up north, you in the world rockin' three-fourths of course/ Never showin' your stuff off boo . . . Valentine cards and birthday wishes, please/ We on another level of plannin' of understandin'/ The bond between man and woman and child/ The highest elevation, cause we above/ All [th]at romance crap you show your love." Meth values the reverence his Earth shows him by always covering herself in her refinement and remaining faithful to him, even if he is serving time in prison. Further, their relationship transcends the average, made-for-television relationships that expect the man to sweep his woman off her feet with flowers and balloons to celebrate European holidays. "Romance crap" is superficial and does not concern Gods and Earths who are more preoccupied with building and uplifting each other on the spiritual plane, especially through the creation of children. And like Masta Killa and J-Live, Method Man reinforces the male hegemony which dictates that his Earth is supposed to "hold him down" when he is not present.[63]

None of the above examples should imply that Five Percenters do not respect or love their Earths. They simply show that like other black men—or most men in general, regardless of race or ethnicity—the Gods' relationships with Earths are complicated and accompanied by socially constructed power relations specific to the mores of a particular time and place. A deeper investigation into the song lyrics from rappers such as Brand Nubian, Busta Rhymes, Leaders of the New School, Jeru the Damaja, and Digable Planets will show opinions that vary as much as the majority of men in the United States. Brand Nubian and Busta Rhymes may appear similar to misogynistic "commercial" rappers who portray women in a negative light, while Doodlebug and Butterfly of Digable Planets have more respectful song lyrics. Although one would hope that by now most men would lean more toward Digable Planets, these varying expressions of manhood reflect the same range of contesting ideologies prevalent during the height of the Black Liberation Movement.

CONCLUSION: TOWARD BOB MARLEY'S SOLUTION[64]

The Five Percenters have been utilizing various means of oral communication to proselytize since the 1960s. In fact, a key to their success in recruiting black youth has been their ability to spread their message through the witty, coded messages in contemporary black slang, while simultaneously dictating its (slang's) trajectory over the years. This eventually led the Five Percenters to Hip Hop, which they dominated until the late 1990s when "shiny suit rappers and flossin' emcees" began gaining their current popularity.[65] Even still, their influence has been so strong that the Hip Hop nation now speaks with language formerly endemic in the NGE without fully understanding the origins of their words. Therefore, we must understand the rhetoric of the Five Percenters in order to realize what many of today's rappers are saying in their songs, and to appreciate fully our own speech patterns.

Understanding the Gods' coded language is also important because it reveals to the listener their beliefs about masculinity, which mirrors black nationalist and American patriarchy. Both of these elements pervade Hip Hop in a relationship that ultimately allows the latter to exploit the former. America has a history of co-opting manifestations of "threatening" radical and African American cultures in order to weaken and manipulate them for profit. Regardless of how we perceive the mass marketing of black culture, it is important to get past the symbols, and—like the Five Percenters' rap lyrics—understand the complex ideas that produced them.

Finally, Five Percenter and "socially conscious" rappers need to understand and embrace their responsibilities as cultural workers. As W. E. B. Du Bois, Langston Hughes, Richard Wright, Angela Davis, Larry Neal, and many other black intellectuals have urged over several generations, black cultural productions are created within the context of oppression; therefore, artists should not attempt to separate their work from the goal of destroying that oppression.[66] Since Five Percenter ideology puts forth a vision of black liberation as their goal, their music should reflect it. One simple step in that direction would be to remove the harmful aspects of their gender discourse and replace them with ideas that affirm men and women's humanity and equality. Five Percenters and "socially conscious" rappers in general need to (re)evaluate how they exploit women in their lyrics, and how they allow the music industry to exploit them and black women, especially in videos. Of course, it is difficult to deviate from the molds set by the corporate forces that distribute their music. Therefore, liberation oriented rappers should unify and collectively utilize their increasing power in the music industry to wage war against their corporate colonizers for more control over their product. Not only is this a viable task for Five Percenter and "socially conscious" rappers (The Coup's music, as well as The Roots' albums *Game Theory* and *Rising Down*, are current examples), it is necessary for them to maintain the legacy of black culture.

However, they probably will not do so until their audiences demand that they stop creating music that brings harm to consumers, especially the youth (whom the Five Percenters consider "the best part").[67] Therefore, listeners also have a responsibility to fight against the corporate-led media assault on African Americans and potentially liberatory black culture. They need to stay conscious of how large corporations dictate the music played on, say Radio One and Clear Channel stations, and Black Entertainment Television through payola and other legal and illegal methods of media control.[68] Most importantly, listeners need to fight against such practices by utilizing strategies and tactics made popular by past and present grassroots social movements, revising them to fit the proper historical and spatial contexts. An essential starting point would be open and honest dialogues between artists, their fans, and critics so that we can work collectively toward creating a better culture. An alternative starting point could be radio and television station boycotts that, if nothing else, will show artists and their corporate colonizers that any music that does not contribute to the betterment of society is not profitable. Even a more moderate demand for balance between the purely entertainment, consumerist musicians and those with a progressive social and political message would be beneficial. In short, the Hip Hop generation needs a mass based cultural revolution. Only then, will we fully realize Hip Hop's potential to aid the social movements necessary to change the oppressive conditions in our society.

NOTES

[1] The quote from the title comes from Method Man, "All I Need," *Tical* (New York: Def Jam, 1994). Suns/Gods and Earths are the men and women who have knowledge of self and belong to the Five Percent Nation. They are those who have attained a certain level of knowledge of self that comes only through doing the proper series of lessons. A fuller explanation of this follows. J-Live quote taken from J-Live, "First Things First," *All of the Above* (New York, 2002).

[2] For a brief overview of the Moorish Science Temple, see Arthur Huff Fauset, *Black Gods of the Metropolis: Negro Religious Cults of the Urban North* (New York, 1974), 41–51. See also Michael Muhammad Knight, *The Five Percenters: Islam, Hip Hop and the Gods of New York* (Oxford, 2007), 14–19.

[3] The terms Five Percenters and NGE are used interchangeably throughout this essay.

[4] As this essay will demonstrate, "cipher" has other meanings.

[5] Jane I. Smith, *Islam in America* (New York, 1999), 101–03; and Yusuf Nuruddin, "The Five Percenters: A Teenage Nation of Gods and Earths," in *Muslim Communities in North America*, eds. Yvonne Y. Haddad and Jane I. Smith (New York, 1994), 109–32.

[6] Ernest Allen, Jr., "Making the Strong Survive: The Contours and Contradictions of Message Rap," in *Droppin' Science: Critical Essays on Rap Music and Hip Hop Culture*, ed. William Eric Perkins (Philadelphia, 1996), 159–81; Charise L. Cheney, *Brothers Gonna Work it Out: Sexual Politics in the Golden Age of Rap Nationalism* (New York, 2005); and Juan Floyd-Thomas, "A Jihad of Words: The Evolution of African American Islam and Contemporary Hip Hop" in *Noise and Spirit: The Religious and Spiritual Sensibilities of Rap Music*, ed. Anthony B. Pinn (New York and London, 2003), 49–70.

[7] Felicia Miyakawa, *Five Percenter Rap: God Hop's Music, Message, and Black Muslim Mission* (Bloomington and Indianapolis, 2005), quote on page 135–36.

[8] Knight, *The Five Percenters*, quote on page 186.

[9] This table follows the model set by James B. Stewart. See James B. Stewart, "Message in the Music: Political Commentary in Black Popular Music from Rhythm and Blues to Early Hip Hop," *Journal of African American History* 90, no. 3 (Summer 2005): 196–225; for Five Percenter rappers Miyakawa, *Five Percenter Rap*, 141–42; for more information on POETREE Chicago, see www.myspace.com/poetreechicago; and for more on Soul Students, see www.myspace.com/soulstudentsthemovement.

[10]See Allen, "Making the Strong Survive"; Cheney, *Brothers Gonna Work it Out* Jeffrey Louis Dekker, "The State of Rap: Time and Place in Hip Hop Nationalism," *Social Text* no. 34 (1993): 55–84; Kalamu ya Salaam, "It Didn't Jes Grew: The Social and Aesthetic Significance of African American Music," *African American Review*, 29, no. 2 (Summer 1995): 351–75. See also Mark Anthony Neal, *Soul Babies: Black Popular Culture and the Post-Soul Aesthetic* (New York, 2002); and Geneva Smitherman, "'The Chain Remain the Same': Communicative Practices in the Hip Hop Nation," *Journal of Black Studies* 28, no. 1 (September 1997): 26–42.

[11]For example, see Patricia Hill Collins, *Black Feminist Thought: Knowledge, Consciousness, and the Politics of Empowerment*, 2nd Ed. (New York and London, 2000); Cherríe Moraga and Gloria Anzaldúa, eds., *This Bridge Called My Back: Writings by Radical Women of Color* (1981; repr., New York, 1983); Beverly Guy-Sheftall, ed, *Words of Fire: An Anthology of African-American Feminist Thought* (New York, 1995); and Filomina Chioma Steady, ed. *The Black Woman Cross-Culturally* (Cambridge, MA, 1981).

[12]For example see Robin D. G. Kelley, "Kickin' Reality, Kickin' Balistics: 'Gangsta Rap' and Postindustrial Los Angeles," in *Race Rebels: Culture, Politics, and the Black Working Class* (1994; repr., New York, 1996), 183–227. Common also challenges the notion that only "gangsta" have lyrics that harm women. In his prelude to "A film Called (Pimp)," a grateful female fan commends him for having positive rap lyrics about women. In response, Common briefly talks about how important it is for rappers to respect the women who birth and raise them. However, another woman whom he apparently pimps angers him, so he proceeds to give her a "smack down" then returns to his soapbox speech about respecting women. This apparent contradiction is worthy of a broad discussion and necessary as scholars and activists debate the role of Hip Hop in today's society. See Common, "The 6th Sense," *Like Water for Chocolate* (New York, 2000). Also, see Jeffrey O. G. Ogbar's recent text, which seeks to include a variety of rappers as he evaluates black masculinity and how it contributes to the construction of the "real nigga" in Hip Hop culture. See Jeffrey O. G. Ogbar, *Hip Hop Revolution: The Culture and Politics of Rap* (Lawrence, KS, 2007).

[13]This mode of analysis follows the work Celnisha L. Dangerfield who applied the principles of understanding values, myths, and fantasy themes to Lauryn Hill's lyrics. Celnisha L. Dangerfield, "Lauryn Hill as Lyricist and Womanist," *Understanding African American Rhetoric: Classical Origins to Contemporary Innovations*, eds., Ronald L. Jackson II and Elaine B. Richardson (New York and London, 2003), 209–21.

[14]For Hip Hop's connections with the Black Arts Movement see Dekker, "The State of Rap," 60–63; and Melvin J. Gladney, "The Black Arts Movement and Hip Hop," *African American Review* 29, no. 2 (1995): 291–301.

[15]John H. Bracey, Jr., August Meier, and Elliot Rudwick, eds., *Black Nationalism in America* (Indianapolis, 1970); Wilson Jeremiah Moses, ed. *Classical Black Nationalism: From the American Revolution to Marcus Garvey* (New York and London, 1996); Alphonso Pinkney, *Red, Black, and Green: Black Nationalism in the United States* (Cambridge, 1976); Sterling Stuckey, ed., *The Ideological Origins of Black Nationalism* (Boston, 1972); and William L. Van Deburg, ed., *Modern Black Nationalism: From Marcus Garvey to Louis Farrakhan* (New York, 1997).

[16]This essay calls for an end to patriarchy and other models of masculinity that depend on dominance over women. In African American communities, especially, where black men and women continue to suffer from varying forms of oppression, black men must recognize their complicity in their own subjugation and take steps to rectify such circumstances. This discussion of Hip Hop hopes to contribute to the current dialogues around this issue.

[17]Beloved Allah, "The Bomb:" "The Greatest Story Never Told" http://trueschool.com/lok/thebomb.html (previously http://www.ibiblio.org/nge/thebomb.html, originally view 14 November 2000). Unless otherwise noted the information about Father Allah is taken from this web document. For an excellent treatment of Father Allah, see Knight, *The Five Percenters*.

[19]There is controversy over the exact date Allah left and whether it was because of his preaching or because of his gambling habits. However, most scholars do agree that Malcolm X officially expelled him. For more information, see Ernest Allen, Jr., "Making the Strong Survive," 165; Anne Campbell, *Girls in the Gang Second Edition* (1984; repr., Cambridge, MA, 1991), 216; and Barry Gottehrer, *The Mayor's Man* (Garden City, NY, 1975), 93.

[20]A wonderful example of how Five Percenters view their role in society comes from the concept behind the Gravediggerz, an offshoot group of the Wu-Tang Clan, whose members include the Rza, Prince Paul, the late Poetic—he died of cancer in 2001—and Fruikwon. The concept behind the name is that their goal is to bring life to the mentally dead (hence the Rza's nickname, the Rza-recta—or resurrector). For the Lost-Found Muslims lessons, see Felicia Felicia Miyakawa, "God Hop": The Music and Message of Five Percenter Rap," Ph.D. diss., 2003, 238.

[21]Allah understood that although people accepted his message, they were reluctant to change their ways of life and thinking. People were able to adhere to the dietary provisions and social/familial framework, and they adopted much of his teaching, but many continued to engage in criminal behavior or alcohol and drug use. As Gottehrer bares witness, Allah himself did not completely follow all of these provisions. See Gottehrer, *Mayor's Man.*

[22]As this research will show, such expectations shaped the relationships Gods and Earths engaged in. One may easily associate the gender framework Allah put forth with religious conservatism. For an overview of this and other ideological trends prevalent in contemporary societies, see Roberta Garner, *Contemporary Movements and Ideologies* (New York, 1996).

[23]The ubiquitous image of Gods being involved in criminal activity is still a major problem for the Nation of Gods and Earth's reputation. See Allen, "Making the Strong Survive," 187 n18; and A. Cortez and C. Goodwin, "In Defense of the Five Percenters," *Black News* 3, no. 13 (October 1976): 21, 31; As one may infer from her title, Anne Campbell considers the Five Percenters a gang and focuses much of her attention on their criminal activity. Campbell, *Girls in the Gang*. Though he does not explicitly consider the Five Percenters a gang, Yusuf Nuruddin does acknowledge the organization's tendency to recruit "street youth," or those who are not unfamiliar with the alternative lifestyle that many underprivileged youth live. See Yusuf Nuruddin, "The Five Percenters," 109–32; some people regard Five Percenters as a problem in prisons and claim they promote terrorism. See Salim Muwakkil, "Hip Hop Hysteria." *The Broward Times* 53, no. 5 (10 January 2003): 3; and Danielle Weekes, "Sniper Suspect in Muslim Sect Link: Muhammad May Have Belonged to Nation of Islam Offshoot," *The Voice* (4 November 2002): 2.

[24]Gottehrer, *The Mayors Man*, 245.

[25]For more details on Allah's work with mayor Lindsay, see Gottehrer, *The Mayor's Man*. For Father Allah's death and analysis on the absence of a predecessor see Felicia Miyakawa, *Five Percenter Rap*, 20–21; and Nuruddin, "The Five Percenters," 113–15.

[26]Knight, *The Five Percenters*, 142–59; and Miyakawa, *Five Percenter Rap*, 33.

[27]Although Gottehrer and Allen provide estimated membership for the Five Percenters during Father Allah's life and immediately following his death, the author has no official estimate at this time. As Nuruddin explains, the lack of formal organization and the prevalence of sympathizers make it difficult to ascertain the exact number of members. See Nuruddin, "The Five Percenters," 109. Beloved Allah, on the other hand, claims, "Today there are thousands of young black men and women who are members of The Nation of Gods and Earths." See Allah, "The Bomb."

[28]The quote in this subtitle comes from Mos Def, "Hip Hop," *Black on Both Sides* (New York, 1999). In this song Mos Def states, "speech is my hammer bang the world in the shape now let it fall."

[29]Frantz Fanon, *Black Skin, White Masks* Trans. Charles Lam Markmann (New York, 1967), 18.

[30]Smitherman, "'The Chain Remain the Same,'" 7; See also Marcyliena Morgan, *Language, Discourse, and Power in African American Culture* (Cambridge, 2002), esp. 2–7; and Sterling Stuckey, *Going Through the Storm: The Influence of African American Art in History* (New York, 1994).

[31]The Rza states that "Islam" can also mean "I Stimulate Light And Matter." Similarly, numbers in the "Supreme Mathematics" contain meanings. For example: one = "Knowledge"; two = "Wisdom"; and three = "Understanding." Adding these numbers together produces six, or "Equality". Accordingly, a God or Earth may use "Equality" to signify a black family or "Cipher." In this case, "Cipher," which also corresponds with the number zero. I do not deconstruct the "Supreme Alphabet" or "Divine Mathematics" in their entirety. See http://www.blackapologetics.com/supremealpha.html for the alphabet; for the mathematics see http://www.blackapologetics.com/mathdetail.html. For a deeper analysis of the two systems, see

Robert F. Diggs (Rza) and Chris Norris, *The Wu-Tang Manual* (New York, 2005), 43–53; and Miyakawa, *Five Percenter Rap*, especially chapter three.

[32] All song lyrics, unless otherwise noted are transcribed by the author. Gang Starr, "Above the Clouds," *Moment of Truth* (1998).

[33] For the relative brain weight of Gods and Earths see Floyd-Thomas, "A Jihad of Words," 58; and The Lost-Found Muslim Lesson in Miyakawa, "God Hop," 238.

[34] Gangstarr, "Above the Clouds."

[35] Melvin J. Gladney, "The Black Arts Movement and Hip Hop," *African American Review* 29, no. 2 (Summer 1995): 292.

[36] Mos Def and Talib Kweli, "K.O.S. (Determination)," *Mos Def and Talib Kweli are Black Star* (1998).

[37] Quote from Mos Def, "Hip Hop."

[38] See Cedric J. Robinson, *Black Marxism: The Making of the Black Radical Tradition* (1983; repr., Chapel Hill, 2000; and Sterling Stuckey, *Going Through the Storm*.

[39] Jeffrey O. G. Ogbar, *Black Power: Radical Politics and African America Identity* (Baltimore, 2004), 31; Trayce Matthews, "No One Ever Asks what a Man's Place in the Revolution Is," in *Black Panther Party [Reconsidered]*, ed. Charles Jones (Baltimore, 1998), 267–304. See also, Kimberly Springer, *Living for the Revolution: Black Feminist Organizations, 1968–1980* (Durham and London, 2005).

[40] See Cheryl Clarke, *"After Mecca": Women Poets and the Black Arts Movement* (New Brunswick, NJ, 2005); and E. Frances White, "Africa on My Mind: Gender, Counter Discourse and African American Nationalism," *Journal of Women's History* 2, no. 1 (Spring 1990): 72–97. It is important to note that since the late 1960s and early 1970s many of these men have turned away from this mode of thinking. For example, see Maulana R. Karenga *Beyond Connections: Liberation in Love and Struggle* (New Orleans and San Diego, 1978). Further, other black nationalists and black activists seriously analyzed black men's treatment of women and began creating paths that deviated from the examples provided here. Groups such as the Black Panther Party, the Revolutionary Action Movement, and the Republic of New Africa attempted to create a more alternative social framework that provided equality for women and homosexuals (at least ideologically) as comrades in struggle. For an excellent treatment of the Panthers and the US Organization, see Matthews, "No One Ever Asks What a Man's Place in the Revolution Is"; For RAM, See Robin D. G. Kelley, "Stormy Weather: Reconstructing Black (Inter)Nationalism in the Cold War Era," in *Is It Nation Time?: Contemporary Essays on Black Power and Black Nationalism*, ed. Eddie S. Glaude (Chicago, 2002), 67–90; and for the RNA, see Imari Abubakari Obadele, *Foundations of the Black Nation* (Detroit, 1975).

[41] For overviews of black masculinity, see Christopher Booker, *"I Will Wear No Chain!": A History of African American Males* (Westport, Conn., 2000); Steve Estes, *I Am A Man!: Race, Manhood, and the Civil Rights Movement* (Chapel Hill, 2005); and Robert Staples, *Black Masculinity: The Black Males Role in American Society* (San Francisco, 1982); for white American manhood see Gail Bederman, *Manliness & civilization: A Cultural History of Gender and Race in the United States, 1880–1917* (Chicago, 1995); Peter Filene, *Him/Her/Self*, 2nd ed. (Baltimore, 1986); Kristin L. Hoganson, *Fighting for American Manhood: How Gender Politics Provoked the Spanish-American and Phillipine-American Wars* (New Haven, 1998); Michael Kimmel, *Manhood in America: A Cultural History* (New York, 1996).

[42] Floyd-Thomas, "A Jihad of Word," 51.

[43] Gladney, "The Black Arts Movement and Hip Hop," 291.

[44] Allen, "Making the Strong Survive," 161; and Bakari Kitwana, "What is the Significance of Malcolm X's Legacy for the Hip-hop Generations?" (lecture, University of Illinois, Urbana-Champaign, 21 February 2005); See also, Cheney, *Brothers Gonna Work it Out*; and Bakari Kitwana, *The Hip Hop Generation: Young Blacks and the Crisis in African-American Culture* (New York, 2002).

[45] Darren W. Davis and Ronald Brown, "The Antipathy of Black Nationalism: Behavioral and Attitudinal Implications of an African American Ideology," *American Journal of Political Science* 46, no. 2 (April 2002): 239.

[46] Davis and Brown, "The Antipathy of Black Nationalism," 239–53. Ronald Brown, Michael Dawson, and James S. Jackson, principle investigators in the NBPS, obtained the data through 1,206 telephone surveys

from November 20, 1993 and February 20, 1994. For a description of the NBPS, see http://www.icpsr.umich.edu/cocoon/ICPSR/STUDY/02018.xml.

[47]Robert A. Brown and Todd C. Shaw, "Separate Nations: Two Attitudinal Dimensions of Black Nationalism," *Journal of Politics* 64, no. 1 (February 2003): 22–44. Quotes on pages 26–27.

[48]Robert Allen, *Black Awakening in Capitalist America: An Analytic History* (1969; repr., Garden City, NY, 1970), especially chapters four and five. Quotes come from page 168.

[49]Angela Davis, "Black Nationalism: The Sixties and the Nineties," *Black Popular Culture: A Project by Michelle Wallace*, ed. Gina Dent, in the series, Discussions in Contemporary Culture/Dia Center for the Arts, no. 8 (Seattle, 1992), 324. In contrast to Davis and Robert Allen, S. Craig Watkins makes a case that young African Americans benefit from and exercise creative agency within corporate America because of the commodification black culture in general. See S. Craig Watkins, "Black Is Back, and It's Bound to Sell!": Black Nationalist Desire and the Production of Black Popular Culture," *Is it Nation Time?: Contemporary Essays on Black Power and Black Nationalism* (Chicago, 2002), 189–214.

[50]Some Boost Mobile ads that have been running in *Vibe* magazine illustrate bring this point back to the Five Percenters. In one issue, Boost Mobile's ad featured a child talking on a cellular phone with the phrase "WORD IS BOND" in white, bold print letters. Father Allah made this phrase popular before his death, and Five Percenters and the Hip Hop nation continue using variations of it. That Boost Mobile appropriated and used this phrase to sell its product to black consumers speaks to how Robert Allen's observations still prevail. Another interesting point about the Boost Mobile ad is that the child with the cellular phone is holding open her hand, as if to symbolize the number five. In "Supreme Mathematics," five correlates to Power/Refinement. "Power is force or creative energy. . . . To Knowledge the Culture of Islam is to have Power." In the case of Boost Mobile, we should read "Power" as the economic capability to profit from their commodification of Five Percenter ideology. See *Vibe*, October 2004, 131; and Miyakawa, *Five Percenter Rap*; for the commodification of black culture, see Watkins, "Black is Back, and It's Bound to Sell"; the quote comes from http://www.blackapologetics.com/mathdetail.html (viewed 11 July 2006). Special thanks to Joshua Clark for bringing this ad to my attention.

[51]We may draw on Nelly and the St. Lunatics to illuminate this point. Although they proudly flaunt the Black Panther Party symbols, these rappers come nowhere near advancing Huey Newton's and Bobby Seale's goals. Newton and Seale created a ten-point platform and program geared toward socialist revolution. On the other hand, the rappers under scrutiny enjoy the fruits of U.S. imperialism. The Panthers created survival programs that fed and clothed poor and oppressed African Americans. Nelly and his crew boast about the ability to buy expensive sneakers and other material luxuries. For more on the Black Panther Party's goals and programs see Charles E. Jones, ed., *The Black Panther Party [Reconsidered]* (Baltimore, 1998); and Kathleen Cleaver and George Katsiaficas, eds. *Liberation, Imagination, and the Black Panther Party* (New York, 2001).

[52]The quote in this subtitle comes from Mos Def and Talib Kweli, "Brown Skin Lady."

[53]For example, he states, "I wouldn't chose any other to mother my understanding" in "Retrospect for Life," *One Day it'll all Make Sense* (New York: 1997); for Supreme Mathematics, see http://www.blackapologetics.com/mathdetail.html.

[54]Erykah Badu, "Orange Moon" *Mama's Gun* (New York: Mowtown, 2000); see also, "Other Side of the Game," *Live* (New York, 1997) for one aspect of relationships between Gods and Earths and good use of Five Percenter rhetoric. Badu is no longer a member of the Nation of Gods and Earths, but still uses their rhetoric in her music; see also Campbell, *Girls in the Gang*, 223.

[55]Yusuf Nuruddin, "The Five Percenters," 128; Jane I. Smith, *Islam in America*, 103; Jeru the Damaja's song "Me or the Papes," help bring home this point. Jeru asserts, "back in the day the devil used to rape her nowadays/ he got her chasing the paper." Jeru the Damaja, "Me or the Papes," *Wrath of the Math* (New York, 1996). It is also interesting to note that while men are also represented by the number seven, or perfection (the God number) women may only reach number six, equality.

[56]Juan Floyd-Thomas, "A Jihad of Words," 60–61.

[57]Campbell, *Girls in the Gang*, 201–02 and 222; see also Beloved Allah, "The Bomb"; and Nuruddin, "The Five Percenters," 115.

[58]I placed emphasis on women toward the beginning of the paragraph for two reasons: first, a God can have as many Earths and non-NGE affiliated girlfriends as he chooses. While I have not seen anything that specifically states the same thing for women, Sun-Africa openly engages in multiple relationships with both Gods and one man who is a part of the Nation. The other reason is that most of the female members of the Nation are young girls in their teens, which may make a difference in their attitude toward submitting to and bearing witness that their men are Gods. See Campbell, *Girls in the Gang*, 196–98.

[59]Knight, *The Five Percenters*, especially "Mothers of Civilization," 208–25.

[60]J-Live, "The 4th 3rd," *All of the Above*.

[61]J-Live, "Get the 3rd," *The Best Part* (2001); Ghostface's song uses similar rhetoric when he disparagingly claims, "you crab bitch, chicken head ho, eatin' heros/ I'm the first nigga that had you watchin' flicks by DeNiro/ you gained crazy points, baby, just bein' with God/ taught you how to eat the right foods, fast, and don't eat lard/ I gave you Earth lessons, I came to you as a blessing/ you didn't do the knowledge that the God was manifestin'." Ghostface Killah, "Wild Flower," *Ironman* (New York, 1996). Hear also, Kool G. Rap, "Truly Yours," *Wanted Dead or Alive* (New York, 1990).

[62]Masta Killa, "Queen," *No Said Date* (2004).

[63]Method Man, "I'll Be There for You/ You're All That I Need to Get By," [Puff Daddy Mix] (New York, 1995).

[64]In "Revolution," Marley claims "It takes revolution/to make a solution." Bob Marley and the Wailers, "Revolution," *Natty Dread* (1974; reissued, New York, 2001).

[65]Quote from De La Soul, "Ooh," *Art Official Intelligence: Mosaic Thump* (New York, 2000).

[66]Davis, using V. I. Lenin, claims that cultural workers should incorporate definite political aims into their work, though without stifling the artists' individual desire to create or their creativity. See Angela Y. Davis, "Art on the Frontline: Mandate for a People's Culture," Joy James, ed. *The Angela Y. Davis Reader* (Oxford, 1998), 236–47; for other assessments of black artists' role in liberatory movements, see Robert Chrisman, "The Formation of a Revolutionary Black Culture," *Black Scholar* 1, no. 8 (June 1970): 2–9; W. E. B. Du Bois, "Criteria of Negro Art," David Leering Davis, ed. *The Portable Harlem Renaissance Reader* (New York, 1994), 100–05; Langston Hughes, "The Negro Artist and the Racial Mountain," *Nation* 122, no. 3181 (23 June 1926): 692–94; Catherine A. John, "Complicity, Revolution, and Black Female Writing," *Race & Class* 40, no. 4 (1999); Lisa Gail Collins and Margo Natalie Crawford, eds. *New Thoughts on the Black Arts Movement* (New Brunswick, 2006); Larry Neal, "Black Art and Black Liberation," *Black Revolution: An Ebony Special Issue* (1969; repr., Chicago: Johnson Publishing Company, Inc., 1970), 30–53; David Lionel Smith, "What is Black Culture?," Wahneema Lubiano, ed. *The House That Race Built: Black Americans, U.S. Terrain* (New York, 1997), 178–94; Richard Wright, "Blueprint for Negro Writing," Davis, *The Portable Harlem Renaissance Reader*, 194–205; and Kalamu ya Salaam, "African American Cultural Empowerment: A Struggle to Identify and Institutionalize Ourselves As a People," Moreno Vega and Cheryll Y. Greene, eds. *Voices From the Battlefront: Achieving Cultural Equity* (Trenton, 1993), 119–34.

[67]Nonliberatory, and even anti-black, music has already taken its toll on the youth. A journey through the Internet community, Myspace, will demonstrate this point. One should simply sample the plethora of rap music put on display by young black (and increasingly white) male rappers. The dominant themes center on frivolous consumerism and wealth accumulation, domineering and misogynistic relationships with women (usually in the forms of free sexual access to women or even more violent acts such as "trains" and "gang-bangs"), and violence usually directed at other oppressed people. Plies, Soulja Boy Tell'em, T-Pain, and Lil Wayne are the commercial manifestations of this problem and, coincidentally, are some of the most popular artists amongst youth.

[68]Davey D's Hip Hop Corner (http://www.daveyd.com) provides a good beginning point for those who would like more information on payola and other corporate scandals.

DEFYING GENDER STEREOTYPES AND RACIAL NORMS: NAMING AFRICAN AMERICAN WOMEN'S REALITIES IN HIP HOP AND NEO-SOUL MUSIC

R. Dianne Bartlow

Music provides a site where African American women challenge the imposition of gender and racial inferiority, and seek instead to define themselves and their experiences on their own terms. The realities reflected in the music of India Arie, Mary J. Blige, and Me'Shell Ndegeocello are premised on several key themes; the need for self-definitions of beauty, respect in heterosexual love relationships, empowerment through self-esteem, and the need to challenge the homophobia that exists in many African American communities.

These songstresses challenge and assert themselves outside the frame of ideological hegemony, which continues to stigmatize African American women by the stereotypes attributed to them. It is well documented that the most controlling and pervasive images of African American women in popular culture include the ever-willing lascivious whore, mammy, sapphire, superwoman, and welfare queen. The myths of African American women are constantly being updated and now include the derogatory terms "Ghetto Bitch," "Hoochie Mama," and "Skeezer."[1] Rap music videos are a key source of the tensions surrounding those images. "The lyrics, images—and attitudes that undergrid them—are potentially harmful to Black girls and women in a culture that is already negative about our humanity, our sexuality, and our overall worth," according to Johnnetta Cole and Beverly Guy-Sheftall. They add music videos "are also harmful to Black boys and men because they encourage misogynistic attitudes and behaviors."[2]

Stereotypes of African American women not only encourage negativity, they also prescribe powerful modes of behavior for them. In *The Black Woman: An Anthology*, Kay Lindsey suggests that when African American women "are defined by those other than ourselves, the qualities ascribed to us are not in our own interests, but rather reflect the nature of the roles which we are intended to play."[3]

Music has also been a site for challenging the dominant images of African American womanhood that prevail in popular culture. The contestation reflected in the music is against the attempt to control the African American woman's behavior by objectifying her as a stereotype "other" than the everyday lived experience of African American women. The challenge is significant when one considers Patricia Hill Collins' assertion that when an individual is objectified, they are viewed not only as different from their counterpart, but as "inherently opposed" to them. Moreover she argues that they are viewed as objects "to be manipulated and controlled." In *Black Feminist Thought: Knowledge, Consciousness and the Politics of Empowerment*,

152

Hill Collins infers that historically, music has been a vehicle through which African American women have been able to define themselves, and empowered to name their own experience.[4]

The songstresses included in this article challenge the notion that they are objects to be manipulated. Instead, they encourage females to take control of their destinies by demanding respect from their significant others, and they define *for* themselves their own identity and challenge homophobia.

They are the supreme heirs of the blues women who came before them. These blues women Angela Davis argues, were "not simply female incarnations of stereotypical male aggressiveness," but rather they used music to mold "an emotional community based on the affirmation of black people's—and in particular black women's absolute and irreducible humanity." In *Blues Legacies and Black Feminism* Davis contends that the blues woman challenged "in her own way the imposition of gender-based inferiority. When she paints portraits of tough women, she offers psychic defenses and interrupts and discredits the routine internalization of male dominance."[5] Moreover, contends Davis, blues women ". . . redefined women's 'place.'" "They forged and memorialized images of tough, resilient, and independent women who were afraid neither of their own vulnerability nor of defending their right to be respected as autonomous human beings."[6] Such is the legacy inherited by the songstresses featured in this article. Through music African American women are able to touch the public consciousness exercising full expression in song and defiance of cultural hegemony.

INDIA ARIE: VIDEO

Arie's song "Video" focuses on the need for a redefinition of self, and the lyrics corroborate Kimberly Springer's apt assessment that Arie is at "the center of her own world"[7] in creating that self-definition. In this reality, unapologetic love of self is espoused, dominant modes of beauty are contested, and the image of the derogatory "video ho" is disavowed:

Sometimes I shave my legs
and sometimes I don't
Sometimes I comb my hair
and sometimes I won't
Depend on how the wind blows
I might even paint my toes
It really just depends on whatever feels good to my soul
I'm not the average girl from your video
and I ain't built like a super model
but I learned to love myself unconditionally
because I am a queen
I'm not the average girl from your video

my worth is not determined by the price of my clothes
no matter what I'm wearing
I will always be
India Arie

—India Arie "Video" from *Acoustic Soul* (2001)

Arie implies that in contrast to conforming to popular beauty standards, being at the center of her own world entails acting for and on behalf of one's self. Arie suggests that depending on the direction of wind, she "sometimes" will shave her legs and comb her hair. Ultimately, her compass for action is dependent on "whatever feels good" to her soul, and not on the currency that the "average girl" from a music video is given in the dominant culture. Nor is her "worth" incumbent upon western consumerism's promotion of pricey fashions as a means to excite and fulfill one's self. Arie's song suggests she is aware of the standard notion of western beauty illumined in the "super model" icon. She suggests she does not fit that image nor does she want to. Neither does she see her "worth" tied to the price of clothes or as an important element in self-definition. Instead, she sees herself as a queen who loves herself unconditionally:

When I look in the mirror
the only one there is me
every freckle on my face is where it's supposed to be
and I know our creator didn't make no mistakes on me
my feet, my thighs, my lips, my eyes,
I'm loving what I see

—India Arie "Video" from *Acoustic Soul* (2001)

The pitch escalates on the last stanza emphasizing with a particular stress that Arie loves what she sees. The emphasis connotes that loving herself and every part of her body is what is important particularly for one's self-esteem. This is a move by Arie to systematically reject popular culture's obsession with an ideal weight for females that hinges on conflating attractiveness with thinness and as the primary means to feel good about one's self. She implies her creator made no mistake on her, or any of her body parts. She knows every freckle on her face "is where it's supposed to be," because she sees herself as whole exactly as she is. Elsewhere in the song, Arie sings "Don't need no silicone, I prefer my own, What God gave me is just fine." She rejects breast augmentation as means to raising self-esteem. She challenges what Naomi Wolf describes as an "unconscious hallucination" that "grows ever more influential and pervasive because of what is now conscious market manipulation," and is one that "contradicts women's real situation." The "unconscious hallucination" of women by "conscious market manipulation," nets the powerful cosmetic surgery industry $300-million, and the diet industry $33-billion-a-year, according to Wolf.[8]

Arie's song calls attention to the ramifications of low self-esteem that is associated with buying into popular beauty standards. For some women, including African American females and Latinas in particular, the "culture of thinness" often results in eating disorders in particularized ways. Becky Wangsgaard Thompson describes the race and class injuries experienced by these women, who are directly impacted by the "culture of thinness." In her essay "A Way Outa No Way:" Eating Problems Among African American, Latina, and White Women," Wangsgaard Thompson observes that

> For some of the Latinas and African American women, racism coupled with the stress resulting from class mobility related to the onset of their eating problems. Joselyn, an African American woman, remembered her White grandmother telling her she would never be as pretty as her cousins because they were lighter skinned. Her grandmother often humiliated Joselyn in front of others, as she made fun of Joselyn's body while she was naked and told her she was fat. As a young child, Joselyn began to think that although she could not change her skin color, she could at least try to be thin. When Joselyn was young, her grandmother was the only family member who objected to Joselyn's weight. However, her father also began encouraging his wife and daughter to be thin as the family's class standing began to change. When the family was working class, serving big meals, having chubby children, and keeping plenty of food in the house was a sign the family was doing well. But, as the family became mobile, Joselyn's father began insisting that Jocelyn be thin. . . . These contradictory messages made her feel confused about her body. As was true for many women in this study, Joselyn was told she was fat beginning when she was very young even though she was not overweight. And, like most of the women, Joselyn was put on diet pills and diets before even reaching puberty, beginning the cycle of dieting, compulsive eating, and bulimia.[9]

From Wangsgaard Thompson's study of women's experiences with eating problems, the ideological apparatus of the family is shown to be complicit in causing low self-esteem.[10] In contrast, in another stanza of the song, Arie provides a solution to this kind of thinking by suggesting that mothers can empower females to feel good about themselves when they encourage their daughters to focus on obtaining knowledge as opposed to being distracted by popular culture's obsession with beauty as the all-defining source of a woman's essence. She sings, "My momma said a lady ain't what she wears but what she knows." This move in her song suggests that knowledge is key to one's self-esteem.

Arie also questions confining gender roles for women and the illusionary perception of what it means to be a woman in our society:

Am I less of a lady if I don't wear panty hose
My momma said a lady ain't what she wears but what she knows
but I've drawn the conclusion
it's all an illusion
confusion's the name of the game
a misconception
a mass deception
something's got to change
Don't be offended
this is all my opinion
ain't nothing that I'm saying long
This is a true confession
of a life-learned lesson
I was sent here to share with y'all
So get in where you fit in
go on and shine
clear your mind
now's the time
put your salt on the shelf
and go on and love yourself
because everything's going to be alright
(refrain)

—India Arie "Video" from *Acoustic Soul* (2001)

The stanzas emphasized with noticeable pitch inflections in this section of the song include "it's all an illusion," "confusion's the name of the game," "a misconception" "a mass deception," and "something's got to change." Here, the mass media is conjured in Arie's song as the medium responsible for creating and disseminating many of the deceptions about African American women that are promoted in popular culture. Arie alludes to the powerful role the media plays in promoting ideologies premised on mass deceptions about African American women. These are the illusions that Toni Morrison suggests are ". . . bizarre and disturbing deformations of reality that... lie mute in novels" and literature regarding Africanist characters,[11] and which Stuart Hall argues are the building blocks for consciousness which have historically contributed to the stereotypes of African Americans in media.[12]

What resonates with Arie fans is the fact the she is effective in countering stereotypical representations of women in so many of her songs. According to Writer Michelle Burford, Arie has connected with "a *legion* of music fans—many of them women" like herself, "weary of the ubiquitous bump-and grind lyrics that insult our intelligence and exploit our bodies . . ." Burford suggests that "it is exactly this honesty, this gut realness from which India both speaks and sings, that prompts sisters around the world to embrace her music. She knows our stories, and she's not afraid to tell." Burford adds that Arie's songs have been "an anthem for *real* women . . ." with

156

many feeling that finally there is an artist who "has . . . the nerve to say what many women of all generations were thinking."[13]

Arie's song "Video" is timely against the proliferation of derogatory images of African American females noted by many scholars and writers in the African American community like Burford, who contend the connection between sex and music has pushed the limits of acceptable representations, and impose an increasing threat to young African American females.[14] The technology of the new generation including TV, MTV and DVD among others creates ". . . a constant climate of stimulation, seduction (sexual, political and economic), and rape masquerading as seduction..." in which "millions of stars and fans in the music world and the athletic world . . ." experience ". . . difficulty in telling the difference between fantasy and reality," according to Writer Lerone Bennett.[15] In his article "Sex and Music Has it Gone too Far?: Backlash Over Lyrics, Violence and Threat to Young Women Grows," Bennett argues these fantasies hold disastrous results particularly since millions of consumers are exposed to them:

> We see this most poignantly in the lives of multimillionaire stars who believe the fantasy they sing and who act out these fantasies in the real world, usually with disastrous results. We see it also in the millions of fans who buy the CDs and music videos and fantasies and try to do to women on their own streets what the stars and the stars' videos and CDs say they do to the women on their street.

> A number of studies indicate that the constant portrayal of young Black girls as sex objects is making them targets for people who are not mature enough to distinguish between video fantasy and reality. The problem is magnified when the recording artist himself can't tell the difference between the two and tries to live his video life even after the camera stops rolling.[16]

The video fantasy immersed in "fancy drinks, "expensive minks," "expensive cars" "Caviar," and guns is rejected in Arie's "Video." Instead, she sings that all she needs is her "guitar." The guitar provides her with the ability to exercise full agency in expressing her voice and experience. In addition, playing the french horn, cello and several other instruments, no doubt contributes to her sense, and mode of expression. The fact that she also writes much of her own material suggests that for Arie, there is a release provided through songwriting that contributes to her wholeness and well being:

> I learned the value of releasing through song writing. . . . My songs are messages to myself while I'm on the spiritual path, and I want people to know that I'm still growing. I want angels to speak through me and my music so that [I] can bring wisdom to people.[17]

Arie sings "This is a true confession of a life-learned lesson I was sent here to share with y'all." The Queen of Hip Hop Soul Mary J. Blige illumines the true confessions, based on life-long lessons, which lead to more wisdom, and sings about in the slow moving ballad "Don't Waste Your Time."[18]

MARY J. BLIGE: DON'T WASTE YOUR TIME (duet with Aretha Franklin)

An instrumental rift commences Mary J. Blige's "Don't Waste Your Time" and sets the tone with an acoustic guitar. Adding emphasis, the song's tempo deescalates and is followed by the overlay of a bass instrumental. Together, the musical sounds connote a sadness. Two more guitar beats deescalate and then simultaneously, the guitar and drumbeat combined give the listener a sense if only briefly, that a collision has occurred. The introductory instrumental comes to an abrupt halt, and then Blige begins singing about a love relationship gone awry. The infidelity of her partner is key to the upset wherein he accuses her as being "the one to blame" for the relationship's problems:

> Lately I've got this funny feeling
> something don't feel the same
> But he's telling me I'm the one to blame
> Yes, I know that he still gives me good loving
> But when he's deep inside,
> there's somebody else on his mind
> —Mary J. Blige "Don't Waste Your Time" from *Mary* (1999)

The stanza "there's somebody else on his mind," illuminates the notion that Blige's partner is not being faithful. It implies she is struggling with letting go because even though she feels the "good loving" by her partner, she nonetheless has a "funny feeling" that the relationship is not the same. The song hints at a "false badge of honor" many heterosexual African American females adhere to which is premised on the need to keep a man who disrespects them. To the demise of many African American women, writer Crystal Sadler suggests that all to often on popular television talk shows too many women spit the line out "I Got a Man . . . as though it proves they are better than a woman who doesn't have a male partner." Sadler notes "The men on these shows seem proud of making conquests, not of having a monogamous relationship. . . ." However, she says she would "like to ask these women if they have any hobbies or interests outside their boyfriend, husband or lover." Sadler wonders what kind of society produces this state of dependency for women even amidst the gains of feminist movements:

> Women's liberation, feminism or whatever you call the Women's Movement did not reach the masses of women. It seems that even the brightest women can end up defining their value to society by whether or not they have a man.

> Whether they're college grads, corporate executives or homemakers, many women put their faith in finding a good man instead of focusing on gaining the

skills and knowledge they need to support themselves. And more often than not these women aren't prepared for when that "good" man leaves them—either because of his new six-figure job, another woman (most likely) or even death.

Thinking this way is dangerous for sisters. Many mentally or physically abusive relationships thrive on this low-self esteem mentality. It's painful to see a woman hanging on to a guy who is a total jerk despite the unhappiness the arrangement causes her—all because she believes it's better to be with someone than to be alone. [19]

Sadler's assessment speaks to the role of the mass media in reflecting and fostering patriarchy where women's focus is on men, and above all "maintaining relationships" with men.[20] Blige sings that she knows "something" in the relationship "don't feel the same" but it is hard to grasp when "he's deep inside." There is confusion because not only does she have a need to maintain the relationship, but also because she conflates sex to genuine loving.

In addition, the "false badge of honor" mindset heralded in the media can be seen as a smoke screen for what really lies beneath the surface in Blige's song. Jill Nelson's contention that too many African American women accept mistreatment from their men at their own expense when they conflate love with sex is instructive:

With all that separates us, heterosexual black women want to love and be loved by a black man. But we are trapped in bad history, negative representations, anger, and miscommunication and this becomes increasingly difficult. In addition, we refuse to face the facts of our situation: that available women far outnumber men, that sexual fidelity from men is largely a myth, and that we tacitly sanction informal and irresponsible polygamy, that most women will not marry and live happily ever after. Instead, we persist in believing in fairy tales. We compete with each other for men to the detriment of ourselves and building a sisterhood. We lie to our daughters and ourselves by holding out the obsolete carrot of the nuclear family. We yearn for an idealized, non-existent notion of marriage, to the detriment of black men, black community, and ourselves. Times are so tough that almost any heterosexual black man with any job, single or married, is besieged by women and held to few if any standards of behavior and responsibility. We twist and reshape ourselves to appeal to men, accept stale crumbs and pretend they're cake, sacrifice ourselves on the altar of the Penis God, to ill effect.[21]

In the song "Don't Waste Your Time," Mary J. Blige is encouraged by the elder Queen of Soul Aretha Franklin to walk away from the relationship even as confusion abounds:

Huh, don't waste your time (Aretha Franklin)
But it gets so hard to know (Mary J. Blige)

Just walk away (Aretha Franklin)
You say that I gotta let go (Mary J. Blige)
Seen it a million times before (chorus)
You shouldn't take his stuff no more (Aretha Franklin)
Can't waste my time (Mary J. Blige)
Girl it's not hard to know (Aretha Franklin)
Should walk away (Mary J. Blige)
Ah, you gotta let him go (Aretha Franklin)
Seen it a million times before (chorus)
Shouldn't take his sh__ no more (Mary J. Blige)
Sister girl, sister girl (Aretha Franklin)
It's much deeper than whatcha thinking ooh (Aretha Franklin)
When something don't feel the same (Aretha Franklin)
Eh you better believe his love has changed (Aretha Franklin)
And I been telling you, telling you (chorus)
And what you've been telling me (Aretha Franklin)
Because it's been hurting me, hurting me (chorus)
Any fool can see (Aretha Franklin)
He's got a sweetie on the side (Aretha Franklin)
Start making truth out of a lie (Aretha Franklin)
                    —Mary J. Blige "Don't Waste Your Time" from *Mary* (1999)

Similar to the true confession theme that Arie alludes to, it also surfaces in "Don't Waste Your Time" with the stanza "And I been telling you, telling you." The assertion acknowledging the hurt and pain associated with love relationships in Blige's song is illuminated with the the stanza "Because it's been hurting me, hurting me" illumines. Franklin suggests it is imperative to "Start making truth out of a lie," and that "It's not hard to know" because she has seen the situation "a million times before." Franklin's sharing of her own experience is a testament to, and confession of her reality and illuminates the importance of autobiography in the music of African American women. Autobiographies "provide entry into the public sphere and give women a chance to tell their stories while making social commentary" and, "the life stories they tell" operate as tools for uplift and improvement in the lives of other Black women," according to Gwendolyn Pough. In *Check It While I Wreck It: Black Womanhood, Hip Hop Culture, and the Public Sphere*, Pough draws on feminist scholar Kimberly Springer's assessment that a dimension of third wave feminism encompasses music with three predominant themes involving relationships. The themes include: "young Black women's relationships with their personal and political histories, their relationships with themselves, and their relationships with Black men."[22]

All three themes emerge in "Don't Waste Your Time." When Blige sings that "it's gets so hard to know" what the truth of her relationship is. She is reflecting on her personal experience in the partnership at the time, and she is gauging that experience against a happier time in the past. She is conscious that she "should walk away," and the stanza illuminates the inner dialogue she uses to make sense of what is occurring presently in the relationship. Franklin comments on Blige's relationship with her man and cautions that "when something don't feel the same . . . you better believe his love has changed." She remarks that "any fool can see" that Blige's man has "a sweetie on the side." Both stanzas hone in on the status of relationships African American women have with the men in their lives, and particularly around the autobiographical narratives they share with one another in coming to the truth of their experiences. The encouragement from the elder Franklin, helps Blige to ferret out the "truth" from "the lie," with the outcome that she "shouldn't take his sh— no more."

In *Blues Legacies and Black Feminism*, Angela Davis argues that "Through the blues, menacing problems are ferreted out from the isolated experience and restructured as problems shared by the community. As shared problems, threats can be met and addressed within a public collective context."[23] Davis contends that the blues song, particularly in the work of Gertrude Rainey and Bessie Smith, "represents the collective woes of the community, along with the determination to conquer them. But at the same time, it acquires a specifically female meaning, furnishing women with one of the rare vehicles through which their agonies, joys, and aspirations may be expressed."[24] In "Don't Waste Your Time," the threat of Blige being blamed for what is wrong in the relationship is ferreted out in song, which then provides her with the determination to conquer the problem.

Drawing upon the work of Angela Davis, Patricia Hill Collins explains that "African American music as an art" has provided a key "location where Black women have found voice."[25] It is a location that Davis suggests involves a process of "confronting the blues, acknowledging the blues, counting the blues, naming the blues through song" which provides "the aesthetic means of expelling the blues from one's life." According to Davis, "This is an expression of the historical role of African American song, whether secular or religious. It also reveals how the blues spirit constantly contests the borders between 'reality' and 'art.'"[26] Moreover, Davis explains that it is through the music of blues women that we can gain a privileged insight:

> The blues songs recorded by Gertrude Rainey and Bessie Smith offer us a privileged glimpse of the prevailing perceptions of love and sexuality in post slavery black communities in the United States. Both women were role models for untold thousands of their sisters to whom they delivered messages that defied the male dominance encouraged by mainstream culture. The blues women openly challenged the gender politics implicit in traditional cultural representations of marriage and heterosexual love relationships. Refusing, in the blues tradition of raw realism, to romanticize romantic relationships, they instead exposed the stereotypes and explored the contradictions of those relationships.[27]

Once the contradictions are exposed in her relationship, Blige comes to a place of empowerment and ultimately, exercises agency. This process of self-identification and naming our realities is central to the music produced by African American women.

Patricia Hill Collins explains that Black women in particular "have been central in maintaining, transforming, and recreating the blues tradition of African American culture. . . ." It is a tradition she notes which has "occupied a special place in Black women's music as a site of the expression of Black women's self-definitions." According to Hill Collins, the "blues singer strives to create an atmosphere in which analysis can take place..." It is an environment that "is intensely personal and individualistic." When Black women sing the blues, we sing our own personalized, individualistic blues while simultaneously expressing the collective blues of African American women."[28]

"Don't Waste Your Time" opens up the space for analysis to take place in love relationships and it is an expression of the collective blues of African American women. It is an expression that has been updated by Blige who has been dubbed "The Queen of Hip Hop Soul," and reflects the currency of her own generation. "As a member of the first generation of Black folks to live through the devastation of crack, AIDS and Black-on-Black violence, Mary sings a different kind of blues," and yet Blige's voice is similar to Aretha Franklin and Chaka Khan according to Joan Morgan. "Like the voices of both Aretha and Chaka, her voice, simultaneously" is "so raw and tender, powerful and vulnerable," that it "conjures up images that chronicle our lives."[29]

"Don't Waste Your Time" is from the album *Mary* which was written and almost entirely conceived by Blige,[30] and it provides further evidence of her artistic agency that resonates with her audience and particularly with females. "She has never fronted when it comes to tumultuous affairs of the heart," according to Morgan. "Instead, she has been right there in the trenches with us, baring her pain. . . . For nearly a decade her visceral, bittersweet vocals have provided a sound track of heartbreak for a generation of sisters. . . ."[31]

Morgan's apt assessment of Blige's music and ability to resonate with her audience speaks to the way in which music is a signifier of meaning. "Like any social discourse, music is meaningful precisely insofar as at least some people believe that it is and act in accordance with that belief," according to musicologist Susan McClary:

> . . . Meaning is not inherent in music, but neither is it in language: both are activities that are kept afloat only because communities of people invest in them, agree collectively that their signs serve as valid currency. Music is always dependent on the conferring of social meaning—as ethnomusicologists have long recognized, the study of signification in music cannot be undertaken in isolation from the human contexts that create, transmit, and respond to it.

> However, this is not to suggest that music is nothing but an epiphenomenon that can be explained by way of social determinism. Music and other discourses do not simply reflect a social reality that exists immutably on the outside; rather, social reality itself is constituted within such discursive practices. It is in accordance with the terms provided by language, film, advertising, ritual, or music that individuals

are socialized: take on gendered identities, learn ranges of proper behaviors, structure their perceptions and even their experiences. But is also within the arena of these discourses that alternative models of organizing the world are submitted and negotiated. This is where the ongoing work of social formation occurs.[32]

The combination of Blige and Franklin in "Don't Waste Your Time" illuminates the experiences of many African American women in heterosexual love relationships. The collective woes of two generations of African American women come together in one song and the knowledge gleaned suggests an alternative model for healthy intimate relationships is sorely needed. The way in which these songstresses deliver a range of emotion vocally, validates the collective experiences of many African American women around heterosexual love relationships. Journalist Laura Randolph suggests that the "natural brilliance" of Aretha Franklin's voice and the mythology that attends it, "has its roots in the *way* that Aretha sings." In her article featuring the elder Queen of Soul, Randolph aptly observes that "Whatever she's singing about— sinking below, rising above, giving up or going on—her emotions are all right there at the surface of her music: raw, naked, laid bare."[33]

In the last stanzas of "Don't Waste Your Time" there is an emotional intensity that reaches its peak as Franklin belts out "Don't you take it." The intensity in the music and its ability to convey meaning particularly for African Americans, can best be understood as the quality and character of "black musical behavior (in Africa and America)" which "is manifestly cultural in terms of its *movement 'with' existence.*"[34] In his essay "Musical Behaviors of Black People in American Society," James Standifer suggests "This behavior, this music, perhaps all black music and music behavior, is to one extent or another a fusion of the African and American experiences." He adds that the "African musical behavior is an extension of the African's natural life activity," whereby the "attention, during aesthetic endeavors, is never diverted from life":

He does not "stop living in his acts of daily life, or stop being directed toward their objects." Moreover, the act of listening (apparently a passive exercise for some cultures) occurs in a dimension that requires the involvement of the African's sense of being and behaving musically—*moving "with" existence.* If African music and music behavior teach a lesson, it is this: such music and musical behavior are about people—the way they move, the way they feel, the things they experience, the sounds they make.[35]

Black musical behavior occurs with music that can be classified as folk music according to Standifer because it "is a product of race," and "reflects feelings and tastes that are communal," and "integrated with a surviving pattern of *community* life." He observes that, "it is also music-made-personal, primarily as a folk singer makes a folk song personal. In the final analysis it is a music (a behavior) in which the realm of ordinary experience fuses with the aesthetic." Crucial to understanding how the African American musical experience confers meaning is its attention to reality and transforming it. Standifer points out that the "black musical experience is frequently a facing of realities and, often, a relieving of the burdens of living." He asserts that "Black musical behavior often chronicles, interprets, and sometimes transforms reality. However, it never loses touch with life, for that, after all, is the very essence of the behavior." Thus, "music and the responses to it become a remaking of reality."[36]

Standifer's analysis helps us to consider the affiliation and impact that culture has in understanding the "creative process—of black musical behavior—as *movement 'with' existence*," that pervades "and continues to shape, and otherwise influence the black musical experience in America." Thus, Standifer contends that the "concept of musical being and behaving makes clearly understandable the resolute and infectious involvement of black people in their experience of music."[37] It is this aspect of Black music that contributes to its formation and signification that McClary's analysis suggests is key in how meaning is constructed.

In the final stanzas of "Don't Waste Your Time," all elements of the African American musical experience are deployed. For this listener who grew up with the African American musical experience, I feel the fusion of experience illuminated by Standifer. By virtue of my involvement in African American culture, of which I am a product, it is indeed deeply personal. I move with every infectious sound in "Don't Waste Your Time." It is a song that leaves no doubt at least for this listener, about the lesson that *must* be learned from this affair gone awry, and the reality that must be transformed:

> Don't you take it (Aretha Franklin)
> What's the point of love (chorus)
> when you've got no trust (chorus)
> What's the point of staying (chorus)
> when you've seen enough (chorus)
> What's the point giving what he don't deserve (chorus)
> He don't deserve it, nah he don't deserve it (Mary J. Blige)
> What's the point of feeling like there's nothing inside (chorus)
> What's the point of saying that you still got your pride (chorus)
> What's the point of giving what he don't deserve (chorus)
> This is a lesson . . . (Mary J. Blige)
> This is a lesson . . . (overlap Aretha Franklin)
> —Mary J. Blige "Don't Waste Your Time" from *Mary* (1999)

The lesson espoused in "Don't Waste Your Time" suggests African American women should be ever cognizant of conflating sex with love. Moreover, they should not deny their own feelings in vain or gauge their worth against the societal expectation that stipulates women "need" to have a man in order to feel worthy. While Arie and Blige call attention to the need for a redefinition of Black Womanhood, more self-esteem, and respect in heterosexual relationships, Me'Shell Ndegeocello challenges the societal mandate that promotes heternormativity. "Leviticus: Faggot" targets the homophobia that creates division in many African American communities, and which promotes violence.

ME'SHELL NDEGEOCELLO: LEVITICUS: FAGGOT

In "Leviticus: Faggot," Me'Shell Ndegeocello calls attention to the homophobia that exists in many African American communities, and thereby disrupts dominant discourses of sex, gender, creed, and more specifically of religion, desire, and sexuality. Her "music consistently rereads, reinterprets, and reconfigures dominant cultural texts while acutely resisting the oppressive meanings generally attributed to marginalized groups through such texts," according to Melisse LaFrance.[38] Ndegeocello's lyrical deployments and compositional strategies also illuminate her musical control and agency, and her ability to tell stories that critique dominant culture in complex ways. In her analysis of Ndegeocello's song "Mary Magdalene," Lori Burns points out that Ndegeocello's "voice alternates between spoken and sung lyrics," which she asserts is conventional to the Hip Hop musical style. Burns assesses that "These two vocal strategies allow the story to be told with different effects and degrees of intensity. Ndegeocello's choice of when to speak and when to sing is significant to the narrative."[39] The vocal strategies Burns refers to are also used in "Leviticus: Faggot" along with a chorus that adds a unique contour to Ndegeocello's music. Both songs along with a number of others with biblical titles are from the _Peace Beyond Passion_ album, which in part explains the consistency of narratives, which is influenced by Ndegeocello's style. I am thankful to Burns for pointing out the two vocal strategies used by Ndegeocello because they are extremely useful in analyzing Ndegeocello's music.

"Leviticus: Faggot" begins with Ndegeocello playing a brief upbeat bass accompanied by a drum set, which is followed by spoken lyrics:

> Hey faggot better run, run, run cause
> daddy's home (sings)
> daddy's sweet lil' boy just a little too sweet
> Every night the man showed the faggot what a real man should be
> but the man and the faggot will never see
> what so many can't even perceive a real man
> tell me
> tell me (chorus)
>
> —Me'Shell Ndegeocello "Leviticus: Faggot"
> from _Peace Beyond Passion_ (1996)

The combination of using spoken words, and sung lyrics in the first and second stanzas of "Leviticus: Faggot" gives the sense that the game of hide-and-seek is being played. The "faggot" is encouraged to "run" and presumably hide as Ndegeocello sings "daddy's home" for emphasis. Yet, as the lyrical narrative progresses we find the "lil boy" in question, must literally hide because he is deemed "just a little too sweet" by his father's standard of heteronormativity. In the father's view, in order to be a "real man," his son must be heterosexual. Heteronormativity is what he has shown his son how to do "every night." The song illuminates what the late filmmaker Marlon Riggs terms "black America's pervasive cultural homophobia." In "Black Macho Revisited: Reflections of a SNAP! Queen," Riggs argues that dominant perceptions of gay black men stipulate that because of their sexuality, they cannot be black or real men:

A strong, proud, "Afrocentric" black man is resolutely heterosexual, not *even* bisexual. Hence, I remain a Negro. My sexual difference is considered of no value; indeed, it's a testament to weakness, passivity, the absence of real guts—balls. Hence, I remain a sissy, punk, faggot. I cannot be a black gay man because, by the tenets of black macho, black gay man is a triple negation. I am consigned, by these tenets, to remain a Negro faggot. And, as such, I am game for play, to be used, joked about, put down, beaten, slapped, and bashed, not just by illiterate homophobic thugs in the night but by black American culture's best and brightest.[40]

In the beginning stanzas of "Leviticus: Faggot, " Ndegeocello questions the normative value given to manhood that the father must teach his son about daily, and the song puts front and center the derogatory stereotypes that are used by dominant culture to characterize gay males. "Faggot" is the very first word she uses to draw our attention to the disdain gay males often face even in their families, which theoretically are supposed to provide unconditional love. Being "put down" if one is deemed to be gay as Riggs aptly surmises, is only par-for-the-course when one is deemed as the "other."

The "other" gains meaning only in relation to their counterparts and stems from either/or dichotomous thinking that "categorizes people, things, and ideas in terms of their difference from one another." Patricia Hill Collins suggests that "Objectification is central to" the "process of oppositional difference," because "In either/or dichotomous thinking, one element is objectified as the Other, and is viewed as an object to be manipulated and controlled."[41]

The notion of the "other" operates with considerable force for black gay men. Marlon Riggs provides an apt assessment of black gay males who are deemed as the "other":

What lies at the heart, I believe, of black America's pervasive cultural homophobia is the desperate need for a convenient Other within the community, yet not truly of the community; an Other to which to blame for the chronic identity crisis afflicting the black male psyche can be readily displaced; an indispensable Other that functions as the lowest common denominator of the abject, the base line of transgression beyond which a Black Man is no longer a man, no longer black; an essential Other which black men and boys maturing, struggling with self-doubt, anxiety, feelings of political, economic, social, and sexual inadequacy—even impotence—can always measure themselves and by comparison seem strong, adept, empowered, superior.

Indeed, the representation of Negro faggotry disturbingly parallels and reinforces America's most entrenched racist constructions around African American identity. White icons of the past signifying "Blackness" share with contemporary icons of Negro faggotry a manifest dread of the deviant Other. Behind Sambo and the SNAP! Queen lies a social psyche in torment, a fragile psyche threatened by deviation from its egocentric-ethnocentric construct of self and society. Such a psyche systematically defines the Other's "deviance" by the essential characteristics that make the Other distinct, then invests those differences with intrinsic defect. Hence, blacks are inferior because they are not white. Black gays are unnatural because they are not straight. Majority representations of both affirm the view that blackness and gayness constitute a fundamental rupture in the order of things, that our very existence is an affront to nature and humanity.[42]

"Leviticus: Faggot" suggests that for "so many" people, it is difficult to really know or "perceive" what a real man is when their reliance for such knowledge is dependent upon derogatory representations particularly of gays in media. The stereotypes have been commodified into commercial hits as evidenced by Madonna's "Truth or Dare" documentary where "Negro faggotry is in vogue," and through the many forms of mass media according to Riggs. He adds, "I am a Negro faggot, if I believe what movies, TV, and rap music say of me. My life is game for play."[43] Against this frame for viewing, Devon Carbado's notes that among the heterosexual privileges represented in television "or at the movies, heterosexuality is always affirmed as healthy and/or normal."[44] Thus, in these early stanzas of "Leviticus: Faggot" Ndegeocello places emphasis on the normative value dominant culture gives to manhood and questions where the frame of reference originates. She challenges her listeners to "tell" her if they have an adequate explanation for what constitutes manhood. The fact that Ndegeocello poses the question twice suggests she wants serious contemplation about the operation of homophobia in many African American communities.

In the next stanzas of the song, heterosexual desire is subverted. The move represents Ndegeocello's agency to put heteronormativity at bay:

It's not that the faggot didn't find a woman fine and beautiful (spoken lyrics)
He admired desired their desires (spoken lyrics)
Wanted love from strong hands (chorus)
The faggot wanted the love of another man (spoken word)
—Me'Shell Ndegeocello "Leviticus: Faggot"
from *Peace Beyond Passion* (1996)

Gay desire is foregrounded and the spoken word used provides the space for the notion of multiple subjectivities. The lyrical strategy moves the marginalized and otherwise demonized "other" to the center frame, providing context for his desire. In *Undoing Gender*, Judith Butler suggests that "desire is implicated in social norms," and that "it is bound up with the question of power and with the problem of who qualifies as the recognizably human and who does not."[45] In these stanzas, by bringing homosexual desire to the forefront, Ndegeocello is exercising agency by insisting that it qualifies for recognition in song. Drawing upon Michel Foucault's discussion of the importance of confession, Butler suggests that "the point is not to ferret out desires and expose their truth in pubic, but rather to constitute a truth of oneself through the act of verbalization itself."[46] The act of verbalization is Me'Shell Ndegeocello's intent in producing her music, and it is her mode of expression. Her genius can be seen in her ability to challenge dominant cultural texts while simultaneously recognizing the existence of multiple subjectivities that each of us has. Gay males who are otherwise deemed to fundamentally rupture the order of compulsory heterosexuality, are particularly illuminated in her music. "Ndegeocello has fulfilled many of the criteria queer theorists now deem necessary for truly 'queer' theorizing and activism," according to Lori Burns. Drawing on Ruth Goldman's work on queer theory, Burns suggests that "queerness, ideally, involves resisting regimes of the normal" and "creates a space for diverse discourses that challenge heteronormativity and the systems that sustain it." Burns points out that "Queerness, if it accomplishes what is was devised for should not only challenge and confuse our understanding and uses of sexual and gender categories but should also provide the theoretical and practical framework within which one can challenge racist, ageist, and classist norms."[47]

How desire can seek and find recognition for itself particularly when one is viewed as the "Other" is "the point of departure for thinking politically about subordination and exclusion," according to Butler.[48] In "Leviticus: Faggot" Ndegeocello suggests that the "lil boy" is subordinated by virtue of having to run and hide because he is deemed "just a little too sweet" by his father. Ndegeocello also provides recognition of gay desire through the metaphor of "strong hands," that the young man is desirous of and which is implied through his need of "love" from a "man." Ultimately, she is urging the homophobic listener to self-reflect even if it threatens their unitary existence. Judith Butler suggests that the process of self-reflection about the "Other" can occur when "One's consciousness finds that it is lost, lost in the Other," that it can "come outside itself," and "find itself as the other or . . . *in* the Other." She adds, "recognition begins with the insight that one is lost in the other, appropriated in and by an alterity that is and is not oneself":

> Recognition is motivated by the desire to find oneself reflected there, where the reflection is not a final expropriation. Indeed, consciousness seeks a retrieval of itself, a restoration to an earlier time, only to come to see that there is no return from alterity to a former self, but only a future transfiguration premised on the impossibility of any such return.[49]

To speak of gay desire from this frame of recognition, Ndegeocello effectively achieves her aim in transfiguring a unitary existence or experience about desire that in dominant culture is deemed to be the exclusive terrain of heterosexuals and which sees heteronormativity as the only compass for morality in love relationships.

Her next move in "Leviticus: Faggot" is to challenge the role of religion in fostering homophobia. The following passages illuminate what Lori Burns refers to as Ndegeocello's ability to subvert and reconfigure biblical texts and discourses:[50]

> His mother would pray-y-y (chorus)
> Save him, save him, save him from this life (chorus) . . .
> Go to church boy (voice)
> Faggot you're just a prisoner of your own perverted world (voice)
> No picket fence acting like a (voice)
> stop acting like a (voice)
> bitch (chorus)
>
> but that's all he sees (Ndegeocello sings)
> Take that you faggot. . . .(chorus)
> —Me'Shell Ndegeocello "Leviticus: Faggot"
> from *Peace Beyond Passion* (1996)

The compositional strategy using spoken word and sung lyrics by Ndegeocello adds a distinct dimension to exposing the homophobia in many African American churches. What is evident in the lyrics "save him from this life," is the notion that homosexuality must be exorcised. The use of the chorus in the first two stanzas, which include sung lyrics, mirrors the musical behavior of many African Americans in church settings, and the connection to religion as an institution, which can and does foster homophobia. James Standifer suggests that "For a long time in American history, the church in particular ways was the primary environment in which most of the unique musical behaviors of black people were born and nurtured." Standifer points out that "religious expression and black musical behavior from the start were one and the same thing":

> Both manifested themselves in the experience of singing (gospels, spirituals, hymns, and the like) and a behavior resulting from this singing called "getting happy." This behavior of being "hit by the spirit" consisted of a variety of behaviors including shouting, dancing, arm-waving, screaming or hollering, swaying back and forth, moaning, singing, fainting, and the like. It is highly individualistic behavior but extremely infectious to other participants. It has its genesis in African musical behavior, and it existed in clandestine gatherings during slavery. As blacks became converted to Protestant religions such as Baptist and Methodist, these behaviors were generally retained unchanged as they were integrated into the doctrines of newly-joined denominations.[51]

Ndegeocello implicates religion in institutionalizing the oppression of gays and lesbians. The young boy's mother tells him if only he will just go to "church" he will be saved from what is deemed to be the "perverted world" and lifestyle. Ironically, while religion has historically "served as a liberating force in the African American

169

community,"[52] Charles Nero points out that some black churches oppress their constituents through the practice of promoting sexism and heterosexism.

In "Signifying on the Black Church," Nero alludes to a minister's homophobic sermon at the funeral of a gay man who had died due to complications from AIDS. Like the title of Ndegeocello's song, the sermon drew upon the book of Leviticus, which provided the minister with justification for denouncing homosexuality:

In Leviticus, Chapter 20 . . . the Lord tell (sic) us: If a man lie with mankind as he lieth with a woman, both of them have committed an abomination: they shall surely be put to death; their blood shall be upon them. There's no cause to wonder why medical science could not find a cure for this man's illness. How could medicine cure temptation? What drug can exorcise Satan from a young man's soul? The only cure is to be found in the Lord. The only cure is repentance, for Leviticus clearly tells us, ". . . whoever shall commit any of these abominations, even the souls that commit them shall be cut off from among their people."[53]

Nero points to the use of religion in oppressing black gays by alienating them from their families but he also notes that the opposite can occur. He suggests when "black families are oppressors," they "are alienated from their gay children, and thus suffer. Black families suffer because their oppression robs them of a crucial sign of humaneness: compassion."[54] In spoken word Ndegeocello's "Leviticus: Faggot" addresses both the alienation black gays experience within the family and also how the family ultimately suffers as well:

No love dreams
Only the favors sweet Michael performed for money to eat
'Cause the MAN kicked the faggot out of the house at 16
> —Me'Shell Ndegeocello "Leviticus: Faggot"
> from *Peace Beyond Passion* (1996)

The three stanzas denote the alienation young Michael experiences from his family. Ndegeocello sarcastically speaks the word "man" with particular emphasis to point out the father's harsh treatment of his own son, which is devoid of humanity and compassion. Young Michael is literally kicked out the house at 16 for expressing his sexuality. He functions as the "Other" that Marlon Riggs alludes to, which views a black gay as the lowest common denominator; neither a man or a black person, only faggot. On his own, young Michael is forced into prostitution as a means of survival and into a hostile environment on the street, which ultimately takes his life. The alienation the family will experience by virtue of losing a son, becomes permanent:

Before long he was crying QUEEN for al-l-l the world to see, his bloody body face down

All hail the queen
The wages of sin are surely death, yes, that's what mama used to say
So there was no sympathy

—Me'Shell Ndegeocello "Leviticus: Faggot"
from *Peace Beyond Passion* (1996)

The stanzas speak to the violent death young Michael has met and they illuminate Marlon Riggs' contention that this is "the terrain black gay men navigate in the quest for self and social identity" which "is to say the least, hostile."[55] The stanzas also illuminate Earl Ofari Hutchinson's assessment in "My Gay Problem, Your Black Problem" that Black gay men continue to feel like men without a people" and who "carry the triple burden of being Black, male, and gay." Hutchinson adds that "They are rejected by many blacks and barely tolerated by many white gays. They worry that the hatred of other black men toward them won't change as long as they (heterosexual black men) continue to believe that gay male identity subverts Black manhood."[56] Hutchinson's analysis speaks to the three ways in which difference is managed and is tied to fear and loathing. We ignore difference, "and if that is not possible, copy it if we think it is dominant, or destroy it if we think it is subordinate," according to Audre Lorde.[57]

The stanzas also illuminate Judith Butler's assertion that "the body implies, mortality, vulnerability, agency: the skin and the flesh expose us to the gaze of others but also to touch and violence." She adds "The body can be the agency and the instrument of all of these as well, or the site where "doing" and "being done to" become equivocal." In "Leviticus: Faggot," young Michael was literally destroyed with his "bloody face down" and "for all the world to see."

In Butler's view, "Although we struggle for rights over our own bodies, the very bodies for which we struggle are not quite ever our own," because "The body has its invariably public dimension; constituted as a social phenomenon in the public sphere." She states "my body is and is not mine."[58] In Butler's discussion of violence against sexual minorities including harassment and murder, she suggests that "On the level of discourse, certain lives are not considered lives at all," and "cannot be humanized" because "they fit no dominant frame for the human." Butler adds "their dehumanization occurs first, at this level," and "then gives rise to a physical violence that in some sense delivers the message of dehumanization which is already at work in the culture":[59]

So it is not just that a discourse exists in which there is no frame and no story and no name for such a life, or that violence might be said to realize and apply to this discourse. Violence against those who are already not quite lives, who are living in a state of suspension between life and death, leaves a mark that is no mark. . . .

The desire to kill someone, or killing someone, for not conforming to the gender norm by which a person is "supposed" to live suggests that life itself requires a set of sheltering norms, and that to be outside it, to live outside it, is to court death.

... This violence emerges from a profound desire to keep the order of binary gender natural or necessary, to make it a structure, either natural or cultural, or both, that no human can oppose, and still remain human.[60]

Even though young Michael has died a violent death there was no sympathy for him from his family because he did not conform to the gender norm by which he was "supposed" to live. As such, he was living in a state of suspension between life and death and was never deemed really human. His death left no mark. Influenced by the force of religion, it was the view of his family that death would be the inevitable outcome since it was deemed young Michael had committed the worst possible "sin" against humanity by simply being himself. He lived outside the heteronormative and in doing so, courted death. Thus, upon his death he would leave no mark, and not being deemed fully human, there would be no sympathy.

Having provided reasons for the mistreatment of gays and lesbians and the ultimate violation against them: murder, Ndegeocello's next move in "Leviticus: Faggot" is to establish compassion for young Michael where none had existed previously. She moves the narrative from third person to first where she herself takes on the subject position of young Michael. The pace of the song slows as the chorus sings "Who will care for me?," "Who will love me?" The following stanzas conclude "Leviticus: Faggot":

Beautiful angels dance around my soul, as I rise (chorus)
Just searching and searching, searching and searching (sung lyrics)
Trying to figure out, life (spoken lyrics)
(Instrumental riff)
Swing low (chorus)
Sweet chariot (sung lyrics)
Let me rise (sung lyrics)
Above my fears (sung lyrics)
Let me rise (chorus)
Above my sadness (sung lyrics)
Let me rise (sung lyrics)
Above my tears (sung lyrics)
Swing low (sung lyrics)
My sweet chariot (sung lyrics)
Let me rise (sung lyrics)
Let your conscious, be clear, as I rise (chorus)
(brief instrumental riff)
As I rise (sung lyrics)
(slow instrumental riff)

—Me'Shell Ndegeocello "Leviticus: Faggot"
from *Peace Beyond Passion* (1996)

Ndegeocello, who has been dubbed the foremother of neo-soul and is the bisexual daughter of a deeply Christian mother,[61] has said that based on the stories about Jesus, she admires him immensely, and that she considers herself on a spiritual path[62] even though she has a problem with the administration of Christianity. Putting Ndegeocello's personal life in context, provides an understanding of how she can sing about "beautiful angels dancing" around her soul in "Leviticus: Faggot." It helps to correlate what she sees as a positive notion of spirituality. It is one that stands in stark contrast to the role that organized religions foster in creating homophobia.

In the last stanzas she sings from a place of reflection: "just searching and searching . . . trying to figure out life." The first instrumental rift provides space in the song for self-reflection. Ndegeocello's next move in "Leviticus: Faggot" employs the old Negro Spiritual "Swing Low." It a mechanism that allows her to situate the band of angels she sings about in a positive frame, and as a model for the kind of spiritually espousing unconditional love that should guide religious beliefs. Her song infers the angels are coming to take Michael to his ultimate home where peace and love reside. It is a compositional strategy by Ndegeocello to establish compassion for him. In this last section of the song, Ndegeocello places young Michael in the first person thereby moving him to the subject position. She sings "let me rise" above my "fears," "sadness," and "tears," that have been bestowed upon her by society. In the song's final move, Ndegeocello wants to make sure listeners are clear about her message. She advises them: "Let your conscious, be clear" or otherwise be free of homophobia and intolerance against gays. The final slow and dreamy instrumental rift, provides the space for that reflection.

CONCLUSION

Ndegeocello has said that having to negotiate her own identity on an ongoing basis has made her feel like a heretic.[63] Like young Michael in "Leviticus: Faggot," she has observed that she feels despised because of the rampant homophobia in many African American communities. In addition, she suggests that because of her bisexuality, some gay people believe she is not gay enough. Being viewed as criminal due to her androgynous look, is one other way she negotiates her identity, according to Ndegeocello. "When I walk down the street, a white woman will clutch her purse. That's the reality I live in."[64] It is the reality that too many African American women know and traverse on a daily basis in varying degrees, and which the music illuminates in a number of contexts that run counter to cultural hegemony. For Ndegeocello, one goal of her music is to challenge homophobia by rereading, reinterpreting, subverting, and reconfiguring dominant cultural texts that are used to oppress African American gays, and that further marginalize them. Exploring the baseline beyond, which a Black man is no longer a Black man, is among the themes she addresses in her spoken and sung lyrics. Her work is focused on moving them from the status of the deviant and inferior "other," to a space of recognizing multiple subjectivities and gay desire in particular. Like Blige and Arie, the tool of confession is utilized to illuminate the importance of autobiography in the lives of African American women vocalists. In Ndegeocello's case, the challenge is focused on the institution of organized religion and its role in fostering homophobia. Her music is also centered on the alienation that separates Black gays from their families, and which contributes to the oppression that also robs the parents of gay children of the ability to express a crucial sign of humanity: compassion. For Ndegeocello, violence against sexual minorities is a cause of grave concern, and particularly when heterosexualized gender norms impede the full expression of one's humanity.

Arie's "Video" suggests that self-definitions are crucial for promoting a love of oneself. They are needed in order to contest western standards of beauty, which can be referred to as unconscious hallucinations that promote consumerism, and an investment in products such as pricey fashions as a false means of raising one's self-esteem. Arie asserts that more than the clothes one wears, knowledge is key to the development of a complete human being. It can be used to challenge gender norms, and the derogatory images of African Americans, as well as a tool parents can use in empowering their children to seek out such knowledge. "Video," illuminates the need to cultivate one's creativity where possible as a measure of fulfillment. Musical instruments provide the outlet for Arie's creativity, and the mode through which she can release stress. Similar to Ndegeocello, music aids Arie in forging the connection between a sense of wholeness and spirituality. It is a connection that ultimately enables Arie to be a conveyor of knowledge and wisdom in promoting the need for self-definition.

How African American women respond to their heterosexual partners' infidelity is the impetus behind Mary J. Blige's call in "Don't Waste Your Time." The transformation needed is to move past a definition of self premised on whether or not a woman has a man. The assertion Blige makes in song illuminates that such a faulty vision is only a smoke screen for what lies beneath the surface of relationships where infidelity exists, and which include at least three factors that influence how partnerships will be played out. These include negative representations of African American women, anger, underlying reasons for denying the reality of infidelity. Similar to Arie, many female fans find Blige's songs to be a soundtrack for their own lives, which helps to explain how they can resonate so deeply with the music produced by both of these vocalists. In Blige's case, knowledge is a key component in moving from an oppressed state, and particularly when the wisdom of elders is embraced as a means to move forward. The combination is useful in conquering the problem of a failed relationship due to infidelity. For Blige, sharing confessions and autobiographies is liberating. Such actions improve and uplift our lives amidst our political history and the relationships we have with African American men. In Blige's "Don't Waste Your Time," music is illuminated as an art form that provides a space where black women have found a voice to acknowledge, confront, and make sense out of their experiences, and to counter male dominance and patriarchy.

For these songstresses, music represents the one path not altogether closed for the expression of black women's experiences. It provides the space for analysis into what influences their worldviews. Music is the rare vehicle indeed, in which black women can speak, and to which attention must be paid.

NOTES

[1]Joan Morgan, *When Chickenheads Come Home to Roost: My Life as a Hip Hop Feminist* (New York: Simon & Schuster, 1999), 100; Kimberly Springer, "Third Wave Black Feminism?" *Signs: Journal of Women in Culture and Society* 27, no. 4 (Summer 2000): 1069.

[2]Johnnetta Cole and Beverly Guy-Sheftall, "No Respect: Gender Politics and Hip Hop," in *Women Images and Realities: A Multicultural Anthology*, Fourth Edition, eds. Amy Kesselman, Lily D. McNair, Nancy Schniedewind (New York: McGraw Hill, 2008), 100.

[3]Kay Lindsey, *The Black Woman: An Anthology*, ed. Toni Cade (New York and Scarsborough, Ontario: 1970), 89.

[4]Patricia Hill Collins, *Black Feminist Thought: Knowledge, Consciousness and the Politics of Empowerment* (New York, 1991), 69–70, 100.

[5]Angela Y. Davis, *Blues Legacies and Black Feminism* (New York, 1998), 36.

[6]Ibid., 41.

[7]Springer, "Third Wave Black Feminism?"

[8]Naomi Wolf, "The Beauty Myth," in eds. Amy Kesselman, Lily D. McNair, and Nancy Scniedewind, *Women, Images, and Realities: A Multicultural Anthology*, 124.

[9]Becky Wangsgaard Thompson, "A Way Outa No Way": Eating Problems Among African American, Latina, and White Women," eds. Susan M. Shaw and Janet Lee in *Women's Voices, Feminist Visions: Classic and Contemporary Readings*, Second Edition (Boston: McGraw Hill, 2004), 226.

[10]Ibid.

[11]Toni Morrison, *Playing in the Dark: Whiteness and the Literary Imagination* (New York: 1992), 23.

[12]Stuart Hall, "The Whites of Their Eyes: Racist Ideologies and the Media," in *Gender, Race and Class in Media: A Text Reader*, eds, Gail Dines and Jean M. Humez (London, 2003), 18–19, 21.

[13]Michelle Burford, "India Arie: The Songstress Talks About Her Difficult Journey to Self-Love" *Essence* (June 2002): 106–07.

[14]Lerone Bennett Jr., "Sex and Music: Has It Gone Too Far?: Backlash Over Lyrics, Violence and Threat to Young Women Grows," *Ebony* (October 2002): 146.

[15]Ibid.

[16]Ibid., 148–150. According to Bennett, a minority of the "new generation" who comprise "youth, raised in an electronic fantasy world exacerbated by a dangerous real world of crack, poverty, low-income family disintegration and racism" coupled with a minority of the new music genre who have "inherited extreme needs (broken families, broken dreams, broken streets) from history . . . are calling history to account in extreme, macho-macho words and images."

[17]Ibid., 174.

[18]Kevin Chappell, "Mary J. Blige: A New Man, A New Career, and No More Drama," *Ebony* (August 2002), 95. Also see Joan Morgan, "What You Never Know About Mary," *Essence* (November 2001): 132.

[19]Crystal Sadler, "'I Got a Man:' A False Badge of Honor?" *Essence* (May 1997): 214

[20]Allan Johnson, "Patriarchy" in *Race, Class, and Gender in the United States: An Integrated Study*, ed. Paula S. Rothenberg (New York, 2004, 2001), 168.

[21]Jill Nelson, *Straight No Chaser: How I Became a Grown-Up Black Woman* (USA: Penguin, 1999), 109.

[22]Gwendolyn D. Pough, *Check It While I Wreck It: Black Womanhood, Hip Hop Culture, and Public Sphere* (Boston, 2004), 111–12.

[23]Angela Y. Davis, *Blues Legacies and Black Feminism* (New York, 1998), 33.

[24]Ibid., 135.

[25]Ibid., 99.

[26]Angela Y. Davis, *Blues Legacies and Black Feminism*, 135.

[27]Ibid., 41.

[28]Patricia Hill Collins, *Black Feminist Thought*, 100.

[29]Joan Morgan, "Hail Mary," *Essence* (April 1997): 76.

[30]Ibid., 140.

[31]Joan Morgan, "What You Never Knew About Mary," *Essence* (November 2001): 132.

[32]Susan McClary, *Feminine Endings: Music, Gender, and Sexuality* (Minnesota, 1991), 21.

[33]Laura B. Randolph, "Aretha Talks About Men, Marriage, Music and Motherhood," *Ebony* (1995): 30.

[34]James Standifer, "Musical Behaviors of Black People in American Society," in *Black Music Research Journal* (1981): 53.

[35]Ibid., 52–54.

[36]Ibid., 55–57.

[37]Ibid., 57–58.

[38]Lori Burns and Melisse Lafrance, *Disruptive Divas: Feminism, Identity & Popular Music* (New York, 2002), 135.

[39]Ibid., 149.

[40]Marlon T. Riggs, "Black Macho Revisited: Reflections of a SNAP! Queen," in *Black Men on Race, Gender, and Sexuality: A Critical Reader*, ed. Devon W. Carbado (New York, 1999), 307.

[41]Patricia Hill Collins, *Black Feminist Thought: Knowledge, Consciousness and the Politics of Empowerment*, 68–69.

[42]Marlon T. Riggs, "Black Macho Revisited: Reflections of a SNAP! Queen," in *Black Men on Race, Gender, and Sexuality: A Critical Reader*, ed. Devon W. Carbado (New York, 1999), 307–08.

[43]Ibid., 306–07.

[44]Devon W. Carbado, *Black Men on Race, Gender, and Sexuality: A Critical Reader*, ed. Devon W. Carbado (New York, 1999), 440.

[45]Judith Butler, *Undoing Gender* (New York, 2004), 2.

[46] Ibid., 163.

[47]Lori Burns and Melisse Lafrance, *Disruptive Divas*, 147.

[48]Butler, *Undoing Gender*, 204.

[49]Ibid., 240–41.

[50]Burns and Lafrance, *Disruptive Divas*, 140–41.

[51]Standifer, "Musical Behaviors," 52.

[52]Charles Nero explains that "Christian churches were some of the first institutions blacks created and owned in the United States." He notes that "From 1790 to 1830 ambitious northern free black men like Richard Allen and Absalom Jones circumvented racism by creating new Christian denominations, notably the African Methodist Episcopal Zion churches." See Charles I. Nero, "Signifying on the Black Church," in *Black Men on Race, Gender, and Sexuality: A Critical Reader* ed. Devon W. Carbado (New York, 1999), 276.

[53]As quoted in Charles Nero, "Signifying on the Black Church," 279–80.

[54]Ibid., 280.

[55]Marlon Riggs, "Black Macho Revisited," 307.

[56]Earl Ofari Hutchinson, "My Gay Problem, Your Black Problem," in *Black Men on Race, Gender, and Sexuality: A Critical Reader*, ed. Devon W. Carbado (New York, 1999), 304.

[57]Audre Lorde, "Age, Race, Class, and Sex: Women Redefining Difference," in *Women, Images, and*

Realities: A Multicultural Anthology, eds. Amy Kesselman, Lily D. McNair, and Nancy Schniedewind, (New York, 2008), 254.

[58]Butler, *Undoing Gender*, 21.

[59]Ibid., 24–25.

[60]Ibid., 25, 34–35.

[61]Asali Solomon, "A Different World," *VIBE*, May 2002: 124.

[62]Robert Hilburn, "She Can't Hide Her Feelings," *Los Angeles Times*, 8.

[63]Ibid., 65.

[64]Ibid.

SCRIPTING AND CONSUMING BLACK BODIES IN HIP HOP MUSIC AND PIMP MOVIES

Ronald L. Jackson II and Sakile K. Camara

. . . Much of the assault on the soulfulness of African American people has come from a White patriarchal, capitalist-dominated music industry, which essentially uses, with their consent and collusion, Black bodies and voices to be messengers of doom and death. Gangsta rap lets us know Black life is worth nothing, that love does not exist among us, that no education for critical consciousness can save us if we are marked for death, that women's bodies are objects, to be used and discarded. The tragedy is not that this music exists, that it makes a lot of money, but that there is no countercultural message that is equally powerful, that can capture the hearts and imaginations of young Black folks who want to live, and live soulfully.[1]

Feminist film critics maintain that the dominant look in cinema is, historically, a gendered gaze. More precisely, this viewpoint argues that the dominant visual and narrative conventions of filmmaking generally fix "women as image" and "men as bearer of the image." I would like to suggest that Hollywood cinema also frames a highly particularized *racial* gaze—that is, a representational system that positions Blacks as image and Whites as bearer of the image.[2]

Black bodies have become commodities in the mass media marketplace, particularly within Hip Hop music and Black film. Within the epigraph above, both hooks and Watkins explain the debilitating effects that accompany pathologized fixations on race and gender in Black popular culture. The title of this essay foretells the consumerist impulse to support images with which the public is familiar *and* the producer's inclination to feed the public's imagination about what Ross and Rose coin "postindustrial urban America(n)" Black bodies.[3] The distribution of these images occurs while being attentive to the general lure—the superintending text of sexuality.

Often when researchers discuss sex and the body in popular culture or everyday human activity, they rightfully make reference to feminist writings for they have been the most perspicacious commentators on this subject.[4] We are convinced, just as Watkins, that there are also numerous other corporeal inscriptions enmeshed with gender and the hypertext of sexuality, including but not limited to race.[5] It is also clear to us that most of the mass media research concerning Black popular culture seems forcibly divided into either audience or producer analyses with not nearly enough examination of how these are entwined. Their inextricable linkage is taken for granted in the following discussion in which we will concentrate on the elaborate sexual inscriptions on Black bodies within Hip Hop music, blaxploitation films, and the resurgent production of pimp movies. When we use the word scripts, scripting, inscriptive, or inscribing, we mean figuratively that the body is socially understood and treated as a discursive text that is read by interactants. The purpose of doing a scripting analysis is not to "point fingers," but to locate a displaced agency and to discover the source of inscriptions existent on Black bodies and prominent in popular media and explore the effects of these inscriptions.

Although this position is principally about the aggrandizement of sexual dysfunction in Black popular culture, we feel compelled to advise the reader upfront that we are neither claiming nor insinuating that black popular culture invented, has a monopoly over, or is the sole proprietor of sexual perversion—only that it is a vehicle through which brilliant Hip Hop and pimp film artists have further impoverished the conditions in which Black bodies are already negatively scripted.

As we explore the sexual and racial scripting of Black bodies in Black popular culture, specifically Black film and Hip Hop music, it is clear that the underlying concern is that producers of popular culture have seduced Hip Hop and Black film artists into a relationship that has become parasitic, one where artists make money, become popular, and remain generally gratified by how the industry courts them. Yet the audience becomes enwrapped in an insidious arrangement where they are pleasured at their own risk. Unfortunately, although these artists are aware these industries have ghettoized blackness, then turned it into a commodity and packaged it for mass consumption, they have been complicit with this stereotype. In fact, it is clear they have facilitated this imagery for profit, fame, and material gain but Hip Hop artists, in particular, are respected and appreciated because of the stylistic ways in which they tell their narratives.[6]

Hip Hop artists consider themselves street raconteurs. Many of these contemporary Hip Hop lyricists consider their role to be aural bridges between the gang, Thug and pimp-related elements of the inner-city's underbelly and the more diverse and well-to-do petit bourgeois and also affluent segments of society. By mimicking sexual freedom, narrating ghetto life, exposing hypermasculine anxieties and elucidating criminally strategic behaviors, gangsta and Thug rappers, whether male or female, vie for an authentic and panoptic blackness designed to expose the essence of Black existence.[7] This implicit competition within the Hip Hop discourse community and in many Black films is signaled by the urban call to "keep it real," which suggests that being down to earth is synonymous with being able to claim and navigate ghetto life despite one's real origins.[8] In fact, if one has grown up in any place other than the projects, very little respect is granted within this discourse community. This automatically allows Black ghetto dwellers comprised of otherwise incarcerated voices to be set free to poetically articulate, dispute, and rhetorically reimagine an urban battleground where dwellers are proud, strong, and most fit to survive.

Nonetheless, while caught up in a digital war to technologically determine who has the top rhythmically impressive billboard hit, most "crunk" booty-shaking video, or most lucid film portrayal of indigent Black life that "keeps it real" while not worrying about getting "props" from music award foundations, artists have become entangled in a moral and ontological crisis.[9] This crisis involves the direction and influence of a public consciousness tainted by industry-driven racial and gendered differences throughout popular culture that have been essentialized. This is the case especially in the interrelated entertainment genres of music and film where exposing ghetto life is the most lucrative kind of Black cultural and corporeal expression.

For example, in a Black Entertainment Television (BET) interview with filmmaker John Singleton after the release of *Baby Boy*, he claimed his movie about a dependent twenty-something adult Black male who lives at home with his mother in a bad neighborhood in Los Angeles surrounded by violence, drugs, and criminal mischief was not sensationalizing ghetto life, but merely presenting one story about the truth of ghetto living. He claimed this is the way he grew up in South Central Los Angeles; this is merely a snapshot of his life. Later in a series of interviews about the movie, he bragged this was the most potent, true-to-form ghetto movie he has ever seen. In an effort to produce, direct, and depict the ultimate ghetto movie, artists like Singleton comply with the controlling gaze and ominous ideological inscriptions of the Black body as a menace, an act that distances blackness from everything conventional and morally familiar so that everyday American citizens are assigned to the position of spectator when observing blackness. They cannot relate to it, because it is not a part of their real world. It appears manufactured. While it represents a real part of someone's life, it is presented as a universal depiction of what it means to be Black. It is carnivalesque in function and hence, it remains a rough, tattered, and vulgar dimension of common public American life.[10] Stuart Hall explains this detachment as a spectator. He points out that since it is not of the elite or high culture but rather "popular" culture, it is merely an escape, though spectators gaze at it to remind themselves of their own comfort.[11] Even still, this distancing conditions audience psyches to associate blackness with civil disobedience, criminal habitats, psycho-sexual dysfunction, dependency, as well as the ghettoized underclass and to be alarmed when these "malignant" Black bodies are performing in alignment with "normal" White bodies. The enormous complexity of this phenomenon is daunting. As David Trend laments:

> Not surprisingly, media villains and political scapegoats are often indistinguishable, whether it is in the implied ethnic criminality of [John Singleton's] *Boyz N the Hood* and *Bugsy* or the foreign menace of *Shining Through* and *The Hunt for Red October*. On one level, it is argued that such films help to coalesce an audience around the fear of a common demon that throws national parochialism into relief. But this analysis fails to account for the complex economies of attraction and desire that also characterize constructions of difference. As Ernesto Laclau has suggested, any entity is both defined and limited by objects of alterity. Because the externalized Other is simultaneously a figure of antagonism and radical possibility, It constitutes a part of the self that the self both wants and fears.[12]

So, within a public sphere where common relational values like love, civility, and morality are bound by popular discourses, the fixed notion that Black bodies are unruly fuels the economy of race relations while satiating audiences' consumptive impulses to be entertained, absorbed, and fascinated by this arcane set of racial differences. This happens in much the same way as lynching, during which members of the lynch mobs pulled out Kodak cameras to preserve the memories of the event.[13] In both cases, the I-Other dialectic is engaged with audience members both co-producing and validating the lynching while remaining its spectators.

Curiously entangled in this dialectic are Black bodies that have come to access themselves via the discursive inscriptions promulgated by popular media.[14] Moreover, they have come to see themselves as victims desiring what appears to be a far-fetched indeterminacy and sense of agency to define and create their own realities.[15] Consequently, estranged Black bodies in popular culture too rarely transcend the surfaces of their imposed inscriptions and thus are forced to cohabitate and become complicit with a manufactured ontological double. If they are not exoticized through popular motifs like singing, dancing, playing sports, or being criminalized, then Black bodies are sexualized.[16]

Popular culture, particularly film and music, is littered with intoxicating hedonistic images, patriarchal imprints, and occasionally aesthetically sanitized inscriptions of Black bodies.[17] In fact, Herman Gray and Paul Gilroy remind us film and music are powerful conduits through which individuals are introduced to localized conceptions of attenuated blackness. These institutionally sanctioned conceptions parade as authentic notions of a Black self.[18] We will explore notions of Black authenticity, a theory of complicity, and Black bodies as sites of sexual eroticism, exoticism, and objectification in Black popular culture.

BLACK AUTHENTICITY AND ESSENTIALISM

In the popular phrases, "I'm representin," "keepin' it real" or "stay Black," the predicates describing who one is representing, how real is defined or what Black means is omitted. This begs the question of authenticity, of what is true, what is real, verifiable, and constitutive of blackness that makes it automatically so. The presumption is that we need not explicate or interrogate issues of representation, the realness or blackness—they are terms already reduced to their immediately interpretable meanings. However, the omission becomes even more conspicuous when we begin the discussion of Black cultural *expression*, or *the* Black *experience*. The glaring fact that there is singularity inherent in each of these constructions, when they both should be rightfully pluralized, is what is meant by essentialism. In defining the immutable essence of a thing, by Western standards, it can be put to a valid test of systematic observation, which will prove its accuracy and veracity. If it does not meet these tests, then it is considered untrue and inauthentic. Certainly, it is clear blackness among Blacks is most well understood within its cultural and cosmological parameters. The primary concern, however, is how Black corporeal inscriptions produced by Blacks sometimes parade as authoritative reflections of *true* blackness when they only repre-

sent a fractional set of what Black means. Examples of this are ghettocentric representations of blackness promoted as being indicative of "real" Black life.[19] For instance,
Thug rapper Trick Daddy raps about his representation of thuggery during a song
entitled "I'm a Thug" on his album *Thugs Are Us*. He states:

> I don't know what this world's gonna bring, but I know one thing that this is the
> life for me baby cause I'm a Thug . . . Could it be my baggy jeans. Or my gold
> teeth. That make me different from ya'll. Ain't trippin dog. But listen dog. I've
> been raised a little different dog. I'm just doing my thang. These are my ghetto
> slangs. And I'm representing Thug shit.[20]

English and Africana Studies Professor Mark Anthony Neal discusses his
exploratory in-class focus group of student perceptions concerning Hip Hop, and
indicates, "Many students feel that 'if you don't have an attitude, if you don't act a certain way, if you aren't from the ghetto, the perception is that you are not Black."[21] He
further comments,

> Some of those who embrace [rapper] DMX include relatively well-off middle-
> class Black young people who may be bound for professional careers, but crave
> acceptance by their Black peers and have also based their perceptions of blackness
> on Hip Hop video and the "ghettocentric noir" cinema. As a result, whatever its
> salutary impulses, there is a cost to this ghettocentric romance, as if Black urban
> youth somehow define the essence of the Black experience.[22]

Neal's reflections concerning the opinions of his students who he calls post-soul
babies are insightful. While trying not to appear didactic or effusive with regards to
what authenticity means, we think it is important to be mindful of encoded commentaries concerning authenticity before framing the following discussion with complicity theory.

In an attempt to decipher and explain what is real in the imaginary, metacommu-
nicative universe of popular culture, Black Hip Hop artists and Black filmmakers have
frequently drawn boundaries between the authentic and inauthentic.[23] These arbitrary
demarcations are well-justified in their minds, since ghetto perpetrators are frustrating-
ly discomfiting to these artists, because *true* Thugs are making money telling their own
true stories while *impostors* lie about ghetto experiences, and make ghetto life experiences seem surreal. For example, while asserting their ownership of an authentic Thug
experience, Thug Hip Hop artists Jay-Z, Ja-Rule, and Earl "DMX" Simmons discuss
their disdain for Thug imposters in their song entitled, "Murdergram":

> I know your type, you hype, all up off that fake shit; You can't understand why a
> man would have to take shit. Or steal shit, but this is that real, niggas kill shit, peel
> shit. I hit you in your head you won't feel shit!!![24]

This comment is also in response to the ever-increasing presence of Black crossover artists who have allegedly "sold out" the Black community and begun writing and performing for a broader market including White audiences. The criticism is concerning the supposedly profligate and undignified nature of crossover artistry, how it taints the artistic elements of Hip Hop production by forfeiting and diluting the essence of blackness. In order to thoroughly understand this indictment, one would have to be acquainted with the humble beginnings of rap music when rappers would sell their homemade rap music cassette tapes out of their trunks.[25] They desired larger distribution, but many of them were not willing to seek this distribution at the cost of their allegiance to maintaining their own voice and "keepin' it real."

Now that rap and Hip Hop music have gained prominence for their straight-no-chaser, hardcore approach to narrating urban life, there are impersonators who want to appear "ghetto" or claim their attachment to ghetto life when in fact they have never lived in the ghetto and have only walked through the ghetto, at most.[26] So, Black authenticity in this regard calls into question discursive points of disarticulation and implies that this mimicry bastardizes blackness. By compromising notions of physical and ontological space and place, impersonating artists jeopardize the authenticity, the realness of Black ghetto life as depicted by *true* Thug-centered rap and cinema. The question is: Who will tell the true ghetto life stories? The controversial and interrogatory reply is, "Does it make them less Black because they tell a different story? Moreover, how do we know what is true and why does it matter who tells the story?"

Authenticity and essentialism issues are neither new in Hip Hop music, nor in Black popular culture. Scholars like Michael Eric Dyson, and Paul Gilroy, among others, have addressed this extensively throughout the years. What is new is how authenticity claims emerge not only in Hip Hop music, but also in Black pimp films, both of which seek to expose Black male sexual domination over Black females and therefore remain complicit with early White hegemonic inscriptions of Black bodies.[27]

A BRIEF NOTE ON COMPLICITY THEORY

According to its progenitor, Mark McPhail, the idea of complicity "manifests itself in terms of an adherence to the problematical ideological assumptions of position and privilege inherent in critical discourse."[28] In addition, Blacks become complicit with negative inscriptions of their bodies when they uncritically adopt structures designed to demean or essentialize blackness.

Toward their recovery from this inscriptive damage, McPhail recommends "coherent integration of similarity and difference," which will result in a more sophisticated, holistic and revelatory understanding of cultural standpoints.[29] This demands that individuals situate notations of self and other on a continuum of thinking about racialized bodies but does not privilege one cultural representative's glance over another. McPhail argues this is especially necessary of popular culture. When examining sexuality in Hip Hop music and film, it is axiomatic to decipher representations of subject and object, elite and subaltern, but also the internal contradictions attendant on these inscriptions.

By using the notion of complicity to analyze Thug personae and the pimp-whore complex, "the Other" is necessarily emphasized as both subject and object when speaking of marginalized group members. McPhail adds to the discussion the following sentiment: "The other illustrates the problem of language in Western culture in its most extreme form, as a figure made flesh that reifies the existence of an essential reality, a reality 'out there,' separate and distinct from the human agents that interact within it."[30] Reclamation of agency is not always liberatory however. Sometimes it can inspire the manufacturing of an equally debased and elitist subjectivity, which leads directly to multitudinous objectifications. Such is the case with the brutish personae of the Thug, Ruffneck, and Pimp, each of whom attempt to retrieve agency only to become complicit with patriarchal inscriptions that deny others their dignity and respect.

THUGS AND ROUGHNECKS AS CONTEMPORARY BRUTES AND SEXUAL PREDATORS

The Thug or Ruffneck is a contemporary manifestation of the contumacious brute image, and the Thug image is enjoying an epoch in which it is able to captivate audiences of rap music throughout the world.[31] Consequently, Thug-related themes have become commonplace in Rap and Hip Hop music. It did not begin with present-day Hip Hop music; it is the contemporary musical brainchild of militant 1960s poet pioneers such as Haki Madhubuti (nee Don Lee), Gil Scott-Heron, and The Last Poets, as well as gangsta rap pioneers N.W.A. (Niggaz wit Attitudes) who are said to be the first to use the term on their song "Gangsta, Gangsta."[32] Their obscene antics may be attributed to forerunner Luke "Skywalker" Campbell, who was probably the first to appropriate and market sex-shock in rap music on a global scale with men and women having sex on stage at his concerts. He was the archetypal rap artist-pimp publicly overseeing sexual coupling. This interloping was recast as simply obscene and become the subject of a high-profile first amendment trial.[33] Regardless of the outcome, which tremendously slowed his multicity tour, almost bringing it to an end, Luke Campbell proved just how potent sexually-charged rap music could and would become, and precociously introduced a new brand of "rump-shaking" that would continue to rise to different levels of aggressiveness with Thug rap.[34]

In fact, as Tricia Rose maintains, "Hip Hop articulates a sense of entitlement and takes pleasure in aggressive insubordination."[35] A spin-off of gangsta rap music, the Thug role is a vivid manifestation of that "aggressive insubordination." Thugs perpetuate the myth of a socially sanctioned Black male warrior, who by mere coincidence, is also sexually-charged. As Trend suggests, it is entirely too uncritical to assert entertainment audiences are so engulfed by the venue and "irresistibly drawn to violence," and sexism that they become completely unaware of their consumption of these hegemonic images.[36] Audiences' attraction to certain pedestrian images is not accidental. People make choices to engage their negative and arguably counterproductive specularity of race and gender. As a result, when we hear Hip Hop music lyrics referring to the Thug, Ruffneck, O.G., or G. (i.e., original gangsta or gangsta, respectively), we should not be surprised that we simultaneously hear laudatory labels like "pimp," "mack,""playa," "big baller" and "dog," several of which refer mainly to his acquisition of cash not just the male's sexual conquest of women and/or the whole mystique of his genital enormity.[37] This is characteristic of popular rappers like Trick Daddy, Tupac, Snoop Doggy Dog, the Lox, Dr. Dre, Cash Money Millionaires, Treach from Naughty By Nature, Nas, Ludacris, and Nelly. Each of their scabrous public personae revolve around a ghettocentric personality that accents material wealth gained by previously struggling urban youth, who have now superseded those despondent and uncertain conditions.[38] As their televised videos demonstrate, they are also lascivious pimps who without fail are surrounded by beautiful, often sculpted, scantily clad females. These females have four primary functions as they gyrate and genuflect throughout the video—to engage the audience's voyeuristic gaze, to embody the apparatus of sexual pleasure, to fuel the fantasies and imaginations about her innately lascivious nature, and to serve as instruments controlled by the Thug. Ja Rule demonstrates this last point in his song, "Bitch Betta Have My Money," in which he states:

> Girl you so hot I feel like Iceberg Slim. I pimp plenty women . . . Game is the topic. And what's between your legs is the product. Use it properly and you'll make dollars biatch.[39]

Ja Rule and Case explain the Thug mentality in another song entitled "Thug Life." In this song, they forthrightly declare their awareness that thuggish behaviors and treatment of women are inappropriate, but they rationalize:

> Everything from the evils to price, from the guns to mic. I'm livin' my life runnin' through hell with no wife. It's a sin, but I tell my lost soul to win . . . Baby, I don't respect shit, with diamonds and live reckless . . . The more resist the better, I'm in it for whatever . . . I respect it cuz niggaz ain't shit, you right.[40]

Thugs seek to re-position the Black male body as being in control of himself and *his* women. We purposefully wrote "women, " to suggest that a Thug never commits to one woman, because then he would not be a "playa"; he would be weak or soft as sensitive, loving, nurturing and monogamous, and it is contrary to the definition of the mack to be weak. One of the hallmark characteristics of a Thug is his desensitization, his emotional paralysis. In other words, a Thug does not feel, except when his territory (i.e., family, physical space, or physical person) is threatened. Thugs see themselves as being committed, not necessarily to the community in terms of enhancing its infrastructure, but to "keeping it real" by remembering the people, the dilapidated housing projects and the "hard knocks" lifestyle and exemplifying this remembrance via their clothing, hair styles, walk, talk, improvisational discourse, dances, and virtually every conceivable dimension of their lives. With exceptions like Jay-Z who has continually returned to his New York community to "give something back," many contemporary rappers who identify with the thug profile somehow have convinced themselves they have taken agency in lifting up their communities by claiming their origins in the ghettoes, which supposedly ensures they have not forgotten their Black heritage. In order to prove this, they make gallant attempts to define their realities and re-script their Black bodies; instead however, they have only complied with the stereo-typical illusions about Black male bodies as violent, irresponsible, and lewd. Even though the mostly oversized prison-inspired apparel, timberland boots, and regional-ly-defined accessories (i.e., bandanas, gold teeth, cornrows in hair, etc.) accompany the Thug image for some and immediately conjure negative images, they are merely the epicenter of a more arcane inscription—the essentialism of the Black male image and presentation of it in consonance with the archetypal minstrel brute belonging exclusively to the underclass.

Mark Anthony Neal tries to unravel the magnetism some segments of the general population, who do not belong to the underclass, have toward performances that glorify Thug life:

> I have plenty of students who embrace DMX as a viable [role] model, and not all of them hail from the ghetto or live the less savory side of life that DMX and his lyrics embody. The natural question is, why working- and middle-class Black college students would embrace such a figure. It doesn't quite take away all the mystery to ask the parallel question: Why do so many White middle- and upper-middle class students embrace the Smashing Pumpkins, Aerosmith or Marilyn Manson.[41]

The Thug is compelling because of his ruggedness and his authentic ghettocentrism. Rappers DMX & Dyme's song "Good Girls, Bad Guys" on DMX's . . . *and then there was X* album explains why some women are attracted to Thugs. Female rapper Dyme, whose name has become synonymous with a sexy and attractive nonghetto "good girl," is in dialogue with DMX (his words are in parentheses):

> Hey yo Boo, I'm diggin you, cause you make me wanna do all them things I was taught I wasn't supposed to. . . . . Attractive to me, wit yo' tactics. Hit it like AHHH! Make me backflip. (What to do? You want the nigga wit the slacks, or the jeans and the boots? You wanna be safe or be laced, cause you can be replaced).[42]

In this exchange, Dyme expresses how DMX's thuggish, edgy, hardcore bad boy image lures her into being a rebel. Everything from his daredevil antics to how he sexes her body to even his Thug uniform of Timberland boots and jeans excites her. He admonishes her to rethink her choices, which apparently are either being with a straight-laced, genteel, law-abiding citizen who probably will not be able to sexually satisfy her or being with a fearless, sexually outrageous Thug who can make her feel safe. Against all odds, she chooses the Thug.

The Thug is a modern brute, which is revered for his Stagoleean disposition and feared for his out-of-control, haphazard and volatile behavior.[43] He is uncontrollable and that aspect of his personality becomes mysteriously attractive to some Dymes. Perhaps it is impulsively connected to their internal desire to feel assured that they will always be protected and safe from external harm and if properly guided by her, the Thug or Ruffneck can prove to be a strong and positive father, and strong husband to the Dyme or "Dyme-piece" as she is sometimes called. Although the sporadic behavior of the Thug does not promise the regularity that child-rearing requires, his bar-none attitude adds a false sense of security that a non-Thug may not be able to supply. This is his lure, but it comes at the price of him being noncommittal, which eventually contributes to the dissolution and incohesion of Black families. It also leads to the steady perpetuation of negative Black masculine scripts.

THUG MISSES

Unlike the weak character disposition of the Dyme, Thug Misses are no domesticated arm pieces to be sported by the Thug, because they too are Thugs. According to Dyson and Rose, these female thugs are prophetic in their unrelenting resistance to the undercurrent of male dominance and female submission.[44] In an effort to formulate and enact a subversive politic that disputes the pandemic paternalism of Hip Hop's old boy's network, the most popular and rising cadre of female rappers and Hip Hop artists have labeled themselves "gangsta bitches."[45] In much the same way Black power and civil rights activists and conscious musicians like James Brown repossessed the until-then negative term "Black" making it positive with the slogan "I'm Black and I'm Proud," or in the same way that Eve Ensler's *Vagina Monologues* rescues women's agency by purging, then claiming initially invective epithets like cunt, bitch, and pussy, "gangsta bitches" have decided to take the derisive term "bitch" and used it to refer to women who are angered by some women's passive resistance strategies or simple acceptance of patriarchal abuse. They are boisterously and boldly exclaiming, "Yeah, I am that bi*** you are talking about, so what's your point?" This is never so clear as it is in Lil' Kim's song "Suck my D***" on her album *The Notorious Kim*. She boldly asserts:

> To all my motherfuckin' gettin' money hoes, and all my ghetto bi***** in the projects. Coming through like bulldozers. No, we ain't sober. . . . Niggas love a hard bitch. What? I'm loving this shit. Queen Bi***! What bi*** you know can Thug it like this? . . . Been doin' this for years, no need to practice. Take lessons from the Queen and you'll know how to mack this. . . .[46]

Lil' Kim is representative of a set of female Hip Hop thug artists that we will call

Thug Misses and Ruff Ryders.[47] They have developed a trendy erotogenic persona of the no-nonsense "around-the-way" or ghettoized girl. The seemingly endless list of such artists include popular rappers Li'l Kim, Foxy Brown, Da Brat, Khia, Eve, Gangsta Boo, Missy Misdemeanor Elliott, and the FlipMode Squad (including Rah Digga, Groove Armada and Trina). The words "hard," "raw," and "sexy" best describe the perverse scripting of Thug Misses' Black bodies. They are reactive, young, Black "down-for-whatever" females who, like their Thug and Ruffneck counterparts, are inviolable ruffians supposedly ready for any kind of confrontation or challenge, physical or otherwise. As they "hit the chronic" and "grip the 40s," and do the things the male rappers do, they are using these gestures as an "alternative economy," perhaps even a "prop," but for them, it is part of the ensemble that constitutes the Thug image.[48] It comes along with the "black net cleavage, flawless skin, and coiffed hair" that bespeaks a certain maturity one might expect of a male-scripted heroine; however, it is their creation.[49] Essentially, they see themselves as warrior-princesses. The mythic Xena, Princess Warrior would be considered too soft for their tastes, but the idea resonates. Instead, Thug Misses are ghetto soldiers with an involutive split personality, both delicate and sexually pornographic as well as courageous and bold. They are not necessarily promiscuous just defined by their raw, sexualized disposition.

Even more profound is the masochism inherent in this sumptuous interplay of difference and devaluation. Black female rap artists have always functioned on the periphery of the rap music industry, so this reproduced image is meant to retrieve her agency and prove her worthiness while formulaically attracting consumers, because it is what consumers are used to viewing—Black women's bodies objectified and sexualized. Of the Thug Misses listed earlier, Rah Diggah, who perhaps is most like Xena, is the least likely to be scantily clad. She intentionally evacuates the site where her Black female body is seen as simply an object of male pleasure and attempts to teach her audience that thugging requires revolution and involves being in control. Self-perceived as one who will lead females away from their colonized location, their site of suffrage, through being a Thug, Rah Diggah calls herself "The Harriett Tubman of Hip Hop" in her song "Do the Ladies Run This." Incidentally, even the title of the album signifies her interest in re-emplacing the anteriority or leadership of Black women in cultural production. In the vein of Homi Bhabha's postcolonial lines of thought, she along with other Thug Misses is attempting "to speak Outside the sentence or the sententious . . . to disturb the causality" and to mount a subaltern rebellion.[50]

Rah Diggah was dubbed by *YRB* fanzine as the "Harriett Thugman" of Hip Hop. She perceives herself as an insurrectionist, re-possessing her Black body by taking control over her own lyrics and Thug persona. In concert with this Thug image, she also has developed a creative gangsta line of clothing called Rugged Apparel, combining cross-stitched jeans with chain-link chokers and sterling zippers and buttons topped off with a half-cocked brim.

On her debut album *Dirty Harriet*, she proclaims, "Black chick with intellect, who wanna match wits? Write my own rhymes so can't no nigga tell me shit."[51] By keeping her persona "gangsta," she ensures audiences will see her as neither weak, tender, nor overly effeminate nor one who is able to be overlooked. As an aside, the audiences she is directing her message at are mostly those that have come to be known as the "Black youth culture" despite the fact that non-Blacks represent the majority of gangsta music consumers.[52] As mentioned previously, Digga attempts to counter the sexualized image that often accompanies the Thug Miss persona, and simply asserts herself as hardcore and lyrically savvy.

Somehow by seizing their own licenses to re-script the Black female body to be able to inflict torment while appearing impervious to pain, Thug Misses accomplish a subversive politic of corporeal representation and see themselves as having arisen as heroines in their own right among rap audiences, rather than forgotten shadows of the Thug or simply objects of sexual commodification. Thug Misses are modern hybrids of the Sapphire, Jezebel, and Brute. They are self-assured, independent, bad girls who supposedly do not tolerate nonsense. Unfortunately, this inversion of a codified patriarchy is underwhelming at times and so slippery, it can be easily be read as unimaginative and counterproductive. Although it is perhaps initially exciting to hear female rappers "rock mics" using the same formula of taunting the competition, exposing bravado, and skillfully rhyming about familiar themes, that does not take away from the fact that the formula is not inventive. Nonetheless, innovative capitalization and enhancement of the Thug image is the principal claim of female thug rappers. By eroticizing a hegemonic Thug fantasy and embodying it with a female standpoint, Thug Misses may have only divested themselves of any possibility of reclaiming true agency. Instead, they put themselves at risk to become lost once again in the shadows, but this time in their own poisoned reinvention of Black female bodies' sexual mystique. To put it plainly, in many ways, the scripting of the Black female body in Hip Hop as a thug is derivative at best. It is merely emblematic of a master narrative—old guard, male representations of women as feisty, overreactive, sexualized mistresses. So, Hip Hop women's counter-narrative occupies a space that simply aligns with the master narrative rather than running against it as we suspected it would.

Whether Thugs or Thug Misses, the contemporary brute image remains well intact. It is pervasive throughout Black popular culture and is one of the most intricate images to be found, because of its admirable resilience in the face of tribulation, yet its frequently demonstrative counter-affectionate, uncivil, unruly, and irresponsible inscriptions. For example, popular cultural images have taught consumers that the average Thug does not see women as potential companions deserving of commitment and love; instead they are considered "bitches," and as such are mere commodities. Rap artists DMX and Sisquo articulate this point in the song "What These Bitches Want" on DMX's sophomore album entitled . . . *and then there was X*. The rap says:

Aiyyo!! Dog, I meet bitches, discrete bitches. Street bitches, slash, Cocoa Puff sweet bitches (WHAT?) . . . I fuck with these hoes from a distance. The instant they start to catch feelings. I start to stealin they shit then I'm out just like a thief in the night. I sink my teeth in to bite. You thinkin life, I'm thinkin more like—whassup tonight? Come on ma, you know I got a wife. . . .[53]

Even while keeping in mind that "rap music is the contemporary stage for the theatre of the powerless," it can also be argued that these artists and their producers are opportunists taking advantage of modern consumptive and voyeuristic audience impulses to witness violence and acquire pleasure from commodified sexual images that excite the senses.[54] Puzzlingly, Dyson is not so severe in his appraisal of these images; he seems to extol them, suggesting there is an evangelical call to arms afoot via Thug rap. In fact, he nimbly apprehends the critical practice of contextualizing and unraveling Thugs' motivations for thuggery. In the same breath in which he admits that gangsta rap music has been rightfully criticized for its vulgarity, commodification, and paralysis of Black women's bodies, he rationalizes that the complexity of these rappers' despondent backgrounds leads them to filter these images to the public so they can feed their families and monetarily uplift their communities.[55] Essentially, all they want to do is escape and give back to the ghetto enclaves from which they emerged. Though true for some artists, we are afraid that Dyson's sonorous critical deconstruction is potentially more damaging than assistive. We agree that all texts should be considered within context and by virtue of pretext, but it is entirely too uncritical to release gangsta and Thug rappers' sexual perniciousness from social critique and intellectual scrutiny. In our reading of his analysis, Dyson appears to have concocted an intellectual elixir that conveniently relieves gangsta rappers and the newer breed/genre of Hip Hop thugs from any responsibility.

It is not that the self-proclaimed Thug artists' experiences are not real; and it is not that the telling of their experiences should be avoided. It is also not the case that Thugs are without viable reason for their gangsta behavior. It is that the hyperfascination with this monolithic industry-driven inscription of blackness exposes many negatively scripted Black stereotypes. The fallout from this suggests a perhaps unintended artistic complicity. Both Dyson and Rose are correct in that Thug rappers and their producers have mutually exploited one another and that their artistry is evolving. The artists have cunningly duped the industry into buying a product that was initially thought to be uninteresting; however their compliance has consensually granted producers the opportunity to commit an even larger grievance via the perpetuation of imagery that is considered far from fantastical in the inscriptive gaze of the guardians of patriarchy.[56] The microcosm of Thugs and Thug Misses as bad boys and bad girls is unfolded via sexually-charged and violent Hip Hop narratives, and these popularized elegies do not exist in a vacuum. Due to the wide appeal of Black cultural expression, they dramatically affect and abet the deleterious inscriptions of Black bodies everywhere.

Rap and Hip Hop have become their own combined enterprise. This industry is a multibillion dollar institution that does generate positive outlets for personal expression, wonderful alternatives for struggling youth, and ameliorative psychological conditions for Black community well-being. It accomplishes this with the music of artists who function on the edge of the genre like Alicia Keys, Mary J. Blige, Erykha Badu, Indie Arie, as well as Jill Scott, and more centrally Sister Souljah, Lauryn Hill, Queen Latifah, Mos Def, Will Smith, Common, The Fugees, Wyclef, and others. However, these artists and their most important "conscious rap" are a relatively small faction comprised of the exceptions, rather than the rule.[57] Thug elegists primarily occupy the contemporary landscape of Hip Hop music—they are the rule, considered the most authentic rap storytellers in the present era.[58]

THE CONTEMPORARY STOCK MINSTREL THUG IN BLACK FILM

The Buck, Brute, or Thug, in all its manifestations, has also seized a distinct sphere of cultural production that serendipitously has been perpetuated in Hollywood blockbuster movies like *New Jack City, Harlem Nights, Boyz N the 'Hood, Crooklyn, Friday, Next Friday, Set It Off, The Wash, Baby Boy,* and a whole slew of Black popular and independent films. Yet the Thug's sometimes maniacal, perennially dystopic "penis-as-animal," behaviors only recapitulate and exacerbate the public paranoia about the beast-like nature of the Black male as brute.[59] The silver screen is exploding with these iconographic images, preoccupied with a Black representational gaze fixated on almost nothing but the ugly aspects of Black existence that celebrate trifling ghetto living and poverty, neither of which are indicative of a composite Black culture, but pretend to be.[60]

Here, it would be easy to cite devastating or optimistic statistics concerning the well-being of Blacks in order to illustrate by comparison actual versus depicted Black life.[61] Additionally, the spectacular consumption of rap music is another avenue of discussion that would permit a segue into conversation about the commodification of Black bodies.[62] It might even be intriguing to talk about the ironies of capitalism and Black youth or expound upon the parallel of Thug life to the self-inflicted and painfully disengaging experience and physical bodily inscriptions imposed via tattooing and body piercing.[63] However, as the citations foretell, this work has already been done, and accomplished exceedingly well we must add. Instead, we have chosen to analyze a heuristic as well as an intriguing extension of the discussion of Thug-related Hip Hop artistry—the Thug-induced "pimp-whore complex" in Black pimp films.

AN ANALYSIS OF *AMERICAN PIMP*: MINSTREL BRUTE PERSONIFIED

The recent proliferation of pimp-related films remarkably reproduces grotesque dialectics between subject and object as well as historical and contemporary corporeal representations. In consonance with the minstrel brute, the Black stud, playa, mack, and pimp images are all Black bucks trying to come to terms with masculinity. A common scapegoat used to justify these roles is emasculation. According to Robert Staples, Black men incurred psychological damage from enslavement, which left them as undignified expatriates in their own homes, removed from familial responsibilities except as breadwinner, and in some severe cases castrated.[64] As a result, he was emasculated, dethroned if you will. Anxious to recapture the ultimate attribute and sign of a man—control—his only recourse was to seize reckless control over every visible

191

aspect of his life from women to materialistic resources.

Ellis Cose counters Staples' redemption logic and contends, "those with a sense of history know that the stud image did not spring from the Black community but originated with Whites searching for signs that Blacks were intellectually inferior and morally degenerate—and therefore suitable for use as slaves."[65] There is little relief resulting from either assertion or rationale especially when Black filmmakers facilitate the perpetuation of the stud, thereby reproducing Black male subjectivity and substituting white hegemony for Black hegemony. The truth is the stud is like the playa and the pimp, both of which are embodiments of masculine representation and regulation. The male pimp, mack, playa, and stud unscrupulously seek out and secure sexual liaisons with multiple consenting, but still very emotionally vulnerable partners. Hence, as in *American Pimp*, it is highly unlikely that two playas will be sexually engaged by one another. That destroys the power-driven sensation, the libidinal thrill, and the rush that the playa experiences when he is able to accumulate multiple partners, then emotionally destabilize and objectify them so that he remains psychically detached from the activity. For him, it is a pimp game, nothing more than a leisurely activity comprised of paternally bound rules and objectives. He chooses to become the master gamesman, rhetorically recasting the dangerous act of prostitution as play. The idea of play, as signified in the commonly used phrase "pimp game," has powerful resonance with sex and pleasure as entertainment devices. It is severely beyond the range of conventional tropes related to men "scoring" with women.[66] Women are treated as mere game pieces, chips, or tokens on the region-bound game boards Thugs use within the game of survival.

Metaphorically, Thugs are the players who mobilize and control the movements of the game pieces. The Thugs set the rules, revise the rules; also, they often play the role of banker. Sometimes Thugs play for large cash rewards and sometimes they do "nickel pimping," which involves mooching off of women for favors, money, shelter, or some other material resource.[67] Thugs are selfish; the primary concern of a Thug is his own survival, so he will do whatever it takes to make that happen. This is evidenced in several pimp films of the late twentieth century.

With the release of White filmmaker Beeban Kidron's *Hookers, Hustlers, Pimps and Their Johns* came a spate of copycat films directed by Blacks who were convinced their depiction of prostitution as a "pimp game" was even more authentic than the last.[68] These movies included Dre Robinson's *Pimps*, Brent Owens' *Pimps Up, Hos Down*, and the Hughes Brothers' Albert and Allen more noted film documentary *American Pimp*, for which motion picture studio executives competed. Common to all of these films, there is a celebration of unmediated misogyny and pandering. With this surge of epics, there is also an energetic embrace of profound masculine anxieties associated with control and domination of mostly Black women; hence the present examination of the Black pimp-Black whore complex. Rather than systematically and intelligently interrogate the abrupt interception of Black agency in defining Black bodies, films like these suggest many Black artists including filmmakers and musicians are vying for elitist subjectivity over portions of the composite community. In centering the masculine *subject* as pimp and marginalizing the female *object* as prostitute, any collective sense of the black body is fractured.

Aware of this, the Hughes brothers explained to an audience of moviegoers why they chose to present the film as they did. One of the bonus tracks of the DVD version of *American Pimp* showed this live interview and discussion with Albert and Allen Hughes, the directors of the documentary. They explained that they purposefully presented the film with a nonjudgmental tone. They also noted they were fully aware of the negative consequences a film like this could have, so they chose a documentary mode that would allow the pimps and prostitutes to speak for themselves while exonerating the directors from responsibility for what was said. The Hughes brothers' interest in directing this film was intricately tied to their childhood during which they witnessed pimping firsthand by a close relative. They wanted to expand the audience's imagination to capture the reality that there are rampant occurrences of prostitution across the United States and this activity often goes unchecked. However, they also wanted to invite outgroup audiences into a world they would probably never come to know. Defying the directorial urge to tidy up filmic endings, the Hughes brothers reveal their conscious choice to leave a resentfully painful denouement with the audience. They intended for the audience to feel as though this situation was unresolved, and it is, especially with each revitalized repetition of pimp imagery.

Just as Black slaves functioned as devices of labor for their master, the reproduction of the machinery of enslavement is exemplified in several pimp films in which the Black male is owner and the Black female is property. Her body and mind is summarily exploited, abused, and treated as an instrument. She is treated inhumanely, denigrated with slurs like "bitch"and "ho," though as the Hughes brothers show us in *American Pimp*, these are allegedly considered affectionate nicknames in the "pimp game."

It does not require a sophisticated analysis to lay testimony to such a transparent straw argument. Just as "nigger" and "boy" were affixed derogatory labels used to describe, besmirch, and refer to Black men during slavery, "bitch" and "ho" function to sabotage and subjugate Black women's bodies, minds, spirits, and hence their identities. But, the more sophisticated question is what does this signify about the economy of the gaze—to name and see her as a female dog or whore? In response to a larger project concerning the dismissal of women's standpoints within a limited range of patriarchal epistemologies, Judith Butler indirectly ruminates on this question and surmises:

Women are the "sex" which is not "one." Within a language pervasively masculinist, a phallocentric language, women constitute the *unrepresentable*. In other words, women represent the sex that cannot be thought, a linguistic absence and opacity. Within a language that rests on univocal signification, the female sex constitutes the unrestrainable and undesignatable. . . . This association of the body with the female works along magical relations of reciprocity whereby the female sex becomes restricted to its body, and the male body, fully disavowed becomes paradoxically the incorporeal instrument of an ostensibly radical freedom.[69]

Consequently, the paradoxically autonomous male body grants itself permission to name, and out of functional necessity, he initiates controlling and persecutory practices that complement his derogatory linguistic rendering of the female body. Remember, in the pimp game, she is merely a token.

Giving credit to the novel *Iceburg Slim*, *American Pimp* is interspersed with excerpts from blaxploitation films like *Willie Dynamite*, *Slaughter's Big Rip Off*, and *The Mack*. *The Mack* has a title character explicating the "game" as follows: "Anybody can control a woman's body, but the key is to control her mind."[70] In fact, in the documentary *American Pimp*, each of the 30 pimps and prostitutes interviewed suggested that the pimping "game" is properly "played" only when the female prostitute understands she is simply a sexual apparatus. As noted with the Thug, the Pimp's hallmark characteristic is desensitization or emotional paralysis. He does not feel, and as hooks asserts with respect to adolescent boys, there is violence in this "abusive insistence . . . that they not feel."[71] In allowing the pimp to control her perceptions and self-esteem, she forces herself into a precarious position where she is unable to experience unconditional and unselfish love. Love only complicates the situation. In excusing the behaviors of pimps, several prostitutes explained the pimp's role as a protector, an overseer, suggesting prostitutes could choose to be free of this enterprise, but then they would be unsafe, especially if they stayed in this profession. One pimp described the archetypal pimp's duty as follows: "I supply the food. I supply the shelter, and I supply the medical bills. I supply everything. All she gotta supply is the money."[72] In this tragicomical synopsis of pimp responsibilities, we return to the Black male's dependency on women to facilitate his survival. All he has to do to fulfill his obligations is be a ruthless, cold-hearted, mind-controlling, objectifying, hypermasculine mack of emotionally and psychologically vulnerable women. Upon closer examination though, this complicit behavior carries with it an implicit interposition of identity negotiation, which suggests a connection between the Thug's anxiety about his socially subjugated masculinity, his maintenance of the pimp image/style, and his psychological investiture in the pimp-whore complex. The disquieting reality, as Cornel West puts it, is

> For most young Black men, power is acquired by styling their bodies over space and time in such a way that their bodies reflect a uniqueness and provoke fear in others. To be "bad" is good not simply because it subverts the language of the dominant White culture but also because it imposes a unique kind of order for young Black men on their own distinctive chaos and solicits an attention that makes others pull back with some trepidation. This young Black male style is a form of self-identification and resistance in a hostile culture; it also is an instance of machismo identity ready for violent encounters. Yet in a patriarchal society, machismo identity is expected and even exalted—as with Rambo and Reagan. In this way, the Black male search for power often reinforces the myth of Black male

sexual prowess—a myth that tends to subordinate Black and White women as objects of sexual pleasure.[73]

West is absolutely correct to suggest that Black macho rigidity is entangled in Black men's quest to be acknowledged, valued, and emotionally secure. He is only secure when he is able to reconstruct knowledge-forms and narratives that fit his fantasies about retrieving custody over his own social and ontological agency. This is evidenced during *American Pimp* with the pimp-whore relationship creation narratives.

The documentary shows pimps who mouth platitudes concerning the origins of and their participation in pimping. These wide-ranging narratives glorified pimping. One "genesis of pimping" story was told of Black male slavehands directing enslaved girls to have sex with the White slavemaster in order to get physically close enough to him to retaliate by stabbing or trying to hurt him. Another pimp suggested pimping began in ghettos as a way to escape the financial ruins of ghetto life while plunging into entrepreneurial endeavors. One pimp from Atlanta named Sir Captain opined that pimping must have evolved from a need to overcome the street life by mastering it. He audaciously remarked, "The street game is the Black man's game. . . . It's the only game he [the White man] can't control. He can control all the dope dealers in the world. He can't control the pimp." These prefatory ruminations lead to a discussion of how pimps were introduced to and how they "play" the "game." Some claimed an innate capacity and drive to be a pimp, while others suggested they learned about it later in life and worked hard to secure respect as a pimp. It should be mentioned that some pimps, like one named "Bishop" from Chicago, who was a pimp for over twenty years before he was ordained as a minister, would take some of their profits and give back to their communities by purchasing and distributing free school supplies to the children and generally ensuring the safety of the families and children in the community. Though his pimping was well-known, his charitable and altruistic acts of kindness salved his relationship with the community and permitted a sort of redemption of his image. Respect is a term that reverberated throughout the documentary—respect from prostitutes, from the pimp's family, from the surrounding community, and from other pimps who validated and uplifted him. As viewers, we play witness to a "Players Ball" in Milwaukee in which hundreds of well-manicured men dressed in fur coats, long hats, and snakeskin shoes attend a gala where they would compete (by showcasing their scantily clad, booty-shaking prostitutes) for trophies as rewards for acquiring and managing a bevy of prostitutes. It is suggested these balls take place throughout the United States each year, from San Francisco and Las Vegas to Milwaukee and New York. The predominant tropes being presented in *American Pimp* are disquieting. The reality is that sexual deviancy, inherent in the pimp-whore complex as exhibited professionally with a pimp and his prostitutes or via interpersonal relationships, robs the transformative potential and liberatory possibilities of vulnerable Black bodies and causes us to regress to the blaxploitation era of filmic caricatures like the Superfly, Mack, Shaft, and Sweetback who perhaps were useful and heroic in their own time, but contemporarily are misfits.

THE RESURRECTION OF THE PIMP IN BLAXPLOITATION FILMS

It is important to recognize that blaxploitation is an intentional anti-establishment genre just as rap music was when it began. It is difficult to make the argument that Hip Hop began this way, but its stylistic elements, swagger and youth appeal, as well as its innovative lexical form and content have significantly transformed a sizeable portion of the present generation of individuals 35 and under, and in that way it may be accurate to say Hip Hop has "bucked the system." As discussed earlier the pure, bottom-line profit generated by mainstream record labels that support Hip Hop alone warrants reconsideration of any claim that Hip Hop has completely bucked the system. Nonetheless, thug-related Hip Hop music seems to have taken notes from blaxploitation films as much of the early images of the smooth-talking pimp were present in these films.

In retrospect or from afar one might think of the wildly clad bevy of film protagonists during this period as nothing more than a gallery of criminal misfits, pimps and prostitutes, and ghetto-dwelling savages trying to assume a position of authority within the underbelly of society just for the sake of having power. Yet, that would be a hasty generalization. While the characters are in fact presented this way, their roles are purposefully scripted this way in order to represent the kind of retaliation that cannot be controlled. No one controls the Superfly, the Mack, Shaft, or Sweetback. Whether they embody the role of a drug kingpin, pimp, detective or whatever, they are not the docile, meek Black male protagonists of the 1960s whose first instinct is deference to Whites and "playing by the rules." Their characters develop their own rules and force the Man to deal with them on their terms. It compels the audience to side with the villain because the villain is presented as the true underdog who seems to have no other options available to escape the trap of a structurally disadvantaged lifestyle but to become the embodiment of the very thing the establishment despises and fears. It is a direct message to White society that if White xenophobia and racism is rooted in this unfounded fear that Blacks are inherently violent, criminal, reckless, savage, intimidating, and flawed just because of how they look, then since there is no way to interrupt that cycle without Blacks becoming a victim of it we will fight back by being the quintessential object of White fear. It is the only domain where Whites lacked control over the Black body, but ironically these representations were so well-aligned with White stereotypes about Blacks that White audiences curiously supported them wholeheartedly at the box office. The same thing is happening with Hip Hop music. Hip Hop artists are contemporarily complying with racial scripts about Black male and female bodies by redefining their bodies as delinquent, unafraid, violent, criminal, and reckless. The unintended consequence of this is that the music has captured the hearts and minds of youth of ALL nationalities and backgrounds, so Hip Hop artists have become the intoxicating symbols of rebellion, fun, self-centeredness, and individualism. At the same time, as their audience grows and with the emergence of every lucrative album slinging ghetto rhymes, the underdog status of thug Hip Hop artists dissipates. Even after we are moved by the necessary coupling of profanity and ghetto narratives, it becomes less and less believable that these artists truly represent the underclass.

In the same way that Hip Hop has been a lucrative enterprise, film studios during the blaxploitation era made millions of dollars and while all-black casts benefited, Black images and representations on film both regressed and movie-going audiences in the 2000s still witness some of the residue and the indelible impact of these pathological images. The blaxploitation era did not as much initiate this line of stereotyping as they did significantly expand it and master it on film. Contemporary thug-related Hip Hop music will leave the same legacy to future generations.

The conflicting nature of both Hip Hop and blaxploitation films is rooted in how and why it should be celebrated. These entertainment utilities represent brands of artistry that are bold, unafraid, energizing, empowering, and supportive of Black artists and actors. Unlike films where Blacks simply played in roles in which they were expected to "act White" prior to blaxploitation, music, from jazz, rock-n-roll, and blues to gospel, reggae, and rhythm and blues (R&B), has always been indisputably influenced and enhanced by Blacks. Although many Black music artists did not own or maintain copyright to their music, and therefore lack creative and financial control, their contributions were clear. Black audiences of both music and film had become both used to and fed up with the servile status given to Blacks. They wanted the kind of respect that White artists and actors seemed to get without asking.

The similarities between Black music and film are not only compelling because of this seizing of agency (which is a major factor), but also simply because Black film has always been influenced by music, and vice versa. For example, it is important to recall that not all blaxploitation films were male-dominated and geared toward the stud, mack, player image. In fact, a slew of films such as *Mahogany*, *Foxy Brown*, *Sparkle*, and *Coffy* introduced a Black heroine who was even more sexy and doubly brutal when compared to the male protagonists in other blaxploitation films. The soundtracks complimented this edgy, yet sensuous tenor to this genre. The music in these films became extremely significant after Earth, Wind and Fire performed the score for *Sweet Sweetback Badaaass Song* and Isaac Hayes was awarded an Oscar for developing the score for *Shaft*. Every studio executive wanted this unique rhythmic sound seemingly most readily available among Black artists like Curtis Mayfield, Marvin Gaye, Quincy Jones, Staples Singers, Donny Hathaway, Aretha Franklin, and others. The soundtracks were produced with the hope that they could achieve the fame and fortune of Hayes' LP. This was never repeated to the same magnitude. Yet the audience excitement and energy in anticipation of these films was unprecedented and that is largely due to this marriage between Black music and Black film.

SUMMARY AND IMPLICATIONS

It is not surprising that contemporary Hip Hop music and Black film resonate with one another. They always have in one way or another. They certainly are commenting on the same cultural reality despite the narrow focus on one type of Black reality—ghetto life. It is significant, however, that they coalesce around certain themes despite the generational differences. Generational legacies are being left with every new iteration, every new Hip Hop elegy, and every new thug film. The fascinating thing is that this thug persona is transcended by the artists themselves. More and more Hip Hop artists like Master P, Jay-Z, DMX, Ja-Rule, LL Cool J, Snoop Doggy Dog, Queen Latifah, Lil Bow Wow, Xhibit, Ice Cube, and others have become prolific actors who continue to vie for the minds and dollars of the larger public. Their messages shift. We get the sex-crazed, wil'in out pimp-player whose anthem calls out for the dogs and the ho's within Hip Hop music, then we see a range of positive and negative images of these artists in film. The ultimate message is to "chase that paper" (i.e., make money) regardless of how you get it, which makes the whole Hip Hop persona seem theatrical and unreal. Nonetheless, the realness of the effects of thug-related artistry is still quite devastating.

To cast it another way, plurisignant hegemonic inscriptions of Black bodies, no matter whether at the hands of White or Black producers, are still tragic. We, the populace of moviegoers, Hip Hop fans, and general consumers of Black popular culture, are still debilitated with the emergence of each reinvented minstrel figure and each recreated and lauded act of misogyny. Indeed, even at its best in popular culture, when paternalism was supposed to make the public feel safe, protected, and affirmed, instead it has shown us hypervigilant, narcissistic, and exploitative metanarratives that contravene any attempt at liberation.[74] It is not that we are doomed, but that we are survivors of epistemic and cosmological violence; yet, the incipient healing from the scars inflicted on us is being routinely interrupted by inscriptive regimes of truth and authenticity in popular culture. We masochistically return to popular culture to be pleasured by its modernized romanticization of heterosexual men's misogyny, hegemony, and colonization. Hence, there is a mutual dependence on one another that may be explained as the I-Other, victimizer-victim, scripter-inscribed dialectic. Audiences' penchant for accepting these images is akin to saying, as singer Bill Withers croons, "if it feels this good gettin' used, then use me up." This involution should stimulate hyper-awareness of the emotive conditions in which the aesthetic is confined; however, we are seemingly apathetic or blinded by the motives, or perhaps just forgiving of the scripters who have exposed us to the destructive mythoforms we now accept as real and verifiable inscriptions.

We also forget about how our sexuality is confounded by this discussion of sex. For heterosexuals, it is easy to overlook the heterosexual tendencies unitarily displayed in filmic depictions of sexuality. This is certainly parallel to Whites overlooking the privileges granted to them and being stupefied by any assertion that others are not equally privileged. Heterosexual experiences possess privileged space in popular culture, and homoerotic experiences are relegated to secondary or tertiary levels of importance. Increasingly, this is changing, but the incontrovertible reality is these ontic relations and their economies are still fairly new to consumers of mass media. We devour the nude when it is presented heterosexually, and we voyeuristically embrace it when it is presented to us in shocking ways, such as with the 2 live Crew or in *Pimps Up, Hos Down*. It directly affects our memory and desire, our fascinations about the sexual object, and potentially our treatment of women. Without our conscious volition, we find ourselves seeing women as objects, gazing at them sexually even when there is no mediated device to stimulate such an observation. We then comply with the hegemonic inscriptions of women's bodies. Again, it is what we do with the inscriptions that is potentially dangerous.

There must be a rewriting of Black male and female bodies in popular media. In seeking this desiderate agency to corporeally re-inscribe culturally progressive meanings, particular attention must be paid especially to patriarchal effacement and materialization of these bodies in the consumptive interests of market values like competition, greed, money, and power. It is hardly enough for artists like N.W.A., Luther Campbell, Lil' Kim, Foxy Brown, P. Diddy, and Master P to own their own record companies and labels. Hip Hop music of the ilk described here is readily accessible to American youth, youth who sometimes are searching for acceptance. This image is popular, and when embraced often comes with a certain degree of respect.[75] Yet, the temperament of thug-related Hip Hop music disengages audiences who are not enchanted by the misogynistic impulses of the genre. Consequently, there is a moral, social, and cultural estrangement experienced by those who first hear Hip Hop music and wonder if its nihilism, sexual perversion, and apolitical tenor is simply the result of a generational shift or if this genre of music really does offer poison to our youth.

Invariably, we are left with romanticized depictions of ghetto life that only seem attractive because of the ghetto dwellers resilience, perseverance, and down-to-earth dispositions. From this menagerie, we come to understand from a middle-class perspective that we can expect a chilling candor that bespeaks courage and fear at the same time—courage to sustain and fear of never being treated as capable, competent, normal human beings. This dialectic emerges and centers around commodified Black bodies that have been scripted as pathological.

For too long, Blacks have looked at themselves through the eyes of others. Historically, Blacks have had to detach themselves from the scripted stereotypes about them that are presented in popular media and elsewhere. As we have explored throughout this paper, two conspicuous effects have surfaced as a result of negative scripts in the popular media: distancing and complicity.

One result has been that Blacks have distanced themselves from the images they see portrayed on film. Yet collectively we are so intrigued by these plastic inscriptions that we support them. Many Blacks still find humor in *Bringing Down the House* and *Head of State*. Furthermore, we are entertained by movies like *Baby Boy* despite their formulaic typecasting, harmful implications, and stereotypical portrayals of Black bodies. In fact, we are left with few filmic alternatives that depict Black lives positively and productively. The sad message we are sending the entertainment industry, when we support these films with our dollars, is that we are prepared to be degraded. When films and music yield millions of dollars in profit, the only way to read this is as a measure of success; hence this leads to even more degrading images.

Another result has been complicity. Producers of negative scripts about Black bodies, some of whom are Black, have constructed a unifocal perspective of blackness that sees it in its most pathologized form. When criticized for having done this, typical responses are that the product is simply for entertainment purposes or that it is representative of a very real and vivid portrait of Black life. They often fail to comment on how this one-dimensional portraiture debilitates Black identities by scripting Black bodies as deviant, criminal, aloof, degenerate, depraved and deprived. No one takes responsibility for the negative effects these images have on Black lives and American race relations. In fact, there appears to be complicity with these images, which only serves to isolate and polarize Black bodies from what can be understood as normal unless we define normal Black identities as universally ghettoized. The result has been Black entertainers and producers who are trading consciousness for profit, and this is not the sole conundrum or fault of Hip Hop music or Black films. This is endemic to the entire entertainment industry where we witness pockets of responsible entertainment between debilitating discourses that disprivilege impressionable minds and succumb to consumerist impulses.

We need positive, healthy, productive, and liberatory discourses to accompany agency. It is not enough to have a Hip Hop clothing line or record label. Perhaps, our saving grace is that although inscribed bodies appear intractable, they can be transformed. What we have sought to illustrate is that transfigurations of Black bodies have essentially rotated hegemony, flipping it on its side; hence the reinventive, or subletting, Black corporeal scripts discussed here have maintained the same posture as the previously inscribed ones produced by Whites; they have moved in place, not forward. Yet the powerful will and resilience of thug rappers to be appreciated for their indigenous experiences is encouraging. There is no salvation in losing connection with one's cultural self. What is most needed is a popular cultural transformation that will couple retrieved agency and potent discourse with emancipatory will.

NOTES

[1]bell hooks, *Rock My Soul: Black People and Self-Esteem* (New York, 2003), 222.

[2]Samuel Craig Watkins, *Representing: Hip Hop Culture and the Production of Black Cinema* (Chicago, 1998), 154–55.

[3]Andrew Ross and Tricia Rose, *Microphone Fiends: Youth Music and Youth Culture* (New York, 1994), 71.

[4]Judith Butler, *Gender Trouble: Feminism and the Subversion of Identity* (New York, 1990); Gwendolyn Foster-Dixon, "Troping the Body: Etiquette Texts and Performance," *Text and Performance Quarterly* 13 (1993): 79–96; Elizabeth Grosz, *Volatile Bodies: Toward a Corporeal Feminism* (Bloomington, 1994); Judith Hamera, "The Ambivalent, Knowing Male Body in the Pasadena Dance Theatre," *Text and Performance Quarterly* 14 (1994): 197–209; M. J. Smythe, "Talking Bodies: Body Talk at Bodyworks," *Communication Studies* 46 (1995): 245–60.

[5]Watkins, *Representing.*

[6]Ibid.

[7]Robyn Wiegman, *American Anatomies: Theorizing Race and Gender* (Durham, 1995).

[8]Michael Hecht, Ronald L. Jackson, and Sidney Ribeau, *Black Communication: Exploring Identity and Culture* (Mahwah, 2003).

[9]One of many laudatory and complimentary words referring to the greatness or splendor of something

being described, David Toop, *The Rap Attack* (Boston, 1984).

[10]Todd, Boyd, *Am I Black Enough for You: Popular Culture from the 'Hood and Beyond* (Bloomington, 1997); Colin MacCabe, *The Eloquence of the Vulgar* (London, 1999); Tricia Rose, *Black Noise: Rap Music and Black Popular Culture in Contemporary America* (Hanover, 1994); Watkins, *Representing*.

[11]Stuart Hall, "What Is This Black in Black Popular Culture?" in *Black Popular Culture*, ed. Gina Dent (Seattle, 1992), 21–36.

[12]David Trend, "Nationalities, Pedagogies and Media," in *Between Borders: Pedagogy and the Politics of Cultural Studies*, ed. Henry Giroux and Peter McLaren (New York, 1994), 231.

[13]James Allen, Leon F. Litwack, Hilton Als, Leon F. Litwack, Hilton Als, *Without Sanctuary: Lynching Photography in America* (Twin Palms Publishers, 2000).

[14]Robyn Wiegman, "Black Bodies/American Commodities: Gender, Race and the Bourgeois Ideal in Contemporary Film," in *Unspeakable Images: Ethnicity and American Cinema*, ed. Lester D. Friedman (Urbana, 1990).

[15]Felipe Smith, *American Body Politics* (Athens, 1998).

[16]Michael Eric Dyson, "Be Like Mike?: Michael Jordan and the Pedagogy of Desire," in *Between Borders*, ed. Henry Giroux and Peter McLaren, 119–26; Nelson George, *Buppies, B-Boys, Baps and Bohos: Notes on Post–Soul Black Culture* (New York, 1992).

[17]Watkins, *Representing*.

[18]Herman Gray, "Television, Black Americans and the American Dream," *Critical Studies in Mass Communication* 6 (Summer 1989): 376–86; Paul Gilroy, "Sounds Authentic: Black Music, Ethnicity, and the Challenge of the Changing Same," *Black Music Research Journal* 10 (Winter 1990): 128–31.

[19]Boyd, *Am I Black Enough for You?*; Mark Costello and David Foster Wallace, *Signifying Rappers: Rap and Race in the Urban Present* (Hopewell, 1990); Adam Krims, *Rap Music and the Poetics of Identity* (New York, 2000).

[20]Trick Daddy. 2001. *Thugs are US*. Slip-N-Slide Records.

[21]Mark Anthony Neal, *Soul Babies: Black Popular Culture and the Post-Soul Aesthetic* (New York, 2002), 188.

[22]Ibid.

[23]Dyson, "Be Like Mike?," 119–26.

[24]DMX, Ja Rule and DMX. 2005. *Murdergram Lyrics*. Def Jam Recordings.

[25]Melbourne S. Cummings & Abhik Roy, (2002). "Manifestations of Afrocentricity in Rap Music," *The Howard Journal of Communications* 13 (2002): 56–79; William Eric Perkins, *Droppin' Science: Critical Essays on Rap Music and Hip Hop Culture* (Philadelphia, 1996).

[26]Bakari Kitwana,*The Hip Hop Generation: Young Blacks and the Crisis in Black Culture* (New York, 2002).

[27]Dyson, "Be Like Mike?,"; Paul Gilroy, "Sounds Authentic: Black Music, Ethnicity, and the Challenge of the Changing Same," *Black Music Research Journal* 11.2 (Autumn, 1991): 111–36.

[28]Mark McPhail, "Complicity: The Theory of Negative Difference," *Howard Journal of Communication* 3 (1992): 5.

[29]Mark McPhail, "From Complicity to Coherence: Rereading the Rhetoric of Afrocentricity," *Western Journal of Communication* 6, no. 2 (1998): 115.

[30]Mark McPhail, "Complicity," 1.

[31]Alex Ogg and David Upshall, *The Hip Hop Years: A History of Rap* (London: 2001).

[32]Nelson George, *Hip Hop America* (New York, 1998).

[33]Perkins, *Droppin' Science*.

[34]Ogg and Upshall, *The Hip Hop Years*.

[35]Rose, *Black Noise*, 60.

[36]Trend, "Nationalities," 138.

[37]"Playa" is the same as player as in someone who plays the field, alternating positions. The metaphor

implies the relational activity of a polygamous male. "Dog" is a term one would think would be considered despicable, but the term, when used among some males has been altered to mean someone who is cool and is part of a posse of males who share similar interests. Playa and Dog are used pretty much interchangeably in Hip Hop music, just as Thug and Ruffneck are. George, *Hip Hop America*.

[38] James Jones, "The New Ghetto Aesthetic," *Wide Angle* 13 (Spring 1991): 32–43.

[39] Ja Rule. 2001. *Bitch Betta Have My Money*. AMG Records.

[40] Ja Rule. 2001. *Thug Life*. Def Jam Records.

[41] Neal, *Soul Babies*, 187.

[42] DMX and Dyme. 1998. *Good Girls, Bad Boys. And then there was X*. Def Jam Records.

[43] Stagolee is the muscular, mythic hero in Black folktales who, armed with rhythmic skill and profanity, intimidates all would-be foes. See Hecht, Jackson and Ribeau's, *Black Communication* and Lester's *Urban Images* for more details.

[44] Dyson, "Be Like Mike?," Rose, *Black Noise*.

[45] Mark Shelton, "Can't Touch This! Representations of the Black Female Body in Urban Rap Videos," *Popular Music & Society* 21 (Spring 1997): 111.

[46] Lil' Kim. 2000. *Notorious Kim*. Undereas/Atlantic Records.

[47] "Thug Misses" is the title of female rap artist and Tampa, Florida native Khia's 2002 album. The instant hit "My Neck, My Back" is a song filled with sexual innuendo. Ruff Ryders is a rap artist syndicate comprised of about a dozen rappers like Eve, Swizz Beats (the producer), Chivon, Wah Dean, Timbaland, Bubba Sparxxx, and JadaKiss.

[48] Shelton, "Can't Touch This!," 111.

[49] Ibid, 113.

[50] Homi Bhabha, "Postcolonial Authority and Postmodern Guilt in *Cultural Studies*, ed. Lawrence Grossberg, Cary Nelson, and Paula Treichler (New York, 1992), 56–68.

[51] Elektra/Wea. 1999. *Dirty Harriet*. Elektra Records.

[52] Philip Brian Harper, *Are We Not Men: Masculine Anxiety and the Problem of Black identity* (New York, 1996).

[53] DMX, *What These Bitches Want*.

[54] Rose, *Black Noise*, 101.

[55] Dyson, "Be Like Mike?"

[56] Ross and Rose, *Microphone Fiends*.

[57] Cummings and Roy, "Manifestations of Afrocentricity in Rap Music," 56–79.

[58] Neal, *Soul Babies*; Watkins, *Representing*.

[59] Susan Bordo, "Reading the Male Body," in *The Male Body: Features, Destinies, Exposures*, ed. L. Goldstein (Ann Arbor, 1994), 270.

[60] Watkins, *Representing*.

[61] William Pinar, *The Gender of Racial Politics and Violence in America: Lynching, Prison Rape and Crisis of Masculinity* (New York, 2001); Peter Lang, Neil Smelser, William Julius Wilson, and Faith Mitchell, *America Becoming: Racial Trends and Their Consequences* (Washington, 2001).

[62] Michael Fenster, "Understanding and Incorporating Rap: The Articulation of Alternative Popular Musical Practices Within Dominant Cultural Practices and Institutions," *The Howard Journal of Communications* 5 (Spring 1995): 223–44; Eric King Watts, "An Exploration of Spectacular Consumption: Gangsta Rap as Cultural Commodity," *Communication Studies* 6 (1997): 42–58.

[63] Watkins, *Representing*.

[64] Robert Staples, *Black Masculinity: The Black Male's Role in American Society* (San Francisco, 1982).

[65] Ellis Cose, *The Rage of a Privileged Class: Why Do Prosperous Blacks Still Have the Blues?* (New York, 1995), 158.

[66] Deborah Borisoff and Dan Hahn, "Thinking with the body: Sexual Metaphors," *Communication Quarterly* 41 (Spring 1993): 253–60.

[67] Joseph Scott and James B. Stewart, "The Pimp-Whore Complex in Everyday Life," in *Crisis in Black Sexual Politics*, ed. Nathan Hare and Julia Hare (San Francisco, 1989), 57–62.

[68] *Pimps and Their Johns* is the only one in the list that is produced and directed by whites.

[69] Judith Butler, *Gender Trouble: Feminism and the Subversion of Identity* (New York, 1990), 9–12.

[70] Michael Campus. 1973. *The Mack*. New Line Home Video.

[71] hooks, *Rock My Soul*, 195.

[72] Albert Hughes and Allen Hughes. 2000. *American Pimp*. 20th Century Fox Home Entertainment.

[73] Cornel West, *Race Matters* (New York, 1993), 305–06.

[74] Michael Awkward, "Black Male Trouble," in *Masculinity Studies and Feminist Theory*, ed. J. K. Gardiner (New York, 2002), 290–304.

[75] Watkins, *Representing*.

CROSSOVER COLLABORATIONS: TOWARDS REALIZING HIP HOP'S POLITICAL POTENTIAL

Bryan R. Bracey

INTRODUCTION

Let's hear it, one for the coons on UPN 9 and WB
Who 'Yes Massa' on TV, what ever happened to Weezy? The Redd Foxx's?
Never got Emmy's but were real to me
Let's hear it, two for the spooks who do cartwheels
'Cause they said they played they parts well
Now they claim caviar, hate that oxtail
Lambda Sigma Phi badge on lapel
Whitey always tell him, "Ooh, he speak so well"
Are you the one we look to, the decent Negro?
The acceptable Negro—hell nah
But they say, "These are our heroes"

—Nas, "These are Our Heroes"[1]

These lyrics represent the hook, or chorus for rapper Nas's "These are Our Heroes" track off of his 2004 *Street's Disciple* album. On the track, originally titled "Coon Picnic," Nas verbally attacks Kobe Bryant, dedicating an entire verse to the much maligned NBA star. His lyrical assault continues however to include, Taye Diggs, Tiger Woods, Cuba Gooding Jr., and O.J. Simpson as well. In reference to the track Nas stated, "I pick out certain guys that's heavy in the media who—whether they're athletes, rappers, whatever—I think [they're] cooning. I don't know if radio and TV are ready for those images, but they should be, because that's what Hip Hop is."[2] Nas's point is not complex and actually quite popular in some circles, as Mark Anthony Neal offers that "words like Sambo and minstrel are used by the 'talented tenth'" to describe rappers.[3] Neal addresses a primary academic motivation to be critical of Hip Hop discourse by stating:

> It shouldn't be surprising then that many black men protect the relative privilege of being black, male, educated, and financially comfortable with a voracity that, in its worst form, creates an animosity toward the image of the Hip Hop thug that rivals the animosities expressed by white racists towards blacks.[4]

Consequently, I am not going to use this essay to dress down the existing popular African American discourse, but rather I am attempting to find ways to address the problems to which the discourse contributes, while looking for ways to reconceptualize our engagement, as academics, with Hip Hop. I recognize the advantages that academia can afford and the associated struggle to protect one's social capital. As such, my goal is to consider some discursive legacies of mainstream African American mediated culture. By critically examining these legacies, I hope to move beyond textual analysis and towards an understanding of the pedagogical potentialities of Hip Hop. By understanding Hip Hop as a "lived curriculum," in which popular culture represents an educational space as it is consumed every day, both the content of Hip Hop as well as the usage of the performative space can be instructive for scholars.[5] Following Bynoe, I am making an effort to move away from bemoaning the shortcomings of Hip Hop and towards a contextual understanding of the place of Hip Hop in contemporary society in an attempt to find new and innovative ways to enact social change.[6] In the words of Russell Simmons at the 2001 Hip Hop Summit, "We're not really here to clean up Rap. . . . I think we have the most important and powerful influence in American culture."[7] Hip Hop is a powerful tool, and for academics, recognizing the power of Hip Hop as well as the contestations facing the world of Hip Hop is paramount.

Nas, in many senses, serves as an exemplar of the many tensions facing contemporary Hip Hop artists. Nas has occupied a strange place in the Hip Hop world as a respected intelligent MC that could be classified as a politically "conscious" rapper while simultaneously a relative staple of the mainstream Hip Hop scene. He is neither a "sellout" nor "underground." However, he also is not defined by his consciousness. As a result, there may not be the same expectations of Nas as there is of say a Mos Def, will.i.am, Common, Talib Kweli, or any other popular MC that demonstrates and/or is noted for a critical bent. It is the lack of affiliation that makes Nas's remarks so fascinating. Nas is making a call to certain celebrities, to stop reinforcing dominant ideology and to be more political. It is a notion that has some currency in the academy as well. Nas extends his critique of Hip Hop in his 2006 album, *Hip Hop Is Dead*, as he laments the commercialization of the mainstream while, in some respects, holding a place in mainstream Hip Hop. In short, he is a surrogate representing the contradictions that seem to surface when one tries to balance capitalistic success and scathing, polarizing social commentary. It is a challenge that many face, including many academics.

THE ROLE OF THE SCHOLAR

The mirror says you are the next American leader
So don't be, acceptin new "We are the World" records
These pickaninnies get with anything to sell records
Cause it's trendy to be the conscious MC
But next year, who knows what we'll see?
Ha-Ha, these are our heroes[8]

In the post-September 11th moment, cultural studies scholars are faced with a major dilemma.[9] As Yvonna Lincoln argues:

> Those who are, or would be, public intellectuals are left with a conundrum: whether to engage, or not. Whether one is better off engaging the war in Iraq and American imperialism abroad, the fight for civil liberties at home, the massive environmental degradation blithely and ominously sanctioned by the Bush administration, corporate pork barreling and greed, the mounting national debt incurred for the war machine, or the conservative far Right's shaping of the social, cultural, and educational agenda. What to police? And where? And in an era of shrinking civil rights protest, what will be the costs?[10]

When discussing policing, Lincoln is referring to this dilemma in the present intellectual moment where the United States, particularly, is policing terror while expanding the surveillance of the American society, thus restricting civil liberties in the name of public safety. Yet as we move further away from 9/11 and the Bush Administration and further into the Obama era, there is an opportunity to contest the notion that "silence, rather than protest, might be the better part of valor."[11]

If we revisit Nas and his criticisms of those "cooning," we have to acknowledge that the obligation of the public intellectual or perhaps more usefully here, the "vernacular intellectual," has to be tempered by the circumstances of the contextual moment.[12] If academics excused their silence out of practicality and fear, it should come as no shock that those with greater financial investment and under even more scrutiny would smile and nod to protect their interests as well.

The fascinating part of the present condition is that while dissent is muted, it is still offered but only in certain terms. As Nas mentioned, it continues to be trendy to be a conscious MC. In other words, in a neoliberal capitalistic sense, there is a place for commodified, sanitized dissent. Perhaps this speaks to the popularity of songs such as Jadakiss's biggest mainstream hit, "Why," or the Black-Eyed Peas, or carefully and selectively, M.I.A.. Take, for example, Kanye West's (another "conscious MC"?) proclamation in his "Jesus Walks" track:

> So here go my single dawg radio needs this
> They say you can rap about anything except for Jesus
> That means guns, sex, lies, video tapes
> But if I talk about God my record won't get played, Huh?[13]

Given the religious agenda of the Bush administration and the fact that West comes with most of the trimmings associated with popular Hip Hop (explicit lyrics, braggadocio, and a debut CD entitled "The College Dropout"), it easy to see how West's "consciousness" could get co-opted into mainstream culture and dominant discourse. Incidentally, his record did get played on the radio. In fact, according to Sean Ross of Edison Market Research, West's single reached 80 million listeners during the first week of August 2004 alone.[14] His record got played quite often, actually. Although it did take some effort on West's part to get his track on the radio, it sort of took the sting out of any anti-establishment message he may be trying to convey. Additionally, given West's lyrical content, it presents Hip Hop music as a space where one is free to "rap about anything," now including Jesus. Most importantly, as Nas suggests, this type of vernacular intellectualism is more likely a trend than the start of a revolution. Pero Gaglo Dagbovie suggests that present-day Hip Hop is increasingly disconnected from the African Diaspora.[15] While the African American experience and its improvement should be inextricably linked to the production of Hip Hop culture, for myriad reasons, that is not necessarily the current case. Not the least of the reasons is the economically and ideologically profitable nature of the popular presentation of a commodified African American culture.

Henry Giroux elaborates on this notion of popular media reinforcing ideology by stating that:

> We are living in dangerous times in which a new type of society is emerging unlike anything we have seen in the past—a society in which symbolic capital and political power reinforce each other through a public pedagogy produced by a concentrated media, which has become a cheerleading section for the dominant elites and corporate ruling interests. This society increasingly marked by a poverty of critical public discourse, thus making it more difficult for young people and adults to appropriate a critical language outside of the market that would allow them to translate private problems into public concerns or to relate public issues to private considerations.[16]

Given Giroux's statement, it becomes imperative to recognize that the ideas and images that make it through to the popular media are likely disseminated with an agenda linked to particular political interests. Not only are those surviving popular ideas and images unlikely to threaten dominant ideology, but they also can seemingly be used to reinforce the virtues of freedom of expression, as well as other traditional American values. Politically, it is not all that surprising that "Jesus Walks" would be placed in heavy rotation while Nas's "These Are Our Heroes" would never be released as a single.

Though entertainers have the audience and reach to make change, given the mediated ideological constraints, even if it were the intention of an artist to be confrontational, it is neither practical nor likely. Nonetheless, Hip Hop's shortcomings are, and will continue to be, a frequent target given its immense and still growing popularity. According to a report in *USA Today*, in 2004, 14 of the 16 most played songs on the radio fell into the category of R&B/Hip Hop.[17] Furthermore, 61% of the radios top 100 for 2004 also fell in the R&B/Hip Hop category.[18] The reach of Hip Hop culture is both vast and obvious. Therefore, it may be a more worthwhile endeavor for academics to work on extending the range of their respective audiences rather than focusing on bashing those with an existing, established following unless, as Neal mentioned earlier, the motive for Hip Hop hating is more self-serving than altruistic.[19] Now, it is important to be careful here. There is a fine line between broadening one's horizons and stepping too far out of one's comfort zone. Perhaps, there is an even finer line between the aforementioned self-serving motivation of capitalizing on Hip Hop's popularity in an effort to bolster one's social capital, much like the ruthless Hip Hop critic, and the humble creative attempt to spread a message. Cornel West, a magnet for both positive and negative attention, opened himself up to significant criticism for his 2001 music CD, *Sketches of My Culture*.[20] Rosemary Cowan goes so far as to pose the question, "So just who is the real Cornel West: a fraudulent intellectual opportunist or one of America's premier intellectuals?"[21] The notion of intellectual "selling out" is going to be a common critique of any foray into the world of popular culture. West may have succeeded with his CD or he may have failed but future attempts to marry the vernacular to the intellectual will only get better and surely yield pedagogical benefits.[22] Hip Hop is just one potential venue and other performative pedagogical approaches may be more useful depending on the scholar. Nonetheless, a recoding of academic ideas and discourses that reach the masses more directly than the existing methods could prove desirable. Norman Denzin echoes the call for a more performative approach to academia by stating that:

We inhabit a performance-based, dramaturgical culture. The dividing line between performer and audience blurs, and culture itself becomes a dramatic performance. Performance ethnography enters a gendered culture with nearly invisible boundaries separating everyday theatrical performances from formal theater, dance, music, MTV, video, and film. But the matter goes even deeper then blurred boundaries. The performance has become reality. . . .

. . . Performance texts are situated in complex systems of discourse, where traditional, everyday, and avant-garde meanings of theater, film, video, ethnography, cinema, performance, text and audience all circulate and inform one another.[23]

If the performance has become reality, it indicates that the significance of performed culture has grown and that this growing significance provides academics with a big opportunity to attempt to make changes that those currently invested may be less inclined to make. Furthermore, the notion of performance becoming reality provides a useful theoretical foundation for understanding the importance a Hip Hop culture before considering a brief discursive history of popular African American discourse.

Jeffrey Ogbar does an admirable job of mapping the evolution of African American imagery in the popular media.[24] My aim is not to rehash Ogbar's work but rather to address two of the discursive legacies, minstrelsy and Stagolee, popularly connected to Hip Hop in academia. The idea here is to develop a conceptual foundation for addressing the discursive constraints imposed upon contemporary Hip Hop.

MINSTRELSY

As Mark Anthony Neal notes:

. . . White male performances of blackness—faces donned with burnt cork in an attempt to "represent" the realities of Black life and culture— became one of the most popular forms of American entertainment in the 19th and early 20th century. In the absence of "real" contact with African Americans, the minstrel stage became the site of authentic blackness for many White Americans, so much so that Mark Twain could remark in his autobiography that the minstrel stage was "the real nigger show—the genuine nigger show—the extravagant nigger show."[25]

Critical to the understanding of the legacies of minstrelsy is the notion that, for white Americans, the minstrels were a look at "real" African Americans. The performances, rooted in stereotypes, served as a mechanism to reinforce dominant notions of African American inferiority for a white audience. Whites, in blackface, performing this brand of African Americanness effectively created a simulated reality in which, as noted by Neal, these displays could somehow be indicative of something genuine. The matter is only made more complex when nonwhites put on the blackface and performed this exotic otherness for white consumption. In one sense, African Americans should profit from the performance of African Americanness. In other sense, it then becomes proof of the realness of the stereotypes. Culture is a two-way street that is both produced and consumed so whether or not minstrels, or certain rappers, believe that they are simply playing a role, feel as if they are hustling an ignorant fan base, subtly poking fun at a stereotype, may not matter if those beliefs are neither widely held nor understood. The value of popular discourse lies in its ability to communicate messages broadly and for academics this is the power of Hip Hop. Louis Chude-Sokei does bring up the important point that discourses like minstrelsy and Hip Hop do change, however, and the change is driven by the participants.[26]

Or, as Shane White critically observes:

Throughout much of African American History, black cultural production has focused primarily on performance: on the development and expression of distinctive African American aesthetic principles at some remove from those prized by the dominant culture. In part, such efforts have been a response to oppression, but, importantly, they have also been the result of choice.[27]

White makes this argument as an explanation for the re-appropriating of certain theatrical culture forms in the case of the African Theater in New York during the early part of the 19th century. It is key, however, that this is done through choice and free will, which suggests, that change is a real possibility through shifting contexts and ideals. There is ideological room for individuals to impact dominant discourse. In some regards, as White may say, this is a form of mimicry or imitation. Perhaps, more specifically, it is a form of "transgression."[28] By subverting or "transgressing" cultural boundaries, one creates new opportunities for resistance while problematizing the existing social order. Yet, the counter-logic to this thinking is that by attempting to problematize restrictions, to transgress boundaries, and to subvert the social order that it, by definition, acknowledges the boundaries and reinforces the status and primacy of the boundaries in question.[29] By attempting to think outside of the box, one recognizes the existence of the box before proceeding to locate one's thinking in relationship to the box. It is critical to keep this in mind when examining the history of images or signs. Yet, while the images may be limited in terms of possibilities of freedom, it is equally as significant to realize that the images and signs have neither fixed nor universally understood meanings.

Leon Litwack notes that for Northerners, "minstrel shows . . . helped to fix a public impression of the clownish, childish, carefree, and irresponsible Negro."[30] Moreover, minstrel shows were a reinforcement of a desired or preferred form of African American culture and not grounded in reality.[31] The result is a scenario in which an ideal form of African Americanness, as perceived by and conceived by whites, is created and disseminated. In this sense, there is a relevant link between contemporary Hip Hop and historical minstrelsy. The content will change and any implications in that regards will always be open for debate. Nonetheless there is a historical location for the white consumption of the exoticized, in this case African American, other. So while, minstrelsy provided a forum for the reproduction of a form of African Americanness from the vantage point of whites, Stagolee represents a form of African Americanness located in African American culture. However, they have similar trappings and enable particular discursive constraints.

STAGOLEE

Stagolee, also known as Stagger Lee, Stack-a-lee, Stackolee or Stacker Lee, was born as an icon. The story goes that, in the 1890s, Lee Shelton or "Stack" Lee shot William Lyons.[32] The facts are unclear but apparently there was a dispute at a bar that resulted in each damaging and seizing the other's hat. Ultimately, Shelton pulled out his gun, which may or may not have been in self-defense, and shot Lyons. Shelton calmly recovered his hat and walked out of the saloon.[33] Lyons eventually died from the shooting and Shelton turned himself over to the authorities when the police came for him.

That was the alleged back-story. The emergent folklore is what represents a new idea of African Americanness. There are marginal changes to the story that accompany oral history, but the general idea is that Billy touched Stagolee's hat and no one touches Stagolee's hat.[34] Stagolee, depending on the version of the story (and there is a panoply of songs and stories), was tough, impulsive, violent, vulgar, and celebrated for being bad. Cecil Brown calls Stagolee "a metaphor that structures the life of Black males from childhood through maturity."[35] Brown goes on to discuss how Stagolee embodies fundamental elements of African Americanness and is a legend that survives because African American men preserve the story.[36] Stagolee is mythical, musical, and an initial sign of the burgeoning "authentic" African American culture. This is a preliminary image constructed for the consumption of an African American population and not created through a white interpretation. Stagolee, in many ways, is the template for future African American popular discourses such as the "Bad Nigger" and later elements of the gangsta imagery in present day Hip Hop.[37] Moreover, as Todd Boyd points out:

> [Bad Niggers] were in a sense heroic, if not revolutionary, for their refusal to be defined by the limited racial reasoning perpetrated by the regressive elements of white society and culture. The bad nigger embodied the notion of resistance at the highest level as his presence defied all acceptable norms of behavior, decorum, and existence.

> On the other hand, the bad nigger was an ambivalent figure in relationship to Black culture at large, especially women. As the code of survival dictates, the bad nigger was, of necessity, equally threatening to both the white community and his own community as well.[38]

As new popular discourses emerge, there are seeds for resistance and revolution while also creating a new set of problematic issues. In addition to any potentially self-destructive consequences, Stagolee (and later the Bad Nigger) exhibits a lack of restraint or a "civilized" nature that serves to reinforce notions of African American subhumanness and inferiority for a white-dominated public. Obviously, it is equally problematic to hold standards of African Americanness to white expectations but, if an argument is for equality in a white-dominated society, one must either fight the battle at the level of perception or at the level of desirability. While threatening, and perhaps even revolutionary, Stagolee has ideological limitations but is extremely significant for his position in early, post-slavery, African American folklore. Much like the case with minstrelsy; Stagolee lives on in the present discourse. The location of such a character persists while, again, the politics of the character's evolution remain open for interpretation.

LEARNING FROM THE PAST:
SPORTING LEGACIES AND THE HIP HOP GENERATION

During the second half of the 20th century, sport served (and continues to serve), much like Hip Hop, as a vehicle that communicates high profile examples of African American social success. Jackie Robinson preceded *Brown v. Board of Education* and sport fueled the problematic notion of an American meritocracy. Yet, like Hip Hop, the political underpinnings of African American participants were quickly quieted in the mainstream. Michael Omi and Howard Winant point out a rearticulation of racial ideology immediately following the Civil Rights Movement.[39] It is a rearticulation that also happens to coincide with the development of a pocket of politically active, confrontational African American athletes in the 1960s.[40] African American athletes were using their relative fame and their visibility to draw attention to the problems facing African Americans. Yet, the rampant commercialization of sport, neoliberal hegemony, and a redefining of the location of race in the United States, contributed to the rapid suppression of any prominent dissent presented in and through popular sport. This is a meaningful lesson for the understanding of Hip Hop and its political potential. This rearticulation of race requires that racial equality comes in the form of a "color-blind" society and the removal of race from any discussion of creating a just society. Consequently, the Hip Hop generation marks the first generation fully constrained in a post-legalized segregation era.[41] However, the impact of segregationist ideology lives on.[42]

The resulting space is one in which African Americans reconcile their "double consciousness" (in the Du Boisian sense) by pursuing an American dream on their own, self-regulated (in a Foucauldian sense) terms. Boyd suggests that Hip Hop culture, which is predicated on authenticity and a genuine African American experience, is seen as that space which combines, as Du Bois might have said, the Negro and the American. Boyd says:

> First of all, considering that basketball and Hip Hop have consistently provided tangible economic opportunities for young Black men, many regard these to be the only viable options in a society where many other opportunities continue to be closed off. With this sense of social mobility at its core, 'ball and Hip Hop redefine the American dream from the perspective of young, Black, and famous.[43]

Boyd also raises several other provocative points in regards to discourse and hegemony. As it pertains to the notion of Hip Hop as being representative of an authentic experience, Boyd does a solid job of recognizing some social elements that prove to be suspect. The idea of an authentic experience and the problems of reconciling the identity of the African American, seems to suggest that Hip Hop may be an attempt to come to terms with what it means to be both African and American. Nonetheless, it is troubling even to make the assumption that a true identity is a fixed and "real" possibility all together.[44] This refers to the tension of the hyperreal and the real. Boyd speaks to this idea of the struggle for identity by saying that:

> Previous generations of African-Americans were thought to have to "sell out," to assimilate, in order to make it in mainstream society. Yet this Hip Hop generation has decided that though they want the money and power offered by mainstream society, they do not want to change in order to get it.[45]

When Boyd says, "they do not want to change in order to get," he is making the conceptual assumption that the "Hip Hop generation" has an authentic experience that they collectively refuse to compromise. It is a bravado that goes back to the Stagolee ideal. In addition, it sets up a linear progression where athletic or entertainment excellence is the way to achieve the African American dream. Hard work and determination leads to success without having to compromise one's own integrity. The irony is that mainstream Hip Hop ideology, as it pertains to materialism, does not differ from mainstream society's ideology. However, the authentic that is championed is based on marketability and, ultimately, consumption. In this regard, the power gained through sporting and entertainment success is attached to one's ability to sell and absent from that equation is political consciousness. Therefore, the manifestation of this power often comes in the form of being a bigger player in the consumptive game whether it is by encouraging consumption or the act of consuming in and of itself.

If O.J. Simpson, if for only a moment in time was able to attain status as "colorless" and racially "transcendent"[46] or at least able to allow for a "racial avoidance,"[47] the result of his apoliticsm, in the face of the Black Power movement, was previously unimagined marketability. Tiger Woods and Michael Jordan were not far behind. Cheryl Cole and David Andrews suggest that Tiger Woods' apolitical nature is essential to the Nike marketing machine in an effort to reach the broadest audience possible.[48] Michael Jordan's case was no different from Simpson's as he famously mentioned that "republican buy Nikes too," when asked about his feelings towards North Carolina Senator Jesse Helms, explicitly communicating his apoliticism. Perhaps Andrews says it best when he notes that Jordan is "vindication of the mythological American meritocracy."[49] Hip Hop with its frequent "rags to riches" stories and privileging of tough upbringings as essential to one's credibility, in many respects, provides even further vindication. Yet, one cannot achieve Jordan-esque or Woods-esque mainstream socio-cultural/economic status while posing any real threat to the dominant social order. Equally as important to that formula, is embodying existing neoliberal ideals. That is not to say that one cannot shed light on power relations and inequality after one establishes an audience. Dave Zirin, frequently highlights contemporary examples of sporting figures who use their relative successes to attempt to enact political change.[50] However, to both attain and retain mass appeal or marketability, one can only be so oppositional. The Hip Hop generation may not want to change to get mainstream money, power, and respect but the fact of the matter is they are not asked to "change" so long as they continue to reproduce the status quo by producing a politically sanitized form of African Americanness that is acceptable for white consumption in the same way that minstrelsy was acceptable to whites. In Gramsci's, or later in Omi and Winant's terms, the process represents a shift from the coerced construction of reality to a more consensual social arrangement.

Using the sporting realm as a template represents a particularly useful tool for understanding the evolution of Hip Hop culture. O.J. Simpson's period of "colorlessness" emerged in the face of Black Power and politically strident athletes culminating with the medal stand protest of Tommie Smith and John Carlos at the 1968 Olympics. Subsequently, sport evolved into a heavily mediated commercialized spectacle in which potential political activist aspirations could be exchanged for endorsement deals. In many respects, the sporting possibility for mainstream economic success took flight in response to the threat of the politically charged minority with access to a stage. Coincidentally or not, MC Hammer's 1990 *Please Hammer, Don't Hurt 'Em* album, which sold over 10 million copies, as rap infiltrated the mainstream, was released within a couple of months of Public Enemy's *Fear of a Black Planet* album. Yet, by looking at the 1968 Mexico City Olympics as an example of political activism and social protest through popular culture, it is also significant to recognize the role of sociologist Harry Edwards and his efforts in organizing the Olympic Project for Human Rights. The pedagogical possibilities that popular culture allows should be cultivated and embraced by the academic community. In this respect, the onus is on the academic community to actively seek ways to help salvage the revolutionary capabilities of Hip Hop culture.

WHAT'S NEXT? FLIPPIN' THE SCRIPT?

For most of Hip Hop's thirty-something years, folk have been compelled to point out the sexism, misogyny, and homophobia that finds a forum in the lyrics of the young black and brown men who have primarily influenced Hip Hop, and the lack of a womanist perspective that could directly counter those lyrics. But I often wonder if it is possible that we are asking Hip Hop, particularly mainstream Hip Hop, to do something that it is fundamentally incapable of doing. . . . But as we make demands of these artists, we also must be clear about what is happening within mainstream Hip Hop. Without doubt, the performance of black masculinity continues to be the dominant creative force in Hip Hop. As numbers have shown fairly consistently over the last decade or so, young white men are the primary consumers—at least in the traditional commercial sense—of the various performances of black masculinity and the pornographic images of black and brown women found in mainstream Hip Hop.

By asking Hip Hop to reform, we are essentially demanding the artists, record labels, and Hip Hop's primary consumer base to produce and consume music that is anti-sexist, anti-misogynistic, and even feminist. In what context have young white men (or black men for that matter) ever been interested in consuming large amounts of black feminist thought? Clearly these young whites are consuming Hip Hop for other reasons.[51]

This lengthy but extremely provocative Mark Anthony Neal quotation addresses several pivotal issues. As Lionel McPherson says "most political rap has not been politically revolutionary."[52] It is essential to realize that the audience of mainstream Hip Hop is primarily white or as Boyd states "the image of Hip Hop in the public imagination is one that is controlled by a dominant White gaze. . . ."[53] Therefore, much like minstrelsy, the idea is to provide a discourse of African Americanness that is both palatable and entertaining for a white audience. That is the function, in many ways, of mainstream Hip Hop. African Americans performing African Americanness as conceived for a white audience lends a new credibility to these "white-created stereotypes."[54] A classic example of this was the highly publicized rap rivalry between 50 Cent and Ja Rule. Rule reached his peak in 2002 and was challenged by 50 on the track "Wanksta," which is 50's slang for fake gangsta. In essence, 50 challenged the authenticity of Rule's performance while simultaneously suggesting that the gunshots and drug dealing that marred 50's past provide a more genuine look at the true African American experience. Part of the reason 50 is critical of Rule is that Rule is "pop" and 50's story is seemingly more real, if not hyperreal, and thus more profitable. The irony, as Neal mentioned, is that the people that 50 is appealing to, in an effort to sell these records, is a predominantly white male audience that finds 50's African Americanness to be more legitimate.[55] Consequently, the standards that inform one's Hip Hop credibility are set by the white audience. Incidentally, Will Smith, who puts the bubble in bubble gum, addresses standards of Hip Hop credibility is his song, "Freakin' It":

Once and for all lets get this straight
How you measure a rapper what make an MC great
Is it the sales? 20 mill
Is it the cars? Bentley's
Is it the women? Jada
Is it the money? Please
Mr. Clean yet the fact remain
Got girls that don't speak English screamin' my name
All you rappers yellin' bout who you put in a hearse
Do me a favor write one verse without a curse[56]

Smith, clearly frustrated with how he is perceived in the Hip Hop world, takes on the traditional categories used by mainstream rappers to assert their own greatness. The perception problem for Smith is that he falls into the transcendent or racially avoidant category with Michael Jordan and Tiger Woods. He is so wildly accepted, popular and marketable that it is virtually impossible to conceive of him as anything other than a neoliberal champion and thus ideologically non-threatening. Conversely, as Neal states, "for much of its sojourn on planet America, Hip Hop has been a primary site for the articulation of distinct forms of black masculinity: urban, hyper-masculine, hyper-sexual, pseudo-criminalized."[57] In essence, Smith draws attention away from his race while a 50 Cent does not. However, 50 Cent as, an embodiment of African American culture who has been authorized by Eminem, is just as comforting for whites as the stripping of one's African Americanness all together. Eric Watts and Mark Orbe suggest that:

The discursive spaces of white privilege must be maintained even as the consumption of blackness intensifies. Spectacular consumption as a critical lens bring into focus how the energy from this dialectic is harnessed by the replication of specific features of the "authentic."[58]

So, while one, Smith, may be a viewed as the "sellout" that Boyd told us the Hip Hop generation refuses to be, the other, 50, is a "Stagolee"-type exuding "genuine blackness." When 50 suggests that the Hurricane Katrina relief effort was handled in an acceptable manner in response to Kanye West's proclamation "that George Bush doesn't care about Black people" while simultaneously offering that he is somehow threatening to the status quo, it is particularly problematic. Additionally, 50 stated that "After 50 Cent (Hip Hop fans) was looking for something non-confrontational, and they went after first thing that came along. That was Kanye West, and his record took off."[59] More to the point, neither would be successful without the approval of a white gaze and both are confined by the mediated, ideological constraints of the current moment. In the case of Smith and 50, in some senses they are just two sides of the same proverbial coin, as both are able to appease a white following for substantial financial gains. At this point, I am not sure which one is more desirable but neither form is leaving the popular discourse any time soon.

CONCLUSION: WHAT MORE CAN I SAY?

You don't ride for the facts like um, say Scarface
You don't know what you feel, y'all too safe
Election done came and went, y'all worked so hard for it
Huh, and in the end we all got d***ed
These are our heroes, thanks a lot public school systems still rot
Still harassed by cops, snitches on blocks[60]

I am not making the argument that Hip Hop is just another case where "the man" has "tricked" us in order to "keep us down." I am also not denying the innovative nature of Hip Hop or its utility as an educational device. What I am hoping to do is point out the discursive constraints on cultural forms in the United States, in particular, for minority groups. There are signs of a developing African American experience, going back to Stagolee, that can inform the popular discourse in African American terms, and not strictly from a dominant white perspective. It is necessary, though, to identify those displays of African American ideological influence as well as the discursive limitations of, in this case, Hip Hop. Both the strengths and weaknesses of Hip Hop are summarized nicely by Nelson George:

While Hip Hop's values are by and large fixed—its spirit of rebellion, identification with street culture, materialism, and aggression—it is also an Incredibly flexible tool of communication, quite adaptable to any number of messages. That's one reason it has endured. That's why no one style has been essential for more than three or four years at a time. That's why it has been so easy to turn every element of the culture associated with Hip Hop into a product. . . ."[61]

Problems for the dominant social order arise when the Nas's of the world can use a powerful vernacular tool and make intellectual contributions. However, in the current neoliberal capitalistic moment, the commodified popular entertainment spectacle has no interest in that which runs contrary to the economic imperative. As Raymond Williams once said, "Most things that we produce have to be sold, or they will not go on being produced."[62] There is too much money involved to expect each individual with entertainment goals to willingly resist. The popular media is so controlling that we need to find discursive locations to establish counter narratives and maybe Hip Hop could be such a space.

The mastery of the vernacular as well as intellectual sophistication is a tough combination especially given the financial motivation to suppress any potentially polarizing ideas. Therefore, we need to appreciate the Nas's, Bob Marley's, Muhammad Ali's[63] et cetera, when they come around while acknowledging that they are a rarity.

Nas's reference to the 2004 presidential election and the "Vote or Die" campaign spearheaded by P. Diddy, Russell Simmons, among others in *These are Our Heroes*, suggests that the project was a failure. That may not be entirely fair in the sense that using economic and cultural capital to register young African American voters is surely a good thing as Derrick Alridge notes.[64] Nas is right, however, if you look at who won that election. One problem with the "Vote or Die" campaign, as Nas would point out, is that the high-profile organizers had conflicting interests on many fronts. Consequently, the campaign was only about getting voters registered without any effort made towards forging a political allegiance, backing a candidate, or even seeking out a representative that would address the issues facing the young African Americans that were asked to register. This is the type of problem that will always confront pop culture icons whose marketability is tied to being, in Andrews's terms, a "black version of a white cultural model."[65] Nonetheless, the "Vote or Die" effort was exactly the place for increased academic involvement in which intellectuals could have assumed a degree of responsibility in both the organization and consequences of a mobilized Hip Hop agenda.

Yet, it seems as if in 2008, some of Nas's challenges were picked up. In just four years, with a firm endorsement from numerous members of the Hip Hop community, Barack Obama was the first African American elected president of the United States. Of particular note is the way in which will.i.am used Youtube as a discursive location to present the immensely popular "Yes We Can" and "We Are the Ones" music videos in support of Obama. In many respects, the election of Obama represents a new opportunity for not only the resurrection of a politicized Hip Hop that Nas proclaimed dead, but for academics to continue to search for new discursive venues, such as Youtube, and techniques for conveying intellectually-informed, political messages. Moreover, this type of political engagement needs to continue post-Obama so that future elections more closely reflect 2008 than 2004.

There will always be elements of Hip Hop and popular discourse that are ideologically problematic and that perpetuate stereotypes as those images will continue to have an audience. As Richard Toll noted, "black minstrels had to work within narrow limits because they performed for audiences that expected them to act out well-established minstrel stereotypes of Negroes."[66] It is in this regard that Hip Hop and its children, at times, follow in the tradition of minstrelsy. The point is however, not that the latter is overtly offensive and the former is an updated, more covertly presented form of racism like so many things are nowadays. Rather, the point is that there has been a space in popular discourse for the presentation of perceived African American culture for mainstream and largely white consumption. Intent is going to be of little significance during this presentation because the mainstream appropriation will invariably be repackaged for a target audience. Or as Langston Hughes offered, "Be stereotyped, don't go too far, don't shatter our illusions about you, don't amuse us too seriously. We will pay you,' say the whites."[67] This is not placing a value judgment on a genre but simply acknowledging the context in which said genre exists. There is always going to be a place in society for the black performance of a white cultural model.

Yet, with the line between the real and the simulated becoming increasingly blurred, gaining some control over the media, or finding alternative mediated outlets, is paramount.[68] The power of Hip Hop is enormous but rather than criticizing mainstream presentations for a white audience, it is up to academics and aspiring academics to find a way to use this tool to help produce and project alternative discourses. I am not sure how this is to be done but it seems worthwhile to focus on how to use Hip Hop, sport, and other vernacular forms to the advantage of academia and our respective agendas. It should be expected that academics make use of all available resources to truly enact change.[69] If we are to follow the lead of Harold Cruse, the "Negro intellectual" has to be critical and vigorously interrogate cultural institutions. As Cruse stated:

> The special function of the Negro intellectual is a cultural one. He [sic] should take the rostrum and assail the stultifying blight of the commercially depraved white middle-class who has poisoned the structural roots of the American ethos and transformed the American people into a nation of intellectual dolts.[70]

In the most general sense, the nation is still in intellectual crisis and popular representations are couched in a discourse of Anglo-Saxon tradition. Intellectually, we must guard against unoriginality, smugness, being "critically tongue-tied," and socially dishonest.[71] These characteristics have dominated the cultural mainstream since the 1920s.[72] It is the role of the intellectual to navigate this cultural terrain without the same investment as those reliant on popular culture for financial reasons (or otherwise). This includes acknowledgement of social context, being critical when appropriate, and both accepting and appreciating contributions from the vernacular while always keeping an eye on the betterment of African Americans. Unless, of course, our agenda is to be critical of popular culture simply to preserve the social capital afforded to academics.

Boyd suggests that the popular media offers a "series of regressive images" of African American males.[73] I would posit that those images have never gone anywhere, will never go anywhere and therefore are not technically regressive especially when you take into consideration the intended audience and the fact that the cultural context is one controlled and established by whites. There has not been a progression from which we are regressing. The discursive change can only come from outside the popular media machine while appreciating any help from within.

NOTES

[1] Nas, "These Are Our Heroes," *Street's Disciple*, Sony Records (2004).

[2] Shaheem Reid, "Nas Takes Aim at O.J., Tiger and Kobe on 'These Are Our Heroes,'" *MTV News*, http://www.mtv.com/news/articles/1494367/20041202/story.jhtml.

[3] Mark Anthony Neal, *New Black Man* (New York, 2005), 15.

[4] Neal, *New Black Man*, 7–8.

[5] Greg Dimitriadis, *Performing Identity/Performing Culture: Hip Hop as Text, Pedagogy, and Lived Practice* (New York, 2001).

[6] Yvonne Bynoe, *Stand and Deliver: Political Activism, Leadership, and Hip Hop Culture* (Brooklyn, NY, 2004), 109.

[7] James G. Spady, H. Samy Alim, and Samir Meghelli, *Tha Global Cipha: Hip Hop Culture and Consciousness* (Philadelphia, PA, 2006), 378.

[8] Nas, "These Are Our Heroes."

[9] Yvonna S. Lincoln, "Who Polices the Crisis?" *Cultural Studies/Critical Methodologies* 4, no. 2 (2004): 269–74; Norman K. Denzin, "The War on Culture, The War on Truth," *Cultural Studies/Critical Methodologies* 4, no. 2 (2004): 137–42; Judith Butler, "Explanation and Exoneration, or What We Can Hear," *Social Text* 20, no. 3 (2002): 177–88.

[10] Lincoln, "Who Polices the Crisis?", 273.

[11] Ibid., 272.

[12] Grant Farred, *What's My Name: Black Vernacular Intellectuals* (Minneapolis, MN, 2003).

[13] Kanye West, "Jesus Walks," *The College Dropout*, Roc-a-Fella Records (2004).

[14] Sean Ross, "Is Christian Radio Meant For So Much More?" *Edison Research*, http://www.edisonresearch.com/home/archives/2004/08/is_christian_ra_1.html.

[15] Pero Gaglo Dagbovie " 'Of All Our Studies, History Is Best Qualified to Reward Our Research': Black History's Relevance to the Hip Hop Generation," *The Journal of African American History* 90 (Summer 2005): 299–323.

[16] Henry A. Giroux, "War Talk, the Death of the Social, and Disappearing Children: Remembering the Other War," *Cultural Studies/Critical Methodologies* 4, 2 (May 2004): 207.

[17] Ken Barnes, "Usher Burned Up the Airwaves in 2004" *USA Today*. 4 January 2005, http://www.usatoday.com/life/music/news/2005-01-04-2004-airplay_x.htm.

[18] Ken Barnes, "Radio Listeners Turn to Hip Hop, R&B," *USA Today*. 4 January 2005. http://www.usatoday.com/life/music/news/2005-01-04-radio-2004_x.htm.

[19]Neal, *New Black Man*.

[20]Rosemary Cowan, "Cornel West and the Tempest in the Ivory Tower." *Politics* 24 (2004): 72–78.

[21]Cowan, "Cornel West and the Tempest in the Ivory Tower," 75.

[22]Tyrone C. Howard, "The Forgotten Link: The Salience of Pre-K–12 Education and Culturally Responsive Pedagogy in Creating Access to Higher Education for African American Students." In *Strengthening the African American Educational Pipeline: Informing Research, Policy, and Practice*, ed. Jerlando F.L. Jackson (Albany, NY, 2007), 17–36.

[23]Norman K. Denzin,"The Practices and Politics of Interpretation," in *Handbook of Qualitative Research* (2nd Edition), ed. Norman K. Denzin and Yvonna S. Lincoln (Thousand Oaks, CA, 2004), 903.

[24]Jeffrey O. G. Ogbar, *Hip Hop Revolution: The Culture and Politics of Rap* (Lawrence, KS, 2007).

[25]Mark Anthony Neal , "The Real Nigger Show," *Seeing Black*, http://www.seeingblack.com/2005/x010705/niggershow.shtm.

[26]Louis Chude-Sokei, *The Last "Darky": Bert Williams, Black-on-Black Minstrelsy, and the African Diaspora* (Durham, NC, 2005).

[27]White, *Stories of Freedom in Black New York*, 67.

[28]Donna Haraway, "A Manifesto for Cyborgs: Science, Technology, and Socialist-Feminism in the 1980s." *Socialist Review* 80 (1985): 65–107.

[29]Brian Pronger, "Post-Sport: Transgressing Boundaries in Physical Culture" in *Sport and Postmodern Times*, ed. Genevieve Rail (New York, NY, 1998), 277–300.

[30]Leon F. Litwack, *North of Slavery: The Negro in the Free States, 1790–1860* (Chicago, IL, 1961), 99.

[31]Litwack, *North of Slavery*.

[32]George M. Eberhart, "Stack Lee: The Man, the Music, and the Myth." In *A Question of Manhood: A Reader in U.S. Black Men's History and Masculinity Volume 2*, ed. Earnestine Jenkins and Darlene Clark Hine (Bloomington, IN, 2001), 387–440.

[33]Ibid.

[34]Cecil Brown, *Stagolee Shot Billy* (Cambridge, MA, 2003).

[35]Ibid.

[36]Ibid.

[37]Dimitriadis, *Performing Identity/Performing Culture*; Todd Boyd, *Young, Black, Rich, and Famous* (New York, NY, 2003).

[38]Boyd, *Young, Black, Rich, and Famous*, 126.

[39]Michael Omi and Howard Winant, *Racial Formation in the United States: From the 1960s to the 1990s* (London, 1994).

[40]David K. Wiggins, "The Year of Awakening: Black Athletes, Racial Unrest and the Civil Rights Movement of 1968," *International Journal of the History of Sport*, 9, no. 2 (1992): 188–208.

[41]Bakari Kitwana, *The Hip Hop Generation: Young Blacks and the Crisis in African-American Culture* (New York, NY, 2002).

[42]Omi and Winant, *Racial Formation in the United States*.

[43]Boyd, *Young, Black, Rich, and Famous*, 15.

[44]Davarian L. Baldwin, "Black Empires, White Desires," in *That's the Joint: The Hip Hop Studies Reader*, ed. Murray Forman and Mark Anthony Neal (New York, NY, 2004), 159–76.

[45]Boyd, *Young, Black, Rich, and Famous*, 16.

[46]Leola Johnson and David Roediger, "'Hertz, Don't It?' Becoming Colorless and Staying Black in the Crossover of O.J. Simpson" in *Reading Sport: Critical Essays on Power and Representation*, ed. Susan Birrell and Mary G. McDonald (Boston, MA, 2000), 40–73.

[47]David L. Andrews, "Excavating Michael Jordan's Blackness," in *Reading Sport: Critical Essays on Power and Representation*, eds. Susan Birrell and Mary G. McDonald (Boston: 2000), 166–205.

[48]Cheryl L. Cole and David L. Andrews, "America's New Son: Tiger Woods and America's Multiculturalism," in *Sport Stars: The Cultural Politics of Sporting Celebrity*, ed. David. L. Andrews and Steven J. Jackson (London, 2001), 70–86.

[49]Andrews, "Excavating Michael Jordan's Blackness," 175.

[50]Dave Zirin, www.edgeofsports.com.

[51]Neal, *New Black Man*, 145.

[52]Lionel K. McPherson, "Halfway Revolution: From That Gangsta Hobbes to Radical Liberals," in *Hip Hop and Philosophy: Rhyme 2 Reason*, ed. Derrick Darby and Tommie Shelby (Chicago, 2005), 173.

[53]Boyd, *Young, Black, Rich, and Famous*, 14.

[54]Toll, *Blacking Up*, 196.

[55]Neal, *New Black Man*.

[56]Will Smith, "Freakin' It," *Willennium*, Sony Records (1999).

[57]Neal, *New Black Man*, 129.

[58]Eric King Watts and Mark P. Orbe, "The Spectacular Consumption of 'True' African American Culture: 'Whassup' with the Budweiser Guys" in *Channeling Blackness: Studies on Television and Race in America*, ed. Darnell M. Hunt (Oxford, 2005), 230.

[59]"50 Cent Disagrees With Kanye West," http://news.yahoo.com/s/ap/20051102/ap_en_mu/people 50_cent.

[60]Nas, "These Are Our Heroes."

[61]Nelson George, *Hip Hop America* (New York, 1998), 155.

[62]Raymond Williams, *Communications* (1970), 104.

[63]Grant Farred, *What's My Name*.

[64]Derrick P. Alridge, "From Civil Rights to Hip Hop: Toward a Nexus of Ideas," *The Journal of African American History* 90 (Summer 2005): 226–52.

[65]Andrews, "Excavating Michael Jordan's Blackness," 174.

[66]Toll, *Blacking Up*, 273.

[67]Langston Hughes, "The Negro Artist and the Racial Mountain (23 June 1926)," in *Burning All Illusions*, ed. Paula J. Giddings (New York, 2002), 57.

[68]Jean Baudrillard, *The Consumer Society* (London, England, 1998).

[69]Yvonna Lincoln. "An Emerging New Bricoleur: Promises and Possibilities—A Reaction to Joe Kincheloe's "Describing the Bricoleur." *Qualitative Inquiry*, 7, no. 6 (2001): 693–705.

[70]Harold Cruse, *The Crisis of the Negro Intellectual*.

[71]Cruse, *The Crisis of the Negro Intellectual*.

[72]Ibid., 456.

[73]Todd Boyd, "The Day the Niggaz Took Over: Basketball, Commodity Culture, and Black Masculinity," *Out of Bounds: Sports, Media, and the Politics of Identity*, eds. Aaron Baker and Todd Boyd (Bloomington, IN, 1997), 140.

COMMERCIAL HIP HOP:
THE SOUNDS AND IMAGES OF A RACIAL PROJECT

Bettina L. Love

Mc's get a little bit of love and think they hot
Talkin' bout how much money they got, nigga all y'all records sound the same
I am sick of that fake thug, R&B, rap scenario all day on the radio
Same scenes in the video, monotonous material, y'all don't hear me though
These record labels slang our tapes like dope
You can be next in line, and signed, and still be writing rhymes and broke
You would rather have a lexus, some justice, a dream or some substance?
A beamer, a necklace or freedom?
Still a nigga like me don't playa' hate, I just stay awake
This real Hip Hop, and it don't stop until we get the crackers off the block.[1]

Hip Hop is a creative muse for an entire generation of talented, ambitious, and artistic individuals who cry out through music to change the world around them, be it directly or indirectly, consciously or nonsocially conscious.[2] Hip Hoppers' cries are political and social because their cries are created and maintained by a capitalistic system that thrives and flourishes on Hip Hoppers' inability to overcome oppression.[3] Historian Manning Marable writes that "Blacks have never been equal partners in the American Social Contract, because the system exists not to develop, but to *underdevelop Black people.*"[4] The counterculture sound that emerged from this oppressive, impoverished, and capitalistic environment was Hip Hop. Hip Hop scholar and historian Derrick Alridge contends that

> For many youth, Hip Hop reflects the social, economic, political, and cultural realities and conditions of their lives; speaking to them in a language and matter they understand.[5]

This means, then, that Hip Hop is a powerful force in shaping the lives of youth, for Hip Hop not only reflects reality, it helps create it. The language that Hip Hop speaks is one that is helping to create a particular notion about the African American race. Because Hip Hop is globally consumed, the ideas it reflects and constructs create what mainstream culture views as African American culture.

One of the four main elements of Hip Hop is emceeing, or rapping. This aspect of Hip Hop culture has grown to unimaginable heights and evolved into a billion dollar commodity. However, the original purpose, struggles, and achievements of Hip Hop music have changed. Due to corporate control of Hip Hop music, much of it is

now informed by Whites. Sociologist Dipannita Basu argues, "major corporate conglomerates control the music industry. . . . Black rap moguls exist, but the industry is
white controlled."[6] The economic power that Whites maintain creates a narrow and
superficial position of power for African Americans in the music industry. Many
African American rap moguls serve as front men for major record labels; their power
as moguls are limited. Basu contends that rap moguls such as Sean "Diddy" Combs,
Shawn Carter (Jay-Z), Jermaine Dupri, and Percy "Master P" Miller are tied to major
record labels like Universal and Sony that receive the majority of profits.[7] For example, Roc-a-Fella records has a 50/50 partnership with Island Def Jam Music Group,
which is a division of Universal Music Group.[8] However, Roc-a-Fella records presents itself as an "independent" record label to the public, especially to the African
American community. Roc-a-Fella's partnership with Universal, a major record label,
provides more than just money; it is a source of power and control. Our African
American youth idolize these rap moguls but, not to downplay their success, their achievements are calculated and determined by Whites. As a result, mainstream, commercial Hip
Hop has become the sounds and images that popular culture internalizes; however, this
sound is driven by Whites' current ideologies of African American culture. The corporate
creators of commercial Hip Hop draw upon their limited, stereotypical, and narrow-
minded understanding of Hip Hop culture to negotiate and disseminate what is popular Hip Hop music and conversely what is African American youth culture. Because
Hip Hop is a language that reflects and creates African American culture, the culture
that is created is often informed by corporate control. This is a key element that
makes Hip Hop a racial project, which maintains racism and White supremacy.

Nevertheless, I do believe that Hip Hoppers negotiate and possess agency
because they articulate their life experiences living and surviving oppressive conditions, which is a key element for advancement. I celebrate emcees' power and courage
to tell their stories and their passion to be heard. As a member of the Hip Hop generation and a Hip Hopper myself, I am thrilled to witness the accomplishments of Hip
Hop music and the impact it has made, not only in African American culture, but also
globally.[9] Hip Hop music popularly provides a space "where control over narratives
and representations passes into the hands of the established cultural bureaucracies;"
commercial Hip Hop "is rooted in popular experience and available for expropriation
at one and the same time."[10] Hip Hoppers' experiences living in oppressive environments have become the narratives and representations for African American youth,
and these representations have propelled African American youth into America's profitable nightmare. The images of commercial rap ignite fear in the minds of
Americans, as African American males are depicted as gangbangers who sell drugs,
wear their pants below their waist, and refuse to assimilate to "American" values. This
nihilistic image has become ubiquitous; however, it is profitable to corporate giants,
who create representations embedded with essentialized notions of Blackness.

When I refer to mainstream, commercial Hip Hop music, I am referring to the
nonsocially conscious rap groups such as the G-Unit, Three Six Mafia, Ying Yang
Twins, and solo artists 50 cent, Jay-Z, T-Pain, Plies, Rick Ross, Mike Jones, and many

more. I define nonsocially conscious rappers as those who produce Hip Hop that primarily serves to further support stereotypical degenerative attitudes about African Americans. For example, those Hip Hop artists whose lyrics encourage senseless sexual promiscuity, violence, and school disidentification, to name a few. Former *Source* magazine editor Bakari Kitwana defines "mainstream Hip Hop" as "aspects of culture that have been packaged, often distorted and then sold in the mainstream."[11] Therefore, I feel compelled to critique some of the more mainstream, commercial Hip Hop or rap music because it perpetuates and glorifies negative stereotypes of African American youth. This commercialized, pre-packaged Hip Hop fosters and preserves the stereotypes of Black male bravado (bellicose, nefarious, materialistic, and hypersexual) and the oversexed Black female. Commercialized Hip Hop is scripted to fit the political, economic, and social agenda of capitalism and White supremacist ideology; therefore, the cultural influence of commercial Hip Hop music on our youth is cleverly calculated to maintain African Americans' subordination. Throughout history, African Americans have been policed in their participation in the entertainment industry. Examples of this include the limited Hollywood roles for African American actors, as well as the long history of White artists stealing songs originally created and produced by African American artists. Whites are able to control the success of African Americans in the entertainment industry because they control the purse strings of the industry; therefore, they control the sound and image. More importantly, their power over the music constructs a stereotypically informed identity for African American youth.

In an interview with *Fish Rap Newspaper* in 2005, one of Hip Hop's most notable scholars Tricia Rose passionately states,

> Hip Hop's initial spirit was about affirmation of collective self in the face of a society that despised the black and brown poor. The excesses in commercialized Hip Hop have limited what we can say, how we imagine ourselves in that space and these limits are designed to normalize and celebrate our dehumanization. It is not violence in Hip Hop, per se, that is the problem; it is violence for what purpose; violence to tell what sort of story about desire and suffering, etc. We need to recognize the crisis in commercial Hip Hop, not just point to underground as a savior. Let's remember, it's underground. We need to recognize that this very large space where virtually all our young people focus their creative energy and dreams for success, has been co-opted. We have to save ourselves from the penetration of the marketplace and its logic. We can do this and still have fun, still enjoy beautiful things. The manipulation of the mainstream can't just be limited to creating another, alternate, underground market, but responding to this one.[12]

I wholeheartedly agree with Rose, and I hope that this theoretical essay contributes to the literature of understanding the current crisis in commercial Hip Hop. The purpose of this paper, therefore, is to understand how commercial rap music has influenced U.S. popular culture and how this effect can be framed as a racial project. Sociologists Michael Omi and Howard Winant define a racial project as "historically situated *projects*

224

in which human bodies and social structures are represented and organized."[13] They add that this project evolves out of hegemony:

> Next we link racial formation to the evaluation of hegemony, the way in which society is organized and ruled. Such an approach, we believe, can facilitate understanding of a whole range of contemporary controversies and dilemmas involving race, including the nature of racism, the relationship of race to other forms of differences, inequalities, and oppression such as sexism and nationalism, and the dilemmas of racial identity today.[14]

Commercial Hip Hop is a contemporary racial project because it constructs the racial identities of African American youth. Albeit globally, many ethnic groups enjoy and embrace Hip Hop culture: African American youth are the established, customary face and sound of Hip Hop. Therefore, African American youth's racial identity is created by the images and sounds of commercial Hip Hop. However, the sound of commercial Hip Hop is created in a society where racism reinvents itself to perpetuate White supremacist ideology; "racism is an integral, permanent, and indestructible component of this society."[15] Hip Hop, unfortunately, plays a large role in the maintenance of destructive images and conceptions about African American youth culture. Such images help perpetuate White supremacy in that they foster notions about who African Americans are and limited ideals of who they can become. Commercial Hip Hop, through the influence of popular culture, has become a primary space for the construction of a racial project, which formulates, organizes, manufactures, and disseminates the social and cultural cynical representations of African American youth. This project is then internalized by mainstream culture and deemed the racial identity of African American youth. Thus, the dilemmas of Hip Hoppers are fostered, created, and perpetuated by White supremacy, politics, and capitalism.

As political platforms rearticulate the meaning of racism, discrimination, and race through mass media, we, as a society, adapt this calculated verbiage to define our racial dynamics and ideologies about one another. The Clinton administration's "hidden agenda" on the topic of racial politics serves as one example. The Clinton administration's contrived racial politics deemed Clinton the "African American president." Adam Fairclough contends,

> When it came to race, Clinton sought to conciliate rather than divide . . . he eschewed liberal polices and swam with the conservative tide. Promising to "end welfare as we know it," he signed a Republican-sponsored bill that ended Aid to Families with Dependent Children, turned welfare over to the states, and cut people from welfare rolls after years. Clinton supported "three strikes and you're out" laws that further swelled the burgeoning prison population.[16]

Thus, the Clinton administration limited economic mobility for people of color and re-established slave labor conditions through prison reform acts, both of which ultimately served to perpetuate White supremacy. The Clinton administration's policies and political rhetoric appealed to African Americans, thus enabling them to collude in their own oppression. Clinton restored African Americans' faith in U.S. politics; however, he simultaneously established laws that institutionally assisted in the continued oppression of people of color. In 1992, Clinton reached out to the African American and Hip Hop community for support during his first run for office. He appeared on the popular Arsenio Hall show wearing dark sunglass and playing the saxophone. Clinton performed on the same stage as Hip Hop performers like Salt-N-Pepa, Public Enemy, Vanilla Ice, and Eazy-E. This political move not only helped Clinton become the 42nd president of the United States; it was also an element of a larger racial project. Clinton's appearance on *The Arsenio Hall Show* reinvented popular culture's contemporary idea of a president and solidified Clinton as "The First Black President," which further mislead African Americans in the political realm. If Clinton was thought of as the "First Black President," his policies clearly undermined this label.

Before Omi and Winant's groundbreaking book *Racial Formation in the United States: From the 1960s to the 1990s*, race primarily evolved around three sociological paradigms: ethnicity, class, and nation. This narrow idea of race negated the idea of race and racism as living, breathing, mutating complex racial misrepresentations, which derives from social and political events throughout history. *Racial Formation's* chronological and descriptive account of U.S. politics and social movements illustrated how race and racism are constructed through multiple lenses to fit the agenda of a particular group.

Omi and Winant's theory of racial formation derives from the notion that race is negotiated, articulated, rearticulated, and constructed around epochal social, political, and historical events. Based on this theory, I argue that commercial mainstream rap music is a racial project much like slavery, Jim Crow, and welfare reform. A racial project such as commercial rap music can be positioned in the political arena because it creates ideologies and attitudes about the African American race and cultivates racial dynamics in the United States. To be clear, I am not arguing that commercial rap music is in any way the same as the physical, psychological, and economical abuses of slavery or Jim Crow. Mainstream rap proliferates and reinforces the historical resentments of African Americans that were established by slavery. In 1994, Rose stated that "rap music is understood as the predominant symbolic voice of black urban males," thirteen years later rap music still defines African American urban youth, now, both male and female.[17] However, this definition of African American urban youth is being constructed by White and Black music executives through rap music and utilized in the destruction of African American culture by the use of symbolic imagery built on relic stereotypes. The ideology of African Americans as hypersexual, misogynistic, and nihilistic transcends the White race. Young African Americans, who are living in an era of global mass media and technological advances such as the creation of Youtube, video games, and MySpace have unlimited access to images and sounds that reinforce negative stereotypes and preserve White supremacist ideology. There are many

226

African American music executives that proliferate White supremacist ideology because they too subscribe to capitalist materialism and hegemony.

The meaning of Hip Hop culture and rap music in popular mainstream culture is one that is fundamentally organized to oppress African Americans and maintain an image that justifies injustice. For example, in order for African American youth to get a record deal, many rap about things that perpetuate White supremacist ideologies and African American inferiority. This can be seen in the abundance of rap songs which glorify drugs, violence, crime and promiscuity. Scholar Michael Eric Dyson contends,

> After all, it's easier to get an album made if you're "pimpin' hoes," "cockin' glocks," or generally bitch-baiting your way through yet another tired tale about how terrible it was to come up in the hood without your father while blaming your mamma for the sorry job she did, than if you're promoting radical black unity or the overthrow of white racism.[18]

The fact that it is easier to get an album made if you are glamorizing crime and promiscuity is an example of how White control of record labels perpetuates commercial Hip Hop as a racial project. In fact, mainstream Hip Hop becomes a site for the construction of a very limited conception of African American youth culture. The corporate control of Hip Hop music gave White America control of the representations of the African American race through the commercialization of Hip Hop music. Arguably, both intentionally and unintentionally, Whites rearticulated and reconstructed the message of Hip Hop music; this is fundamentally a racial project. According to Queeley, "From *Birth of a Nation* to *Amos 'n' Andy* to *Good Times* to *Family Matters*, the television and film industries are notorious for disseminating stereotypical depictions of Black people created by White writers and directors."[19] White writers and directors disseminate negative and sectarian images of African American culture, of which all viewers make meaning. Whites' conscious and dysconscious racism are now embedded in commercial Hip Hop music.[20] The music of the people has turned into the music of the oppressor, who uses the music to rationalize his pathologic ideas of the African American race and maintain the status quo. Commercial Hip Hop as a racial project is largely invisible because the faces of the oppression are African American.

THE ORIGINAL VISION V. THE CAPITALIST APPROPRIATION

One of Hip Hop's original purposes was to serve as a vessel for the oppressed and the silenced. Hip Hop's grandfathers, such as Afrika Bambaataa, Melle Mel, and The Furious Five, expressed the social, economic, and political ills of the African American community. These artists also expressed the beauty and strength of African American culture. The excerpt below by Grandmaster Flash, Melle Mel, and the Furious Five from their legendary song "New York, New York," illuminates the struggles of many African Americans then and now:

A castle in the sky, one mile high
Built to shelter the rich and greedy
Rows of eyes, disguised as windows
Lookin down on the poor and the needy
Miles of people, marchin up the avenue
Doin what they gotta do, just to get by
I'm livin in the land of plenty and many
But I'm damn sure poor and I don't know why.[21]

However, in the 1980s rap music and its message left the inner-city streets and entered mainstream America.[22] The hit single "Rapper's Delight" by The Sugar Hill Gang is arguably rap music's first major crossover hit. Rose states,

Rap went relatively unnoticed by the mainstream music and popular culture industries until independent music entrepreneur Sylvia Robinson released "Rapper's Delight" in 1979. Over the next five years rap music was "'discovered'" by the music industry, the print media, the fashion industry, and the film in industry, each of which hurried to cash in on what was assumed to be a passing fad.[23]

The popularity of "Rapper's Delight" outside the urban community changed Hip Hop forever. Before "Rapper's Delight," rap music was not seen as a profitable music genre and many thought that the sound of Hip Hop would fade—much like disco music. However, by the mid-1990s, rap music could be heard almost everywhere and with the creation and popularity of Music Television, better known as MTV; there was now a face to rap music—the African American face. During the time period of 1986–1993, commonly known as the golden age of Hip Hop, socially conscious groups such as Public Enemy, Native Tongues, and Boogie Down Productions changed rap music with their militant and politically charged lyrics, which criticized and exposed racism, White supremacy, and the current state of African Americans due to the above issues. As Public Enemy and other conscious Hip Hop acts challenged White America's power structures, they were also being challenged by commercial and gangsta rap. The release of NWA's (Niggaz With Attitude) album *Straight Outta Compton* in 1988 and in 1992 the overwhelming success of Dr. Dre's album *The Chronic* and Snoop Dogg's album *Doggystyle* legitimated gangsta rap and, for many people, established rap music as violent and a threat to society. However, gangsta rap generated billions of dollars and appealed to White audiences much like jazz, blues, and R&B. Therefore, White record companies monopolized Hip Hop. Scholar Mark Neal reports, "six major record companies, all owned by whites, produce eighty percent of all music made in the U.S."[24] These six companies control the sound of Hip Hop and the ideological images that are transmitted to mainstream America. The white dominated music industry not only controls mainstream Hip Hop and music, it also controls the images of African American youth. Current mainstream Hip Hop videos shown on BET and MTV often depict

African American women and men in stereotypical roles. Gender and adolescent development scholars Ward, Hansbrough, and Walker write,

> As a visual, story-telling format with little time to devote [to] deep characterizations, music videos often rely on shortcuts and cultural stereotypes working to a point with a quick cut, image, or gender role cue.[25]

Through commercial Hip Hop videos, African American women are portrayed as "opportunistic gold diggers, aggressive gangsters, bitches, freaks, divas, and dykes."[26] African American males are depicted as oversexed criminals who objectify women and pose a serious danger to society. Media outlets that program commercial Hip Hop videos have a direct relationship to the socialization of African American youth. It is reported that African American children between the ages of 8 and 18 watch 5 hours of television daily.[27] A large majority of these five hours are spent watching their race be redefined as oversexed, uneducated, and non-contributors to society. The racial project of commercial rap music is the presentation of negative images of African American youth to blacks and whites. This learning about the limited roles African American youth can play in society further reifies racism and perpetuates White supremacy.

This remarkable music that originated as the sound of inner-city life is now being proscribed by White and Black America; the very nature of capitalism has put rap music in a "chokehold." Historian Robin D. G. Kelley contends that capitalism is African American "youths' greatest friend and greatest foe."[28] Hip Hop scholar Andrea Queeley adds that "Through the corporate takeover of [H]ip [H]op culture, multiconsumerism masquerades as multiculturalism, and in the process, white supremacist ideology has been re-released onto a global terrain."[29] Commercial Hip Hop is the primary global tool for fostering White supremacist ideology and manipulating young African Americans' value systems. This racial project has rearticulated commercial Hip Hop into a co-opted art form that maintains white supremacist oppression and defines African American youth culture.

MANIPULATION & MULTIPLE MEANINGS OF POPULAR CULTURE

As I begin my critique of commercial Hip Hop in popular culture, I write from the standpoint of feminist cultural studies, which posits that textual representations matter and that most popular culture texts articulate ideologies of race, gender, class, and sexuality.[30] In addition, consumers of a text enter into a relationship with that text, especially texts that are popular such as commercial Hip Hop.[31] Furthermore, Hip Hop has made an impact on all mechanisms of popular mainstream culture, above all the advertising industry. Bakari Kitwana writes,

> Hip Hop is a three billion dollar a year industry . . . the top selling music format . . . and its pervasiveness in advertisement for mainstream corporations like AT&T, The Gap, Levi's, and so on.[32]

229

The pervasive influence that Hip Hop culture has on popular culture provides a space for the interpretation of Hip Hop by mainstream culture. Stuart Hall contends, "Black popular culture is a contradictory space. It is a sight of strategic contestation."[33] Arguably, there are three groups waging the struggle for control of Hip Hop music: the socially and politically conscious rappers who speak out against racial and social injustices; the nonsocially conscious commercial rapper (one who utilizes negative notions about African American culture for profit) who spits lyrics of denigration because he or she is either unaware of his or her role in the racial project or is consumed by capitalism; and major white owned record labels who, through economic means, seductively subdue African American rappers, producers, and record executives into perpetuating negative African American stereotypes. Unfortunately, Hip Hop artists, producers, and record executives have to choose a side; the road most often taken leads to subjecting oneself and one's people to media mutilation. bell hooks writes that "Much of Hip Hop culture is mainstream because it is just a black minstrel show—an imitation of dominator desire, not a rearticulation, not a radical alternative."[34] Part of this minstrel show aspect of Hip Hop is created by corporate White America's control over record labels. As previously stated, African American artists have always been limited in their roles in the entertainment industry. The fact that commercial Hip Hop has limited roles is a testament to a contemporary racial project. This racial project has historical roots as "Black performers have always been pressured to perform the Blackness of the white imagination, and the Blackness is most often in the service of white supremacy."[35] The text of commercial Hip Hop teaches mainstream culture that African American youth are sexually promiscuous, criminally minded, and materialistic. For instance, 50-cent's song P.I.M.P, illuminates the depictions of African American as nihilistic:

> I told you fools before, I stay with the tools
> I keep a Benz, some rims, and some jewels
> I holla at a hoe til I got a bitch confused
> She got on Payless, me I got on gator shoes
> I'm shopping for chinchillas, in the summer they cheaper
> Man this hoe you can have her, when I'm done I ain't gon keep her
> Man, bitches come and go, every nigga pimpin know
> You saying it's secret, but you ain't gotta keep it on the low
> Bitch choose with me, I'll have you stripping in the street
> Put my other hoes down, you get your ass beat
> Now Nik my bottom bitch, she always come up with my bread
> The last nigga she was with put stitches in her head
> Get your hoe out of pocket, I'll put a charge on a bitch
> Cause I need 4 TVs and AMGs for the six
> Hoe make a pimp rich, I ain't paying bitch
> Catch a date, suck a dick, shit, trick.[36]

These lyrics perpetuate injustice towards African Americans and validate White America's stereotypical attitudes about crime and race. Manning Marable contends, "The driving ideological and cultural force that rationalized and justifies mass incarceration is the White American public's stereotypical perceptions about race and crime."[37] For instance, in 2003 African Americans comprised only 12.2% of the population and 13% of drug users; yet, they made up 38% of those arrested for drug offenses and 59% of those convicted of drug offenses.[38] Currently, there are over two million Black men incarcerated. Ninety-three percent of New York's imprisoned drug offenders are Black or Latino, despite the fact that drug use and sales are equally distributed across the races.[39] Political artist and prolific scholar Angela Davis writes,

> As prisons proliferate in U.S. society, private capital has become enmeshed in the punishment industry. And precisely because of their profit potential, prisons are becoming increasingly important to the U.S. economy. If the notion of punishment as a source of potentially stupendous profits is disturbing by itself, then the strategic dependence on racist structures and ideologies to render mass punishment palatable and profitable is even more troubling.[40]

One example of this exploitation is the "1979 Prison Industry Enhancement certification program (CPI), which gave private companies access to prison laborers."[41] Criminologist Niles Christie suggests, "crime control, rather than crime itself, is the real danger for our future, especially since humans are seen as products that can be controlled for billions of dollars a year."[42] The negative images that mainstream Hip Hop music disseminates legitimate the exploitation of African American males. Commercial Hip Hop has become a vehicle for corporate America to perpetuate negative stereotypes of African American males, which justifies politicians' and mainstream America's views on incarceration. Commercial Hip Hop music and videos glorify incarceration and an illegal lifestyle. Rick Ross' song "Hustlin" is a prime example of this celebrated criminal lifestyle:

> Who the fuck you think you fuckin' with, I'm the fuckin' boss
> Seven forty-five, white on white that's fuckin' Ross
> I cut 'em wide, I cut 'em long, I cut 'em fat (What)
> I keep 'em comin' back (What), we keep 'em comin' back
> I'm in the distribution, I'm like Atlantic
> I got them motherfuckers flyin' 'cross the Atlantic
> I know Pablo, Noriega, the real Noriega
> He owe me a hundred favors
> I ain't petty nigga, we buy the whole thang
> See most of my niggas really still deal cocaine
> My roof back, my money rides
> I'm on the pedal, show you what I'm runnin' like

When they snatch black I cry for a hundred nights
He got a hundred bodies, servin' a hundred lifes.[43]

This fantasy world of crime, money, and drugs that Rick Ross and other nonsocially conscious rappers like him disseminate to young African Americans through
their videos and lyrics assists in the oppression and self-destructive mindset of many
young African American males. Hall writes, "black men continue to live out their
counter-identities as black masculinities and replay those fantasies of black masculinities in the theaters of popular culture."[44] Because White supremacist ideologies limit
positive versions of African American masculinity, the fantasy versions presented in
music videos are seductive because they are portrayed not as fantasies but as viable
options for African American youth. As millions of African American youth, especially males, tune into MTV and BET everyday and internalize the negative images of
commercial rap music, the fantasy world in which rappers exist becomes a reality for
African American men who swell prisons and become even more disenfranchised from
a system that capitalizes on their demise.

HEGEMONY & COMMERCIAL HIP HOP

Race scholar Eduardo Bonilla-Silva argues that Hip Hop is a counterculture and
"will lead the fight against modern racism."[45] Bonilla-Silva further argues that Hip
Hop has the power to become a political movement and draws parallels to the Civil
Rights Movement, seeing both as vehicles to stop oppression and racism. Bonilla-
Silva contends that young African Americans in the Hip Hop industry have the
power and resources to mobilize a movement with Hip Hop being the "cultural
foundation."[46] Similar arguments have been made about the power of Hip Hop as a
political movement, with events such as the Million Man March, Russell Simmons'
Annual Hip Hop Summit, Sean "Diddy" Comb's 2004 Vote or Die campaign, and,
most recently, will.i.am's song, "Yes We Can," in support of Barack Obama, which
encouraged young Americans, especially young African Americans, to vote. On the
surface, it seems that Hip Hop culture has made a substantial impact on American
politics. Kitwana writes,

> Given Hip Hop's tremendous influence (as American pop culture and as a $3-4
> billion a year force in the music industry), expanding into the political arena is
> inevitable. But who will emerge as the Hip Hop generation's power brokers? This
> question is critical to whether Hip Hop's foray into politics will be about social
> change for the many or enrichment for the few.[47]

I agree with Kitwana that Hip Hop's role in the political arena is inevitable; however, the question of who will be the power brokers and who will profit from the economic success of Hip Hop is answered by bell hooks, who writes,

Patriarchal Hip Hop ushered in a world where black males could declare that they were "keeping it real" when what they were doing was taking the dead patriarchal protest of the black power movement and rearticulating it in forms that, though entertaining, had for the most part no transformative power, no ability to intervene on politics of domination, and turn the real lives of black men around.[48]

hooks expresses how commercialized rap music is unable to exercise effective political power because it cannot exercise control over the messages that are propagated. Control of rap music maintains the status quo, perpetuates White supremacist ideology, and patriarchal ideology because of the limited versions of African American youth culture it displays. For instance, the more socially conscious artists such as dead prez, Talib Kweli, Lupe Fiasco, and Michael Franti have not been able to achieve a wide spread audience because their lyrics passionately and unapologetically address the injustices in the world. These lyrics could possibly awaken our youth and lead them to question their socially constructed position in our society; but it is not an accident that the music of dead prez, Michael Franti and others are underground and dismissed by mainstream radio stations. Contrast this to the popularity and economic success of 50 Cent, Piles, and Ying Yang Twins whose lyrics glorify promiscuity and violence.

Such negative ideology about Hip Hop is constructed and internalized by a large majority of African Americans, especially African Americans who feel they are "keeping it real." Negative African American stereotypes are reaffirmed through commercial Hip Hop music and become "common knowledge," which is a vital component of hegemony. Omi and Winant refer to Italian theorist Antonio Gramsci's argument that

> in order to consolidate their hegemony, ruling groups must elaborate and maintain a popular system of ideas and practices—through education, the media, religion, folk wisdom etc.—which he called "common sense," this ideology (in the broadest sense of the term), that a society gives its consent to the way in which it is ruled.[49]

White corporate America transmits negative images of African Americans to society through the media, which makes African Americans' social and economic failures "common knowledge." Mainstream America has come to understand African American oppression as "common knowledge." Basically, this "common knowledge" understanding of African Americans legitimates the social and economic oppression of African Americans. In addition, it legitimates racist thinking because society defines what is and what is not African American based on the "characters" found in mainstream Hip Hop videos, lyrics, and magazines. Race scholar Charles Gallagher reported that in 1991:

> A National Opinion Research Center study found that 78 percent of whites believed that blacks were more likely to prefer to live off welfare, 62 percent

believed that blacks were less hard working, 56 percent responded that blacks were violent, and 53 percent believed blacks were less intelligent.[50]

The ideologies above expressed by Whites derive from various places; however, popular culture plays a significant role in Whites' and mainstream culture's understandings of African American culture and values. Commercial Hip Hop is a site of education that presents White supremacist ideas of African American culture and values. However, the African American culture and values that are demonstrated through commercial Hip Hop are not accurate representations of African Americans. Although many forms of popular culture have contributed to the degradation of African Americans, right now commercial Hip Hop is in the forefront of perpetuating this view. Through this genre, Whites believe that African Americans are less intelligent, enjoy living on welfare, and shy away from hard work because popular Hip Hop music glorifies street life, prison, and disidentifying with formal education. This hegemony also leads to what sociologists some call laissez-faire racism.[51] As an example, Gallagher contends, "Whites blame blacks for high rates of poverty by using stereotypes to justify their beliefs while ignoring the structural conditions that perpetuate such inequality."[52] Due to the pathological stereotypes that commercialized rap music encourages, Whites to believe that these African Americans are violent and unintelligent, among many other negative attributes, and these ideas become "common knowledge." This is a key element of hegemony and a racial project. As a result of the ideologies imbedded within the psyche by these "common knowledge" stereotypes, Whites dismiss talk of institutional racism and discrimination "as excuses by blacks for not engaging in the type of work and thrift needed to achieve the American Dream."[53] This perpetuates the idea that African Americans are not successful because of poor choices and lack of ambition, not because racism limits African American achievement.

Conversely, these negative images of African Americans are made a reality by African American viewers through "lived" experiences; however, America's judicial system continually tyrannizes African Americans for portraying the images they (corporate America) disseminate to mainstream culture. African American youth internalize the pessimistic ideologies of Hip Hop culture, and their failures become "common knowledge" or a way of life. Psychologist Claude Steele defines what I am describing as the "stereotype threat." Steele argues that marginalized groups internally feel "the threat of being viewed through the lens of a negative stereotype, or the fear of doing something that would inadvertently confirm that stereotype."[54] For instance, in testing situations when students felt they were being judged by stereotypes, they performed poorly on standardized tests. In this case, Hip Hoppers are aware of the stereotypes that label them uneducated, lazy, and shiftless; nevertheless, they internalize these stereotypes in society because of the seductive nature of a racial project. Commercial Hip Hop's message of sexual promiscuity, criminal lifestyle, and cultural degeneration woos young Hip Hoppers and renders them incapable of social change. Furthermore, the life experiences of African American youth depicted in mainstream

Hip Hop music and videos become the social representations of the African Americans' culture to mainstream culture. Bonilla-Silva contends that these representations are "conscious and nonsocially conscious sum of ideas, prejudices, and myths that crystallize the victories and defeats of the races regarding how the world is and ought to be organized."[55] Through mass media, African American youth deliberately and involuntarily consume commercial Hip Hop, which manifests into the cultural representations of the generation.

CONCLUSION

Arguably, there is no other sound that resonates with our youth like Hip Hop music. Its influence and its message, whether positive or negative, is one that is apparent and infectious. Hip Hop music has become the language, culture, and sound African American youth use to communicate with the rest of the world. However, before they use their microphone to speak to the world they are interrupted and subdued by major record labels operated by Whites. Their message is then diluted and reconstructed to fit the agenda of white supremacist ideology, while they employ African Americans as moguls to run their racial project. Rap moguls such as Sean "Diddy" Combs and Shawn Carter (Jay-Z) are marketing tools: they lack the power and control of Hip Hop music to empower our youth. Through the media's influence and corporate America's contrived marketing of African American rappers, society has come to believe that African American youth lack the intelligence and determination to achieve anything other than becoming a rap star. These stereotypical beliefs are then internalized by African American youth and manifested in society through poor education and the prison systems. Mainstream commercial Hip Hop encourages, provides, and maintains the oppression of African Americans through language and imagery. Popular Hip Hop music is saturated with profanity, sexual exploitation, and violence. There exist countless social and educational implications of Hip Hop as a racial project. No one could know the negative impact commercial Hip Hop has had on African American youth and the ramifications its perceptions have ingrained in mainstream culture, nor the negative psychological effects that African American youth display in schools and society at-large as they perform what they believe to be Hip Hop culture.

For me, this racial project becomes a lived experience every time I see a child in the back of his parent's car trying to mimic the foul language in rap music that is being blasted from his parent's vehicle. Every time a young teenage boy turns on BET and learns how to treat women from the videos that slide a credit card down a women's backside, and signifies that a purchase has been or can be made, a racial project has become a lived and defining experience.[56] As young African American girls dream about one day becoming strippers and young African American boys fantasize about becoming pimps, the language and images that popular culture circulates to our youth maintain their oppression for generations to come.[57]

So what can be done, what now? Parents, educators, community leaders, and Hip Hop scholars have to start a dialogue with our youth to help them understand who is controlling the sound and image of commercial Hip Hop and their contrived interest in the control of the music. In addition, we must start to struggle with the questions of what is liberating and what is oppressive in Hip Hop. Is the story of a man that sold drugs and started his "own" record company from drug money to become the CEO of Def Jam liberating or oppressive when our sons strive to follow in his footsteps? Is the idea of women rappers declaring their sexual freedom by broadcasting the sexual acts they perform liberating or oppressive when it is heard and internalized by our daughters? Furthermore, how liberating or oppressive is commercial Hip Hop when it is pre-packaged and sent to our children in the form of a racial project? If we are to challenge the assumptions encouraged by the detrimental consequences of nonsocially conscious Hip Hop music, racism, and White supremacist ideology, we must ask these questions and actively seek answers that will provide the foundation for our children to become critical thinkers in a time when cultural representations can be bought and sold to the highest bidder.

Also, further research must be done to understand how youth make meaning of commercial Hip Hop music. Youth need to be interviewed and observed to examine their consumption of Hip Hop and how the music becomes part of their lived experiences. It would be important to study numerous racial groups, especially White communities to determine the impact mainstream Hip Hop culture has played in their constructions of African American youth culture. I am aware that these suggestions only provide a band-aid to the larger problems that exist in our society. However, I suggest them as a start, a launch pad for ideas that will help youth develop a disposition of inquiry and critical thinking skills. So as our youth listen to commercial Hip Hop they understand that they are listening to music that has been manufactured to assist in their oppression and that truly "keeping it real" is questioning who is "keeping it real."

NOTES

[1] dead prez, "Hip Hop," *Dave Chappelle's Block Party*, Geffen Records (2006).

[2] I define rappers who rap about the social, political, economical plight of the oppressed as conscious rappers. For a more informative definition of conscious rappers, see Derrick Alridge "From Civil Rights to Hip Hop: Toward a Nexus of Ideas," *The Journal of African American History* 90 (Summer 2005): 226–52.

[3] When I use the term Hip Hoppers, I am referring to inner city youth, individuals that are a part of the Hip Hop generations and primary African American youth. I am aware that not all inner city youth listen to Hip Hop and identify with the Hip Hop culture. However, I am making this generalization due to my experience growing up as an inner city youth; I was surrounded by Hip Hop culture, as were all of my peers.

[4] Manning Marable, *How Capitalism Underdeveloped Black America* (Boston, 1983), 2.

[5] Derrick P. Alridge and James B. Stewart, "Introduction: Hip Hop in the History: Past, Present and Future," *The Journal of African American History* 90 (Summer 2005): 190–95.

[6] Dipannita Basu, "A Critical Examination of the Political Economy of the Hip Hop Industry" in *African Americans in the U.S. Economy* (Maryland, 2005), 258.

[7] Ibid.

[8] See the chart on page 264 of the Dipannita Basu article listed above.

[9]See Baraki Kitwana, *The Hip Hop Generation: Young Blacks and the Crisis in African-American Culture* (New York, 2002). Kitwana contends that African Americans born between 1965 and 1984 make up the Hip Hop generation.

[10]Stuart Hall, "What is this "Black" in Black Popular Culture," in *Black Popular Culture*, ed. Michelle Wallace (New York, 1983), 22.

[11]Bakari Kitwana, *Why White Kids Love Hip Hop* (New York, 2005), xiii.

[12]Tricia Rose, interviewed by Lauren Kennedy, Staff Writer, *Fish Rap Newspaper*, http://www.tricia rose.com/.

[13]Omi and Winant, *Racial Formation in the United States: From the 1960s to the 1990s* (New York 1994), 56.

[14]Ibid.

[15]Derrick Bell, *Faces at the Bottom of the Well: The Permanence of Racism* (New York, 1992), x.

[16]Adam Fairclough, *Better Day Coming: Blacks and Equality, 1890–2000* (New York, 2001), 333.

[17]Tricia Rose, *Black Noise: Rap Music and Black Culture in Contemporary America* (Connecticut, 1994), 126.

[18]Michael Eric Dyson, *Race Rules: Navigating the Color Line* (New York, 1996), 114.

[19]Andrea Queeley, ""Hip Hop and the Aesthetics of Criminalization," *Souls* 5 (Winter 2003): 1–15.

[20]The term dysconscious racism is derived from Joyce King "Dysconscious Racism: Ideology, Identity, and the Miseducation of Teachers," *Journal of Negro Education* 60 (Spring 1991): 133–46.

[21]Grandmaster Flash, Melle Mel, and the Furious Five, "New York, New York," *Message from Beat Street: The Best of Grandmaster Flash, Melle Mel & The Furious Five*, Rhino (1994).

[22]I utilized the definition by Richard Alba and Victor Nee to define mainstream America. They contend that mainstream is not limited to the middle class, "it contains a working class and even some who are poor, not just affluent suburbanites." See Richard Alba and Victor Nee, *Remaking the American Mainstream: Assimilation and Contemporary* (Massachusetts and England, 2003), 12.

[23]Tricia Rose, *Black Noise: Rap Music and Black Culture in Contemporary America* (Connecticut, 1994), 3.

[24]Mark Neal, "Sold Out on Soul: The Corporate Annexation of Black Popular Music," *Popular Music and Society* (Fall 1997).

[25]L. Monique Ward, Edwina Hansbrough, and Eboni Walker, "" Contributions of Music Video Exposure to Black Adolescents' Gender and Sexual Schemas, *Journal of Adolescent Research* 20, no. 2 (2005): 143–66.

[26]Dionne P. Stephens and Layli D. Phillips, ""Freaks, Gold Diggers, Divas, and Dykes: The Socio-historical Development of Adolescent African-American Women's Sexual Scripts," *Sexuality and Culture* 7, no. 1 (2003): 3–49.

[27]Donald Roberts, Ulla Foehr, Victoria Rideout, and Mollyanne Brodie, ""Kids and Media at the New Millennium," *Henry J. Kaiser Family Foundation* (1999).

[28]Robin D. G. Kelley, "Looking to Get Paid: How Some Black Youth Put Culture to Work," in *Yo' Mama Disfunktional! Fighting the Culture Wars in Urban America* (Boston, 1998), 77.

[29]Queeley, ""Hip Hop and the Aesthetics of Criminalization," *Souls* 5, 1–15.

[30]Angela McRobbie, *Feminism and Youth Culture: From "Jackie" to "Just Seventeen"* (Boston: 1991).

[31]Douglas Kellner, *Media Culture: Cultural Studies, Identity and Politics Between the Modern and the Postmodern* (London and New York, 1995).

[32]Kitwana *The Hip Hop Generation*, 10.

[33]Stuart Hall, "What Is This "Black" in Black Popular Culture," 26.

[34]bell hooks, *We Real Cool: Black Men and Masculinity* (New York, 2003), 33.

[35]Andrea Queeley, ""Hip Hop and the Aesthetics of Criminalization," *Souls* 5 (Winter 2003): 1–15.

[36]50 cent, "P.I.M.P," *Get Rich or Die Tryin*, Interscope Records (2003).

[37]Manning Marable, "Racism, Prisons and the Future of Black America"—Part Two of Two August 1, 2000, http://www.freepress.org/columns/display/4/2000/506.

[38]See *Drug Policy Alliance* website for statistics at http://www.drugpolicy.org/homepage.cfm.

[39]Ibid.

[40]Angela Y. Davis, *"Masked Racism: Reflections on the Prison Industrial Complex,"* http://www.arc.org/ C Lines/CLArchive/story1 2 01.html.

[41]Bakari Kitwana, *The Hip Hop Generation: Young Blacks and the Crisis in African-American Culture.* (New York, 2002), 73.

[42]Niles Christie, *Crime Control as Industry* (Norway, 2000), 173.

[43]Rick Ross, "Hustlin" *Career Criminal*, Def Jam (2006).

[44]Hall, "'What Is this "Black" in Black Popular Culture," 22.

[45]Eduardo Bonilla-Silva, *White Supremacy & Racism in the Post–Civil Rights Era* (Colorado, 2001), 203.

[46]Ibid.

[47]Kitwana, *The Hip Hop Generation*, 193.

[48]hooks, *We Real Cool*, 182.

[49]Omi and Winant, *Racial Formation*, 67.

[50]Charles A. Gallagher, "Playing the White Ethnic Card: Using Ethnic Identity to Deny Contemporary Racism." In Ashley W. Doana and Eduardo Bonilla-Silva, *White Out: The Continuing Significance of Racism* (New York, 2003), 150.

[51]Ibid.

[52]Ibid.

[53]Ibid., 151.

[54]Theresa Perry, Claude Steele, Asa Hilliard III, *Young, Gifted and Black: Promoting High Achievement Among African-American Students* (Boston, 2003), 111.

[55]Bonilla-Silva, *White Supremacy*, 64.

[56]I am describing a scene from the controversial video "Tip Drill" by commercial rapper Nelly.

[57]One of the most popular commercial Hip Hop songs of 2006 is a song by T-Pain called "I'm in Love with a Stripper," and there are countless songs that glorify the pimp lifestyle.

HIP HOP AND GLOCAL POLITICS IN CARIBBEAN MUSIC: DEBATES IN TRANSNATIONALISM AND RESISTANCE IN CARIBBEAN HIP HOP

Lesley Feracho

The relationship between the universal and the particular, between the global and the local, while historically enacted as part of social and economic development, has reached greater levels of relevance in the current climate of globalization and transnationalism. The question of how communities respond to the external economic and cultural forces that influence local discourses—both economic and social—is an important part of understanding ongoing struggles for autonomy. Roland Robertson's theory of interdependence has been particularly cited as a helpful way of understanding the dynamics of these struggles. As he states:

> . . . we should consider globalization, in and of itself, to be simultaneously *homogenizing*—making things the same—and *at the same time*, making things different. . . . I think we have to get used to this *interpenetration*, this relationship between universality and particularity, or else we are going to continue to produce a distorted image of what is happening in the modern world.[1]

Borrowing from the Japanese economic term *dochakuka*, Robertson has described this interdependence through the term *glocalization*:

> This is a word, incidentally, which has played an increasingly important part in my own writings . . . about globalization. Because "glocalization" means the simultaneity—the co-presence—of both universalizing and particularizing tendencies. . . . But the basic idea of glocalization is the simultaneous promotion of what is, in one sense, a standardized product, for particular markets, in particular flavors. . . .[2]

More specifically, glocalization is defined as "combining the global with the local, to emphasize that each is in many ways defined by the other and that they frequently intersect, rather than being polarized opposites."[3] In a historical and social moment where technology and reigning economic systems move different communities toward not only a sharing of information, but an increasing homogenization, how does the particular remain and continue to develop under such pressure? While Robertson sees a move towards fundamentalism on one hand, the process is also important for specific communities' understanding of the world, their place in it, and the implications of their particular historical moments. As he states:

. . . the current phase of very rapid globalization facilitates the rise of movements concerned with the "real meaning" of the world, movements (and individuals) searching for the meaning of the world as a whole. The universalization of the particular refers to the global universality of the search for the particular, for increasingly fine-grained modes of identity presentation.[4]

For disenfranchised communities across the globe, this "search for the meaning of the world" is a process that must deal with issues of marginalization, disempowerment, and possibilities for agency. While political movements, particularly grass roots movements in communities ranging from African Americans and Chicanos in the United States, blacks and indigenous communities throughout Latin America to women's workshops throughout Africa, have had varied levels of success in providing effective strategies for mobilization and empowerment, cultural movements have increasingly taken on this responsibility. Hip Hop, as a increasingly global phenomenon of the past three decades is one such example of a cultural engagement that has provided a forum for addressing the concerns of those who do not benefit from the promises of globalization and progress. As Tony Mitchell notes in *Global Noise: Rap and Hip Hop Outside the U.S.*, Hip Hop culture in all its facets has, in specific communities, served the purposes that formalized party based political movements have not been able to:

> In its recombination into local linguistic, musical, and political contexts around the world, rap music and Hip Hop culture have in many cases become a vehicle for various forms of youth protest. They are also used in different local contexts to espouse the causes of ethnic minorities (e.g., in the Basque Country or Aotearoa-New Zealand) and to make political statements about local racial, sexual, employment, and class issues (e.g., in France, Italy, Germany and elsewhere).[5]

As Mitchell notes Hip Hop culture has become a bridge form that links the artistic with the political, the local with the global (exemplifying in the ways I have pointed out, the "glocal" characteristics Robertson has delineated) and cultural discourses with the economic realities of the possibilities of and obstacles to financial advancement. In studies of Hip Hop, questions not only of globalization, but also transnationalism have become issues around which critics of cultural studies, music, and sociology like Flores, Fernandes, Baker, and Pacini-Hernández have gathered to understand the ramifications of this musical and political form.

While Hip Hop is reaching almost every inch of the globe, from the aforementioned France, Italy, Spain, and Germany to the Caribbean, South America, Hawaii, Israel and the African continent (in countries like Senegal, South Africa, and Tanzania) this study will focus on the nations of the Spanish Caribbean, Cuba and Puerto Rico, where Hip Hop, and particularly rap, have taken on these roles of protest and political engagement while also in some cases serving the conflicting role of vehicle for social advancement. Rather than provide a systematic overview of the complex history of rap as it connects both to the United States, and the larger world, I will examine how Hip Hop can be a means of engaging transnational processes in the cultural sphere, particularly in areas of social contestation and compliance.

In this study, I will demonstrate how Hip Hop can address local issues that resonate on a global scale, particularly with other disenfranchised communities seeking a voice. By looking at examples in both island nations, specifically "Se contamina el barrio" by Cuban Hip Hop group Explosión Suprema, "Resistiendo" by Las Krudas, a Cuban feminist Hip Hop group, and "Loiza" by Tego Calderón from Puerto Rico, I will look at ways in which Hip Hop has been used as a "glocal" form of expression to engage issues of citizenship, identity politics, and social justice. In particular, my focus on Caribbean Hip Hop will illuminate strategies of social critique and resistance as navigations of local and global socio-cultural and (to an extent) political spaces. This essay will also briefly touch on representations of larger diasporic communities and their participation in these cultural and social flows of knowledge and mobilization.

I will begin with a brief history of the development of rap on both islands and focus on examples of their musical and lyrical navigation of glocal identity politics and social injustice as projects of contestation that unite them with other marginalized groups. I have chosen to study the cases of Caribbean Hip Hop and in particular Cuban and Puerto Rican rap because of their transnational histories shaped by migrations and their importance in the development of Hip Hop as a musical form. I will use Sallie Westwood's definition of transnationalism alongside Damián Fernández's study of its application to Cuba. For Westwood transnationalism considers the physical and emotional importance of the nation as well as ". . . those processes such as cross-border migration . . . each of these processes is constituted in racialised, gendered and class relations which are by no means static, not least because of the ways in which individuals and collectivities contest certain boundaries and carve out new spaces of identity and control for themselves. . . ."[6]

One of the most common historical accounts of the genesis of Hip Hop locates it in the urban areas of New York City in the 1970s. However, sociologists like Tricia Rose trace its origins back to the spoken word and experimental artists of the 1960s and 1970s such as The Last Poets and Gil Scott-Heron. In addition to musical influences, Rose also cites the impact of political activists such as Malcolm X and the Black Panthers in the development of Hip Hop's vernacular language.[7] However, while Rose's primary accounts define Hip Hop as "a black cultural expression that prioritizes black voices from the margins of urban America," recognizing the partnership nonetheless of Afro-Caribbean youth, the history of Hispanophone Caribbean and Latino participation in the genesis of Hip Hop is underrepresented. Mitchell, takes the representation of Latinos and Caribbeans further by acknowledging the importance not only of breakdancing's and graffiti's Latino members (e.g., Futura 2000, Rock Steady Crew), but the participation of rappers such as Disco Wiz, DJ Charlie Chase, Ruby Dee, and Devastating Tito in creating a musical form that was cross cultural from its inception.[8] Later seminal studies by Juan Flores and Raquel Rivera most specifically rewrite this history of Hip Hop by highlighting the collaborative work of African Americans and Caribbean youth and musicians in order to recognize the pioneers outside of the Black community and counteract the cultural "amnesia" that both have noted. As Flores states:

Not only is the social context wider, but the historical reach is deeper and richer: the black and Puerto Rican conjunction in the formation of rap is prefigured in doo-wop, Latin jazz, Nuyorican poetry, and a range of other testimonies to intensely overlapping and intermingling expressive repertoires. . . . In addition to these more obvious associations, the formative years of rap follow closely the development of both salsa and Nuyorican poetry, expressive modes which, especially for the young Puerto Ricans themselves, occupy the same creative constellation as the musical and lyrical project of bilingual and bicultural rap.[9]

The recognition of Puerto Rican collaboration is in part further proof of the "long history of cultural interaction with African Americans . . . a sharing that once again articulates their congruent and intermingling placement in the impinging political and economic geography."[10] However, the earlier lack of recognition of these shared social, political, and cultural locations is also representative of larger questions of race and nationality in the United States vs. the Caribbean. As Rivera has noted in her study *New York Ricans from the Hip Hop Zone* regarding perceptions of Puerto Rican and African American identity:

> . . . their Hip Hop stories challenge some of the prevailing assumptions regarding Puerto Rican creative practices and identities. . . . I argue in these pages that New York Rican hip hoppers have certainly not abandoned but simply stretched the boundaries of *puertorriqueñidad* (Puerto Ricanness) and *latinidad* (Latinoness) and questioned the assumption that these categories do not intersect with blackness.[11]

As I will expand later in my discussion of Puerto Rican Hip Hop, the migratory relationship of African Americans and Caribbeans, of Puerto Ricans on the mainland and those on the island provide a necessary historical basis for contemporary understandings of Caribbean Hip Hop that predate labels of global and transnational. Given these earlier histories, both islands' contemporary participation in Hip Hop provide opportunities to continue to look at this musical form beyond the scope of the U.S. context and beyond earlier perceptions of it as a transitory phenomenon.

While the participation of Nuyoricans in early Hip Hop is becoming increasingly acknowledged and analyzed, that of contemporary Hip Hop musical production on the island is in fact second to its hispanophone neighbor, Cuba. In part, the saliency of U.S.-Cuban relations, and Cuba's political and economic status after its Special Period make it a revelatory subject in studies of globalization, international relations, and its impact. As Damián Fernández observes:

> Cuba, like most nations, was born transnational; colonialism, capitalism, and slavery marked the national experience structurally as well as cultural. . . . Cuba is a good case study because it reveals that despite physical insularity and political barriers (domestic and international), globalization and transnationalism are part and parcel of the contemporary physical and cultural landscape.[12]

The attention paid to Cuban music in general makes growing studies of Cuban rap a revealing avenue into larger issues of political agency, relations with the Cuban State, globalization and the cultural navigations of power dynamics. However, as Fernandes notes in her study *Cuba represent!* the growth of Hip Hop as a means of addressing pressing social issues or espousing different aspects of collective pride makes this cultural process a forum that has at times proven more effective than State politics in engaging these topics:

> Issues that were earlier relegated to political organizations and mass rallies are increasingly being addressed in the spheres of culture and consumption. Within the arts and popular culture, Cubans debate questions of socialism and democracy, legality and illegality, tourism, emigration, and issues of racial and sexual discrimination.[13]

It is this ability of Hip Hop to become a vehicle for socio-political awareness and critique that demonstrates its global linking of local responses to social injustice. Cuba's political history with the United States, for example, is a complex study in the tensions of control and autonomy, as evidenced by the end of the War for Cuban Independence (known in the United States as the Spanish American War) in 1898 where, upon its defeat, Spain granted Cuban independence, only to see the United States engage in a military occupation it termed "enlightened intervention" and the "Platt Amendment," allowing intervention in Cuban domestic politics should any threat of instability arise.[14] This political relationship with the United States is, however, historically only one part of the story. The relationship of Cubans with the African American community is decades old and reaches outside political coalitions. In her collection of essays *Between Race and Empire: African Americans and Cubans before the Cuban Revolution*, Lisa Brock reminds her readers that:

> It became increasingly clear to us that these black, mulatto, Latin American, West Indian and Latino peasants, sharecroppers, ministers, immigrants, artists, workers and socialists had in fact centered themselves; these men and women had consistently subverted their nations' elites and created a universe in which they cohabited.[15]

This history of "centering" and subversion between these communities is one that will continue through later coalitions with Black writers and underground musicians as Hip Hop develops on the island and represents the expansion of the revolution and of the Hip Hop community along the lines of current understandings of transnationalism. One example of this is the "Black August Collective," "a network established during the 1970s in the California prison system as a way of linking up movements for resistance in the Americas" that would later sponsor visits by "conscious" rappers like Paris and Talib Kweli to interact with "underground" Cuban rappers as a sign of racial, social, and political solidarity.[16] This relationship between Cuban and U.S. artists is one example of the transnational, migratory character of Cuba, in opposition to its falsely perceived isolation yet also demonstrates how concepts of blackness and Cubanness interact and are challenged through different cultural discourses.

Such a reevaluation of race and nation in Cuba is of course not solely connected to Cuban-U.S. relations but can be seen in the early years of the revolution when Castro's initial silence on the lack of racial advancement is turned into a confrontation of the relationship between Black Cubans and the promises of the Revolution. Carlos Moore charts Castro's relationship with Blacks and racism in Cuba in the early years of the Revolution when he observes that:

> Racial segregation both in public and private establishments was still pervasive when the Revolution overthrew Batista. . . . Castro nonetheless pointedly mini-mized the racial question in Cuba in those early weeks of euphoria. In answer to a foreign journalist's question during a press conference on January 23, he even reiterated standard white Cuban platitudes. . . . There is racial discrimination in Cuba, but to a much lesser degree. We feel that our Revolution will help to elim-inate those prejudices and injustices that remain latent.[17]

This breach between the rhetoric of progress of the Revolution and the reality of dis-enfranchisement, here a racialized one, would be seen in later years in other social spheres.

In 1990, Cuba is thrown into a period of uprooting and political and economic reassessment known as the Special Period, due to the collapse of (1) the U.S.S.R in 1989, and (2) in many ways its economic base and the continuing U.S. embargo.[18] The Cuban population as a result was confronted with the exacerbation of its eco-nomic and social vulnerabilities evidenced by the lowered living standards and "rationing quotas," fuel shortages, a greater necessity for "hard currency" and greater class disparities in part worsened by the unequal flow of remittances and the resur-gence of discriminatory practices. It is especially during this Special Period that soci-ologists and historians studying Cuba point to the increased marginalization and dis-satisfaction that is experienced by the Cuban population, and as a result, a growing tension between the continued promises of the Revolution, the pressures and influ-ences of outside, capitalist economic systems, and the attempts by the disenfranchised to give voice to the inequalities and privations they face. It is within this time of eco-nomic, social, political, and class upheaval that Cuban rap is truly born.

As Sujatha Fernandes has noted, Cuban Hip Hop illuminates the fight for agency and empowerment in isolated communities within Cuba as well as the tense relation-ship where "cultural producers negotiate, subvert, and reproduce aspects of state power in the context of a socialist system."[19] This dual subversion and reproduction is an important aspect of Cuban rap that distinguishes it from U.S. models to which it is too often compared. While Hip Hop is initially distanced from the State, by the early 90s it is embraced as a musical form capable of transmitting revolutionary ideals. By 1991 rap music was beginning to be organized in concerts or peñas in Casas de la Cultura, a precursor to its incorporation into the open air stage known as La Piragua.

This placement of rap music on a larger stage signaled a greater acceptance and legitimization by the State, represented by the institutional support given by the *Asociación Hermanos Saiz* (Brothers Saiz Organization, AHS) and the "youth cultural wing" of the official Cuban youth organization, *Unión de Jóvenes Cubanos*.[20] By organizing such an event the Cuban government recognized the importance of Hip Hop as part of its musical landscape and equally importantly, as a useful and marketable social tool.

While part of a complex relationship to the state, the element of social contestation in Cuban rap comes from its beginnings in the relocated housing projects in the Alamar district and other mainly black, working class communities like Old Havana, Central Havana, Sancto Suarez, and Playa.[21] Unlike older Black Cubans who experienced a level of Revolutionary progress, the younger generation of Black Cubans in these districts were born after "the early period of revolutionary triumph" and are the hardest hit by the failure of the institutions that promised racial equality.[22]

Cuban youth's interaction with Hip Hop falls in line with the musical form's roots as a form of social protest and rejection of official discourses and stereotypes of gendered and racial behaviors:

> Cuban rap musicians use their lyrics, style, and performance to play with stereotypes of blacks as delinquents and criminals. . . . Rappers appropriate these dominant stereotypes, employing a posture of aggression to turn fears of the "urban black threat" back upon those who have created such myths and stereotypes. . . . Afro-Cuban youth use rap music as a way of asserting their voice and presence, in contrast to attempts by state officials to play down the salience of race in Cuban society.[23]

Rap therefore becomes a cultural tool of expression for an increasingly silenced generation: "Cuban Hip Hop emerged as a local response to experiences of displacement and relocation, as well as impoverishment and discrimination."[24] It is within this context that groups like Explosión Suprema and Las Krudas used Hip Hop to assert a collective voice that speaks to a Cuban and global reality of resistance. Explosión Suprema, from the neighborhood of Alamar, East Havana where Cuban Hip Hop had its beginnings, was made up of four friends who formed their group in the late 1990s as a way of addressing the concerns of their generation. As Fernandes notes, some underground Hip Hop artists navigate the line between resistance to institutional silencing and forms of oppression while supporting larger State criticisms of foreign neoliberal policies: "Rappers associate the Cuban nation with the underground condition, with its connotations of political awareness and rebellion. Local actors comply with and reinforce official narratives in strategic and self-conscious ways." [25]

As Geoffrey Baker notes, Cuban rappers have been able to occupy a space of a "revolution within the Revolution," presenting music as rebellion yet a form also accepted by the State.

. . . rappers made a name for themselves both at home and around the world because of the elaboration and commitment of their lyrics, something which ultimately made their work comprehensible or even attractive to the state. Rap has been successfully assimilated in part because of the many points of coincidence between the philosophy of underground Hip Hop and the revolutionary ideology of the Cuban state.[26]

Groups like Explosión Suprema exemplify this attitude: "We are the Cuban underground, almost without a chance, but with the little we have we are not dissenters."[27] As Sue Herrod notes in her blog on Cuban Hip Hop their third album *La Injusticia Tiembla* won the Cuerda Viva independent music award in 2007 and continues its critique of oppression with a musical mixture that incorporates not only rap but Cuban timba and jazz.[28] This musical crossing of boundaries is accompanied by a lyrical placement of their struggle within larger ones by those disenfranchised outside of the Caribbean, as evidenced by their song "Se contamina el barrio." In this song, the neighborhood (or barrio) is represented as a site of contamination, invaded by forces seen as threatening. However, while the language of the first lines (and title) could seemingly point to a condemnation of the community's infiltration by dangerous influences, the observation is followed by a declaration of a release that is achieved. What follows is an explanation of what has penetrated the community: a musical and lyrical presence that sees itself as a voice for the marginal, calling for change, be it social or economic.

> Se contamina el barrio, se contamina (repeat 3x)
> Aún mi estética personal camina por las paredes, por las esquinas
> Se contamina el barrio (se contamina)
> (la) música negra entre callejones, barrios marginales haciendote una escuela y se respira se respira la adrenalina que corre por mi cuerpo buscando la forma de atraer la . . . suerte para que provoque una hemorragia económica en mi vida

> The neighborhood is contaminated, it is contaminated
> Even my personal aesthetic walks along the walls, through the streets
> The neighborhood is contaminated, it is contaminated
> . . . black music in side streets, marginalized neighborhoods making you a school and you breath in, you breath in the adrenaline that runs through my body looking for the way to attract the . . . luck in order to cause an economic hemorrage in my life [all translation by the author]

The subject highlights the presence of black music that inhabits the marginalized places—yet speaks through them—providing alternate knowledge to more official discourses. While the first few stanzas do not specifically place the voice within the Caribbean, the 3rd stanza's reference to two musical styles—the rumba and guagancó—that provide a release of sorts to all who hear it (Y se respira, y se respira, mi rutina rumbera , . . . y mi guaguancó; And one breathes, one breathes, my rumba-like routine . . . and my guagancó [translation mine]), ultimately alert the listener to the Cuban context within which he speaks. However, the geographic location is secondary to the social themes addressed which are an example of a transnational call for change. The references to an unnamed neighborhood where black music and the disenfranchised fight to be heard demonstrate the song's reach outside of its national context to other marginalized communities struggling to move forward. While the subject's desires for change include the economic—later verses foreground the goal to represent the collective and bring awareness, as evidenced in the second stanza:

Pues mi barrio me necesita
Soy yo quien le da vida cada fantasia que se converse en cada esquina cuando me pongo a cantar
Todos sabemos que esto no anda, no funciona, no camina, pero aún así lo tenemos que lograr

Well, my neighborhood needs me
It is I who gives life, each fantasy that may be spoken in each corner when I start to sing
Everyone knows that this doesn't run, it doesn't work, it doesn't walk, but even so we have to achieve it [all translation by the author]

The speaker is aware that the individual mission is connected to a larger community, bringing to life the hidden, unspoken, or silenced desires and thoughts. On one hand the exhortation to continue to strive despite obstacles and failures can be read within Cuban Hip Hop's indictment of the failures within the revolutionary system—particularly post-Special period—where promises of equality and change were soon seen by Afro-Cubans in particular as flawed. As Fernandes notes:

Through their texts, performances, and styles, Cuban rappers demand the inclusion of young Afro-cubans into the polity and they appeal to the state to live up to the promise of egalitarianism enshrined in traditional socialist ideology. . . . Rappers recase street life and the experience of marginal communities as a valid and real part of Cuban society, in contrast to official reports that want to claim the eradication of marginal communities and ways of life.[29]

However, it can also be seen as a general call to fight regardless of the location. This struggle is not only economic but also against discrimination as evidenced by the condemnation of those who prosper while the subject suffers—both artistically and racially: "y usted sonriendo y yo sufriendo imitaciones verbales, tales opiniones en cuanto a los negros salvajes"; "and you smiling and me suffering verbal imitations, opinions such as those of the black savages. . . ."[translation by author]

In this act of creative resistance the subject's weapon of choice is the word and solidarity: "Que aprendan mis frases como artes marciales/Y que sientan por mí amor/Como aquel amor que nunca podrá olvidarse [Let them learn my phrases like martial arts/ and feel love for me/like that love that can never be forgotten] [translation mine]. The song's return in the last stanza to the declaration of the "contamination" as a process of infiltration and release throughout the neighborhood closes the subject's journey with a return to a larger, general space that underscores the larger community of marginalized to which it refers. The words of resistance that the subject releases move throughout all the disenfranchised barrios, connecting the Cuban struggle and the musical vehicle through which it is carried with larger global movements for change and resistance.

Such processes are not, however, solely masculine projects of contestation, as evidenced by the growing presence of Cuban women in Hip Hop and their critique of gender and racial discrimantion. While critical studies by Baker and West Durán speak somewhat to the role of women in Cuban rap, citing particularly the husband and wife led group Obsesión, later studies by Fernandes and scholars such as Ronni Armstead focus more heavily on the female space within Cuban rap. Armstead points to the Black, female group Las Krudas as an example of an openly feminist agenda whose representation of "the emergence of a strongly oppostional, Black, feminist activist art in Cuba" questions all encompassing ideas of Cubanidad, revealing the spaces where race and gender together are excluded. As she notes:

> Unlike their North American counterparts, Las Krudas readily identify themselves as feminists and refuse to relinquish their strong critiques of the nature and effects of Cuban patriarchy on the lives of marginalized women. Las Krudas' lyrics encourage Black women to reject the racism and sexism of patriarchal notions of femininity, and they seek to raise the self-esteem of their female audiences.[30]

It is within these critiques of patriarchy and calls for women to mobilize against silence and oppression while recognizing their worth that Las Krudas operate on a glocal level, creating songs that speak to local oppressions and strategies while reaching out to the larger community of women engaged in similar struggles. Songs like "Vamos a Vencer" with its statements of resistance despite difficult times ("Vivimos moments difícules/pero seguimos pa'lante/. . . No obstante el camino estrecho/. . . Krudas, !prender la mecha!") and "Pa'ketenteres" that references *jineteras* and other survival roles women take on ("Pa'ketenteres, asére/y sepan el juego jugamos las mujeres") are ways in which Las Krudas carve out a female voice of contestation. Similar to their male counterparts, groups like Las Krudas focus on gender inequalities and the possibilities of feminist responses to the disparities in the socialist vision:

> Las Krudas's rap lyrics reveal a very keen political analysis, one that recognizes that the viability and livelihood of the very state that oppresses Black women is dependent upon their sexual, domestic, and emotional labor. . . . New awareness of the gap between official proclamations and living reality has led to unofficial

radical movements such as Cuban Hip Hop and the feminist, oppositional lyrics of Las Krudas.[31]

In their song "Resistiendo" the struggle of Cuban women, and particularly Black Cuban women, is extended to oppressed women throughout Latin America and the world. The first line "Krudas, de Cuba, para el mundo" [Krudas, from Cuba, for the world] explicitly frames their song of resistance as one meant to go beyond national struggles for power and voice and is supported by the combination of Hip Hop beats and classical Indian strings that give the song an international sound.

The first stanza highlights the song's international, transnational dialogue through the listing of all the groups who engage in acts of resistance like Las Krudas:

Las mujeres, resistiendo,	The women, resisting
This is Hip Hop, resistiendo	This is Hip Hop, resisting
Black people, resistiendo	Black people, resisting
Emigrantes, resistiendo	Emigrants, resisting
Latinoamérica . . ., resistiendo	Latin America, resisting
Revolucionarias, resistiendo	Female revolutionaries, resisting
Krudas . . . Cubensi, resistiendo	Krudas, Cubensi, resisting
Aquí siempre, resistiendo	Always here, resisting

The references to women, Black people, Latin Americans, those who emigrated from Cuba and those women who are revolutionaries highlight the coalition that Las Krudas musically creates in their fight against oppression. While primarily intented to unite women, the reference to Latin America suggests that their struggle is not only against sexism and other gender-based discrimination but is a response to abuses of power to which those within the region have historically been subject. This extension beyond a gendered act of resistance is supported in the fourth stanza where the list of those who fight oppression includes "the Caribbean." Throughout the song, las Krudas refer to movement and their constant efforts to go outside of any attempts to enclose them: "Sí . . . querían que yo me quedara allí/Nada de eso, yo me fui. . . . /Por muchas partes yo representé. . . ."[Yes . . . they wanted me to stay there/None of that, I left . . ./In many places I represented. . . .] [translation mine] This constant movement and refusal to be controlled by another is in service to their overall mission: "llegaron las Krudas para cambiarte la vida"/[The Krudas arrived to change your life] [translation mine] As Dr. Tanya Saunders observes in her blog essay "This is not the feminism of Gloria Steinem," Las Krudas project unites several projects of contestation: "Through employing underground Hip Hop as a revolutionary cultural aesthetic, Krudas has developed an emergent discourse that blends revolutionary, Afro-Cuban and feminist discourses into underground Hip Hop."[32] This intersection of multiple subjects fighting marginalization and seeking a voice of empowerment is highlighted further by the second to last stanza, when the call to mobilize is extended globally to include those struggling under economic, political, racial, and sexual oppression—"Black people, resistiendo; Cuban people, resistiendo; Queer people, resistiendo" [Black people, resisting; Cuban people, resisting; Queer people, resisting"] [translation mine]. Just as Carole Boyce Davies sees Black women's writing and expression as one of multiple subject positions and "migrations of the subject" which she defines as ". . . the many locations of Black women's writing, but also to the Black female subject refusing to be subjugated"[33] Las Krudas transnational coalition refuses to geographically limit itself. While the Cuban struggle is always the central point, ultimately, ideologically, what they promote is a larger, transnational ideology of empowerment, what they describe within the song's last stanza as "the new Caribbean feminist. . . ." The alternation of Spanish and English also underscores the constant crossing of boundaries (in this case linguistic) that is part of what Las Krudas sees as "nuestra lucha"/"our fight" that musically unites Hip Hop to social justice on a global scale. I will now turn to Puerto Rican Hip Hop and specifically the artist Tego Calderón, as an example of the "glocal" contestation of social, and political discourses of oppression.

While Cuban rap's engagement with international, migratory forces in part is the continuation of a long history of collaboration alongside larger political histories of intervention vs. national independence, Puerto Rico's political and cultural situation have been tied to the international through migration and intervention in ways that continue to develop. As with Cuba, the end of the Cuban war for Independence (Spanish American War) in 1898 signalled a defeat of Spain by the United States that forced the colonial power to cede its territory. While Cuba did receive its independence, albeit with provisions for U.S. intervention, Puerto Rico was channeled towards interdependence (with a constant military presence) with the United States: (1) Declaratio of Puerto Rico as a U.S. protectorate under the 1900 Foraker Act; (2) U.S. citizenship for Puerto Ricans in 1917; (3) provisions for controlled self-government in 1947; and (4) "commonwealth" status.[34] While other Caribbean nation-states like Cuba saw the sugar economy as a means of bringing the country out of a rural peasant economy, the Puerto Rican road to progress would come through "technological innovation" creating an ambiguous national, social, and cultural state.[35]

The economic development undertaken in the 1950s and 1960s under "Operation Bootstrap" was an important historical moment in the already longstanding history of U.S.-Puerto Rican relations and migration. Under this plan the U.S. government would encourage foreign investment small labor-focused in businesses through tax breaks and other incentives. As Skidmore notes, what was especially created as a result was a dual island population: "In a sense there are now two Puerto Ricos: one on the island and one on the mainland. There is movement and communication back and forth, of course, but social tensions and cultural differences separate the two communities."[36] Despite the tensions that Skidmore and others note in island-mainland relations another side to their relationship exists, one that has created a diasporic relationship of Puertoricanness that does not position its citizens on one side of the "charco" (puddle; Atlantic Ocean) or the other negating economic, political, and cultural ties. This diasporic connection instead shows the existence of community and difference. As other scholars like Juan Flores have noted, this tension of a community that has been geographically and culturally uprooted, creates another, connected sense of home, that is at the same time in conflict with what he terms the "lite colonial" state of Puerto Rico.[37]

The history of Hip Hop in Puerto Rico therefore, unlike Cuban Hip Hop, is born out of not only a geographically fixed island dynamic but a migratory one that connects it to the experiences of Puerto Ricans (and particularly Nuyoricans) on the mainland. In this sense, Puerto Rico's cultural navigation of the island and mainland through the development of Hip Hop and the issues it addresses serves as a different example of the "glocal." For Rivera this diasporic musical dialogue is key not only for understanding accurately the genesis of Hip Hop as a musical and social collaboration but also provides important insights into the navigations of race, ethnicity, and national identity of New York Puerto Ricans in particular in ways that still refer to ties with the island:

> I believe that the meanings given to blackness and *latinidad* by the young New Yorkers involved in Hip Hop have had a complex relationship with those meanings common among the older Puerto Rican and African American generations as well as with media and academic representations of these ethno-racial identity fields. Through Hip Hop's creative expressions, young Puerto Ricans and African Americans, among others, have partly deconstructed and reconstructed "official" ethnic and racial categories. Simultaneously, they have been deeply influenced by the dominant formulations, by which they abide at times.[38]

The "deconstruction" and "reconstruction" of categories of identity that Rivera cites through Hip Hop is another example of the contestatory nature of the musical genre that is present in all its North American and global manifestations. However, the transition from community-based accounts of urban experience to globalized mass media production that she references exemplifies the tensions of global exposure and musical development that go beyond one-way exercises of power and compliance.[39] Due to its fluid nature Rivera eschews the term "Hip Hop community," preferring instead a larger social and spatial term—"Hip Hop zone" that recognizes its border crossing nature:

> Hip Hop is a fluid cultural space, a zone whose boundaries are an internal and external matter of debate. A profoundly diverse, translocal, multiethnic and multiracial cultural phenomenon, hip hop expressions also can present themselves as exclusionary for aesthetic, regional, gender . . . or myriad other reasons. The dynamic tensions within Hip Hop and its constant drawing and crossing of borders are better addressed by the somewhat ambiguous concept of a "Hip Hop zone" than by frequently adopted but more limiting . . . terms like "Hip Hop community" and "Hip Hop nation."[40]

The origins of Puerto Ricans in New York participating in this multiethnic phenomenon date back to the beginnings of Hip Hop in New York in the late 1960s and early 1970s where dance styles like "rocking"/"uprocking" performed in particular by Puerto Rican men influenced later styles of breaking while MCing over musical foundations developed not only within the African American community but in cultural manifestations that connect it, according to Rivera and others with Puerto Rican musical traditions of *plena, bomba, and música jíbara*.[41]

Despite these ties, Hip Hop in its early days was seen and represented in many mediums as an African American form. However, some of the seminal Puerto Rican figures of its early development and into its first years as a more mainstream product (from 1979 to 1984) include DJ Charlie Chase of the Cold Crush Brothers, the Fearless Four's Devastating Tito and Dj Master OC, the Fantastic Five's Prince Whipper Whip, Prince markie Dee Morales of the Fat Boys and the Real Roxanne.[42] While Rivera sees freestyle as a more New York-based musical style with heavy Puerto Rican participation, she points to later developments of "Latin rap" as a more West Coast based production with less participation (in part due to the historical patterns in Latino populations in the Northeast vs. the Southwest or the West Coast) by Puerto Ricans and more by Chicanos and Cubans like Kid Frost and Mellow Man Ace.[43]

An interesting element of this Afro-diasporic practice that Rivera notes is a link between African American, Puerto Rican, and other Caribbean musical expressions in ways that Cuban rap does not have. One such example is the development of *reggaetón*: the incorporation of reggae rhythms with rap and other Caribbean musical traditions.

While cultural and music scholars like Flores, Rivera, Giovanetti, and Baker have together provided important histories of U.S. Puerto Rican participation in Hip Hop, scholarship on the island has also paid increasingly more attention to the Puerto Rican importance and development of rap. Building on Rivera's study *Para rapear en puertorriqueño: discurso político y cultural* Puerto Rican writer and cultural critic Mayra Santos Febres traces Puerto Rican Hip Hop's growth in order to demonstrate its representation of a specifically pan-Caribbean musical and social aesthetic. The history of rap in Puerto Rico that she cites stresses the importance of the social and economic developments on the island, and their failures, as impetus for rap's musical critique. Like their Cuban counterparts, Puerto Rican rap in part found a common language to express the disillusion of failed economic and social programs: "La pobreza, la falta de recursos sociales y la experiencia del 'inner city' o lo urbano se convirtieron en referentes obligados que fueron fomentando el desarrollo de un lenguaje simbólico común."/"Poverty, lack of social resources and the inner city or urban experience were converted into obligatory references that fed the development of a common symbolic language" [translation by author].[44]

However, Febres emphasizes a double movement that is in part similar to the concept of "glocalization" with which I opened this essay: the revision of local symbolic language in dialogue with homogenizing global forces:

Frente a la globalización de la cultura (de la cual, obviamente el género participa) la voz rapera se ancla en lo específicamente regional/territorial, y, a partir de ese enraizamiento en las comunidades residenciales marginales busca comunicación con otros territorios de igual condición y de paso añade otro punto de tensión en la batalla sobre lo que conforma la cultura nacional.[45]

In the face of the globalization of culture (in which, obviously, the genre participates) the rapper's voice anchors itself in the specifically regional/territorial, and, from this rooting in the marginal residential communities looks for means of communication with other territories in equal conditions and as such adds another point of contention in the battle over what comprises national culture. [translation mine]

As part of this crossing of the local yet also transnational movement Febres, like Baker of Cuban rap and urban space as protest, points to greater understandings of rap territory as key to amplifying our engagement with rap as more than just social phenomenon. Therefore, Puerto Rican rappers references to sites like La Colectora, Puerta de Tierra, Las Acacias, sections of Santurce, Carolina, Cataño, Bayamón, Puerto Nuevo, the U.S. ghetto, the street, prison, and death are a way of creating community outside of officially acceptable sites.[46] Part of this reimagining of local and national space occurs in the function of the chorus:

El corillo es una sinécdoque del barrio y de Puerto Rico, que es el lugar que valida y recoge a todo este contingente de raperos que cantan en el cd #39 de Playero. Cada uno rapea para "representar" a los suyos. Al crear equivalencias entre nación y corillo, el discurso rapero criminaliza la nación y la hace partícipe de las experiencias del corillo, la redefine y reubica en otra geografía distinta de la oficial estatal. De esta manera, la recupera, invirtiendo los discursos legales y gubernamentales que los marginan a ellos de la nación legal.[47]

The chorus is a synechdoque of the neighborhood and of Puerto Rico, which is the place that validates and recovers this entire contingent of rappers that sing in the cd#39 of Playero. Each one raps in order to "represent" his own. By creating equivalence between the nation and chorus, the rap discourse criminalizes the nation and makes it a participant in the experience of the chorus, redefines it and resituates it in a different geography from that of the official state. In this way, it recuperates it, inverting the legal and governmental discourses that marginalize them from the legal nation.

In contemporary examples of 21st century Puerto Rican rap this confrontation and redefinition of the nation along the lines of race, gender, and class can be seen in Puerto Rican musicians like Ivy Queen and Tego Calderón. According to Ejima Baker Ivy Queen's musical development engages in similar discussions of racism and sexism:

"Although musical hybridization between blacks and Latinas/os was already quite common in the 1990s, the idea of latinidad and blackness were still separate. . . . As a black/Latina, Ivy has to defend herself, especially when confronted with most images of women in music videos."[48]

Her development within rap and reggaetón, together with her critique of race and gender in particular in a musical genre, often characterized as promoting hypersexualized images of women, stands as an example of the ways in which Hip Hop continues to avoid simplistic binaries.

I will end this study with Tego Calderón, an artist who also refuses to adhere to the lyrical or musical limitations of any genre: be it reggaetón or rap. Alongside songs that celebrate his lyrical prowess, or explore the nuances of relationships, Calderón is also know for his treatment of social themes of injustice and racism. I will briefly look at one example where his critique of discrimination subtlely exemplifies the "glocal" politics of Hip Hop through its applicability to peoples of the African diaspora and to its overall presentation of strategies of resistance in critique and celebration. In the song "Loiza" from the first album *El Abayarde* (released in 2002), Calderón uses the history of the Northeastern seaside town of Loiza as a backdrop for a critique of contemporary practices of alienation of Black Puerto Ricans in order to ultimately call for not only awareness but also contestation. While explicitly framing the song within specific locations and historical realities, its overriding critique of racism and celebration of black pride creates a message of resistance that can be applied to other communities throughout the African diaspora, similar to Explosión Suprema's "Se contamina el barrio" or Las Krudas' "Resistiendo."

The town of Loiza is known historically as the embodiment of the African tradition in Puerto Rico, a site where slave communities were settled, resulting in cultural expressions of Africanness and its connection to Puerto Rican identity in religion, celebrations such as the Festival of Santiago Apostol in Las Cuevas and the musical form known as bomba.[49] It is this implicit reference to the African history of Loiza— although regarded by some as purely folkloric—where Tego is able to establish the first part of his dialogue: the contemporary voice of Puerto Rican Black youth with the African past that has marked that very geographical space. At the same time, the reference opens up a space to dialogue with other members of the African diaspora, regardless of their geographical location. As his song states:

Oye!
Esto es pa' mi pueblo! . . .
Pa' mi pueblo, que tanto quiero!
De Calderon, pa' Loiza entero!
Oye!

Listen !
This is for my people!

254

For my people, that I love so much!
From Calderón, to all of Loiza!

In the last stanza Calderón emphasizes that Loiza is in fact a community, but one that in part has suffered through a criminalization of its residents where marginalization is most effectively realized through incarceration.

Me quiere hacer pensar
Que soy parte de una trilogia racial
Donde to' el mundo es igual, sin trato especial

Entre otras cosas
Cambiaste las cadenas por esposas
No todos somos iguales en terminos legales
Y eso esta probao en los tribunales

You want to make me think
That I am part of a racial trilogy
Where all the world is equal, without special treatment

Among other things
You changed the chains for handcuffs
We aren't equal in legal terms
And that is proven in the courts

For Calderón this aspect of the link to Loiza's slave past is not a focus on the legacy for African-descended peoples through a celebration of the African culture but through a focus on the oppressors who "changed the chains for handcuffs," where justice is never fully achieved, only in parts, and the legal sentence is in fact a condemnation to a second-class defense.

The history of enslavement is therefore one that continues with modern ramifications for Black Puerto Ricans who have been abandoned by the system yet can also be seen as part of larger critiques of racism by Hip Hop artists throughout the Diaspora, such as the Cuban Hip Hop artists discussed earlier, others like Anónimo Consejo and Hermanos de la Causa (particularly, as West-Durán notes, in their song "Tengo"/"I Have" which dialogues with Nicolás Guillén's poem of the same name), and Brazilian Hip Hop artists like MV Bill and Nega Gizza).[50] This critique of social division is therefore a transgression of these borders and can be read on a local and global scale: as resistance to the historical, economic, and cultural colonization of Black Puerto Ricans (not by only Europe but also the United States) and ultimately a challenge to the idea of the Puerto Rican nation that such limits not only implied but protected, and a symbolically similar act of resistance by others of African descent marginalized in their own communities. This strategy of confronting discrimination that Calderón's lyrics articulate however, extends its reach beyond the African diaspora to marginalized communities globally using different cultural forms to confront their oppressions.

The last element of Calderón's message to his people is one of celebration by placing the challenge to these dominant discourses alongside important racial and national affirmations:

Yo soy niche
Orgulloso de mis raices
De tener mucha bemba y grandes narices

I am niche
Proud of my roots
And of having thick lips and a large nose
[translation by author]

Reminiscent of the poems of Cuban Negrismo poet Nicolás Guillén like "Negro Bembón" and "La mulata" where the latter points to specific African facial features as a source of pride: "mulata, ya sé que dise que yo tengo la narise como nudo de cobbata"/"Mulata, I know that they say that I have a nose like the knot of a tie," and Puerto Rican poet Julia de Burgos' "Cry for a Kinky Haired Girl" where she states "Ay, ay, ay que soy grifa y pura negra; grifería en mi pelo, cafrería en mis labios; y mi chata nariz mozambiquea"/"Ay, ay, ay I am black, pure black; kinky hair and Kaffir lips and a flat Mozambian nose. . . ." Calderón uses the term niche as a signifier of the identity whose African roots and facial features are a source of pride and not shame. This culminates in the last stanza where the community is united with the contested and expanded national identity:

Boricua!
Este es el Abayarde!
Trayéndola como es!
Metiéndole fuertemente, pa' depertar a mi gente! . . .
Oye, que bonito es mi Loiza!
Mira que bonito es!

Boricua
This is el Abayarde!
Bringing it like it is!
Giving it to you strong, to wake my people up
Look at how beautiful my Loiza is!
Look at how beautiful it is! [translation mine]

256

Ultimately, Calderón's crossing and transgression is demonstrated locally in three important ways: (1) a musical representation of the crossing of rhythms such as bomba with Hip Hop; (2) a rejection of Loiza as solely a site of folkloric ideas of blackness; and (3) a challenge to more exclusive notions of Puerto Rican identity that diminished the representation and contributions of peoples of African descent. Globally, the strategies of musical migration represented, alongside the challenge to hegemonic discourses of equality that mask discrimination culminating in a celebration of difference, strength, and community give the song a larger subtext of resistance that allows it to dialogue transnationally with other protest movements.

In both Caribbean representations of Hip Hop examined here the revision of an exclusionary national identity through racial, gendered, and class mobilization both inside and outside national boundaries demonstrates the fluidity of Hip Hop as a musical genre that rhythmically, lyrically, and socially continually adapts to other social, historic, and political factors. The result is a constant resistance and realignment that at times subverts, at others manipulate dominant discourses. This movement outside national boundaries can be extended even further when placed within the context of diaspora studies. Scholars like Carole Boyce Davies, Michelle Wright, Michael Gomez, and Patrick Manning are only some within the field who explore the historical, political, and cultural processes of people of the African diaspora particularly as we begin the 21st century of transnationalism and technology. Hip Hop, as a cultural project that has global significance for marginalized communities, has added an important element to these studies by revealing nuances of resistance and appropriation. Alongside the study of Hip Hop in the Caribbean one can raise questions about its role in the diaspora of Caribbeans migrated to other parts of the world, as well as what some georaphers now define as the greater Caribbean (which according to Thomas Boswell includes the islands between North and South America, east of Central America and Mexico, Belize and northern South American territories Guyana, Suriname and French Guiana.)[51] What do we discover when we connect discussions of Cuban and Puerto Rican Hip Hop, and reggaetón in the Dominican Republic, with artists like Arianna Puello, born in the Dominican Republic yet raised in Spain and Chocquibtown, an Afro-Columbian Hip Hop group from the Pacific Coast of Columbia (specifically Quibdó), who represents the black Columbian culture of the Pacific and Caribbean coasts of the country?[52] For Puello, her Dominican roots are an important part of her identity, despite her geographical positioning in Europe. In songs like "Así es la Negra," she states:

No soy morena, soy negra . . .
Si vuelvo a nacer quiero ser lo que ahora soy,
De la misa raza, mismo sexo y condición

I'm not brown, I'm black . . .
If I am born again I want to be what I am now,
The same race, same sex and condition . . . [translation mine]

257

Similar to Calderón's assertions of Black pride that reach beyond Loiza's boundaries, and Las Krudas' strategies of global collective resistance, Puello's declarations extend her celebration of race, gender and class to communities of women and blacks around the world. For Chocquibtown, particularly in the title song of their album *Somos Pacífico* [We are Pacific], a title that dually refers to their geographical location and messages of peaceful celebration and resistance, their assertions of racial and regional pride locate their message both within the Colombian Pacific Caribbean space and to larger cultural spaces of communities within the African Diaspora, particularly in the Americas:

> Somos pacífico, estamos unidos
> Nos une la región
> La pinta, la raza y el don del sabor . . .
> Unidos por siempre, por la sangre, el color
> Y hasta por la tierra. . . .
> Con un vínculo familiar que aterra
> Característico en muchos de nosotros
> Que nos reconozcan por la mamá y hasta por los rostros
>
> Étnicos, estilos que entre todos se ven
> La forma de caminar
> El cabello y hasta por la piel
>
> We are pacific, we are united
> We are united by the region,
> The color, the race and the magic of the flavor . . .
> United forever, by the blood, the color
> And even by the land . . .
> With a family tie that terrifies some
> Characteristic in many of us
> That recognize us by our mother and even by our faces . . .
> Ethnic style that is seen by all
> The way we walk,
> Our hair, and even by our skin [translation by author]

For Chocquibtown, their Afro-Colombian community is connected to a larger one, united not only by physical markers of blackness like skin color and hair, but by deeper ties, like the culture, the land, and their parentage—be it their biological mother or symbolically, their motherland Africa. Artists like Puello and Chocquibtown extend our understandings of Caribbean and diaspora while providing important points of connection with the artists I have studied as representatives of Hip Hop's transnational navigation of the local and global musical, social, and political spaces of celebration and critique, contestation, appropriation, and change.

NOTES

[1]Roland Robertson, "Comments on the 'Glocal Triad' and Glocalization," in *Globalization and Indigenous Culture*. ed. Inoue Nobutaka (Kokugakuin University, 1997).

[2]Ibid.

[3]Cited in Toni Mitchell, "Introduction: Another Root-Hip Hop Outside the USA," in *Global Noise: Rap and Hip Hop Outside the U.S.A.* ed. Tony Mitchell (Middletown, 2001), 11.

[4]Roland Robertson, *Globalization: Social Theory and Global Culture* (London, 1992), 178.

[5]Mitchell, *Global Noise*, 10.

[6]Salli Westwood and Annie Phizacklea. *Trans-nationalism and the Politics of Belonging* (London, 2000), 2.

[7]Tricia Rose, *Black Noise: Rap Music and Black Culture in Contemporary America* (Hanover, NH, 1994), 55.

[8]Mitchell, *Global Noise*, 4.

[9]Juan Flores, "Puerto Rocks: New York Ricans Stake Their Claim," in *Droppin' Science: Critical Essays on Rap Music and Hip Hop Culture*, ed. William Eric Perkins (Philadelphia, 1996), 87, 138.

[10]Ibid., 138.

[11]Raquel Rivera, *New York Ricans from the Hip Hop Zone* (New York, 2003), 2–3.

[12]Damián Fernández, "Cuba Transnational: Introduction," in *Cuba Transnational*, ed. Damián J. Fernández (Gainesville, FL, 2005), xv–xvi.

[13]Sujatha Fernandes, *Cuba Represent! Cuban Arts, State Power, and the Making of New Revolutionary Cultures* (Durham, 2006), 2.

[14]Thomas Skidmore, *Modern Latin America*, 5th ed. (Oxford, 2001), 261.

[15]Lisa Brock, "Introduction: Between Race and Empire," in *Between Race and Empire: African-Americans and Cubans Before the Cuban Revolution*, eds. Lisa Brock and Digna Castañeda Fuertes (Philadelphia, 1998), 2.

[16]Fernandes, *Cuba Represent!*, 91.

[17]Carlos Moore, *Castro, the Blacks and Africa* (Los Angeles, 1988), 15.

[18]Thomas Skidmore, *Modern Latin America*, 5th ed. (Oxford, 2001), 286.

[19]Fernandes, *Cuba Represent!*, 3.

[20]Sujatha Fernandes, "Island Paradise, Revolutionary Utopia or Hustler's Haven? Consumerism and Socialism in Contemporary Cuban Rap," *Journal of Latin American Cultural Studies* 12 (2003): 361.

[21]Sujatha Fernandes, "Fear of a Black Nation: Local Rappers, Transnational Crossings, and State Power in Contemporary Cuba," *Anthropological Quarterly* 76, no. 4 (2003), http://search.ebscohost.com/login.aspx?direct=true&db=aph&AN=11583974%site=ehost-live, 3–4.

[22]Ibid., 4.

[23]Ibid., 7–8.

[24]Fernandes, "Island Paradise," 361.

[25]Fernandes, *Cuba Represent!*, 121.

[26]Geoffrey Baker, "The Politics of Dancing: Reggaetón and Rap in Havana, Cuba," in *Reggaeton*, eds. Raquel Z. Rivera, Wayne Marshall, and Deborah Pacini Hernandez (Durham, 2009), 169.

[27]Cited in Fernandes, *Cuba Represent!*, 121.

[28]Sue Herrod, "Cuba Absolutely: Cuban Hip Hop, Rap and Reggaeton." http://www.cubaabsolutely.com/music/hip/ hop.htm.

[29]Fernandes, *Cuba Represent!*, 96, 99.

[30]Ronni Armstead, "'Growing the Size of the Black Woman': Feminist Activism in Havana Hip Hop," *National Women's Studies Association Journal* 19 (2007): 110.

[31] Ibid., 115.

[32] Tanya Saunders, Krudas blog, "This is not the feminism of Gloria Steinem," comment posted November 7, 2007, http://blogs.myspace.com/index.cfm?fuseaction=blog.view&friendId =127583057&blogId=326249654.

[33] Carole Boyce Davies, *Black Women, Writing and Identity: Migrations of the Subject* (London, 1994), 36.

[34] Skidmore, *Modern Latin America*, 309.

[35] Ibid.

[36] Ibid., 310.

[37] Juan Flores, *From Bamba to Hip Hop: Puerto Rican Culture and Latino Identity* (New York, 2000), 38.

[38] Raquel Rivera, *New York Ricans*, 9.

[39] Ibid., 14.

[40] Ibid., 15.

[41] Ibid., 38–9.

[42] Ibid., 66.

[43] Ibid., 93.

[44] Mayra Santos Febres, "Geografía en decibeles: utopías pancaribeñas y el territorio del rap," in *Sobre Piel y Papel* (San Juan, 2005), 97–98.

[45] Ibid., 99.

[46] Ibid., 106.

[47] Ibid., 107.

[48] Ejima Baker, "A Preliminary Step in Exploring Reggaetón," in *Critical Minded: New Approaches to Hip Hop Studies*, eds. Ellie Hisama and Evan Rapport (New York, 2005), 112–13.

[49] Samiri Hernández Hiraldo, "If God Were Black and from Loiza: Managing Identities in a Puerto Rican Seaside Town," *Latin American Perspectives* 33 (2006): 66–79.

[50] Alan West-Durán, "Rap's Diasporic Dialogues: Cuba's Redefinition of Blackness," in *Cuba Transnational*, ed. Damián J. Fernández (Gainesville, FL, 2005), 135–39.

[51] Thomas Boswell, "The Caribbean: A Geographic Preface," in *Understanding the Contemporary Caribbean*, eds. Richard S. Hillman and Thomas J. D'Agostino (Kingston, 2003), 19.

[52] Carlos A. Quiroz, "Chocquibtown: The Musical Voice of Urban Afro-Colombians," Carlos in D.C. Blog," (accessed August 31, 2009).

GLOBALIZATION AND THE RADICAL IMPACT OF AFRICAN AMERICAN HIP HOP CULTURE AND RAP IN THE PEOPLE'S REPUBLIC OF CHINA

Bernard W. Bell

As a Fulbright Senior Scholar in the People's Republic of China (PRC) in 2004 and 2006, I discovered that most Chinese adults and authorities I met, like many pre-Civil Rights era adult Americans, misguidedly thought that all rap music glorifies violence, sex, and drugs. So, many American and African American parents and authorities might envy China for accomplishing what they could not: regulating the social and moral values of an indigenous Hip Hop culture. Although African American Hip Hop culture, especially rap, has opened the floodgates of freedom of expression and individualism for the youth generation in PRC, the Chinese government has set guidelines and limits to this freedom. In explaining how this was accomplished, I begin with a definition of globalization, a brief summary of my Fulbrights in China, an outline of the impact of African American culture in PRC, and a brief history of the roots of rap and Hip Hop in the United States. I then move to the Chinese government's censorship of Hip Hop, the major characteristics of Chinese Hip Hop, the major rap stars and styles in PRC, the promotion of Hip Hop dance in China, and conclude with my perspective on the future development of an indigenous Chinese Hip Hop culture.[1]

WHAT IS GLOBALIZATION?

"Economic 'globalization,'" according to the Western dominated International Monetary Fund (IMF) staff, "is a historical process, the result of human innovation and technological progress. It refers to the increasing integration of economies around the world, particularly through trade and financial flows. The term [which came into popular use in the 1980s] sometimes also refers to movement of people (labor) and knowledge (technology) across international borders."[2] But globalization means more than the international economic integration of developed, developing, and formerly Communist nations. In addition to its "economic roots and political consequences," David Rothkop argues in "In Praise of Cultural Imperialism? Effects of Globalization on Culture," that globalization "also has brought into focus the power of culture in this global environment—the power to bind and to divide in a time when the tensions between integration and separation tug at every issue that is relevant to international relations. The impact of globalization on culture and the impact of culture on globalization merit discussion. The homogenizing influences of globalization that are most often condemned by the new nationalists and by cultural romanticists are actually positive; globalization promotes integration and the removal not only of cultural barriers but of many of the negative dimensions of culture."[3] Disagreeing with the IMF staff and Rothkop, the Nobel Prize-winning economist Joseph Stiglitz argues in *Globalization and Its Discontents* (2002) and *Making Globalization Work* (2006) "that globalization holds out great promise as a force for good, but that the rules of the present international economic order are designed and enforced by the rich nations to serve their interests."[4]

Some critics also fear that the globalization of American culture leads more to the marginalization or extinction of indigenous traditional cultures than to cultural diversity and multiculturalism. When I was a Fulbright scholar in 1982 at the University of Coimbra, one of my brightest Portuguese students poetically expressed the negative economic and cultural impact of what she viewed as American imperialism on the indigenous economy and culture of Portugal with the declaration, "Coca Cola is the dirty water of American capitalism." I don't believe that this is exactly what philosopher and sociologist Max Weber had in mind when he published *The Protestant Ethic and the Spirit of Capitalism* (1905). In 2006 when I was a Fulbrighter at Southwest University of Science and Technology (SWUST), one of my Chinese assistants expressed ambivalence about the impact of American fast-food chains on Chinese youth. She was most concerned about her four-year-old daughter's crying tantrums whenever the family passed a McDonald's without stopping for fries. Many youth in pursuit of new freedoms today, however, are unaware or unconcerned, despite government censorship, that the growing practice of hanging out at Kentucky Fried Chicken, eating at McDonald's, drinking Coca-Cola, watching *Desperate Housewives,* and listening to Tupac Shakur, Snoop Doggy Dog, and 50 Cent can become "a threat to one's culture . . . to one's God or one's ancestors and, therefore, to one's core identity."[5]

Unlike the devastating, systematic purges of Western cultural and economic imperialism by Mao and the Red Guard during the Cultural Revolution, Deng Xiaoping, a dedicated, controversial post–Cultural Revolution reformer, promoted a bold new policy toward globalization in PRC. Although, as Todd Crowell and Thomas Hon Wing Polin remind readers, he "persecuted thousands of intellectuals during Mao's Anti-Rightist Campaign of 1957," Xiaoping also began the radical economic and cultural reformation of his society into "one country, two systems" with exhortations between 1979 and 1992 that "to get rich is glorious." He promoted the spirit of capitalism by encouraging small businesses to develop in Guangdong Province, by negotiating the return of Hong Kong to PRC from the British, and by allowing 750–800 million peasants of 1 billion, 300 million people in 55 ethnic groups to grow any crops they wished so long as they delivered specific amounts to the central government. But he also called out the tanks in 1989 against protesting students, in Tiananmen Square, who adopted as their anthem the song "Nothing to My Name" by Ciu Jian, the father of Chinese rock music.[6]

ON BEING A BLACK AMERICAN FULBRIGHT SENIOR SCHOLAR AND SPECIALIST

Proposed to the U.S. Congress in 1945 by Senator J. William Fulbright of Arkansas, the Fulbright Program, as many readers know, is the principal international cultural and academic exchange activity sponsored by the Bureau of Educational and Cultural Affairs of the United States Department of State. Its purpose is "to enable the government of the United States to increase mutual understanding between the people of the United States and other countries . . . and thus to assist in the development of friendly, sympathetic, and peaceful relations between the United States and other countries of the world." Of the five Fulbright awards that I have received (China 2006 and 2004, Spain 2003 and 1996, and Portugal 1982–1983), the most recent have been in PRC. Although there are more than ten American Studies Centers in PRC, I am honored and humbled by the news from Chinese scholars and administrators that my scholarship has been the primary inspiration and guide for the only African American Studies Center in China. It was founded in 1994 at Mianyang Teachers College in Sichuan Province by Dean Liu Jie, the primary translator in 2000 of my 1987 study, *The Afro-American Novel and Its Tradition*. In October 2006 I returned to China after an earlier lectureship in 2004 to deliver the keynote address at the Twelfth Anniversary of the Center, now located at the SWUST in Mianyang, and to celebrate the bilingual publication in Beijing of my book, *The Contemporary African American Novel: Its Folk Roots and Literary Branches* (2005).

When I first went as a Fulbrighter to PRC in 2004, my primary goal was to teach postgraduate students and faculty at Beijing Foreign Studies University (BEIWAI) and Peking University (BEIDA), two of the most prestigious universities in PRC, how African American history, vernacular culture, especially the blues and Hip Hop, as literature can become a model for Chinese youth under thirty-five years old struggling to resist the cultural assimilation of Western globalization. The Maoist anti-Western, anti-Confucian Communist Cultural-Revolution (1966–1976) generation that rejected jazz and rock music as degenerate forms of American art, as well as the Xiaoping (1977–1997) urban generation that began cautiously to sanction the individualism of capitalism with the slogan "one country, two systems," are particularly struggling with the inequities, injustices, anxieties, and alienation of unprecedented rapid rates of migration, urbanization, industrialization, and technologization. My lectures and seminars at BEWAI and BEIDA suggested that African American history and culture, especially music, could be a model for the validation and valorization of the resiliency and resourcefulness of Chinese youth and postgraduate students in peacefully harmonizing both the lessons of the past with the present and the tensions of their ethnic, regional, and national cultural identities in the emergence of the power of a new China and world.

As an internationally respected African American literary critic and specialist in vernacular theory (Germany 1974–1975, Nigeria 1977, France 1980, Portugal 1982–1983, Spain 1996 and 2003, and China 2004 and 2006), I am fully aware of the influence of the indigenous oral traditions of different peoples on their literatures. In imaginative literary narratives and poetry, the validation and valorization of distinctive racial, ethnic, national, and cultural languages and identities are evident from the King James *Bible*, Geoffrey Chaucer's *The Canterbury Tales*, and Miguel de Cervantes Saavedra's *Don Quijote* to Mark Twain's *Huckleberry Finn*, William Faulkner's *Go Down, Moses*, Ralph Ellison's *Invisible Man*, N. Scott Momaday's *House Made of Dawn*, Chinua Achebe's *Thing Fall Apart*, Amos Tutola's *The Palm-Wine Drinkard*, and Gabriel Garcia Marquez's *One Hundred Years of Solitude*. But it was not until transcultural exchanges with my Chinese postgraduate students that I discovered the folk and ver-nacular roots of Chinese literature. It was only after my students introduced me to *Journey to the West*, a fantastic multivolume classic Chinese novel published around 1592, that I began to understand the transcultural, wryly humorous adventures of the Native American trickster character in Gerald Vizenor's *Griever: An American Monkey King in China* (1986) and to appreciate the bicultural roots of Maxine Hong Kingston's *Tripmaster Monkey: His Fake Book* (1989). Based on the Chinese vernacular tradition, including myths, legends, fables, tales, sayings, and popular beliefs, *Journey to the West* is the allegorical journey of a legendary Chinese monk, Xuan Zang (602–664) to find and translate the *Sutra*, the Buddhist holy book, into Mandarin.

THE IMPACT OF AFRICAN AMERICAN CULTURE IN PRC

Turning to the impact of the globalization of African American culture on Chinese youth in the pre-Mao Communist triumph of 1949, post–Cultural Revolution of 1976, and Xiaoping reforms of 1979, let me begin by acknowledging that two of the most well-known global signs of American cultural and economic power are Coke and African American culture, especially blues, jazz, and Hip Hop. Unlike Coke, however, rather than displace indigenous youth cultures and their authentic music, African American musicians and music from the 1930s to 1990s have inspired cultural innovation and political independence movements globally because they have been historically more spiritually liberating and widely respected interna-tionally than nationally. In 1873 the Fisk Jubilee Singers performed a command con-cert for Queen Victoria and toured for a decade in several troupes nationally and internationally in order to help prevent the economic collapse of the religion-found-ed black university. It is unsurprising that neither the cultural tradition of Confucianism nor the political history of Communism made the pre-Deng Xiaoping era in China a welcoming site for African American spirituals, gospel, blues, and jazz music.

The freedom and individualism of American cultural expression, especially African American music, were introduced to the urban PRC of Deng Xiaoping pri-marily by international programs of the Department of State of the United States like the Fulbright exchanges of scholars and tours by famous jazz artists, as well as by tapes, radio, CDs, films, television, records, video, and the Internet. Three schools in PRC teach modern jazz and pop music: the JZ School in Shanghai, the Midi School of Music in Beijing, and the Beijing Contemporary Music Institute. Founded in 1993 with just 100 students, Beijing Contemporary Music Institute is the first, largest, and most popular music academy with more than 3,000 students studying jazz, blues, rhythm and blues, rock, pop, country, Hip Hop, world music, and street dancing in a college setting. Because rappers like the Wu-Tang Clan, Chuck D, Dr. Dre, Tupac, Biggie Smalls, Jay-Z, and 50 Cent were either banned or censored by the PRC government as too political, vulgar, or violent as recently as 2007, when Jay-Z's Shanghai concert was cancelled, their influence on rappers in Beijing and Shanghai was largely by CDs and Internet rather than by live performances.

A BRIEF HISTORY OF THE ROOTS OF RAP AND HIP HOP IN THE UNITED STATES

"Hip Hop," according to African American cultural critic Tricia Rose, "is an Afro-Diaspora cultural form which attempts to negotiate the experiences of marginalization, brutally truncated opportunity and oppression with the cultural imperatives of African American and Caribbean history, identity and community. . . . Worked out on the rusting urban core as a playground, Hip Hop transforms stray technological parts intended for cultural and industrial trash heaps into sources of pleasure and power. These transformations have become a basis for digital imagination all over the world."[7] In light of the brutal anti-Western restrictions and oppression by Mao Zedong's youthful Red Guard of Westernized institutions and leaders during the Cultural Revolution of 1967–1976 in communist China, an examination of the impact of African American Hip Hop on youth culture in PRC will illuminate the limitations and possibilities of globalization. Hip Hop "which grounds black cultural signs and codes in black culture and examines the polyvocal languages of rap as the 'black noise' of the late twentieth century—will foster the development of more globally focused projects," Rose predicted in her highly influential academic study, *Black Noise*.[8] She finds the polyvocal roots of rap in such African American oral traditions and artists as the toast, Last Poets, Gil Scott-Heron, Malcolm X, 1950s radio disc jockeys like Douglas "Jocko" Henderson, and soul singer Millie Jackson. Unlike Rose, Anglo-Jamaican and British critics Paul Gilroy and David Toop, respectively, provide a more culturally diverse history. While both highlight the importance of diasporic influences, Gilroy stresses his discovery of the roots of rap in hybrid cultural exchanges of black Americans with Jamaican toasters and sound systems in the black Atlantic world in his study, *The Black Atlantic*. "The musical components of Hip Hop are a hybrid form nurtured by the social relations of the South Bronx where Jamaican sound system culture was transplanted during the 1970s and put down new roots," Gilroy writes. "In conjunction with specific technological innovations, this routed and re-rooted Caribbean culture set in train a process that was to transform black America's sense of itself and a large portion of the popular music industry as well."[9]

Toop also outlines the influential role of Jamaican DJs who rapped over the records they played. But, as British critic Tony Mitchell notes, Toop reveals that such

DJs as "Count Machouki, U Roy, and King Stitt . . . were themselves influenced by the jive of 1950s African American radio DJs such as Dr. Jive and Douglas 'Jocko' Henderson via the Jamaican producer Coxsone Dodd."[10] Most importantly and convincingly, Toop concludes that "Rap's forebears stretch back through disco, street funk, radio DJs, Bo Diddley, the bebop singers, Cab Calloway, Pigmeat Markham, the rap dancers and comics, the Last Poets, Gil Scott-Heron, Muhammed Ali, acapella and doo-wop groups, ring games, skip-rope rhymes, prison and army songs, toasts, signifying and the dozens, all the way to the griots of Nigeria and the Gambia. *No matter how far it penetrates into the twilight maze of Japanese video games and cool European electronics, its roots are still the deepest in all contemporary Afro-American music.*"[11]

In his article "Cultural Synchronization: Hip Hop with Chinese Characteristics?" media critic Jeroend de Kloet challenges the consensus of most black American cultural critics and insiders that the roots of rap and Hip Hop are essentially African American. He draws on Michel Foucault, Arjun Appadurai, and Rey Chow to support his outsider's view that because of "a constant synchronization with the West, Chinese Hip Hop is not only intrinsically cosmopolitan—it can also be read as an act of sonic betrayal of both assumed origin and of the context in which it is appropriated."[12] Similarly, Mitchell argues in *Global Noise* that "these roots are as culturally, eclectically, and syncretically wide ranging as they are deep."[13] With chapters on rap music in the United Kingdom, France, Germany, Bulgaria, Spain, Italy, Canada, Japan, Korea, Australia, New Zealand, and the Netherlands, *Global Noise* reveals that rap music and Hip Hop culture are an industry "driven as much by local artists and their fans as by the demands of global capitalism and US cultural domination."[14] However, except for the discussion in his introduction of the now dissolved expletive-named LMF, the radical hard-core Cantonese rap group that was popular between 1998–2000 in Hong Kong, whose lead rapper MC Yan was influenced by the Wu-Tang Clan, Mitchell neglects to include Hip Hop culture and rap music in PRC in his collection of essays.

As most American youth know, Hip Hop has four interrelated forms: disc jockeying, mcing (master of ceremony)/rapping, breakdancing/b-boying, and graffitiwriting/painting. But rapping is globally the corporate billion-dollar money-maker. Two of the most inventive and popular digital techniques of rap disc jockeys are sampling and scratching. Sampling is the digital use and blending of sounds and voices from other records and sources into a song, performance, or video. Scratching is sliding needles across records on two or more turntables by a DJ to create original rhythms and sounds to blend with samples of bars or lyrics from other records.

Despite its legendary, transcultural origin in the South Bronx in the 1970s, rap music was intended for neither a mass nor a global audience. The founding fathers of Hip Hop culture and rap music are Clive "DJ Kool Herc" Campbell, Bambaataa "Afrika Bambaataa" Kahim Aasim, and Joseph "Grandmaster Flash" Saddler. "Hip Hop pioneers such as Kool Herc, Afrika Bambaataa, and Grandmaster Flash and the Furious Five, among others," as historian Derrick P. Alridge notes, "articulated the post–civil rights generation's ideas and response to poverty, drugs, police brutality, and other racial and class inequities of post-industrial U. S. society."[15] According to DJ Kool Herc, a Jamaican-born disc jockey, Hip Hop was born on August 11, 1973, at 1520 Sedgwick Avenue in the West Bronx, not the South Bronx. With an innovatively constructed, huge, booming new sound system, he began spinning records at a back-to-school party promoted by Cindy Campbell, his sister, in the community room of their building before moving Hip Hop out into nearby parks and streets. He mixed James Brown, soul, R&B, and the phrase "Get Down" to describe the type of beats he used in between song breaks and during choruses. In 2007, he says retrospectively, "It wasn't a black thing, it was a we thing. . . . We played everything."[16]

Although the other two founding fathers of Hip Hop are also the sons of Caribbean immigrants, they were native-born bi-cultural black Americans who introduced distinctive styles to rap music. The consensus of rap fans and cultural historians is that Afrika Bambaataa was the most dynamic pan-Africanist founder of the Hip Hop movement. The son of transplanted Jamaican and Barbadian parents, Bambaataa was a gang warlord, poet, disc jockey, and founder of the Universal Zulu Nation crew, who was not only influenced by Kool Herc's new sound system and beats. He also promoted a distinctive black nationalist message in the Hip Hop movement of the 1970s by experimenting with the recitation of poetry and excerpts from speeches by such black nationalists as Malcolm X over the electronic beat and breaks of funk music. Grandmaster Flash, also the son of Barbadian immigrants, moved beyond the power of Kool Herc's sound systems and Afrika Bambaataa's innovative black nationalist programming with his original theories, techniques, and styles on the turntable and with mixing. He "came up with the Quick Mix theory, which was like cutting, the backspin, and the double-back. . . . While the MCs kept the energy high, Flash unveiled eye-catching tricks—cutting while flipping around, scratching with his elbows, cross-fading with his back-bone."[17] Inspired by these fathers of Hip Hop, fans and artists began around 1978 calling their music and uncensored mixed tapes rap.

Rap is generally classified in three types. The first is lyrically soft, playful, primarily dance rap to loud drum machines like that of Grammy Award winners (1989 and 1992) D.J. Jazzy Jeff & The Fresh Prince (Will Smith) and the more radical award-winners Run DMC. The latter is a trailblazing crew of three Hollis Queens friends wearing Adidas sneakers without shoelaces, black hats and leather jackets, and outfits with large gold chains hanging around their necks. The second is hard core, political, aggressive black nationalist rap like that of Chuck D, the incomparable social messenger of Public Enemy, and Rakim (Ra King Islam Master Allah), a Five Percenter (a 1963 splinter sect of the Nation of Islam) millenarian poet, saxophonist, and legendary rapper who was as "serious as cancer." The third and most controversial type is the profane, boastful, sexist, violent, radical gangsta rap that glorifies the hustling life of crime, sex, drugs, and living large in the ghetto like that of NWA, Tupac Shakur, Snoop Dogg, and 50 Cent. Some contemporary rappers, such as Common and Mos Def, draw on all three categories through their imaginative mix of wryly humorous lyrics, live instrumental music, and compelling images of street culture to relay powerful socio-political messages. Black nationalist and gangsta rap have been criticized and censored, most effectively in PRC, for their graphic celebration of sex, violence, drugs, thug-life, and anti-homosexuality.

The first rappers to sell over 500,000 records, to perform on MTV, and to make the cover page of *Rolling Stone Magazine* was Run DMC. In 1979 the Sugar Hill Gang (Michael "Wonder Mike" Wright, Guy "Master Gee" O'Brien, and Henry "Big Bank Hank" Jackson) from New Jersey was auditioned by Sugar Hill Records to cut *Rapper's Delight*, the first chart-busting rap record to sell two million copies globally. In 1983 Sugar Hill Records' production of "The Message," the grim and gritty downbeat record about the social and psychological impact of institutional racism by Duke Bootee and Melle Mel of the Furious Five, became the fifth rap single to reach the gold status for sales of over 500,000. And in 1989 the playful, dancing rap era of Will Smith and Jazzy Jeff was transformed into the West Coast gangsta rap of Niggaz With Attitude (NWA), led by Ice Cube, Eazy-E, and Dr. Dre, in *Straight Outta Compton*, which sold over 500,000 albums in six weeks. Although such white rappers as the Beastie Boys and 3rd Bass were early cultural bridges for white fans, Dr. Dre's sponsorship of Eminem broke not only new sonic ground in the reinvention of the art form but also sales records in the industry. Taking it to another level in 2003 was Jin, the English and Cantonese-rapping Chinese-American shining star in the new wave of free-style rappers. He was showcased in Black Entertainment Television's "Freestyle Friday" Hall of Fame "for going undefeated seven straight weeks in the network's '106 and Park: Top 10 Live' rap battle in which the best barbs and rudest rhymes often win in spontaneous head-to-head duels."[18] Although Jin has released five rap albums, including one largely in Cantonese (ABC/American Born Chinese), major national awards for rap have been recently won by Ludacris, Common, TI, and Lil' Wayne.

THE GOVERNMENT'S CENSORSHIP OF HIP HOP CULTURE IN PRC

The growth of rap and Hip Hop culture in PRC is a relatively new phenomenon. Because of political and cultural differences in China and the United States, it didn't develop in PRC until legendary popular singers like rock stars Cui Jian, Dai Bing, and Li Xiaolong began experimenting with the new music genre in the mid-1980s and 1990s. Cui Jian included a rap song on his mid-1980s album, and Dai Bing started rapping in 1986. The release by Li Xiaolong in 2000 of his first album *Li Shao Long* marks the beginning of solo performances by Chinese rappers. Contrary to the conventional belief that Chinese language is not congenial for rap, Li Xiaolong believes that Chinese characters with rich connotations are better for rap than English language. His rap is marked by an authentic sense of Mandarin tonal changes and various traditional Chinese musical instruments. In 2003 the release of the compilation album *Xi Ha Now China* significantly increased the number of Hip Hop and rap bands in Beijing and Shanghai. It demonstrates that Hip Hop was gradually gaining more ground in PRC.

Scream Records released the first albums by Yin T'sang, Sketch Krime, and Kungfoo in 2004. In April of the same year, MC Black Bubble from Shanghai battled

MC Webber from Beijing, a member of Yin T'sang's rap crew, in the finals in Shanghai. Dramatizing the power struggle over nonmainstream music between Beijing and Shanghai, similar in a less violent manner to the conflict between West Coast and East Coast rappers, MC Webber won the battle. The atmosphere during the battle was inspiring; the crowd—dressed in Hip Hop outfits—sang "Welcome to China 2008" along with Kungfoo during his performance and shouted encouragement to the female rappers from Wuhan that joined the battle. Reflecting the realities of the political and cultural differences and government control in PRC, the common outfits of rock artists and some rappers in the United States and the United Kingdom—the long hair, tie-dyed shirts, bling, body piercings, and tattoos—were absent at the event.

Although authorities in PRC never accepted hard rock, heavy metal, and punk music because it fostered rebellious disruptive moral and social behavior among the younger generation, they have supported the development of a highly regulated Hip Hop culture. Rap is even "heard on commercials and public service announcements aired over the government-controlled television network." However, "before appearing in concert or releasing a record," a reporter for the *Los Angeles Times* writes, "Chinese artists must submit their lyrics for approval by the Ministry of Culture, which vetoes anything deemed obscene or politically unacceptable. Enforcement has been inconsistent, and the more 'radical' elements of Chinese rap still find their way onto the Internet . But the policing of tunes has forced commercial groups and their record companies to give rap a certain wholesomeness."[19]

In rap battles at Hip Hop parties, clubs, and concerts in Beijing and Shanghai, according to Dana Burton, an African American promoter of a national freestyle rap contest, the new generation of "Chinese rappers copy the hard-edged attitude [and flows shared primarily on the Internet] of their American counterparts . . . but only to a point. . . . This is China," Burton reminds us." Glorifying street culture doesn't translate. Here. It's cut and dried. If you have a gun and you shoot someone, you're going to be executed. You sell drugs, you're gone."[20] Sexually provocative clothing and politically radical staging are not as popular as retro sports jerseys, designer's sports outfits, baggy trousers, and dyed hair in PRC. Recently, the *Los Angeles Times* reports, "the State Administration of Radio, Film and Television and local affiliates issued guidelines calling on TV anchors to stop dying their hair strange colors, wearing bizarre clothes, showing too much skin, using Hong Kong or Taiwanese accents, displaying their navels or cleavage, and wearing plunging necklines or short skirts." Some Chinese youth believe these guidelines and regulations are signs of a big generation gap. "What the older generation sees as the loss of traditional culture," a Chinese student explains, "reflects a more integrated China. . . . What elders see as brash behavior is a more confident outlook needed in a fast-paced world. And what they see as a lack of respect for elders is a healthy questioning of authority." A member of a popular Hip Hop group laments that "government censorship forces artists and record companies to turn out 'Socialist Hip Hop.'"[21] Although government censorship has tamed the radical freedom of speech and individualism of hard core

African American Hip Hop culture in PRC, the Internet cafes are major outlets for the growing celebration of freedom of cultural expression and radical individualism by the younger generation.

MAJOR CHARACTERISTICS OF HIP HOP IN PRC

In "Cultural Synchronization: Hip Hop with Chinese Characteristics?" cultural critic Jeroen de Kloet reveals five major characteristics of Hip Hop culture in PRC: (1) the involvement of non-Chinese, (2) the lyrics of the bands, (3) the role of the Internet, (4) the intricate link between Hip Hop subculture and mainstream popular Chinese culture, and (5) the increasing variety of dialects.[21] First, foreigners play a conspicuous role in Chinese Hip Hop. For example, only one of the four members of the Yin T'sang crew is a Chinese national: the lead rapper MC Webber is a Beijing resident. Two members are white Americans, and one is a transplanted Chinese performer from Canada. Sketch Krime, the lead rapper of Dragon Tongue Squad, who moved from Yunan to Beijing, works with four MCs from France, Britain, Japan, and the United States. The two groups therefore regard rap in PRC differently. Although the membership of both crews include national diversity, Yin T'sang seems to be more committed to affirming the authority and authenticity of a Chinese identity by adopting a Chinese name for their band and by rapping in Mandarin, the standard national dialect in PRC. In contrast, the guest MCs on Sketch Krime's CD rap in English, French, and Japanese. Increasingly, however, more native Chinese Hip Hop groups began appearing as the first generation of hip hoppers, most of whom were born in the 1980s, grew up and became eager fans.[22]

Secondly, the lyrics of both bands focus on everyday life in Beijing and Shanghai. However, while the Mandarin lyrics of Yin T'sang obscure whether they express a foreign or Chinese perspective, the language choice on Sketch Krime's CD is clearly from the vantage point of nonnative Chinese outsiders. Supported by the government, the impetus to localize rap is obvious in such songs by Yin T'sang as "Welcome to Beijing," "Beijing Bad Boy," "SARS," and "Yellow Road." In "SARS," for example, Yin T'sang raps about the days when the SARS virus seemed to control Beijing:

> Frequently wash your hands. Wear a mask, stay away from me, wear gloves, stay physically fit, don't use your hands to touch your face. I have come to invade. Call me SARS. I was born in Guangzhou. In that climate I developed a vicious demeanor. Who would have guessed that it would go this far, that little old me could make everyone so scared?[23]

In contrast, Kungfoo's lyrics focus mainly on the problems of teenagers in a rapidly changing Chinese culture with a mixed communist and capitalist system in which problems of drug addiction, sexual violence, ethnic conflict, and crass materialism are far less conspicuous. The language and lyrical reflections upon everyday life in Beijing and Shanghai thus nationalizes the sense and sound of Hip Hop in PRC.

Third, the Internet plays a decisive role in the proliferation and popularity of Chinese Hip Hop culture. Internet cafes are very popular in PRC even though they are monitored closely and occasionally shut down by authorities for frequent violations of their license. Through websites, hip hoppers get in touch with one another to exchange news and their latest raps. Fourth, urban magazines carry the latest images in Hip Hop fashion, the tours of new bands from the United States, and photos of graffiti in Guangzhou. Compared to Japan and South Korea, Hip Hop culture in PRC is still marginalized in the mainstream Chinese culture, but its popularity among the youth is increasing. However, a large part of the Hip Hop culture movement in PRC, de Kloet writes, "represents a fashion statement more than a 'real' Hip Hop identity."[24] Unlike de Kloet, I do not interpret the radical impact of African American and transcultural Asian rap in PRC as a "cultural pollution" of Chinese nationality. The fifth and final major characteristic is the increasing use of some of the 1,500 local dialects, especially Shanghainese, rather than English or Mandarin by rappers.

The production and language of Chinese Hip Hop culture reveals that the national identity, especially among the youth generation, is in transition in its authority, authenticity, and agency. Primarily because of the Internet, despite censorship in PRC, and the illegal sale of cheap copies of foreign CDs, the production and promotion of Hip Hop in China demonstrate the dominant impact of the West, especially America and African Americans. However, Chinese Hip Hop rejects or resists such key elements of African American Hip Hop culture as ethnicity, rebellion, class divisions, profanity, and violence. In a sense, Hip Hop in PRC challenges what constitutes global Hip Hop culture, as well as what constitutes the cultural identity of contemporary Chinese youth.

SOME MAJOR RAP STARS AND STYLES IN PRC

Similar to the convenient historical and geographical division in the United States of Hip Hop culture into East and West Coast stars and styles, Hip Hop culture in PRC is most conveniently examined by dividing it into two schools: Northern and Southern. Both regions emulate African American styles, but the Northern school, which began around 1990 with Dai Bing's English single in "Rap Man," is more bowdlerized, didactic, danceable, playful, commercial, and indigenous; the Southern, which began with the first Iron MIB Rap Battle of 2002, is more innovative, satirical, creative, dynamic, transnational, and multilingual.

The two most popular bands of the Southern school are Hi-Bomb and Bamboo Crew, both starting in Shanghai in 2002. Hi-Bomb has only two members: Little Lion, who was born in Shanghai but raised in the United States, and Shanghao, who was born and raised in Shanghai. Their first single, which won them a contract with Bacardi Carta Blanca, is influenced by the East Coast rap style. The main theme and tone of the lyrics are a moderately satirical examination of the daily lives of Chinese youth, especially in Shanghai, but the lyrics avoid the socially offensive and morally objectionable language, topics, and issues of their African American models. They have achieved several top ten hits by rapping not only in English, but also in Mandarin and Shanghaiese. Bamboo Crew, the other popular Shanghai rap team, is a crew of five members, including a female: Blakk Bubble, Masta Loop, Zeero (a female), Mummy-C, and Shout Dogg. After competing successfully in national battles with other rap groups, they released their first album, *Shanghai Rap*, in 2005, and their second, *Cheer Up*, in 2006.

Probably the three most important Northern rap stars and groups in PRC inspired by African American Hip Hop culture and rap music are Dai Bing, Kungfoo, CMCB, and Yin T'sang, all based in Beijing. Dai Bing is generally considered the Father of rap in PRC. Before graduating from the Institute of Diplomacy in 1990, he began singing rhythm & blues songs that he learned from an African American friend. Fascinated by West Coast gangsta rappers like Ice Cube and East Coast militant political rappers like Chuck D, Dai Bing learned the moves and sounds of the pioneers of the hard core style, but softened their angry, radical, boastful lyrics about racial, ethnic, and underclass life in the black inner city, the hood, in his first English single release, "Rap Man," in 1990. "Rap Man" was so successful in receiving approval of government censors and gaining popularity with fans that some of the censored tracks encouraging social and environmental responsibility and reform were used in advertising campaigns for sports and food products. With friends D. D. Rhythm and Tianbao, Dai Bing then started the first indigenous rap band in PRC in 2000. Because his album *Hot Rhythm* earned rap a respected place in popular Chinese music, he is honored by participation in nearly all the rap concerts in PRC.

Organized in 2001, Kungfoo, whose leader, Yang Fan, is a Chinese opera fan who raps in the clear, distinct four tones of Mandarin, was the first Hip Hop group to receive the approval of the government to perform in the mammoth People's Hall in Beijing. The three-member band view themselves as a modern Hip Hop continuation of traditional Chinese culture that promotes wholesome social values and national pride. In contrast to African American gangsta rap, their lyrics are distinctly pronounced, bland, rhythmic statements about such themes as teenage love, respect for elders, social responsibility, and patriotic duty. Some youthful fans therefore consider their indigenous rap to be like hotpot, an extremely spicy meal in Sichuan Province, without pepper. Scream Records, a leading producer of rock and rap in the nation, released *Impulsion*, their first album, in 2004 with a sticker on the cover asking teenagers to recommend it to their parents. The title track of the album "warns against acting on teenage impulse like a distraught student who commits suicide."[25] With sales of more than 100,000, which surpassed the sales of Yin T'sang's *For the People* in 2003, the album earned the band the title of the most popular new band in China.

Formed in 2002 by seven residents from various obscure underground bands in Beijing, CMCB (China MC Brother) is perhaps the largest Hip Hop band in PRC. They rely primarily on the colloquial Beijing dialect to express directly and humorously their anger at social problems and injustice. Hence, their songs were more popular among teenagers than government censors. With the release of their first album

Gongfu by Scream Records, they won the nomination for the best new rock/rap star in 2002. In 2004 they released their second album *who moved my noodle* with Yin T'sang as their guest artists, which marked a new development for Hip Hop in PRC with two powerful crews joining together to market the album.

Although Yin T'sang is the most famous indigenous Hip Hop group based in Beijing, it was the first multinational Mandarin rap group in history. Wang "MC Webber" Bo, its lead rapper and co-founder in 2000 with Foenix XIV, is the only one of the four-member transnational crew who was born in PRC. Watching a video of MC Hammer, he was influenced to become a rap star at fifteen years old.[26] Foenix XIV and Heff are white Americans from New York and Chicago respectively, while Sbazzo is a Chinese Canadian from Toronto. They nevertheless have a unique flow and rhyme style in Mandarin that ranges from underground to Top 20 Chart-selling tracks. After their live freestyle performances, influenced by major West and East Coast African American rappers, in the major party spots and clubs in Beijing became highly popular in 2001, MC Webber and Foenix IV began writing songs over commercial beats for Nike, CASIO, Philips, White Rabbit TaiShan Beverage Company, and the Chinese Basketball Association.

Instead of highlighting the racial and ethnic discrimination and the glorification of drugs, sex, and violence in African American gangsta rap, the focus of Yin T'sang's themes and lyrics in such songs as "SARS," "Beijing Bad Boy," and "Welcome to Beijing" is on everyday health, moral, environmental, and commercial issues of life in Beijing. "SARS," for example, is a cautionary warning about the personal responsibility of everyone to control the spread of the deadly virus in Beijing. The release in 2003 of Yin T'sang's first album, *For the People*, featured their hit single "Welcome to Beijing," which invites everyone to visit PRC and experience its rich history and friendly people. Written by Hong Kong lyricist Lam Jik, the song became so popular that the government adopted it as the theme song for the 2008 Summer Olympics in China. The following bilingual excerpt in English and Pinyin rather than Chinese script illustrates the appeal of its simple lyrics, melody, and rhythm:

We promised to get together here. So welcome!
Xiang yue hao le zai yi qi, wo men huan ying ni.

We cultivate Chinese evergreen in the garden. All the time, it is producing a new legend.
Wo jia zhong zhe wan nian qing, kai fang mei duan chuan qi.

In the soil rich in traditions, we plant. Hope everything we plant here leaves you a great experience.
Wei chuan tong de tu rang bo zhong, wei ni liu xia hui yi.

Our guests, no matter if we've met before or not, please feel at ease.
Mo sheng shu xi dou shi ke ren, qing bu yong ju li.

Even if you have been here many times, you won't feel bored 'cause we have vast new things for you.
Di ji ci lai mei guan xi, you tai duo hua ti.

Welcome to Beijing; we've done a lot for your visit.
Bei jing huan ying ni, wei ni kai tian bi di.

Its charm in ever changing is full of life.
Liu dong zhong de mei li, chong man zhe chao qi.

Welcome to Beijing; let's breathe together in the sunshine.
Bei jing huan ying ni, zai tai yang xia fen xiang hu xi.

Let's establish new records here in China.
Zai huang tu di shua xin cheng ji.[27]

Even though *For the People* sold only 70,000 copies locally, very low sales by American standards, it established the Yin T'sang crew as leaders of the Hip Hop movement in PRC.

MC Webber also achieved fame and street credit as "the best MC in China by winning the National Iron Mic Freestyle Competition in Shanghai three years in a row." This led to his sharing the MC stage with San Francisco's Ugly Duckling and rap legends The Jungle Brothers. In addition to performing collaborations and concerts with Hong Kong's famous LMF crew and DJ Tommy, Toronto native MC Vandal, and Beijing's Dragon Tongue Squad, MC Webber continues to be the most recognized MC in PRC. Foenix XIV continued to DJ in Beijing's biggest and hottest clubs (Vics, Mix, Solutions, Orange, and Tango) until he opened Lush, voted #1 new live venue among students in the university district of Beijing in early 2004, and he landed major roles in two television series, *Admirers Fate* and *Dazzled*.

In addition to pursuing individual interests, Yin T'sang has traveled PRC as a group performing in major cities across the mainland. Making appearances at the Pepsi Music Awards, where they were nominated for Best New Rock-Rap Group of 2003, and the China National Radio Music Awards, where they won Best New Group of 2003. In addition to full-length articles by the *LA Times*, the *China Daily* and *Music Magazine* (China), the group also made special appearances on CCTV-1, PBS, and Stir TV (cable). Yin T'sang then recruited two new members to increase their versatility and to make the crew even more well-rounded. Chen Mingyu, the pianist and vocalist who was featured on "For the People" track, helps to add an R&B feel to many of the new songs, and Young Kin, aka Kinetic Raw, who recently returned from a concert tour with superstar Jay Chao, is the new link to the streets. Yin T'sang encompasses Chinese Hip Hop from the underground to the charts, where their last single "Welcome to Beijing" hovered in the Top 20 for sixteen weeks.

Sbazzo, with his unique flow and rhyme style, wrote and recorded commercials for Nike, CASIO, Philips, White Rabbit, TaiShan Beverage Company, and the Chinese Basketball Association (CBA) in addition to making guest appearances on Dragon Tongue Squad's #1 single "The Game is On" and CMCB's "Put Your Hand's Up." Heff managed the business side, lining up Yin T'sang to open for Canada's DJ Kid Koala, and, with the help of Society Skateboards, bringing together the Hip Hop community every last Saturday of the month for Section 6, Beijing's only real Hip Hop party. These parties feature Yin T'sang on the mics, with Shanghai's DJ V-Nutz, and Beijing DJ's Shorty-S and Wordy (all national DMC finalists) on the cuts.

THE PROMOTION OF HIP HOP DANCE IN PRC

As a part of youth culture, Hip Hop dance gained a great number of followers throughout the world. The youth in PRC discovered Hip Hop dance in the 1980s movie *Breaking*. After the release of the movie, break-dancing became popular among the teenagers and youth in their twenties. With the rapid increase of migration, urbanization, and industrialization, many urban households could afford VCRs, and the teenagers could use video to develop their break-dancing styles. Many break-dance centers sprang up in various big cities, and break-dance competitions were often held. It even became a featured item of nationwide dancing competitions.[28]

Unfortunately, the craze for break-dancing seemed to vanish from the whole country overnight at the end of 1980s. This may be attributed to several factors. First, the excessive commercialization of break-dancing in the United States resulted in it losing its former appeal, and it suddenly became outdated and was discarded. B-boys and B-girls, who wished to identify themselves by the break-dance, seemed to disappear overnight all over the world. Hence in China, the inspiration for the break-dancers suddenly dried up. Second, because most people believed that it was the cultural fashion of school drop-outs and rebellious bad boys or girls, breaking did not gain social recognition. Third, there was not an ideal environment for the development of break-dancing in PRC. Most of the hip hoppers could not get financial support. Therefore, break-dancing soon lost its vitality and appeal among the young people.

But in the 1990s, as Hip Hop culture swept the whole world and won many new followers in the United Kingdom, France, Spain, Italy, Japan, Korea, Taiwan, and Hong Kong, break-dancing regained its popularity. Because it is near Hong Kong and shares the same language and regional culture, Guangzhou was the first city to welcome the coming of Hip Hop. Soon it permeated all the major cities in the whole Guangdong Province. At that time hip hoppers in Guangdong led Hip Hop dance in PRC. Meanwhile, Shanghai, influenced by Japanese Hip Hop culture, quickly generated its own Hip Hop dancers. The new school of Hip Hop took the lead in the whole nation. Dedicated fans adept at locking, popping, and breaking could be found in Shanghai. Yet the B-boys and B-girls in the capital city Beijing, chiefly influenced by Korean Hip Hop dancers, lagged behind those in Guangzhou and Shanghai. In 2002, a dancing group named Northern Dancing Group was established to promote Hip Hop culture, which enriched both the organization and the individuals financially and culturally. Quickly the group recruited all the top hip hoppers in Beijing and made a name for itself among the hip hoppers on the Mainland.

Hip Hop not only became widely popular in the big metropolitan cities, but it also started to develop in the inland areas, like Zhenzhou, Henan Province. Different from the hip hoppers in the big cities, who were mainly influenced by the Japanese, Korean, and Hong Kong performers, dancers in Zhenzhou borrowed some of the martial arts techniques and concepts for their Hip Hop dance. Shoppers and workers could see hip hoppers on the city squares practicing or perfecting their dancing skills at night or on weekends in all the cities. Most of them were middle-school students, university students, and professional dancers, and a small number are young white-collar workers. Before long, the hip hoppers in PRC began organizing regional and nationwide competitions to improve their dancing skills.[29]

Around 2000, various kinds of Hip Hop dance competitions were held all over the country. In February 2002 the first Hip Hop dance competition was held in Guangzhou, which attracted many dancers from the province. In September, Jiangxi Province held a Hip Hop dance competition to promote the sale of Everyday Fresh Vc Orange Juice. In 2003, CCTV and the Chinese Aerobic Association jointly spon-sored the first national Hip Hop competition. All the contestants were divided into three groups: aerobics Hip Hop, skating Hip Hop and, the most demanding and pro-fessional, popular Hip Hop. At the competition, the viewer could see that Hip Hop was being innovatively localized in several ways. First, unlike most international Hip Hop contestants, who were dressed in Hip Hop fashions, some of the hip hoppers were dressed in martial arts outfits or flowing white silk Taiji overalls. They also incorporated the martial art skills and Taijing techniques in their Hip Hop dance. Second, the music they used in their competition was not rap, but pop songs or even classical music played by Guzheng or traditional Chinese three-stringed Erhu. Third, some of the contestants adopted facial designs from Beijing Opera in their make-up. The competition revealed the inadequate knowledge of and experience with the ori-gins and development of African American Hip Hop culture by both the participants and the judges. The overall impression was that the competition was only for ama-teurs. In contrast, the university participants in the China Mobile, who held the M-Zone Hip Hop Competition on Campus were much more talented and impressive.

The second national Hip Hop competition was held in 2004. Since there were so many hip hoppers wishing to show their talent in this competition, they had to go through the preliminary, second round, and final competition in one of the ten ven-ues. The most outstanding hip hoppers could enter the final in Beijing. Compared with the national competition, all the contestants demonstrated much more knowl-edge of and experience with Hip Hop. In 2005, the most influential World Annual Hip Hop Battle Competition established a venue in China. This was the first time that an international Hip Hop dance competition was held in China. It inspired the top Chinese hip hoppers to participate in the competition. This competition paved the way for the Chinese hip hoppers to go international. Increasingly, since the late 1990s, some world-renowned hip hoppers, especially African Americans, could sometimes be seen break-dancing in the clubs in Beijing, Shanghai, or Guangzhou. All have made major contributions to the promotion of Hip Hop in PRC. Now hip hoppers can be seen not only in all cities in PRC, but also in clubs nightly from Ningxia to Beijing. Recently, Star Club in the capital had a dynamic show with a Japanese DJ spinning the newest hits to an adoring crowd of young, rich, and powerful Chinese.[30]

THE FUTURE OF HIP HOP CULTURE IN PRC

Hip Hop in PRC reveals the limitations and possibilities of cultural globalization. On one hand, many Chinese rappers strive to emulate, nationalize, and localize rap; on the other hand, most attempt to imitate and catch up with African American Hip Hop. Each cultural phenomenon has to undergo a certain degree of localization when it is introduced to a new culture. Hip Hop subculture is no exception. Hip Hop in PRC has several unique features. First, in most of the Western countries and some of the Asian countries, like Japan and Korea, Hip Hop is not tightly regulated by governmental organizations. In PRC, hip hoppers at first organized by themselves for individual expressive freedom and fun. Now the Physical Culture and Sports Commission at the various levels from the provincial to the national attempt to control Hip Hop as a kind of aerobics. So not only are many teenagers fond of hip hopping, but also some members of the over thirty-five-year-old generation are fans. The deceased comic star Zhao Lirong, for example, was often seen on TV performing Hip Hop dance. However, some of the older generation made it their own by including Taijing or martial art skills and techniques, which contributes to the indigenization of Chinese Hip Hop.

Second, because it is a kind of avant-garde lifestyle and vogue, the spread of Hip Hop is regulated along with the ability of young people to purchase the associated Hip Hop cultural items. Baggy pants, wide sunglasses, retro-basketball shirts, multicolored hair, and lots of hair gel are the popular fashion items of hip hoppers in PRC seeking to look cool and express personal cultural freedom. Although most of the teenage hip hoppers are unaware of the origin and history of Hip Hop culture, many adopt it as a good way to show the independence and individualism of their new identity in a rapidly changing Chinese culture as a result of migration, urbanization, industrialization, and technologization. Because some universities have even offered Hip Hop courses for their students, hip hoppers are often seen in the university fitness center, in dance classes, at New Year's parties, at art festivals, and even at weekend public dance balls. While lecturing in 2006 as a Fulbright Senior Specialist at the SWUST in Mianyang, I introduced the origins and history of African American rap and Hip Hop culture to my seminars and assistants.

Assistant Professor Lamei Xiao, my principal assistant, and her colleagues Xiong Tingting and Wu Linlin outlined three major problems that confront the future of Hip Hop in PRC.[31] First, rap language is the major problem for Chinese artists. Some of the rappers attempt to localize Hip Hop by rapping in Chinese. But many DJs or MCs do not bother to rap in Chinese; instead, they prefer the more "rappable" English. Some attribute it to the fact that English and Chinese belong to different language systems. The tonal Chinese language, I learned, hinders the creativity of rappers in Chinese. Yet some of the singers like Jay Chou (Zhou Jielun) try to rap in Chinese by leaving out the tone of the Chinese characters. This is a bold attempt. Yet most of the lyrics cannot be understood by the audience. Consequently, some fans contend that he does not contribute to the popularity of Hip Hop and that only HotDog and Shawn (Song Tingyue) can be regarded as the "real" Chinese rappers. However, many fans do not agree that the Chinese language is not suitable for rap. In Chinese cross talk or comic dialogue, for example, the audience can easily understand the humor in it no matter how fast the performers speak. So these fans believe that the key problem is that there are few good lyric writers.

Second, government censorship is a problem. In rap, the themes of the lyrics are as important as the rhythm. However, in PRC, the government censorship keeps the songs off the air if the lyrics contain profanity, sexism, drug use, or violence. So popular rap in Chinese like, "Life's a Struggle" by Shawn, has been prohibited from being broadcast in PRC, for his song reveals the dark, disturbing impact of migration, urbanization, and industrialization on the rapidly changing society.

Third, rap crews have problems with recording and distribution. One of the biggest hurdles to local outfits is getting recording and distribution deals. Independent record labels are a relatively new concept in PRC, but finding record shops to stock minority-taste local products is even more difficult. "Fans are always coming into our office looking for our CDs," says Shen Lihui, general manager of Modern Sky, the largest recorder of Indie avant-garde, rock, and alternative music. "The big problem is we have no direct sales circulation of our recordings," explains Shen.[32]

Looking at the continuing development trends of Hip Hop in Asia, especially in Japan, Korea and Taiwan, rappers and fans say that there is a bright future for Hip Hop culture in PRC and that Yin T'sang, Hi-bomb, Dragon Tongue Squad, CMCB, and Kungfoo are at the forefront. Whereas five years ago there were only two Hip Hop nightclubs in Beijing, there are currently at least four venues that exclusively play Hip Hop, and almost every bar has at least one urban music night per week. Oversized team jerseys and baseball caps can be found in most boutiques. Hip Hop now takes up one whole rack at the local CD stores. People between the ages of 15 and 45 can be found dancing to rap music at Tango, the most successful new high-capacity super club in Beijing. Support for Hip Hop is encouraged through street basketball (Nike and Reebok), extreme sports (Society Skateboards, NanShan Ski Resort, Siemens X-treme Games), and even major corporations (McDonald's advertising campaign, Meters Bourn, and Nokia). By adapting it to their social conditions, including censorship, and cultural imperatives, Chinese youth have demonstrated that African American Hip Hop culture has had a radical impact on Hip Hop by spreading freedom of expression and individualism in PRC.

NOTES

[1]This article was conceived in 2006 while I served as a Fulbright Senior Specialist at Southwest University of Science and Technology in Mianyang, China. I am indebted to Assistant Professor Lamei Xiao, my inexpendable assistant in Mianyang, and her colleagues Xiong Tingting and Wu Linlin for the invaluable research and translations of twenty-eight academic papers from the online data bank by physical education teachers and professors in the universities or in the Physical Culture and Sports Commission.

[2]IMF Staff, "Globalization: A Brief Overview," *International Monetary Fund*, May 2008, http://www.imf.org/external/np/exr/ib/2008/053008.htm.

[3]David Rothkop, "In Praise of Cultural Imperialism? Effects of Globalization on Culture," *Global Policy Forum*, http://www.globalpolicy.org/globaliz/cultural/globcult.htm.

[4]Jeffry A. Frieden, "To Have and Have Not," *The New York Times Book Review*, 24 December 2006, 19.

[5]Rothkop, "In Praise of Cultural Imperialism?".

[6]Todd Crowell and Thomas Hon Wing Polin, "Deng Xiaoping," *Asia Now*, http://www-cgi.cnn.com/ASIANOW/asiaweek/features/aoc/aoc.deng.html; Calum MacLeod, "Rolling Stones Tour Brings Hot Rocks to Shanghai," *USA Today*, 7 April 2006, 10A.

[7]Quoted in Mark Magnier, "A Style Nobody Can Deal with: Politics, Style and the Postindustrial City in Hip Hop," *Microphone Fiends: Youth Music and Youth Culture*, eds. Andrew Ross and Tricia Rose (New York, 1994), 71.

[8]Tricia Rose, *Black Noise: Rap Music and Black Culture in Contemporary America* (Hanover, NH, 1994), iv.

[9]Paul Gilroy, *The Black Atlantic: Modernity and Double Consciousness* (Cambridge, MA, 1993), 2–4, 33–34, 85.

[10]David Toop, *Rap Attack 2: African Rap to Global Hip Hop* (London, 1991), 4.

[11]Ibid., 19 (emphasis mine).

[12]Jeroend de Kloet, "Cultural Synchronization: Hip Hop with Chinese Characteristics?" *Norient*, 4 June 2007.

[13]Tony Mitchell, "Another Root—Hip Hop Outside the USA," in *Global Noise: Rap and Hip Hop Outside the USA*, ed. Tony Mitchell (Middletown, CT, 2001), 4.

[14]Ibid., 2.

[15]Derrick P. Alridge, "From Civil Rights to Hip Hop: Toward a Nexus of Ideas," *Journal of African American History* 90 (Summer 2005): 226–52.

[16]Quoted in David Gonzalez, "Will Gentrification Spoil the Birthplace of Hip Hop?" *The New York Times*, 21 May 2007, A17.

[17]Jeff Chang, *Can't Stop Won't Stop: A History of the Hip Hop Generation* (New York, 2005), 112–14.

[18]Erin Chan, "Slim Shady, Watch It: Asian Rapper's Got It," *The New York Times*, 12 Aug 2003, http://query.nytimes.com/gst/fullpage.html?res=9F04E5D71031F931A2575BC0A9659C8B63.

[19]Ralph Frammolino, "You Can't Get a Bad Rap Here: Hip-Hop Has Caught on in China," *Los Angeles Times*, A1.

[20]Quoted in Frammolino, "You Can't Get a Bad Rap Here."

[21]Mark Magnier, "China's Newest Cultural Revolution Worries Elders," *Los Angeles Times*, 3, A1.

[22]de Kloet, "Cultural Synchronization."

[23]Ibid.

[24]Ibid.

[25]Frammolino, A1.

[26]Ibid.

[27]Angie Ryan, "Welcome to Beijing Lyrics—English Translation of Official Song of 2008 Olympics," *GoArticles*, http://www.goarticles.com/cgi-bin/showa.cgi?C=1057727.

[28]This sub-section on Hip Hop dance is based primarily on conversations with students and a report "A General Survey of Hip Hop Culture in Mainland China" by Xiong Tingting, Xiao Lamei, and Wu Linlin, currently in my private collection.

[29]Ibid., 11.

[30]Ibid., 13.

[31]Ibid., 15.

[32]Ibid., 10.

"JUST BECAUSE I AM A BLACK MALE DOESN'T MEAN I AM A RAPPER!": SOCIOCULTURAL DILEMMAS IN USING "RAP" MUSIC AS AN EDUCATIONAL TOOL IN CLASSROOMS

Ayanna F. Brown

Working at Diamond High School exposed me to a youth culture unlike anything I had ever experienced when I was in high school. First, the high school was predominantly African American. I, on the other hand, attended a multiethnic, multilingual, yet predominantly white and affluent, high school that was situated in an affluent predominantly white community. My high school's nonwhite student population was bused in because the city in which we lived did not have the infrastructure to fund or maintain a public high school. This was in the 1990s and yes, I was bused. So, my only experience in a predominantly African American high school was through my experiences as an educator in the South. One thing I learned while living in the South was that many of these black high schools modeled much of their social and cultural identities from Historically Black Colleges & Universities (HBCUs). Socially, football games, the band, half-time culture, fraternities, and sororities exist in an enclave of higher education that is unparalleled. Within popular culture and more prevalent in recent films, we have seen black college culture magnified. Films like *School Daze*, *Drumline*, and *Stomp the Yard* illustrate the array of activities and intracultural dynamics that exist uniquely within black colleges that make them intriguing, to say the least.[1] When I was in high school and living in a state where black colleges did not exist, my only connection to these schools and this culture was through the television sitcom, *A Different World*.[2] I was greatly influenced by these images when I chose to attend an HBCU despite my school administrators near plea for me not to. It was my experiences with culture and community at an HBCU that allowed me to explicitly connect African American culture and education. As such, when my tenure at Diamond High School began, I quickly noticed how my students' high school and community cultures were complementary or more profoundly, when they collided.

Diamond High School, located in the Southern region of the United States, was filled with varying degrees of black southern culture. For example, three HBCUs were less than three miles from the school. The historical role of these institutions was the epicenter for pride and resilience for the black community. The Diamond High community was regarded with nostalgic remembrances of the nearby University football games, the Homecoming Parades, and long days of Fall, when the neighborhood park was filled with barbeque grills and "sounds of blackness" that made them feel good about the community.[3] And yet, even today, as the community is not as strongly connected, and urban sprawl has enticed families to consider the suburbs of the city—Diamond High School remains, and the rich history of the community and school bring families back annually for football games, street festivals, and parades.

The year that I entered Diamond High School, I saw black and white teachers fighting to retain and enhance what Diamond High School had to offer the city. And too, there were a handful of teachers who were challenged by the poverty, limited curriculum, and low expectations. I held a position that was designed to work closely with the faculty and the school's administration. This position allowed me to work closely with the students, parents, and the curriculum in ways that were not necessarily available to the classroom teachers or guidance counselors. I had the opportunity to walk in classrooms unannounced, sit among students during lunch and afterschool, conduct home visits, and participate in extracurricular activities.

After two years working at Diamond, I decided to examine the cultural wealth that made Diamond so unique and yet perilous in its academic success compared to more affluent schools and communities within the school district. One of the unique components of its high school curriculum was that it included an African American History course. Here is where I began my inquiry into what it meant to study black history, and particularly at a predominantly black high school. Would this course examine a broad array of what constitutes black history? Would that inquiry reflect an African diaspora? How would students engage in these historical discussions differently than in other humanities classes? In addition to these questions, I was wondering whether the students would take the African American History course content for granted because much of it was written on the historical landmarks that created the perimeter of the school, itself. Quite frankly, the course content might be considered *passé* to the students because the community was inundated with tangible artifacts and relics of black history in a physical and sociopolitical way.

To my surprise, an assignment for the students in the African American History class unveiled several paradoxes. The students were asked to write, "Black History Raps," and the construction of *blackness*, black music, and *maleness* new challenges emerged. This article will focus on these and the tensions created in the classroom as the students attempted to discover what it means to first, write a rap and secondly how to represent black history within this genre. The questions that guide my examination of this event were grounded in the student-teacher interactions during the time of the study. I use transcripts from the class events to disentangle the nuances of these interactions that illustrate the tension between what constitutes black history and equally what constitutes writing a rap. What was central in this study was the implications of the attempt to infuse popular culture into an academic setting. My questions are as follows (1) Are we asking students to use Hip Hop culture to "cross over" to academic literacy while some schools and teachers have yet to value or validate Hip Hop as a culture? And secondly, if schools and teachers are un-accepting of "organic" Hip Hop culture (language, style, dress, and its resistance to the status quo) can Hip Hop be used substantively in schools? In order to begin addressing these questions, there is also the responsibility for both scholars and practitioners to unveil the racial and gender constructions that are minimally, the core of what makes Hip Hop so powerful. The perception of Hip Hop is largely relegated to discussions about authorship, audience, and performance in ways that (re)construct stereotypical notions of race and gender. There are potential assumptions about race and gender that when critically examined, exploit ideology about what it means to be both black and male and the cultural norms that are thought to be a part of this racial and gender paradigm.

The data for this essay come from a micro ethnographic study conducted in a secondary African American History classroom in the southern portion of the United States. I use cultural discontinuity as a heuristic to describe the intersection of Hip Hop culture and school culture.[4] The nuances of this intersection are that arguably, black youth culture embodied in Hip Hop music is at odds with school culture. This is not to suggest that black youth culture does not include academic achievement. On the contrary, there are many successful African American students in predominantly African American school communities where blackness is not negotiated in order to access academic achievement. HBCU's are excellent examples in which racial and cultural identity are used as sources of empowerment and not tropes for racial stereotyping.[5] However, Hip Hop culture is not inherently black and not the given culture of all black males. The tension that exists between culturally relevant pedagogy and these constructions of race and gender is made visible in the classroom interactions between teachers and students.

RAP MUSIC AND THE CLASSROOM: "CHECK THE RHYME"

Within the last ten years, teachers and researchers have been investigating ways to use popular culture media as a tool for learning in classrooms.[6] Some teachers, particularly in secondary language arts and English classrooms, have included rap music in instruction for at least two specific purposes.[7] One purpose for using rap music in classrooms is to motivate seemingly uninterested students in writing activities. In this way, teachers use rap music as a catalyst for students to think about how writers use themes to discuss topics. The goal for these activities has been to promote and enhance students' access and participation in academic literacy. I define academic literacy as the use of written and oral language reflective of academic discourse and the educational standards validated by "the academy." However, to what extent has Hip Hop culture been used with the intent of making academic literacy more accessible without much, if any, pedagogical, social, cultural, or linguistic responsibility on the part of teachers for their students? What social and cultural assumptions are teachers guided by that encourage them to believe that rap music can be a useful bridge to academic literacy?

Several classroom teachers and researchers have used rap music pedagogically, tapping into the brilliance and creativity of their students, which is often ignored in traditional literacy activities. These teachers have taken risks using a "culturally relevant" pedagogical framework for making learning fun. Additionally, these teachers have sought out an African American youth art form and identified it as a valuable tool for representing artful style and linguistic prowess. However, I suggest that there is a challenge before practitioners and researchers alike with regard to how using rap in schools may lead to simplistic and stereotypical misgivings about our students as well as the cultures they may or may not embrace.

The purpose of this essay is to examine the sociocultural dilemma of using "rap" music in the classroom environment and the sociocultural tensions connected to its usage for African American secondary students who participate in Hip Hop culture outside of school. The attempt to insert "writing a rap" in the classroom where the academic discourse does not model or reflect the rap discourse was both an imposition and a "dis" to Hip Hop.

WHAT IS RAP?

Lyrically, rap music profoundly influenced how race and economics are viewed. It created a response from the music industry, which couldn't deny the popularity of rap and its sense of raw display of African-American and Latino urban street culture.

The roots of rap tap into how African-American males use street knowledge, African heritage and syncopations, politics, and the complexities of language to create what is referred to today as rap music and Hip Hop culture. Scholar Tricia Rose posits, "the politics of rap music involves the contestation over public space, expressive meaning, interpretation, and cultural capital"[8] In short, it is not just what one says, it is where one can say it, how others react to what one says, and whether one has the means with which to command public space. Rap music as a political sounding board for otherwise voiceless, alienated, and exploited people has created an awakening in society where the status quo has had to pay close attention to lyrics and lyricist.

Sociolinguist Geneva Smitherman, suggests that the talent displayed in rap music's artful and linguistic reflections of life is a sociocultural "disturbance" of the American middle class.[9] Scholarly inquiry is needed regarding the effects of rap music when it enters the classroom considering its provocative nature to create social and culture upheaval. Questions we might consider are (1) What type of rap is being considered for learning activities and (2) How is rap music being represented as a tool for teaching and learning? It is important to know whether rap is intended to be a "feel good" lyrical rhyme, which utilizes syncopation to help students memorize facts or a politically terse and rhythmic critique of life experiences textualized by the rapper using critical literacy, intertextuality, and other socially constructed literacy practices.[10] If these clarifications are not made, students who socially and culturally identify with rap music and its lyrical content may not know how to respond to the lesson or appropriate rap discourse in a classroom environment that implicitly contests these uses of language.[11]

An important aspect for appropriating rap discourse in classrooms is first, understanding the linguistic and social interactional discourses that define rap, and secondly, understanding the language features and bravado that define rap as an art form and as a means to communicate or challenge social identity. These discourses are not merely words written or spoken, but they include the context and concept for Hip Hop that makes it distinct from Blues or Rock and Roll. Despite the similarities that may exist between genres of music like The Blues and country, and Rock and Roll, identifying the nuances between genres is critical to understanding what makes music meaningful and more provacatively, how these genres represent and reflect the communities and cultures from where they emerged. The study of Hip Hop allows us to examine language, culture, race, class, and gender _in situ_, which makes Hip Hop so much more than merely hard bass beats, gutsy sexual images, and provocative language.

THE DISCOURSE OF RAP

Discourse is defined in a multitude of ways. Scholar Norman Fairclough describes discourse as "more than _just_ language use: it is language use, whether speech or writing, seen as a type of social practice."[12] Jaworski & Coupland describe discourse as

> language in use relative to social, political and cultural formations—it is language reflecting social order but also language shaping social order, and shaping individuals' interaction with society.[13]

Sociolinguist, James P. Gee, distinguishes between discourse as big "D" or little "d." Big "D" discourse (<u>D</u>) encapsulates the social and political meanings conveyed with the use of language and the embodiment of that language, as little "d" discourse (<u>d</u>) isolates meaning to the words written or spoken, literally.[14] Rap music would be comprised of <u>d</u>iscourse practices that illuminate music, rhythm, and sound. Hip Hop culture would be the <u>D</u>iscourse that gives rap music its life. Using this description of discourse as a heuristic for language, culture, and power, the <u>D</u>iscourse of Hip Hop is what makes rap music the powerful language that has transcended generations, ethnicities, and languages.

"Rap music is rooted in Black oral tradition of tonal semantics, narrativizing, signification/signifying, the dozens/playin the dozens, Africanized syntax, and other communicative practice."[15] Playing the dozens, referred to in different urban regions as checkin,' crackin,' and or burnin,' is when individuals or groups create insults about one another, family members (commonly known as "ya mama jokes"), socioeconomic status, social capital, and/or political ideologies. The use of humor and signifying takes creating narratives to another level where the narrative can be constructed around a common idea that is rooted in playin' the dozens.

Using specific African American Vernacular English (AAVE) characteristics, rap music can be distinguished from stylized poetry or simply a story that rhymes.[16] Before entering the specifics of rap music and AAVE, it must be noted that in order to be respected as a rapper, or to be "given props for "havin' skillz," the rapper must be verbally gifted. He or she is expected to hold the mic (or floor) with an arrogant confident command of his or her language. In short, he or she is expected to "come wit it," which includes rate of speech, tone, cadence, body and facial expressions. These abilities are what create the discourse of rap. Within Hip Hop culture, clairvoyance is an expectation and anything less than this generates questions as to whether or not a rapper is "true to da game."

Performances are key in rap music, for they convey messages, create imagery, and bring home the ironies and word play that makes rap music entertaining and enlightening. Smitherman's model of AAVE and its correlations to rap address the linguistic patterns in rap and the discourse modes of rap, which are significant for two reasons.[17] First, the recognition of linguistic speech patterns authentic to African Americans specifically and Africans who speak English diasporically, has been highly controversial over the past thirty years.[18] While AAVE, BE (Black English), and Ebonics are terms used to clarify the philosophical distinctions regarding whether "talking black" is a part of a formal language system or a dialect of English, the debates about whether "black talk" is *appropriate* language has not been settled.[19] The very core of the debate raises racial, political, cultural, and economic questions of language and power. This was made evident in the public "Ebonics Debate" regarding Oakland Public Schools in 1996. The highly public and political debate centered around Oakland teachers and community members advocating for using *Ebonics* as a bridge to teaching standard English. Part of this effort was the discussion of *Ebonics* as legitimate language, considering that vast numbers of African American school-aged children used similar features in their communication. A key controversy was rooted in questioning whether or not this "bastard speech" was indeed a language. This debate did not begin in 1996 with the Oakland case. In actuality, researchers, scholars, and teachers more than twenty years earlier had begun examining *black talk*.[20] Secondly, the acceptance of rap Discourse in classrooms directly connects back to the appropriateness of black speech patterns in school. The linguistic characteristics of rap are rooted in black speech patterns. Teachers who desire to use rap as a means to encourage and create learning activities will be challenged to consider the Discourse of rap, as well. For example, many students pace back and forth during presentations or they stand at a podium and read. Many students raise, increase, and decrease their tone while using body language that mimics these inflections or they use a consistent voice tone. These small characteristics of what it means to "rap" encourage or discourage students from bringing these discourses to school.

LINGUISTIC PATTERNS OF RAP

There are no set boundaries for what constitutes rap music; however, there are particular linguistic features of rap music that are significant in connecting the tenuous relationship between rap music and the classroom.

The grammatical and phonological forms of rap have three specific features.[21] These features are: (1) the habitual be; (2) zero copula; and (3) consonant word reduction. Each of these features refers to a grammatical structure that shifts the action or sound of a verb.

First, the habitual "be" is what is described as a continuum of time where the verb "to be" is not conjugated. "She be trippin'" is an example of how the speaker is suggesting that she always or typically "trips" (or behaves unpredictably). The habitual be is featured typically in rap in an attempt to express the habits of one person to another. For example, Kanye West's rap _All Falls Down_ utilizes the habitual be to emphasize pattern and habit, whereas a conjugated form of "to be" would suggest action but not continually or without provocation.

> And **she be dealing** with some issues that you can't believe
> Single black female addicted to retail and well.[22]

Next, zero copula is what is described as the absence of the verb "to be," where action is implied but not stated with the verb. Consider Talib Kweli's use of the zero copula, where action is implied as constant through the absense of the verb "to be." This absense places emphasis on the subject of the sentence rather than the behaviors of the subject.

> **This a beautiful situation** right here
> Given birth on the track cuz the cypher stay pregnant with ideas
> **And we rockin it**—rock, rock, rockin it
> Tell the hater players put a sock in it![23]

Finally, the consonant word reduction describes the dropping of the final consonant sound of a word. For the example in a gerund, the "g" is deleted or dropped from the pronunciation of a word. The first selection is not a rap, but a radio spot advertising the new Hip Hop station. What is iterated in this selection is the acknowledgment that there is a Discourse that represents Hip Hop and that this discourse is more than language but represents life. Notice in the language the word construction and the deletion of the letter "g," which changes the /ing/ sound to /en/.

> Yo, dig this! Most radio stations talk, but can they walk the walk. **Talkin'** Hip Hop is not enough. You got to live it to be it. Don't speak about it—be about it. For real. The Beat walked in **carryin'** a big stick. **And they wasn't sayin' nothin**. It's about time—ya damn skippy. Bout time [Middleville] had a station that lives the live, real, proof and uncensored, uncut Hip Hop.[24]

The Discourse of rap is represented in Hip Hop culture and in the stage performances of rappers. There is an inextricable link between the use of rap Discourse for musical and artistic purposes and the very culture lived by African American and Latino youth. It is within the minority youth culture that rappers target their audience and attempt to engage youth in a dialogic exchange around politics, economics, social justice, sexual promiscuity, philosophy, popular culture, and fashion. Each of these alone does not represent Hip Hop culture, yet all of these intertwined create a synergistic exchange that is rap.

Hip Hop culture is dynamic and is constantly being redefined. The creative structures, inconsistencies and presuppositions of identity make rap music unpredictable yet rule-governed by the sociocultural nuances of American street life. Clearly, there is an unspoken understanding that authenticity as a MC is rooted in the core of the Discourse of rap. Given the linguistic characteristics of rap and the social discourses that connect rap to the social, political, economic, and racial tenor of American life, why would the classroom environment inhibit the construction of a rap for African American students? There is a unique crossroads between rap and academic discourse that tacitly includes issues of culture, power, and language that need to be considered in attempting to understand why the intersection between the two cultures are complex.

I use ethnography as a means to understand this complexity focusing on the experiences of several African American students. I use sociolinguistics offered to the ethnography of communication as a means to analyze the data focusing on two themes: (1) students' perception of rap and (2) sense making of appropriating rap in schools. I will specifically look at one speech event dividing it in two sections corresponding to the above-stated themes.[25]

RESEARCH METHODOLOGY

This research is based on a year-long ethnographic study conducted in an inner city high school African American history course located in the southern United States. I draw on the traditions in sociolinguistic ethnography, ethnography of communication, and discourse analysis both as methodologies for data collection and analysis.[26] I served as the participant observer in the classroom, which included participating in class discussions and leading class lessons and activities. Research data included field notes, videotaped class lessons, audiotapes and videotapes of student interviews, and collections of classroom artifacts and student work. Formal and informal ethnographic interviewing processes were used with the students and the instructor throughout the data collection period.

The Curriculum

The classroom curriculum included an examination of African and African American History that followed a historical chronological pattern. Topics included the Transatlantic Slave Trade, chattel slavery in the United States, Reconstruction, and the Civil Rights Movement. A significant portion of the class included discussions of African American historical figures like Frederick Douglass, Harriet Tubman, Martin Luther King Jr., Malcolm X, and Bobby Seale. In many respects, the course content was "typical" in that it covered the icons of black history and the major social political movements. There was unique culture created in the classroom. Students often came to class discussing various topics from their own out-of-class social communities. These discussions were often encouraged by Ms. Smith, the teacher. She would ask questions about the students' experiences and then attempt to use them as transitions to the "official curriculum." While the class was dynamic in that it was student-centered and there was a place for student-culture in the class, the course content was often presented as fixed or static. The students did not actively participate in deconstructing what constituted blackness or history. I partly believe this was an assumed *given* notion because of the school demographics and the demographics of the class. However, in the lack of description and definition of these concepts, opportunities to construct the ideas with the writing of black history raps were missed.

The African American History Classroom and Participants

The African American History class is located on the third floor in the corner of the first corridor. The room is set up in a traditional manner. There are posters of world maps, famous African Americans and world leaders affixed to the walls, bulletin boards, and podium. The room is very colorful and filled with various resources including a computer that sits behind the teacher's desk.

The participants in this study were the African American History class instructor and the fourteen students in the class. Three of the fourteen students did not attend class regularly, and one of the fourteen students did not join the class until the fourth month of the study. All of the fourteen student-participants in the study were African American. Twelve of the students were males between 16- and 18-years-old. The two female students were between 15- and 18-years-old. The instructor was an African American woman in her mid-fifties and had taught for more than fifteen years in the same school district. She initiated getting the African American History course at Diamond High School by attending workshops and by earning a certificate to teach African American History. This effort was made independent of her preparedness to teach a secondary social studies curriculum. Ms. Smith was always prepared and engaged in whatever was centering in the lives of her students. She appreciated them and communicated her interests in their lives. As a teacher, she embraced her students, but she also believed in the traditional structures that defined student and teacher. I believe it was this traditional belief that separated her intentions with the rap assignment from the students' ability and willingness to create a product.

The Speech Event: "Write a Black History Rap"

The data are based on one particular speech event. It is important to note that while the greater research project involved case studies, these data are being analyzed by looking at the interactions and dialogue between all of the research participants, not solely case study participants.

In this particular event, the students were asked to write a "black history rap" and were given "rap" as a model. The "rap" the students were given, entitled, "African American History Rap" was a "list" of famous African Americans or historical events ordered alphabetically. The teacher referred to this piece as a "model" and expressed the direct expectation that the students' rap should do the following: (1) include some of the people from the model; (2) not use explicit language; and (3) try to do or say something positive. The students were given a copy of the "rap" and were told to be ready with their raps in the next two weeks. Additionally, the students needed to be prepared to present their raps in front of the class. The presentation, according to the teacher, needed to be performed.

The following field notes capture my observations and inquiries about how the teacher and the student were communicating, specifically about the black history rap.

#1 February 14, 2002
Martin gets Ms. Smith's attention. He is asking her about the raps. He wants to distinguish his rap from the ABC format. Ms. Smith is listening to him but doesn't appear to understand the idea of distinguishing his rap from the handout. He says, "How should I frame my rap so it's not culturally biased? I need to talk about some issues that may come off like-culturally biased?" What is cultural bias to Martin? What perspective of black history is he interested in presenting that would be biased?

#2 February 14, 2002 (five minutes later)
Ms. Smith is being overwhelmed with lots of questions about the task. Each student who seemed halfway interested in the assignment had a question. What is it about this assignment that is so complex? Ms. Smith stops the class states while holding the handout up in the air, "Are these people in your raps? You need to put these people-facts in your raps." I wondered, wow, are these people black history? Is black history about people or historical events or what? Can a rap be a rap with so many limitations and standards?

#3 February 18, 2002 (notes written immediately after leaving the field)
Ms. Smith, Martin, and I were in the room after the rest of the class departed. I am taking down the video camera. Martin kept looking back and forth—sort of glancing at me then Ms. Smith. I reminded Ms. Smith that I wanted to video the rap presentations. Ms. Smith immediately turns to Martin and says, "Please have black history facts in your rap." She doesn't seem to get the notion that his rap can be his words, his style, and include whatever information that fits the rap context. Martin glanced back at me as she was speaking. Is he hoping I will chime in and/or rescue him from her "cultural bias?" What do I say? Ms. Smith concluded the conversation by stating, "You are smart, intelligent—do what you'd like for your rap, but be creative." He never even got a word in edgewise. Did he have a question? Martin packed his bag and walked out of the classroom saying nothing.

The field notes were my first forms of documentation that suggested there were tensions brewing in the classroom around this assignment. Without a sense of how the students were interpreting the task and their true understanding of the assignment, videotape data were needed to support my own observations. On February 19, 2002, the students were scheduled to present/perform their raps in front of the class. The students entered the classroom and immediately engaged in a conversation with Ms. Smith about the weekend and some activities that had transpired with one of their classmates, Bret. Their conversation takes up forty minutes of the class period and leaves no time for the rap presentations. The avoidance of presenting or mentioning the rap assignment and the focus on weekend activities can be interpreted as a strategic move by the students. Creating a distraction for the instructor is an example of the students' behavior when there is an assignment they had not completed or if there is a test for which they were not prepared. During the last five minutes of class, Ms. Smith reminded the class to "be ready with your raps tomorrow." At this time, none of the students responded to Ms. Smith affirming or declining their readiness.

The transcript below is from the following day, February 20, 2002. Ms. Smith initiates class by requesting volunteers to come forward to present the raps. The transcripts represent one speech event that has been divided among two themes: (1) students' perception of rap and (2) sense making of appropriating rap in schools. I will analyze each transcript according to the theme illustrating the difficulty involved in appropriating rap Discourse in an academic setting.

Theme 1: Students' Perception of Rap
Transcript 1

1. Teacher: Klark, did you make an effort?

2. Klark: I don't rap.

3. Teacher: Did you make an effort? (Elevates tone and emphasizes effort) Did you even read it? (Says while waving the African American History rap paper)

4. Klark: I read it! (Klark does not look directly at teacher)

   (Klark looks away)

5. Teacher: Did you even try (says with emphasis) toooo (hesitates to complete phrase) put it in your own words—no.
   (time lapse)

6. Carlos: I read it and tried to write—but I couldn't put it in my own words.

7. Teacher: You couldn't put it in your own words. You couldn't think of any kind of Black history—with these Black people on here (holding the paper). You couldn't think of any (says with stress) way (moving the paper in a swooping motion) to change it around and include the Black history and make it into a rap. You couldn't write anything down at all. O.K. Michael, did you put forth any effort?

(Time lapse: Nnamdi is at the board writing a rap. He makes it seem as if he wrote this at home, but is actually composing at the board.)

8. Teacher: There ain't no bad words up there now.

9. Bret: (puts his face in his hands) I don't think everybody likes this project.

10. Teacher: It wasn't hard. You had the information all week.

11. Bret: It's kinda hard.

12. Teacher: All you had to do is read it and put it in your own words (undecipherable) don't make excuses because you didn't do it. Now be quiet.

13. Bret: (in a low tone) You wouldn't let anybody talk about it.

Transcript 1 represents the complexity of the students' resistance, where their silence represents their opposition to the assignment itself. The nature of the assignment requires the students to compose a rap. The notion of composing a rap aligns the student with taking a genre of music, which they listen to and of which they are consumers, and produce their own piece of music. Klark's initial comment, "I don't rap," in Line 2 explicitly addresses the assumption that because the students listen to rap and even come in class rapping (reciting raps to which they listen), he is not a rapper. Klark interprets this notion of not being a rapper as also being incapable of composing a rap.

The teacher questions Klark's effort and his work ethic. In Line 3 and Line 5, she asks bluntly, "Did you make an effort?" Klark is silent and does not respond. In Line 4, Klark responds to the teacher's question about whether he read the "rap" (the handout). Klark responds that he read it, but does not add any information regarding why he did not write anything. Klark and his classmates' silence led me to attempt to understand more deeply the students' perspective of the assignment and what were the possible factors that impeded their ability, interest, or desire to complete the assignment. Before illustrating the students' perspective of the assignment, I want to note Line 7 and 8, where Carlos emphasizes he read the assignment but could not put it into his own words. This statement re-emphasizes Carlos' understanding that he had to use his own words to rewrite someone else's rap, which in the Hip Hop community, creates an ethical dilemma. Unlike sampling, where a rap artist creates his own music or rap by borrowing the music or a beat from another song, the rap content is not duplicated. Line 7 demonstrates the teacher's lack of knowledge of rap culture or rules when she laments, "You couldn't put it in your own words. You couldn't think of any kind of Black history—with these Black people on here. . . . You couldn't think of any way to change it around and include the Black history and make it into a rap." Again, re-arranging someone else's words does not constitute writing a rap.

Additionally, the limitations placed on the students to reword the model "rap" and also to "use the black people" mentioned in the "rap" neither allows the students to authentically use their own creativity nor does it afford them the opportunity to define black history.

Lines 11 and 13 are particularly significant. Bret states he doesn't believe anyone likes the project and that the teacher wouldn't let anybody talk about it. Bret is expressing the sentiment that the students needed to talk about the assignment because there were issues that were not clear. His statement also suggests that their attempt to initiate a dialogue about what constitutes writing rap would have been helpful. The lack of dialogue between the students and the instructor is examined and how it affects the students' willingness to participate in the lesson. Bret concludes, "I don't think everyone likes this project," which speaks to the students' lack of voice and power in constructing knowledge around the parameters of appropriating rap in school.

Theme 2: Sense Making in Appropriating Rap Discourse in School
Transcript 2

1. Martin: Let's record it. Let's record it and like play it. . . .

2. Teacher: Look, this—(begins listening to Martin). . . .

3. Martin: And play it on tape.

4. Teacher: (teacher is obviously frustrated with class) This is the 2nd week (begins holding up the paper) that I gave you this paper last week. This is into the 2nd week and I have not heard from you yet. Now what's the excuse? Now you're talking about let you record it first?

5. Martin: And then just play it. That's embarrassing. You can't stand up—

6. Teacher: (teacher breaks in) What's embarrassing? Embarrassing to whom?

7. Bret (adding): Scared.

8. Teacher: (teacher quickly responding) Scared of what?

9. Bret: Our fellow classmates.

10. Teacher: Teacher: Look! Stop handing me those little first grade excuses and stop behaving like that—you know better.

(All of the students' body posturing is sunken. Either their heads are in their hands and they are looking down or they are leaning their bodies forward in a subordinate position.)

11. Martin: All I'm sayin' Ms. Smith—it's different. A rap is different from an essay or a speech. It's a rap. (Emphasizes rap.) You know—you have ta—its ya own personal style. However you want to display it.

12. Teacher: (teacher nodding head as if to agree) Exactly.

13. Martin (continues): And you getting' up in front of a crowd (begins to lightly chuckle) and bustin' out—

14. Carlos (breaks in at Martin's pause): You always elaborate.

15. Teacher: Shhh! Let one person talk at a time. (Not turning her attention from Martin)

16. Nicole: (mumbling softly) I'm ready to go home. (Nnamdi begins stretching elaborately in his seat)

17. Martin: Now, if we would be able to record it and bring it and just play it.

18. Teacher: Well, why?

19. Martin: We can walk out of the room. And you know whatever—You know what I'm sayin.' People feel uncomfortable just standin' in front of people period just saying hello—let alone just sayin rap. He stresses the word "rap."

20. Bret: I agree.

21. Teacher: I, o.k., well I gave you—(holding up the papers; then responds to Nnamdi) You can erase that (waving the paper upwards).

22. Nnamdi: Ah man, I'll do mine. (Nnamdi gets up from his seat approaching the dry erase board while asking the teacher) "Can I erase this?"

23. Martin: I'm not trying to make up no excuses—this is the truth. I know how I feel about it. (Martin states in a low tone) I should have recorded it.

24. Teacher: (Interrupting Martin) That's the best thing you could have said (tapping the papers against the desk) because this like I said the 2nd week. I gave this paper to you last week. So that's the best thing you could have said. "I should have (puts emphasis on "should have") already done it." Now—uhhh.

Transcript 2 is an interesting moment in the speech event because the students and the instructor are at an impasse. Martin speaks up first to address the difficulties of presenting the raps in class. Although he presents his argument around the idea of performing the rap, he is conveying an idea that rap Discourse encompasses an appropriated setting for rapping that is not regimented, like a classroom, and allows for students to *transform* their school identity to a nonschool identity. This inability to transform is representative of the manifestation of the cultural discontinuity between rap music and schools. Line 11 exemplifies Martin's position that a rap requires an allowance for style that is inconsistent with a classroom environment. He expresses the notion that a rapper has to rap in his own style, unlike an essay, which conforms to a standard that is appropriate for the classroom environment. This statement is significant because it illustrates how Martin is keenly aware of academic discourse and nonacademic discourse. Additionally, his comment also suggests there are ramifications for when students have appropriated AAVE and different types of stylized discourse in school. It appears that he might be looking for a "pass" from the teacher in order to begin thinking about how to infuse one culture into another. Considerations might be whether there would be any risk associated with performing a "rap" in class. Would the teacher view him positively if his rap included "edgy" or controversial ideas. Line 17 reflects Martin's early position that recording the rap at home and bringing the tape in allows the student to retain a student identity while the rap can be listened to in class. The student who records his or her rap can play the student role and act as a participant in the class while the rap is playing, which does not threaten or challenge the school identity. Ultimately, Martin attempts to negotiate the complexities of rapper identity versus student identity by suggesting another format.

Martin's suggestion along with Bret's support and Carlos' attempt to provide additional support for the argument signifies the shared belief of the students that the classroom is a difficult place to perform a rap. The teacher only seems to recognize the length of time the students had to complete assignment, unable to recognize the correlation between writing a rap, performing it, and the Discourse required to authentically support the genre.

"Maybe I didn't see this clearly"

One of the significant aspects of social science research is to ensure that your perspective as the researcher is not being used to interpret the events that you have observed or recorded. In an effort to make sure that my interpretation of events were shared by the students, I conducted several follow-up interviews. In a conversation with Klark and Carlos, they explained why he didn't do the assignment.

Carlos said," I ain't no—I'm not a rapper, so I can't just—you know what I'm saying. Say somethin' off the top of my head and then put it together and make it sound like a real good rap. I'd have to really take out a lot of time or just ask my brother, cause he raps."

Klark also shared this sentiment in his comments. "Because I don't rap and then on the other hand we had to stand up in front of everybody and read it. And you know, if it don't sound right . . . (begins shaking his head)"

It is the voices of Klark and Carlos that resonates with the social and cultural implications when considering the role of Hip Hop culture in schools. One of the operating assumptions is that black youth or blackness is synonymous with Hip Hop or at least relates to it. This assumption is taken up by Klark and Carlos explicitly as they express candidly that they listen to and like rap, but they do not qualify as rappers. Klark and Carlos also do not believe their peers identify themselves as rappers.

There are several issues embedded in this data set that can be analyzed and further discussed. Perhaps the issue of why the "ABC Rap" was so easily constituted as rap by the teacher was because rap music has been commodified and reduced to rhyme schemes and music. During an era where Hip Hop culture is so heavily embedded in everyday life, what aspects of this "rap" other than its title, seemed akin to what Hip Hop is all about. One might suggest that in the teacher's attempt to embrace Hip Hop culture, she begins with what she considers "safe," and academically oriented rhyme, not considering a preemptive discussion among her students about what rap is and how one might go about creating one. The intention to continually support a culturally responsive environment is derailed because of a greater challenge. The usurpation of society's interpretive frame of "appropriate" Hip Hop against Hip Hop culture's understanding of a social and cultural way of life has created a tension that plays itself out in mainstream spaces. For example, black youth rhyming or checkin' (playin' the dozens) in the hallway of school or even in the middle of class quickly warrants suspension, particularly if the event itself generates a "hype crowd." Most schools regard this behavior negatively and resort to disciplinary action because it "appears to be violent, disruptive or potentially hazardous." When I taught middle school, it was customary to hear my African American male students making beats by tapping their pencils or pounding their fists on the tops of their desks. The girls would crowd around or dance on the side. Frequently, this was done while waiting for my instructional directions. Albeit disruptive in the sense that it was often loud and the boys would jump and shout when a beat was "on point," I was challenged to recognize that these events were creative, bonding, and useful for their social and cultural relationship building. As an agent of the school, I found myself spewing the discourse of *appropriate* and *untimeliness* when alerting my students that I was ready to begin. It is through my own reflective lens and as a participant observer in this study that I now question whether classrooms are ready to embrace Hip Hop culture at all.

DISCUSSION OF RESEARCH FINDINGS

It is evident from the transcripts that the instructor's intentions were taken up by the students, as they suggested alternative creative ways to accomplish the same goal. The tension among the students that lead to the class conflict manifested in how the students interpreted how rap was being constituted by the teacher and how black history was subsequently being framed. In other discussions with the participants in the study, they found it complicated to challenge why the people in the "ABC Rap" represented black history and not others. Subsequently, this study helps raise new questions about the consequences of superimposing Hip Hop, a space that African American males by and large define on school curricula. In essence, Hip Hop is countercultural to school and therefore inherently problematic. What forms of power exist in school settings where the authority on a cultural form (traditionally, in this case African American males and Hip Hop) is not empowered to use this authority in school? There are layers of issues involved in how cultural authority is tacitly usurped by the hegemony of the institution itself. To be done well, there is an explicit intentionality that is required of teachers that is as explicit as the genre itself. Students should know what constructions are valued and which will be "taken up" in the classroom even if and when they defy the status quo of formalized academic systems.

Next, the teacher's emphasis on _appropriate_ behavior for the young men represents her alliance with school culture and the cultural norms, which are expected for students. Even in the context of an assignment she created, there was emphasis placed on all things moral and ethical unlike in other class assignments. The students may have found the teacher's matriarchal dialogues and subsequent enforcement of school rules and regulations indicators that she would **not** approve of any behavior, language, word play, or references that appeared antithetical to those beliefs even if they were in fulfillment of her assignment. The students' power as African Americans and males who self identify as members of Hip Hop culture, while affirmed frequently in the context of the course, is neglected in the context of this assignment, which includes content and form.

Next, these data reflect social constructions of literacy and history that are now gaining a great deal of attention in schools.[27] The use of popular culture, film, music, sitcoms, and prime time animated cartoons as tools to discuss traditional school texts is gaining momentum. The use of intertextuality as a means to increase critical thinking, comprehension, and textual awareness has added to the scholarship of literacy in secondary classrooms.[28] While this research field is growing and the use of popular culture and intertextual teaching methods are being introduced in schools, there are still questions about what forms of popular culture (e.g., rap music) are appropriate for academic engagement or more profoundly, how might teachers' knowledge of popular culture impact the success of its use in academic learning environments? Rap music has been stigmatized as being violent, sexually perverse, and laden with racial overtones and often ignored for its potential as critical pedagogy. Furthermore, because rap music reflects overwhelmingly African American and Latino culture, using it in schools requires an acceptance of not only the music, but the Discourses of African American and Latino communities. This requires a tremendous shift in schools' ideologies about academic discourse and appropriate language.

THE COMMODIFICATION OF RAP

Rap music and Hip Hop culture have been commodified and commercialized to an extent that its high profile visibility has made it virtually invisible to many 1970s era hip hoppers that originated the music and culture. White middle-class youth have responded to rap music and influenced the market significantly. Rap has become a commodity used for material gain—not just within the Hip Hop community, but also by large corporations who have invested large amounts of money into marketing mainstream products. Everything from bread, soda, cars, cell phones, even potato chips have been marketed using rap discourse or Hip Hop cultural forms, more broadly. One of the consequences for the mass marketing of rap has been its dilution. In short, rap has been made palatable to fit the social consciousness of mainstream society and has lost the essence of many of the issues and messages it once conveyed. In some cases, rap no longer encompasses an edge, which keeps the pulse of urban society and the sociopolitical challenges for African American and Latino youth. For many hip hoppers, hip hop presently uses funky beats and rhyme schemes for relatively superficial topics. Additionally, many rap artists have limited the command for complex language usage and ability to connect the present and the past using allegory to overly simplistic repetitive words and ideas. Sadly, this minimalist rap gains favor on the airways while more thoughtfully orchestrated beats and rhymes are left to the black market and underground radio shows. Subsequently, the commodification of rap has made it more acceptable for dominant society ultimately creating a demarcation between its consumption and its appreciation. This research presents data that illuminates the question of whether classroom activities contribute to this type of commodification? Do teachers have a sense of why "we" rap at all?

CONCLUSION

In a provocative skit on *The Chappelle Show*,[29] comedian Paul Mooney expressed the notion that being black is popular. American society has blossomed partly because of its access to and reproduction of black art, music, language, and culture. One interesting aspect of Mooney's comment is that while much of black culture has been mimicked, replicated, and in some cases denigrated, there are other aspects of black culture that have been "sold." We have seen the black churches placed on display for entertainment in chicken commercials, television award shows, and movies. We have witnessed the wisdoms of our mothers and grandmothers turned into minstrels and performed in transgendered fashion. Placing rap music on a proverbial platter for society to consume is miniscule in scale when considering the many other ways black life and culture have been consistently commodified. Mooney's comedic critique posits that society will market black life without relative interest in the essence or preservation of black culture. Concomittant to this are the discussions of "race" that likely centralize both black and youth culture, which presently remain submerged under colorblind and colormute praxis.[30] Yet, the gate keepers of Hip Hop culture, the youth of our society who are often scorned for their seemingly careless attitude about black history have spoken up to defend, if not preserve the integrity of Hip Hop. This data illustrates that even in their silence, these youth have claimed Hip Hop to be theirs.[31] As practitioners and researchers, we must consider the possible emerging questions that challenge the notion of bringing students' social and cultural identities into academic spaces, particularly when these identities are generally undervalued by the larger society and marginalized by schools. It is essential that as we begin an attempt to embrace our students' interests, we simultaneously (co)construct ways to think about what is required of us and our students to thrive. This does not suggest that black and Latino cultures are not ideal for schools any more than Asian of white culture. One must note that this complexity and challenge rarely exists for Asian and white students. Perhaps one of the many entangling webs that disturb the relationship between Hip Hop and classrooms is the acknowledgement that although Hip Hop culture and rap music can be adopted, replicated, and performed by many people representing many ethnic and racial backgrounds, Hip Hop culture and its authenticity will always be measured and validated by the black Hip Hop community, and as illustrated in this study, black youth.

NOTES

[1] *School Daze*, DVD, directed by Spike Lee (1988; US: Sony Pictures, 2001); *Drumline*, DVD, directed by Charles Stone III (US: Twentieth Century Fox, 2003); *Stomp the Yard*, directed by Sylvain White (US: Sony Pictures, 2007).

[2] See, for example, *"A Different World,"* DVD, numerous directors (1987; US: Urban Works, 2002).

[3] Cynthia H. Willams, "The 'Sound of Blackness': African American Language, Social and Cultural Identities, and Academic Success in a Middle School Language Arts Classroom Environment." Ph.D. diss. Vanderbilt University, 2007.

[4] John Ogbu. "Cultural Discontinuities and Schooling," *Anthropology and Education Quarterly*, 14 (Fall 1982): 291–306.

[5] Sonia Nieto, *Affirming Diversity: The Sociopolitical Context of Multicultural Education*. Fourth Edition (Boston, Massachussetts, 2004).

[6] Ayanna F. Brown, "'I Am Black and Male, But I Am Not a Rapper': An Ethnographic Study of Intra-group Cultural Discontinuity in a Secondary African American History Classroom," paper presented at the annual meeting of the American Education Research Association, Chicago, Illinois, April 21–25, 2003.

[7] Jeff Duncan-Andrade and Ernest Morrell, "Turn Up That Radio, Teacher: Popular Cultural Pedagogy in New Century Urban Schools," *Journal of School Leadership* 15 (2005): 284-308; Jabari Mahiri and Soraya Sablo, "Writing for Lives: The Non-School Literacy of California's Urban African American Youth," *The Journal of Negro Education* 65 (Spring 1996): 164–80.

[8] Tricia Rose, *Black Noise: Rap Music and Black Culture in Contemporary America* (New England, 1994).

[9] Geneva Smitherman, "The Chain Remain the Same: Communicative Practices in the Hip-Hop Nation," *Journal of Black Studies* 28 (Fall 1997): 3–25.

[10] David Bloome and Ann Egan-Robertson, "The Social Construction of Intertextuality in Classroom Reading and Writing Lessons," *Reading Research Quarterly* 28 (Summer 1993): 305–32; Elaine Richardson "'To Protect and Serve': African American Female Literacies," *CCC* (Winter 2002): 675–703; John Gumperz and Jenny Cook-Gumperz, "Introduction: Language and the Communication of social Identity," in *Language and Social Identity*, ed. John J. Gumperz (Massachussetts, 1982), 1–21; Shirley Brice Heath, "What No Bedtime Story Means: Narrative Skills at Home and at School," *Language in Society* (1982): 49–76.

[11] Elaine Richardson, "To Protect and Serve," 675–703.

[12] Norman Fairclough, *Critical Language Awareness* (London, 1992).

[13] Adam Jaworski and Nikolas Coupland, *The Discourse Reader* (London, 1999), 1.

[14]James Paul Gee, *Social Linguistics and Literacities: Ideology in Discourse* (London, 1996).

[15]Nancy Guevara, Women Writin' Rappin' Breakin' in *Droppin' Science: Critical Essays on Rap Music and Hip Hop Culture*, ed. William E. Perkins (Pennsylvania, 1996).

[16]Baugh, 198; Richardson, 2002.

[17]Geneva Smitherman, "Black English/Ebonics: What It Be Like?" in *The Real Ebonics Debate: Power, Language, and the Education of African American Children*, eds. Theresa Perry and Lisa Delpit (Massachussetts, 1988): 29–37.

[18]Theresa Perry and Lisa Delpit, *The Real Ebonics Debate: Power, Language, and the Eduction of African American Children* (Massachussetts, 1988): 225.

[19]John Baugh, *Black Street Speech* (Texas, 1983); Cynthia Williams, *The 'Sound of Blackness': African American Language, Social and Cultural Identities, and Academic Success in a Middle School Language Arts Classroom Environment* (Tennessee, 2007); John Rickford, *African American Vernacular English* (England, 1999).

[20]Cynthia Williams, *The 'Sound of Blackness': African American Language, Social and Cultural Identities, and Academic Success in a Middle School Language Arts Classroom Environment* (Tennessee, 2007); John Rickford, *African American Vernacular English* (England, 1999).

[21]Genevera Smitherman, "The Chain Remain the Same: Communicative Practices in the Hip-Hop Nation," 3; Geneva Smitherman, "Black English/Ebonics: What It Be Like?" in *The Real Ebonics Debate: Power, Language, and the Education of African American Children*, 29; Walt Wolfram and Erik Thomas, *The Development of African American English* (United Kingdom, 2002), 237.

[22]Kanye West, "All Falls Down," *The College Dropout*, Roc-A-Fella Records (2004).

[23]Talib Kweli, "Put it in the Air," *Quality*, Rawkus Entertainment (2002).

[24]WUBT 101.1 commercial excerpt, Clear Channel Communications.

[25]Dell Hymes, *Foundations in Sociolinguistics: An Ethnographic Approach* (Pennsylvania, 1974), 260.

[26]David Bloome and Ann Egan-Robertson. "The Social Construction of Intertextuality in Classroom Reading and Writing Lessons," 305–32; Jenny Cook-Gumperz, "Dilemmas of Identity: Oral and Written Literacies in the Making of a Basic Writing Student," *Anthropology and Education Quarterly* (Spring 1993): 336–56.

[27]David Kirkland, "The Boys in the Hood: Exploring Literacy in the Lives of Six Urban Adolescent Black Males," Ph.D. diss. Michigan State University, 2006.

[28]Elizabeth Mojie and David O'Brien, *Constructions of Literacy: Studies of Teaching and Learning In and Out of Secondary Schools* (New Jersey, 2001), 357.

[29]David Chappelle. First broadcast in January 2003 by Comedy Central.

[30]Ayanna F. Brown, "Constructing 'Race' Through Talk: A Micro-Ethnographic Investigation of Discussions of 'Race' among African American Secondary Students," Ph.D. diss., Vanderbilt University, 2008, 308.

[31]Stephanie Power Carter, "She Still Would've Made That Face Expression": The Use of Multiple Literacies by Two African American Young Women," *Theory into Practice* 45 (November 2006): 352–58.

TRANSFORMING THE *CARMEN* NARRATIVE:
THE CASE OF *CARMEN THE HIP HOPERA*

Paula Marie Seniors

The many interpretations of *Carmen* reflected Orientalism and always revolved around the outsiders' gaze on the exotic beginning in 1845 with French writer Prosper Merimee's racy novella set in Seville, Spain in 1820 and narrated by a French archeologist.[1] Voyeurism continued to dominate the story with French composer George Bizet's 1874 opera *Carmen* and white writers Richard Rodgers and Oscar Hammerstein's interpretation of Southern African American life in *Carmen Jones* (1943/1954). These versions gave whites an avenue to leave the constraints of European mores of civility behind as voyeurs of the exotic, and they exploited caste systems. Bizet and Merimee's *Carmen* offered audiences two ethnicities—the Romani and the Basque—both outsiders in Spanish culture, while *Carmen Jones* exploited African American class differences.[2] But what happens to the story of *Carmen* when the outsiders gaze disappears and the interpretation is from an insider's perspective?

In 2000 MTV writer Michael Elliott IV, lyricist Sekani Williams, and director Robert Townsend (all African Americans) decided that *Carmen* needed a modern retelling and envisioned *Carmen the Hip Hopera* for television with a Hip Hop audience in mind. Set in North Philadelphia it starred an all African American cast led by singer Beyoncé Knowles as Carmen Brown, actor Mekhei Phifer as Liutenant Derrick Hill, and rapper Mos Def as the villain Sergeant Frank Miller. In *Josephine Baker in Life and Art: The Icon and the Image*, contemporary scholar Benetta Jules Rosette analyzed Baker's life through A. J. Greimas and Vladimir Propp's master narrative structure, which presents an excellent research model to study the *Carmen* narrative. Using this theoretical model, historical analysis, the Hip Hop study of T. Denean Sharpley-Whiting, and Hip Hop film arguments of Norma Manatu, S. Craig Watkins, and Paula J. Masood, I will compare the earlier versions of *Carmen* to *Carmen the Hip Hopera* to discuss whether Carmen is transformed when the producers, writers, directors, and performers are all African American.[3]

In *Hip Hop in American Cinema* Melvin Donalson maintains that Hip Hop—rap, music, dance, dee jaying, and graffiti art fit nicely into the Hollywood movie musical model. Donalson contends that movie musicals relied heavily on popular music during each historical period. The popularity of Hip Hop in the 1980s led filmmakers to make *Beat Street* (1984), *Krush Groove* (1985), and *School Daze* (1988) to capitalize on the genre.[4] In the 1990s Broadway delved into Hip Hop with *Bring in Da Noise Bring in Da Funk* (1995), the story of Africans in America, and in 2000 Danny Hoch founded the Hip Hop Theater Festival in New York City.[5] *Carmen the Hip Hopera* fits into the Hip Hop musical genre. To understand whether the *Carmen* narrative is transformed, we must consider the novella.

Prosper Merimee's *Carmen* revolved around the exploits of brown skinned-Moorish Carmen, a lascivious Romani woman, an outcast in Spanish culture, a liar, a cheat, and a seducer of men.[6] The story unfolds with her seduction of Don Jose the fair-haired, blue-eyed Basque, a corporal in the Dragoons, another outsider in Spanish culture.[7] When she grows tired of him she callously casts him aside. Distraught by this turn of events Don Jose murders Carmen. Bizet's opera follows the story of the novella, as does *Carmen Jones*, while *Carmen the Hip Hopera* appears more benign given that Derrick Hill, Don Jose's counterpart foregoes committing murder.

Through the master narrative structure we discover that *Carmen the Hip Hopera* departs from the caste system due to the all African American cast and protagonists who belong to the same socio-economic class. Jules Rosette's analyzed Josephine Baker's life through the master narrative structure functions of the tests that the hero must take for success in the narrative. For this study I will examine *Carmen the Hip Hopera* through the initial situation, what Propp and Greimas define as the point in a story where the family is introduced.[8]

The film exposes the urban landscape of North Philly, a decrepit and rundown neighborhood, rife with crime and graft, a victim of discriminatory Federal policies, including the Federal Housing Act of 1934, urban renewal, and discriminatory housing practices which led to this decay.[9] It is in this environment that the family is introduced—Derrick Hill/Don Jose, a Lieutenant in the Philadelphia police force. He personifies African American middle-class stability and upward mobility due to his government job.[10] The characterization of Sergeant Hill as middle class replicates Don Jose, his upper middle-class Basque counterpart from the novella whose ethnicity positions him on the margins of Spanish society, and Joe the fly-boy from *Carmen Jones*. Although Derrick Hill is a good cop whose manhood remains intertwined with his job—"becoming a cop is like becoming a man to me," we must consider that his cop status marks him as an outsider in the African American community given the sometimes-contentious relationship between African Americans and the police. Ultimately, he holds the same marginal position as Don Jose, an insider yet on the outside.[11] The initial situation reveals that the film is not really about Carmen Brown but rather it is about Derrick Hill/Don Jose.

The centering of the story on Hill reproduces trends in rap, Hip Hop music, and film. S. Craig Watkins argues that Hip Hop fails to respect the African American girl and woman and that it lacks emancipatory and "empowering images of African American women," by concentrating wholly on the plight of the African American male.[12] In *African American Women and Sexuality in the Cinema* Norma Manatu contends that African American male filmmakers portray black female sexuality more negatively than white filmmakers, which supports Hip Hop feminist filmmaker Rachel Raimist's argument that films like *Boyz n the Hood* replicate virulent stereotypes about African American females. Raimist maintains that affirmative representations of African American women and girls like Michael Jackson's *Thriller* written by Jackson and video director white filmmaker John Landis, or African American female filmmaker Darnell Martin's *I Like it Like That* (1994), which both centered the story on African American women remain few. S. Craig Watkins maintains that Hip Hop erases the real lived "cultural" experiences of African American women and girls by erasing their interests, desires, dreams, and stories.[13] The initial situation reveals that *Carmen the Hip Hopera* duplicates this trend and also introduces the viewer to the villain, Sergeant Miller.

"BLACK COP"—THE VILLAIN IS PRESENTED

The master narrative structure dictates that a villain must exist in the story, with a primary and secondary motivation for his/her vendetta against the hero.[14] In *Carmen the Hip Hopera* we meet the corrupt Lieutenant Miller who typifies the bad cop on the take in an unmarked police vehicle extorting money from Pockets, the drug dealer (Jermaine Dupri).

This scene illuminates the realities of urban renewal and its effect on the African American community. From 1967 to 1976 a million retail, manufacturing, and wholesale jobs disappeared in Philadelphia, New York, Chicago, and Detroit, where by 1982 over a quarter of the nation's poor lived.[15] The loss of blue-collar jobs held by African American males led to their massive unemployment and by 2006 their situation remained dire as their work opportunities and social advancement diminished.[16] Some found low wage work as janitors, in hospitals, as deliverymen, and food outlets. Many found themselves feeling hopeless, without job prospects, and some turned to crime, drug dealing, and drug use.[17] The scene with Pockets, the drug dealer and Lieutenant Miller illustrates this reality of African American urban life.

This scene also makes clear that Lieutenant Miller typifies the criminal cop, the unwelcomed interloper in the African American community. The rapper KRS-One discusses the shortage of African American police officers in "Black Cop."

Black cop!! Black cop black cop Black cop
Thirty years, there were no black cops
You couldn't even run, drive round the block.[18]

The lack of African American cops in Philadelphia further complicated the already bad situation that African Americans experienced when they came in contact with white cops.[19] When African American police officers joined the force this also caused tensions in African American neighborhoods due to the strained relations between the African American community and the cops. KRS-One states:

Recently police trained black cop
To stand on the corner, and take gun shot
This type of warfare isn't new or a shock
It's black on black crime again nonstop.[20]

Many of the newly appointed African American police officers appeared upstanding, although their status as law enforcers further problematized the already tenuous situation with African Americans given the potential of "black on black crime again nonstop."[21] Other police officers like Lieutenant Miller in the film replicated their corrupt white counterparts.

Lieutenant Miller's character represents police corruption and its influence on the African American community. Miller in a sense reproduces all the negative attributes of dishonest police officers such as Detective Julio C. Vasquez of the New York City Police force. In 2003 the state arrested Vasquez for stealing $169,000 from a drug dealer and selling cocaine over a five-year period.[22] He was on the take like his fictional counterpart Lieutenant Miller who replicated real-life police corruption.

After Miller's extortion of Pockets he and Sergeant Hill answer a call concerning a stolen Durango. Miller arrives before Hill only to discover Jalil, the mini criminal played by a prepubescent Lil' Bow Wow running away from the truck. Lieutenant Miller gives chase and when he finally catches Jalil in an alley he plants drugs at his feet. This scene illuminates the criminalization of African American youth and the aversion that many African Americans hold for the "Black Cop," due to these types of negative interactions. In 2000 both African American and white Philadelphia police officers shot and brutally beat African American Thomas Jones. Despite evidence including a videotape of the beating, the criminal justice system found these officers innocent.[23] So it is no wonder that Jalil runs when he sees the "Black Cop." Miller represents the worst element, the immoral police officer of KRS-One's "Black Cop."

> Black Cop!! Black cop black cop black cop
> Stop shootin black people, we all gonna drop
> You don't even get paid a whole lot
> So take your M-60 and put it 'pon lock
> Lookin' for your people when you walk down the block.[24]

"Black Cop" demonstrates the precarious relationship between the African American community and the African American cop. Miller embodies all the attributes of the debased and dangerous "Black Cop," with his harmful interactions with Jalil. This scene sheds lights on the disturbing trend in Hip Hop culture to criminalize African American youngsters. Hip Hop equates this type of peccancy to "authentic Blackness," in order to encourage children to liken lawlessness to heroism.

JALIL, THE MINI CRIMINAL— CRIMINALIZING AFRICAN AMERICAN YOUTH

In the film we see a nine- or ten-year-old Jalil in the prison yard with grown men, a licentiously charged environment. They lift weights while Jalil uses highly sexualized language for a young child. Upon observing the victim of Miller's vendetta, Derrick Hill, imprisoned due to Carmen's transgressions, writing to Carmen says,

"Got a Jones, huh?" which presents this child as a little sexualized man.[25] The scene while humorous in the context of the film, remains jarring and harsh in the portrayal of the child as a sexually knowledgeable felon and exposes sexual abuse of young African American boys, a very real experience for those in the Hip Hop community. In *Vixens Diaries* Karrine Steffans identifies African American male singer Norwood Young as a kindred spirit due to their shared experience as child sexual abuse survivors. Steffans draws the connection between abuse, lack of self-esteem, and promiscuity; which for some can lead to prison. The filmmaker's cavalier portrayal of Jalil as a sexually knowledgeable convict remains irresponsible and reprehensible.[26] The scene also brings to light the history of the creation of the African American as felonious.

The criminalization of African Americans took on added meaning during and after Reconstruction with the emergence of Black codes—vagrancy and apprentice laws, and the prison system with its convict and contract labor. All of these painted African Americans as delinquent, reestablished them as a serf class, and prevented them from voting.[27] The drawing of African American youth as lawless continued into the twenty-first century with African Americans receiving higher conviction rates than whites for offenses connected to drugs. In 2002 Pennsylvania incarcerated 3,108 African Americans compared to 281 whites. African Americans experienced disenfranchisement because one out of seven ex-felons lost the right to vote in Florida and Georgia due to these convictions. Racial profiling also proved a potent strategy for ensuring their criminalization.[28]

Jalil's scenes uncover the emergence of African American "disconnected youth" with 5.5 million of them without jobs and few opportunities for financial or social advancement. Angela Davis notes that U.S. schools act as conduits to prison as the government moves away from a commitment to education and building schools to growing the prison industrial complex. Administrators pushed struggling students out of school leading to high dropout rates, and programs to train young people for the job market disappeared. This created an environment in which few job opportunities exists for the African American working class youth except the military; which as in the Vietnam War has led to African American overrepresentation in all U.S. wars including the Iraq and Afghanistanian Wars. This legacy of neglect of the African American working class by the State, the government, and social welfare organizations remains shameful.[29] In *Carmen the Hip Hopera* Jalil's presence tenders a romanticized vision of prison life over educational attainment, as we never see him in school, but rather in a fantasy adult jail. We don't see the reality of the African American prisoner, the loss of freedom, innocence/virginity, and the right to vote.

In *Tragic Failure* Tom Wicker contends that an apparent conspiracy to criminalize African American men and boys exists given how the laws for drug possession were created, and the severity of the punishment for non-violent drug offenders whose sentences in many cases exceed those who commit murder, robbery, or rape.[30] I would like to argue that contemporary Hip Hop music remains a co-conspirator in propagandizing African American youth as lawless. Hip-hop glorifies youthful peccancy with songs like "Beautiful Girls"(2008) by the seventeen-year-old African American singer Sean Kingston. "Beautiful Girls" (2008) not only trivializes suicide, a rising problem in the African American community, but the video set in the "innocent" 1950s teen soda shop and the bouncy tune obscure the throwaway lyrics that promote youthful illegal activity.[31]

> It was back in '99,
> Watchin' movies all the time,
> Oh when I went away,
> For doin' my first crime.[32]

Kingston's lyrics let the listener know that his recalcitrant behavior continued after his "first crime." Similarly, African American "Ghetto" R&B singer Jaheim's "Put Your Woman First" also aggrandizes malfeasance and jail culture to a catchy beat.

> If it wasn't for parole
> Steady duckin' my P.O. [Parole officer]
> Girl You Know . . .
> Tell me how could I ever forget to be your lover[33]

These types of lyrics contribute to the insidious nature of promoting criminal activity over education and create an environment where African American youth aspire to going away for doing their "first crime" and "duckin' my P.O." as opposed to dreaming of erudition through higher education. Comparably, *Carmen the Hip Hopera's* filmmakers cynical drawing of Jalil as a mini criminal remains just as specious as Kingston's and Jaheim's lyrics and contribute to the conspiracy that Wicker points to of criminalizing African American youth, especially given the very real-lived experiences of African American men and boys. Jalil in effect replicates hip-hop's elevation of the African American male as a convict without offering the viewer the consequences of malfeasance, undereducation, incarceration, sexual abuse, overrepresentation in war, and in many cases death. As *Carmen the Hip Hopera* progresses we *finally* meet Carmen Brown.

CARMEN THE INTERDICTION

The master narrative analysis of *Carmen the Hip Hopera* reveals Carmen Brown as what Vladimir Propp and A. J. Greimas call the interdiction—the prohibition by decree.[34] In the novella and the opera Carmen is marked as an outsider in Spanish and European society given that she is a "copper-skinned" Romani, defined as an outcast of Europe due to the Romanies dark skin, nomadic lifestyle, language, practice of the occult, and non-Christian status. The Romani remain on the margins of white mainstream society because of racism and discrimination. Erroneously named gypsies by whites when they arrived in Europe 1,000 years ago, Europeans initially treated them with deference and respect.[35] This soon changed with the rise of anti-Romani sentiment and laws. The Romani soon found themselves enslaved in places such as the Balkans in the 1300s and Spain in the late 1700s, coerced into forced labor; and forcibly removed from France and Spain in the 1600s.[36] To justify their oppression, Europeans created stereotypes that deemed Romanies thieves, criminals, immoral, unclean, hypersexual, and practitioners of the occult.[37]

In the novella Carmen represents all these stereotypes. She personifies hypersexuality, she fights, steals, and seduces every man who crosses her path including Don Jose while brashly flouting her marriage to a fellow Romani. Carmen embodies all the attributes of the ultimate bad girl. Carmen begins her seduction of Don Jose by speaking Basque and attributes her mastery of the language to her nomadic lifestyle.[38] Carmen cuts a woman at the cigar factory who called Carmen the "adopted daughter of Satan," she is so bad that she runs a group of bandits and contrabandists; and smuggles a knife in bread for Don Jose's escape from prison.[39] This is one bad chick.

Carmen Brown of *Carmen the Hip Hopera* appears to emulate her doppelganger in the novella. Dressed in a very form-fitting red dress with a high slit, which references Dorothy Dandridge's *Carmen Jones* and Merimee's Carmen; Carmen enters the bar at the top of the stairs to Bizet's "Habanera," a reference to the opera.[40]

Beyoncé Knowles' Carmen appears bold, bad, and sexy, the object of overt lust from the men in the bar but not nearly as dangerous as Merimee's *Carmen*. Just one gaze from Carmen Brown and the men cannot resist her. She causes a minor ruckus by catching the eye of a police officer who looks at her a little too long for his wife's/girlfriend's taste, causing an argument between the couple. The wife/girlfriend confronts him, "What are you doing? She's not all that."[41] Carmen responds by throwing her head back in laughter and states "Please, its all here baby."[42] Lieutenant Miller sets his sights on Carmen offering his secondary motivation for his vendetta against Hill, he covets both Carmen and Hill's fiancée Cayla. Carmen rejects Miller in rap.

Man you may be mumbling
See I have dreams and with a man
What will become of them?
There's not a kid out here who can make me believe
I should postpone my goals
He's got tricks up his sleeves
Whole bar full of cuffs
And you ain't locking me down.[43]

Earlier versions of *Carmen* relied on the outsiders' literary construction of the exotic—French composer Bizet, and French lyricists H. Meilhac and L. Halevy's interpretation of Romani and Spanish culture, and Rodgers and Hammerstein's rendering of African American Southern life. *Carmen Jones* featured dialect reminiscent of Black faced minstrelsy.[44] James Baldwin contended that in *Carmen Jones* "Negro speech [was] parodied out of its charm and liberalized . . . the result is that they sound ludicrously false and affected like ante-bellum Negroes imitating their masters."[45] *Carmen Jones's* audiences heard a foreign tongue when sophisticated African American performers Harry Belafonte and Dorothy Dandridge, made strangulating sounds of "de's," "dems," and "dat," in the film which caught conspicuously in their throats.[46] Thankfully, this form of speech remained absent from *Carmen the Hip Hopera* as lyricist Sekani Williams and writer Michael Elliott IV emancipated the characters through articulated English in speech, rap, and song.[47] *Carmen the Hip Hopera's* African American creative staff and cast discarded the voyeur's gaze on "the other." Carmen remains an intriguing character given earlier interpretations, but how is she represented in *Carmen the Hip Hopera*?

What remains interesting about the film is that Carmen really does not come off as a hypersexual Jezebel lusting after men, but more like an impetuous child playing games. This Carmen does not embody a salacious hypersexual persona; she actually appears conflicted about the role of the Jezebel. Carmen Brown actually fizzles as the object of lust in the remainder of the film. She is a good girl in comparison to her unrepentantly debauched counterpart in the novella, Carmen Brown foregoes sleeping around and commits herself to Derrick Hill even when he is imprisoned due to her misdeeds.

When Carmen catches Blaize the rapper's attention, she ultimately rejects him as a lover due to her pledge to Derrick, although she confides in Blaize about her desire to become a thespian. "I have dreams, plans. I want to move to LA, I want to be an actress, a STAR." She remains faithful to Derrick Hill until the tarot cards mark her for death and Derrick dismisses her theatrical dreams—"Even the most talented Black actresses get the hootchie girl roles."[48] It is only when the tarot cards foretell her death and Hill rejects her dreams that she chooses Blaize. Despite her flirtation with the bad girl model and her tentative pursuit of Blaize, Carmen does not symbolize the ultimate hypersexual bad girl, given her redeeming qualities, and her unabashed love of Derrick Hill.

CLASS DIFFERENCES

The nearest thing in our modern American life to an equivalent of the gypsies in Spain is the Negro. Like the gypsy, he expresses his feelings simply, honestly, and graphically. Also as with the gypsy there is a rhythm in his body, and music in his heart.

—Oscar Hammerstein II 1945[49]

The class and racial differences so intrinsic to the story of *Carmen* vanish with an all-African American cast and creative team and because of Carmen and Derricks' middle-class status, offering one of the major transformations to the *Carmen* narrative. While Carmen appears to live a life of leisure with no visible means of income, her dress throughout the film signifies the middle class. Her rap signifies her independence and self-reliance "See, I have dreams, and with a man what will become of them?"[50] The lived experience of the Romanies and African Americans also remains integral to both productions. Because the Romani people still live as outcasts in European society and African Americans are fundamentally intertwined within the fabric of American society the class differences between Carmen and Derrick Hill/Don Jose so entrenched in *Carmen* disappear as well.[51] African Americans remain linked to U.S. society, they participated in every aspect of U.S. culture from Jewel Plummer Cobb a cell biologist and the president Emirata of California State University, Fullerton, to holding the highest political office—Barack Obama, the first African American President of the United States, to physically building cities such as Washington, DC, and Philadelphia, and designing structures such as the Philadelphia Museum of Art.[52] African Americans belong to all the socio-economic classes of U.S. society. Unfortunately, the Romanies *still* face extreme marginalization, violence, and oppression in cities across Europe. This is not to say that issues of class don't materialize in *Carmen the Hip Hopera*, they do, but matters of class and race between Carmen and Derrick Hill/Don Jose simply don't exist in the film given their middle-class status, their African American heritage, and the United States filmsetting. The initial situation continues after Carmen's grand entrance and several issues arise. Carmen brawls with the police officer's wife/girlfriend who she held a flirtation leading to her arrest. Lieutenant Miller compels Derrick Hill to escort Carmen to jail, which reveals Carmen as a malefactor.

CARMEN AS A MALEFACTOR

While the film deals sparingly with Carmen as immoral, the criminalization of African American women remains a disturbing trend in Hip Hop culture given their overrepresentation in the prison system, the rise in their incarceration rates, their representation in Hip Hop music as low-life malefactors; and the historical background of these depictions in the media.[53]

African American singers Alicia Keys, Beyoncé, and rapper Lil' Kim's characterization of African American woman as malefactors follows this fad. Keys's 2001 music video "Fallin," directed by African American Chris Robinson, features a chorus of African American female convicts, while, Keys acts as a voyeur. Images of African American women in orange prison uniforms in the field, reminiscent of the chain gang and forced and slave labor dominate the video. This scene exposes the actual humiliation of incarceration during and after slavery, and inexplicably defies the lyrics depiction of a woman struggling to reconcile herself with her love of a man, "I keep falling' in and out of love with you, I never loved someone the way I love you."[54]

Alicia Keys's role as a spectator distances her from the negative portrayal of the African American women as prisoners and positions her as their superior. Robinson's pessimistic representation of African American women supports Norma Manatu's contention that African American filmmakers portray African American women more negatively than their white counterparts.[55] Comparably, Beyoncé's 2006 music video "Ring the Alarm" depicts the African American female prisoner, but Beyoncé plays the jailed malefactor—extremely unmanageable, wildly sexual, and in need of control— offering a shift from performer as onlooker to performer as criminal. Lil Kim's appropriation of the malefactor took it to a whole other level given her shameful delineation as a diablerie rebel felon, after her 2006 jail time for perjury. She flaunted her prison experience as a badge of honor, at the 2006 Video Music Awards, dressed in an orange prison jumper and was escorted on stage by "prison guards."[56] These performances signaled a disturbing trend in Hip Hop given how the African American female malefactor image affects the lives of African American women and girls, and their demonization in U.S. culture and the prison justice system. Manatu suggests that African American girls' self-esteem drops when confronted with negative African American female film images especially given the more balanced images of white women and girls in film.[57] T. Denean Sharpley-Whiting reported that an African American female college student challenged African American rap impresario Russell Simmons's support of corrosive images of African American women, and hurtfully stated that these images "impinged upon her sense of womanhood."[58] Defining African American women as depraved and felonious is not new, but what is new is the heralding of this image by African American female performers. While the portrayal of Carmen Brown as a convict remains small, and her misdeeds remain benign compared to her unlawful Romani counterpart, her criminalization brings into focus the very lived experiences of some African American women. Carmen Brown remains multifaceted as she represents the malefactor, and the African American middle class, while also personifying the good girl, but questions arise as to whether she fits the other model—the Gold Digger stereotype.

CARMEN AND THE GOLD DIGGER STEREOTYPE

> I don't think that for the most part black men respect black women the way they are supposed to be respected. Rap, music for example, I can't stand listening to it because the whore thing, bitch—that it's always about sleeping around. Women who have too much sex, they always portray them as whores, bitches. It's just unbelievable to me how we're disrespected.
>
> —Anondra, twenty-two[59]

Historically, the relegation of African American women to what Peter Stallybrass and Alon White describe as the "low other" characterized as "something that is reviled by and excluded from the dominant social order as debased, dirty, unworthy, but that is simultaneously the object of desire and/ or fascination" gained popularity at the infancy of U.S. slavery.[60] According to Stallybrass and White the exclusion of the "low other" from political and social organization occurred due to their status in society. The creation of the asexual mammy happy in slavery, the oversexed Jezebel, and the Mulatto who due to the one drop of Black blood remains "not white" originated to justify the brutalization and rape of African American women and girls during slavery.[61] All of these stereotypes including the Gold Digger embody the "low other" model. According to Hazel Carby in all of these stereotypes "Black women repeatedly failed the test of true womanhood because she survived her institutionalized rape, whereas the true heroine (white women) would rather die than be sexually abused."[62] Hip Hop culture labels Gold Diggers groupies who African American male rappers vituperate, disparage, and immortalize in vulgar and contemptuous lyrics; and who they treat "[l]ike wet wipes, are convenient and disposable."[63] The disproportionate representation of the image of African American women as the hypersexual Gold Digging Jezebel in the media continues to consign African American women as unworthy of true womanhood and *Carmen the Hip Hopera* includes this stereotype.

Carmen the Hip Hopera diverges from previous renderings by including Gold Diggers. The novella and the opera showed women who worked in the tobacco factory with Carmen, as well as her band of smugglers/Romanies, communities in which Carmen the outsider fits in and belongs. These characters helped to establish class differences and tensions between the Spanish elite and the outcast Romani.[64] *Carmen Jones* offered women who worked in the parachute factory with Carmen. Although *Carmen the Hip Hopera* and *Carmen Jones* remain interesting to watch they are not nearly as exciting as the novella or the opera with its groups of contrabandists and tobacco workers, Carmen's people. We never see Carmen of *Carmen the Hip Hopera* in a work environment, or group of people related to her who remain on the margins of society like the Romani and the contrabandist. We do meet a tiny band of two, Nikki played by Joy Bryant and Rasheeda played by Rah Digga, the Gold Diggers as their rap illustrates.

You know how we do cats
And keep runnin'
Standing on Sunset
Air Force One-in.[65]

Like Carmen, Nikki and Rasheeda appear to live a leisure life with no discernible jobs. As the rap demonstrates they look for unsuspecting "cats" and take them for their money to support their idle life. They reveal themselves as Gold Diggers as they set their sights on traveling to California with Blaize the rapper, and encourage Carmen to join them.

Carmen Why you buggin'
This ain't the time for lovin'

311

Blaize got the dough
We should stick it in the oven.[66]

Carmen appears mindful and refuses their proposal to take advantage of men. Carmen raps:

It might seem
but everything
that glitter don't bling
I ain't never met those brothers
How is that the right thing?[67]

Carmen exhibits moral fortitude in her refusal to profit from men and her dedication to Derrick Hill becomes apparent in her response. "Well you watch Derrick try to love me and hold me. Sounds nice but I need to see what love has got to show me."[68] Carmen's rap reinforces her good girl persona as her love for Derrick emerges, which dispels the notion that she fits the Gold Digger mold.

While Nikki and Rasheeda amuse the audience in their rap, the repercussions of the reality of the Gold Digger and the stereotype for African American women and girls prove incredibly detrimental. In *Pimps Up, Ho's Down: Hip Hop's Hold on Young Black Women*, T. Denean Sharpley-Whiting contends that participation in the Hip Hop groupie/Gold Digger lifestyle can lead to sexual assault, gang rape, and HIV/AIDS.[69] Nikki and Rasheeda's real-life counterpart, rape and child abuse survivor Karrine Steffans, chronicled her life in *Confessions of a Video Vixen* and *Vixen Diaries*. Steffans traded sex with rappers for social and financial gain, but experienced sexual humiliation, low self-esteem, drug addiction, and homelessness.[70] Norma Manatu found that African American female film stereotypes reinforce the idea that African American women are lazy, uninterested in working, welfare dependent, and antithetical of the very real-lived experiences of many African American women who are more likely to attend and graduate from college than African American men.[71] The maintenance of this image by white and African American performers, music videos, the print media, and record companies remains damaging to African American women and girls. Pamela Weddington of Motivational Educational Entertainment conducted a ten-city study of African American girls from 16 to 20 years old and asked them about music videos and sexuality. She found that videos taught girls that their minds remained inconsequential in relationship to their bodies and that they should use their bodies to obtain things in life. In a study conducted in 2003, in rural Alabama, by Dr. Ralph DiClemente, associate director of the Center for AIDS Research at Emory University in rural Alabama, the researchers asked girls about their habits watching music videos and found that girls who watched them more than 21 hours a week were "60 percent more likely to have contracted a STD that year, twice as likely to have multiple sex partners and 60 percent more likely to use alcohol and drugs."[72] The dominance of light-skinned uber-mulatto types in videos can also lead some African American girls to reject their beauty like the surgically enhanced rapper Lil Kim, or the eighteen year old who stated "[w]atching the videos, you see the long curly hair [and] think, 'Man that would be nice to have some long, curly hair.'"[73] This all points to the corrosive effects music videos have on African American girls' lives and self-esteem.

Magazines such as *King*, *XXL*, and *Smooth* feature African American women on their covers in various states of undress promote the stereotype of the African American woman as hypersexual Jezebel/Gold Digger. While the editors of these magazines profess to change the image of African American women, in reality they ultimately reinforce the Jezebel/Gold Digger stereotype.[74] This perception of African American woman in many cases can lead to unwanted attention, violence and abuse from both white and African American men and boys. Patricia Hill Collins notes in *Black Feminist Thought* that due to these stereotypes African American women rarely escaped rape by both white and African American men. Sharpley-Whiting argues that African American women are 10 percent more likely to face sexual assault than white women; less likely to report the crimes, and those who commit violence against them serve less times than those who commit violence against white and Latina women.[75]

Both African American and white male performers promote the African American woman as the Gold Digging Jezebel. African American rapper Nelly's 2004 video "Tip Drill" typifies the direction in which rap videos headed in the twenty-first century. The video shows Nelly swiping a credit card down an African American woman's rear end, and young women gyrating topless simulating lesbian sexual acts. Despite widespread protests against "Tip-Drill" by young African American women at Spelman College in 2003, these types of images remain prominent in rap and Hip Hop music.[76] Several distraught African American mothers across the country addressed the devaluing of African American women and girls in music videos, and discussed how these depictions affect their daughters. In 2006 Michelle Goodwin tackled the issue in the *Christian Science Monitor*. She recalled that her eleven-year old daughter informed her that a "new class mate from the Philippines, unprovoked, called my daughter a 'stupid ho' and 'b-ch,' terms of "endearment" used by some African American men in videos and rap music. When confronted by the principal, the boy admitted addressing my daughter that way, but argued in his defense that he learned it from African American men on TV."[77] Diane Weathers, the former editor of *Essence Magazine* recounted a similar incident when a classmate called her eleven-year old daughter a "ho."[78] While the images of Carmen Brown's Gold Digger girl-friends appear inane and harmless, African American girls and women suffer the consequences of these stereotypes.

In 2003 depicting the African American females as the "low other," Jezebel/Gold Digger took on added meaning when *Source* magazine published rap lyrics written by white rapper Eminem that portrayed African American girls as Gold Diggers and as inferior to white women. "Black girls only want your money . . . black girls are dumb and white girls are good chicks. White girls are good, I like white chicks"[79] Eminem eventually apologized for the content of the lyrics, but surprisingly Russell Simmons and Dr. Benjamin Chavis the former president of the National Association for the Advancement of Colored People came to Eminem's defense as opposed to safeguarding African American women and girls. Russell Simmons asserted that while the lyrics proved "regrettable," instead of anathematizing Eminem or making clear that the lyrics caused damage to African American women and girls, he stated "[w]e Believe Eminem's apology is sincere and forthright." Dr. Benjamin Chavis stated, "Hip Hop culture transcends race. We therefore must be careful as to how the race card is played to divide people rather than to encourage unity in the struggle for freedom and equality for all."[80] It appears that Chavis believes that *Source* magazine played the "race card" against Eminem in publishing the toxic lyrics that maligned African American girls, he in effect champions Eminem rather than protect African American womanhood. Both Simmons and Chavis condoned the denigration of African American women by the white rapper. Chavis basically asserts that the "struggle for freedom and equality" does not include African American women and girls. It remains interesting that they both would align themselves with a white man who publicly defamed African American females, and that Chavis would argue that the "race card was played," given the history of African American men's attempt to protect African American womanhood during and after slavery. Simmons and Chavis response magnifies Hazel Carby's assertion and furthers her argument that African American women and girls continue to fail the test of true womanhood, and remain unworthy of protection, while white women are upraised to mythic proportions of womanhood.

After seven cases of sexual harassment and child pornography were lodged against African American singer R. Kelly, and he faced the accusation that he raped and humiliated several young African American girls and was eventually acquitted of child pornography in Chicago, we heard no public out cry or protest in support of these young girls, rather the overwhelming sound of silence from both the African American and white community flooded the air.[81] The perception that enacting brutality against African American women and girls proves an acceptable sport took on new and added meaning with the most popular video games, where 86 percent of the African American female characters experience savagery, with none of the harmful outcomes of violence shown in these videos.[82]

Music videos that portray African American females as hypersexual Gold Diggers/Jezebels remain incredibly harmful to their psyche and well being and this type of representation lends credence to the rejection of the African American female by the African American male as viable partners. The steady drop in marriage rates of African American women also offers some weight to the effects of these stereotypes. Patricia Hill Collins contends that out-marriage of African American men outnumbers the out-marriage rates of African American women. Nell Painter notes that African American men are three times more likely to marry outside of their race than

African American women; while Sam Roberts reports in the January 16, 2007 *New York Times* that 70% of African American women remain single.[83] bell hooks contends that because the media emphasizes the undesirability and unsuitability of African American women as marriage partners and friends for many, marriage proves unattainable.[84] The rendering of Nikki and Rasheeda as Gold Diggers may seem innocuous, innocent and fun, but this depiction proves deleterious and ultimately wreaks havoc on the lives of African American women and girls.

Finally, is the *Carmen* narrative transformed when the creative team and cast are all African American? The creators of *Carmen the Hip Hopera* transfigured the *Carmen* narrative by discarding the voyeur and abandoned the foreign languages of French and Black minstrel dialect in favor of articulated English. They presented the tale from an insiders' perspective in the segregated landscape of North Philly, thus exposing structural racism, urban renewal, and how they affect African Americans.

The master narrative reveals that like previous versions of *Carmen*, *Carmen the Hip Hopera* remains firmly centered on the travails of the male protagonist Derrick Hill, thus replicating trends in Hip Hop culture, which devalues African American women and girls. Class differences so entrenched in the original story between the protagonists disappeared given Carmen and Derrick's Blackness and middle-class status. Another transformation occurred with the villain, Lieutenant Miller, the "Black Cop," whose presence and immoral acts illuminated the "Black Cop's" threat to African American communities. Through Miller, the audience viewed the African American working class and their lack of social and economic opportunities in urban environs. Miller's harassment of Jalil, the mini criminal uncovered the "disconnected youth," with few economic or social opportunities except military service, and their classification as lawless, which promoted trends in Hip Hop culture that encourages criminalization over education. Jalil's sexualized language in jail alludes to child sex abuse and unmasks another nasty trend in Hip Hop, the characterization of African American children as salacious. The Master narrative reveals the radical transformation of Carmen Brown as a good girl not a Jezebel committed to Derrick Hill, with scant hints of a diablerie, which brought into focus African American female Hip Hop performers' use of the malefactor. The malefactor shed light on the criminalization of African American women and girls and the rise in their incarceration rates. The master narrative also exposed the Gold Digger stereotype, which uncovered the debasement of African American women and girls in Hip Hop culture through hypersexualization, sexual, physical and verbal victimization, and the effects of the Gold Digger stereotype on marriage rates, womanhood rights and self-perception. While transformations occurred within *Carmen the Hip Hopera*, unfortunately the creative staff reinforced stereotypes of African Americans as inherently reprobate and replicated sexism and harmful fads in Hip Hop music and culture.

NOTES

I would like to thank Dr. Gloria Dickinson of the Association for the Study of African American Life and History for encouraging me in writing this project. I would also like to thank Clarence Henry Seniors, Dr. Derrick Alridge, Dr. V. P. Franklin, and Dr. James Stewart for their continued support of my scholarship, and Dr. Matt Baumer for his comments on the manuscript. Finally, I would like to thank the anonymous readers of the manuscript for their thoughtful comments and critique in shaping this chapter.

[1]Invented by Europeans, Orientalism is the construction of an imagined Asia.

[2]Prosper Merimee, *Carmen* (1845), 1, 13, 6; Joseba Gabilondo, "Uncanny Identity: Violence, Gaze, and Desire in Contemporary Basque Cinema," *Constructing Identity in Contemporary Spain: Theoretical Debates and Cultural Practice*, ed. Jo Labanyi (Oxford, 2002), 263; *Carmen: Opera in Four Acts* (New York, 1958), 1–3; Susan McClary, *Georges Bizet: Carmen* (New York, 1992), 22; Nicholas John, *Carmen* (London, 1982). According to Ian Hancock in *We Are The Romani People* the word Gypsy is offensive to the Romani people because outsiders gave them the name. It remains offensive in large part because of the negative imagery and stereotypes that it represents, therefore for this study I will use Romani (see Ian Hancock, *We Are the Romani People* [Centre De Recherches Tsiganes, United Kingdom, 2002], XVIII).

[3]Benetta Jules Rosette, *Josephine Baker in Art and in Life: The Icon and the Image* (Urbana, 2007), 44; Vladimir Propp, *The Morphology of a Folktale* (Austin, 1968), 25; A. J. Greimas, *Structural Semantics* (Lincoln, 1983), 228.

[4]Melvin Donalson, *Hip Hop in American Cinema* (New York, 2007), 8–9; Paula J. Massod, *Black City Cinema* (Philadelphia, 2003), 123–25; S. Craig Watkins, *Representing: Hip Hop Culture and the Production of Black Cinema* (Chicago), 1998), 139–46; Kate Taylor, "Assault on the Gentrifiers and the Audience," *NYTimes.com*, 16 November 2008, 1–2. *Beat Street* (1984) was written by white writer Andrew Davis, directed by African American Stan Lathan, and produced by African American actor Harry Belafonte. *Krush Groove* (1985) was written by African American Ralph Farquhar and directed by African American Michael Schultz, while African American Reg E. Gaines wrote *Bring in Da Noise Bring in Da Funk*. African American George C. Wolfe directed the show, African American singer Ann Duquesnay, African American composer Daryl Waters, and Zane Mark wrote the music.

[5]*Bring in Da Noise, Bring in Da Funk*, Playbill 1995; Ben Brantly, "Theater Review; Story of Tap as the Story of Blacks," *New York Times*, 16 November 1995; Taylor, "Assault on the Gentrifiers, and the Audience," *NYTimes.com*; Jeff Chang, *Total Chaos: The Art and Aesthetics of Hip Hop* (New York, 2006), 79, 301.

[6]*Carmen: Opera in Four Acts*, 1–3.

[7]Merimee, *Carmen*, 13, 6; McClary, *George Bizet's Carmen*, 22; Nicholas John, *Carmen* (London, 1982).

[8]Propp, *The Morphology of a Folktale*, 25; Greimas, *Structural Semantics*, 240; Rosette, *Josephine Baker*, 44–46.

[9]Andrew Wiese, *Places of Their Own: African American Suburbanization in the Twentieth Century*. (Chicago, 2004), 20–21.

[10]Melvin L. Oliver & Thomas M. Shapiro, *Black Wealth White Wealth: A New Perspective on Racial Inequality* (London, 1997), 83–84; Joe R. Feagin, Melvin P. Sikes, *Living with Racism: The Black Middle Class Experience* (Boston, 1994), 27.

[11]Sekani Williams, *Carmen the Hip Hopera*, 2000.

[12]S. Craig Watkins, *Hip Hop Matters* (Boston, 2005), 219–20.

[13]Ibid., 219–20; Norma Manatu, *African American Women and Sexuality in the Cinema* (Jefferson, 2003), 182–183; "Put Your Camera Where My Eyes Can See—Hip Hop Video, Film and Documentary: A Roundtable Curated by Erik K Arnold with Rachel Raimist, Kevin Epps and Michael Wanguhu" in Jeff Chang, *Total Chaos: The Art and Aesthetics of Hip Hop* (New York, Basic Books, 2006), 312.

[14]Propp, *Morphology of a Folktale*, 68; Greimas, *Structural Semantics*, 223, 231. A. J. Greimas advanced Propp's analysis and coupled vilany with the function that signifies that the protagonist is lacking something in their lives. Greimas, *Structural Semantics*, 223, 231.

[15]Tom Wicker, *Tragic Failure: Racial Integration in America*. (New York, 1996), 124.

[16]Erik Eckholm, "Plight Deepens for Black Men, Studies Warn: Growing Disconnection from the Mainstream," *The New York Times*, 20 March 2006, A1, A18.

[17]Wicker, *Tragic Failure* (New York, 1996), 125.

[18]KRS-One, "Black Cop," *Return of the Boom Bap*, Jive Records, 1993.

[19]Karl E. Johnson, "Police-Black Community Relations in Postwar Philadelphia: Race and Criminalization in Urban Social Spaces, 1945–1960," *The Journal of African American History* 89, no. 2 (Spring 2004): 122–23.

[20]KRS-One, "Black Cop."

[21]Ibid.

[22]William K. Rashbaum, "Ex Detective Turned Drug Dealer Gets 6-Year Prison Sentence," *The New York Times*, 6 October 2006, B3; "A Virginia Sheriff Is Charged with Selling Drug Evidence," *The New York Times*, 3 November 2006, A24.

[23]Renford Reese, *American Paradox: Young Black Men* (North Carolina, 2004), 36.

[24]KRS-One, "Black Cop," *Return of the Boom Bap*, Jive Records, 1993.

[25]*Carmen the Hip Hopera*, 2000.

[26]Karrine Steffans, *Vixen Diaries* (New York, 2007) 3–4, 6. In *Confessions of a Video Vixen* Steffans details her physical abuse at the hands of her mother, her rape at the age of thirteen, her career as a sixteen-year-old stripper in Arizona, her sexual promiscuity for social and economic gain with rappers, music executives, and athletes like Ice T. and Fred Durst of Limp Biskit fame, and her ultimate ascension in Hip Hop as a Video Vixen in music videos Karrine Steffans, *Confessions of a Video Vixen* (New York, 2005), 18–19, 32–33, 29–30, 48–50, 88, 89, 106.

[27]W. E. B. Du Bois, *Black Reconstruction in America* (New York, 1935, 167, 674); John Hope Franklin, *From Slavery to Freedom* (New York, 1947), 342.

[28]Fox Butterfield, "2 Studies Find Laws on Felons Forbid Many Black Men to Vote," *The New York Times*, 23 September 2004, A21; Nell Painter, *Creating Black Americans: African American History and Its Meanings 1619 to the Present* (New York, 2006), 245; Renford Reese, American *Paradox*, 155.

[29]Bob Herbert notes that racial profiling leads to tragic consequences for African Americans. He points to the case of New Jersey State Troopers who pulled three African American men and one Latino man over and opened fire on them Bob Herbert, "Truth Telling On Race? Not In Bush's Fantasyland," *The New York Times*, 25 August 2005, A.23.
The images shown in numerous *New York Times* articles concerning the war signify that African American men and women remain overrepresented in the war in Iraq and Afghanistan, and face few options of upward mobility besides the army. One example is Aubrey Bell who grew up impoverished in Alabama with hardly any opportunities but to join the military. Bell died in Iraq in 2003. Jeffrey Gettleman, "Deaths in Iraq Take a Steady Toll at Home," *The New York Times*, 2 Sunday November 2003, A10; Bob Herbert, "Locked Out at a Young Age," *The New York Times*, 20 October 2003, A19; Gettleman, "Deaths in Iraq Take a Steady Toll at Home," A1, A10; Bob Herbert, "Letting Down the Troops," *The New York Times*, 29 October 2003, A23; "The Reach of the War: The Deadliest Day," *The New York Times*, 31 January 2005, A12; Robert Steinback, "'60s Figure Calls for End to Prisons in FIU Speech," *The Miami Herald*, 20 September 2003, 5B; Reese, *American Paradox*, 153, 150; Wicker, *Tragic Failure*, 124–25; Karen W. Arenson, "Colleges Struggle to Help Black Men Stay Enrolled," *The New York Times*, 30 December 2003, A1, A21; Painter, *Creating Black Americans*, 245.

[30]Wicker, *Tragic Failure*, 124–25.

[31]Sean Kingston, "Beautiful Girls," Sony BMG Music Entertainment; Nicholas Bakalar, "Suicide Rate High in Violent Death Data," *NYTimes.com*, 10 June 2008; Pam Belluck, "Black Youths' Rate of Suicide Rising Sharply, Studies Find," *NY Times.com*, 20 March 1998.

[32]Kingston, "Beautiful Girls."

[33]Jaheim, "Put Your Woman First," Video directed by Darren Grant.

[34]Propp, *The Morphology of a Folktale*, 26; Greimas, *Structural Semantics*, 224–25; Jules Rosette, *Josephine Baker*, 44.

[35]Hancock, *We Are the Romani People*, 2002; Betty Alt and Silvia Folts, *Weeping Violins: The Gypsy Tragedy in Europe* (Kirksville, MO, 1996), 2; Bertha Quintana, Lois Gray Floyd, *Que Gitano: The Gypsies of Southern Spain* (New York, 1972), 13–14.

[36]Angus Fraser, *The Gypsies* (Oxford, 1992), 144, 169, 164–65; Alt and Folts *Weeping Violins*, 4. Over time the Romans faced enslavement in several countries in Europe including the Balkans in the 1300s and Spain in the late 1700s where Europeans impelled them into forced labor. Europeans used them in forced labor in North Africa for the naval arsenal and in the mercury mines of Almaden (Fraser, *The Gypsies*, 164–65; Alt and Folts, *Weeping Violins*, 4). In Romania the Romanies faced enslavement from 1855–1856. According to Zoltan Barany emancipation came in 1864 one year after African American enslavement, because of France's criticism of Romanian slavery (Zoltan Barany, *The East European Gypsies: Regime Change, Marginality and Ethnopolitcs* [London, 2002], 95, 86.

[37]Hancock, *We Are the Romani People*, 94, 103, 100, 102; Fraser, *The Gypsies*, 124, 125, 160.

[38]Merimee, *Carmen*, 23.

[39]Ibid., 22.

[40]According to Susan McClary, Georges Bizet "borrowed" Sebastian Raider's "El Arregelito," a musical selection based on Afro-Cuban music, for the "Habanera." See McClary, *Georges Bizet*, 51–52.

[41]*Carmen the Hip Hopera, 2000.*

[42]Ibid.

[43]Sekani Williams, *Carmen the Hip Hopera*, 2000.

[44]Martin Cooper, "Opera-Comique," in Nicholas John's *Carmen*, 13, 16.

[45]James Baldwin, "Carmen Jones: The Dark Is Light Enough," *Notes of a Native Son* (1955; reprinted New York: 1963), 48–49.

[46]I am sure that I read a version of this phrase and attribute it to James Baldwin, although I cannot find the quotation.

[47]While *Carmen the Hip Hopera* departed from the type of speech representation, which rendered African American speech a foreign tongue, MTV's 2005 *Hustle and Flow* brought a strange Black dialect back into the American imagination.

[48]*Carmen the Hip Hopera, 2000.*

[49]McClary, *George Bizet's Carmen*, 133.

[50]*Carmen the Hip Hopera, 2000.*

[51]"Two Killed in Attack on Roma Houses in Hungary," 3 November 2008, *Reuters.com*; "Racism in Italy? Roma Crackdown Draws Critics," 29 July 2008, *Reuters.com*; "Italy Deploys Troops in Cities to Fight Crime,"4 August 2008, *Reuters.com*; Agnieszka Flak and Julie Breton, "Finland's Roma Face Threat of Losing Children," 31 July 2008, *Reuters.com*; Serge Schmemann, "Gypsy Protesters Driven from a Nazi Camp," October 4, 1989, *NYTimes.com*.

[52]"President Obama," *Newsweek*, 17 November 2008; *Time Commemorative Issue*, 17 November 2008; Jewel Plummer Cobb, interview by author, 2005.

[53]Painter, *Creating Black Americans*, 245; Adam Liptak, "1 in 100 U.S. Adults Behind Bars, New Study Says," *NYTimes.com*, 28 February 2008; Amnesty International USA, amnestyusa.org. Amnesty International USA reports that "Over a five-year period, the incarceration rate of African American women increased by 828%. (NAACP LDF Equal Justice Spring 1998.) An African American woman is eight times more likely than a European American woman is to be imprisoned; African American women make up nearly half of the nation's female prison population, with most serving sentences for nonviolent drug or property related offenses." (Amnesty International USA, www.amnestyusa.org/women/womeninprison.html)

[54]Alicia Keys, "Fallin," from *Songs in A. Minor* (J. Records, 2001).

[55]Manatu, *African American Women and Sexuality in the Cinema*, 182.

[56]Lola Ogunnaike, "Much to Do Before Checking into Prison," *The New York Times*, 19 September 2005,

E1, E7; Lola Ogunnaike, "The Big House Didn't Break Lil' Kim," *The New York Times*, 31 August 2006, B1, B7; Brian Orloff, "The VMAs' Top 5 Most Shocking Moments," *People Magazine*, 31 August 2006.

[57]Manatu, *African American Women and Sexuality in the Cinema*, 166.

[58]T. Denean Sharpley-Whiting, *Pimps Up, Ho's Down: Hip Hops Hold on Young Black Women* (New York, 2007), 3.

[59]Tricia Rose, *Longing to Tell: Black Women Talk About Sexuality and Intimacy* (New York, 2003), 292.

[60]Peter Stallybrass and Allon White, The Politics and Poetics of Transgression (Ithaca, NY: 1986), 191–93; Robert C. Allen, Horrible Prettiness (Chapel Hill, University of North Carolina Press, 1991), 26.

[61]Deborah Gray-White, *Ar'n't I a Woman? Female Slaves in the Plantation South* (New York, 1985), 28–29; Donald Bogle, *Toms, Coons, Mulattoes, Mammies, & Bucks: An Interpretive History of Blacks in American Films* (New York, 2004) 9, 168; Hazel Carby, *Reconstructing Womanhood: The Emergence of the Afro-American Woman Novelist* (Oxford, 1987), 31.

[62]Carby, *Reconstructing Womanhood*, 34.

[63]Denean Sharpley-Whiting, *Pimps Up, Ho's Down*, 88–89, 13.

[64]McClary, *George Bizet's Carmen*, 47.

[65]*Carmen the Hip Hopera*, 2000.

[66]Ibid.

[67]Ibid.

[68]Ibid.

[69]Sharpley-Whiting, *Pimps Up, Ho's Down*, 2007, 71–75, 105, 59, 79. Sharpley-Whiting details the mentality of Tupac Shakur's lyric "First let my nigga fuck then I fuck," with some rappers who faced sexual assault charges like Mystikal's gang rape of his hair stylist and Shakur's complicity in the gang rape of Ayana Jackson. Sharpley-Whiting, *Pimps Up*, 2007, 59, 79.

[70]Steffans, *The Vixen Diaries*, IX–IX, 1–6; Steffans, *Confessions of a Video Vixen*, 18–19, 32–33, 29–30, 48–50, 88, 89, 106.

[71]Manatu, *African American Women and Sexuality in the Cinema*, 165.

[72]Jeannine Amber, "Dirty Dancing," *Essence*, March 2005: 165–66.

[73]Sharpley-Whiting, *Pimps Up, Ho's Down*, 23.

[74]Lola Ogunnaike, "New Magazines for Black Men Proudly Redefine the Pinup," *The New York Times*, 31 August 2004, B1, B6.

[75]Sharpley-Whiting, *Pimps Up, Ho's Down*, 57, 81–82, 68.

[76]Kristin Wyatt, "Black Women in College Take Aim at Rap Artists," *The Herald*, 24 April 2006; "It's Gettin' Hot in Here: An Explicit Video by a Rap Superstar Draws Criticism at Spelman College," *The Chronicle of Higher Education*, 4 June 2004, 1–4.

[77]Michelle Goodwin, "Taking the Debate over Degrading Rap Videos Off Mute," *The Christian Science Monitor*, 11 August 2006, 1. I experienced something similar in 2006 when I traveled to Central Asia to give lectures for the United States State Department. At a university in Tajikistan a male student called me a Nigger. I informed him that him calling me this pejorative remained unacceptable. He informed me that he heard black rappers used the term and others when referring to African American women; therefore it was okay. I learned firsthand across the world of the far-reaching scope of the demeaning depictions of African American women.

[78]Diane Weathers, "Why We're Taking Back the Music," *Essence Magazine*, March 2005, vol. 35, no. 11, 34.

[79]Kelefa Sanneh, "Unguarded Lyrics Embarrass Eminem," *The New York Times*, 20 November 2003, B1.

[80]*Miami Herald*, 21 November 2003; *NYTimes.com*, 23 March 2005.

[81]*NYTimes.com*, 14 August 2003, B 3; David Streitfeld, "R. Kelly Is Acquitted in Child Pornography Case," 14 June 2008, *NYTimes.com*.

[82]*Essence*, May 2002: 40.

[83]Patricia Hill Collins, *Black Sexual Politics* (New York, 2004), 261; Sam Roberts, "51% of Women Are Now Living Without Spouse," *NYTimes.com*. 16 January 2007. Patricia Hill Collins notes that African American men who date or marry white women receive acceptance within the black community and even receive sly "winks" while black women face strong opposition and "are accused of being race traitors" from black men when they date or marry white men. A prohibition and resistance exists concerning African American women (Collins, *Black Sexual Politics*, 261).

[84]bell hooks, *Ain't I a Woman: Black Women and Feminism* (Boston, 1981), 67.

"OF ALL OUR STUDIES, HISTORY IS BEST QUALIFIED TO REWARD OUR RESEARCH": BLACK HISTORY'S RELEVANCE TO THE HIP HOP GENERATION

Pero Gaglo Dagbovie

Each generation, depending on its problems and needs, must select and arrange the specific facts which form the best system for its own inspiration and guidance. It is because the past is a guide with roads pointing in many directions that each generation and epoch must make its own studies of history.

Earl E. Thorpe, 1957[1]

Every generation has the opportunity to write its own history, and indeed it is obliged to do so. Only in that way can it provide its contemporaries with the materials vital to understanding the present and to planning strategies for coping with the future. Only in that way can it fulfill its obligation to pass on to posterity the accumulated knowledge and wisdom of the past, which, after all, give substance and direction for the continuity of civilization.

John Hope Franklin, 1986[2]

History inspires. History teaches. History also guides. . . . We, as a Hip Hop people, must come out of the past and into our present. We, as a Hip Hop people, must re-create ourselves. True freedom for us Hiphoppas is to create and live a lifestyle that uniquely empowers us. . . . True freedom is self-creation. . . . We Hiphoppas will be busy at work creating a history that simply works better for our children.

KRS-One, 2003[3]

The meaning, purpose, and function of black history as a field of academic inquiry, a philosophy, and "as a weapon in the fight for racial equality" has undergone a host of significant transformations and stages since the antebellum era and the professionalization of the black historical enterprise during the early 20th century.[4] Building upon the institutions and paradigms created by Carter G. Woodson and other contributors to the early black history movement, black and white historians and scores of black activists during the Black Power era significantly transformed the systematic study and day-to-day application of black history. Black Power era historian William Van Deburg has pointed out the manner in which the masses of young blacks from about 1965 to 1975 collectively drew upon black history as "a wellspring of group strength and staying power."[5] Likewise, in their exhaustive study on the black historical enterprise, August Meier and Elliott Rudwick argued that by the late 1960s "Afro-American history had become fashionable, a 'hot' subject finally legitimated as a scholarly specialty."[6]

Challenging the widely accepted thesis of black history's unprecedented growth, centrality, and legitimization during the Black Power era, in his 1967 classic *The Crisis of the Negro Intellectual*, recently deceased cultural critic Harold Cruse indicted young black intellectuals for being tragically "uninterested in history." On the last page of his mammoth study, Cruse concluded, "The farther the Negro gets from his historical antecedents in time, the more tenuous become his conceptual ties, the emptier his social conceptions, the more superficial his visions. His one great and present hope is to know and understand his Afro-American history in the United States more profoundly. Failing that, and failing to create a new synthesis and social theory of action, he will suffer the historical fate described by the philosopher who warned that 'Those who cannot remember the past are condemned to repeat it."[7] In the "Foreword" to a 1984 edition of Cruse's opus, Bazel E. Allen and Ernest J. Wilson pronounced that "the message of this book remains painfully apt today."[8] Cruse's observations are still relevant and especially applicable to the Hip Hop generation.

This essay concerns the relationship between the Hip Hop generation and black history and is written by a Hip Hop generation historian who shares Thorpe and Franklin's sentiments that each generation of African American historians must leave their distinct marks on the profession, the production of scholarship, and the debates surrounding the functions of black history. My discussion is guided by the premise that Hip Hop culture is the single most widespread preoccupation among today's African American and African diasporan youth and has the potential to play an important role in rejuvenating the modern black history movement and raising the Hip Hop generation's cultural and historical consciousness. African American historians, especially those of the Hip Hop generation, could help advance approaches to teaching and popularizing black history by using elements of Hip Hop culture while helping the Hip Hop generation better understand its peculiar position within the broader scope of black history. Articulating the ideas of more than a few Hip Hop scholars, in an important 2004 issue of *Black Issues in Higher Education*, Scott Heath astutely remarked that Hip Hop is "an area where we might see theory and practice coming together inside African American intellectualism, where we might see an attempt to develop innovative approaches to using Hip Hop as a method for organizing African American youth around issues that are important to their survival."[9]

Many broad, interconnected questions help frame my analysis. How do we best conceptualize, subdivide, and historicize the Hip Hop generation? How has black history been interpreted in popular, "commercial" Hip Hop culture within the last several years? Generally speaking, how do some of today's most popular mainstream Hip Hop magazines, emcees, and current Black History Month celebrations present black history to today's black youth? How do these popular representations of black history compare to those of the Black Power era, a period which is often romanticized by, and compared to, the Hip Hop generation? How can Hip Hop generation black historians historicize their generation's experiences and worldviews while explaining and reintroducing black history to black youth culture? Theoretically, in the tradition of Carter G. Woodson, I maintain that black history can still help foster healthy black

322

youth identity and contribute to American social and educational reform. Black history can help the Hip Hop generation develop a better appreciation of the once more common values of sacrifice, service, unity, and historical consciousness. Woodson's mission of popularizing and ritualizing black history could be especially useful for the Hip Hop generation who actively samples from past musicians, fashions, cultural icons, and other phenomena from "back in the day" and the "old school." Historical dialogues of some sort are common in even today's most "commercial" rap music. A central component of Hip Hop culture and rap music involves Hip Hop artists who routinely recount their own personal histories of resilience, which mirror the overall theme of perseverance against the oppression that dominates the African American experience. Many commercially successful emcees also make passing references to black history in their rhymes, videos, and self-presentation. Nonetheless, African American historians have not played a leading role in analyzing Hip Hop or critically tapping into Hip Hop culture as a viable discursive space for the black historical experience.[10] Given the tradition of "historical revivalism" in rap's heyday, African American historians' underrepresentation in Hip Hop scholarship is surprising.

CONCEPTUALIZING THE HIP HOP GENERATION

Within the last decade, scholarship on rap music and Hip Hop culture has skyrocketed. Several dozen books were published on facets of Hip Hop during the 1980s and 1990s.[11] As Kendra Hamilton has noted, 1994 represented a landmark year in the legitimization process of Hip Hop scholarship with the publication of Tricia Rose's *Black Noise: Rap Music and Black Culture in Contemporary America* and Robin D. G. Kelley's *Race Rebels: Culture, Politics, and the Working-Class*.[12] Adhering to rigorous scholarly standards, these works historicized and theorized dimensions of Hip Hop culture in a discourse that would probably seem foreign to most of the MCs whose art Rose and Kelley analyzed. In 2000 the Brooklyn Museum of Art presented a first of its kind multimedia exhibition on Hip Hop. "Hip Hop Nation: Roots, Rhymes, and Rage," in one reviewer's words, portrayed Hip Hop "as a cultural wealth of America to be appreciated by a larger crowd than the hip-hop fans."[13] Other critics believed that the museum's liberalism crept in too much at the expense of watering down Hip Hop's political message and radicalism. In 2002 one scholar published a dictionary on Hip Hop terminology and at the dawning of the 21st century many scholarly studies on Hip Hop had been published by mainstream presses.[14] Hip Hop studies, perhaps soon to be called "Hiphopology," is one of the newest fad-fields in American, African American, and cultural history, and in critical studies and ethnomusicology. Major universities have been offering courses on Hip Hop for several years. The courses are popular and have been legitimized in the mainstream academy by established black scholars such as Todd Boyd, Michael Eric Dyson, Mark Anthony Neal, and Tricia Rose, who was recently dubbed the "Ph.D. Diva" of Hip Hop by the *New York Times*.[15] Nonetheless, as one scholar noted in 2002, while a significant "rap and Hip

Hop canon" exists, there is room for expanding this discourse.[16] Inquiries into Hip Hop as representing a generation deserves to be elaborated upon.

In *The Hip Hop Generation: Young Blacks and the Crisis in African American Culture* (2002), journalist and cultural critic Bakari Kitwana provides a provocative definition of the Hip Hop generation that expands upon what scholars have called, in Robin Kelley's words, "a lot of things: the post-soul generation, the post–civil rights generation, the postindustrial generation," and even "soul babies."[17] Kitwana uses the Hip Hop generation "interchangeably with black youth culture." He designates the Hip Hop generation as including those African Americans born between roughly 1965 and 1984 who share a common worldview concerning "family, relationships, child rearing, career, racial identity, race relations, and politics." Shaped by the rise of multinational corporatism, globalization, neo-segregation, racialist public policy, the expanding media, and an overall poor quality of life for black youth, members of the Hip Hop generation are linked mainly by the fact that we were born after the major struggles of the Civil Rights Movement and have collectively inherited a great deal from the battles waged by our elders.[18] Echoing others, Kitwana noted that the Hip Hop generation seems cut off from the social activist tradition associated with the Civil Rights-Black Power era. I agree with Kitwana's critiques in this instance.

In his benchmark study *The Origins of the Civil Rights Movement* (1982), Aldon Morris argued that civil rights activists recognized that they were part of a "rich tradition of protest." Many members of the Hip Hop generation seem alienated from the important influences of previous generations, those—in Morris's terms—traditionally "transmitted across generations by older relatives, black educational institutions, churches, and protest organizations."[19] To add to Morris's argument, African American historians have also historically played a significant role in passing on historical epistemologies for the "tradition of protest."

According to Kitwana, the Hip Hop generation, with some exceptions of course, seems to be self-consumed, individualistic, and not willing to sacrifice for the advancement of "the tradition of protest." "For us," Kitwana contends, "achieving wealth, by any means necessary, is more important than most anything else, hence our obsession with the materialistic and consumer trappings of financial success." Kitwana adds that one of the greatest problems facing the Hip Hop generation is the fact that we have abandoned the positive cultural values held by our parents, elders, and ancestors. We have exchanged what Elijah Anderson has called "old head" values for ideals promoted by a capitalistic, individualistic, and racist society.[20] The "fact remains that when many Hip Hop generation youth have to choose between personal financial success, or what the older generation considers communal cultural integrity, individual gain comes first."[21]

Beyond what some might consider overgeneralizations, Kitwana's analysis is problematic in delineating such a large generation spanning nearly twenty years. As he admits in passing, his Hip Hop generation could be further broken down into at least "three distinctive subgroups."[22] Nelson George and Todd Boyd have both discussed how being born at certain points during the Civil Rights Movement has impacted their analyses of Hip Hop. I would at minimum highlight that there is a significant difference between the ideologies of those born between 1965 and the mid-1970s and those born in the late 1970s and the 1980s. Those young African Americans born in the 1980s, for instance, were not being molded as adolescents and young adults by the same types of black cultural nationalist stimuli that shaped those of us born between 1965 and the mid-1970s and socialized during the late 1980s and early 1990s, arguably the "Golden Age" of Hip Hop and rap music. I call those young African Americans born between 1965 and the mid-1970s Black Power era born (hereafter BP) hip hoppers. Those African Americans born during the late 1970s and the early to mid-1980s constitute the post–Black Power era Hip Hop generation (hereafter PBP). These young African Americans have largely been socialized by "commercial" Hip Hop culture. The BP Hip Hop generation was shaped by social and cultural forces that were more conducive to black cultural nationalism than the PBP Hip Hop generation. The gap in historical consciousness between the BP and PBP Hip Hop generations exists and is noteworthy.[23]

The most recent significant resurgence and upsurge of black cultural consciousness and nationalism occurred during the late 1980s and the early 1990s until perhaps as late as 1995 or 1996, marked by the Million Man March and the death of Tupac Shakur respectively. Though this period was not nearly as lively, widespread, and progressive as the well-known cultural revitalization of the Black Power era, during the late 1980s and especially the early 1990s there existed meaningful stimuli promoting black consciousness among the BP Hip Hop generation. As Robin D. G. Kelley has attested, "the decade of the 1990s was a period of resurgent black nationalism."[24] Many examples in black popular culture demonstrate this historical trend.

Perhaps most importantly, aboveground (nonunderground), popular, "nation-conscious," "reality rap," and analytical rap music was more common during the late 1980s and the early 1990s than it is currently. In order to be a "conscious" rap artist, one must devote the majority of his/her lyrics to discussing "empowerment through politics and knowledge," social change and/or nonsuperficial aspects of black history, and the problems facing the black communities in critical areas.[25] In the late 1980s and early 1990s, the Golden Age of Hip Hop, there were many of these types of rap artists, including Public Enemy, KRS-One and Boogie Down Productions, De La Soul, Brand Nubian, at times Ice Cube, A Tribe Called Quest, Jungle Brothers, Goodie Mob, Paris, X-Clan, Black Star, Poor Righteous Teachers, Queen Latifah, and others. In one of his first articles on Hip Hop culture, written in 1989, Michael Eric Dyson highlighted the "historical revivalism" of rap during its golden years, arguing that it "retrieved historic black ideas, movements, and figures to combating the racial amnesia that threatens to relegate the achievements of the black past to the ash heap of dismemory." More importantly, Dyson asserted that this "renewed historicism" permitted members of the BP Hip Hop generation to "discern links between the past and their own present circumstances, using the past as a fertile source of social reflection, cultural creation, and political resistance."[26] The PBP era Hip Hop generation was not being exposed to historically conscious "nationalist rappers" as was the case for the BP era Hip Hop generation when we were coming of age.

Though variations of 1970s "blaxploitation films" continued through the 1980s and 1990s, Spike Lee's films particularly from 1988 through 1992 played a major role in socializing young African Americans by addressing important and often controversial issues in their lives and in black history. In 2001 black film historian Donald Bogle commented that Lee's *Do the Right Thing* (1988) "remains the most controversial and provocative film by an African American filmmaker" and that "no other black film drew as much attention or had as great a cultural impact as this drama."[27] In 1991 John Singleton produced *Boyz N the Hood* for the BP Hip Hop generation. He openly discussed important issues facing black urban America during the Reagan years, such as HIV/AIDS, racism, black male-female relationships, community development, and black leadership. A decade later, for the PBP Hip Hop generation, he produced the much less analytical *Baby Boy*.

There have been a few black films that PBP Hip Hop generation could have gravitated towards, but chose not to. For instance, Spike Lee's *Four Little Girls* (1997) and *Bamboozled* (2000) failed to attract a large young black viewership. *Bamboozled*, Lee's magnum opus, which he directed as an amateur, public historian, could have become a rites of passage cinematic experience for the PBP Hip Hop generation. Instead, in 2002 the PBP Hip Hop generation witnessed Halle Berry and Denzel Washington receive Oscars for Best Actress and Best Actor for their stereotypical roles in *Monster's Ball* (2003) and *Training Day* (2003) respectively. Berry's character had no socially redeeming qualities, and embodied the image of the black woman as the oversexed, promiscuous Jezebel, a stereotype which, as Deborah Gray White has demonstrated, dates back to the days of slavery.[28] Denzel Washington earned his Oscar for Best Actor forty years after Sidney Poitier earned the same award for his role in *Lilies of the Field*. Washington played the role of a corrupt black cop and deadbeat dad. This was especially interesting given the history and the recent acts of police brutality against African Americans at the hands of white policemen. Washington could have very easily won an Oscar for Best Actor for his historically relevant roles in *Malcolm X* (1992) and *The Hurricane* (1999). Jamie Fox's Oscar winning performance as Ray Charles in *Ray* (2004) is promising. Fox is a member of the Hip Hop generation and *Ray* draws from elements of black history.

Afrocentrism, popularized by Molefi Kete Asante beginning in the 1980s, attracted a large following among the BP Hip Hop generation. Afrocentric thinkers and black scholar-activists routinely lectured at major colleges and universities throughout the nation in the late 1980s and early 1990s. The roll call of these speakers is long, including Na'im Akbar, Jawanza Kunjufu, Yosef ben-Yochanan ("Dr. Ben"), Ivan Van Sertima, Frances Cress Welsing, John Henrik Clarke, Oba T'Shaka, Asa Hilliard, Wade Nobles, Angela Davis, Haki Madhubuti, Leonard Jeffries, Jr., Sister Souljah, and many others. Such types of speakers are not popular among the PBP Hip Hop generation. Africa medallions, ankh pendants, and all sorts of Afrocentric gear were in style in the 1980s and were easily purchased in every major U.S. city. Imitating Hip

Hop video fashion, many members of the PBP Hip Hop generation today wear the red, black, and green wristbands without any knowledge of Marcus Garvey.

The popularization of Malcolm X was very important in fostering a black historical consciousness within the BP Hip Hop generation. Malcolm X was resurrected by Boogie Down Production's album *By All Means Necessary* (1988) and by Spike Lee's lengthy film *Malcolm X* (201 minutes). In the 1990s, X hats, tee shirts with Malcolm and other black leaders, and other sorts of black historical memorabilia were popular and fashionable. Lee's film was criticized by cultural critics such as bell hooks, and by black activists who knew Malcolm such as Dick Gregory. But, the film did spark within the BP Hip Hop generation an intense interest in Malcolm X, black history, and militant black ideologies. Using Malcolm X as a spiritual advisor and building upon the black student movement of the Black Power era, in the late 1980s and early 1990s thousands of black students at various predominantly white colleges and universities engaged in many meaningful, well-organized protests and sit-ins. In May 1989 black students at Michigan State University and Penn State University initiated two of the largest student protests of the decade, which closely resembled those organized by black students who demanded Black Studies programs during the 1960s and 1970s. Nationwide, expressions of black student unity during the late 1980s and early 1990s resembled that of the Black Power era. The college students of the PBP Hip Hop generation have collectively not been as politically active as previous generations.

The Million Man March on 16 October 1995 signaled the last stage in the steady decline of the black cultural pride movement that began in the late 1980s and early 1990s. While this "Holy Day of Atonement" did little to solve the major problems facing African America and went against many of the fundamental principles of black economic nationalism espoused by Louis Farrakhan and the Nation of Islam, it cannot be denied that the Million Man March served as a key turning point for many black men, raised black consciousness among young black men who attended it or heard firsthand accounts, created a sense of black unity, and countered some of white America's racist stereotypes about black men.[29]

The collective ethos of young blacks who were coming of age during the late 1980s and early 1990s seemed to draw upon Aldon Morris's black "tradition of protest" and historical consciousness in ways reminiscent of the Black Power era. Our consciousness was not something created independently of the external social forces of our times. Those of us coming of age in the late 1980s and early 1990s were stimulated to become active by not only various forces in popular culture, but also by a host of post–Civil Rights Movement struggles.[30] The PBP Hip Hop generation is living in an era which, despite great progress, resembles what Rayford W. Logan called the "nadir" of black life, especially in terms of health.[31] Yet, unlike previous generations, they have not responded collectively to black oppression or made distinctive contributions to the black "tradition of protest." Because racial oppression has become increasingly sophisticated and dangerously subtle to the layperson, critical thinking is needed more than ever before by the PBP Hip Hop generation. Despite the significantly different sets of circumstances which molded and socialized BP and PBP Hip Hop generations, today, beginning mainly in the mid- to late 1990s, members of Kitwana's broad Hip Hop generation appear to share a general lack of concern for and knowledge of black history. Currently, members of both Hip Hop generations live at a time when it is far too easy to undervalue or fail to appreciate the value of African American history. Contemporary black youths are distracted by a multitude of media-generated images and messages with which no previous younger black generation has had to deal. While earlier generations of black youth have drawn great knowledge and inspiration from black history and cross-generational dialogues, the Hip Hop generation has largely failed to recognize the potential value of employing black history. Those African Americans born after the Civil Rights-Black Power Movement need to study black history in order to understand their unique status and position among African people in the world and in the evolution of African America's struggle for advancement.

THE HISTORICISM OF THE HIP HOP GENERATION'S MAGAZINES

What makes the Hip Hop generation's current disregard for black history especially perplexing is that, comparatively speaking, this cohort has more access to information on black history than any other previous generation of African American youth. Currently, there are countless books on black history, numerous websites, and many very useful videos, especially those produced by California Newsreel and the Public Broadcasting System (PBS). College and university students can regularly enroll in courses focusing on African American history. Among the repositories of knowledge, popular media significantly molds black youths' views of black history. It is therefore useful to look at African American history as portrayed in popular magazines. Currently, the five most popular magazines among African Americans between roughly 18 and 34 years old are the *Source*, *Vibe*, *Ebony*, *Jet*, and *Essence*. Many other Hip Hop magazines are attempting to generate followings, such as *XXL*, Marc Ecko's *Complex*, *Urb*, *Ballin'*, *Owners Illustrated*, *Undercover*, *Scratch: The Science of Hip Hop*, the *Ave Magazine: A Street Movement in Print*, as well as a variety of Internet magazines. The majority of these publications largely ignore black history.[32]

For fifteen years, the *Source* has detailed the lives, struggles, and music of countless Hip Hop artists. The history of the magazine is nothing short of remarkable, a modern-day rags to riches story that embodies the struggles and successes of countless Hip Hop artists. Founded as a one page newsletter in 1988 by two young whites and one black, by 1997 the editorial staff of the magazine was dominated by African Americans and Hispanics and sold more than any other music periodical in the United States.[33] In 2003 the *Source* boasted nine million readers each month. The average issue is about two hundred pages and contains slightly more than one hundred advertisements per month. In 1988 the *Source* sold for $2.50. The price of placing an ad in the *Source* in 2003 was $32,000.00. According to its editors, it is "the most respected and most read" magazine for urban African Americans between ages 18 and 34 years old.[34] *Vibe* makes the same claim. It is safe to say that the *Source* and *Vibe* are, give or take some thousand readers, equally as popular. The *Source*, however, seems to deal more critically with issues relevant to African America's status, past and present, than its chief competitor.

Writers for the *Source* have adroitly kept their readers abreast of the latest developments and drama within the community of Hip Hop artists and musicians. They often provide a forum for discussions relating to the state of Hip Hop. In a few feature articles and in the "Ear to the Street" and "Central Booking" sections of the magazine, writers for the *Source* have critically addressed relevant aspects of African American life, past and present, as well as issues pertaining to the African diaspora, such as HIV/AIDS, female circumcision in Africa, reparations, Black Studies, police brutality, and black leadership. These commentaries, however, represent only a very small part of the magazine. *The Source* is nonhistorical for the most part, unless speaking about the not-so-distant history of Hip Hop music and culture or the personal histories of Hip Hop artists. The feature length articles pertaining to black history are uncommon. When the editors have decided to deal with historical issues, the results have often been positive. The potential for igniting historical consciousness among its readers is great and has been revealed in more than a few instances.

The March 2001 issue serves as a pertinent and revealing example. This issue discussed the life of Gwendolyn Brooks based upon an interview with Haki Madhubuti, the history of police brutality in Oakland, California, and the life of former Black Panther Dhuruba bin Wahad, and also addressed the Detroit race riot of 1943. The six page article featured rare photographs and easy to read historical prose. The author Dan Frosch traced the history of black resistance in Detroit, mentioning the city's Underground Railroad, the black newspaper the *Plain Dealer*, the famous Ossian Sweet case in the 1920s, the riots of 1943 and 1967, Motown, and the leadership of Coleman Young. One photo in the article is particularly shocking and instructional. Blown up on a full page under the heading "Horrifying scene from the 1943 riot," the article presents a photo of a nicely dressed middle-aged black man bleeding profusely from the face and being held up by two young white men who were looking directly into the camera as if the scenes had been carefully constructed by them. One of the white youths was wearing a U.S. Army sweatshirt and a pair of bloodstained khaki pants. In his right hand he held a blood soaked handkerchief of some sort, which he had apparently used to wipe off the victim's face. The other young man was smiling proud, sporting a suit and tie. More than previous black generations, the Hip Hop generation relates to history as revealed through visual images. These images certainly helped the *Source's* black readers better understand the police brutality their community faced. Similar historically relevant articles are scattered throughout issues of the *Source*. More articles such as these are needed, especially as feature articles, since it is easy to overlook such knowledge among the onslaught of ads and distracting images.[35]

Vibe is also an interesting case study. Founded in the early 1990s by Quincy Jones and Time-Warner, *Vibe* is more mainstream in its appeal than the *Source*. In 2002, *Vibe* beat out the *New Yorker*, *Jane*, *Wired*, and *Gourmet* in winning the General Excellence award from the National Magazine Awards, sponsored by the American Society of Magazine Editors. According to *Vibe's* former Editor in Chief Emil Wilbekin, "it's the first time a magazine that covers urban music, with a large African American audience, has won in the award's 37-year history."[36] *Vibe* focuses upon Hip Hop artists, fashion, and music; and it rarely focuses on issues related to black history and cultural consciousness in critical manners. Nationalist rappers like dead prez and "underground" and other socially conscious artists have received some coverage, but much less than in comparison to the attention given to "commercial" artists.

In the one-page "What's Up" section of the magazine, which is easy to overlook, the editor in chief routinely discusses important issues relevant to the black community. In May 2002 Wilbekin called upon African American men to stop emulating "the posturing, the clothing, the jewelry, the womanizing, and the lifestyle of the gangster high life," all dynamics that the magazine directly glorifies. He has also criticized Hip Hop's self-destructive elements. In another instance, evoking history, Wilbekin asserted that Hip Hop artists were not correctly laying the foundations for future generations as earlier ones had. "Back in the day, Hip Hop had political consciousness . . . we need to get involved and make more powerful statements, as our forefathers did."[37] However, such ideas are significantly contradicted by other views. When making references to black history for inspiration and comparisons, there has been a tendency among the Hip Hop generation to turn to the Black Power era because it is fresh in African America's collective memory, many of the activists from this period are still alive, it is more appealing than the nonviolent direct action strategies of the Civil Rights Movement, and it provides an obvious form of militancy and radicalism with which many hip hoppers (especially those self-proclaimed "thugs" and "gangstas") can relate. In a 2002 issue, Wilbekin asserted: "There's a new Black Power in America. Secretary of State Colin Powell and National Security Advisor Condoleezza Rice are the most powerful of any African Americans in government. Russell Simmons is politicizing the Hip Hop nation. . . . Tiger Woods, Venus and Serena Williams, Shaquille O'Neal and Kobe Bryant are flexing athletic prowess and reigning as champions. . . . We won . . . but we need to keep on fighting, working, demanding equality . . . creating powerful music, and keeping our eyes on the prize."[38] The brief commentary also featured a photo of Denzel Washington and Halle Berry with their Oscars in hand. Wilbekin's version of Black Power is ahistorical, cliché at best, and equates Black Power with African American "firsts" and ideological and political conservatism. Of all Hip Hop generation entertainers, dead prez has done one of the most thorough and accurate jobs of historicizing and memorializing the Black Power era with their countless tributes to the Black Panther Party on *let's get free*.

In the September 2002 volume of *Vibe*, another article equated Black Power with the economic gains and conspicuous consumption of a few Hip Hop moguls. The photo accompanying the article is of a black male executive's clenched fist imitating the traditional Black Power symbol. It is easy to decipher the Rolex mark on the man's watch. The author Audrey Edwards opens by defining Black Power in a simple, misleading, ahistorical manner: "Back in the day, black power was about the symbols, not the benjamins. Black leather jackets and black beats. Dashikis and towering Afros. . . . We marched and sat in. We had clear leaders then, diverse and often divided, but each with a following and a vision." Edwards claimed that, "though many of us never really thought about what Black Power actually looked like once we had it, we were always pretty clear on what it meant: the freedom to mix and mingle with whites as equals. To sit beside them in the classroom or on the bus or at a lunch counter, to live next to them in integrated neighborhoods, to work with them in racially diverse job settings." Edward's description of "Black Power" sounds more like an oversimplification of the goals of the Civil Rights Movement. The proponents of Black Power (the Black Panther Party, Stokely Carmichael, Malauna Karenga and US, Angela Davis, George Jackson, Amiri Baraka, the Republic of New Africa, D.R.U.M., and many others) did not see integration with whites as their ultimate goal. Black cultural autonomy was central to Black Power activists. Further clouding the history of the Black Power era, Edwards claimed that "entertainment is driving American culture to Black Power."[39]

Popular magazines are not expected to provide deep historical analyses of African American history. This is the job of professional historians. But, if widely read magazines decide to delve into history, they should be accurate in their presentation. Hip Hop generation historians need to be actively involved in promoting and popularizing the study of black history among the Hip Hop generation by tapping into the Hip Hop ethos. A popular black history magazine administered by Hip Hop generation historians is long overdue. We are in need of an updated, Hip Hop version of Woodson's the *Negro History Bulletin,* first started in 1937 as a means of broadening black history's clientele.[40] The *Crisis,* founded by the NAACP and Du Bois in 1910, continues to address crucial issues relating to the African American community, past and present. However, it has not attracted a large following among the Hip Hop generation. Published from October 1989 until June 2000, a magazine like *Emerge* needs to be reintroduced.[41] There currently exists one major, widely circulated magazine, which is devoted to democratizing the complex study of black history. A quarterly founded in 1998, *American Legacy: The Magazine of African-American History and Culture* is thorough, informative, reader friendly, and covers a wide range of interesting topics in every issue. This magazine does not possess the political flavor that the *Crisis* does or that *Emerge* did, and unfortunately it does not seem to have attracted a large following within the Hip Hop generation. Each issue of *American Legacy* does, however, contain informative, easy to read articles concerning vital issues of African American history. Such a magazine with a Hip Hop culture flavor could help restore black history's important function in black youth culture.[42]

In the not so distant past, especially during and shortly after the Black Power era, *Ebony* and *Essence* were vital in promoting black history. Their recent histories could help guide future hip hoppers' efforts. Lerone Bennett, Jr.'s, numerous articles throughout the Civil Rights-Black Power era not only exposed *Ebony* readers to important historical events and personalities, but he also challenged his readers to

331

acknowledge their relationship to the past. In a paper delivered at an annual ASALH meeting, which was published in *Ebony* in 1980, Bennett declared, "We are responsible, totally responsible, not only for ourselves but for the whole of the Black experience. For it is only through us that the dreams of the past can be fulfilled. It is only through us that the first slave can reach the finish line."[43] During the 1970s *Essence* featured informative articles on Africa and African culture, Black Studies, black male-female relationships, black literary figures, and black history and culture in general. In the early 1970s, John Henrik Clarke published several articles on African Women's history more than a few years before it became a major subfield for Africanists. During the mid- to late 1970s, *Essence* featured a history section called "Family Tree." In July 1976, Anita King challenged her readership with a "Her-Story Quiz," proclaiming that throughout the course of history, black women "were not just standing on the sidelines cheering our men on."[44] This leading black women's magazine still continues to address issues pertinent to black women, and like *Ebony* and *Jet*, it deals with black history from time to time, usually during Black History Month. Echoing Na'im Akbar, the February 2005 volume of *Essence*, in its "Black History Special," critically discusses various incarnations of "post-traumatic slave syndrome" and how African Americans can liberate themselves.[45] Yet, overall *Essence* no longer possesses the overt political and historical flavor that it did during its formative years.

"HISTORICAL REVIVALISM?": RECENT COMMERCIAL HIP HOP'S PORTRAYAL OF BLACK HISTORY

Though Todd Boyd adamantly argues that the Hip Hop generation cannot mimic the struggles and approaches of the Civil Rights Movement and that Hip Hop better informs us about the present state of black America than the black historical record, he also acknowledges that "Hip Hop is defined by a strong sense of historical identity," that it's "all about history."[46] Many of today's most popular Hip Hop artists' modern Horatio Alger stories and personal histories are inspirational to black youth and significant local and underground black history-centered Hip Hop exists; yet, the rap music that dominates today's airwaves does little to spark young people's interest in black history. In previous generations, even during the so-called heyday of Hip Hop from the 1980s until the early to mid-1990s, young African Americans could readily turn to nonunderground black music for insightful discussions about the state of African people, past, present, and future. Prior to the Black Power era, music was especially functional in African American culture. The Spirituals, Jazz, the Blues, Soul music, and R&B have all functioned in constructive, therapeutic ways in black communities.[47] Certainly, black musical expressions have been exploited for hundreds of years.[48] Yet, within the last decade, rap has reached unprecedented levels of commodification and commercialization, all the while extolling "the virtues of conspicuous consumption."[49] In his insightful assessment of the "black popular music tradition" over the last fifty years, *What the Music Said*, Mark Anthony Neal identifies the recent shift in Hip Hop's historicism: "In less than a decade, Hip Hop culture had been transformed from a subculture primarily influenced by the responses of black urban youth to postindustrialization into a billion-dollar industry in which such responses were exploited by corporate capitalist and the petit bourgeois desires [and interests]." As a result, Hip Hop has become increasingly disconnected from "the real communal history of the African American diaspora."[50] Recent widely embraced, "commercial" rap is not concerned with black history in any meaningful sense. Several examples are revealing.

In "The Jump Off" from her *La Bella Mafia* album, Lil' Kim likened herself to the Black Panthers. She rhymed: "I'm the wicked bitch of the east, you better keep the peace, or come out like the beast. We the best, still there's room for improvement. Our presence is felt like the Black Panther movement."[51] Commercial Hip Hop has in a few cases revived Emmett Till and the modern Civil Rights Movement. In his hit "Through the Wire," which recounts his October 2002 near fatal car accident, Kanye West recounted: "And just imagine how my girl feel, on the plane scared as hell that her guy look like Emmett Till." West's personal triumph over tragedy is inspirational. Still, it would be refreshing if a major, rising mainstream Hip Hop artist could discuss the brutal lynching of Till more directly. In a few more stanzas, West could have very easily schooled young African Americans about what Till represents for the black struggle. In another track with Jay-Z on the 2003 *College Dropout* CD, West mentions how his mother and grandparents' sit-in activities influenced him. A more complete set of verses about the meaning and realities of the Civil Rights Movement's strategies is easily within West's range and would be very instructive to his young listeners. As Fayemi Shakur has observed, Remy Ma, who mentioned Till on Terror Squad's "Yeah, Yeah, Yeah," admitted that she only used Till in her rhyme because West did. "Had I known more about the history behind it, I probably would have done it differently," Remy told *The Ave*.[52] Mississippi native David Banner has more seriously attempted to memorialize Till. He remembers Till in his music and videos, and has honored Till by "launching a line of jerseys in the boy's honor." A pragmatist, Banner rationalizes this act of homage: "To get information out to our people sometimes means we have to get down at a level they're at. And in Hip Hop, that means you got to thug it out."[53] Hip Hop artists certainly have the right to define their own agendas. But, they clearly have the power and potential to influence many black youths by injecting facts and symbols from black history into their rhymes, which are ritualistically memorized by millions. Nelson George's observation from 1998 is still very relevant: "Hip Hop's major problem is that MCs are not social activists by training or inclination."[54]

Nas (Nasir Jones) presents an interesting case. He was almost universally praised for his 2002 hit "I Can." One reviewer noted that in "I Can," Nas blows black youths' minds with "a fact-filled verse about African empires and the dawn of European colonial aggression."[55] Given the state of commercial Hip Hop, Nas's anthem was refreshing. Nas declares in a series of verses: "Africa was almost robbed naked. Slavery was money, so they began making slave ships. . . . Still goes on today, you see?

If the truth is told, the youth can grow. Then learn to survive and gain control. Nobody wants to be gangstas and hoes. Read more, learn more, change the globe. Ghetto children, do your thing. Hold your head up, little man, you're a king." The children's background vocals, like those that appear in Trick Daddy's thug anthem and Jaheim's "Fabulous," help draw in young listeners. Though inspirational, positive, and original, Nas's "I Can" contains a few factual inaccuracies about ancient African history. In other tracks from "God's Son," Nas demonstrated the ability to successfully include tidbits from black history. He should also be applauded for his history-relevant lyrics on the re-mix of Jadakiss's "Why?" and his 2004 *Street's Disciple* double CD, which contains several socially conscious and historically relevant tracks.

In "These Are Our Heroes," Nas chastises the Hip Hop generation's icons for not praising the sacrifices of elder black entertainers and leaders such as Stokely Carmichael (Kwame Ture), Nikki Giovanni, Jim Brown, Fela Kuti, and Mariam Makeba. Echoing Spike Lee's tactics in "Bamboozled," Nas compares today's black entertainers with those of the past: "You Homey the Clown, bowtie, apple pie, Bo Jangles. But we love Bo Jangles, we know what he came through, but what's your excuse? . . . You don't ride for the facts. . . ." In "U.B.R. (Unofficial Biography of Rakim)," Nas demonstrates his ability to clearly articulate the personal life history of a pioneer Hip Hop artist. Such an approach would work well with all major personalities in African American history. In "Bridging the Gap," a track he recorded with his father jazz trumpeter Olu Dara, Nas delves into the history of black music, making relevant connections between himself and the past: "Bridging the gap from the blues to jazz to rap. The history of music on this track. The blues came from gospel, gospel from blues. Slaves are harmonizin' them ah's and ooh's. Old School, new school, know the rules. All these years I been voicin' my blues. . . ." There are several other instances where Nas has historicized Hip Hop.[56]

Yet, when compared to KRS-One's flow from the late 1980s and early 1990s about African and African American history, Nas's black history conscious rap, however impeccable, seems perhaps a bit less advanced. KRS-One, who recently published an insightful study entitled *Ruminations* (2003) in which he discusses the meaning of black history for the Hip Hop generation, rapped about African and African American history in greater detail than any of today's mainstream rappers. His approach was clearly a reflection of the Golden Age in the late 1980s and early 1990s, his upbringing, and the pre-hyper commercial phase of Hip Hop. In his hit "You Must Learn," from Boogie Down Production's *Ghetto Music: The Blueprint of Hip Hop* (1989), a nineteen year old KRS-One schooled his listeners: "When one doesn't know about the other one's culture, ignorance swoops down like a vulture. 'Cause you don't know that you ain't just a janitor. No one told you about Benjamin Banneker, a brilliant man who invented an almanac. . . . Granville Woods made the walkie-talkie. Lewis Latimer improved on Edison. Charles Drew did a lot for medicine. Garrett Morgan made the traffic lights. Harriet Tubman freed the slaves at night. Madame C. J. Walker made the straightening comb, but you won't know this if you weren't shown. The point I'm gettin' at, it might be harsh, 'cause we're just walkin' around brainwashed. . . . You must learn."[57] A year later on his *Edutainment* album, KRS-One discussed facets of African American history in the form of brief lectures. He continues to lecture throughout the country and has shared the podium upon several occasions with Cornel West.[58]

There are artists whose rhymes contain detailed black history and socially conscious lyrics and are found at the present time in the works of Talib Kweli, dead prez, Immortal Technique, Mos Def, and many others. Their music, however, does not receive the type of airplay and support needed to have a large scale impact on those who do not buy their CDs. The challenge becomes how to make black history socially conscious Hip Hop without becoming overly commercial. Rejecting the label of role model that is often placed upon them by American society, most Hip Hop artists probably do not view themselves as being responsible for changing their listeners' consciousness, especially concerning black history. But imagine if all the major "commercial" Hip Hop artists agreed to devote at least one major track of every album to black history. Imagine if Hip Hop artists agreed to collaborate with historians on a black history CD.

HISTORICIZING THE HIP HOP GENERATION'S BLACK HISTORY MONTH CELEBRATIONS

In February 1966 John Hope Franklin wrote a brief article in *Negro Digest* in which he chronicled the contributions of black historians from James W. C. Pennington's 1841 *A Text Book of the Origins and History of Colored People* to the early works of Du Bois and Woodson. In an uncharacteristically emotional manner, Franklin concluded his essay on "Pioneer Negro Historians" by declaring: "One of the most cruel things that one could do today would be to forget or ignore pioneers such as these early Negro historians. One of the most praiseworthy things one could do would be to recognize the enormous importance of their keeping the light of truth flickering until it could be kindled by greater resources and many more hands."[59] Franklin's forty-year-old sentiments are still relevant.

Hip Hop generation black historians could benefit from critically revisiting how black historians from the Woodson era through the Black Power movement actively transformed history into a social force and reforming agent. Since the unofficial end of the Black Power movement in the mid-1970s, the pragmatic Woodsonian vision of black history seems to have been co-opted. This is epitomized by the increasing commercialization of Black History Month, Kwanzaa, and the Martin Luther King, Jr., Holiday.[60] Let's look briefly at Black History Month. As a result of the ASALH's efforts at popularization, beginning in 1976 Woodson's week-long celebration became Black History Month. The exact point at which Black History Month became intimately linked with American capitalism and commercial life is unknown, but it was an inevitable transition. Profit seekers very likely began exploiting black history during the Negro History Weeks of Woodson's times.

By the late 1970s many U.S. corporations capitalized on Black History Month and the vestiges of black cultural pride leftover from the Black Power era. A perusal of *Essence* and *Ebony* demonstrates how advertisers used black history and Black History Month to target middle-class black consumers. United and American Airlines, Chrysler, and Bell Telephone were among the first to feature ads in these magazines that used elements of black history as marketing hooks. By the mid-1980s, Black History Month was being directly used by countless corporations to sell products. For instance, in the February 1986 issue of *Ebony*, there were several pages of special "Black History Month Money Saving Coupons." *Essence* followed similar trends, featuring many advertisements that used black history and Black History Month to target black consumers.[61]

Currently, companies like Campus Marketing Specialists, Inc. are seeking to make profits off of the history of the African American struggle by mass marketing Black History Month posters, pens, notepads, buttons, key tags, bookmarks, stadium cups, and faux Kente cloth scarves. Some may argue that this publicity helps popularize black history. Memorabilia can indeed help publicize Black History Month. But, it can also trivialize black history and the millions of dollars made off of this type of marketing should, as Woodson championed, be invested into the black history movement. Black consumers should also be aware of these disrespectful marketing ploys. U.S. popular culture and media has increasingly commodified Black History Month, distancing it from the day-to-day lives of young African Americans and thereby going against the Woodsonian paradigm.

During the 1990s various black historians and scholars, including John Hope Franklin, Earl Ofari Hutchinson, Robert L. Harris, Jr., Bettye J. Gardner, Harold Cruse, and Darlene Clark Hine, collectively voiced their concerns regarding the commercialization of Black History Month.[62] The Hip Hop generation suffers from the changes these scholars described. In 1997 writers for the *Journal of Blacks in Higher Education* discussed how Black History Month had been "usurped by large corporations" and greedy book publishers.[63] Franklin chastised marketers and lecturers for capitalizing on the celebration. "The commercialization of the 'month,'" Franklin declared, "provides the hucksters with a longer period in which to sell their trinkets and souvenirs, corporations a greater opportunity to display their special brand of 'civic awareness,' and lecturers the golden chance to show off their knowledge of black history."[64]

Cruse recounted that the Negro History Weeks of Woodson's times profoundly impacted him, but he openly criticized contemporary black historians for adding "very little, if anything" to Woodson's contributions. In his classic iconoclastic style, Cruse challenged young black historians to innovate new ways of conceptualizing Black History Month: "The bulk of the new bunch of black historians has little to say that is really new, inventive, or revealing."[65] Cruse's harsh critiques of black historians coming of age in the late 1990s could have very well represented unresolved issues carried over from *The Crisis of the Negro Intellectual*. Nonetheless, Hip Hop generation historians should respond to his challenges by attempting to incorporate Black

History Month into Hip Hop culture. Given the overall ahistorical mainstream culture in the United States when it comes to dealing with the African Americans, making black history practical and popular among the masses of black youth today would certainly be something—in Cruse's terms—"new, inventive" and "revealing." In order to successfully accomplish this, black historians could benefit from immersing themselves in Hip Hop culture in order to reach the youth. This immersion must be monitored and balanced so as not to render oneself unproductive and disrespected as a professional historian. As various Hip Hop intellectuals have demonstrated, it would be useful for Hip Hop generation historians to speak several languages and be able to code-switch. This code-switching, as cultural critic Adolph Reed, Jr., has warned, must be genuine and not merely entertainment.[66]

The Negro History Week celebrations of Woodson's times are instructive for current conditions. They were much more pragmatic than many more recent Black History Month celebrations. Though living in times when the study of African American life and history has been legitimized in the academy and widely accessible, the members of the Hip Hop generation do not enjoy the same types of black historical celebrations as many black youths did during the first half of the twentieth century. Many of Woodson's colleagues believed that Negro History Week was Woodson's "most characteristic creation." Luther Porter Jackson called Negro History Week "the feeder for every other activity of the Association." L. D. Reddick added that Woodson's "greatest influence upon the public came through Negro History Week." In 1926 Woodson created Negro History Week essentially to integrate the teaching of black history into the curricula of U.S. elementary and secondary schools while also exposing the black masses, especially the youth, to black history. He also believed that whites' exposure to black history could help to eliminate racial prejudice. In pamphlets, *The Journal of Negro History*, and especially the *Negro History Bulletin*, Woodson routinely detailed how Negro History Week celebrations could be best carried out.[67]

For Woodson, it was of the utmost importance for the people themselves, especially the children, to directly participate in the black historical process. In October 1941 he offered the following advice to school teachers: "Do not call in some silver-tongued orator to talk to your school about the history of the Negro. The orator does not generally have much in his head. His chief qualification is strong lungs—a good bellows. He knows very little about things in general and practically nothing about the Negro in particular, except how to exploit the race. Let the children study the history of the race, and they will be the speakers who will put the spellbinder to shame."[68] As Negro History Week became more popular, Woodson also routinely warned about those "impostors" and "mis-informants," mainly entertainers, who, under the name of the Association, made large profits during mid-February. At one point, he even demanded that they turn over their earnings to the Association.[69] Black History Month commemorations are currently plagued by the problems Woodson described decades ago.

Activist-columnist Earl Ofari Hutchinson has pinpointed the dilemmas with the Hip Hop generation's exposure to Black History Month. "Seventy-four years ago, pioneer black historian Carter G. Woodson initiated . . . Negro History Week. He wanted to rescue black people's accomplishments from the netherworld of American history and make them a source of pride for blacks and all Americans. Today Black History Month is an established tradition. Politicians designate special days, issue proclamations, and sponsor tributes to African American notables. TV networks shove in most of their specials, documentaries, and features on African Americans. Then February ends, and it's back to business as usual. Black achievements vanish from the screen, the concert halls, and the speeches of politicians." Hutchinson concluded his critique by declaring that "It's time to end this annual disappearing act. Black contributions to society should be celebrated every month. . . . When the experience of blacks is accepted as central to the American story, black history will be what it always should have been—American history."[70]

EMBRACING "SANKOFA" WHILE TAPPING INTO HIP HOP CULTURE: THE NECESSITY OF HIP HOP GENERATION HISTORIANS' PERSPECTIVES

Young black historians cannot simply imitate Woodson and his co-workers' visions and efforts.[71] I am not calling for the blind return to some utopian black historical past. Our efforts must be reflective of the distinct times in which we live. Armed with our knowledge and distinct interpretations of history, we need to address a host of serious problems in the black community, all of which have concrete historical roots in a past marked by racial oppression and discrimination. Vincent Harding's eloquent articulation of the responsibilities of black scholars to "direct as much of their writing, their speaking, their teaching, and their singing" to the black community is instructive.[72] We need to embrace, engage, and speak to the young in the Hip Hop generation, whose culture is at the present time defining and directing youth cultural movements around the world. As pioneering Hip Hop scholar Tricia Rose has convincingly argued, rap music and Hip Hop culture have the potential to "revitalize American culture."[73]

Black historians, especially those of the Hip Hop generation, need to consider creating effective, innovative, and appealing media with which to popularize and transmit black history throughout black communities, especially among the Hip Hop generation and the youth. The recent development of various online black history websites as well as the movement to publish easy-to-read textbooks, biographies, thematic studies, and juvenile literature are necessary steps in making black history popular and accessible. Rap music, Hip Hop culture's most characteristic creation, could serve as an effective transmitter of black history. Cheryl Keyes has highlighted the relationship between emcees and griots—oral historians from bardic West African traditions—suggesting that modern rappers were influenced by their African oral history predecessors.[74] Rose has defined the role of the rapper in the black community in a manner that is strikingly similar to the role of the black historian: "Rap music is a black cultural expression that prioritizes black voices from the margins of urban America. Rap music is a form of rhymed storytelling accompanied by highly rhythmic, electronically based music. . . . From the outset, rap music has articulated the pleasures and problems of black urban life in contemporary America. . . . Rappers speak with the voice of personal experience, taking on the identity of the observer or narrator. . . . Rappers tell long, involved, and sometimes abstract stories with catchy and memorable phrases and beats that lend themselves to black sound bite packaging, storing critical fragments in fast-paced electrified rhythms. Rap tales are told in elaborate and ever-changing black slang and refer to black cultural figures and rituals, mainstream film, video and television characters, and little-known black heroes."[75] As academic MCs, Hip Hop generation historians must continue to develop innovative ways to share with black youths their communal history. We are, after all, competing with a very attractive group of musicians and artists. Of the utmost importance is that we approach our craft with the passion and energy of the four main pillars of Hip Hop: MCing, DJing, graffiti art, and dancing.

Scores of Hip Hop scholars have acknowledged the pragmatism of embracing dimensions of Hip Hop. Several elder scholars from a generation largely alienated from their progeny have transcended divisive generational boundaries and have also recognized this. In his recent study *Great Wells of Democracy* (2002), Manning Marable called for cross-generational dialogues and the usage of Hip Hop "as a matrix for black empowerment."[76] On his debut 2001 CD, *Sketches of My Culture*, Cornel West attempted to speak to the Hip Hop generation by marrying Hip Hop instrumentals to his intellectual discourse. Harvard University president Lawrence Summers failed to understand the importance of West's pragmatic approach to black history and West's CD did not gain any following among the Hip Hop generation. Tapping into Hip Hop culture, a central part of many young black adults' existence, could be very useful for upcoming generations of black historians. Black historians could help restore Hip Hop's "historical revivalism." If mainstream Hip Hop artists in conjunction with black historians produced a CD with a dozen tracks, which recounted black history from the shores of Africa to the present, millions of black and white youths alike would be able to recite black history, feel the black past, and internalize aspects of the enduring black struggle for liberation. Given the present crises facing black youth, such creative means are warranted. Hip Hop generation historians could also help the present and future Hip Hop generations fully appreciate where they fit in the black struggle. They should be routinely reminded that their generation follows in the footsteps of a black history characterized by struggle.

A student of black history himself, Malcolm X served as the "archetype, reference point, and spiritual advisor in absentia" for Black Power activists. Similarly, during the late 1980s and early 1990s, especially following Spike Lee's 1992 film, youths of the Hip Hop generation looked to Malcolm X for great inspiration. Malcolm understood that "of all our studies, history is best qualified to reward our research," and believed adamantly that African and African American history were central to the formation of African Americans' collective identity.[77] While he was not a professional historian, it is timely to reflect upon Malcolm's straightforward ideas pertaining to the significance of black history in African peoples' struggles for freedom and advancement. In a speech to members of the Organization of Afro-American Unity a month before he was assassinated, Malcolm X argued that African Americans lacked a knowledge of their history, which contributed directly to their oppression. He defined black history in direct relation to the present: "When you deal with the past, you're dealing with history, you're dealing actually with the origin of a thing. When you know the origin, you know the cause. If you don't know the origin, you don't know the reason, you're just cut off, you're left standing in mid-air. It is so important for you and me to spend time today learning something about the past so that we can better understand the present, analyze it, and then do something about it."[78]

NOTES

[1] Earl E. Thorpe, "Philosophy of History: Sources, Truths, and Limitations," *The Quarterly Review of Higher Education Among Negroes* 25 (July 1957): 183.

[2] John Hope Franklin, "On the Evolution of Scholarship on Afro-American History," in Darlene Clark Hine, ed., *The State of Afro-American History: Past, Present, and Future* (Baton Rouge, LA, 1986), 13.

[3] KRS-One, *Ruminations* (New York, 2003), 145, 154–55.

[4] Earl E. Thorpe, *Black Historians: A Critique* (New York, 1971), 18. For discussions of the black historical profession, see Thorpe's study as well as Michael R. Winston, *The Howard Department of History: 1913–1973* (Washington, DC, 1973); Franklin, "On the Evolution of Scholarship in Afro-American History," 13–22; August Meier and Elliott Rudwick, *Black History and the Historical Profession, 1915–1980* (Urbana, IL, 1986); Carter G. Woodson, "Negro Historians of Our Times," *Negro History Bulletin* 8 (April 1945): 155–59, 166; Benjamin Quarles, "Black History's Antebellum Origins," *American Antiquarian Society* 89 (1979): 89–122; John Hope Franklin, *George Washington Williams: A Biography* (Chicago, IL, 1985); Wilson Jeremiah Moses, *Afrotopia: The Roots of African American Popular History* (Cambridge, MA, 1998); Julie Des Jardins, *Women and the Historical Enterprise in America: Gender, Race, and Politics of Memory, 1880–1945* (Chapel Hill, NC, 2003); Pero Gaglo Dagbovie, "Black Women Historians from the Late 19th Century until the Dawning of the Civil Rights Movement," *The Journal of African American History* (Summer 2004): 241–61.

[5] William Van Deburg, *New Day in Babylon: The Black Power Movement and American Culture, 1965–1975* (Chicago, IL, 1992), 280.

[6] Meier and Rudwick, *Black History and the Historical Profession*, 161.

[7] Harold Cruse, *The Crisis of the Negro Intellectual* (New York, 1984), 565.

[8] Bazel E. Allen and Ernest J. Wilson, "Foreword," to Harold Cruse, *The Crisis of the Negro Intellectual* (1967; reprinted New York, 1984), vi.

[9] Scott Heath quoted in Kendra Hamilton, "Making Some Noise: The Academy's Hip Hop Generation," *Black Issues of Higher Education* 21 (22 April 2004): 35.

[10] Robin D. G. Kelley is an exception. He first addressed Hip Hop in the 1990s. Other black historians have recently addressed Hip Hop as well. These references, however, have been in passing in textbooks on the African American experience.

[11] Some of these books include: Steven Hager, *Hip Hop: The Illustrated History of Break Dancing, Rap Music, and Graffiti* (New York, 1984); Houston Baker, Jr., *Black Studies: Rap and the Academy* (Chicago, IL, 1993); S. H. Fernando, *The New Beats: Exploring the Music, Culture, and Attitudes of Hip Hop* (New York, 1994); Tricia Rose, *Black Noise: Rap Music and Black Culture in Contemporary America* (Middletown, CT, 1994); Russell A. Porter, *Spectacular Vernaculars: Hip Hop and the Politics of Postmodernism* (Albany, NY, 1995); Nelson George, *Hip Hop America* (New York, 1998); Alan Light, ed., *The Vibe History of Hip Hop* (New York, 1999). For a comprehensive list of sources dealing with Hip Hop from the 1980s and 1990s, see the bibliography in Cheryl L. Keyes, *Rap Music and Street Consciousness* (Urbana, IL, 2002), 260–80. For a brief review of the historical scholarship on Hip Hop, see Murray Forman and Mark Anthony Neal, eds., *That's*

the Joint: The Hip Hop Studies Reader (New York, 2004).

[12]Hamilton, "Making Some Noise," 34.

[13]Untitled document, *Dergi: The Magazine*, http://www.instanbulmuseum.org/muze/dergi/magazine/hiphp.htm.

[14]For instance, see Alonzo Westbrook, *Hip Hoptionary: The Dictionary of Hip Hop Terminology* (New York, 2002); Jim Fricke, *Yes Yes Y'all: The Experience Music Project Oral History of Hip Hop's First Decade* (Cambridge, 2002); Todd Boyd, *The New H.N.I.C. (Head Niggas in Charge): The Death of Civil Rights and the Reign of Hip Hop* (New York, 2002); Murray Forman, *The 'Hood Comes First: Race, Space, and Place in Rap and Hip Hop* (Middletown, CT, 2002); Anthony Pinn, *Noise and Spirit: The Religious and Spiritual Sensibilities of Rap Music* (New York, 2003); Oliver Wang, ed., *Classic Material: The Hip Hop Album Guide* (Toronto, Canada, 2003); Todd Boyd, *Young, Black, Rich, and Famous: The Rise of the NBA, the Hip Hop Invasion, and the Transformation of American Culture* (New York, 2003); Kevin Powell, *Who's Gonna Take the Weight?: Manhood, Race, and Power in America* (New York, 2003); Ian Maxwell, *Phat Beats, Dope Rhymes: Hip Hop Down Under Comin' Upper* (Middletown, CT, 2003); Forman and Neal, eds., *That's the Joint*; Gwendolyn D. Pough, *Check It While I Wreck It: Black Womanhood, Hip Hop Culture, and the Public Sphere* (Boston, 2004).

[15]Rachel Raimist, "You Must Learn: Hip Hop Academics Are Now on the Rise at Most Colleges," *The Source: The Magazine of Hip Hop Music, Culture and Politics* No. 168 (September 2003): 57. Raimist appears to have coined the term "Hiphopology." On 18 October 2003, *The New York Times* featured a lengthy article on Rose in its "Arts and Ideas" section.

[16]Forman, *The 'Hood Comes First*, xix–xx.

[17]Robin D. G. Kelley and Earl Lewis, eds., *To Make Our World Anew: A History of African Americans* (New York, 2000), 613. Mark Anthony Neal has called what Kitwana's calls the Hip Hop generation "soul babies."

[18]Bakari Kitwana, *The Hip Hop Generation: Young Blacks and the Crisis in African-American Culture* (New York, 2002), xiii, 4.

[19]Aldon Morris, *The Origins of the Civil Rights Movement: Black Communities Organizing for Change* (New York, 1984), x.

[20]For a more detailed discussion of "old head" black men, see Elijah Anderson, *Streetwise: Race, Class, and Change in an Urban Community* (Chicago, IL, 1990).

[21]Kitwana, *The Hip Hop Generation*, 6–8.

[22]Ibid., xiii, xiv; Jeff Chang does not agree with Kitwana's conceptualization of the "hip-hop generation," and he has openly challenged Kitwana. See Chang, *Can't Stop Won't Stop: A History of the Hip Hop Generation* (New York, 2005), 1–3.

[23]It must be noted that there are certainly those who do not fit neatly within the two general categories of Hip Hop generations that I offer. I am not arguing for a dichotomy between the BP Hip Hop generation and the PBP Hip Hop generation. I offer this subdivision to contribute to a dialogue about defining the Hip Hop generation.

[24]Kelley and Lewis, eds., *To Make Our World Anew*, 604.

[25]For a brief definition of "conscious" rap, see Yvonne Bynoe, "How Ya' Like Me Now?: Rap and Hip Hop Come of Age," in Herb Boyd, ed., *Race and Resistance: African Americans in the 21st Century* (Cambridge, MA, 2002), 89–99. Also see Cheryl L. Keyes, *Rap Music and Street Consciousness* (Urbana, IL, 2004); Joseph D. Eure and James G. Spady, *Nation Conscious Rap* (Philadelphia, PA, 1991).

[26]Michael Eric Dyson, *The Michael Eric Dyson Reader* (New York, 2004), 408–409.

[27]Donald Bogle, *Toms, Coons, Mulattoes, Mammies, and Bucks: An Interpretive History of Blacks in American Films* (New York, 2001), 318, 319, 323.

[28]Deborah Gray White, *Ar'n't I A Woman?: Female Slaves in the Plantation South* (New York, 1985), 27–61; see also Patricia Hill Collins, *Black Feminist Thought: Knowledge, Consciousness, and the Politics of Empowerment* (New York, 1990).

[29]For discussions of the impact of the Million Man March, see Roberto Gibral-Tarik, *One in a Million: Messages of the Historic Million Man March* (Berkeley, CA, 1996); Haki R. Madhubuti and Maulana Karenga,

eds., *Million Man March/Day of Absence: A Commemorative Anthology* (Chicago, IL, and Los Angles, CA, 1996).

[30]For a discussion of the harsh realities facing young blacks during the 1980s and 1990s, see Robin D. G. Kelley's essay, "Into the Fire," in *To Make Our World Anew*.

[31]Logan first defined the "nadir" in African American history as stemming from 1877 until 1901. He then extended it until 1923. See Rayford W. Logan, *The Negro in American Life and Thought: The Nadir, 1877–1901* (New York, 1954); Logan, *The Betrayal of the Negro from Rutherford B. Hayes to Woodrow Wilson*, New, Enlarged Edition (New York, 1968). For a contemporary discussion of African American health and its relationship to the past, see W. Michael Byrd and Linda A Clayton, eds., *An American Health Dilemma: A Medical History of African Americans and the Problem of Race, Beginnings to 1900* (New York, 2000); W. Michael Byrd and Linda A Clayton, eds., *An American Health Dilemma: Race, Medicine, and Health Care in the United States, 1900–2000* (New York, 2002).

[32]*The Ave Magazine: A Street Movement in Print* is not among the "majority of these magazines."

[33]For a discussion of the *Source*, see George, *Hip Hop America*, 16, 17, 67, 71–72.

[34]http://www.thesource.com.

[35]Dan Frosch, "Slum Beautiful," *The Source* (March 2001): 174–79.

[36]Emil Wilbekin, "In It to Win It," *Vibe* (September 2002): 70.

[37i]Emil Wilbekin, "No More Drama," *Vibe* (May 2002): 42; Wilbekin, "Follow the Leader," *Vibe* (June 2003): 26.

[38]Wilbekin, "In It to Win It," 70.

[39]Audrey Edwards, "Black Power," *Vibe*, September 2002, 188. For a recent discussion of Black Power see Jeffrey O. G. Ogbar, *Black Power: Radical Politics and African American Identity* (Baltimore, MD, 2004).

[40]For a discussion of *The Negro History Bulletin* during Woodson's times, see Pero Gaglo Dagbovie, "Making Black History Practical and Popular: Carter G. Woodson, the Proto Black Studies Movement, and the Struggle for Black Liberation," *The Western Journal of Black Studies* 27 (Winter 2003): 263–74.

[41]*Emerge* was one of the most recent black magazines devoted to important issues, historical and contemporary, pertaining to the African American community, covering topics such as "affirmative action, economic empowerment, religion, the criminal justice system, civil rights, sexism, education, and much, much more." The articles in *Emerge* were at times hard-hitting, often times historical, and could be easily digested and understood by lay members of the Hip Hop generation. In 2003, former editor George E. Curry announced that he hopes to soon publish the magazine again. One did not need to search through advertisements, photos of half-naked models and Hip Hop video "divas," celebrities' mansions and cars, as well as biographies of Hip Hop artists, celebrities, and entertainers in order to find historically relevant articles, as seems to be the case with today's popular black magazines. See George E. Curry, ed., *The Best of Emerge Magazine* (New York, 2003).

[42]For a good example of *American Legacy*'s commitment to black history, see "10th Anniversary Issue" (Fall 2005).

[43]Lerone Bennett, Jr., "Listen to the Blood: The Meaning of Black History," *Ebony* 36 (February 1981): 36, 38, 42.

[44]Anita King, "Her-Story Quiz," *Essence* 7 (July 1976): 20.

[45]Na'im Akbar, *Chains and Images of Psychological Slavery* (Jersey City, NJ, 1984); "Breaking the Chains," *Essence* 35 (February 2005): 150–53.

[46]Boyd, *The New H.N.I.C.*, 88. Throughout his diatribe, Boyd talks about how blacks of the Hip Hop generation should not turn to the past for guidance. He argues that the Hip Hop generation must create its own programs. At the same time, he claims, with limited evidence, that the Hip Hop generation is also very historical in its orientation.

[47]For an interesting discussion of the history of black music, see Samuel A Floyd, Jr., *The Power of Black Music: Interpreting Its History from Africa to the United States* (New York, 1995).

[48]In every stage of African American history, expressions of black music have been commercialized in varying degrees. For instance, during the middle passage it was not uncommon for African musicians to be used

for entertainment purposes. Likewise, during the antebellum and postbellum periods, minstrel shows and black groups like the Fisk Jubilee Singers existed and were very popular.

[49]Bynoe, "How Ya' Like Me Now?," 93.

[50]Mark Anthony Neal, *What the Music Said: Black Popular Music and Black Public Culture* (New York, 1999), 150, 154.

[51]The lyrics of Kim, West, Nas, KRS-One, and all the other Hip Hop artists cited in this article come from http://www.ohhla.com, one of the most reputable websites for Hip Hop lyrics.

[52]Fayemi Shakur, "Divided We Fall," *The Ave: A Street Movement in Print* Issue #05 (2004): 46.

[53]Ibid.

[54]George, *Hip Hop America*, 154–55.

[55]Akiba Solomon, "Record Report," *The Source* (No. 161), February 2003. 128.

[56]For a further discussion of Nas' view of history, see Saptosa Foster, "Bridging the Gap," *The Ave: A Street Movement in Print* Issue #05 (2004): 48–54.

[57]Boogie Down Productions, "You Must Learn," *Ghetto Music: The Blue Print of Hip Hop*, Jive/Novus (1989).

[58]For a sample of KRS-One and West's collaboration, see the audio CD by Front Page Entertainment in KRS-One, *Ruminations*.

[59]John Hope Franklin, "Pioneer Negro Historians," *Negro Digest* 15 (February 1966): 8–9.

[60]Beginning in the late 1990s, Malauna Karenga has responded to the commercialization of Kwanzaa in several articles in major papers such as the *Philadelphia Tribune*. For an insightful critique of the commercialization of Martin Luther King, Jr., Day, see Michael Erica Dyson, *I May Not Get There with You: The True Martin Luther King, Jr.* (New York, 2000), 286–306.

[61]The ads that I have discussed here appear in *Essence* and *Ebony* from about 1975 until 1979. United Airlines released an ad in *Essence* in 1975 and 1976 which told blacks to "celebrate yesterday's heroes" by visiting historical sites related to black historical figures such as Jean Baptiste Point Du Sable, Peter Salem, Bose Ikard, and Harriet Tubman. Several years later, in 1977 one of United's competitors, American Airlines, featured an ad featuring images of Frederick Douglass, James Beckworth, and Crispus Attucks. "Relive American History on an American Fly-Drive," American Airlines declared. "Now you can visit the historical places you've read and heard about. Places where great men spoke out for what they believed in." In the same year, the U.S. government urged *Essence* readers to purchase U.S. savings bonds in memory of Benjamin Banneker's surveying of the nation's capital. Chrysler used a black man with a big afro and dashiki to sell its vehicles. Bell Telephone marketed their products by claiming that they understood and respected blacks' unique history of communication and oral history, from the griots in West Africa to the present, and blacks' success in the motion picture and television industries. An obscure company named SOIL based in Mississippi offered *Essence* readers "genuine African earth encased in clear acrylic" "direct from Nigeria" for $10.50. This company claimed that the dirt was inspected by the U.S. government and represented "the soil on which trod the forefathers of Black America." Though educational, several companies, at least one of which was black-owned, marketed black history board games in *Essence*. Similar ads also appeared in *Ebony*. By the mid-1980s, many corporations were using Black History Month to actively market their products. For instance, in the February 1986 issue of *Ebony*, there were several pages of "Black History Month Money Saving Coupons." Businesses such as Duncan Hines, Tide, Tylenol, Uncle Ben's Rice, Aunt Jemima, Artra Skin Tone Cream, Sinutab, LaxCaps, Carefree Panty Shields, and many others joined the Black History Month bandwagon by strategically offering token salutes to famous black pioneers and inventors on coupons for their products. *Essence* carried similar coupons. Since the mid- to late 1980s, Philip Morris, Anheuser-Bush, Coors, McDonalds, Coca-Cola, Nissan, and many others have also been involved in Black History Month marketing. Some department stores have even had Black History Month sales.

[62]"How to Celebrate Black History Month 12 Months of the Year," *Ebony* 50 (February 1995): 62–66.

[63]"Black History Month: Education or Tokenism?," *The Journal of Blacks in Higher Education* 3 (Spring 1994): 30–31; "Black History Month: Serious Truth Telling or a Triumph of Tokenism?," *The Journal of*

Blacks in Higher Education 18 (Winter 1997–1998): 87.

64"Black History Month: Serious Truth Telling or a Triumph in Tokenism?," 88.

65Ibid., 90.

66Adolph Reed, Jr., criticized public intellectuals, namely Dyson, hooks, and Kelley, for what he deemed code-switching. In essence, Reed argued that they exploited, commodified, and trivialized elements of black popular culture in order to make names for themselves in the mainstream academy. See Reed, "What Are the Drums Saying, Booker?: The Current Crisis of the Black Intellectual," *The Village Voice*, 11 (April 1995): 31–36.

67L. D. Reddick quoted in Dagbovie, "Making Black History Practical and Popular."

68Carter G. Woodson, "Start Now Negro History Year in Order to Have a Negro History Week," *Negro History Bulletin* 5 (October 1941): 24.

69Carter G. Woodson, "Negro History Week," *The Journal of Negro History* (April 1936): 106–07.

70Earl Ofari Hutchinson, "Black History Is U.S. History: It's Time to Put the Role of Blacks on Center Stage," *San Francisco Chronicle*, 8 February 1999.

71"Sankofa" (pronounced sang-ko-fah) belongs to a larger group of the Akan people's adinkra symbols. Beginning several hundred years ago, these symbols originally functioned as cultural signifiers in adinkra cloths often worn by the Akan peoples during funerals. The cloth was decorated with different adinkra symbols and "in a specific manner to convey a parting message to the deceased." Though not as prevalent as in pre-colonial times, adinkra symbols still function in their traditional capacity. They have been transformed, often reinterpreted, reconfigured, and incorporated into facets of Ghanaian, West African, and even African American popular culture. Throughout West Africa, adinkra symbols have been fused into textiles, clothing, buildings, drums, furniture, jewelry, and many other material items. In African American culture, many have shown appreciation for these symbols in similar ways. In major U.S. cities and over the Internet, it is not difficult to purchase tee shirts, books, jewelry, and clothing which incorporates adinkra symbolism. Many young black cultural nationalists and Afrocentric thinkers have also gotten tattoos of adinkra symbols. "Sankofa" means "go back to fetch it," "go back to the past in order to build for the future," and "we should not forget our past when moving ahead." In a popular version of this symbol, a bird with its head facing backward, often searching through its feathers, is used. These symbols should be embraced by African Americans, especially by members of the Hip Hop generation. Black history and the strategies and philosophies of our ancestors should be a part of our daily lives, helping guide our actions, decisions, and thought in the present and future. For more detail on "Sankofa" and adinkra symbols in general, see W. Bruce Willis, author of *The Adinkra Dictionary: A Visual Primer on the Language of Adinkra* (Washington, DC, 1998).

72Vincent Harding, "Responsibilities of the Black Scholar to the Community," in Hine, *The State of Afro-American History*, 279–81.

73Rose, *Black Noise*, 185.

74Keyes, *Rap Music and Street Consciousness*, 18–19.

75Rose, *Black Noise*, 2–3.

76Manning Marable, *Great Wells of Democracy: The Meaning of Race in American Life* (New York, 2002), 269–70.

77George Breitman, ed., *Malcolm X Speaks: Selected Speeches and Statements* (New York, 1965), 8.

78Malcolm X, *Malcolm X on Afro-American History* (New York, 1988), 4–5.for nonviolent drug or property related offenses." (Amnesty International USA, www.amnestyusa.org/women/womeninprison.html)

CONTRIBUTORS

Derrick P. Alridge is Professor of African American Studies and Education at the University of Georgia. He is author of *The Educational Thought of W.E.B. Du Bois: An Intellectual History*. His areas of scholarship include the history of African American education, African American intellectual history and the history of ideas, and civil rights studies.

R. Dianne Bartlow is Associate Professor in the Department of Gender and Women's Studies at California State University, Northridge. Her research focuses on representations of African American women in popular music, culture, and film, and violence against women. Her published work includes "'No Throw-away Woman': Maria W. Stewart as a Forerunner of Black Feminist Thought," in *Black Women's Intellectual Traditions: Speaking Their Minds*, edited by Kristin Waters and Carol B. Conaway, and she is co-author of "Exploring New Frontiers: Women of Color in Academia," in *Women in Mass Communication* (Second Edition), edited by Pamela Creedon. Bartlow has also worked extensively in television production and is a multiple Emmy Award winning director/writer/producer. She is currently producing the documentary *Justice Denied*.

Bernard W. Bell is a Liberal Arts Research Professor of English and Professor of African American Studies at The Pennsylvania State University, University Park, PA. The recipient of five Fulbright-Hays Scholar Awards, his most recent prize-winning book is *The Contemporary African American Novel: Its Folk Roots and Modern Literary Branches*.

Bryan R. Bracey is a Lecturer in the Department of Sport Management at the University of Massachusetts—Amherst. His research emphasizes the relationship between sport, race, and mediated technologies.

Ayanna F. Brown is Assistant Professor of Education and Cultural Studies at Elmhurst College. She has authored several journal articles and book chapters in the areas of Language and Literacy with specific emphasis of "race" and education.

Sakile K. Camara is Assistant Professor of Communication Studies at California State University Northridge. Her research emphasizes the relationship between communication, power, and culture in a variety of contexts. The foundation of her research interests includes issues of uncertainty and anxiety management in interpersonal interactions.

Charise Cheney is Associate Professor of Ethnic Studies at the University of Oregon. She is author of *Brothers Gonna Work It Out: Sexual Politics in the Golden Age of Rap Nationalism*. Her areas of research include African American popular and political cultures, Black nationalist ideologies and practices, gender and sexuality.

Aimee Meredith Cox is Assistant Professor in the African American and African Studies Department at Rutgers-Newark. She is currently the co-editor of *Transforming Anthropology*, the journal of the Association of Black Anthropologists. Her research interests include youth cultural productions, black girlhood, urban ethnography and performance.

Pero Gaglo Dagbovie is Associate Professor of History at Michigan State University in East Lansing, Michigan. He has published numerous articles in *The Journal of African American History*. His books include *Black History: Old School Black Historians and the Hip Hop Generation* (2006), *The Early Black History Movement, Carter G. Woodson, and Lorenzo Johnston Greene* (2007), and *African American History Reconsidered* (2010). As the Principal Investigator for the Carter G. Woodson Home, NHS, his current project is the Historic Resource Study entitled *"Willing to Sacrifice": Carter G. Woodson, the Father of Black History, and the Carter G. Woodson Home*, NHS (National Park Service, U.S. Department of Interior, Washington, D.C., June 2010).

Lesley Feracho is Associate Professor in the Department of Romance Languages and the Institute for African American Studies at the University of Georgia. She specializes in identity politics, gender, race and cultural studies in contemporary narrative of Latin American, the Hispanophone Caribbean and African Diaspora. She is the author of *Linking the Americas: Race, Hybrid Discourses and the Reformulation of Feminine Identity*.

V. P. Franklin holds a University of California Presidential Chair and is Distinguished Professor of History and Education at the University of California, Riverside. He currently serves as the Editor of *The Journal of African American History*. He is the author of *The Education of Black Philadelphia: The Social and Educational History of a Minority Community, 1900–1950* (1979), *Black Self-Determination: A Cultural History of African American Resistance* (1984, 1992), *Living Our Stories, Telling Our Truths: Autobiography and the Making of the African American Intellectual Tradition* (1996), and *Martin Luther King, Jr.: A Biography* (1998). He is the co-author of *My Soul Is a Witness: A Chronology of the Civil Rights Era, 1954–1965* (2000); and he is the co-editor of *New Perspectives on Black Educational History* (1978), *African Americans and Jews in the Twentieth Century: Studies in Convergence and Conflict* (1998); *Sisters in the Struggle: African American Women in the Civil Rights–Black Power Movement* (2001), and *Cultural Capital and Black Education: African American Communities and the Funding of Black Schooling, 1860 to the Present* (2004).

Ronald L. Jackson II is Professor and Head of the Department of African American Studies and Professor of Media and Cinema Studies at the University of Illinois at Urbana-Champaign. He is author of nearly 75 articles and chapters in various disciplines in addition to ten books including the recently released *Encyclopedia of Identity* (Sage). He currently serves as co-editor (with Kent Ono) of the academic journal *Critical Studies in Media Communication*.

Bettina L. Love is Assistant Professor in the Department of Teacher Education at Northern Kentucky University. She is the author of the forthcoming book *Hip Hop's Li'l Sistas Speak*. Her research focuses on youth perceptions of popular culture and the ways in which race, class, and gender impact those perceptions.

Edward Onaci is a PhD student in the Department of History at the University of Illinois, Urbana-Champaign. His research interests include 20th century black radicalism and independence movements throughout the African Diaspora. His dissertation is focused on the Republic of New Afrika, specifically how social movement participation impacts activists.

Kerri Reddick-Morgan received her BA in English Composition & Rhetoric in June of 1995. After a six-year hiatus from academia she returned to complete her MA graduate certificate in Women's Studies, with a concentration in adolescent girls. Simultaneously, she was awarded the Ethel Draper Fellowship for the Study of Adolescent Girls (2003–2004) and the Diane L. Fowlkes Unsung Hero Fellowship (2003–2004). Prior to completing her MA studies she published an article in *Globalization* (2004) and co-authored an article in *The Journal of African American History* (2005). She remains a consummate networker in the marketing and political arenas, actively involved in National Women's Studies Association (NWSA) and Public Policy Network—International, which allow her to continually advocate for the less privileged, upholding ideals of integrity, leadership, accountability and excellence.

Layli (Phillips) Maparyan is Associate Professor of Women's Studies and Associated Faculty of the African American Studies Department at Georgia State University. She edited *The Womanist Reader* (Routledge, 2006) and is at work on a follow-up volume, *The Womanist Idea* (Routledge, 2011). She has published several articles on women and Hip Hop. Currently, she is working with the University of Liberia to develop its inaugural Gender Studies Program, as well as researching women and spiritual activism.

Paula Marie Seniors is Assistant Professor in the Africana Studies and Sociology Departments at Virginia Tech and won the Letitia Woods Brown Memorial Prize from the Association of Black Women Historians for her book *Beyond "Lift Every Voice and Sing": The Culture of Uplift, Identity, and Politics in Black Musical Theater*. Her area of expertise is comparative Ethnic Studies.

Dionne Patricia Stephens is Assistant Professor with a joint appointment in the Department of Psychology and the African Diaspora Studies Program at Florida International University. Her research examines socio-historical factors shaping racial/ethnic minorities' sexual script development and sexual health outcomes. She was awarded the American Psychological Association's Carolyn Payton Early Career Award and the National Council on Family Relations' Jessie Bernard Award for Outstanding Feminist Scholarship in recognition of her work in these areas. A recipient of the Blackboard Greenhouse Exemplary Online Course Award, Dr. Stephens teaches Psychology of Women, Psychology of Health, and Race, Gender & Sexuality in Hip Hop.

James B. Stewart is Professor Emeritus at The Pennsylvania State University where he earlier held the positions of Vice Provost for Educational Equity and Director of the Black Studies Program. His eleven books include the co-authored *Introduction to African American Studies, Transdisciplinary Approaches and Implications* and he has published over seventy-five articles in Economics and Black Studies professional journals. He has served as editor of *The Review of Black Political Economy*, President of the National Economic Association, and President of the National Council for Black Studies. He is currently national President of the Association for the Study of African American Life and History.

INDEX

2 Live Crew 198
"4th 3rd, The" (J-Live) 143
50 cent 122, 127, 215, 223, 230, 223, 262, 265, 267
"A Change is Gonna Come" (Sam Cooke) 14
A Different World 281
A Salt with a Deadly Pepa 94
"A Song for Assata" (Common) 39, 40
A Tribe Called Quest 40, 50, 325
Across 110th Street 19, 20
Adelphi University 70
Adinkra necklaces 54
Adler, Alfred 74
Aerosmith 186
African American History 209, 263; relevance to Hip Hop generation 328, 331, 334, 335, 342n31, 342n48; in school curriculum 282–91
African American Vernacular English (AAVE) 285, 295
African Blood Brotherhood 72
African Diaspora 53–4, 67, 72, 90, 96, 207, 265, 282, 322, 329; and the Caribbean 254, 256, 257, 258
African storytelling 54
Afrobeat 56
Afrocentricity 79, 81, 102, 139, 166, 326, 344n71
"Ain't No Stoppin' Us Now" (McFadden and Whitehead) 21
"Ain't Nuthin' but a She-Thing" (Salt-n-Pepa) 102
Akbar, Na'im 326
Ali, Muhammad 217, 266
All Falls Down 287
All Hail the Queen 94, 103
Allen, Bazel E. 322
Allen, Jr., Ernest 132, 133, 139, 148n27, 229

Alridge, Derrick 66, 217, 222, 266
American Legacy: The Magazine of African-American History and Culture 331
American Pimp 192–4
AmeriKKKa's Most Wanted 77–8, 84
Amos 'n' Andy 227
Anderson, Elijah 324
Andre 3000 46, 126
Andrews, David 213, 217
Angela Davis: The Prison-Industrial Complex 40
Antebellum era 321, 343n48
Appadurai, Arjun 266
Appeal 73, 77
Aquemini 39, 46
Archie Bell and the Drells 22
Aretha Franklin 158–60, 162–4, 197
Arie, India 145, 153–8, 160, 164, 173–4, 190
Arkansas 263
Armstead, Ronni 248
Asante, Molefi Kete 326
Asheru 134 table 1
"Así es la Negra" (Puello) 257–8
Asociación Hermanos Saiz (Brothers Saiz Organization, AHS) 245
Association for the Study of African American Life and History (ASALH) 332, 335
Atlanta, Georgia 24, 39, 41, 94, 195
audience segmentation, 9
auditory imagery 7
authenticity 130n4, 181–3, 198, 212, 215, 281–2, 288, 296, 299
Autobiography and the Making of the African American Intellectual Tradition 66
Autobiography of Malcolm X 66
Ave Magazine: A Street Movement in Print 328

Axelrod, Beverly 64
Baby Boy 191
Bacardi Carta Blanca 271
Badu, Erykah 40, 46, 94–5, 105, 134
table 1, 141, 190
Baduizm 95
Baker, Ejima 253
Baker, Ella 54
Baker, Geoffrey 245–6, 248, 253
Baker, Josephine 302
Baldwin, James 308
Bambaataa, Afrika 35, 44, 54, 66, 74, 93,
227, 266–7
Bamboo Crew 271, 272
Bamboozled 326, 334
Banneker, Benjamin 48
Banner, David 333
Bar Kays, 21
Baraka, Amiri 73, 139, 331
Baraka, Ras 75
Basu, Dipannita 223
Beale, Frances 133
Beastie Boys 53, 268
Beat Street 93, 301
"Beautiful Girls" (Kingston) 306
Bee Side 93
Beeban Kidron 192
"Beijing Bad Boy" (Yin T'sang) 270
Beijing Contemporary Music Institute
265
Beijing Foreign Studies University
(BEIWAI) 263
Beijing, China 263, 265, 268–78
Belafonte, Harry 308
Bennett, Lerone 157, 331–2
Benson, Reynaldo 16
ben-Yochanan, Yosef ("Dr. Ben") 326
Berry, Halle 130n1, 326, 330
BET 59n27, 146, 180; and the depiction
of black women 125, 128, 129,
130n9, 228–9, 232, 235
Beyoncé 127, 301, 307, 309
Big Boi 46, 126

Big Rube 46
Biggie Smalls 94
bin Wahad, Dhruba 329
Birth of a Nation 227
bisexuality 173
Bizet, Georges 301, 308
Black Arts Movement 2, 83, 133, 135,
139, 143
Black August Collective 243
Black body, exploitation of in Hip Hop
and film 178–200; *see also* sexuality
Black Commentator 27
"Black Cop" (KRS-One) 303–4
Black English 286
Black Enterprise 53
Black entrepreneurship 50–3
Black film 80, 178, 179, 182, 191–200,
326–7, 339; Hip Hop film history
301; *see also* blaxploitation films
Black Freedom Struggle 35, 36, 38–9,
41–2, 49–53; 67 and Pan-African
solidarity 54
black history 49; and school curricula
282, 288–90, 293, 296, 298; and
321–340, 343n61
Black History Month 322, 332; commercialization of 335–8, 343n61
Black Issues in Higher Education 322
black nationalism 11, 42, 70–3, 76–9, 95,
133, 135, 138–40, 147, 267, 325, 330
Black Panther Paper 62
Black Panther Party 23, 36, 39, 51–2,
62–8, 70, 80, 84, 140, 241, 329–31,
333
Black Panther Party Reconsidered, The 65
Black Power Movement *see* Civil
Rights–Black Power Movement
Black Scholar, The 64
black self-determination 17, 40–7,
49–50, 55, 66, 67, 71–2, 135, 138;
and women 95; and athletics 211–13
Black Star (Mos Def and Talib Kweli)
45, 325

Black Star 45
Black Star Line 45
"Black Star-K.O.S. (Determination)"
   (Kweli) 45
Black Thought 41
"Black Women in Defense of
   Ourselves" statement 96
"Black Zombie" (Nas) 28
Blackalicious 36, 56
Black-Eyed Peas 206
blackness, *see* authenticity
Blakk Bubble 272
blaxploitation films 18–19, 21, 28, 80,
   178, 194–5, 326; character of the
   pimp in 196–7; *see also* Black film
Blige, Mary J. 94, 152, 190; as role model
   121, 123; and women's perspective in
   Hip Hop 157–63, 164, 173–4
Blondie *see* Deborah Harry
Blow, Kurtis 74
blues 5, 6, 43–4, 197, 228, 263, 264,
   264, 285, 332, 334; and black femi-
   nism153, 161–2; as musical back-
   ground for Hip Hop 118, 120,
   121–4; political commentary in
   13–15, 24–5, 26, 27
Bo Diddley 266
Bogle, Donald 326
Bomb Squad 77
Bond, Angelo 17
Bonilla-Silva, Eduardo 232, 235
"Bonnie and Clyde" anthems 106
"Bonnie and Clyde Theme, The" (Yo-
   Yo) 106
Booba 56
Boogie Down Productions 33n112, 70,
   74–5, 80, 84, 228, 325, 327, 334
Booker, Chris 65
Boston, Massachusetts 24, 56
Boswell, Thomas 257
Boyd, Todd 37, 58n9, 76, 211–19, 323,
   324, 332, 343n46
Boyz 'n the Hood 180, 191, 302, 326

Brand Nubian 44, 46, 66, 80, 131, 134
   table 1, 144, 325
Break Dancing 118, 275, 277; b-boys
   266, 275
Breaking 275
"Breaks, The" (Kurtis Blow) 74
Brent Owens 192
"Bridging the Gap" (Nas) 334
Bring in Da Noise Bring in Da Funk 301
"Bring the Boys Home" (Johnson, Perry
   and Bond) 17
Bringing Down the House 199
Brock, Lisa 243
Bronx, New York City 54, 90, 92,
   109n1, 118, 265–7
Brooklyn Museum of Art 323
Brooks, Gwendolyn 329
Brother D 74
Brother J 71
Brown v. Board of Education 211
Brown, Elaine 65
Brown, H. Rap 77, 80
Brown, James 17, 22, 36, 38, 56, 187,
   267
Brown, Jim 334
Brown, Ronald 140
Brownies' Book 49
Bryant, Joy 311–12
Bryant, Kobe 204, 330
Bureau of Educational and Cultural
   Affairs, U.S. Department of State
   263
Burford, Michelle 156
Burns, Lori 165, 168, 169
Burton, Dana 269
Bush, George W. 123–4, 206, 216
Busta Rhymes 131, 134 table 1, 144
Butler, Judith 167–8, 171, 193
Butterfly 144
By All Means Necessary 75
Cade, Toni (Bambara) 133
California Newsreel 328
Calloway Cab 266

Campbell, Anne 142

Cannon, Nick 128–9

capitalism 11, 35, 40, 44, 52–3, 67, 96, 132, 178, 189, 191, 205–6, 217, 242, 244, 262–3, 266, 270, 324, 333, 335 336; and the commercialization of Hip Hop 222–36; black 140–1; *see also* commodification

Carbado, Devon 167

Carby, Hazel 314

Caribbean contribution to Hip Hop 3, 55, 87n10 239–58, 265, 267

Carmen Jones 301, 308

Carmen the Hip Hopera 301–15

Carmen: and orientalism 301; original novella 301; 1874 Bizet version 301, 308

Carmichael Stokely 73, 77, 79, 80, 331, 334

Carson, Sonny 71

Casas de la Cultura 244

Cash Money Millionaires 185

Castro, Fidel 244

CBS Records 21

Cee Lo 39, 46, 134 table 1

censorship 124, 126; in China 261, 262, 269, 272, 278

Center for AIDS Research at Emory University 312

"Chain Gang" (Sam Cooke) 14

Chaka Khan 162

"Change the Beat" (Bee Side) 93

Chappelle Show 298

Charles Drew, 48

Charlie Chase 241

Chase, Clifton 27

Chavis, Benjamin 314

Cheer Up 272

Chen Mingyu 274

Cheney, Charise L. 67, 132, 133

Cheryl the Pearl 92

Chicago, Illinois 13, 24, 93, 134, 137, 195, 273, 303, 314

Chi-Lites 9, 17

China, People's Republic of 261–79

"Chocolate City" (Clinton, Collins and Worrell) 24

Chocquibtown 257–8

"Choice of Colors" (Mayfield) 14

"choreopoetry" 133

Chow, Rey 266

Christian Science Monitor 313

Christianity 22, 173

Chronic, The 228

Chuck D 39, 70, 75, 77, 85, 94, 265, 267, 272

Church Commission Report, U.S. Senate 62

Ciu Jian 262, 268

Civil Rights Commission (CRC) 26

Civil Rights–Black Power Movement 5, 7, 9, 67, 68, 69n25, 85, 111n20, 133, 140, 187, 206, 213, 232–3, 288; and the Black Panther Party, 70, 72–3, 77; comparison to Hip Hop era 321–340, 342n41; failures of 14, 23; and Pan-African solidarity, 54; post–Civil Rights era 79, 81–3, 212, 266, 324, 327, 328; pre–Civil Rights era 113, 261; relationship to socially conscious Hip Hop 35–42, 46, 47, 50, 52–3, 56–7, 66; and song lyrics 11–18

Clarke, Cheryl 133

Clarke, John Henrik 326, 332

classism 91, 105, 108

Clear Channel 145

Cleaver, Eldridge 64–5, 68n11, 77, 79, 80, 331, 334

Cleveland, Al 16

Cleveland, Ohio 24

Clinton, George 24

Clinton, William Jefferson, administration of 225–6

"Cloud Nine" (Whitfield and Strong) 23

CMCB 272, 275, 278

Coca-Cola 262, 264
Cocaine Song, 20–21
Coffy 197
Cold Crush Brothers 252
Cole, Cheryl 213
College Dropout 206, 333
Collins, Patricia Hill 133, 152–3, 161–2, 166, 313, 314, 320n83
Collins, William 24
"Colonial Mentality" (Kuti) 56
Coltrane John 140
Combahee River Collective 133
Combs, Sean "Puffy" *see* Puff Daddys
commercialization, *see* commodification
commodification 7, 207, 217; of hip hop, 70, 118, 119–120, 130, 135, 140–141, 150n49, 206, 222–36, 296, 297–99, 332; of black culture 167, 179, 336, 344n66; of black bodies 124–130, 178, 189–90, 191, 199
Commodores 22
Common 28, 39, 40, 56, 134 table 1, 147n11, 190, 192, 205, 267, 268
Common Sense (rapper) *see* Common
community theaters 9
Complex 328
complicity theory 183–4
"Concrete Schoolyard" (Jurassic 5) 28
Confucianism 263, 264
Congress of African People, 73
Congress of Racial Equality (CORE) 37
Consejo, Anónimo 255
Cooke, Sam 14, 22
Cookie: The Anthropological Mixtape 40
Cooper, Anna Julia 48, 50, 54
CORE see Congress of Racial Equality
"Corner, The" (Common and the Last Poets) 28
Cosby, Bill 130n1
Cose, Ellis 192
Count Machouki 266
Coup, the 28, 36, 51, 134 table 1, 145

Coupland, Nikolas 285
Cowan, Rosemary 208
Cox, Oliver
CRC see Civil Rights Commission
criminal justice system, *see* law enforcement, police
Crisis of the Negro Intellectual, The 322
Crisis, 331
Crooklyn 191
Crowell Todd, 262
Crummell, Alexander 50, 73
crumpin' 118
Cruse, Harold 218, 322, 336–7
Cuba 240–58
Cubans, contribution to Hip Hip 239–58; *see also* Latinos
cultural diversity 262
Cultural Revolution 262, 263, 264, 265
D. D. Rhythm 272
D.R.U.M. 331
Da Brat 94, 188
Dagbovie, Pero Gaglo 207
Dai Bing 268, 271, 272
Dandridge, Dorothy 308
Dara, Olu 334
Davies, Carole Boyce 250, 257
Davis, Angela 36, 40, 79, 326, 331; on culture and black liberation, 140–1, 145, 150n49, 151n66; and black music 153, 161; on prisons 231, 305
Davis, Darren 140
Davis, Miles 81, 140
de Kloet, Jeroend 266, 270, 271
de la Causa, Hermanos 255
De La Soul 40, 325
dead prez 36, 37, 134 table 1, 233, 330, 335; and black liberation struggles 46, 47, 49, 51, 52, 55, 56; and sexism 85
Death Certificate 73
Death Row Records 94
DeBarge 75
Debbie Dee 93

Deborah Harry 92, 93
Def Jam Records 53, 223, 236
Def Poetry Jam 53
Dekker, Jeffrey Louis 133
Delaney, Martin R. 37, 72
Deng Xiaoping 262–4
Denzin, Norman 208
Desperate Housewives 262
Detroit race riots: 1943 329; 1967 329
Detroit, Michigan 13, 22, 24, 32n78,
    303, 329; study of homeless women
    in 114, 116, 119, 122
Devastating Tito 241, 252
Diaspora, African *see* African Diaspora
Dibango, Manu 56
DiClemente, Ralph 312
Die Nigger Die 80
Digable Planets 134 table 1, 139, 144
Diggs, Taye 204
Dirty Harriet 188
dis tradition, compared to signifyin' 93
Disco 24
Disco Wiz, DJ 241
disconnected youth 305, 315
Discourse 118, 121, 137, 145, 287, 288,
    291, 293, 295; defined 285; feminist
    109n7
discrimination *see* race discrimination
disenfranchisement 90; and African
    Americans 75, 232, 305; and
    Latinos 240, 244, 246–7, 248
Disposable Heroes of Hiphoprisy 76
Dixon-Gottschild, Brenda 122
Dizzee Rascal 56
DJ Charlie Chase 252
DJ Master OC 252
DJ Tommy 274
DJ Yella 94
DMX 53, 106, 182, 186, 189, 198
Do the Right Thing 326
"Dog Match" (DMX) 106–7
Doggystyle 228
Dolemite 80

"Don't Call Me Nigger, Whitey"
    (Stewart) 23
"Don't Waste Your Time" (Blige) 158,
    159–60, 161–3, 164
"(Don't Worry) If There's a Hell Below
    We're All Gonna Go" (Curtis
    Mayfield) 16
Donald D. 92
Donalson, Melvin 301
"Doo Wop (That Thing)" (Hill) 104
Doodlebug 134 table 1, 144
Doug E. Fresh and Slick Rick 94
Douglass, Frederick 38, 288, 343n61
dozens 266, 285, 296
Dr. Dre 94, 185, 228, 265, 268
Dragon Tongue Squad 270, 274, 275,
    278
Dre Robinson 192
drugs 11, 12 table 1, 16, 18, 35, 47,
    52–3, 114, 117, 180, 231, 266; dis-
    proportionate imprisonment for,
    231; glorification in Hip Hop cul-
    ture 196, 215, 223, 227, 232, 236,
    261; in song lyrics 20, 23, 44, 97,
    106; use by rap musicians 121
Drumline 281
Du Bois, W. E. B. 6, 29n4, 36, 48, 145,
    331, 335; and Black economic
    empowerment 49–50, 52–3; and
    Pan-African solidarity 54, 59n32;
    and double-consciousness 72, 212
Duke Bootee 268
Dungeon Family 41–2, 46
Dupree, Jermaine 94, 223, 303
Durán, West 248, 255
Durham, North Carolina 51
Dyme 186–7
Dyson, Michael Eric 76, 86, 183, 187,
    190, 227, 323, 325, 344n6
Earth, Wind, and Fire 23, 197
East Coast, school of rap 75, 78, 94,
    269, 271, 272, 273
Eazy-E 94, 226, 268

Ebonics 286
Ebony magazine 328, 331, 332, 336, 343n61
economic disparities: poverty 18, 35, 36, 38, 47, 51, 52, 53, 57, 57n3, 83, 114, 175n16, 191, 234, 266, 282; job loss/deindustrialization 26, 51, 303; exploitation 72; wage inequity 51
economic solidarity, for African Americans 51–3, 327; for African American women 95
Edison Market Research 206
education system, U.S.: failures of 47
Edutainment 335
Edwards, Audrey 330–1
Edwards, Harry 214
EEOC see Equal Employment Opportunity Commission
El Abayarde 254
Elliott, Missy 94, 188
Emerge 331
"Emergency on Planet Earth" (Jamiroquai) 28
Eminem 215, 268, 313–14
Ensler, Eve 187
Enter the Wu (36 Chambers) 132
Equal Employment Opportunity Commission (EEOC) 26
Eric B. 131
Essence Magazine 313, 328, 331, 332, 336, 343n61
Estelle 56
ethnography 208, 288
ethnomusicology 323
Eve 94, 100, 101, 106–7, 188
"Everyday People" (Stewart) 23
Exodusters 72
Explosión Suprema 241, 245–6
"Fabulous" (Jaheim) 334
Fairclough, Adam 225
Fairclough, Norman 285
"Fallin" (Keys) 309

Family Matters 227
Fanon, Frantz 37, 137
Fantastic Five 252
Fard, W. D. 135
Farmville, Virginia 50
Farrakhan, Louis 75, 76, 327
Fat Boys 252
Fatback 26
Father Allah (a.k.a. Clarence Smith or Clarence 13X) 131, 133–37, 143, 147n19, 148n21, 148n22, 148n27, 150 n50
Faussart , Celia 55
FBI see Federal Bureau of Investigation
Fear of a Black Planet 38, 70, 214
Fearless Four 252
Febres, Mayra, Santos 252–3
Federal Bureau of Investigation (FBI) 62
"Fela Mentality (Intro)" (Kuti) 56
female circumcision, in Africa 329
femininity 248; and black nationalism 78–79
feminism 95–108, 117, 109n7, 133, 158, 178, 214, 229, 302; in the Caribbean, 241, 248–50; compared to womanism, 109n8, 111n27
feminist scholarship 89n61, 92, 94–6, 98, 107, 108, 133, 160
Fernández, Damián 240, 241–8
Festival of Santiago Apostol 254
Fiasco, Lupe 233
"Fight the Power" (Public Enemy) 38, 70
film *see* Black film, blaxploitation films
Final Call 66
Fish Rap Newspaper 224
Fisk Jubilee Singers 264
Five Percent Nation of Islam, 44, 66, 131-151, 267; *see also* Nation of Gods and Earths
Flack, Roberta 15
Fletcher, Ed 27
FlipMode Squad 188

Flores, Juan 240, 241–2, 250–52
Floyd, Samuel 6
Floyd-Thomas, Juan 132, 139, 142
Foenix XIV 273
folklore 6
"(For God's Sake) Give More Power to the People" (Eugene Record) 9, 17
For the People 273
Foraker Act 250
Foucault, Michel 76, 168, 266
Four Little Girls 326
Four Tops 14
Foxx, Jamie 130n1
Foxy Brown [film] 197
Foxy Brown [rapper] 94, 107, 188, 199
Franklin, Aretha 197; with Mary J. Blige 158, 159–60, 162, 163
Franklin, John Hope 321, 322, 335, 336
Franklin, V. P. 43, 72
Franti, Michael 28, 36, 37, 54, 233; and Disposable Heroes of Hiphoprisy 76; and Spearhead 35
"Freakin' It" (Smith) 215
"Freddy's Dead" (Mayfield) 19
"Free Huey Newton" (Chuck D) 39
Freedman's Bureau 47
freedom schools 47
Fresh Start Shelter, Detroit 114–30
Friday 191
"Friendship Train" (Whitfield and Strong) 14
"Fuck tha Police" (NWA) 28
Fugees 54–5, 94, 190
Fulbright Program 263
Fulbright, J. William 263
funk 5, 22–4, 27, 266
"Funk You Up" (MC Angie B) 93
Funkdafied 94
Funky 4 + 1 more 92
Futura 2000 241
Gallagher, Charles 233–4
Gambia 266
Gamble, Dee Dee Sharp, 22

Gamble, Kenny 14, 17, 22
"Game is On, The" (Dragon Tongue Squad) 275
"Game Time" (Ishues) 48–9
Gang Starr 134 table 1, 137–8
Gangsta Boo 188
gangsta rap 58n8, 117, 147n12, 211, 215, 228, 267–8, 330, 334; and black nationalism 44, 67, 70, 77, 86n5; in China 272–3; takeover by commercial interests 78, 178–203; west coast 78, 94, 268
"Gangsta, Gangsta" (NWA) 184
Gardner, Bettye J. 336
Garnet Henry Highland 73
Garvey, Marcus 36, 37, 38, 45, 75, 76, 327; and black nationalism 54, 72
Gaye Marvin, 16–17, 18, 19, 41, 42, 197
Gee, James P. 285
Geeche language 43–4
Gender inequality: within black nationalist groups, 73; in Black Power movement, 73
"Gentleman" (Kuti) 56
George, Nelson 21, 22, 24, 28, 31n61, 82, 84, 109n5, 216, 324, 333
"Get Out of the Ghetto Blues" (Scott-Heron) 25
"Get out the Vote" initiative 28
ghetto 14, 20, 22, 25, 44, 49, 74, 78, 106, 130n1, 253, 267, 306, 334; used as an adjective 114, 116; as subject for rap music and black film 179–200
Ghetto Music: The Blueprint of Hip Hop 334
Gilbert, Cary 22
Gilroy, Paul 181, 183, 265
Giovanni, Nikki 334
"Girl, Don't Be No Fool" (Yo-Yo) 101–2
Giroux, Henry 207
"Give the People the Power They Want" (Gamble and Huff) 17

Gizza, Nega 255
Gladney, Melvin 139
Gladys Knight and the Pips 14
globalization 1, 3, 11, 35, 225, 263, 324;
    defined 261
globalization of Hip Hop 90, 118, 127,
    184, 222, 223, 225; in Caribbean,
    239–58; in People's Republic of
    China 261–71, 277
Glover, Melvin 27
God's Son 334
"Golden Age" of Hip Hop/rap 67,
    70–86, 132, 228, 325, 334
Goldman, Ruth 168
Gomez, Michael 257
Gongfu 273
"Good Girls, Bad Guys" (DMX and
    Dyme) 186
Good Times 227
Goodie Mob 36, 39, 41–2, 325
Gooding Jr., Cuba 204
Goodwin, Michelle 313
Gordy, Berry 17–19, 22
gospel 197, 264, 334
Gottehrer, Barry 136
Grady-Willis, Winston
Gramsci, Antonio 233
Grand Puba 44
Grandmaster Flash and the Furious
    Five 27, 35, 51, 58n14, 74, 227,
    266–7
Gray, Herman 181
Gray, Macy 56
Great Society 90
Gregory, Dick 327
Greimas, A. J. 301, 302
*Griever: An American Monkey King in
    China* 264
griots 6
Groove Armada 188
Guangzhou Province, China 271, 275,
    276
Guillén, Nicolás 255

Gullah language 43–4
gun violence 67–8
G-Unit 223
Hall, Arsenio 226
Hall, Perry 13
Hall, Stuart 156, 180, 230
Hamilton, Kendra 323
Hammerstein, Oscar 308
Hansbrough, Edwina 229
Haralamabos, Michael 11
Harding, Vincent 42, 338
Harlem Nights 191
Harold Melvin and the Blue Notes *see*
    Melvin, Harold
Harris, Robert L. Jr. 336
Harry Belafonte 93
Harvard University 339
"Hat 2 Da Back" (TLC) 103
Hathaway, Donny 15, 197
Hayes, Isaac 21, 197
Haymes, Stephen 47
Head of State 199
Heath, Scott 322
Heff 273, 275
Helene 55
Helms, Jesse 213
Henderson, Douglas "Jocko" 265,
    266
Herrod, Sue 246
heteronormativity 73, 79, 166, 172
heterosexuality 73, 198; and Hip
    Hop/Neo-Soul music 152, 158–74;
    and rap nationalism, 84–86; as
    theme in *Carmen the Hip Hopera*
    307, 308
Hi-Bomb 271, 278
Hieroglyphics 36, 51
Hill, Lauryn 50; and the Fugees 55, 94,
    106, 147n13, 190; and black
    empowerment 104
Hilliard, Asa 326
Hilliard, David 63
Hine, Darlene Clark 95, 336

Hip Hop film, *see* Black film
Hip Hop Generation 1, 2, 3, 58n11,
    59n32, 70, 75, 77, 97, 107, 146,
    211–13, 216, 223, 232, 236n3, 340-
    2; and the Civil Rights era 36–8, 53,
    55–7; and the Black Panther Party,
    62–8; defined, 57n4, 324; and histo-
    ry 321–40
Hip Hop Is Dead 205
Hip Hop musicals 301
Hip Hop Nation 131, 145, 251, 323;
    and capitalism 135, 138, 140, 141;
    and the Five Percent Nation of
    Islam 150; and gender roles 81, 82,
    83, 89n55; and rap nationalism 73,
    76, 79 87n12, 137
Hip Hop Nation: Roots, Rhymes, and Rage
    323
Hip Hop nationalism 135, 140; *see also*
    Hip Hop Nation *and* rap nationalism
Hip Hop Soul 94, 97, 157, 162
Hip Hop Summit 53, 57, 61n81, 205,
    232
Hip Hop Theater Festival 301
"historical revivalism" 323, 325, 332,
    339
Historically Black Colleges and
    Universities (HBCUs) 281
HIV/AIDS 55, 56, 79, 102, 162, 170,
    312, 326, 329
Holliday, Billie 124
Hollywood 18
homophobia 67, 73, 78, 85, 141, 152,
    153, 214, 268; addressed in the
    music of Me'Shell Ndegeocello
    165–74
homosexuality 165–73, 268
Hong Kong, China 262, 266, 269, 273,
    274, 276
Hong Kong, return from British control
    262
Hookers, Hustlers, Pimps and Their Johns
    192

hooks, bell 178, 194, 230, 232–3, 315,
    327, 336, 344n16
"Hot Night" (Ndegeocello) 40
Hot Rhythm 272
HotDog 278
"How We Gonna Make the Black
    Nation Rise" (Brother D) 74
Huff, Leon 14, 17, 22
Hughes, Albert and Allen 192–3
Hughes, Langston 24, 145, 218
Hurricane, The 326
Hurston, Zora Neale 5
"Hustlin" (Ross) 231–2
Hutchinson, Earl Ofari 171, 336,
    337–8
Hutson, Leroy 15
"I Can" (Nas) 49, 333–4
I Like It Like That 303
Ice Cube 28, 94, 106, 198, 268,
    272, 325; as participant in rap
    nationalism 70–84
Iceburg Slim 194
Ice-T 44
Illmatic 49
imaging (musical technique) 37–40, 42;
    defined 38
Immortal Tecnique 36, 59n27, 134
    table 1, 335
imperialism 28; cultural 261; U.S. 35,
    36, 150n51, 206, 262
Impressions 9
imprisonment, *see* law enfocement
Impulsion 272
incarceration *see* law enforcement
income levels, for African Americans 26
Industrialization, in China 263, 275,
    277, 278
Ingram, Luther 14, 21
"Inner City Blues (Make Me Wanna
    Holler)" (Gaye and Nyx) 16
inner city conditions 114; *see also* eco-
    nomic disparities, ghetto
internal statism 72

Internet 56, 151n67, 264, 265, 269, 271, 328; Internet cafés, in China 269, 271
Intruders 22
Iraq War 41
Iron MIB Rap Battle 271
"Is This the Future?" (Fatback) 26
Ishues 48–9
Islam 22, 80, 132, 134 table 1, 137, 148n31, 150n50; *see also* Nation of Islam *and* Five Percent Nation of Islam
Isley Brothers 17
It Takes a Nation of Millions to Hold Us Back 70, 75
Ivy Queen 253–4
J. J. Fad 94
jackanapes 62–8
Jackson, George 331
Jackson, Jesse 38
Jackson, Luther Porter 337
Jackson, Michael 75, 302, 305
Jackson, Millie 265
Jackson, O'Shea 78
Jackson, Sharon *see* Sha-Rock
Jadakiss 206
Jaheim 306, 334
Jamiroquai 28
Ja-Rule 182, 185, 198, 215
Jasper, Chris, 17
Jaworski, Adam 285
Jay Chao 274
Jay-Z 53, 94, 107, 122, 125, 182, 186, 198, 223, 235, 265, 333
jazz 2, 55, 197, 228, 263–5, 332, 334; as background for Hip Hop 118, 122–3; Latin 242, 246
Jazzy Jeff 40, 267–8
Jean Grae 134 table 1
Jean, Wyclef 55, 94, 190
Jeffries, Leonard Sr. 326
Jeremiad 10, 12 table 1, 13, 15–16, 28
Jeru the Damaja 80, 134 table 1, 144, 150n55

"Jesus Children of America" (Wonder) 15–16
"Jesus Walks" (West) 206–7
Jet magazine 328, 332
Jiangxi Province, China 276
Jim Crow 10, 13; 43, 226; *see also* segregation
Jin 268
J-Live 131, 134 table 1, 143–4, 146n1
Johnson, J. J. 20
Johnson, Norman 17
Johnson, Ollie A. 65
Jones, Charles E. 65, 66
Jones, Mike 223
Jones, Quincy 197, 329
Jordan, June 133
Jordan, Michael 213, 215
Journal of African American History 66
Journal of Blacks in Higher Education 336
Journal of Negro History 337
Journey to the West 264
judicial system *see* law enforcement
"Jump Off, The" (Lil' Kim) 333
Jungle Brothers 79, 325
Junior M.A.F.I.A. 94
Jurassic 5, 28, 36
JZ School, Shanghai, China 264
Kahim Aasim 266
Kam 75
Karenga, Maulana (Ron) 32n82, 72–3, 139, 149n40, 331, 343n60
"Keep on Pushing" (Mayfield) 9, 14
"Keep Your Head to the Sky" (White) 23
"Keeper of the Castle" (Lambert and Potter) 14–15
"keepin' it real" 181–5; 190, 230, 233, 236 see also authenticity
Kelley, Robin D. G. 35, 229, 323 344n66, 340n10; and black nationalism 324; and women's equality 78–9, 82
Kenneth "Babyface" Edmonds 94

kente cloth 54, 336
Kentucky Fried Chicken 262
Keyes, Cheryl 338
Keys, Alicia 123–4, 190, 309
Khia 188
Khujo 42
Kid Frost 252
Kid Koala 275
Kilson, Martin 36
Kinetic Raw 274
King Stitt 266
King, Anita 332
King, Martin Luther Jr., 15, 36, 37, 38, 51, 140, 288, 334, 343n60; Martin Luther King, Jr. holiday, 335; and masculinity 74, and Pan-African solidarity 54; and the Vietnam War 41
Kingston, Maxine Hong 264
Kingston, Sean 306
Kitwana, Bakari 57n4, 139, 224, 229–30, 232, 324, 328
Knight, Michael Muhammad 132, 143
Knowles, Beyoncé *see* Beyoncé
Kool G. Rap and Ghostface Killah 143
Kool Herc 35, 44, 58n14, 92, 93, 266–7
K-Os 56
Kraemer, David 7
KRS-One 33n112, 36, 46, 51, 54, 66, 70, 74, 84, 94, 134 table 1, 325; on black police officers 303–4; critique of the U.S. educational system 48, 49; on history 321, 334–5; and rap nationalism 84–5
Krush Groove 301
Kungfoo 268, 269, 270, 272, 278
Kunjufu, Jawanza 236
Kuti , Fela Anikulapo 55–6, 334
Kwanzaa 335
Kweli, Talib 56, 76, 134 table 1, 138, 205, 233, 243, 287, 335; and black nationalism 45–7
L. A. Reid 94
L'Ouverture, Toussaint 42

La Bella Mafia 333
La Face Records 94
La Injusticia Tiembla 246
"La mulata" (Guillén) 256
La Piragua 244
Laclau, Ernesto 180
"Ladies First" (Latifah) 103
Lady B, 92
Lady of Rage 94
Lady Sings the Blues 19
Lady Tee 93
LaFrance, Melisse 165
Lam Jik 273
Lambert, Dennis 14
Lamei Xiao 277
Landis, John 302
Las Krudas 241, 245, 248
Las Vegas, Nevada 195
Last Poets, *see* Scott-Heron, Gil
Latimer, Louis 48
Latinos 70, 317; contribution to Hip Hop 83, 90, 91, 93, 98, 231, 239–58, 284, 287, 297, 298, 299
Lavong, Reggie 6
law enforcement 11; and the Black Panther Party 65; use of death penalty, 35; judicial system 44; disproportionate imprisonment 26, 42, 225, 231–5, 243, 266, 304, 305, 308–10 318n51; *see also* police, Federal Bureau of Investigation
Leaders of the New School 144
LeBlanc's, Keith 74
Lee, Spike 326–7, 334, 339
Les Nubians 55–56
Let's Clean Up the Ghetto 21
let's get free 46–7, 330
"Let's Talk about Sex" (Salt-n-Pepa) 102
Lethal Injection 70
"Letter to the Academy" (Hughes) 24, 25
"Letter to the Firm (Holy Matrimony)" (Foxy Brown) 107

Levine, Lawrence 43
"Leviticus: Faggot" (Ndegeocello) 164, 165, 166, 167, 168, 169, 170–72, 173
Lewis, John 41
Lewis, John Miles 41
Li Xiaolong 268
"Liberation" (OutKast) 46
"Life's a Struggle" (Shawn) 278
Like Water for Chocolate 39
Lil Bow Wow 198, 304
Lil' Kim 94, 123, 187, 188, 199, 309, 310, 313, 333
Lil' Wayne 268
Lilies of the Field 326
Limbaugh, Rush 77
Lincoln, Yvonna 206
Lindsay, John V. 136
Lindsey, Kay 152
Little Lion 271
Litwack, Leon 210
Living for the City (1973) 16
LL Cool J, 34n113, 53, 108, 198
LMF 266, 274
Locke, Alain 6, 13
Logan, Rayford W. 327
"Loiza" (Calderón) 241, 254–5, 256–7
Lord Jamar, 46
Lorde, Audre 133
Los Angeles Times 269
Los Angeles, California 21, 24, 77, 180; relocation of Motown Records to 22, 32n78
Lott, Tommy L. 80
"Love Is Blind" (Eve) 100–101
"Love Train" (Gamble and Huff) 14
Lovebug Starski and DJ Hollywood 93
Lox 185
Lubiano, Wahneema 72
Ludacris 185, 268
Luke "Skywalker" Campbell, 184, 198
lumpen proletariat 64; "black lumpen" 65
Lynch, Monica 93

lynching 181, 333
lyrics 5; political messages in 8, 9–10, 12, 35–6; 39–40; 45–6; 48–9; 51
M.I.A. 206
M-1 51
Ma Rainey, a.k.a. Gertrude Rainey 122, 124, 161
Maal, Baaba 56
Mack, The 80, 194
Madhubuti, Haki (a.k.a. Don Lee) 139, 184, 326, 329
Madonna 167
Mahogany 197
Makeba, Mariam 334
Malcolm X [film] 326
Manatu, Norma 301, 302, 310, 312
Manning, Patrick 257
Mao Zedong 262
Marable, Manning 223, 230, 339
Marilyn Manson 186
Marley, Bob 145, 217
Martin, Darnell 303
Marxism 52
"Mary Magdalene" (Ndegeocello) 165
masculine protest 74
masculinist discourse, 73, 76, 78
masculinity 2, 91, 98, 103, 128, 211, 214–15, 224, 232, 248, 282; and black sexual stereotypes 179, 187–94; and black nationalism 70, 73–82, 84, 85, 86; and the Nation of Gods and Earths 131–5, 139–40, 144–5, 147n16; *see also* masculinist discourse
Masood, Paula J. 301
Masta Killa 143–4
Masta Loop 272
Master P 94, 53, 94, 198, 199, 223
Mayfield, Curtis 197; political messages in music 13, 14–16, 19, 20–21, 28
Mbonisi, Talibah 52
MC Angie B *see* Stone, Angie 93
MC Black Bubble 268

MC Hammer 214
MC Lyte 94
MC Ren 94
MC Vandal 274
MC Webber 269, 270, 273, 274
MC Yan 266
McClary, Susan 162, 164
McClary, Thomas 22
McDonald's 262
McFadden, Gene 21
McPhail, Mark 183
McPherson, Lionel 214
Medina Green 134 table 1
Melle Mel 51, 227, 268
Mellow Man Ace 252
Melvin, Harold 22
Memphis, Tennessee 13
Mercedes Ladies 92
Merimee, Prosper 301
"Message from a Black Man"
    (Temptations) 9
"Message to the Grass Roots" 72
"Message, The" (Grandmaster Flash)
    27, 51, 74, 268
Method Man 53, 144
Mia X 94
Mianyang Teachers College, Sichuan,
    China 263
Michael, Pras 55
Michigan State University 327
Middle Passage 42
Midi School of Music, Beijing, China
    264–5
Miller, Kelly 50
Million Man March 229, 325, 327
Milwaukee, Wisconsin 195
minstrelsy 78, 186, 191, 198, 204,
    208–19, 230, 298, 308, 315,
    342–3n48
Miseducation of Lauryn Hill, The 94, 104
Mis-education of the Negro 48
misogyny 78, 79, 81, 85, 86, 117, 214;
    in film 192, 198; *see also* sexism

Mississippi 333
Mitchell, Tony 240–1, 265, 266
Miyakawa, Felicia 132
Modern Sky 278
Monie Love 103
Monster's Ball 326
Montgomery, Alabama 7; bus boycott, 39
Mooney, Paul 298
Moore, Carlos 244
Morgan, Garrett 48
Morgan, Joan 78, 162
Morris, Aldon 324, 327
Morrison, Toni 156
Mos Def 28, 36, 134 table 1, 148n28,
    190, 205, 267, 301, 335; and black
    self-determination 45, 47, 51–52
Moses, Wilson Jeremiah 72
Motivational Educational
    Entertainment 312
Motown Records 13, 19, 23, 28, 329;
    relocation to Los Angeles 22, 32n78
Move Experiment, The 115–30
Mr. Lif 36
Ms. Dynamite 36, 56
Ms. Jade 95, 99
Ms. Melodie 94
MTV 59n27, 129, 157, 208, 268, 301;
    and the depiction of black women
    228, 232
Muhammad Speaks 66
Muhammad, Elijah 77, 135
Mummy-C 272
"Murdergram" (Jay-Z, Ja-Rule and
    DMX) 182
music videos 8, 28, 85, 217, 229, 232,
    309–10, 312; portrayal of women
    in, 122, 124, 125, 152–7, 254,
    313–14; *see also* MTV, BET
MV Bill 255
MySpace 226
NAACP *see* National Association for
    the Advancement of Colored
    People

Nas 28, 134 table 1, 185; and black self-determination, 49, 204–7, 217, 333–4;

Nation Conscious Rap 74

Nation of Gods and Earths (NGE) 131–46; *see also* Five Percent Nation of Islam

Nation of Islam 22, 44, 51, 65–6, 79, 267, 331; Father Allah's apostasy of 131, 135; overlap with Five Percent Nation of Islam, 135–6; and gender roles 139, 141

National Association for the Advancement of Colored People (NAACP) 37, 314, 331

National Basketball League *see* NBA

National Black Feminist Organization 133

National Black Politics Study (NBPS) 140

National Magazine Awards 330

Native Tongues 228

Natural High 22

Naughty By Nature 185

NBA (National Basketball League) 204

Ndegeocello, Me'Shell 36, 40, 56, 152, 168–74; *see also* homophobia

Neal, Larry 83, 145

Neal, Marc Anthony 8, 182, 186, 204, 208–9, 214–15, 228, 323, 332–3

"Negro Bembón" (Guillén) 256

Negro Digest 335

Negro History Bulletin 331

Negro History Bulletin 49, 337

Negro History Week 335

Nelly 28, 127, 139, 150n51, 185, 313

Nelson, Jill 159

Neo-soul 2, 95, 97; and African American women, 152–75

Nero, Charles 170

"New Day, New World Comin'" (Gamble, Huff and Gilbert) 22

New Jack City 191

New Jersey 61n81, 140, 268, 317; *see also* Newark, New Jersey

New Negro Movement 67

New Orleans, Louisiana 94

New York City 24, 76, 77, 186, 195, 209, 235, 273, 301; black police officers in 303–4; and the origins of Hip Hop 90, 92–4, 109n1; and the origins of the Nation of Gods and Earths, 131, 133, 135–7; and Puerto Rican contributions to Hip Hop 241–2, 251–2

New York Times 74, 315, 323

"New York, New York" (Grandmaster Flash and Melle Mel) 227–8

New Yorker 330

Newark, New Jersey 54; black and white mayors of 75

Newton, Huey 39, 65, 80, 141, 150n51; and the recruitment of Black Panther members 62–4

Next Friday 191

Nigeria 55–6, 263, 266, 343n61

"Nigga You Love to Hate, The" (Ice Cube) 77, 78

Niggaz With Attitude (NWA) 28, 44, 77, 184, 198, 228, 267–8

No Limit Records 94

"No Sell Out" (LeBlanc) 74

Nobles, Wade 326

Northern Dancing Group 276

"Nothing to My Name" (Ciu Jian) 262

Notorious BIG 67

Notorious Kim, The 187

"Now Is the Time to Do It" (Gamble, Huff and Gilbert) 22

Nuruddin, Yusuf 132

Nuyoricans 242, 251

NWA see Niggaz With Attitude

Nyx, James 16

O'Jays 14, 22

O'Neal, Ron 19

O'Neal, Shaquille 330

Oakland, California 62, 80, 286, 329
Obama, Barack 3, 206, 217–18, 232, 309
Obsesión 248
Ogbar, Jeffrey 208
"Oh My God" (Franti) 35–6
Olympics, 1968: protest of Tommie
    Smith and John Carlos 214; 2008 in
    China, 273
Omi, Michael 212, 224, 226, 233
Orbe, Mark 215
Organization of Afro-American Unity
    339
"Other Side of the Game" (Badu) 105
OutKast 39, 41, 46, 125–6, 134 table 1
Owners Illustrated 328
Oyewole, Abiodun 25
P. Diddy, *see* Puff Daddy
"P.I.M.P" (50-cent) 230
Painter, Nell 314
Pan-African Conference, London 1900
    53–4
Pan-Africanism 42, 53–6; and Afrika
    Bambaataa 267
Paniccioli, Ernie 44
Pareles, Jon 74
Paris 71, 74–5, 243, 325
Parks, Rosa 39
Parliament 24
"Party for Your Right to Fight"
    (Chuck D) 70
patriarchy 73, 98, 159, 174, 233, 248;
    and the treatment of women in Hip
    Hop 178, 181, 184, 187, 189, 190,
    193, 194, 199; and the Nation of
    Gods and Earths 135, 136, 142,
    144, 145, 147n16; *see also* sexism,
    misogyny
Paul, Billy 22
Paulette Tee and Sweet Tee 92
P-Diddy 53
Peace Beyond Passion 165, 167, 169,
    170–72
Peebles, Melvin Van 80

Peking University (BEIDA) 263
Pendergrass, Teddy 22
Penn State University 327
Pennington, James W. C. 335
"People Get Ready" (Mayfield) 14
Perkins, Eric 38
Perkins, William Eric 80
Perry, Greg 17
Pete Rock and C.L. Smooth 134 table 1
phallocentrism 73
Phifer, Mekhei 301
Philadelphia International All-Stars 22
Philadelphia International Records
    21–22, 29
Philadelphia, Pennsylvania 13, 24, 40,
    92, 94, 313; black police officers in
    301–4; as setting for *Carmen the Hip
    Hopera*, 301–15
Philly Sound 13
Physical Culture and Sports
    Commission, People's Republic of
    China 277
Pigmeat Markham 266
Piles 233
"Pimp Juice" (Nellie) 28
Pimp: The Story of My Life 80
Pimps 192
Pimps Up, Hos Down, 192
Plain Dealer 329
Platt Amendment 243
Please Hammer, Don't Hurt 'Em 214
Plies 223
POETREE Chicago 134 table 1
police 16, 25, 26, 42, 75, 100, 210,
    307, 309; and the Black Panther
    Party 63–4; brutality 35, 42,
    44–5, 47, 57n3, 62, 80, 266,
    304, 326, 329; in New York City
    303–4; in Philadelphia, 301–4;
    see also Federal Bureau of
    Investigation
Polin, Thomas Hon Wing 262
Poole, Thomas 24

Poor Righteous Teachers 50, 54, 57n3, 70, 131, 134 table 1, 136, 325
"Pops' Rap . . . All My Children" (Common) 40
Portugal 262
post–World War I era 2, 67
post–soul generation 182, 324
post–World War II era 13, 97
Potter, Brian 14
Potter, Russell A. 76-7
Pough, Gwendolyn 160
poverty see economic disparities
Powell, Colin 330
Powell, Jr., Adam Clayton 38
Powell, Kevin 76, 83, 84, 85
"Power to the People" (Chuck D) 70
Pras 94
Predator, The 72
Prince 75, 148n20
Prince Markie Dee Morales 252
Princesses Nubiennes 55
prison(s) see law enforcement
Professor X 66, 71
Project Hip Hop 56
Propp, Vladimir 301, 302
Prosser, Gabriel 42
Protestant Ethic and the Spirit of Capitalism, The 262
"Proud to be Black" (Run DMC) 74
Psychedelic Soul 5, 23
Public Broadcasting System (PBS) 328
Public Enemy 94, 139, 214, 226, 228: and civil rights, black self-determination 36, 37, 38–9, 46–7, 54, 57n3; and economic empowerment 51, 53; as socially conscious rap artist 66, 267, 325; and rap nationalism 70–85
Puello, Arianna 257
Puerto Ricans 55; contribution to Hip Hop 93, 126 239–58 see also Latinos
Puerto Rico 55, 93, 126, 240–2; 250–8
Puff Daddy (P. Diddy) 53, 94, 199, 217, 223, 232, 235

Purvis, Charles 50
"Put Your Hands Up" (CMCB) 275
"Put Your Woman First" (Jaheim) 306
Queeley, Andrea 227, 229
Queen Latifah 54, 134 table 1, 139, 190, 198, 325; as female Hip Hop pioneer 94, 99, 103, 123; and rap nationalism 81–82
Queen Lisa Lee 93
"Queen" (Masta Killa) 143-4
Queens, New York 267
R&B see Rhythm and Blues
R. Kelly 314
race discrimination 57, 72; increase during Reagan administration 26; see also racism, segregation
racism 35, 36, 47, 57, 57n3, 91, 104, 105, 108, 113, 137, 176n52, 196, 218, 268, 307, 315, 326; in the Caribbean 244, 248, 253, 254, 255; and commercial Hip Hop 225–26; and gender politics in rap nationalism 73, 77, 82, 86
radio 8; disc jockeys 9, 18, 27; AM 18; FM 18; decline of black news 27
Radio One 145
Rah Digga 188-9, 311–12
Raimist, Rachel 302
Rainey, Gertrude see Ma Rainey
Rakim 131, 267, 334
Ramsey, Guthrie 9, 18
Randolph, A. Philip 38
Randolph, Laura 163
rap as literacy tool, 283–99
"Rap Man" (Dai Bing) 271, 272
rap nationalism/"raptivism" 2, 67, 70–86, 88n55, 132, 140 see also Hip Hop nationalism, Hip Hop Nation
"Rapper's Delight" (Sugarhill Gang) 92, 228, 268
"Rapture" (Deborah Harry) 93
Rawls, Lou 22
Ray 326

Reagan, Ronald 26
Reagan-Bush era, 75, 326
Real Roxanne, The 93, 98–9
Reality Flow 48
Reconstruction 50
Record, Eugene 17
Records: shift from single to LP
    format, 18
Red Hot + Riot: The Music and
    Spirit of Fela Kuti 55–6
Reddick, L. D. 337
Reed, Adolph Jr. 337
reggae 35, 55, 197, 252
reggaetón 252, 254
Remy Ma 333
reparations 329
Republic of New Africa 72, 87n10,
    149n40, 331
"Resistiendo" (Las Krudas) 241, 249–50
"Respect Yourself" (Rice and Ingram)
    14
"Revolution Will Not Be Televised,
    The" (Scott-Heron) 9, 25–6
Rhone, Sylvia 92
Rhythm and Blues (R&B) 2, 40, 55, 75,
    92, 111n20, 121, 127, 130n1, 197,
    207, 222, 228, 265, 267, 272, 274,
    306, 332; political commentaries
    in 5–9, 13–26, 29n2; typology of
    political commentaries in 10–12;
    transition to Hip Hop 26–9
Rice, Condoleeza 130n1, 330
Rice, Mark 14
Rick James 93
"Ride the Fence" (The Coup) 28
Riggs, Marlon 86, 166–7, 170, 171
"Ring the Alarm" (Beyoncé) 310
Ritchie, Lionel 22
Rivera, Raquel 241, 242, 251–2
Rize 118
Roberts, Sam 315
Robertson, Roland 239
Robeson, Paul 24, 38

Robinson, Chris 309
Robinson, Jackie 211
Robinson, Sylvia 27, 92, 228
rock 'n roll 97, 111n20, 197, 285, 287;
    in China 263, 265, 268, 269, 272–3,
    274, 278, 285
Rock Steady Crew 241
Rock-a-fella records 94, 223
Rodgers and Hammerstein, 308
Rolling Stone Magazine 268
Romani 301, 302, 306–15, 316n2,
    318n36
Roots Manuva 56
Roots, The 40, 41 59n26 134 table 1,
    145
"Rosa Parks" (OutKast) 39
Rose, Tricia 79, 84, 90, 178, 224, 226,
    228, 241, 265, 284, 323, 338; and
    thug rappers 184, 187, 190
Rosette, Benetta Jules 301–2
Ross, Andrew 178
Ross, Rick 223, 231
Ross, Sean 206
Roxanne Shanté *see* Real Roxanne
"Roxanne, Roxanne" (U.T.F.O) 93, 98
"Roxanne's Revenge" (the Real
    Roxanne) 93, 98–9
Ruby Dee 241
Ruff Ryders 94
"Ruffneck" (MC Lyte) 94
Rugged Apparel 188
Ruminations 334
Run DMC 74, 267–8
"Runaway Child Running Wild"
    (Whitfield and Strong) 23
Rush Productions 53
Sabbath schools 47
Sade 56
Sadler, Crystal 158
salsa music 242
Salt-n-Pepa 94, 99, 102–3, 105
sampling 37–8, 40, 42, 132, 266, 292;
    defined 38, 266

San Francisco, California 195
sankofa 338
"SARS" (Yin T'sang) 270
Saturday Night Live 92
Saunders, Tanya 248
"Save the Children" (Gamble and Huff) 22
Sbazzo 273
School Daze 281
Scott, Jill 106, 190
Scott-Heron, Gil 5, 9, 25, 26, 36, 184; and the Last Poets, 24, 28, 241, 265–6
Scratch: The Science of Hip Hop 328
scratching 37–8, 42, 58n14, 92, 266–7; defined 38, 266
Scream Records 268
"Se contamina el barrio" (Explosión Suprema) 241, 246–8
Seale, Bobby 62, 63, 64, 150n51, 288
Second Reconstruction 75; *see also* Civil Rights–Black Power Movement
segregation, racial 9, 26, 43, 96, 212, 324; in Cuba 244; in housing and schools, 23–4; *see also* Jim Crow
Seize the Time: The Story of the Black Panther Party and Huey P. Newton 62
Sellers, Cleveland 56
Set It Off 191
sexism 47, 78, 170, 184, 214, 225, 248–9, 253, 267, 278, 315, 342n41; and participation of women in Hip Hop 95–108; and socially conscious Hip Hop 81–2, 85, 86, 141; *see also* gender inequality, misogyny
sexuality 73, 77, 95, 102, 226, 230, 234, 285, 287–8, 312, 315 320n83; in rap music 178–84, 192–99, 224, 261, 267–8, 273, 288, 297; of Black men 73–4, 80, 84–5, 105, 143, 151n67, 184–7, 215, 229, 304–5, 319n69; of Black women 73, 79, 80, 99, 100, 102, 152, 158–165, 174, 187–90, 224, 236, 254, 302, 307, 308, 310–15, 317n26, 326; in videos 124–30, 157; and health 312; *see also* heterosexuality, heteronormativity, homophobia, homosexuality, stereotypes
Shaft 197
Shakur, Assata 39–40
Shakur, Fayemi 333
Shakur, Mutulu 52
Shakur, Tupac 28, 66, 81, 185, 262, 265, 267 319n69, 325; ideas on capitalism 52–3, murder of 67
Shange, Ntozake 133
Shanghai Rap 272
Shanghai, China 265, 268–77
Shanghao 271
sharecropping, 43
Sha-Rock 92, 93
Sharpley-Whiting, T. Denean 301, 312, 313, 319n69
Shaw, Todd 140
Shawn 278
Shen Lihui 278
Shout Dogg 272
"Show Stoppa (Is Stupid Fresh)" (Supernature) 94
"Show, The" (Doug E. Fresh and Slick Rick) 94
"Shuffering and Shimiling" (Kuti) 56
signifying 167, 170, 266, 285
Simmons, Russell 33n112, 34n113, 53, 205, 217, 232, 330; and the depiction of black women 310, 314
Simpson, O.J. 204, 213
Sisquo 189
Sister Souljah 36, 37, 50, 75, 79, 82, 85, 88–9n55, 94, 190, 326
Sketch Krime 268, 270
Sketches of My Culture 208, 339
Skidmore, Thomas 250
Slater Fund 47
Slaughter's Big Rip Off 194

slavery 8, 43, 46, 47, 72, 161, 169, 226, 288, 326, 333; education under 47; punishment under 47; stereotypes perpetuated by 193, 309, 311, 314
Slim, Iceberg 80
Sly and the Family Stone 23
Smashing Pumpkins 186
Smith, Bessie 124, 161
Smith, Jane I. 132
Smith, Will 190, 215, 216, 267, 268
Smitherman, Geneva 137
SNCC *see* Student Nonviolent Coordinating Committee
Snoop Dogg 81, 185, 198, 228, 262, 267
So So Def Productions 94
socially conscious music 19
Socially/politically conscious Hip Hop 66, 108, 117, 132, 133, 138–40, 145, 222–4, 228, 230, 232–3, 235–6, 330, 334; 335; and women 141
sociolinguistics 288
"Somos Pacífico" (Chocquibtown) 258
Sony records 223
"sorrow songs" 6
soul [music] 6, 7, 10, 21, 55, 94, 265, 267, 332
"soul babies" 324, 341n17
Soul on Ice 64
Soul Students 134 table 1
Souls of Black Folk, The 6
Source magazine 224, 313–14, 328–9
South Africa 24
South Carolina 93
Southwest University of Science and Technology, Mianyang, China (SWUST) 262, 263, 277
Soviet Union (U.S.S.R.) 244
Spain: as setting for *Carmen* 301, 302, 306, 308, 311
Spanish American War (a.k.a. War for Cuban Independence) 243, 250
Sparkle 197
Sparky D 93

Spearhead *see* Michael Franti
Speech Debelle 56
Spelman College 313
spirituals 8, 43–4, 169, 264, 332
Springer, Kimberly 160
"Square Biz" (Lady Tee) 93
Stagolee 187, 208, 210–19; myth defined 202n43, 210
Stallybrass, Peter 310–11
"Stand" (Stewart) 23
Standifer, James 163–4, 169
Staple Singers 14, 21, 197
Staples, Robert 191
Starr, Edwin 17
Stax Records 13, 21
"Stay Human (All the Freaky People)" (Franti) 28
Stay Human 35
Steele, Claude 234
Steffans, Karrine 305, 312
Stepney, Charles 23
stereotypes 103, 105, 113, 156, 161, 179, 190, 196, 199, 209, 215, 218, 283–4, 307, of African American men 186; of African American women, 95, 152–3, 310–15; 315n2; in commercial Hip Hop 222–36; in Cuba 245; in film 197, 302, 326; of gay men 166, 167; Jezebel/Gold Digger 189, 229, 308, 310–15, 326
Stiglitz, Joseph 262
Stomp the Yard 281
Stone, Angie, a.k.a. MC Angie B 93
"Stop the Violence" movement 28–9
"Stop the War Now" (Whitfield) 23
Straight Outta Compton 228, 268
Strange Fruit Project 134 table 1
Street's Disciples 49
Strong, Barrett 14, 23
Stuart, Mel 21
Stuckey, Sterling 43, 72
Student Nonviolent Coordinating Committee (SNCC) 37, 56, 59n32

"Suck my D***" (Lil' Kim) 187
Sugar Hill Records 92, 268
Sugarhill Gang 92, 228, 268
Summers, Lawrence 339
Supa Dupa Fly 95
Superfly 19
Supernature *see* Salt-n-Pepa
Sutra 264
Sweet Sweetback Badaaass Song 197
"Sweetest Thing, The" (Hill) 106
"Swing Low Sweet Chariot" 8
T'Shaka, Oba 326
"Teacha, The" *see* KRS-One
technology: computers and Pan African
    Hip Hop 56
Teena Marie *see* Lady Tee
Tego Calderón 56, 241, 250, 253, 254–8
Temptations 9, 15, 23
"Tengo" (Hermanos de la Causa) 255
"Ten-Point Platform and Program [of
    the Black Panthers]" 64
Terrell Robert 50
Terror Squad 333
"That's the Way of the World" (White)
    23
"These are Our Heroes" (Nas) 204,
    205, 207, 216, 217, 334
"they schools" (dead prez) 49
third world 11
This Side of Glory 64
Thomas, Rufus 21
Thompson, Becky Wangsgaard 155
Thorpe, Earl E. 321, 322
Three Degrees 22
Three Six Mafia 223
Thriller 302
thug culture 67, 106, 113, 166, 179–200,
    201–2n37, 204, 222, 268, 330, 333,
    334; thug misses 187–91; 202n47;
    see also gangsta rap
"Thug Life" (philosophy) 52–3, 67,
    185–6, 191
Thugs Are Us 182

TI 268
Tiananmen Square 262
Tianbao 272
Till, Emmett 333
Timbaland 95
"Tip Drill" (Nellie) 313
Tipping Point, The 40
TLC 94, 102
"To the Beat Y'All" (Lady B) 92
Toast, The 265
Toll, Richard 218
Tommy Boy Records 93
Too Short 80
Toop , David 265, 266
Toronto Sun 70
Tour of a Black Planet 75
Toure, Kwame 36
T-Pain 223
Training Day 326
"Tramp" (Salt-n-Pepa) 99
transnationalism 3, 239–58
Treach 185
Trend, David 180, 184
Trick Daddy 94, 182, 185, 334
Trina 94, 100, 101, 116, 188
Tripmaster Monkey: His Fake Book 264
"Troublesome 96" (Shakur) 28
"Truth or Dare" [documentary] 167
"Tryin' Times" (Hathaway and Hutson)
    15
Tubman, Harriet 38, 48, 188, 288, 334,
    343n61
Turner, Bishop Henry McNeal 72
Turner, Nat 42, 77
U Roy 266
"U.B.R." (Nas) 334
"U.N.I.T.Y." (Latifah) 99
U.T.F.O. 93
"Umi Says" (Mos Def) 28
Undercover 328
Underground Railroad 8, 40, 329
underperforming schools 26, 44, 216,
    281–99, 305

unemployment, for African Americans *see* economic disparities

Unión de Jóvenes Cubanos 244

Universal records 223

University of Coimbra 262

"Unpretty" (TLC) 103

Urb, Ballin' 328

urban renewal 303

urban schools 44, 49; see also education system, U.S.

Us Girls 93

US Organization 72–3

Vagina Monologues

"Vamos a Vencer" (Las Krudas) 248

Van Deburg, William L. 6, 9, 10, 11, 71, 321

Van Sertima, 326

Vanilla Ice 226

Vasquez, Julio C. 304

Vesey, Denmark 42

Vibe magazine 328, 329

"Vicious Beat" (Starr) 93

"Vicious Rap" (Paulette Tee and Sweet Tee) 92

"Video" (Arie) 153–4, 156

Vietnam War 17, 23, 41, 44, 305

"Visions" (McClary and Ritchie), 22

"Visions" (Wonder) *15*

Vixens Diaries 305

Vizenor, Gerald 264

"Vote or Die" campaign 217

"Wake Up Everybody" (McFadden and Whitehead) 21

"Wake Up" (reprise) (Brand Nubian) 44

Wale 56

Walker, Alice 133

Walker, David 73, 77

Walker, Eboni 229

Walker, Madame C. J. 48

"Wanksta" (50 cent) 215

"War (What Is It Good For)" (Whitfield and Strong) 17

War for Cuban Independence *see* Spanish American War

War: effect on African Americans 17–18, 305, 306, 317n29

Ward, Brian 6–7, 9, 10, 11

Ward, L. Monique 229

Wash, The 191

Washington, Booker T. 50, 53

Washington, DC 24

Washington, Denzel 326, 330

"Watch Yo Back" (Trina) 100

Watkins, S. Craig 150n49, 178, 301, 302, 303

Watts [neighborhood of Los Angeles] 25, 130n6; riots of 1965 21, 23

Watts Summer Festival, 1972 21

Watts, Eric 215

Wattsax 21

Weathers, Diane 313

Weber, Max 262

Weddington, Pamela 312

"Welcome to Beijing" (Yin T'sang) 270, 273–4

welfare 40, 117, 152, 225, 226, 233, 234, 305, 312

Wells-Barnett, Ida B. 36, 37

Welsing, Frances Cress 326

West Coast (of the United States) 23, 118; school of rap 75, 78, 94, 252, 268, 269, 271

West, Cornel 194–5, 208, 335, 339

West, Kanye 28, 36, 123, 206, 216, 287, 333

Westood, Sallie 241

What's Going On (Album) 19

"What's Going On" (Al Cleveland, Marvin Gaye, and Renaldo Benson) 16–17

"What's *Happening* Brother" (James Nyx and Marvin Gaye) 17, 18

WHAT-FM, Philadelphia 92

"Whatta Man" (Salt-n-Pepa) 105

"When the Revolution Comes"
(Oyewole) 25
Whipper Whip 252
White supremacy 77, 83, 130n1, 141;
and the commodification of Hip
Hop 223–36
White, Alon 310–11
White, Deborah Gray 326
White, Maurice 23
White, Shane 209
White, Verdine 23
Whitehead John, 21
Whitfield, Norman 14, 23
"Why You Tell Me That?" (Ms. Jade)
99–100
"Why? (What's Going On?)" (the
Roots) 41
"Why" (Jadakiss) 206, 334
Wicker, Tom 305
Wilbekin, Emil 330
Wild Style 93
will.i.am 205, 217, 232
Williams, Raymond 217
Williams, Sekani 301
Williams, Venus and Serena 330
Willie Dynamite 194
Wilson, Ernest J. 322
Winant, Howard 130 n4, 212, 213, 224,
226, 233
Winfrey, Oprah 130n1
Witchdoctor, The 41–2
Withers, Bill 198
Wolf, Naomi 154
Womack, Bobby, 19, 28
womanism 92, 94–109, 133, 214; com-
pared to feminism 109n8, 11n27
Women in Hip Hop 90–109
women of color 95–108; sexual stereo-
types of 95; themes in music by 98;
empowerment of 98, 101–4, 108; in
the Carribean 239–58; *see also* femi-
nism, mysogyny, sexism, womanism
Wonder, Stevie 15, 16, 22

Woods, Clyde
Woods, Granville 48
Woods, Tiger 204, 213, 215, 330
Woodson, Carter G. 1, 48, 49, 57, 321,
322–3, 331, 335–8
World Annual Hip Hop Battle
Competition 276
Worrell, Bernard
Wright, Michelle 257
Wright, Richard 145
Wu Linlin 277
Wu-Tang Clan 132, 134 table 1, 137,
148n20, 265, 266,
X, Malcolm 36, 37, 38, 41, 44, 51, 54,
72, 74, 76, 140, 147n19, 288; and
early Hip Hop 241, 265, 267; and
economic self-determination 139;
and masculinity 75, 138; influence
of Spike Lee's film *Malcolm X* 327,
339–40; transformation from
"Detroit Red" 66
X-Clan 54, 325; and rap nationalism
70–1, 75; and feminism 81–2
Xena 188
Xhibit 198
Xi Ha Now China 268
Xiong Tingting 277
Xodus 71
ya Salaam, Kalamu 133
"Yeah, Yeah, Yeah," (Terror Squad) 333
"Year of Decision" (Kenny Gamble,
Leon Huff, and Cary Gilbert) 22
"Years of Tears and Sorrow" (Kuti) 56
"Yellow Road" (Yin T'sang) 270
"Yes We Can" (will.i.am) 232
Yin T'sang 269
Yin T'sang, 268–78
Ying Yang Twins 223, 233
"You Can't Fade Me" (Ice Cube) 78
"You Make Your Own Heaven & Hell
Right Here on Earth" (Whitfield
and Strong) 15
"You *Must* Learn" (KRS-One) 334

Young, Coleman 329
Young, Norwood 305
youth culture 3, 44, 97, 113, 117–18,
     189, 265, 275, 281, 283, 287, 298,
     322, 324, 331; and commercial Hip
     Hop 223, 225, 227, 229, 233, 236
YouTube 217, 226
Yo-Yo 94, 101–2, 106
YRB fanzine 188
Zeero 272

Zero copula 286–87
Zhao Lirong 277
Zhenzhou, China 276
Zhou Jielun 278
Zirin, Dave 213
Zulu Nation 54, 93
Zulu Nation Crew 93, 267
"Zulu Nation Throwdown"
     (Queen Lisa) 93
Zulu tribe 54

CPSIA information can be obtained at www.ICGtesting.com
Printed in the USA
LVOW032309110112

263499LV00001B/63/P